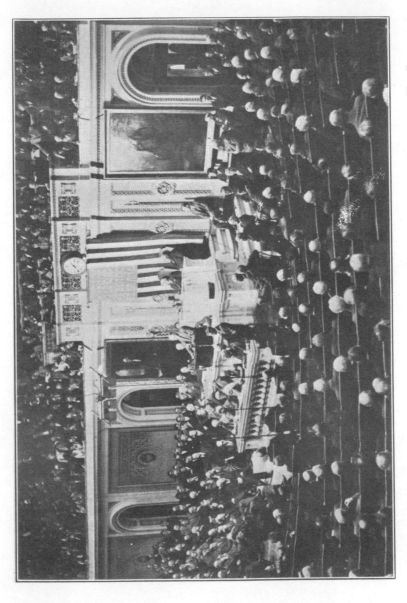

Vice-President John N. Garner (left) and Speaker Henry T. Rainey (right) Presiding at the Joint Session of the Two Houses of the Seventy-Third Congress, January 3, 1934, With President Franklin D. Roosevelt Delivering His First Annual Message.

A HISTORY

OF THE

Vice-Presidency

of the United States

---

by *Louis Clinton Hatch*, PH.D.

REVISED AND EDITED BY

Professor EARL L. SHOUP, *Department of Political Science, Western Reserve University*

GREENWOOD PRESS, PUBLISHERS
WESTPORT, CONNECTICUT

Originally published in 1934
by The American Historical Society, Inc., New York

First Greenwood Reprinting 1970

Library of Congress Catalogue Card Number 72-109744

SBN 8371-4234-2

Printed in the United States of America

Prefatory Note

D R. LOUIS C. HATCH long had in mind the project of writing a treatise on the Vice-Presidency of the United States. The subject had attracted even less attention from historians than does the office from the generality of American citizens. Professor H. B. Learned had written three or four short articles on the subject; there were short incidental studies on its legislative aspects in works on the Senate; but, other than an occasional newspaper or popular magazine sketch, this was all. Dr. Hatch had long been known through his historical contributions, the more important of which are: *The Administration of the American Revolutionary Army* (Harvard Historical Studies, 1903), *Maine: A History* (3 vols., 1919), and *The History of Bowdoin College* (1927). He began active work on this manuscript about six years ago (1927) and continued until illness in the summer of 1931 forced him to discontinue it. The work was uncompleted at the time of his death in December of 1931.

The typewritten manuscript came to my hands in June, 1932. All the chapters had been proof-read by the author and long-hand corrections and supplementary text had been indicated. Throughout all but two or three of the chapters were blank spaces for material which the author had expected to supply later, such as dates, quotations, titles of books, and in some cases entire paragraphs of text. These I have supplied in such amount and style as seemed fitting and most consistent with the text and the author's method of presentation. My objective was simply to fulfill the plan of work as conceived by the author, not to modify or elaborate. The difficulty of the task was greatly increased by the unavailability of his original notes and long-hand text. Every effort was made, however, to correct those errors in details which inevitably appear in transferring text from written notes and original sources to typewritten manuscript. It goes without saying that my scrutiny has extended only to textual matters and not to judgments on men and events. These, with the exceptions to be noted below, remain entirely those of the author.

Chapter XVIII was incomplete and fragmentary and considerable sections of text were necessarily added. Chapter XIX, except for a half dozen scattering paragraphs relating to the elections of 1920 and 1924, all of the short concluding Chapter XX, and the chapter-headings are my work.

The book's subject matter falls naturally into two parts: the first, a study of the origin, nature, and functions of the office of Vice-President; the second, a chronological, historical study of Vice-Presidential nominations and elections. The elections are all treated on much the same plan. There is an account of the national party nominating conventions; a short biography and characterization of each candidate; the popular reaction of the time to each nomination; a description of the campaign; and an account of its outcome. The book in content, therefore, forms for the student of American political history, a useful companion-piece to the older work of Mr. Edward Standwood, *A History of the Presidency*.

The editor must give grateful acknowledgment to the officers and assistants of the Hatch Library of Western Reserve University, the Cleveland Public Library, and the Library of the Western Reserve Historical Society, for their unvarying cheerfulness in complying with the exacting demands which he has made on their time in the course of his work. Acknowledgment, also, is due Mr. Elmer T. Boyd, of the Bangor Public Library, Mr. Thomas P. Martin, of the Congressional Library, Professor P. S. Flippin, of Coker College, Hartsville, South Carolina, Miss Esther U. McNitt, of the Indiana State Library, and Mrs. Edith F. Greenwood, of Lynn, Massachusetts, for the supplying of valuable information; and to Miss Harriet Towne, of Flora Stone Mather College, Western Reserve University, for her painstaking care in typing and otherwise preparing the manuscript for publication.

                                                    EARL L. SHOUP.

Contents

Illustrations

PART ONE

Various Aspects of the Office of Vice-President

CHAPTER I.

The Constitutional Convention

of 1787

W HY did the Convention which drew up the Constitution of the
United States create the office of Vice-President? Probably at
least nine out of ten persons would answer, to provide a successor
for the President. But this, though a partial cause, was not the chief reason.
A mere heir apparent is likely to be either a dignified loafer, or a center of
opposition to the head of the state. This seems to have been realized by the
Convention. Three important sketches of a Constitution were presented by
Edmund Randolph of Virginia, William Patterson of New Jersey, and Alexander Hamilton of New York. Mr. Patterson vested the executive power
in a council. Mr. Randolph left this point undetermined, and therefore
neither plan provided for a Vice-President. Mr. Hamilton proposed an
elected "Governor" to serve during good behavior; when a vacancy existed
his authority was to be exercised by the President of the Senate.

The Convention held its first business session on May 25, 1787; on July
26, a draft constitution was referred to a committee of detail which reported
on August 6. It provided for a President to be selected by the Legislature and
to hold office for seven years. In case of disability or vacancy, the President
of the Senate was to act as President. When the report was considered by
the Convention there was strong objection to vesting in the Senate the power
of naming the temporary President. Gouverneur Morris suggested that the
Chief Justice should act. Madison proposed an "executive council."[1] Williamson of North Carolina desired that the Legislature should provide for the
matter by law and moved that the clause be postponed. Dickinson of Delaware seconded the motion and it was passed unanimously.

---

[1]There was under consideration, though not then before the Convention, a recommendation for the establishment of a Privy Council consisting of the Speaker, President
of the Senate, Chief Justice, and certain heads of departments, when established, to advise
the President if he should request it.

The Convention was ready to accept the recommendation of placing the supreme executive power in a single person, but it had great difficulty in deciding how this important officer should be chosen. To give the right to the Legislature was to violate a principle which the Convention held to be of the first importance, that of the separation of powers; but if the people were to choose, it would be possible for the inhabitants of the large states to control the election. Madison, indeed, pointed out that there was no fundamental difference of interest between the larger and the smaller states, that the real division was that of free and slave; but the smaller states were very apprehensive lest they should be made the serfs of the larger, and it was almost certain that unless ample guarantees for their safety and welfare were given them, they would refuse to ratify the Constitution. Moreover, the difficulty of communication between remote states, and the scarcity of newspapers made it hard for the bulk of the people to know much of men who lived in other sections of the country and it was feared that a choice by general suffrage would result in the scattering of the votes among a number of small men of merely local reputation.

Williamson of North Carolina proposed that three candidates be voted for. He said that probably each state would vote for its favorite citizen but take the remaining two from other states, and as likely from the small as the large. Gouverneur Morris approved of the idea but suggested that only two men be chosen and that the voters should be required to name at least one man from a state other than their own. "Mr. Madison thought something valuable might be made of the suggestion with the proposed amendment of it. The second best man in this case would probably be the first in fact. The only objection which occurred was, that each citizen after having given his vote for his favorite fellow-citizen, would throw away his second on some obscure citizen of another state, in order to ensure the object of his first choice. But it could hardly be supposed that the citizens of many states would be so sanguine of having their favorite elected, as not give their second vote with sincerity to the next object of their choice."

Dickinson of Delaware said: "The greatest difficulty, in the opinion of the House (Convention), seemed to arise from the partiality of the states to their respective citizens. But might not this very partiality be turned to a useful purpose? Let the people of each state choose its best citizen. The people will know the most eminent characters of their own states; and the people of different states will feel an emulation in selecting those of whom they will have the greatest reason to be proud. Out of the thirteen names thus selected, an executive magistrate may be chosen either by the national legislature, or by electors appointed by it." But the Convention by a vote of six states to five[1] refused to postpone the question then under consideration in order to take up the matter.

On September 4 a committee to whom all unsettled questions had been referred, reported a method of electing a President and here for the first

---

[1]The Convention voted by states, each state having one vote.

time a Vice-President appeared. By this arrangement each state would appoint, as its Legislature might direct, a number of electors equal to the number of Senators and Representatives to which the state was entitled. The electors were each to vote for two persons, the one having the most votes to be President, provided that he received a majority of the whole number cast; if two received an equal majority, the House would decide between them. If no one obtained a majority, then the House would choose a President from the five highest on the list. After the choice of the President, the remaining candidate who had the greatest number of electoral votes should be Vice-President; in case of a tie the Senate was to decide.

This section of the report was discussed at some length; little was said about the creation of a Vice-President, but Mr. Gorham of Massachusetts objected to making the second highest man Vice-President unless he had a majority of the votes, since by reason of the great scattering which might take place, it would be possible for a very obscure man who had received only a few votes to be elected. Mr. Gorham believed that, failing a majority, the choice should be left to the Senate. A member of the committee who made the report, Roger Sherman of Connecticut, said that he had no objection to the choosing of the Vice-President, if there was no electoral majority, as the President was chosen. The debate revealed a great apprehension of the added power which the House would receive by allowing it to choose the President.

Although the Constitution was finally adopted, it met with a tempest of criticism which spared scarcely a single provision; but its opponents were generally ready to acknowledge that the method of choosing the President was well guarded. Yet this apparent success of the new plan was to prove its most obvious failure. The supposedly independent Presidential electors quickly became mere agents with just enough freedom to give opportunity for intrigue. Moreover, if the electoral vote were solidly partisan, the candidates of the victors would be tied, with a chance of the person intended for Vice-President being chosen President by the House of Representatives, voting by states. If, in order to prevent this, the stronger party scattered its electoral votes, the minority could, by voting solidly, obtain the Vice-Presidency. Furthermore if party lines were not absolutely drawn or the party choice designations not absolutely clear,[1] in a close contest a few of the majority electors who were influenced by personal or local feeling might join with the minority in voting for some half-and-half candidate who had been put forward to attract support; and so give the chief office to a man confessedly of the second class and intended for the second place.

In November, 1799, the Legislature of Vermont passed a resolution favoring an amendment of the Constitution requiring separate votes for President

---

[1]For forty years candidates were selected, sometimes by a general understanding, but usually by a meeting of the party Senators and Representatives in a caucus which carefully avoided claiming anything but a right like that of other meetings of citizens to recommend.

and for Vice-President, and in February, 1800, the Legislature of Massachusetts endorsed the resolution; but Congress took no action. In the Presidential election of that year the "Republican" candidates, Thomas Jefferson and Aaron Burr, received an equal electoral vote. In the House their opponents, the "Federalists," for a time prevented a choice, their hope being to win over a few Republican Representatives and elect Burr, or perhaps to make a Federalist officeholder, President *ad interim*. The attempt failed and thanks to the patriotic conduct of some Federalists who either did not vote or cast blank ballots, Jefferson was chosen President. Burr automatically became Vice-President. The crisis had been safely passed, but the country had been threatened with civil war, and the Republicans had been near seeing their sincere and very popular leader displaced by a man whose loyalty both to the party and to the country was a matter of doubt. Under these circumstances it was natural that measures should be taken against the recurrence of such dangers. In New York both parties, or perhaps one should say, both Federalist and Republican anti-Burrites united in favor of a radical change in the mode of electing the President and Vice-President. In 1801 Alexander Hamilton drew an amendment like that which had been proposed by Vermont, and a second providing for the choice of electors by districts.

These resolutions were introduced into the New York Legislature by DeWitt Clinton and were passed on January 30, 1802. They were presented to the Senate by one of the New York Senators, Gouverneur Morris, but the Senate took no action. On May 1, the House of Representatives in Committee of the Whole approved an amendment to the Constitution requiring the Electors to vote for President and Vice-President separately. The Speaker ruled, contrary to what is now the established principle, that all motions relating to an amendment to the Constitution require a two-thirds vote to pass and that therefore the committee had rejected the amendment. But on the same day, the House passed it by a vote of 47 to 14. There was little debate on the parliamentary question, and less on the merits of the resolution itself. But those who opposed it protested loudly against rushing through an amendment to the Constitution at the end of a day and the end of a session.

In general the Republicans favored the amendment and the Federalists opposed it. Roger Griswold of Connecticut, a thorough-going member of the latter party, said that if the amendment were adopted the Vice-Presidency would be carried to market to purchase the support of particular states. Mr. Dana of Connecticut thought that a question might arise if there remained any use for a Vice-President; he said that he believed that an examination of the records of the Constitutional Convention would show that no provision was made for a Vice-President until a double election was introduced.

The longest speech appears to have been made by James A. Bayard of Delaware, one of the less extreme Federalists. He did not absolutely condemn the resolution but opposed immediate action. The Republicans had urged that the bill had been under real though not formal consideration for a long time. Bayard replied that he had heard it spoken of but, expecting that it would be regularly brought up, he had not given it the consideration that its magnitude deserved. Mr. Bayard admitted that he was "puzzled to account for the rules laid down for choosing a President but said that his regard for the talents of the framers of the Constitution convinced him that there must have been strong reasons for their course. But he believed it very improper at this late hour to agitate the subject, and he considered it a bad precedent at the end of a session to make any innovation in the Constitution. . . . . He was therefore in point of time against taking up the resolution; he thought it improper when the members were occupied in preparing to depart, in packing up their clothes, with which they had packed up many of their ideas; when we are here, barely to go through the formalities attending the passage of bills." But the House refused to postpone by a vote of 44 to 28.

The resolution was considered in the Senate on the last day of the session and failed, by a single vote, to receive the two-thirds majority necessary for passage. Among those voting in the negative was Gouverneur Morris, who had introduced a similar resolution by direction of the Legislature of his state. Although not recognizing the right of instruction, he felt that an explanation was due, and on December 25, 1802, he wrote to the presiding officers of the New York Senate and House giving the reasons for his action. They were (1) that frequent amendments would weaken the moral authority of the Constiution; (2) that, generally speaking, it is better to bear an evil which is known, than hazard those with which one is unacquainted; and (3) that the proposed change would degrade the Vice-Presidency and was therefore unadvisable if considered by itself. Mr. Morris alleged that the Constitutional Convention foresaw that if a discrimination were made in the ballots of the Electors, the Presidency would be fought for by two rival leaders "while there would be numerous candidates for the other office; because he who wished to become President would naturally connect himself with some popular man of each particular district, for the sake of his local influence so that the Vice-Presidency would be but a bait to catch state gudgeons. The person chosen would have only a partial vote, be perhaps unknown to the great part of the community, and probably unfit for those duties, which the death of the President might call on him to perform."

The next Congress met in October, 1803, and on the twenty-seventh of that month, the House passed an amendment providing that the Electors should vote for President and Vice-President separately; if there should not be a majority for President, the House voting by states should elect from the five highest as originally provided; the person receiving the most votes for Vice-President should be Vice-President but in the case of a tie the Senate should choose. However, the Senate was already considering an amendment of its own. On October 21 an amendment similar to that of the House but leaving blank the number of candidates from whom the House might select, if the choice should devolve upon it, was offered by DeWitt Clinton, then Senator from New York.

There was a prolonged and sharp debate which was not confined to the abstract merits or demerits of the resolution. Senator Dayton of New Jersey moved to abolish the Vice-Presidency, and with other Senators desired to refer the resolution to a select committee. There was barely time for the State legislatures to act upon the amendment before the ensuing Presidential election; the legislatures of Vermont and Tennessee were in session but were about to adjourn. If they were called in special session, it would cause inconvenience and expense; if their votes were delayed, the election might be held under existing law and the Federalists get the Vice-Presidency, which would be specially displeasing to DeWitt Clinton, as it was probable that his uncle would be the Republican candidate.

There was another reason for haste: DeWitt Clinton was about to vacate his seat in the Senate to become mayor of New York, and the contest over the resolution was so close that the loss of a single vote might prevent the obtaining of the necessary two-thirds. His anxiety for an early vote, therefore, quite naturally led him to attribute delaying tactics to the opposition. Clinton said that the obvious intention of the new amendment proposed by the gentleman from New Jersey was to put off or get rid of the main question; it would more comport with the candor of the gentleman to meet the question fairly. This was strong language.

Dayton denied the charge of wilful procrastination with much heat, saying "while he was on the floor he would take the liberty of saying that he had not thought proper to answer the honorable member from New York, because his high respect for the Senate restrained him from replying in those terms which were due to such rudeness and such indecency of language as that in which that member had indulged himself. There would be a fitter time and a fitter place for taking that notice of it which it merited." On the following day, Senator Wright of Maryland read what John Quincy Adams described as "a handsome apology" by Clinton. Wright said that as Clinton had acted by direction of the Legislature of New York, he thought it his duty to press for a decision in order that the mover of the resolution might vote for it, but that as Clinton had gone home he was now willing to give time for the consideration of such an important question as the amendment.

If Mr. Dayton and other Federalists had been playing for delay with a view to affecting the Presidential election, Republicans also had been influenced by regard to party. Cocke of Tennessee said in the debate that he acted from an earnest wish to prevent the election of a Federalist as Vice-President. Other Republicans were not so frank and to their credit be it said some were not so partisan. Butler of South Carolina opposed the amendment. He alleged that it would prevent the citizens of the smaller states from attaining the Presidency. He also said that, in conversation, the chief reason given for the amendment by the Republicans was that it would exclude the Federalists from the Vice-Presidency, and he put the pertinent question, "When we, as Republicans, were out of power did we not reprobate such conduct? Shall we then do as they did?"

The Republicans put forward as a great objection to the existing system that the majority in order to elect their candidate for President must abandon the Vice-Presidency to their opponents. Senator Jackson of Georgia, a man noted for the vehemence of his language, declared that this was to put a price on the head of the President. But Senator Hillhouse of Connecticut, a staunch Federalist, told the Senate that in a government of checks like that of the United States, it was well to have the President and Vice-President of different parties, that political persecution in the matter of assignment of offices would be diminished if the Vice-President were of another party than the President.[1]

The critics of the amendment, like Gouverneur Morris in his letter of the preceding December, urged that it would degrade the office of Vice-President and cause it to be given to inferior men. Senator Plumer of New Hampshire said that the Vice-President "will be voted for not as President of the United States but as President of the Senate, elected to preside over forms in this House. In electing a subordinate officer the Electors will not require those qualifications requisite for supreme command. The office of Vice-President will be a sinecure. It will be brought to market and exposed to sale to ambitious, aspiring candidates for the Presidency. Will his friends and favorites promote the election of a man of talents, probity and (general) popularity for Vice-President, and who may become his rival? No! They will seek a man of moderate talents, whose ambition is bounded by that office, and whose influence will aid them in electing the President."

Senator Bradley of Vermont was of the same opinion as Senator Plumer. He said that "he should not be surprised to hear of as many candidates for Vice-President as there are states, as the votes for President would be offered in truck for votes for Vice-President and an enterprising character might employ his emissaries through all the states, to purchase them, and your amendment lays the foundation for intrigues. He was desirous that he who is to be set up should as at present be equally respectable, or that there should be none—that at least he should be the second man in the Nation; adopt the designating principle without the most guarded precautions and you lose that assurance." Senator Butler thought that the present method by which an aspirant for the Presidency might find himself relegated to the comparatively unimportant second place would prevent an unduly ambitious and powerful man from seeking the chief office.

Mr. Dayton's amendment abolishing the Vice-Presidency was defeated by a vote of 19 to 12. After much debate over the number of candidates from

---

[1]Mr. Hillhouse seems to have overrated the influence of the Vice-President as a party leader, and also that of his right to a casting vote in the confirmation of nominations.

whom the Representatives might choose if the election devolved upon them, it was fixed at three, instead of five as in the existing Constitution.   Instead of the Senate being limited in choosing a Vice-President in the case of a tie, it was provided that it should choose between the two highest candidates, if no one obtained a majority of the electors appointed, two-thirds of the whole number of Senators voting being necessary for a quorum and a majority for an election.   It was also provided that if, when the election devolved upon the House, that body failed to elect before the fourth of March, the Vice-President should "act as President as in the case of death or other Constitutional disability of the President."   The amendment was passed by a vote of 22 to 10.

The House of Representatives discussed the resolution at considerable length, but the debate threw little new light on the question at issue.   The amendment was passed by a bare two-thirds majority, the vote of the Speaker being required to make up the number.   The states, however, promptly ratified the amendment, only three of the sixteen—Massachusetts, Connecticut, and Delaware—dissenting.

CHAPTER II.

The Oath and the Inauguration

THE Vice-President is usually thought of as a shadowy creature only important as a possible successor of the President. But there is attached to the Vice-Presidency another office by nature wholly independent, that of President of the Senate; and because of this union the country had a Vice-President exercising his functions before it had a President; and, technically speaking, such has been the case until the present day. The members of the old Congress of the Confederation had been extremely dilatory in their attendance, and their successors at first followed the bad example. Although March 4, 1789, had been fixed for the meeting of the first Congress under the Constitution, yet a quorum of both houses did not appear at New York, the temporary capital, until April 6. The votes were then duly counted and George Washington and John Adams were declared elected President and Vice-President.

The House of Representatives left it to the Senate to notify these gentlemen and the Senate did so in a ceremonious manner which, though respectful to both, yet marked the superiority of the President to the Vice-President in official rank, and also the special esteem in which the former was held personally. Letters of announcement were written by John Langdon, who had been chosen presiding officer of the Senate for the sole purpose of carrying out the count of the electoral vote, and dispatched by special messengers to Washington and to Adams at their residences at Mt. Vernon, and Braintree (now Quincy), Massachusetts. To Washington, Langdon wrote: "I have the honor to transmit to your Excellency the information of your unanimous election to the office of President of the United States of America. Suffer me, Sir, to indulge in the hope that so auspicious a mark of public confidence will meet your approbation, and be considered as a sure pledge of the affection and support you are to expect from a free and an enlightened people." To Adams there was no intimation that he might possibly refuse the second place. Langdon followed the notice of election[1] with the words, "Permit me, Sir, to hope that you will soon safely arrive here, to take upon you the

---

[1] He kindly refrained from giving the number of votes, which would have shown that Adams had just failed of obtaining an absolute majority.

discharge of the important duties, to which you are so honorably called by the voice of your country." The Secretary of the Senate, Mr. Charles Thompson, who had been Secretary to the Continental and Confederation Congresses, was chosen as the messenger to Washington; to Adams was sent Mr. Sylvanus Bourne.

The Senate voted that three Senators and five Representatives should meet the President when he embarked to cross from New Jersey to New York, and informally conduct him to the house previously occupied by the President of Congress; and that two Senators and three Representatives should wait on the Vice-President when he should come to the city, and in the name of Congress congratulate him on his arrival. The House in effect concurred. Major Bourne reached Braintree on April ninth. On the thirteenth, Adams left for New York, receiving various honors in places through which he passed. On April 18, 1789, he was met at the New York line by a troop of the Westchester Light Horse and conducted to the city, where lodgings had been prepared for him. On April 21, he was introduced into the Senate Chamber by a committee of two Senators, and was met on the middle of the floor by President Langdon, who said, "Sir, I have it in charge from the Senate to introduce you to the chair of this house and also to congratulate you on your appointment to the office of Vice-President of the United States of America," and conducted him to the chair. The Vice-President then made a formal and very complimentary address to the Senate.

The President-elect had not yet reached New York. Accordingly, Mr. Adams had the pleasure of being the chief figure at his own inauguration and of knowing that it was the event of the day. Later Vice-Presidents have been obliged to content themselves with the rôle of leading men in a curtain-raiser to the real play.

Washington, who lived at a greater distance from New York, and who received more public attentions on his way than Adams, did not reach the capital until April 23. There were still some finishing touches to be given to "Federal Hall," the old City Hall, which, thanks to the generosity of private citizens, was being restored and remodelled for the use of Congress, under the direction of Major L'Enfant. Consequently, Washington was not sworn in until April 30. The Constitution provides a specific oath or affirmation for the President, but only requires one pledge to support the Constitution from other officers, and Congress could not establish a form nor authorize persons to administer oaths until there was a President legally qualified to approve a bill or resolution. The Senate would appear to have strained at a gnat and swallowed a camel; accordingly, neither Vice-President nor Senators took any oath until legal provision had been made.

Yet they proceeded to transact business without being sworn in at all.[1] On June 1, President Washington signed the first law passed under the Con-

---

[1] The House of Representatives held a different view of its duty. In April 6, it directed the bringing in of a bill providing an oath, and on April 8, at the request of the House, the Chief Justice of New York swore in the Speaker and the members in the manner provided by the bill.

JOHN ADAMS, MASSACHUSETTS, THE FIRST VICE-PRES-
IDENT OF THE UNITED STATES, 1789-1797.

stitution, one for administering oaths. It provided that the then Vice-President should, within three days after its enactment, be sworn in by a member of the Senate and that his successors, if they had not previously taken an oath, should be sworn in in like manner. On June 2, in compliance with the law, Adams was sworn into the office whose duties he had performed for over a month, by President *pro tempore* John Langdon.

In 1793, it was felt that as the President and the Vice-President succeeded themselves, there was little need of an inauguration. Jefferson and Hamilton, agreeing for once, advised Washington to take the oath privately and send a certificate that he had done so to Congress; but the other members of the Cabinet differed from them, and on March 4 the President quietly entered the Senate Chamber and in the presence of some Senators, Representatives, and private citizens, took the oath and delivered an address. Vice-President Adams took his oath, when entering on his duties as President of the Senate, in the following December.

Jefferson sincerely disliked formality; he also knew the political value of displays of "Republican simplicity"; and on his election as Vice-President, he took prompt measures to prevent his induction into the office from suggesting either monarchy or aristocracy. On January 22, 1797, he wrote to Henry Tazewell, a Republican Senator from Virginia, expressing the wish that he be notified of his election by mail; and on January 30 he wrote Madison: "I hope I shall be made a part of no ceremony whatever. I shall escape into the city as covertly as possible. If Governor Mifflin should show any symptoms of ceremony, pray contrive to parry them."

The House, as it had done eight years before, requested the Senate to take charge of the notification. The Senate might have preferred to follow the ceremony of 1789, but after some consideration directed its Secretary to sign a certificate of election in a prescribed form and requested the Secretary of the Senate to give by letter to the Vice-President-elect, a notification of his election, the President of the United States to cause the notification to be transmitted to Mr. Jefferson. On the second of March Jefferson quietly entered Philadelphia, and on the fourth appeared as unobtrusively in the Senate Chamber and took the oath of office, which was administered to him by the President *pro tempore*.

The example set by the inauguration of Jefferson has in the main been followed at those of subsequent Vice-Presidents. The most important variation from earlier custom is in the administering of the oath. Until 1861, this was usually done by the President *pro tempore* of the Senate, but there were many exceptions. In 1809, Vice-President Clinton and, in 1833, Vice-President Van Buren, were sworn into office by Chief Justice Marshall, immediately after he had administered the oath to the President. On March 4, 1825, the President *pro tempore*, Mr. Gaillard, had resigned; the retiring Vice-President, Mr. Tompkins, was absent from Washington; and Vice-President Calhoun was sworn in by the oldest Senator present, Andrew Jackson of Tennessee. There is no record of either Clinton or Calhoun taking an oath on beginning their second terms. Possibly they believed that their first oath was sufficient. It will be remembered that Tyler was of the opinion that his oath as Vice-President rendered the taking of another oath, when he became President by succession, unnecessary.

Three Vice-Presidents have been sworn in away from Washington, one of them in a foreign country. The first two cases presented no difficulty, because the law relating to the Vice-Presidential oath had been changed so that it might be administered by any officer who was authorized either by laws of the United States or of his State or locality to administer oaths of their respective jurisdiction. In the winter of 1813, Vice-President-elect Gerry was at his home in Massachusetts; and, since a special session of Congress was called for the May following the beginning of the new administration, he avoided a second trip over the difficult roads of the time by taking the oath there before the United States District Attorney. Tompkins, at the beginning of his second term, probably took the oath at his home on Staten Island, and took it twice. In 1821, March fourth fell on Sunday. He therefore took the oath on March third; then, having heard that Monroe would be inaugurated on March fifth, was himself sworn in over again on that day.

The health of William R. King became so seriously impaired after his election as Vice-President in November, 1852, that in December he resigned his position as President *pro tempore* of the Senate, and in January, 1853, sailed for Cuba. On March 2, a law was passed allowing him on March 4 or on any subsequent day to be sworn in in Cuba by the American consul, and a copy of the law was immediately sent to Havana by a United States war steamer. Mr. King was then at a plantation near Matanzas, called *La Cambre* because of its situation on the hills overlooking the city. There, in a setting unique among all Vice-Presidential inaugurations, the oath was administered to him by Consul Rodney of Matanzas, who had been deputized for the purpose by Consul-General Sharkey. The Vice-President was in the last stages of consumption and, unable to stand alone, was supported on either side by Representative George W. Jones of Tennessee, and the American consul. One of the American witnesses of the ceremony wrote of the beauty of the scene, "the clear sky of the tropics over our heads, the emerald carpet of Cuba beneath our feet, and the delicious sea breeze of these latitudes sprinkling its coolness over all of us." Even at the time of the taking of the oath the Vice-President knew that the end was not far off. He lingered in Cuba yet a few weeks, took ship for Mobile, and died at his plantation April 18, only a day after arriving.

In 1861, the oath was administered by the retiring Vice-President, and this has been done at subsequent inaugurations except the nine when the Vice-Presidency has been vacant because of the death of its holder or his succession to the Presidency, or when he has succeeded himself.

It is customary for the Vice-President, like the President, to make an inaugural address, but as his strictly Vice-Presidential service is chiefly to stand and wait, he speaks to the Senators before him as their President, and not to the country. In these salutatories the Vice-President praises the Senate and tells the members how much he appreciates the honor of being their presiding officer and how greatly he will need their forbearance and assistance. He has sometimes added that their wisdom and magnanimity will prevent his errors from injuring the country (by over-ruling his decisions.) At the close of his service the Senators present him with a vote of thanks for the manner in which he has performed the duties of his office. He thanks them in return for the help which they have given him and extends to all his good wishes. In recent years the officers of the Senate have sometimes been included in his thanks, which is most suitable, as their prompting and advice are often very useful to him. Marshall says in his *Autobiography* that it is the custom for the Senate to lay a trap for a new Vice-President by endeavoring to cause him to call a Senator to order for not speaking to the question. It would seem that enough publicity has been given to Senatorial filibustering for every Vice-President, however green, to know that a Senator has the right to talk as long as he pleases on whatever subject he pleases; but Marshall says that he would have fallen into the snare had he not been warned by the Assistant Secretary of the Senate. Mr. Coolidge has recently told us that it is not necessary for the Vice-President to be acquainted with the technicalities of Senate procedure, because the Assistant Secretary will give him all the information which he may need.

At times the retiring Vice-President compliments his successor and begs for him the favor of the Senate, or the incoming Vice-President eulogizes the man whose place he takes. Sherman told Fairbanks: "I accept, Sir, from your hand the gavel with the earnest hope that I may measure up to the standard you have set, and if I do so I feel that I shall have met every expectation." Dawes said: "To my successor in office, and the dear friend of us all, Senator Curtis, I wish the great success which his fine character, his ability, and his long experiences in this body make certain."

The practice of extreme laudation of the Senate was begun by the first Vice-President, the vain and combative John Adams. He said: "I should be destitute of sensibility, if, upon my arrival in this city, and presentation to this Legislature, and especially to this Senate, I could see, without emotion, so many of those characters, of whose virtuous exertions I have so often been a witness; from whose countenances and examples I have ever derived encouragement and animation; whose disinterested friendship has supported me, in many intricate conjunctures of public affairs, at home and abroad; those celebrated defenders of the liberties of this country, whom menace could not intimidate, corruption seduce, nor flattery allure; those intrepid asserters of the rights of mankind, whose philosophy and policy have enlightened the world, in twenty years, more than it was ever before enlightened, in so many centuries, by ancient schools or modern universities. I must have been inattentive to the course of events if I were either ignorant of the fame, or insensible to the merit, of other characters in the Senate, to whom it has been my misfortune to have been hitherto personally unknown." In his retiring speech Adams said: "Within these walls, for a course of years, I have been an admiring witness of a succession of information, eloquence, patriotism, and independence, which . . . . would have done honor to any Senate in any age."

A note like this, if not quite so high, was sounded a hundred and forty years later by Vice-President Curtis. Mr. Curtis said: "The United States Senate is today one of the greatest legislative bodies in the world, one of the greatest actual and potential powers for the promotion and advancement of civilization. Its personnel is of a calibre the equal if not the superior of any previous body heretofore assembled." It is unnecessary to describe in detail the pæans of praise, usually of the same general nature, which one Vice-President after another has sung in honor of the Senate in the days between the Dogeships of Adams and of Curtis. As might be expected from the character of the minstrels, those of Gerry, Tompkins, R. M. Johnson, and Dallas were specially loud and full. There is one note which recurs continually and is particularly delightful to Senatorial ears. This is the description and defense of the Senate as the balance wheel of the government, the protector of the Constitution and of liberty. John Adams said that the character and abilities of the Senators afforded "a consolatory hope (if the Legislatures of the states are equally careful in their future selections, which there is no reason to distrust) that no council more permanent than this (the extreme Federalists desired a life-Senate, as a branch of the Legislature) will be necessary to defend the rights, liberties, and properties of the people, and to protect the Constitution of the United States, as well as the constitutions and rights of the individual states, against errors of judgment, irregularities of the passions, or other encroachments of human infirmity, or more reprehensible enterprise, in the Executive on one hand, or the more immediate representatives of the people on the other." Burr said that the Senate would be the last refuge of the Constitution and of liberty. Tyler echoed the sentiments of Adams and of Burr. Other Vice-Presidents spoke in a similar strain. In the last half century, their praise of the Senate as a conserving body has usually been united with a defense of its custom of permitting unlimited debate.

But at times there has been mingled with this profusion of compliment a gentle recognition of the fact that angelic as the Senate may be, its treasure is preserved in earthen vessels. Tyler praised the Senate for the dignity which has *for the most part* (italics are the author's) marked its proceedings. Dallas in his speech of withdrawal said that the few transient disturbances on the floor of the Senate were due to the importance of the questions before it, and "only exhibited in a stronger relief the grave decorum of its general conduct."

Many Vice-Presidents on taking the chair have begged the indulgence of the Senate because of their lack of knowledge of parliamentary law, and their inexperience in performing duties such as would now devolve upon them. With some this was not simply a humility required by etiquette.

Arthur had never been a member of any legislative body. Jefferson had not sat in one for twenty years. Others, though active in lawmaking, had given little attention to rules of procedure. Both the Johnsons specifically mentioned this circumstance. Fillmore claimed the forbearance of the Senate because he had never been a presiding officer. He had, however, been Whig floor leader in the House of Representatives and must, therefore, have had some practical knowledge in the application of parliamentary law, or perhaps one should say, in the evasion of it. On the other hand, there have been two Vice-Presidents, Colfax and Sherman, whose long success as presiding officers would have made a profession of unfitness blatant hypocrisy. Colfax, however, found reason for diffidence in the circumstances that he was younger than most of the Senators, and that he was not chosen by the body whose head he was. Sherman endeavored to commend himself to the Senate by saying: "Two decades of service in the Capitol though not in this Chamber, have impressed me with the weight of Senatorial responsibility and the value of Senatorial duty well done."

But some Vice-Presidents, so far from pleading ignorance, have almost vaunted their previous experience as a guarantee of the proper performance of duty. Hamlin began his address by saying: "Senators, an experience of several years as a member of this body has taught me many of the duties of its presiding officer which are delicate, sometimes embarrassing and always responsible." Wilson told the Senate: "In passing from the seat I have held for more than eighteen years, to this chair, I trust I comprehend something of its just requirements; something too of the tone and temper of the Senate." Wheeler said that service in analogous parliamentary spheres[1] "has taught me how delicate and at times difficult and complex are the duties which the oath I am about to take will impose on me." Curtis said: "My service among you has impressed me with the responsibilities of every Senator, and at the same time it has given me a clear understanding of the duties and obligations of the Vice-President."

The Vice-Presidential addresses have always been short, at times extremely so,[2] and they have generally been confined to the subject of the Senate and the duties of its President. Jefferson and Richard M. Johnson expressly stated that they considered themselves as held in strict limits by the proprieties of the occasion. Jefferson proclaimed his fealty to the Constitution and the Union, but said: "I suppose these declarations not pertinent to the occasion of entering an office whose primary business is to preside over the forms of this house. . . ." Johnson said: "Contemplating the duties and ceremonies of this day, it might be considered improper in me to consume any more of your time by adverting to other subjects however relevant to the new position which I now occupy. I shall therefore, close my remarks by informing the

---

[1]Wheeler had been an efficient President of a recent New York constitutional convention, and had sat in the national House for several terms.

[2]Probably Wheeler, Hamlin and Sherman have the best record for brevity.

Senate that I am now ready to proceed with them to the business for which we are assembled (the inauguration of the President)." A few Vice-Presidents have allowed themselves more liberty. It is noteworthy that two of these instances occurred in time of war. In 1813, Gerry made a rather heavy pro-war speech declaring victory certain. In 1917, Marshall, in his valedictory at the end of the first session of the Sixty-fifth Congress, said that it would be his duty when called on for public speeches, to voice his belief in the justice and necessity of the war in which the country was engaged, and stated that he was requested by the Secretary of the Treasury to ask Senators, when they addressed American citizens, to call attention to the fact that the war must be finally fought out with dollars and cents, and to urge the necessity of buying Liberty bonds.

Marshall, in other addresses, delivered what might be described as pious and platitudinous confessions of moral beliefs. Hendricks spoke in somewhat the same manner. Fillmore took office when the Revolution of 1848 was raging in Europe, and he called attention to the different methods of changing government abroad and at home, the one by bloody revolution, the other by a quiet, matter-of-course submission to the expression of the will of a free people.

The addresses have been uniformly grave and dignified with the exceptions of those of 1865 and 1917. The former is discussed on a succeeding page. The latter, though in the main lofty in tone, contained a bit of Marshall's characteristic humor. He said: "The present occupant of this chair wants to thank the Senate of the United States for the resolution (of thanks) just adopted, and for the patience and forbearance with which they have dealt at many times with my irascible conduct. I want to assure them that the outbursts that now and then have taken place from the Chair were not real in character. They were simply intended to call the attention of the Senate to the fact that they did have a presiding officer, not one that perhaps they wanted, but one that an ignorant electorate had thrust upon them."

Two Vice-Presidential speeches are preëminent by the impression which they made, one of solemn admiration, the other of horror and disgust. The first was the farewell of Aaron Burr, the other the inaugural of Andrew Johnson. Burr's address was delivered to the Senators alone, for the Senate was in executive session and the galleries were therefore empty. Burr wrote his daughter that he had prepared nothing, but that "it was the solemnity, the anxiety, the expectation and the interest which I saw strongly painted on the countenances of the auditors, that inspired whatever was said." The address is thus summarized by Gales and Seaton in their *Annals of Congress*:

> "Mr. Burr began by saying that he had intended to pass the day with them, but the increase of a slight indisposition (sore throat) had determined him then to take leave of them. He touched lightly on some of the rules and orders of the House, and recommended, in one or two points, alterations, of which he briefly explained the reasons and principles.

He said he was sensible he must at times have wounded the feelings of individual members. He had ever avoided entering into explanations at the time, because a moment of irritation was not a moment for explanation; because his position (being in the chair) rendered it impossible to enter into explanations without obvious danger of consequences which might hazard the dignity of the Senate, or prove disagreeable and injurious in more than one point of view; that he had, therefore, preferred to leave to their reflections his justification; that, on his part, he had no injuries to complain of; if any had been done or attempted, he was ignorant of the authors; and if he had ever heard, he had forgotten, for, he thanked God, he had no memory for injuries.

He doubted not but that they had found occasion to observe, that to be prompt was not therefore to be precipitate; and that to act without delay was not always to act without reflection; that error was often to be preferred to indecision; that his errors, whatever they might have been, were those of rule and principle, and not of caprice; that it could not be deemed arrogance in him to say that, in his official conduct, he had known no party, no cause, no friend; that if, in the opinion of any, the discipline which had been established approached to rigor, they would at least admit that it was uniform and indiscriminate.

He further remarked, that the ignorant and unthinking affected to treat as unnecessary and fastidious a rigid attention to rules and decorum; but he thought nothing trivial which touched, however remotely, the dignity of that body; and he appealed to their experience for the justice of this sentiment, and urged them in language the most impressive, and in a manner the most commanding, to avoid the smallest relaxation of the habits which he had endeavored to inculcate and establish.

But he challenged their attention to considerations more momentous than any which regarded merely their personal honor and character—the preservation of law, of liberty, and the Constitution. This House, said he, is a sanctuary; a citadel of law, of order, and of liberty; and it is here—it is here, in this exalted refuge; here, if anywhere, will resistance be made to the storms of political phrensy and the silent arts of corruption; and if the Constitution be destined ever to perish by the sacrilegious hands of the demagogue or the usurper, which God avert, its expiring agonies will be witnessed on this floor.

He then adverted to those affecting sentiments which attended a final separation—a dissolution, perhaps forever, of those associations which he hoped had been mutually satisfactory. He consoled himself, however, and them, with the reflection, that, though they separated, they would be engaged in the common cause of disseminating principles of freedom and social order. He should always regard the proceedings of that body with interest and with solicitude. He should feel for their honor and the national honor so intimately connected with it, and took his leave with expressions of personal respect, and with prayers, and wishes."

The Vice-President then with quiet dignity left the Chamber, closing the door behind him with a vigor which was the only sign he gave of the intense feeling hidden beneath his calm exterior. A man of courage, ability, and much personal charm, his career was closing in utter defeat. He was bankrupt in fortune, an outcast politically, and in the eyes of religious men of his own section of the country stamped with the mark of Cain. The Senate felt all this. The touch of sermonizing in the address and the personal note gave no offense; the call to be worthy of their high position and the description of themselves as the last guardians of liberty, still more the thought of what might have been a great career closing in difficulty and darkness, went to their hearts. For several minutes they sat silent, some actually weeping. They elected a President *pro tempore,* and then unanimously voted Burr their thanks for his impartiality and ability, and their entire approbation of the manner in which he had discharged his duties as President of the Senate, and sent the resolution to him by a committee of two Senators. Burr replied: "Gentlemen: Next to the satisfaction derived from the consciousness of having discharged my duty,. is that which arises from the favorable opinion of those who have been the constant witnesses of my official conduct, and the value of this flattering mark of their esteem is greatly enhanced by the promptitude and unanimity with which it is offered. I pray you to accept my respectful acknowledgements, and the assurance of my inviolable attachment to the interests and dignity of the Senate."

The answer sounds priggish and hypocritical. Present historians judge Aaron Burr more leniently than did either his contemporaries or the writers of the nineteenth century, but neither his private nor his public life was such as to warrant him in prating of his conscience.

Andrew Johnson, at the time of his election as Vice-President, was Military Governor of Tennessee, and was busily engaged in reconstructing his domain as a free state in the Union. In the winter he was prostrated by an attack of typhoid fever. Therefore, both for personal and public reasons, he desired to remain in Tennessee. He wrote of his wish to President Lincoln and also to Mr. Forney, the Secretary of the Senate, and asked the latter if there were legal precedents for taking the oath away from Washington. Lincoln telegraphed Johnson: "Several members of the Cabinet with myself considered the question today (January 24, 1865) as to the time of your coming on here. While we fully appreciate your wish to remain in Tennessee until her state government shall be completely reinaugurated, it is our unanimous opinion that it is unsafe for you not to be here on the 4th of March. Be sure to reach here by that time."

Secretary Forney replied that he saw no objection to Johnson's taking the oath in Tennessee and the next day sent a list of Vice-Presidents who had taken the oath at a different time from the President. But with it he wrote a letter declaring that it was absolutely necessary for Johnson to come to Washington in order to save "the great Union party," that is, to secure ample recognition of the war Democrats who had supported the reëlection of Lincoln. Johnson yielded to these arguments and arrived at Washington about March 1, stopping at his favorite hotel, the Kirkwood. On the evening of March 3 he attended a party in his honor given by Secretary Forney, where "the wine flowed as freely as the oratory." Johnson was not intemperate, but like most public men of his day, neither was he a tee-totaller; and he may have indulged somewhat freely. In the morning he awoke much shaken. About half-past ten Senator Doolittle of Wisconsin, one of the committee appointed by the Senate to make arrangements for the inauguration, and Vice-President Hamlin called at the Kirkwood, and drove with Johnson to the Capitol, where all three went to the Vice-President's room. There Johnson spoke of his enfeebled condition, said that he was not fit to take the journey from Tennessee to Washington, and asked for a stimulant. Hamlin, as Vice-President, had forbidden the sale of liquor in the Senate restaurant, but he sent for some whiskey or brandy (accounts differ) and Johnson took two or three drinks, with disastrous results.

Probably at the best his speech would have been offensive to good taste. Mr. Winston gave his life of Johnson the extremely appropriate sub-title, *Plebeian and Patriot*. Lincoln rose above his origin, remembering it not with shame, but only as something which had deprived him of desirable opportunities; and his speeches on great occasions were marvels of nobility of thought and beauty of expression. The unfortunate Johnson, on the other hand, was the backwoods stump orator engaged in a rough and tumble fight with his enemies. As has been well said, he suffered from an inferiority complex; with all his vigor and courage he was of a sensitive nature and he met those who looked down on him because he had once been an illiterate tailor, by bragging in season and out of season that he was one of the masses. Only a man of the finest nature could have avoided pride at the thought that he, once a penniless boy, a runaway apprentice, was to assume the second office in the land. The Senate Chamber was very hot and the liquor which Johnson had taken went to his head. He had prepared no notes which might have guided and restrained him,[1] and shaking his fists he bellowed out a tirade that shocked the hearers and the country.

There are reports in various newspapers and in the Congressional *Globe*. The latter is the official account and there Johnson appears to least disadvantage, but it was not printed until some days after the delivery of the speech and there is no doubt that the reporter cut out portions and reshaped the rest of what was a confused, egotistic, demagogical, drunken harangue. John-

---

[1] Johnson's papers, unlike his speeches, are well-reasoned and well-expressed.

son announced that he was a plebeian and was proud of it. He proclaimed the sovereignty of the people, said that their will, not his own effort, had made him Vice-President and informed the Senate, the Supreme Court, and the Secretaries of State, War and Navy specifically, being obliged, however, to ask who held the last office, that they were the creatures of the people. He gave the same information to the foreign ministers sitting together in their brilliant uniforms, and it is probable that he addressed them as "you, gentlemen of the Diplomatic Corps, with all your fine feathers, and gewgaws." Like other Vice-Presidents he professed ignorance of parliamentary law and dependence on the courtesy of Senators, but he unfortunately added with scornful pride: "I have only studied how I may best advance the interests of my state and of my country, and not the technical rules of order." Quite unnecessarily the Vice-President pronounced on a question the President was most anxious to avoid, that of the constitutional status of the seceded states, by declaring that Tennessee was a member of the Union, that her suspended government was about to be restored, and that her representatives must of right be admitted to sit in the House and Senate.

The distinguished audience which filled the Senate Chamber listened first in surprise and disapproval and then with amazement and horror, and perhaps in the diplomatic seats, with ill-concealed amusement. It is said that Lincoln's head dropped in humiliation, and that on leaving the building for his own oath and address, the immortal second inaugural, he said to the marshal: "Do not let Johnson speak outside." Sumner and other Republican Senators hid their faces. Some reporters were too ashamed to write the news to their papers. The three great Republican dailies of New York, the *Tribune, Times,* and *Post,* made no reference to Johnson's condition. But the *Independent,* a powerful anti-slavery and reforming *Weekly* which might be regarded as the political representative of a great section of the Christian Church, blamed their conduct and insisted that unless the press was to abandon its right of criticising men in office, Johnson must be publicly condemned. The Bangor *Jeffersonian,* which was in a measure the organ of the retiring Vice-President, Mr. Hamlin, declared "ridiculous if not scandalous, the attempt of a few Union papers to deny that Vice-President Johnson on inauguration day was under the influence of intoxicating drink. What is the object of having a party respectable and honest if such public obliquities of conduct are to be whitewashed?"

Others told the story not with fitting gravity and sadness, but with gleeful exaggeration and partisanship. Doggerel lines describing the affair were sung at a Washington theatre. The *New York World* called Johnson "an ignorant drunken brute in comparison with whom Caligula's horse (that the crazy emperor made a consul) was respectable." Such attacks brought sharp retort. To the attempt of the Democratic papers to make the Republicans responsible for Johnson's conduct, the *Jeffersonian* replied that the Republicans did not know when they nominated him, that he had kept his love of rum when he got rid of his other Democratic principles. It added that "two of the leading Democrats in the United States Senate were continually drunk but that the papers 'which now so conspicuously parade Mr. Johnson's recent disgraceful conduct' had never said a word about that." This criticism was doubtless correct, but Democrats did not demand virtue of Republicans alone.

The Senate had been much shocked by what had happened on March 4, and on March 6, when electing its standing committees, excluded from places thereon the two Senators to whom the *Jeffersonian* had referred. Actually, though not formally, each party chose its own committee members and the exclusion was therefore the act of the Democrats. The Senate also, on the motion of a future Vice-President, Senator Wilson of Massachusetts, directed the Sergeant-at-Arms forthwith to remove all liquor from the Senate wing of the Capitol, and to exclude it in every form in future. Hitherto, ardent spirits had been obtainable in the Senate Chamber itself. A bar well supplied was kept in an adjoining room and, thanks to an opening famous as "the Hole in the Wall," Senators without leaving the floor of their place of meeting could and did thoroughly moisten their parched throats.[1]

Mr. Johnson had the mortification of hearing the motion for the exclusion of liquor put and of declaring it carried. It is, indeed, usually said that he was taken at once to the country house of the Blairs, Silver Spring, Maryland, but this appears to be an error. The *Senate Journal* shows that he presided at the session of Monday, March 6, and the correspondent of the *New York Tribune* wrote his paper that the Vice-President attended the inauguration ball that evening and was especially attentive to Mrs. Lincoln; but, on March 7, Mr. Johnson was absent from the Senate and remained so throughout the session. It is probable that he went to Silver Spring on that day, and it is certain that he stayed there about a fortnight until after the Senate had adjourned, the excitement over his inauguration had died down, and his health had improved.

At Silver Spring Johnson made a complete conquest of the senior Blair, who, like himself, was an old Jackson Democrat, a strong Unionist, but no consolidationalist. On March 2, Blair told Albert E. Browne, the private secretary of Governor Andrew of Massachusetts, that Johnson was not a drunkard nor had he been drunk at his inauguration, that he had been ill with typhoid fever, had taken a little whiskey that day, and was a little disordered by the situation and all the other things; that he did not say anything that was bad sense but only bad taste, and that it would not have been nearly so much of a thing if Sumner had not been so egoistic about it.[2]

Blair is not the only one to blame Sumner for being "unco guid." Mr. George Fort Milton in his *Age of Hate* speaks of "the virtuous Sumner" hiding his face during Johnson's speeches. It is true that Sumner was vain,

---

[1]This new self-denying ordinance provoked satirical comment, it being regarded as a mere gesture. In substance time soon justified the belief, though the hole in the wall did not reappear.

[2]It has been said that Sumner offered a resolution in a Republican Senatorial caucus asking Johnson to resign.

pedantic, and sadly lacking in breadth of view, but he was filled with a noble idealism and was the dear friend of some of the best and most progressive men of his time; if he was deeply shocked when he saw "the second official of the Nation—drunk—*drunk* (italics in the original) when about (to) take his oath of office, bellowing and ranting and shaking his fists at Judges, Cabinet and Diplomats," so were many others, including the always gently-judging Lincoln. Browne suggested to Blair that Sumner might have felt specially responsible for Johnson because the Massachusetts delegation at the Republican convention had supported him in preference to Hamlin, the New England candidate. Few went as far as Mr. Blair in defending Johnson, but many found excuses or reasons for forgiveness. Gail Hamilton wrote to a friend that during the speech Johnson's better self seemed struggling with a demon.[1]

During the speech members of the Cabinet exchanged whispered comments which passed from surprise and disapprobation to bewilderment and horror. At the beginning of the address Johnson did not appear to be intoxicated. He was known to be a nervous man and his stammering was attributed to this cause. Seward at first thought that it was due to the emotion aroused by his return to the Senate Chamber, the scene of the dramatic proceedings ushering in the war just four years ago, in which Johnson had played so conspicuous a part. Seward himself was much affected. Attorney-General Speed at first believed Johnson guilty only of wretchedly bad taste, but soon concluded that he was out of his head. Welles consider d him drunk or crazy, but when writing in his diary, took a more gentle view. He said: "The Vice-President-elect made a rambling and strange harangue, which was listened to with pain and mortification by all his friends. My impressions were that he was drunk"; then struck out the last word and substituted "under the influence of stimulants, yet I know not that he drinks; he has been sick and is feeble; perhaps he may have taken medicine or stimulants, or his brain from sickness may have been overactive in these new responsibilities. Whatever the cause it was all in very bad taste." Under March 7, he wrote: "The meeting at the Cabinet was interesting, the topics miscellaneous. Vice-President Johnson's infirmity was mentioned. Seward's tone and opinions were much changed since Saturday (the fourth). He seems to have given up Johnson now but no one appears to have been aware of any failing. I trust and am inclined to believe it a temporary ailment, which may, if rightly treated, be overcome."

In this judgment Welles was right and more than right. There is an enormous preponderance of evidence that Johnson was never an intemperate man. Lincoln, when Secretary of the Treasury Hugh McCulloch expressed alarm because only one life stood between Johnson and the Presidency, replied: "I have known Andy for many years; he made a bad slip the other

---

[1] There is no other evidence that Johnson was conscious of his condition and fighting against it.

day, but you need not be scared. Andy ain't a drunkard."[1] Hamlin in an interview said that "Andrew Johnson is not an intemperate man. He is sober and in his right mind—" and seemed to blame himself for assisting Johnson to obtain the liquor. A friend of Johnson published a long article in a Nashville paper which described the Vice-President's services to the Union, and asked if it were right to condemn him to eternal infamy for a single lapse.

Some papers, though filled with righteous indignation, were willing that the sinner be forgiven on condition of public repentance followed by reform. The *Jeffersonian* declared that the Nation was "disgraced, and that Mr. Johnson should apologize as publicly as the offense was committed, ask forgiveness of the Senate, the President and Cabinet and the Nation, and solemnly promise that hereafter he would totally abstain from the use of all intoxicating liquors. If he failed to do this he should be expelled or impeached."[2] The *Independent,* in the name of an insulted people, demanded that the Vice-President atone for his affront to the dignity of the Republic by apology or resignation.

It was not in Johnson's nature to apologize or sit on the stool of repentance and reform. He did, indeed, write to the chief reporter of the Senate: "As I understand there has been some criticism upon the address delivered by me in the Senate Chamber, will you do me the favor to preserve the original notes and retain them in your possession, and furthermore at your earliest convenience bring me an accurate copy of your report of what I said upon that occasion?"; and there was a story in Washington that a conference of physicians would be held and they would declare that the Vice-President had been insane. But Johnson made no excuse and after a stay at Silver Spring had restored his health, left his refuge and mixed in the world as before.

---

[1]This is a surprising statement. Lincoln could have had little or no personal acquaintance with Johnson, though he had met him during the campaign. Probably McCulloch, who retired from the Cabinet after his breach with the Republicans, unconsciously did Johnson the favor of strengthening his statement. McCulloch's autobiography was written and published in his old age, thirty-three years after the incident.

[2]The Vice-President is not a Senator and cannot be expelled.

CHAPTER III.

President and Vice-President

THE relations between the President and the Vice-President have been sometimes close and cordial, sometimes merely formal. In the Constitutional Convention, Elbridge Gerry had objected to making the Vice-President, President of the Senate, saying: "We might as well put the President himself at the head of the Legislature. The close intimacy that must subsist between the President and the Vice-President makes it absolutely improper." Gouverneur Morris replied: "The Vice-President then will be the first heir apparent that ever loved his father," and the pithy retort has often been quoted.

The previous relations between the first President and Vice-President, and the personal character of the latter were such as to make a coolness probable. Adams had been very critical of Washington during the Revolution, and, though patriotic, honest, and able, he was conceited and jealous. He now believed that he stood on the same plane as the President. In his view, the Constitution provided that the electors should choose the two worthiest citizens; the one who had the most votes, provided that they were a majority of the whole, should be President, the other, Vice-President; and America should be in form a kind of two-headed State, like Sparta with its Kings, Rome with its consuls, and Carthage with its judges.

Adams' theory of the equality in rank of the two chief officers of the Nation was manifested in a curious way at the beginning of the new government. He anxiously inquired of the Senate where his place should be when the President visited the Senate Chamber for his inauguration. The possibility seems to have occurred to him that the giant Washington and his short, fat self[1] might squeeze themselves together into the commodious chair of the President of the Senate. When William and Mary were crowned as joint sovereigns of England, Mary sat in a replica of the ancient coronation chair specially made for the occasion; and Peter the Great and his weak-minded brother used as co-Czars of Russia a double throne. But Adams, though a

---

[1] While the subject of giving titles in addressing high officers of state was being discussed, Senator Izaard in private conversation called the Vice-President, His Rotundity.

well-read man and a great respecter of precedents and etiquette, was perhaps ignorant of these recognitions of divided sovereignty; at least he made no reference to them and sat at the head of a line of Senators on the right of the great chair, which Washington occupied in solitary dignity.

Adams was by nature unfitted for a second place, and he chafed at his own inactivity. But apparently he never vented his ill humor on Washington. When taking the chair of the Senate, he had praised the President-elect in the highest terms, saying: "Were I blessed with powers to do justice to his character, it would be impossible to increase the confidence or affection of his country, or make the smallest addition to his glory. This can only be effected by the discharge of the present exalted trust, on the same principles with the same abilities and virtues, which have uniformly appeared in all his former conduct, public or private. May I nevertheless be indulged to inquire if we look over the catalogue of the first magistrates of nations, whether they have been denominated presidents or consuls, kings or princes, where shall we find one, whose commanding talents and virtues, whose overruling good fortune[1] have so completely united all hearts and voices in his favor, who enjoyed the esteem and admiration of foreign nations and fellow-citizens with equal unanimity? By those great qualities and their benign effects has Providence marked out the head of this Nation with a hand so distinctly visible as to have been seen by all men, and mistaken by none."

On taking leave of the Senate, Adams spoke of Washington as one with whom he had coöperated, "though in less conspicuous and important stations, and maintained an uninterrupted friendship for two and twenty years," and said that it would be a lifelong comfort that "in a government constituted like ours," he had for eight years held the second situation under the Constitution of the United States, in perfect and uninterrupted harmony with the first, without envy in one or jealousy in the other." It might be suspected that Adams did protest too much, but there is no doubt that his valedictory description of the relations between President and Vice-President is absolutely correct as far as it concerns Washington, and probably it is reasonably so in regard to Adams himself. Washington was without ambition for office or political power and if duty to the country had permitted it, he would at any time gladly have exchanged the dignities and burdens of the Presidency for the pleasures and comparative ease of a planter at Mt. Vernon. Adams had the satisfaction of being consulted by the President, and of being regarded by many as his destined successor at an early date. Adams' casting vote as President of the Senate had been very useful to the Federalists; Hamilton and his followers looked on him with more favor than formerly, and on his

---

[1]Does the last phrase reveal a little of the old prejudice which, during the war, led Adams to rejoice that it was not by Washington that Burgoyne was overcome, because then "idolatry and adulation would have been unbounded—so excessive as to endanger our liberties, for what I know. Now we can allow a certain citizen to be wise, virtuous and good, without thinking him a deity or a saviour."

reëlection as Vice-President, he had a good majority and the united support of his party.

Adams and Jefferson came into the Presidency and Vice-Presidency as leaders of contending parties; yet at first there was on both sides thought of an alliance. Adams was angry at the narrowness of his escape from defeat by Jefferson, to whom he considered himself greatly superior, but he was infuriated at the thought that, thanks to the management of Hamilton, he had nearly been outrun by Pinckney. Jefferson was always on the watch for an opportunity of winning allies, and was a master in the art of doing so. He was now busy assuring his friends that he did not desire the Vice-Presidency, and had the strongest repugnance to the Presidency and the conflicts which it would bring. He and Adams had been leaders together in the fight for independence, and as Mrs. Adams said, there had never been "any public or private animosity" between them. Under these circumstances, a reunion of the old comrades seemed not unfitting.

Jefferson prepared to make the first advance. He asked Madison if the electoral votes should be tied, or if there should be a division (a tie?) in the House of Representatives, to make it known that he desired that Mr. Adams should have the preference because "he has always been my senior; from the commencement of our public life, and the expression of the public will, being equal, this circumstance ought to give him the preference." He also prepared a letter for Adams himself, expressing the hope and belief that he would be President in spite of "a trick worthy of the subtlety of your arch friend from New York who has been able to make tools of your real friends to defeat their and your just wishes."

On January 1, 1797, Jefferson sent the letter to Madison with a request that it be returned to him should Madison consider its delivery inadvisable; at the same time he made the rather startling suggestion, "If Mr. Adams can be induced to administer the government on its true principles and to relinquish his bias to an English constitution it is to be considered whether it would not be on the whole for the public good to come to a good understanding with him as to his future elections. He is perhaps the only sure barrier against Hamilton's getting in."

Madison replied that he feared that it would be unwise to send the letter. He said that Adams was now well disposed toward Jefferson, and that Jefferson's feelings toward him "have found their way to him in the most conciliating form"; that there was danger that Adams might think that Jefferson was attempting to make a tool of him, that Jefferson's earnest partisans would dislike anything tending to depreciate the importance of the cause in which they fought; that indeed some of them were "already sore on this head"; and that as it was probable that Republicans would feel obliged to oppose Adams, it might be embarrassing for him to have in his hands so complimentary a letter as Jefferson proposed to send. Accordingly, Madison advised that the letter be withheld, and Jefferson readily agreed.

But he did not cease his endeavor to maintain friendly relations with Adams. He called on him promptly on his arrival in Philadelphia, and paid him a high compliment on taking the chair of the Senate, saying that "the Presidency has been justly confided to the eminent character which *(sic)* has preceded me here, whose talents and integrity have been known and revered by me through a long course of years and have been the foundation of a cordial and uninterrupted friendship between us."

At first Adams seemed to welcome Jefferson's advances. In the preceding winter he had spoken well of Jefferson, and had expressed pleasure at the prospect of administering the government in conjunction with him. He promptly returned Jefferson's call, tendered him the position of minister to France, and on his declining the offer expressed the intention of sending Madison as Commissioner in conjunction with Gerry and Minister Pinckney, and requested Jefferson to find out if Madison would accept.

A few days later, Adams and Jefferson were returning from a dinner at General Washington's. Jefferson reported that Madison declined. Adams answered that his own friends had raised some objections to Madison's appointment; and was explaining with some embarrassment what these objections were. When the physical paths of President and Vice-President diverged, their political ones did the same, and there was no further consultation between them during Adams' Presidency. Indeed his offer to Jefferson had been made most unwillingly. Adams wrote Knox, who had advised it, that the Vice-President was too high in the government to be used as an envoy, and that he had made a great stretch in proposing it, to accommodate the feelings, views, and prejudicees of a party.[1]

In the excitement of the campaign of 1800, when Adams and Hamilton were fighting a duel to the death, Adams was reported to have spoken somewhat favorably of Jefferson, and to have declared that he would rather be Vice-President under him "than owe the Presidency to such a being as Hamilton." But when Jefferson called on Adams after his own election, Adams received him bitterly, and he hurried away from Washington rather than attend the inauguration of the man who had defeated him.

Jefferson and Burr were of the same party. On December 15, 1800, Jefferson wrote him regretting that arrangements had not been made to prevent throwing away so many votes (to secure his own election) "as to frustrate half the Republican wish," and rather inconsistently saying that Burr's probable choice as Vice-President would leave a gap in the Cabinet, which he had intended to compose of men "whose talents, integrity, names and dispositions, should at once inspire unbounded confidence in the public mind, and insure a perfect harmony in the conduct of the public business."

Burr at the same time wrote a letter to Senator Smith of Maryland, to be used if necessary, stating that he would not do so dishonorable a thing as to

---

[1]Meaning a number of persons of similar views. Parties in the modern sense were as yet not fully organized and defined.

allow himself to be run in the House against Jefferson. But the Federalists voted for him for thirty-five ballots without protest from Burr or his friends. When Jefferson was officially informed of his own election by the committee of notification, he replied, "I receive, gentlemen, with profound thankfulness, this testimony of confidence from the great Representative Council of our Nation: It fills up the measure of that grateful satisfaction which had already been derived from the suffrages of my fellow-citizens themselves, designating me as one of those to whom they were willing to commit this charge, the most important of all others to them. In deciding between the candidates whom their equal vote presented to your choice, I am sensible that age has been respected rather than more active and useful qualifications."

But this was only the official lie of courtesy which Jefferson believed that the circumstances required. He would have felt outraged and justly so, had the House elected over him a man whom neither party wanted for President. Early in his administration Jefferson manifested a great coldness toward Burr. He gave many of the Federal offices in New York to his enemies; and when the Congressional caucus kicked Burr downstairs by refusing him a renomination, Jefferson declined his petition for an appointive office as a sort of mattress to break his fall. Burr on his part often acted in a manner irritating to the administration, and roused general suspicion of his party loyalty.

George Clinton was rough and independent by nature. He and the New York Republicans generally were restive under the Virginia Dynasty; he had little love for Jefferson and none for Madison, whom he fought for the Presidency. Probably the Madisonians set traps for Clinton and he, by his casting vote, defeated a measure most important to the Administration, the recharter of the First Bank of the United States. He also joined in factious and unwarranted attacks on Albert Gallatin, the Secretary of the Treasury. Gerry died early in his term and Tompkins neglected his duties. Each was anxious to be on good terms with his chief, and spoke most highly of him in his inaugural address to the Senate.

With the austere Calhoun there came a change. Adams and Jackson men had joined in electing him. When the Republican party, now swollen and faction-riven, divided into National Republicans and Democratic Republicans under the leadership of Adams and Jackson, respectively, Calhoun entered the Jackson camp, and his failure as President of the Senate to call John Randolph to order when he was pouring abuse on the President and the Secretary of State, bitterly angered Adams, who attributed this inaction to partisanship as well as fear of Randolph.

Calhoun accepted the support of the Jacksonians for reëlection, shared their triumph, and probably expected to succeed the elderly Jackson, perhaps in only four years. The President was not unwilling, and he recognized the value of Calhoun's alliance by putting several of his friends in the Cabinet, but the Vice-President would have been better pleased if other men had been selected. Calhoun was defending Nullification, which was anathema to Jackson in practice, however he may have regarded it as a theory; and what was equally offensive, Calhoun approved of and Jackson came to believe that he was the leader in the social boycott of "Peggy" Eaton, wife of Jackson's friend and Secretary of War, on the ground that she had been immoral.

Moreover, the characters of Jackson and Calhoun though resembling each other in some ways, were antipathetic in others. Professor Bassett says in his life of Jackson: "Calhoun, seen from a distance, was a man after Jackson's own heart. He had courage, vigor, and candor; and these qualities won the Tennessean. But closer contact showed a man who was cold, correct, and intellectual, a public man of the old Virginia manners, and one who could not bend to the will of a leader."

There was a similar difference between the supporters of the two men. The close friends of Jackson were ultra-democratic; in education, feeling, and manners they wore the stamp of the frontier. Calhoun's chief supporters, perhaps one should rather say allies, belonged to the old aristocracy who had taken up Jackson to check the revival of nationalism under John Quincy Adams. In 1828, many of the Jackson leaders had been unwilling to renominate Calhoun for Vice-President, and might have turned to DeWitt Clinton, had he lived. After his death, some looked toward another New Yorker, Martin Van Buren; but he lacked strength outside his own State, and public opposition to Calhoun was abandoned as useless.

Scarcely, however, had Jackson been elected, when among the politicians, though not among the masses, the next Presidency became the subject of earnest discussion. The anti-Calhounites got certain men into the Cabinet to aid them against the Vice-President, and selected Van Buren as their candidate when Jackson should leave the White House. "The New Yorker had the social availability which they lacked and (he) soon won the strong personal friendship of the President." But Calhoun was still too strong to be defeated by Van Buren, and it was decided to persuade Jackson that it was his duty to yield to the demand of the people to take a second term; also it was determined to kindle his wrath against Calhoun.

The first plan was probably carried out easily, though the exact time and place of its execution are unknown. The second scheme was more difficult and was accomplished by a slow and careful use of the Seminole-Florida affair. In 1818, General Jackson had followed raiding Seminole Indians into the then Spanish province of East Florida, seized Spanish towns, and acted with the untamed vigor characteristic of him. He believed that he had the definite though informal authorization of the President, which Mr. Monroe later denied. Jackson's action came at a most inopportune time, for the United States was trying to induce Spain to sell Florida; and there was a proposal in the Cabinet to censure or disavow him. But John Quincy Adams, then Secretary of State, opposed, saying that there was no real, though an apparent, violation of his instructions, and that his proceedings were justified by the necessity of the case, and by the misconduct of the Spanish commanding officers in Florida.

These views had such weight that it was decided merely to restore the towns, and evacuate Florida. The President wrote to Jackson in most conciliatory language, but Jackson was very angry at there being any thought of blaming him for what he considered a proper and patriotic action previously authorized by the President. He believed that Secretary Crawford had been the chief offender, and Calhoun his advocate. In fact, Calhoun, who was Secretary of War, had regarded Jackson's conduct as disrespectful to himself and had shown special irritation. But Cabinet discussions were confidential. Calhoun could not with honor have given a full account, and he remained completely silent. Crawford, who hated Calhoun, and the Tennessee Jackson group contrived that the facts, and perhaps something more, should be reported to the President. Calhoun had professed the greatest admiration for Jackson, and the honest old soldier felt that he had been deceived by a hypocrite. Friends interposed; neither Jackson nor Calhoun wished to appear to be the aggressor and responsible for splitting the party, and complete breach was for a time avoided; but in the end there was a public and bitter quarrel between the President and the Vice-President.

Van Buren's election to the Vice-Presidency was a personal triumph for Jackson in a contest where his opponents were mighty and many of his friends half-hearted; it strengthened the union between the two men, already very close, and probably no other Vice-President was so highly esteemed by his chief and had such influence with him.

Van Buren's Vice-President, Richard M. Johnson, had been a rival, but his office gave him hopes of the succession. He was "regular"; both men were supported by the national wing of the party and had their chief strength in the North; among the "old stagers," each was of a conciliatory disposition; and King and Prince seem to have lived together in harmony. Dallas on his nomination wrote Polk that he felt highly honored at being associated with him; the letter suggests that of Frelinghuysen to Clay in the same campaign, but is more flowery and less pious. Immediately after the election, Dallas was overwhelmed by letters from office-seekers, the writers appearing to believe that the Vice-President would be all-powerful. This was far from the truth. The leader of another faction in Pennsylvania, James Buchanan, was appointed Secretary of State and his position gave him great influence. But Mr. Polk remembered that he was the head of the whole party; the friends of Dallas were allowed a portion of the Federal offices in the State; and Dallas stood firmly by the administration in spite of great pressure to take an opposite course. Polk wrote in his *Diary* that Buchanan, because of his seat in the Cabinet, received more than his share of patronage, but that he was displeased because he was not given full control of appointments in Pennsylvania.

Polk consulted Dallas on the important parts of his first message, and Dallas declared himself highly pleased with them. Polk also informed Dallas of the proposal of the British Minister for settling the Oregon boundary question, and of his own intention of taking the advice of the Senate before acting on it, a course which Dallas approved. The President, likewise, conferred freely and frankly with Dallas when a Philadelphia lawyer, an agent of the Queen of Spain, made the Vice-President an intermediary in regard to negotiations for the purchase of Cuba. Dallas on his part supported the administration bill for a sweeping reduction of the tariff, although it was extremely unpopular among his constituents. Dr. Learned says in his book, *The President's Cabinet,* that the coöperation of Polk and Dallas is one of the three chief instances of intimate relations between President and Vice-President. The others, where the union was perhaps stronger, were those of Jackson and Van Buren, and McKinley and Hobart.

President Taylor, at the time of his election, had the most cordial feeling toward his Vice-President and in his ignorance, which may have been shared by others who ought to have been better informed, believed that the Vice-President sat in the Cabinet.

The question of the status of slavery in the territory just acquired from Mexico was a pressing and difficult problem, but perhaps a more immediate and dangerous one for the new Administration was that of the distribution of the spoils. William H. Seward, who had just been elected Senator and had come to Washington to attend the inauguration, enter on his new duties and look out for his fences, soon found the capital so full of hungry Whigs that he "jocosely remarked a little later, that the world seemed to be divided into two classes; those going to California in search of gold and those going to Washington in quest of office." The most important patronage was that of New York, and if Taylor should take the Vice-President for chief counsellor in dispensing it, he would give great offense to its only Whig Senator,[1] to Thurlow Weed, and to the majority of the Whig party in the Empire State; but if he neglected Fillmore, he would offend many valuable supporters.

Fillmore and Seward were both anti-slavery men and had begun political life fighting under the banner of Thurlow Weed, the Whig boss. But Seward's union with the party manager had become closer with the years, while Fillmore's had weakened. This had happened partly because Weed, in his desire to win back the New York "Conservatives," old National Republicans who joined the Democrats because of the Whig inclination to anti-Masonry and had been alienated from their new friends by Van Buren's sub-treasury scheme, had successfully supported the reëlection of Tallmadge for United States Senator in 1839, notwithstanding the strong claims of Fillmore himself

---

[1]Seward's colleague, Daniel S. Dickinson, was a Democrat.

and of the other steadfast Whigs. There had been a half concealed rivalry between Seward and Fillmore, which still remained in 1848, though the party had found a prominent place for each.

There was a miscellaneous but able and vigorous opposition to Seward, led by John A. Collier, to whom the nomination of Fillmore as Vice-President was chiefly due. Collier had contested the nomination for Senator with Seward and bore him a personal grudge of long standing. Whig politicians of New York City had planned to win Taylor's favor as he passed through New York. Weed was well disposed toward Fillmore, and he wished to avoid a breach in the party. Accordingly, he invited the Senator and the Vice-President-elect to a dinner and patched up a truce. But Taylor's first nominations for New York custom-house offices were made without consulting Seward, and were all given to friends of Fillmore. Seward, as a loyal Whig, quietly voted to confirm them. He did, however, report the matter to his ally, Weed; and Fillmore soon found himself out-maneuvred.

Taylor had referred appointments to the member of the Cabinet under whom the officer would serve, thus avoiding being personally involved in the Fillmore-Seward contest. This rule, as it worked out in practice, gave Fillmore a powerful voice in making some of the best appointments in the State. But Weed arranged for an invitation to Washington and persuaded Taylor, who had some embarrassing non-partisan notions, that the will of the people and the welfare of the country required him to turn Democrats out of office and to put Whigs in. The members of the Cabinet were told that the object of changes in New York was to strengthen the party there, that the Whig Governor was its head, and that by taking his advice they would avoid the embarrassment of deciding between Vice-President and Senator.

The Governor, Hamilton Fish, was an ally of Seward and Weed. He owed his nomination to their influence and efforts, and the Seward men saw the gates of the Promised Land open wide before them. Far different was the fate of the Fillmoreites. Frederic C. Bancroft, in his life of Seward, calls him a combination of John Quincy Adams whom he revered, and of Thurlow Weed who was so friendly and useful to him. Bancroft says that as long as Seward had political ambitions, though he "desired to be true to Adams' example, he thought it necessary to keep Weed as a guide and ally." So now, though Seward wrote that he detested and loathed running to the President every day to protest against this man or that, evidently he did it.

Weed had made overtures to the Vice-President, but Fillmore proved irresponsive, and the time came when he could not obtain the nomination of two friends to offices in Buffalo, his home city. Seward finally won the heart of the President by writing for the benefit of the Free Soilers, a vindication of Taylor's conduct in regard to the Wilmot Proviso. Mr. Bancroft says, "Fillmore's candle was not entirely snuffed out, but it soon ceased to be counted as one of the lights of the administration. Seward's politic suggestions, his readiness, and his *savoir faire* inspired the President's confidence and won his friendship. Fillmore was suave and prepossessing in manner, but a Vice-President has neither power nor constituents."

Differences of policy also helped to separate the President and Vice-President. General Taylor favored the admission of California as a free State without reference to other measures, and in this he had the hearty coöperation of Seward. But Fillmore, though he had belonged to the anti-slavery wing of the Whigs, was a devoted unionist, a natural conservative, and a loyal party man. Personal pique and more honorable motives finally made him a supporter of Clay's Compromise and, therefore, an opponent of the President. However, he took no open stand, believing that his position as President of the Senate required neutrality; but he privately told the President that if called on to give a casting vote, probably it would be in favor of Clay's bill.

Vice-President King died before taking his seat. The relations of Breck-inridge and Buchanan were polite but distant.

Hamlin and Lincoln at the time of their nomination had never met, though Hamlin had been a Senator during Lincoln's single term in the House. Each, however, had heard the other speak and had not forgotten the circumstance. In July, Mr. Lincoln wrote a pleasant note as "a sort of introduction to Mr. Hamlin." On September 4, he wrote again saying that he had heard that Hamlin had written Schuyler Colfax that the Republicans would lose two Congressmen in Maine and elect their candidate for Governor by only a small majority, that he feared that the moral effect would be disastrous, and that Hamlin must not allow it. Hamlin went vigorously to work, the Maine Republicans elected all their Congressmen, and gave their Governor a reasonably satisfactory majority.

After the election Mr. Hamlin, by Mr. Lincoln's request, met him at Chicago. Lincoln said that he would always accept in the best spirit any advice which the Vice-President might give, and Hamlin pledged friendship and "the best advice and assistance in my humble power." Lincoln avoided a close discussion of the question of what was to be done in South Carolina, but took up that of the Cabinet. He told Hamlin that he had decided that the latter should name the New England member; but he himself mentioned three men, Charles Francis Adams, and Nathaniel Banks, of Massachusetts, and Gideon Welles, of Connecticut. No decision was reached at the time. Circumstances eliminated Adams, and Hamlin, personally, objected to Banks because of his theatrical manner and trimming attitude in politics. Welles showed up in a much better light. Hamlin received many endorsements of him; finally recommended him to the President; and the appointment was duly made.

Hamlin and Welles soon quarrelled, the former declaring that the latter had broken his word in relation to the allotting of a contract. They have left differing accounts of Welles' appointment, and the exact amount of Hamlin's influence is hard to determine. Lincoln did not intend merely to sign on a dotted line, nor Hamlin to take more liberty than Lincoln wished to give. Lincoln left to Hamlin, in conjunction with Senator Trumbull of Illinois, the power to forward or withhold a letter which he had prepared offering the Secretaryship of State to Seward.[1]

After the inauguration Lincoln frequently consulted Hamlin, at first in conference with Cabinet and high military officers, and then individually. But the two men were of somewhat different temperaments and their policies differed. Each was a good politician, neither was a weakling; but Lincoln preferred to walk softly, Hamlin was more ready to wield the big stick. He disapproved of Lincoln's failure to take vigorous action before the attack on Sumter, and of the slow development of his anti-slavery policy. He, however, defended the President in private correspondence, and refused to contest the nomination with him in 1864 when approached by the Radicals.

Lincoln frequently advised with Hamlin as he did with many others, and Hamlin worked cordially in securing delegates from Maine to the Republican National Convention who were favorable to the President's renomination. Yet the Vice-President had felt that he was neglected. In 1863, Mrs. Frémont requested Hamlin to use his influence to obtain a command in the field for her husband. Mr. Hamlin replied: "What can I do? The slow and unsatisfactory movements of the government do not meet my approbation, and that is known and of course I am not consulted at all, nor do I think there is much disposition in any quarter to regard any counsel I may give much if at all."

Johnson succeeded Lincoln too early for any special relation between them to develop, but it is probable that they would have been on the best of terms. Both were of the country-born proletariat, without formal education, sons of their own works. Lincoln had highly approved of Johnson's conduct as Military Governor of Tennessee, and had judged leniently his intoxication at the inauguration. Johnson as President adopted Lincoln's tentative policy of Reconstruction, but unhappily he had not Lincoln's breadth of view, charity for opponents, and flexibility in non-essentials.

In the first years of the administration, the relations between Colfax and Grant seem to have been cordial enough, although the former was never taken into the latter's confidence. Colfax explicitly stated that he expected to show that, contrary to the rule of the past, a Vice-President and President could remain friends; and he announced his intention to attempt in no way to meddle in the President's patronage. But Colfax, after all, was unable to prove the exception to the rule. In the winter and spring of 1872, it was believed by many people that he was more than receptive to the suggestion that he be placed forward as a candidate for the first place in opposition to Grant. Grant himself seems to have sensed the situation, and a coolness

---

[1]It will be remembered that in the convention at Chicago, while the Seward men refused to make any recommendation for the Vice-Presidency, they let it be known that they would be pleased by that of Hamlin.

developed between the two which was one factor in the denial of a renomination to him for the second place on the ticket.

Wilson, though an old anti-slavery man, disapproved of Grant's radical Southern policy, and had a low opinion of him as a civilian. Hayes and Wheeler were strikingly similar in origin and nature. One was born in Vermont; the parents of the other were born and bred there, and moved to the "Western Reserve" of Ohio only four years before his birth. Each attended a first-class "small college." Both were honest, industrious, generous, temperate, pure, and religious, true New Englanders of the best type, though, like the Hellenes of Italy or Asia Minor, they did their work, died, and were buried far from the Motherland. Between them and their families there quickly grew up a close intimacy. Mr. Wheeler was one of a small group which was accustomed to gather at the White House Sunday evenings for singing hymns and "genial conversation." "No cant, no assumed solemnity marred the hour. It was a time of Christian cheerfulness." Apparently the music was not wholly religious, since we are told that Wheeler sang "folk songs."

At the time of Wheeler's death, Hayes wrote of him in his diary, "He was one of the few Vice-Presidents who were on cordial terms—intimate and friendly with the President. Our family were heartily fond of him. He came often to the White House, and often expressed in strong language the pleasure his visits gave him. In character he was sterling gold."

Between Garfield and Arthur there came a definite separation almost from the first days of the administration. President Garfield and Senator Conkling quarrelled over New York patronage; Arthur unqualifiedly remonstrated against two of Garfield's appointments, and when the breach was complete Arthur supported Conkling. He is reported by an active New York politician to have told him that the President weakly truckled to Secretary Blaine and used tortuous methods. " 'Garfield has not been honorable, nor square, nor truthful with Conkling!' said Arthur in so many words. 'It is a hard thing to say of the President of the United States but it is, unfortunately only the truth. Garfield, spurred by Blaine, by whom he is easily led, has broken every pledge made to us; not only that but he seems to have wished to do it in the most offensive way.' "

This was unjust to the President. There is not space here for a full account of the affair, which may be found in the twenty-eighth chapter of Theodore C. Smith's *Life of James Abram Garfield*. Professor Smith makes a strong defense against most of the charges brought by the Stalwarts while admitting, perhaps minimizing, some errors of the President.

Vice-President Hendricks died after about only eight months' service, but already there were reports of dissension between him and Mr. Cleveland. The President represented the new reform; the Vice-President the old machine wing of the party, which, it was said, was planning to nominate Hendricks for President four years later. It was also reported that there had been friction between the two leaders over appointments. Hendricks' biographers, however, deny this and maintain that, though he made recommendations on proper occasions, he carefully avoided interfering.

Harrison and Morton lived on good terms, and the President favored the renomination of his Vice-President; but, like many leaders in Republican politics, Morton found Harrison unpleasantly independent. Harrison knew that he was the official head of his party and of the Nation, and intended to fulfill the duties and exercise the powers of his position. After the election, he wrote Morton, "desiring that he would approach him with the utmost frankness," and Morton replied, in effect, demanding that Messrs. Platt and Miller be made Secretaries of the Navy and of Agriculture, respectively. But the President-elect did not wish to do this. Morton then suggested that the choice for the Navy Department be postponed until a conference could be held in Washington. Harrison reluctantly agreed, but said that he must consider these appointments as national not State matters, that his New York friends were forgetting this, and that they must present for his consideration for Cabinet office not one but several candidates without mention of any special place. In the end Platt, as well as Miller, was omitted entirely, to the great wrath of the New York boss, who charged breach of faith.

Cleveland's second Vice-President, Adlai E. Stevenson, was even more a politician than Hendricks, and though the relations with his chief were outwardly friendly, they can hardly have been cordial.

McKinley and Hobart had their first meeting during the campaign. They were pleased with each other, but Hobart in his letter of acceptance and in his speeches defended the gold standard with more vigor and frankness than McKinley and Hanna thought wise.

When just before the inauguration Hobart reached Washington, he found McKinley's secretary waiting at the station with a request that he call. Hobart, of course, complied and his biographer[1] states that though the meeting was short," from that hour their hearts were knit together in mutual esteem and confidence. Their friendship was never broken by envy or jealousy." Hobart and McKinley were both tactful and conciliatory men. Hobart had taken up his residence in a mansion near the White House, a propinquity which made frequent and informal conferences easy. He was regarded by the President and the public as a junior colleague and was often referred to as the Assistant President. In the politics of Washington as in those of New Jersey, Hobart proved an excellent liaison officer. He gave a dinner to the Senate which McKinley attended. The Senators were seated at small tables where they could engage easily in conversation. The President passed from table to table in a friendly, informal way, and relations were better from that night.

Hobart kept the President and the Senate in touch. In 1898, he told him that unless he recommended war with Spain, the Senate would act independently. After the war began, the army in Cuba suffered from the con-

---

[1]David Magie, Life of *Garrett Augustus Hobart*, p. 168.

fusion and lack of supplies common at the beginning of every war and almost unavoidable when an army must be increased and sent abroad on the instant. The public turned in wrath upon the Secretary of War, General Alger. Alger was no Carnot or Stanton, but he was blamed for what was really due to a truly American reluctance to prepare for war in advance, and for the inherent difficulties of his problem. The gentle McKinley, however, shrank alike from facing the popular anger and from becoming its direct agent, and he induced Hobart, who was an intimate friend of the Secretary, to break the news to him that his resignation was desired.

The union between the President and the Vice-President was strengthened by that between their wives. Mrs. Hobart was both a kind-hearted woman and an experienced hostess, and she gladly assisted "The First Lady in the Land," whose health was feeble, in bearing the burdens of her many and onerous social duties.

The relation between Fairbanks and Roosevelt perhaps may be best described as one of covert hostility. In 1900, Fairbanks had begun to seek support in the Middle West as McKinley's successor, but accomplished little because of the strength of the sentiment for Roosevelt. Fairbanks was allied with the Old Guard and probably shared their fear of Roosevelt's "wildness." The friends of Roosevelt were inclined to regard Fairbanks as undesirable, timid, and hypocritical. "Mr. Dooley" ended a plea to Roosevelt not to go down in a submarine with the word, "If you do, take Fairbanks with you." Roosevelt read to Major Butt a reply of President Monroe to some clergymen of Portland, Maine, in which he said that religion in general would always have his support. Butt wrote his sister: "Why, by the side of these speeches, the remarks of our estimable Vice-President, Mr. Fairbanks, would seem most indiscreet if not positively indecent."

In 1904, Fairbanks told Lodge that he did not want the Vice-Presidency, and Lodge wrote Roosevelt that this convinced him that he did want it. It may be that Roosevelt himself used the sword, or dagger. Mr. Einstein says in his *Roosevelt—His Mind in Action*: "As he (Roosevelt) did not sympathize with Vice-President Fairbanks' ambition to succeed him, he felt intense pleasure when he discovered an opportunity to have cast on the latter a censorious ridicule because of the cocktail which the unfortunate Vice-President had been unwary enough to drink in his presence."

The situation when Taft and Sherman became President and Vice-President, respectively, had some resemblance to that of four years earlier. Sherman was Old Guard through and through. Taft was the choice of Roosevelt, and moderately Progressive. But Taft and Sherman, like McKinley and Hobart, were genial men who preferred the ways of peace; and matters began well. Taft made Sherman one of his golf companions and though Sherman's play was poor, and Butt warned his chief that his constant companionship with the Vice-President was giving offense in various quarters. Taft refused to hurt Sherman's feelings by dropping him.

On his part, Sherman gave the President shrewd counsel about getting legislation he wanted through Congress. Taft was very anxious for the passage of a postal savings bank bill. Sherman advised him to announce that as the party had declared in convention in favor of such legislation, no Republican Senator who voted against the bill would be allowed an atom of patronage. But Mr. Taft was inclined to be independent and to favor changes. Mr. Sherman, who was willingly a cog in the party machine, did not do so in the least. Taft desired a reduction in the tariff. Sherman and his friends were ultra-protectionists, and there came a rift between President and Vice-President, slight at first, then wide and deep, though not fully known to the world at large.

On July 30, 1909, Butt expressed a fear that the tariff conference report would prove a humiliation for Sherman. On May 8, 1911, he wrote his sister that at the theatre Taft had promptly sent some telegrams which he had received concerning the Mexican situation to Sherman and had talked with him in a very friendly way. But he added: "The President feels very badly over the report that the Vice-President is playing him false in New York but he forgives everything on the ground of human weakness."

After Roosevelt's return from Africa, he and Taft slowly and unwillingly opposed each other, to the great grief of mutual friends like Major Butt. Before the separation had become complete, there was sharp conflict between Roosevelt and the Republican organization in New York, and each looked to the President for aid. Mr. Taft endeavored to be neutral and worked for conciliation, with the result that he offended both sides. Sherman was bitterly angry and it is probable that Taft did not realize the impression which his action or non-action would give, and that Sherman could not be blamed for thinking him guilty of duplicity.

Roosevelt and his friends demanded that the President break utterly and forever with the Vice-President. Butt wrote his sister that Taft could not accept such terms, but prophesied that he would so act toward Sherman in the future as to alienate him completely without doing any good to himself. Taft shortly after published a letter which Butt thought most people would construe as an apology to Mr. Roosevelt and an insult to the Vice-President. Taft failed to attain a reconciliation with Roosevelt, but the two at least joined in vigorous condemnation of Sherman. President, Vice-President, and ex-President attended a banquet in honor of Cardinal Gibbons. All three spoke. The Vice-President adorned his oratory with quotations from the Bible, whereat Roosevelt said to Taft in a stage whisper: "When Jim Sherman quotes Scripture the devil must shake all hell with laughter"; and Taft replied: "I should think it would make the Cardinal feel like going out of business."

Wilson and Marshall remained on good terms, the latter acquiescing in the President's view that he was not "disabled" when absent in France or confined to his bed by a shock. Harding and Hoover invited Vice-Presidents

Coolidge and Curtis, respectively, to sit in their Cabinets; which invitations were loyally accepted, although both had been nominated by men opposed to their chiefs, and Curtis had had strong hopes of obtaining the nomination himself.

The relations between Messrs. Coolidge and Dawes were only outwardly harmonious. Dawes announced that he would not accept a seat in the Cabinet, which Coolidge had done from Harding, and though his statement was couched in terms most courteous to the President and gave excellent reasons against the Vice-President's holding such a place, politicians suspected that Mr. Dawes wished to keep himself morally free to work for the succession in 1928. On taking his seat, the Vice-President made a violent attack on the Senate rules, an action of which former Vice-President Coolidge disapproved, both because of its substance and its form.

While Mr. Dawes did not definitely and publicly approve the McNary-Haugen bill for an equalization fee on farm exports, he was credited with favoring it, and it was understood that he initiated a combination of the friends of the McNary bill and those of an act allowing branch banking, which passed both. The President approved the bank bill but was compelled by his judgment, conscience, and the political situation to veto the relief bill, a course which could not fail to injure him in the West. According to the *Outlook,* "Mr. Coolidge, it has been said, nearly got apoplexy when he realized how neatly the buck had been passed to him. A mutual distaste [Silent Cal and Hell-and-Maria must have been somewhat antipathetic] was considerably heightened, and this may eventually cost Dawes the Republican nomination and the Presidency."

At first thought, it may seem very strange that the Vice-President, who may at any moment become the head of the Nation, should not sit in the Cabinet as, to use a European term, Minister without portfolio, and so obtain a personal knowledge of the problems he may be called upon to solve. There is no legal obstacle. The Cabinet is the creation of custom, not law. No provision in the Constitution or the statutes requires the chief administrative officers to sit together as a council, though some of the wisest members of the convention foresaw such a result; and no date can be fixed for the establishment of the American Cabinet. At first, President Washington did not treat his heads of departments as a well-defined and standing council. He talked matters over with them individually, and in a few cases he asked the advice of all in writing on matters of general, rather than departmental, policy.

There are instances of the Vice-President being included in this group, but all of them occurred during the first five years of Washington's administration, before the members of the Cabinet had been clearly marked out as the official advisers of the President. In one of these cases the opinion of Madison was also sought, and in another that of Chief Justice Jay. Probably Adams sat in the evolving "Cabinet" but once. This was at its first session on April 11, 1791. Washington, who had begun a Southern tour. wrote to request that if business of importance should arise, the Vice-President and the Secretaries[1] should meet to consider if it were advisable for him to return to the capital. On April 11, 1791, the gentlemen named assembled, but decided that there was no reason for a change of plan.

When Adams was elected President, he expressed pleasure at the prospect of administering the office in conjunction with Jefferson, and this probably led some to believe that the latter would be offered a seat in the Cabinet. Such action, however, would have been a serious mistake. The Federalist-Republican feud would have at once manifested itself, and while a Cabinet may properly be a council of war whose members hold and defend contrary plans for defeating the common enemy, it should not itself be a field of battle. There was, however, no danger of so incongruous a union. The Hamiltonian Secretaries would have resigned at once had Adams attempted to thrust Jefferson among them.

Probably Adams himself would not have been willing to go so far, and to Jefferson the idea was abhorrent. He was a skillful chief of staff, who liked planning a campaign in his office, but he had none of that joy of the conflict which drives the born soldier into the thickest of the fray. Moreover, as often, he had constitutional theories which were in harmony with his personal desires. On January 22, 1797, he wrote to Madison concerning his taking a seat in the "executive Cabinet," "Both duty and inclination will shut that door to me. I cannot have a wish to see the scenes of 1793 revived as to myself and to descend daily into the arena like a gladiator to suffer martyrdom in every conflict. As to duty, the Constitution will know me only as the member of a legislative body; and its principle is that of a separation of legislative, executive and judiciary functions except in cases specified. If this principle be not expressed in direct terms yet it is clearly the spirit of the Constitution and it ought to be so commented and acted on by every friend to free government."

Jefferson found no reason, when he himself became President, to change his opinion of the proper place of the second officer of the government. Both his Vice-Presidents, Burr and Clinton, were opposed to Southern dominance. Burr's party loyalty soon became suspect, and the rough, narrow, and domineering Clinton would have been quite out of place in the Cabinet of the diplomatic, cultured Jefferson. There were similar objections, as far as loyalty was concerned, to Clinton's sitting in the Cabinet of Madison, with the added one that he had opposed Madison for the Presidency, even bolting what might fairly be described as the regular ticket. Moreover, the Cabinet was coming to be a well-recognized body of which the Vice-President was not a member. As early as 1800, Jefferson in a polite letter to Burr, assumed as a matter of course that the Vice-Presidency excluded the holder from the Cabinet.

Yet, many years later, this was not known to all. Taylor, whom Webster is said to have described as "an ignorant frontier Colonel," supposed, when

---

[1]Why the Attorney-General was excluded is not known. Perhaps the omission was due to the fact that it did not seem probable that there would be need of attending to any politico-legal question.

elected, that Vice-President Fillmore would be, *ex officio,* a member of his Cabinet; and, what is more surprising, when Hannibal Hamlin was nominated for Vice-President, the New York *Evening Post* said that ". . . . his long familiarity with public affairs will make him a wise and safe adviser in the Cabinet."

After the Civil War, there was consideration and discussion, from time to time, of how the Vice-Presidency might be made more attractive to first-class men. Three Vice-Presidents had succeeded to the chief place, and all had been condemned as traitors to party or principle. The most recent instance was that of "Andy" Johnson of Tennessee, whom the mass of the Republicans regarded as an ignorant drunken boor who bit the hand that fed him, and did his best to deliver the country and the helpless Freedmen into the hands of unrepentant rebels. Fillmore was moderate, refined, and courteous—so thoroughly a Whig that he may be said to have remained one after his party had dissolved. But the more radical wing that helped form, and gave the tone to, the Republican party, felt that he had turned away from righteousness, and they never forgot that he had approved the Fugitive Slave Law. Tyler had been formally repudiated by the Whigs; he was bitterly scorned and hated by the followers of Henry Clay; Webster finally turned against him; stories, exaggerated or false, which made him appear ridiculous, were widely circulated and believed; and when in 1886, young Mr. Roosevelt, the rising historian-politician, in his life of Thomas Hart Benton, described Tyler as the smallest of the Presidents, he expressed the general feeling at the North. It might be thought that if the Republicans denounced, the Democrats would praise. But Tyler and Johnson were deserters from their ranks. Fillmore fought against them all his life, and all three reached the Presidency by beating Democratic candidates. Later services might bring forgiveness for this, but not championship.

In 1877, President Hayes spoke strongly to Mr. Talcott Williams of the burden which the President had to carry, and his need of an assistant. But it was difficult to find a means of making the Vice-Presidency more attractive. To give him more power in the Senate would be considered contrary to the principle of equality of states. Moreover, he might be opposed to the dominating party. In October, 1896, an article by the Honorable Walter Clark in the *Green Bag* proposed that the Vice-President be placed at the head of a new Department of Interstate Commerce, in which would be grouped the work of the existing Interstate Commerce Commission, and of the bureaus dealing with the Pacific railroads and the Nicaragua Canal. It was urged that the plan would serve to make the office of Vice-President attractive to capable and ambitious men, and it was pointed out that no constitutional amendment would be necessary for putting it into practice. President McKinley's frequent and well-known consultations with Vice-President Hobart were partly due to a wish to increase the prestige of the second office of the government.

During the campaign of 1908, Mr. Bryan announced that if the Democrats won, he would invite the Vice-President, Mr. Kern, to become a member of the Cabinet. The advisability of such a course was widely discussed in the newspapers, but the victory of the Republicans made the promise a gesture merely. Presidents Taft and Wilson paid no such compliment to their Vice-Presidents, but during the campaign of 1920, Mr. Harding, following the example of Mr. Bryan, said that if elected, he should request Mr. Coolidge to sit in the Cabinet. After the election, Mr. Coolidge visited Mr. Harding, the invitation was renewed personally and cordially, and after some hesitation from fear, was accepted.

Talcott Williams wrote in the January 1, 1921, issue of the New York *Independent,* highly approving the experiment which Mr. Harding was to make. He said that the Vice-President could review the opinions of different Secretaries on bills which affected matters in their several departments, and represent the President in policy as well as in ceremonial speeches. "For these duties Vice-President Coolidge is precisely suited. He is a glutton for work in digging up all there is to be known about bills awaiting approval, and about departmental differences. He has the gift of expression. His speeches have many phrases, utterances and pithy pregnant sayings that move the public and yet bring no trouble. He can present a policy so that it commands attention and approval. He has dignity and weight. He may be dry but he never slops over. Lastly he is exactly the kind of silent, judicious, prudent mixer who brings people together, and such a link between the White House and the cloak-rooms of the Senate is greatly needed to fill the duties of an assistant President."

The death of President Harding, a scant year and a half after his inauguration, prevented the experiment from being tried for the natural four-year period, and the man who was responsible for it, from giving a calm judgment in retrospect. Mr. Coolidge, however, has stamped it with his approval, though only in part for the reasons given by Mr. Williams. He says in his *Autobiography*: "If the Vice-President is a man of discretion and character so that he can be relied upon to act as a subordinate in that position, he should be invited to sit with the Cabinet, although some of the Senators, wishing to be the only advisers of the President, do not look on that proposal with favor. He may not help much in its deliberations, and only on rare occasions would he be a useful contact with the Congress (House), although his advice on the sentiment of the Senate is of much value, but he should be in the Cabinet because he might become President and ought to be informed on the policies of the Administration. He will not learn all of them. Much went on in the departments under President Harding, as it did under me, of which the Cabinet had no knowledge. But he will hear much and learn how to find out more if it ever becomes necessary. My experience in the Cabinet was of supreme value to me when I became President."

It will be noted that Mr. Williams stresses the special, personal qualifications of Mr. Coolidge for sitting in the Cabinet; and that Mr. Coolidge differs somewhat from Mr. Williams in postulating a willingness on the part of the Vice-President to take a subordinate place, in the usefulness of a Vice-President in the Cabinet, and in laying special stress on the advantage to a President by succession of having had personal knowledge of the actual working of the Executive branch of the government. Of this there can be no doubt, but only six Vice-Presidents have been Presidents in the century and a quarter since the adoption of the Twelfth Amendment.[1] It has chanced also that three of them, Tyler, Johnson, and Arthur succeeded almost at the beginning of the Presidential quadrennium, and so would have derived very little benefit from experience in the Cabinet of their predecessor. Moreover, while Mr. Coolidge was ready to efface himself, it must be remembered that he was a calm, restrained man, and that he owed his seat to Mr. Harding. Later Vice-Presidents may be of a more assertive disposition, and may feel no gratitude for an invitation which custom has made mere form.

The Vice-President who followed Mr. Coolidge, Charles G. Dawes, deemed it best to remain outside the Cabinet. His reasons were an excellent summary of the objections to the inclusion of the Vice-President in that council. In an interview after his election as Vice-President, he said: "Long before I had any thought that I would have an individual interest in the question, I said the plan of having the Vice-President sit with the Cabinet was unwise. The Cabinet and those who sit with it always should do so at the discretion and inclination of the President. Our Constitution so intended it. The relationship is confidential and the selection of a confidant belongs to him who would be injured by the abuse of confidence, however unintentional. No precedent should be established which creates a different and arbitrary method of selection. Should I sit in the Cabinet meetings, the precedent might prove injurious to the country. With it fixed, some future President might face the embarrassing alternative of inviting one whom he regarded as unsuitable into his private conferences, or affronting him in the public eye by denying him what had been generally considered his right."

It remains to be seen whether the inclusion of Messrs. Curtis and Garner in the Cabinet has yet established such a custom.

------

[1]Tyler, Fillmore, Johnson, Arthur, Roosevelt, and Coolidge.

CHAPTER IV.

Social and Ceremonial Questions
of the Vice-Presidency

ALTHOUGH the second officer of the government frequently has had little to do with the first, yet in one respect he has become a true *vice;* he performs much service as substitute for the President in social affairs. From the beginning the Vice-President's political rank gave him precedence of all except the President, but his actual part in society varied with the personalities, tastes, and financial means of the different holders of the office. For the last fifty years, however, as society at Washington has grown more official and more ceremonious, the Vice-President has become the prize decoration for the tables of lion-hunting hostesses who are fortunate enough to catch him.[1]

He is also called on to play the host, himself, to distinguished visitors after the President has done so; and in his own right, to those whose position entitles them to special attention, but not to the great compliment of dining at the White House. He also does the honors to royal guests. Vice-President Stevenson paid this respect to the Infanta Eulalie, aunt of Alfonse XIII of Spain, when she represented her country and the royal family at the Columbian Exposition. Probably his duty was not over-pleasant. The Princess had exalted notions of her position, cared nothing about being on time, was rather fond of liquor, and rejected a suggestion that when Stevenson came to her she should rise and give him her hand. When, in 1931, the King of Siam arrived in Washington, the Vice-President and the Secretary of State met him at the station and also saw him off. Edwin G. Lowry, in his *Washington Close-Ups,* says of the Vice-President: "His day's work really begins when he gets to his hotel in the evening and finds his dress clothes laid out on the bed, His dress clothes are his working clothes; the overalls of a Vice-President.

---

[1]The President is not accustomed to dine out except twelve times in one season— once with each of the ten Cabinet members, with the Vice President, and the Speaker of the House respectively.

"By tradition and precedent the Vice-President is the diner-out of the Administration. Every night from November until May he must sally forth in his glad raiment, and eat for his party and his chief."

Yet the matter has its serious side. The choice foods, as well as the drinks, of Washington may be dangerous when indulged in to excess. There were rumors that the dinners which Vice-President Hobart gave and attended, broke down his health and caused his death. But rumors and even the written words of witty newspaper correspondents are often more interesting than reliable. The biographer of Mr. Hobart, David Magie, not an unbiased authority it is true, classes all these rumors as baseless. Although the Hobarts did entertain and go out to dinner often, even this was exaggerated by the newspapers. As the official diner-out for the President and practically always the highest ranking guest, he and Mrs. Hobart had the privilege of retiring early; and they almost always managed to be at home by half past ten. Mr. Hobart's temperament, too, was such that he particularly found rest and recreation, rather than a strain, in social life.

Ex-President Coolidge states in his *Autobiography* that the Vice-Presidential dining out is less than is supposed, that even in the season it does not on the average occur oftener than three times a week, that the Vice-President as the guest of honor has the privilege of arriving last and leaving first, and that he himself was usually home by ten o'clock. The testimony of this self-restrained scion of Vermont is good evidence that the Vice-Presidency need not be dangerous.

To some the social opportunities and duties of the place have been attractive; to others the reverse. Roosevelt wrote Lodge that Timothy Woodruff had told him frankly that he wanted the Vice-Presidency chiefly because he had plenty of money and could entertain. Morton and Hobart were even wealthier men than was Timothy of the glorious vest, but they were millionaires, accustomed to associate with persons of intelligence and culture; they dispensed a refined and liberal hospitality and doubtless enjoyed the social leadership which their office gave them, and their means and experience enabled them to maintain. Mr. Fairbanks' situation was somewhat similar. Vice-Presidents Stevenson, Marshall, and Coolidge were used to living modestly, and they cheerfully resigned themselves to occupying a suite at a hotel. Mr. Roosevelt felt differently. On February 2, 1900, he wrote to Lodge: "I have not sufficient means to run the Vice-Presidency as it ought to be run. I should have to live very simply and would always be in the position of 'poor man at a feast.' I would not care a snap of my finger for this if I went into the Cabinet or as a Senator or was doing a real bit of work but I should want to consider it when the office is in fact merely a show office."

But something more than money is needed to make the social throne of the Vice-Presidency a wholly easy seat. Its possessor is a high officer of a democracy called on to lead an aristocratic life. Such a situation is a difficult and dangerous one. The masses demand that equality be maintained, the classes that strict lines be drawn. An attempt to comply, in a measure, with the latter requirement was, perhaps, the chief cause of the defeat of Vice-President Colfax for renomination. Fairbanks and Sherman adopted what seemed to the Four Hundred a policy of the open door and so offended the elite. Major Butt wrote his sister that Fairbanks and his wife always desired political popularity, and "one cannot have this and cachet in the fashionable set at the same time." Later, in describing a reception of Sherman's, he said that such a one had not been seen since the days of Fairbanks; and Mr. Taft remarked as they passed the house: "It looks like a regular Vice-Presidential evening."

But society has troubles of its own. Publicists may ask: "Why is a Vice-President?" Masters of ceremonies ask: "Where?" As regards other citizens of the United States, indeed, his position has been fixed without difficulty. But what of Ambassadors? In monarchies they represent the person of the sovereign; republics are entitled to equal treatment for their legates and the claim may reasonably be made that Ambassadors should rank with heads of states.

For over a century the question did not arise in Washington; the United States sent no Ambassadors and therefore received none. But in 1893, immediately after the two countries had mutually raised the rank of their diplomatic representatives from that of Minister to Ambassador, Mr. Olney, President Cleveland's Secretary of State, allowed the British Ambassador, Sir Julian Pauncefote, to take precedence over Vice-President Stevenson. But when Sir Julian made a like claim in President McKinley's term, he was firmly resisted by Vice-President Hobart, and a war was on. In Society the person of inferior position makes the first call, and neither Vice-President nor Ambassador would do so. Sir Julian invited Mr. Hobart to a reception; Mr. Hobart's secretary replied that there must be a mistake as Sir Julian had not called on the Vice-President. The Ambassador declined invitations to various parties because he could not be assured of being placed above the Vice-President. He did, however, accept a carefully planned equality at a musicale at the Austrian Embassy.

President McKinley supported the Vice-President, and placed him in his own carriage at the dedication of Grant's tomb. The committee of arrangements had evaded the question of precedence by inviting the Ambassadors and Ministers not in their official capacity, but as distinguished guests. Hobart and Pauncefote brought no personal rancor into their official war, but neither would take the responsibility of yielding, since, by doing so, he would establish a precedent and, in effect, tell his successors to go way back and sit down. In 1897, Sir Julian had occasion to visit London, and he was there told that the government, while approving of his claim, would not insist upon it. Accordingly, on returning to Washington, he, Sir Julian, called on Mr. Hobart, and then through an intermediary requested President McKinley to give his final decision on the matter. The President replied: "Make my kind regards to Sir Julian and tell him there has never been a question that the Vice-President comes after me."

The reason for Great Britain's giving way was said to be that at European Courts the Heir Apparent takes precedence even of Ambassadors. The United States Government may have held, like John Adams, that there was a double headship of the State. During the contest Mrs. Hobart said sharply to President McKinley: "I thought the ticket elected was McKinley and Hobart, not McKinley and Pauncefote," and the President entirely concurred with her. The other Ambassadors who had been waiting for a settlement of the Hobart-Paunceforte matter now called on the Vice-President.

The precedent was generally regarded as authoritative for Washington society, but it did not absolutely establish a rule. In President Roosevelt's first term there was no Vice-President; in his second term Vice-President and Mrs. Fairbanks absolutely refused to accept invitations unless they were assured of first place in the absence of the President. The claim was usually admitted, but Congressman Draper said in his *Recollections of a Varied Career,* published in 1908, that a wise man would not ask the Vice-President to dinner at the same time as an Ambassador.

Another question has recently arisen which has convulsed Washington and the Nation with mirth. A husband *ipso facto* confers his rank upon his wife. But what if the Vice-President has no wife? May he appoint an official one to act as his hostess, and is she entitled to the honors of a spouse? Moreover, if the lady is married, where does her husband get off, or get on?

Former Vice-President Curtis is a widower. For some years his half-sister, Permelia Curtis, known to her friends as "Dolly," and wife of a Washington patent lawyer, Edward Everett Gann, called "Billy" by his wife and intimates, was a model sister, as duteous in life as in fiction. She was accustomed to act as her brother's careful, industrious, and efficient secretary; and, like other secretaries, she composed as well as typed many of the letters which bore her chief's signature. When Mrs. Curtis' health failed, she loyally took over many of the invalid's household and family cares and after her death, Mr. Curtis, his motherless children, his sister, and her husband made their home together. Mrs. Gann is described as a very energetic woman who enjoys being high up on the social ladder; and her brother was glad to show his appreciation of her help and affection by assisting to place her just below the topmost round.

But it is an inescapable fact that a sister is not a wife, and there was a dispute which recalled Jefferson's famous rule of pêle-mêle whereby regular seating at dinner was abolished, and when the meal was ready, each gentleman took the lady who was handiest and escorted her to the table. Mrs. Gann may be said to have spurred her horse to the fray before the trumpet sounded. Being invited to a dinner in honor of the wife of the retiring Secretary of Agriculture, although Mr. Curtis was not yet Vice-President, Mrs. Gann demanded and obtained assurance that she should be given precedence of the Cabinet lady. There is an important social organization, the Senate Ladies Luncheon Club, which is accustomed to choose the wife of the Vice-President as its President. The club now refused to choose Mrs. Gann, on the ground that she was only an honorary member, not being the *wife* of a Senator.[1] At an Easter Breakfast at the house of Mrs. Edward R. McLean, where most of the guests found places for themselves at small tables and a few of the élite were seated at a special table, Mr. Gann, who had supposed that the hostess of the Vice-President would be placed in a seat of the mighty, discovered too late that this was not the case and was obliged to leave his own quiet, well-selected table to rescue his abandoned and desolate wife and struggle with the herd for manger and fodder.

But there was a triad of the gods to compose social quarrels on Olympus. The greatest but least active was the President of the United States; next came the Secretary of State who must face those stirrers of strife, the diplomats and their wives; and last but greatest, the Supreme Judge of the Court of Etiquette, Alvin A. Adee, Assistant Secretary of State. To the out-going Secretary Mr. Kellogg, who was holding over until the arrival from the Philippines of his successor, Mr. Stimson, Mr. Curtis brought his tale of woe. Mr. Kellogg suggested that he submit a written statement that his sister was his official hostess, and when he did so, without giving an opportunity for further discussion, he ruled that international usage had long since established the rule in such matters; that while Mrs. Gann should be recognized as the hostess of the Vice-President, when entertaining in their own home, and so rank above all others, on other occasions she should rank below the wives of Ministers and Ambassadors.

But soon a new judge sat in the social court and to him Mr. Curtis appealed for a reversal of the Kellogg decision.[2] But, departing utterly from recent custom and especially from that of his immediate predecessor, Judge Stimson refused to take jurisdiction of this mighty cause, saying, "The State Department . . . . has no authority to determine questions of precedence among American officials nor of general social precedence in Washington, and it is my belief that it should no longer assist in such questions. I am therefore instructing the Department to give no further advice or suggestions in such matters."

On the day of this letter the Diplomats at Washington sent the Dean of their body, that is, the Ambassador of longest service, Sir Esme Howard, to Secretary Stimson with a memorandum stating that they hoped to have the honor of entertaining Mr. Curtis and Mrs. Gann very soon, and asking if the ruling of Secretary Kellogg was in force. The Secretary talked for an hour

---

[1] The Club considers the Vice-President as entitled to Senatorial privilege.

[2] It is said that the Vice-President's action in this affair was due not only to fraternal and personal feeling, but to a belief that he was a soldier in the eternal war between high officers of the United States and the Diplomatic Corps.

with the Ambassador, consulted President Hoover, and informed Sir Esme of what he had written the Vice-President, that the order of precedence in the houses of the diplomats rested with them, but he added that "any courtesy which they may show the Vice-President and to Mrs. Gann will be most agreeable to me." Sir Esme wrote in reply: "In these circumstances my colleagues and I, desirous, as already stated, of showing all possible courtesy to the Vice-President, will with great pleasure accord to his sister, Mrs. Gann, at all official and ceremonious diplomatic entertainments, until we can obtain some definite ruling on this point from a constituted American authority, the precedence due to the wife of a Vice-President of the United States."

The day was won and soon the victory was made manifest to all and sundry. The Chilean Ambassador gave a very elaborate dinner and took in Mrs. Gann, doing her the same honor that he would have paid to Mrs. Hoover. But few triumphs are absolutely complete, and Mrs. Gann found a lady who was very prominent in Washington society playing Mordecai to her Haman. This was Mrs. Alice Roosevelt Longworth, wife of the Speaker of the House. Kings in the persons of their Ambassadors might bow down, but not she. No longer "Princess Alice," she made no claim as daughter of a President, but the Speaker of the House was almost, if not quite, the equal of the Vice-President; his spouse might come after the wife of the Vice-President, but if that gentleman did not possess one, he must take, shall one say, the bitter with the sweet; no "official" substitute should go before the real thing. It was reported that Mrs. Longworth avoided parties where Mrs. Gann would attend. Yet, in this day of world-conferences to establish peace, even ladies' wars may end, and the fighters are said to have met in society and proclaimed their reconciliation with a cordial "Hello Dolly" and "Hello Alice," before "death threw down the warder."

Mrs. Gann doubtless enjoyed her triumph, but from the public she received not cheers, but laughter. Tom Heflin, indeed, paused in his attack on the Pope to proclaim that the official hostess of the Vice-President should not step down for any foreigner. "This is a serious issue—and if it aint settled the country is gone." But he was alone or nearly so in his treatment of the question. Arrows of sarcasm flew from all quarters. The Springfield *Union* in mock approbation of Heflin, asked: "Shall a lady who represents the best in the democratic social traditions of Kansas stand aside for those who have brought to America the artificial atmosphere of decayed monarchical courts? Shall a lady in whose veins flows the blood of the American Indian[1] take a second place to the descendants of European lords?" There were many references to Gilbert and Sullivan's opera of the *Mikado*. A cartoon in the Portland *Morning Oregonian* represented the "Social Precedence Storm" carrying away men and hats and "Farm Relief" and staggering Uncle Sam,

---

[1]This is an error. Mr. Curtis was of rather remote Indian descent through his mother, not his father.

while the Research Department of the Supreme Court was examining books on etiquette, and a man was studying "Etiquette by Cleopatra."

Senator Norris, who seems to enjoy ridiculing Vice-Presidents, wrote an open letter to the Secretary of State urging him to pass on the awful question at once. He said: "Until it is known definitely where the Vice-President's sister is going to sit, it will be impossible for many socially-minded Washingtonians to properly shine in society in accordance with their social and financial ambitions.

"The League of Nations, the World Court, the maintaining of a big Navy, the conducting of a war in Nicaragua, are all important and may affect the peace of the civilized world, but they sink into insignificance and fade into oblivion when compared with the great question that is now agitating the whole world as to where the Vice-President's sister shall sit at the dinner table.

"Either decide it without delay or officially report a disagreement on your part to the President of the United States and ask him to submit it to the World Court."

The *Literary Digest* said: "While the bulk of the comment throughout the country ran to ridicule, the Gann imbroglio was recognized in Washington as a threat of serious embarrassment to the Administration. Strong men shuddered at the possibility that the Vice-President might go on strike against his traditional job as the Government's representative diner-out. On the other hand, it was politically unthinkable to slap Mr. Kellogg on the wrist by reversing his ruling, and then there were the Diplomatic Corps and the Cabinet wives. However, the resourceful Mr. Stimson, after some days of suspense and agitated consultation, engineered a compromise which seemed to promise to bottle up the trouble for the time being."

Some, however, condemned the settlement as un-American. The Cleveland *Plain Dealer* wished precedence to be settled by a grand scramble. The Chicago *Tribune* expressed a similar view. It said: "Mr. Jefferson when President had a question of precedence on his hands but he, a true democrat, would have none of it. Mr. Merry, the British Minister, was sore, nearly unto war, but Mr. Jefferson stood by his point that the 'pêle-mêle' should prevail and he would have no other. When the dining room doors were open, and the bell invited the guests to come and get it, they went for it on their own. It was the system which prevailed for years on the American river steamboats. The ablest citizen got most of the butter and the largest part of the chicken.

". . . Precedence, with the pêle-mêle code governing, would be authentic and valid. The protocol is at variance with every true American conception of individual worth. The boarding house rush would conform to the simple nobility of the Republic."

Much anxiety was expressed concerning Mr. Gann. Senator Norris in his letter to the Secretary of State urged that officer to decide his fate also. Later, in another letter, the Senator said that, as he had feared, Mr. Gann "was left wholly unprovided for," but "I refuse to abandon him in this crisis. I do not intend to let this matter rest until I am assured he will have at least a snack wherever he goes."

William Hard, however, maintained in the Washington *Evening Star* that reason showed that Mr. Gann stood on the heights. He said: "Mrs. Gann, however, is but the beginning of the misery of the State Department in this matter. The swelling climax of it is Mr. Gann. A wife is equal to her husband. An 'official hostess' is equal to a wife. Therefore, an official hostess is equal to a husband who has chosen her for his official hostess. But a husband, conversely, is equal to a wife. Mr. Gann, therefore, is equal to Mrs. Gann. Mrs. Gann, however, is equal to a Vice-President. Things which are equal to the same thing are equal to each other. Therefore, Mr. Gann must precede Ambassadors. Can you find any weakness in that reasoning? You can not! It is simply a case where the extreme of logic is the extreme of insanity.

"It is only hoped that Mr. Gann, finding his wife 'the official hostess' of the Vice-President and quite busy at the job, will not go and adopt some nice lady to be his own official hostess in Washington official society. Then on the principle that things that are equal to the same things are equal to each other, Mr. Gann's official hostess being equal to him and therefore to Mrs. Gann and therefore to the Vice-President, would have to precede Ambassadors' wives, too."

It will be observed that men who have described the social duties of the Vice-President have often written in a rather frivolous vein and with little respect for the office, nor are they the only ones to treat it lightly. Indeed, the very holders of the position themselves have frequently spoken of it as an almost worthless thing, a kingdom for a *roi fainéant*. The first Vice-President, John Adams, wrote to his wife: "My country has in its wisdom contrived for me the most insignificant office that ever the invention of man contrived or his imagination conceived." Jefferson also recognized the emptiness of the Vice-Presidency, but professed to find this a recommendation. He wrote to Doctor Benjamin Rush that he preferred his home to any public office. "If I am to act, however, a more tranquil and unoffending station could not have been found for me nor one so analogous to the dispositions of my mind; it will give me philosophical evenings in winter and rural days in the summer." (When Congress was not in session.) The victorious candidate then proceeded to thank the Philosophical Society of Philadelphia, of which Dr. Rush was a prominent member and vice-president,[1] for some bones of "an animal of the lion kind but of a most exaggerated size," and to express his own astonishment at the creature. One is reminded of the famous letter, written four years later, in which President-Elect Jefferson joined an offer of the Secretaryship of the Navy with a description of the bones of a supposed mammoth and a report of a story of a mountain of salt.

---

[1] The term philosophy was then applied to natural science as well as metaphysics.

Roosevelt, while considering the question of accepting the nomination for Vice-President, expressed an opinion of the nature of the office like that of Jefferson, but, as would be expected of the apostle of the strenuous life, differed with him entirely as to its desirability. He wrote to Lodge: "The chance of a Vice-President to do anything is really infinitesimal. I suppose that I should have leisure to take up my historical work again but that is about all." Years afterward he told the New York Historical Society: "In fact, gentlemen, I came to the conclusion while in Europe that a constitutional monarch has the same place in government as a perpetual Vice-President and that is rating them pretty low."

This appraisement doubtless amused its hearers, and Roosevelt is not the only Vice-President who has made a jest of his own insignificance. Breckinridge and Stevenson laughed at it, though perhaps with a tinge of bitterness. It is said that "James S. Sherman smiled a good deal over being Vice-President; and Thomas R. Marshall was the author of a whole catalog of Vice-Presidential jokes. He delighted in the self-inflicted epigram, 'I come from Indiana, the mother of Vice-Presidents, the home of more second-class men than any other state.'" He also said: "Since the days of John Adams there has been a dread and fear that some Vice-President of the United States would break loose and raise Hell and Maria[1] with the Administration. Everything that can be done, therefore, is done to furnish him with some innocuous occupation. They seek to put him where he can do no harm. Among the other nameless, unremembered things given him to do is the making him a Regent of the Smithsonian Institution. There if anywhere he has an opportunity to compare his fossilized life with the fossils of all ages."

Other men in public life, the press, politicians and students of American government have joined with Vice-Presidents in treating their position as insignificant. When, in 1789, the question of using titles in addressing high officers of state was much discussed, Franklin is said to have proposed calling the Vice-President "His Superfluous Excellency," and the joke has often been repeated. When, in 1804, the method of electing the Vice-President was changed, a Senator said in debate: "It has of late become fashionable to attach very little importance to the office of Vice-President, to consider the matter of small consequence whoever the man may be, to view his post merely as an idle post of honor, and the incumbent as a cypher in the government or, according to the idea expressed by an honorable gentleman from Georgia, quoting I believe some Eastern politician, as a fifth wheel to a coach."

In the House, Representative Thomas Lowndes of South Carolina said that the Vice-Presidency was a situation certainly not calculated to inspire or satisfy the aspirations of an ambitious man. When, in 1822, the younger Patrick Henry urged Henry Clay to make DeWitt Clinton President with

---

[1] A reference to the famous exclamation of future Vice-President Dawes when testifying before a Senate committee which was investigating expenditures during the war.

certainty of the succession, he told the Kentuckian that meanwhile he would have the choice of the Vice-Presidency or the Secretaryship of State, and that "the former would keep you out of turmoil and responsibility, and perhaps be the safest place. You would be happy in it, honored and supported by everybody."

Hendricks' biographers say of him that "he never sought or aspired to the position he held (the Vice-Presidency) and its quiet and negative functions far more suited to his active genius." Instances have been noted in previous chapters of the use of the Vice-Presidency as a cushioned seat for elderly retired statesmen, or as small change to buy off minor candidates for the Presidency, or to secure local support for the Presidential nominee.

Quips on the nonentity of Vice-Presidents have appeared in the newspapers repeatedly. One ran somewhat as follows:

> *Reporter.* I have accidentally discovered that the late Mr. Jones
> was at one time Vice-President; shall we mention it in his obituary?
> *Editor.* Oh, no! Notice only important matters.

After the election of Hobart in 1896, the Chicago *News* said that he "will not be seen nor heard from until after four years when he emerges from the impenetrable vacuum called the Vice-Presidency." Half a century later, the *New Republic* expressed a similar opinion, saying: "According to Hoyle the Vice-President is entitled to one squawk (on taking the chair of the Senate) before the total eclipse; after that he gets about as much attention as a book-agent in Hollywood." A popular hit on the stage was a reference to a man whose two brothers disappeared; one went West and was never heard of again; the other became Vice-President.

Publicists have been very severe in their condemnation of the Vice-Presidency, because of its insignificance. Bryce called the office "ill-conceived," and Woodrow Wilson said that "the chief embarrassment in describing it is that in saying how little there is to be said about it one has evidently said all that there is to say." In a later book Mr. Wilson expressed the opinion that "the Vice-President of the United States has become even more insignificant than the Constitution seemed to make him."

It is natural that the holder of this dignified, but not specially onerous position, has received a salary and perquisites much less than those allowed the President. In 1789, the President's salary was fixed at twenty-five thousand dollars, that of the Vice-President at five thousand. Probably the Federalists would gladly have been more liberal to the second officer. Gouverneur Morris wished to give him eight thousand dollars, alleging that he must entertain the foreign ministers, since the dignity of the President would not allow him to do so.

In 1791, Hamilton wrote Adams that he hoped that "the starvation policy will not continue fashionable." But there was no change in salary until 1853 when the salaries of the Vice-President and the members of the Cabinet were raised to eight thousand dollars.[1] In 1873, the Vice-President was given the benefit of the notorious Salary Grab Act, his salary being raised to ten thousand dollars a year, from the beginning of the Congress passing the law. But in 1874, the act was repealed; and the Vice-President was obliged to content himself with the former salary until 1907 when he was given twelve thousand dollars. In 1925, the salary was made fifteen thousand.

There have been proposals to give the Vice-President not only a salary but a residence. Wealthy Vice-Presidents have bought or leased some of the finest houses in the capital; others of modest means have taken rooms at the New Willard which have come to be known as the Vice-Presidents' Suite. Mr. Coolidge in his *Autobiography* says that he was well satisfied with living at the Willard, but that the American principle of equality requires that all Vice-Presidents should be on the same footing. An aged lady, Mrs. John B. Henderson, the wealthy widow of a Speaker of the House of Representatives, has offered to give her mansion to the United States for a Vice-Presidential home, but it remains to be seen if Congress will accept what might prove to be a white elephant of the largest size. Unless the Vice-President is always to be a rich man the government would be called on to maintain and furnish the junior White House and the cost would be heavy.

The President stands in a class by himself; but once furnish residences to other officials at Washington, and there would always be a clamor for more and more. The House of Representatives is unwilling to acknowledge that the Senate is superior and might demand that its presiding officer, who has considerable social duties, be placed on an equality with the President of the Senate. The Secretary of State is brought into constant social relations with foreign diplomats and guests of high position; why should he not be enabled to entertain them in the manner practiced by other great countries? But the Cabinet is a unit; the Secretary of State is at most only *primus inter pares,* if he is that; should not his colleagues also be provided with homes? What of the Chief Justice of the Supreme Court, the head of the most august and powerful judicial body in the world, which stands on an equality with the President and Legislature in our triplex government, and which, within limits, can annul the acts of both; shall not he be given a suitable home where he can live in the dignity and ease so appropriate to his office?

---

[1]Heretofore Cabinet officers did not receive equal amounts. But after this date, all of them and the Vice-President were allowed the same compensation.

CHAPTER V.

The Succession to the Presidency

IF THE custom of the Vice-President's sitting in the Cabinet becomes fixed, the importance of the office will be considerably increased. Moreover, the Vice-President is *ex officio* President of the Senate, a position of some power and, for a pleasant, tactful man, of considerable influence. The duties of a "spare" in the Executive Department and of the chairman of a branch of the Legislative have no natural relation, and the part played by the Vice-President as President of the Senate will be considered in the following chapter. But whatever the importance of the Vice-President while he retains his office, all agree that his real significance is in his possibility of transformation. This has taken place six times and it is a curious fact that on three of these occasions the Vice-President was at a distance from the place where the President died.

The first vacancy in the Presidency was that caused by the death of William Henry Harrison, which took place in the city of Washington on April 4, 1841, at 12:30 a. m. Vice-President Tyler was then at his estate near Williamsburg, Virginia. Members of the Cabinet immediately issued a formal announcement of the death, which stated that they believed it was their duty so to do as Congress was not sitting and the Vice-President was absent from the capital. They also signed a letter addressed to "Vice-President Tyler," informing him of what had happened. It was at once sent by the hands of Fletcher Webster, the chief clerk (then the second officer) of the Department of State, who was accompanied by Robert Bealle, assistant doorkeeper of the Senate.

Such good speed was made by these gentlemen and by Mr. Tyler himself, that the latter arrived at Washington on April 6 at 4 a. m., having covered two hundred and thirty-one miles in twenty-one hours. He went immediately to Brown's Hotel, where he had stayed at the inauguration. At noon he was waited upon by all the members of the Cabinet except the Secretary of the Navy, George E. Badger, who was on a visit to his home in North Carolina. Mr. Tyler made a very brief speech expressing his grief at the death of Harrison, his sense of the responsibilities which had devolved upon him, and his wish that the heads of departments should retain their places. He then took and subscribed the oath of office before the Chief Justice of the District of Columbia, William Cranch, who made a formal written certificate of the act.

The Chief Justice of the United States, Roger B. Taney, was at Baltimore and refused to come to Washington because he had not received a direct official invitation. Notice of the death of President Harrison had been sent to him immediately, and on the following day the clerk of the Supreme Court, Mr. Carroll, wrote to him by request of Secretary Webster "to say not only that it would be highly gratifying that you would be present on Wednesday, at the funeral, but also that the Cabinet would be pleased to see and confer with you at this most interesting moment." Judge Taney replied that he believed that the head of a coördinate branch of the government should not attend the funeral without a special invitation from the Cabinet or the Vice-President. He protested, however, that he did not think that there was any disrespect or unkindness intended by the omission, and forbade Carroll to mention his letter to the Vice-President or to the Cabinet; it was intended, Taney said, to answer such inquiries as Carroll might think proper, and so prevent a misconstruction of his own motives.

It will be noted that there was not the extreme haste in taking the oath which has been thought advisable on similar occasions in recent years. Indeed Tyler himself believed the act to be unnecessary, and that the oath which he had taken as Vice-President was sufficient. He only took a second oath for greater precaution and because doubts might arise, and a statement to this effect was incorporated by Judge Cranch in his certificate. Chief Justice Taney had been consulted by Carroll on this matter, but had declined giving an opinion for reasons similar to those which prevented him from attending the late President's funeral.

President Lincoln was shot the evening of April 14, 1865, a few minutes past ten, while sitting in his box at Ford's Theatre. The assassin, John Wilkes Booth, had gained access to the President's box and shot him at short range. It was seen at once that the wound was mortal, and the President was hastily removed to a house across the street.

While the theatre was in the utmost of confusion, there was at least one in the audience who showed an admirable presence of mind. Ex-Governor Farwell of Wisconsin, realizing at once the need of informing the Vice-President and of caring for his safety, rushed to the Kirkwood House where Mr. Johnson was staying; called to clerks to place guards at the door, the stairway, and Johnson's room; and ascending to the Vice-President's chamber, pounded on the door crying: "Governor Johnson, if you are in, I must speak to you." Johnson, who had retired, admitted his visitor without stopping to dress and was overcome by emotion at the news.

About two in the morning, Mr. Johnson, in spite of the remonstrances of friends, insisted on visiting the house where Mr. Lincoln had been carried.

Refusing an escort, he went on foot, accompanied by Farwell, who could serve as a guide, and Major O'Beirne, the commander of the Provost Guard. His one precaution was to partly conceal his face by pulling down his hat and turning up his collar. After remaining about half an hour, Johnson and O'Beirne returned to the hotel.

A few years later, Moorfield Storey, then the secretary of Charles Sumner, was at supper with his employer and Stanton. The latter told him that he had sent for Johnson, and Sumner said that he had got him away as Mrs. Lincoln disliked him. But these were the recollections of men who had become bitter enemies of Johnson. All the other evidence indicates that the Vice-President went of his own initiative. Sumner's statement is, however, of some importance because a story that Johnson was under the influence of liquor when he and the President visited Richmond after its surrender and that Lincoln wished to avoid him, ultimate y rests on Mrs. Lincoln's authority.

President Lincoln expired the morning after he was shot, at twenty-two minutes past seven. All the members of the Cabinet were at the death bed except the wounded Secretary of State, William H. Seward, and the Secretary of the Treasury, Mr. McCulloch, who had helped keep the vigil throughout the night, but had departed shortly before. After Rev. Doctor Gurley had offered prayer, the Cabinet officers withdrew to another room and signed a paper drawn by Attorney-General Speed informing the Vice-President of the death of Mr. Lincoln, and advising that he take the oath of office at once. Mr. Speed, as the law officer of the government, and Secretary McCulloch who, next to Mr. Seward, was ranking member of the Cabinet, were chosen to carry the paper to Mr. Johnson. But they were anticipated at the Kirkwood by General Halleck, who called for a moment to tell Johnson that he must not go out without a guard, and Johnson understood by this warning that Lincoln was dead.

When Messrs. McCulloch and Speed arrived at the hotel, they found Chief Justice Chase there, and there was some discussion of the time and place of administering the oath of office to the new President. It was agreed, in accordance with the wish of Mr. Johnson, that the place should be the parlor of the hotel and ten o'clock the time. The Chief Justice and the Attorney-General then went to the latter's office to look up the precedents furnished by the accessions of Tyler and Fillmore, and to examine the Constitution and the laws.

At ten or a little later, a group of some twelve or fourteen gentlemen, including the Vice-President and the Chief Justice, the members of the Cabinet, two or three Senators and ex-Senators who had remained in Washington after the close of the special session of the Senate, Francis P. Blair, Sr., and his son Montgomery, gathered in the parlor of the Kirkwood. Mr. Chase pronounced the oath of office word by word. Mr. Johnson repeated it and solemnly kissed an open Bible. His lips touched the twentieth verse of the eleventh chapter of Ezekiel, "But *as for them* whose heart walketh after the heart of their detestable things and their abominations, I will recompense their way upon their own heads, saith the Lord God." As Mr. Johnson believed that treason should be made odious and some of the leading rebels executed, there was a grim appropriateness in the passage. Mr. Johnson's biographer, Lloyd Paul Stryker, in his *Andrew Johnson, A Study in Courage,* says the ceremony ended, "the Greenville tailor was President of the United States." Chase, who himself had so earnestly and vainly desired the Presidency, wrote in his diary: "He (Johnson) was now the successor of Mr. Lincoln. I said to him, 'May God guide, support and bless you in your arduous labors.' The others then came forward and extended their sad congratulations."

〔 President Garfield was shot at the railroad station in Washington on July 2, 1881. Vice-President Arthur was then on his way by steamboat from Albany to New York, and heard the news on his arrival. He also received a notification from the Cabinet that he should be prepared to take the oath at any moment, and late the same day proceeded to Washington. There he was waited on by Mr. Blaine, the Secretary of State, with a similar message; but a little later there came word by an orderly that the immediate danger had passed 〕

Mr. Blaine, however, made it a practice to call daily and report the condition of the President. For a while this seemed to improve but the infection caused by the wound spread, and on August 26 and 27 the physicians abandoned hope. They informed the Cabinet that death was near, and Arthur was notified. Then there was another rally; and on September 6, to gratify a longing of the President for the sea and to take a last desperate chance for recovery, Mr. Garfield was moved to the sea coast at Elberon near Long Branch, New Jersey. But the change was of no avail, and on September 19 he died.

Those members of the Cabinet who were at Elberon telegraphed Mr. Arthur, who had returned to New York when it had seemed that the President might recover. "It becomes our painful duty to inform you of the death of President Garfield and to advise you to take the oath of office as President of the United States without delay. If it concurs with your judgment, we will be very glad if you will come here on the earliest train tomorrow morning." Preparations had been made, and on September 20 at 2 a. m., the new President was sworn in at his house by Justice John R. Brady of the Supreme Court of the State of New York in the presence of members of the family and friends, among whom were District Attorney Rollins and Elihu Root. Notice was at once sent by telegraph to Long Branch and Washington.

〔 At nine, Secretaries Blaine, Lincoln, and Postmaster-General James, who lived in New York City, had called on President Arthur and later in the day all proceeded to Elberon.〕 On the twenty-first they accompanied the remains of the late President to Washington. On September 22 the President went to the Vice-President's room at the Capitol, and in the presence of a small group of distinguished men, which included ex-Presidents Grant and Hayes, was again sworn into office by Chief Justice Waite.

A double oath by the President was not unprecedented. In 1821 and 1877, March fourth fell on Sunday, and the public inauguration was held on Monday. Monroe and Hayes, however, were privately sworn in on March 3 and 4, respectively, by the Chief Justice before a few witnesses. But in 1853, when the fourth of March also fell on Sunday, Pierce took no oath until the fifth, and, unless the requirement that the President take an oath or affirmation to protect the Constitution be directive only, it would appear that the United States was a day without a President.

President McKinley was shot on September 6, 1901, while holding a reception at the Buffalo Exposition. The news reached Vice-President Roosevelt when he was concluding a speech near Burlington, Vermont. He hastened at once to Buffalo and remained there two days. Then, informed that the President was out of danger and wishing to calm the public mind, he joined his family in the Adirondacks. On September 13, while they were picnicking on Mount Tahawus, a guide appeared with two telegrams from the President's secretary. The first stated that Mr. McKinley was much worse; the second, that Mr. Roosevelt should come to Buffalo at once.

The Vice-President and the guide walked ten miles to a club house, arriving after dark. There, with difficulty, they obtained a horse and wagon and drove at high speed through the dark over a thirty-five-mile road that was little more than a trail, changing horses wherever possible. It was a rash act. Probably there would be little harm if the country should be without a President for a few hours. It might be serious if the Vice-President should be killed as well as the President, and still more so if he should be badly injured and lie between life and death for months as Garfield did. True, Mr. Roosevelt had been assured that the President would recover, and a show of optimism on his part helped business; but doctors are not infallible, and the Vice-President should have remained close to the telegraph and railroad.

At the station Mr. Roosevelt found awaiting him his private secretary, Mr. Loeb, a special train, and news that President McKinley was dead. At Buffalo, by advice of Elihu Root, the Secretary of War and one of the leading lawyers of the country, the new President took the oath at once. It was administered at the house of Ansel Wilcox by Judge John R. Hazel. All constitutional and legal requirements had been fulfilled, and President Roosevelt did not repeat the oath at Washington.

The last and the most dramatic of the accessions of a Vice-President to the Presidency was that of President Coolidge. On the morning of August 2, 1923, Mr. Coolidge, his wife, and his two sons were visiting his father, John C. Coolidge, at the old home in the hamlet of Plymouth Notch, one of several small villages which made up the town of Plymouth, Vermont. President Harding was ill at San Francisco, and the Associated Press, the United Press, and several metropolitan papers had sent representatives to the town of

Ludlow, a few miles from Plymouth. These gentlemen arranged for a high-powered automobile to be ready at their call that they might rush to the Coolidge farm at any moment. But soon the news from Mr. Harding's bedside made these preparations seem wholly unnecessary. Half the visiting journalists were withdrawn and on August 2 Mr. Coolidge, when passing through Ludlow, expressed his surprise that any were left, and his belief that all would be gone by nightfall. All did depart the next day, but for a very different reason from that which moved Mr. Coolidge to his prophecy.

The Vice-President spent the evening quietly with the family, and made the remark, casually, to a member of the company, shortly before retiring, that he believed the President now entirely out of danger and on the road to recovery. A little before one (Daylight Saving Time), he was awakened by his father's coming up the stairs and calling his name in an unsteady voice. The elder Coolidge was a man of great self-control, and his son felt at once that something of much importance had occurred. It had, indeed. John Coolidge had always cherished high ambitions for his son, and had shrunk from no effort or hardship to give the boy an education which would fit him for a great place; now he was rewarded by the solemn privilege of informing him that he was President of the United States.

The news had been brought by W. A. Perkins, of Bridgewater, who owned and operated a small private telephone line from Bridgewater to Plymouth. He carried two telegrams, one from the late President's secretary, G. C. Christian, the other from the New York *Times*. Each stated the fact of President Harding's decease. The secretary briefly mentioned the circumstances and the probable cause of the death. The newspaper with true journalistic enterprise added: "We will appreciate any statement you care to have us publish." The reporters at Ludlow reached the Coolidge home about five minutes after Mr. Perkins, a paper in Boston having telephoned Ludlow on receipt of the news.

Upstairs, Mr. and Mrs. Coolidge were dressing, and Mr. Coolidge tells us in his *Autobiography* that "before leaving the room I knelt down and, with the same prayer with which I have since approached the altar of the church, asked God to bless the American people and give me power to serve them." About fifteen minutes after receiving the news, Mr. and Mrs. Coolidge came downstairs. Mr. Coolidge says: "My first thought was to express my sympathy for those who had been bereaved and, after that was done, to attempt to reassure the country with the knowledge that I proposed no sweeping displacement of the men then in office and that there were to be no violent changes in the administration of affairs."

The telegrams which had been received were read aloud by Mrs. Coolidge, and the messages to Mrs. Harding and to the American people were dictated by Mr. Coolidge; the first was signed by Mrs. Coolidge, also. Mr. Coolidge gave great attention to the drafting of the second document, "took much time in preparing it," wrote the impatient *Times* correspondent. But after spending ten minutes waiting for an interview, and half an hour with Mr. Coolidge, the eager reporters were able to jump into their automobile and rush back to Ludlow and a telegraph office, leaving Mr. Coolidge in perplexity and isolation. He may have been uncertain whether he was President or Vice-President. Secretary Christian had avoided the question by sending his telegram to "Mr. Calvin Coolidge"; the New York *Times,* however, had given him the benefit of the doubt, if indeed it felt any, and addressed him as "President Coolidge."

The Constitution requires the President to take a specific oath before exercising the duties of his office, and what were the precise words of that oath? At the end of his statement to the people the new chief executive had said, "It is my intention to remain here until I can secure the correct form for the oath of office, which will be administered to me by my father, who is a notary public, if that will meet the necessary requirement." Plymouth Notch had an independent telephone company, a farmers' line with a station in a near-by general store formerly carried on by Mr. Coolidge's father; but the long distance connection was often unsatisfactory. However, a broken conversation was held with Washington, and the advice of the Attorney-General that the oath should be taken at once, and the information that the President might be sworn in by any person who was legally competent to administer oaths, was obtained.

Meanwhile, the elder Coolidge had found in his library a book containing the oath; and there followed an act unparalleled in history, the induction into office of the head of a republican nation by his father. Mr. Coolidge says in his *Autobiography*: "Where succession to the highest office in the land is by inheritance or appointment, no doubt there have been kings who have been inducted into office, but in republics, where the succession comes by an election, I do not know of any other case in history where a father has administered to his son the qualifying oath of office which made him the chief magistrate of a nation. It seemed a simple and natural thing to do at the time, but I can now realize something of the dramatic force of the event."[1]

The *mise-en-scène* and the act itself were thus described in the New York *Times* of August 3 and 4. The furnishings are "those of the ordinary New England farm house of the better class. The faint light of an old fashioned kerosene lamp with a fluted top chimney and etched sides, was sufficient to throw the faces of the President and his father into bold relief. Back of the President was a large framed portrait of himself which occupies the position of honor in his father's home . . . . although there are several small, well chosen prints of figures and landscapes. . . . .

---

[1]Mr. Coolidge need not have excluded monarchies, provided they were Christian. Kings may have officiated at the coronation ceremonies of their sons, but the actual crowning has been done by an ecclesiastic. The oath, too, has been administered by an ecclesiastic except in Aragon where it was given by the Justiciar, who was never the father of the King.

"The President's father, sturdy and active, despite his years [78] stood at the south side of a small centre table that held the lamp, the family Bible and a number of other books." The Bible, which had belonged to Mr. Coolidge's mother, was not officially used, as "it is not the practice in Vermont or Massachusetts to use a Bible in connection with the administration of an oath."

At the swearing in of every other Vice-President as President, there have been witnesses who were persons of high official rank and of present or future national reputation. Among the little group in the country sitting room, watching a plain farmer induct his son into an office which for combined dignity and power has no equal in the temporal world, there were Mr. Coolidge's wife, his secretary, stenographer, chauffeur, and by a sort of chance, a representative of the press, of the bureaucracy, and, technicalities being waived, of the National Legislature. These were Joseph H. Fountain, editor of the Springfield (Vermont) *Reporter,* S. L. Lane, a superintendent of the mail service and president of the Railway Mail Association of New England, and ex-Congressman Porter H. Dale, who had just resigned his seat in the United States House of Representatives to become a candidate, a successful one as it proved, for a vacant Senatorship. Mr. Dale lived, and Mr. Lane was visiting, in a neighboring town. They had heard the news over the radio and hastened to the Coolidge home. Outside, looking through the open doors and windows, were friends and neighbors of the hamlet, who had been roused by the coming and going of autos and had learned of the honor which had come to their former townsman. Curiously enough, neither of Mr. Coolidge's sons was present. The elder had gone to a military training camp the afternoon before and the younger, a boy just fifteen, was sleeping so soundly that it was thought best to leave him undisturbed.

The oath was taken at 2:47 Eastern Standard Time, four hours and seventeen minutes after the death of President Harding. Mr. and Mrs. Coolidge then withdrew to their room, and the little company broke up. The isolation of the new President did not last long. At three-thirty full telephone connection had been made with the outside world, and Mr. Coolidge was talking with his private secretary, Edward T. Clark, in Washington. Special precautions were also taken for the safety of the President. S. L. Lane, president of the Railway Mail Association of New England, declaring that the people of the United States would wish their President to be protected, kept guard at the door nearly all night. He was relieved toward morning by a United States Marshal, A. M. Harvey of Chester, who, while pursuing bootleggers, had heard of the death of Mr. Harding, and on his own responsibility proceeded to Plymouth. He in turn was relieved by a member of the National Secret Service.

A vacancy in the Presidency may be caused not only by death but by removal, as the result of conviction on impeachment, or by resignation. As yet, no such cases have occurred, although President Johnson narrowly escaped conviction, and there were rumors that Washington, who had accepted the Presidency unwillingly from a sense of duty to the country, and Wilson, who had been prostrated by a shock, intended or contemplated resigning. It was alleged by President Jackson's enemies during the campaign of 1832 that he sought reëlection only as a "vindication"; that immediately thereafter, because of his frail health, he would resign and go home, leaving the Presidency to Mr. Van Buren. There seems, however, never to have been the slightest foundation for such an assertion.

There is another power and duty of the Vice-President of the most delicate nature—that of acting as President when the President is disabled. This has never been done though it can not be said that the question has never arisen. The Constitution provides no means of determining if a disability exists. The omission was pointed out in the convention. Dickinson of Delaware asked: "What is the extent of the term 'disability,' and who is to be the judge of it?"

Every effort has been made to avoid deciding these questions, and it has so happened that circumstances have been specially favorable for evasion. Nearly all executive duties are performed by Cabinet and subordinate officers subject to the direction of the President when he chooses to exercise it. He must indeed use his personal judgment in approving or vetoing bills. But during the last sicknesses of Presidents Harrison, Lincoln, Garfield, and Harding, Congress was not in session. Taylor's illness was of a few days only, the Senate was absorbed in the struggle over the Compromise of 1850, there were no bills needing his signature, and no other duties sufficiently pressing to raise the question of disability.

The last illnesses of all the Presidents who died in office, except that of Mr. Garfield, were short. His extended from the second of July to the nineteenth of September. The doctors forbade him to attend to public affairs. On the one occasion when the members of the Cabinet spoke to him on the subject, they saw him separately and by agreement among themselves, all made entirely favorable reports. The President performed but one official act. With difficulty and by using an apparatus that had been specially prepared, he affixed his name to a warrant for extradition which would have been invalid without his signature.

It would seem that Vice-President Arthur had a full right to act as President, but from an honorable delicacy and perhaps from regard to the feelings of the people, who would have regarded such an assumption of power as an outrage on the helpless President, he refrained from doing so. The Cabinet also acted with moderation. Miss Helen Nicolay says in her book, *Our Capital on the Potomac*: "Every day during Garfield's illness Blaine conscientiously visited Vice-President Arthur, to report on the condition of the invalid and on the political outlook. The two men were by no means in accord, but each deferred to the other, Blaine giving Arthur every opportunity to make suggestions, as he had a constitutional right to do, the President being incapacitated, while Arthur as scrupulously refrained from interfering with the policy of the Administration as carried out by the Secretary of State."[1]

A President may suffer from a grave illness, which is not mortal, and such a one has raised the most recent and the most difficult question of Presidential disability. On September 2, 1919, President Wilson suddenly abandoned a speaking tour in the West and returned to Washington, arriving there next morning. The capital was full of rumors, but the President's wife and his physician, the Surgeon-General of the Navy, Admiral Cary Grayson, adopted and maintained a policy of secrecy. No direct and authoritative information was given, even to members of the Cabinet.

On Friday, October 3, Secretary of the Treasury Houston found Secretary of War Baker in extreme alarm at the state of affairs. Next day Private Secretary Tumulty told Houston in strict confidence that the President was paralyzed in one leg and one arm. On Sunday, Houston, on speaking with Vice-President Marshall in the dining room of the Shoreham Hotel, found him angry with the doctors for not taking him into their confidence, anxious at the thought of assuming the responsibilities of the Presidency, and especially so because he would be placed at the head of a government with which he had not been kept in touch.

Adequate evidence is not yet available as to whether or not any one in authority seriously thought of raising the question of the President's inability to perform the powers and duties of his office. Joseph Tumulty, the President's secretary, asserts that Secretary of State Lansing did broach the question; and a reading between the lines in one section of Secretary Houston's *Eight Years in Wilson's Cabinet* would seem to bear him out. There are others who say that no such action was ever contemplated. Whatever may have been the facts, no such plan ever proceeded far. Although Mr. Marshall was entirely free of such odium as attached to Mr. Arthur at the time of Garfield's illness, he was so overshadowed in the public estimation by the personality of Woodrow Wilson, that any serious proposal to place him in the Presidential chair while the latter was alive would have seemed shocking.

---

[1]Legally, he had no right to suggest but only a right and also a duty to command, if a certain contingency had arisen.

CHAPTER VI.

The Presidency af the Senate and Its Rules of Procedure

IT IS the duty of a presiding officer to conduct the business of the body over which he presides, but the modes of doing this vary in different Legislatures and other deliberative bodies. The Constitution specifically gives to each House of Congress the right to "determine the rules of its proceedings." Under these circumstances it is not surprising that the powers of the Vice-President have been subject to question and to change. Ordinarily a presiding officer, even when a member, does not take part in the debates, for such action would interfere with his duties and throw doubt on his impartiality; on the rare occasions when he intervenes in discussion he calls another member to the chair, obtains the floor in the usual manner, and speaks from it on an equality with his colleagues. But though he does not debate in the chair, he may give from it the reasons for his decisions on questions of Parliamentary law.

The Vice-Presidents have followed this custom and have occasionally extended it by explaining the reasons for their casting votes. John Adams, at least during the first part of his Vice-Presidency, did far more. The Senate sat with closed doors until February 20, 1794. But Senator Maclay of Pennsylvania, who served from April 24, 1789, to March 3, 1791, kept a journal from day to day in which he recorded the proceedings of the Senate and summarized the speeches. Consequently, we have a detailed and interesting account of the secret sessions. Maclay, however, was a radical Democrat, severe in his judgments of those who opposed him, and especially hostile to John Adams; therefore in reading his diary one must be very careful to allow for the personal equation of the writer. Adams appears to have interfered frequently in debates and to have played the schoolmaster far more than Aaron Burr, to whom a Federalist diarist, Plumer of New Hampshire, later applied the term.

On May 9, 1789, the Senate considered the report of a committee recommending that the President should be officially addressed as, "His Highness the President of the United States, and Protector of the Rights of the Same."

Maclay says in his diary tnat when the Senate was ready for the question: "Up got the Vice-President, and for forty minutes did he harangue us from the chair. He began first on the subject of order, and found fault with everything almost, but down he came to particulars, and pointedly blamed a member for disorderly behavior (for reflecting on the House of Representatives) . . . . All this was only prefatory. On he got to his favorite topic of titles, and over the old ground of the immense advantage, of the absolute necessity, of them . . . . The above I recollect with great precision, but he said fifty more things equally injudicious which I do not think worth mentioning."

The frequency, as well as the matter of Adams' addresses, irritated Maclay. On May 12 he thought it worth while to note that "this day, the Vice-President gave us no set speech from the chair"; but under May 14 comes the entry: "It was here that the Vice-President made us his speech for the day." Adams displayed great earnestness in behalf of the grant of an annuity to Baron Steuben or, as Maclay puts it, "Bonny Johnny Adams[1] took uncommon pains to bias us . . . ."

The Vice-Presidents who followed Adams refrained from mingling in discussions unconnected with Parliamentary questions, although during the great Nullification Debate between Webster and Hayne, Calhoun is said to have several times sent to the latter written suggestions concerning his argument.

There are a few instances of Senators addressing or referring to the Vice-President in debate. The first was on May 8, 1789. Maclay writes in his journal for that day: "Here he (Richard Henry Lee) began to enumerate many nations who gave titles—such as Venice, Genoa, and others. The Greeks and Romans, it was said, had no titles, 'but' (making a profound bow to the chair), you were pleased to set us right in this respect to the Conscript Fathers the other day.' Here he repeated the Vice-President's speech of the 23d ultimo (April), almost verbatim all over."

In 1828, during the discussion of a rule giving the Vice-President the right to call to order for words spoken in debate, Benton told Calhoun that "the steps of disagreement were fully stated by you, sir." The most famous case of personal address is that of Clay to Van Buren during the struggle over the recharter of the United States Bank. There were many "distress petitions" describing in vehement language the misery caused by Jackson's attack on the bank and begging that this most necessary institution might have its life prolonged. On March 7, 1834, Webster presented a petition from workmen of Philadelphia for the recharter of the United States Bank and moved that it be printed. Clay seconded the motion, advanced as if unconsciously toward the Vice-President's desk, and begged him to inform the President of the actual conditions of the country. "Those in this chamber who support the administration (he said) could not render a better service

---

[1]Adams had at times a simpering expression not unlike that of an embarrassed boy who wishes to avoid offense.

than to repair to the Executive Mansion, and placing before the chief magistrate the naked and undisguised truth, prevail upon him to retrace his steps and abandon his fatal experiment. No one, sir, can perform that duty with more propriety than yourself. To you, then, sir, in no unfriendly spirit but with feelings softened and subdued by the deep distress which pervades every class of our countrymen, I make the appeal." Then in most forcible and moving language Clay described the suffering which he declared had been caused by the measures that the President had been induced to take.

Benton says in his *Thirty Years in the United States Senate* that "during the delivery of this apostrophe, the Vice-President maintained the utmost decorum of countenance, looking respectfully and even innocently at the speaker, all the while as if treasuring up every word he said to be faithfully repeated to the President. After it was over and the Vice-President had called some Senator to the chair, he went up to Mr. Clay, and asked him for a pinch of his fine Maccoboy snuff (as he often did) and, having received it, walked away." To "snuff," like to "sniff," meant to express contempt; a thing of trifling value used to be described as not worth a pinch of snuff, and Van Buren was intimating that he cared nothing for Clay's buncombe. But there were Whigs who did not choose to treat their leader's burst of rhetoric as mere political "snuff." A public meeting at Philadelphia adopted a resolution that "Martin Van Buren will deserve and receive the execration of all good men, should he shrink from the responsibility of delivering to Andrew Jackson the message sent by the Hon. Henry Clay."

On December 21, 1870, a somewhat similar appeal was made to Vice-President Colfax. Senator Sumner was speaking against the annexation of Santo Domingo and, turning toward the chair, he said: "Sir, I appeal to you, as Vice-President. By official position and by well-known relations of friendship you enjoy opportunities which I entreat you to use for the good of your country and, may I add, for the benefit of that party which has so justly honored you. Go to the President, I ask you, and address him frankly with the voice of a friend to whom he must hearken. Counsel him not to follow the example of Franklin Pierce, James Buchanan, and Andrew Johnson; tell him not to allow the oppression of a weak and humble people; ask him not to exercise War Powers without authority of Congress, and remind him kindly that there is a grandeur in Justice and Peace beyond anything in material aggrandizement, beyond anything in war."

As early as April 16, 1789, the Senate adopted a few simple rules, but left most questions of Parliamentary law to be decided by the Vice-President without debate and without appeal. Adams doubtless believed himself qualified for the task, though Senator Maclay was of a different opinion. But Jefferson shrank from such grave responsibilities. He felt that there ought to be some recognized system of rules so that the President, to quote his own words, "may neither leave himself free to indulge caprices or passion, nor open to the imputation of them." Accordingly, he took the rules of the Senate, the customs of Parliament, which had been the foundation of those of most of the State Legislatures, and a commonplace book of his own compiled many years before; he then gradually worked out a manual of parliamentary law which he deposited in the archives of the Senate, and which, though never formally adopted by that body, was continually referred to, and treated as an ultimate authority.

But though Jefferson became, as it were, the Lycurgus of the Senate, he did not evoke the enthusiasm aroused by his successor, Aaron Burr. About a month after Burr took his seat, Senator Plumer wrote in his diary: "Burr presides in the Senate with great ease and dignity, he always understands the subject before the Senate, states the questions clearly and confines the speakers to the point."[1] At the close of Burr's term, Senator Mitchill of New York described him as "one of the best presiding officers who ever presided over a deliberative assembly," and Plumer recorded his full approbation of Burr's conduct as President of the Senate.

These commendations were the more honorable to Burr because his position was unusually difficult. It was during his term as Vice-President that he fought his fatal duel with Hamilton. This brought him a storm of reproach, but he did not flinch. The Senate rules gave the Vice-President the right to appoint committees, but it was the custom for him to be absent during the first days of the session, thereby leaving the appointment of committees to the Senate itself. But when the Senate assembled for the first session after the killing of Hamilton, it found its President in the chair. Plumer wrote to his son: "Colonel Burr seems determined to browbeat and cajole public opinion . . . . His manners and address are very insinuating."

The Federalists kept aloof from the man who had killed their idolized leader. Some had hoped for his impeachment. Those from New England did not call on him. Plumer made "a very formal bow" when Burr passed in the Senate Chamber but held no conversation with him. Pious men, especially those from New England, were deeply shocked by the situation. Plumer wrote to a friend that it was the first time "(God grant it may be the last) that ever a man indicted for murder presided in the American Senate. We are indeed fallen on evil times. To a religious mind, the aspect of public affairs is veiled in darkness. The high office of President is filled by an *infidel;*[2] that of Vice President by a *Murderer.*" (Italics in the original.)

But the Republicans and President Jefferson, who had denied Burr a renomination and even refused him an office which would permit him to march out with the honors of war, now showered attentions upon him. Madison took him up in his carriage to call on the French Minister. Jefferson not only invited him to dinner, but even gave three important offices to members of his clan. Lesser chiefs of the party took a like course. John Quincy

---

[1] In later years such confinement would have been regarded as a gross infringement of Senatorial privilege.

[2] The term was often applied by the Federalists to Jefferson.

Adams wrote to his father: "The Vice-President is treated by his former friends with a degree of distinction and respect to which he had before this session long been a stranger. His case is held out as being eminently entitled to compassion." And Adams added, justly or unjustly: "He seems to be under a deeper personal obligation to one member of the Senate than from his situation he ought to be and the effect of this obligation is too perceptible on his conduct as President."[1]

Probably this attention was chiefly due to a desire to conciliate Burr because he was to preside over the impeachment of a judge of the Supreme Court whom the Democrats were very anxious to drive from the bench. But violent partisans were grateful to Burr for ridding them of an enemy. Mr. Wright of Maryland said on the floor of the Senate: "The first duel that I ever read of was that of David's killing Goliath. Our little David of the Republicans has killed the Goliath of Federalism, and for this I am willing to reward him."

The rough, uncultured Clinton was in striking contrast to Burr, and on the January 15 following his induction into office, John Quincy Adams wrote lamenting that the new Vice-President was "totally ignorant of all the most common powers of proceeding in Senate," that "a worse choice than Mr. Clinton could scarcely have been made." Gerry was a man of great politeness and of a very conciliatory disposition, and during the year and a half that he lived to preside over the Senate his course was doubtless satisfactory on the whole. To give entire satisfaction to the partisan and factious Senate would have been a task for an angel. Tompkins was of much the same type as Gerry, and we may believe that the Senate might have been highly pleased with their chairman if only he had been oftener in the chair. But, broken by unjustifiable charges of embezzlement, by loss of fortune, and by intemperance, he frequently absented himself from the Senate for long periods. During the latter part of his second term, his affairs and his habits both improved, and he was more frequently at his post.

Mr. Tompkins was succeeded by John C. Calhoun, the only American statesman of the first or second rank who held the Vice-Presidency in the century between its occupancy by Jefferson and by Roosevelt. As would be expected from a man of Mr. Calhoun's high character, and respect for law, he was most strict in the performance of the duties of his office. He came to Washington early in the sessions and remained in the chair until the time of adjournment was near when, according to custom, he would withdraw, the purpose being to give the Senate an opportunity to choose a President *pro tempore* who by law would succeed to the Presidency in case of the death or disability of both the President and the Vice-President.[2]

---

[1] The reference is probably to a leader in the obtaining of the signatures of nineteen Senators to a letter urging Governor Bloomfield of New Jersey to dismiss an indictment for murder which had been brought against Burr in that state.

[2] He was, however, a mere *locum tenens,* provision being made for a special election. The law was changed in 1886 and the succession was made to run through the Cabinet beginning with the Secretary of State.

Calhoun was equally conscientious in retaining his place when once occupied. He stated in an anonymous article that during the session of 1827-28 he was not absent a moment and that he often remained in the chair from eight to twelve hours. Vice-President Calhoun departed from the custom of his predecessors of calling the persons before him "Gentlemen" and, as befitted the champion of States' Rights, addressed them as "Senators." His example was followed by the members themselves in referring to each other, and it is still the practice.

All must praise Calhoun's regularity of attendance; the term "Senator" is more appropriate, if less honorable, than the vaguer "gentlemen," and the Senate gave it the sanction of imitation; but a third change was less approved, and rightly so. John Randolph, now a Senator, had repeatedly assailed the administration with his accustomed violence, and in a famous speech had described Adams and Clay as a combination of "Blifil and Black George, the blackleg and the Puritan." He also accused or seemed to accuse Clay of falsity in connection with his conduct as Secretary of State. There was a violent clash between Senator Lloyd of Massachusetts, who defended the President, and Randolph. Clay and Randolph fought a bloodless duel; Adams countered the Blifil and Black George comparison, which Randolph had taken from Chatham, by entering in his *Diary* a quotation from Ovid describing the man filled with jealousy and envy.

Calhoun had allowed Randolph to pour out his vituperation without restraint, defending himself on the ground that the Senate had the right to fix the rules of its own procedure, that none gave the Vice-President the power to call a Senator to order for words spoken in debate, that he could only act when a point of order was made by a Senator, and that for him to do otherwise would be to limit the freedom of debate. The matter was discussed in the Senate, without anything being done, and also by the newspapers. One of them printed articles by "A Western Senator" defending Calhoun. Thereat "Patrick Henry" arose from his grave and fiercely arraigned both Calhoun's decision and his supposed motives. But ghost met ghost. "Onslow," the most distinguished Speaker the House of Commons ever had, answered the Virginia orator with an ability equal, if not superior, to his own. The public followed the debate with much interest, the more as it was confident that the masked warriors were none other than the President and Vice-President themselves.

There is no reasonable doubt that "Onslow" was Calhoun; whether "Patrick Henry" was Adams is less certain. Mr. Worthington C. Ford wrote Mr. William C. Meigs, when the latter gentleman was preparing his life of Calhoun, that he believed that Adams and "Patrick Henry" were entirely different persons. Mr. Meigs, however, thinks that much weight is due to the fact that contemporaries believed "Patrick Henry" to be Adams. "Henry's" mode of argument is very like that of Adams, and Mr. Meigs inclines to the theory that Adams supervised the articles. But whether he did or not, we know his opinion of the affair from a caustic and prejudiced entry in his diary, two years later. He says that Calhoun "permitted John Randolph, day after day, in speeches of ten hours long, to drink himself drunk with bottled porter, and in raving balderdash of the meridian of Wapping, to revile the absent and the present, the living and the dead. This was tolerated by Calhoun because Randolph's ribaldry was all pointed against the administration, especially against Mr. Clay and me, and because he was afraid of Randolph."

In the session of 1827-28 the Senate appointed a committee to revise its rules. Adams gives as the reason that "the opposition party having a majority in the Senate, and wishing to hold up Calhoun again for the Vice-Presidency, have been trying by various means to get a vote of the Senate sanctioning his abdication of his duty." A kind of sanction was obtained, but only technically and in Calhounesque manner. When the committee reported, Senator Tazewell of Virginia, a high priest of the States' Rights faith, asked if there had been any alteration of the rules by whose authority the Vice-President had decided, correctly as the speaker believed, that he had no right to call to order for words spoken in debate. Mr. Tazewell was informed that no change had been made but that one member of the committee had differed from his colleagues in the matter; whereupon Senator Foote of Connecticut announced that he was the member and that, having been thus alluded to, he should offer in the Senate the motion which had been voted down in committee.

The amendment gave to the Vice-President the power to call to order for words spoken in debate, but to the Senator, thus halted in his speech, a right to appeal to the Senate. The Vice-President was also permitted, if he desired, to take the opinion of the Senate on the question of order. A long debate ensued which was participated in by three future Vice-Presidents—Van Buren, Tyler, and King.[1] Each side endeavored to show that the principles of its opponents would or might lead to the gravest consequences.

The friends of the amendment urged that only a few cases were provided for in the rules and that if the President of the Senate could not keep order by virtue of his office, he could not prevent a riot on the floor. Mr. Chambers of Maryland said that "on some of the plainest as well as the most important rules of legislative order the Senate had no written rule whatever. He believed in every legislative body it was held necessary to restrain the speaker from subjects wholly and obviously foreign and irrelevant to the matter in hand. But yet, unless it had eluded his research, there was no written rule of the Senate to secure this necessary result. Not one word on the subject. If he were now to leave the subject of the rules and practice of this body and indulge himself in a history of the beauty, the splendor, and the utility of the Chesapeake and Delaware Canal, he would deny the authority of any individual in this Chamber, whether president or member, to charge upon him a

---

[1]Tyler, however, merely took his seat, having succeeded to the Presidency before the Senate met for business, and King died without sitting at all.

violation of order on the hypothesis that the *lex scripta* is the only rule of this House."[1]

It was urged that order in debate would be much better preserved by the President than by the Senators individually because what is everybody's business is nobody's business, that the person attacked would not wish to appeal to Parliamentary usage lest he might seem to fear discussion, and that other Senators might be unwilling to object lest they should draw the assailant on themselves with the demand: "By what right do you interfere when all your colleagues see no reason to do so." It was also pointed out with much reason that quarrels on the floor usually originated in slight criticism growing fiercer and fiercer as retort followed retort, and that no one was so fitted to resist the beginnings as the presiding officer whose duty it was to watch the debates. The friends of the amendment appealed to precedent as well as reason. They said that Jefferson's manual, which had become a sort of Bible of Parliamentary procedure, directed the Vice-President to call to order, and that from the beginning of the government until 1825 this power had been recognized as belonging to the President of the Senate.

For the period between 1811 and 1825, the deaths of Clinton and Gerry and the frequent absences of Tompkins had made a president *pro tempore* necessary for the greater part of the time. This position usually had been held by Senator Gaillard of South Carolina, and he had not hesitated to call to order members who had manifestly wandered from the question, even though their language was of the most decent and orderly nature. Much was made of these precedents and it was pointed out that they were of the greater value because Gaillard was a modest, unassuming man, not given to grasping at power, and that he was deeply learned in parliamentary law.

Opponents of the change in the rules did their best to break the force of such arguments from precedent. They said that Jefferson's manual only provided that words should be taken down at the close of a speech, when the mischief would be done, and reminded the Senate that the manual had never been formally adopted as a rule of procedure. It was hinted that what was proper in Gaillard who was elected and could be removed by the Senate, might not be so in a President imposed on it from without. Calhoun himself twice intervened in the discussion. He said that he had only refrained from calling a Senator to order when to do so would have interfered with the freedom of debate, that he had repeatedly called to order for a violation of the rules of the Senate, which was a purely ministerial act. Great stress was laid by the supporters of the existing rules on the difference between ministerial and original power. Tyler compared the President of the Senate to a court which can construe but not make laws. "He defined the powers of the chair to be ministerial, and properly exercised under the rules originating

---

[1] Such conduct then supposed as a mere *reductio ad absurdum* is now allowed by the Senate.

from the Senate, and he contended, at great length, that no other power was or could be given to the chair, by implication, or by the *Lex Parliamentaria.*" Great horror was expressed at allowing the Vice-President despotic authority to suppress debate at will. Something had been said of the inherent power of a presiding officer and this revived the old quarrel concerning a grant of implied powers by the Constitution.

The friends of the amendment replied with much reason that they were the true defenders of liberty, that if the presiding officer wished to suppress a debate he could almost certainly find one Senator to raise a point of order against it, and that by the present rules the Vice-President could decide a member to be out of order without debate and without appeal; but that by the amendment the speaker whom it was desired to silence might appeal to the Senate itself. Yet the argument from the danger of the doctrine of inherent power was two-edged. "Mr. Van Buren spoke at considerable length, in opposition to the opinion expressed that the powers delegated, in the Constitution, could be enlarged to so great an extent as was claimed, by implication," and defended the democratic principle of drawing power from the head to the sources, but announced his intention of voting against his Democratic friends because, although he had considered it inexpedient for the Vice-President to have the right under discussion, he believed that there was no better way of rebuking the doctrine of inherent power than by giving it to him, and thus proving that he did not hold it by virtue of his office.

When at last the amendments were put to a vote, the right to call to order for words spoken in debate was conferred on the Vice-President by thirty-one yeas to fifteen nays; the privilege of appeal was given with substantial unanimity. "The Vice-President then rose, and said, that he took this opportunity to express his entire satisfaction with that portion of the amendment giving to Senators the right of appeal from the decision of the chair, as it was not only according to strict principle but would relieve the chair from a most delicate duty. As to the power conferred upon the chair, it was not for him to speak; but he assured the Senate that he should always endeavor to exercise it with strict impartiality." Calhoun, in accordance with his nature, talked of the limitation of powers, and others also said much of this principle.

But disputes on abstract theory usually have some concrete cause, and members were thinking of Calhoun's failure to stop Randolph. Senator Dickerson of New Jersey spoke of the occasion "two years ago, when two Senators (Randolph and Lloyd) by the violence of their remarks upon each other totally interrupted the business of the Senate." Benton defended Randolph's conduct as within the limits of Parliamentary privilege. Calhoun participated in the debate to the extent of an explanation of the grounds for his non-action. He made it plain that he had not decided against the power of the chair to call to order in general, but only that he had no power under the rules to call to order for *words used in debate*. For instance, there was a Senate rule forbidding one Senator to speak to another, read a newspaper, or otherwise interrupt the proceedings of the Chamber; this gave the chair authority to tap on the desk for order. There was another rule prescribing an order of business for the day; this was a sufficient basis for the chair's declaring motions inconsistent therewith. But neither in the Constitution nor in the Senate rules did there exist a phrase which conferred the power to call a Senator to order for words used in debate. It was inconceivable that the Constitution would have vested in the Vice-President so despotic a power. "Who is a Senator," he asked, "that the right of uttering his sentiments within these walls should be placed under the will of an officer connected, in a certain measure, with the executive branch of the government? He is the representative of a state in its sovereign capacity, and, in the larger states, is the organ of the will of more than a million of constituents. It would then be absurd to suppose that the right of determining what he should say, and in what manner, should be placed by the Constitution in the power of an officer wholly irresponsible to this body."

When the amendments had been passed and then slightly modified, Noble of Indiana spoke the final word by hoping "that under the present regulations, the flood gates of the waters of Roanoke would never be opened to inundate the Senate Chamber again."

Van Buren came to the Vice-Presidency under trying circumstances. The Senate had insultingly refused to confirm his nomination as Minister to England, and President Jackson had replied by using the blunder as a means for placing him over the body that had rejected him. The Opposition Alliance was in control of the Senate and it was led by the great triumvirate, Calhoun, Clay, and Webster. Political feeling was most bitter. At one time there was some danger that the conflict would not be verbal merely, but that there would be an anticipation of the Brooks-Sumner episode, perhaps a fatal one. One of the most violent of the Whig Senators was Poindexter of Mississippi. Intemperance and financial and domestic troubles had dulled his once brilliant intellect and inflamed his temper. Van Buren had presided at the convening of the Senate, and a Newburgh (N. Y.) paper had stated and other papers had repeated, that "this early attendance was due to a wish to keep the chair from the disgrace of being occupied by that bloated mass of corruption— Poindexter."

Poindexter wrote to Van Buren that he would not believe that he had so unworthy a purpose, that he would prefer to regard his presence as due to an anxiety to perform his duties with promptness and industry. Poindexter concluded his letter with the threatening sentence: "It is now in your power to give me the assurance which I consider *absolutely* (italics in the original) necessary to avert the consequences of an opposite conclusion." That evening Jackson, Van Buren, and Senators Forsyth of Georgia and Wright of New York held a consultation. All agreed that the letter was a preliminary to violence. A brief reply was prepared in which Van Buren told Poindexter that he was correct in believing that he had no intention of interfering with

MARTIN VAN BUREN, NEW YORK, EIGHTH VICE-PRES-
IDENT OF THE UNITED STATES, 1833-1837.

the right of the Senate to choose its presiding officer and that "your very proper and explicit disclaimer of all idea of holding me responsible for the commentaries and constructions of the public press has enabled me so far to respect the official relations existing between us, and to which you refer, as to give you this answer." It was feared that so cold a disclaimer might be regarded as insufficient by the hot-headed Southerner and Van Buren, who had never before carried arms, next morning took the chair of the Senate "with a pair of pistols loaded and cocked, concealed on his person." But Poindexter did not press the matter further; it is said that his return to reason was due to the advice of Henry Clay.

Van Buren's successor was the amiable and conciliatory Richard M. Johnson who did his duty as a deferential, courteous figurehead. John Tyler, whose strong States' Rights views and previous service in the Senate might have led him to minimize his authority over the ambassadors of sovereign states, was called to the Presidency within a month after his accession. Mr. Dallas was praised for the gracefulness with which he presided over the Senate. His inaugural speech had indicated a wish to avoid responsibility, and though he was obliged to give a most important and embarrassing casting vote on the tariff law of 1846, he was as far as possible the very humble servant of the Senate. His successor, Millard Fillmore, though not wholly unlike Dallas, was a stronger man. His biographer says: "As Vice-President, Mr. Fillmore was an ideal presiding officer. Always urbane, dignified, judicial in bearing as in habit of mind, he ruled with impartiality and imbued his associates with a new sense of the dignity of their office and the services they were looked upon to perform." A year's experience of the Vice-Presidency convinced Mr. Fillmore that the Senate needed a firmer hand.

The amended rules, adopted in 1828 after so much debate, had fallen into disuse and partial forgetfulness. On April 3, 1850, after a series of disorderly scenes caused by the unchecked use of unparliamentary words, Vice-President Fillmore addressed the Senate on the matter of the presiding officer's responsibility and powers in that respect. He stated that he had inquired of some of the Senators to know what had been the usage on this subject, and was told that the general practice had been, since Mr. Calhoun had acted as Vice-President, not to interfere unless a question of order was made by some Senator. He continued:

> "I was informed that that distinguished and now lamented person had declined to exercise the power of calling to order for words spoken in debate, on the ground that he had no authority to do so. Some thought that the rule had been changed, and others not, but there still seemed to be a difference of opinion as to the power. Under these circumstances, though my opinion was strongly in favor of the power—with or without a rule to authorize it—I thought it most prudent not hastily to assume the exercise of it, but to wait until the course of events should show that it was necessary. It appears to me that the time has now arrived, and that the Senate

should know my opinion on this subject, and the powers which, after mature reflection, I think are vested in the chair, and the corresponding duties which they impose. If I am wrong in the conclusions at which I have arrived, I desire the advice of the Senate to correct me. I therefore think it better to state them now, when there is an opportunity for a cool and dispassionate examination rather than wait until they are called into action by some scene of excitement which may be unfavorable to dispassionate deliberation and advice. . . . ."

Mr. Fillmore then stated his belief, and the reasons therefor, that it was both his right and his duty to call to order for words spoken in debate. He said: "I know how difficult it is to determine what is and what is not in order, to restrain improper language and yet not abridge the freedom of debate. But all must see how important it is that the first departure from the strict rule of parliamentary decorum should be checked, as a slight attack, or even insinuation, of a personal character, often provokes a more severe retort, which brings out a more disorderly reply—each Senator feeling a justification in the previous aggression. There is therefore no point so proper to interpose for the preservation of order, as to check the first violation of it."

Mr. Fillmore expressed full confidence in the judgment of the Senate, and gently called its attention to the frequency of the infraction of certain minor rules which it might be unwise always to strictly enforce. He expressed his disapproval of a practice which had grown up of interrupting a Senator, and his hope that it would be done only for urgent reason and then by addressing not the Senator who was speaking, but the chair, as the rules required.

The Senate gave no opinion on these remarks of its President, but on motion of its leading parliamentarian, William R. King, unanimously ordered that they be entered in the Journal, and on the motion of another Democrat, James W. Bradbury of Maine, also directed that they be printed. What developments might have followed had Mr. Fillmore served out his term it is difficult to say. But in the ensuing July the death of General Taylor called him to the Presidency; and for seven years the Senate was presided over by one of its own choice, since William R. King, who was elected Vice-President with Pierce, did not live to take his seat. A formal man, learned in and highly esteeming the science of parliamentary law, he might have played the part of schoolmaster to the Senate, though probably, like Calhoun and Tyler, he was too great a devotee of States' Rights to have relied on the doctrine of implied powers to justify an exercise of authority.

Buchanan's Vice-President, John C. Breckinridge of Kentucky, was so strong an advocate of States' Rights that he joined the Confederacy, although his State did not secede, and presumably he was inclined to think himself when President of the Senate, as chairman of a council of Ambassadors.

Of the subsequent Republican Vice-Presidents, Johnson sat for only a single day, and Wilson was absent for a considerable period because of ill health, and died in office. Hamlin, Colfax, and Wheeler were specially versed in Parliamentary law. Colfax and Wheeler were remarkably gentle and courteous in manner, and had already been very successful as presiding officers. Senator Cullom, in his memoirs, mentions Wheeler as one of the Vice-Presidents who was peculiarly successful in guiding the Senate without seeming to do so.

Vice-President Hendricks, the only Democrat who held the Vice-Presidency in the period of thirty-two years between 1861 and 1893, died before Congress met in regular session. Under Levi P. Morton came a demand that the Vice-President should be not a moderator but a czar. The Democrats were filibustering against the Force Bill, and Mr. Morton was urged to suppress debate on the ground that it had become dilatory; he refused to do so and the Force Bill was laid aside. Many Republicans, though they voted for the proposed law, did not wish to see the South under ignorant negro rule. The Democrats were, of course, delighted at their triumph. Mr. Morton had shown poise, moderation, and courtesy in the performance of his official duties, and all the Senators of both parties united in giving him a dinner as a mark of appreciation and respect.

The question of allowing unlimited debate in the Senate and thereby permitting "a little group of wilful men," as President Wilson later called the filibusters against the declaration of war with Germany, to defeat the wishes of a great majority, had been much discussed in the country and the Senate rules had been freely condemned and ridiculed. But they had been of great service to the Democrats in defeating the Force Bill.

The new Vice-President, Adlai E. Stevenson, was a Democrat. In his inaugural address he did not refer to the rules, but assured the Senate that he assumed the duties of presiding with no feeling of self-confidence. Senator Cullom says in his reminiscences: "Adlai E. Stevenson became much beloved by the Senate. He also fell in love with the body. Hence he left us with benedictions." The benedictions were mutual. They consisted on the part of the Senate of the gift by its members of a silver service; on the part of their President, of a farewell speech in which he unstintedly praised the much criticized rules, saying:

> "It has been my earnest endeavor justly to interpret, and faithfully to execute, the rules of the Senate. At times the temptation may be strong to compass partisan ends by a disregard or a perversion of the rules. Yet, I think it safe to say, the result, however salutary, will be dearly purchased by a departure from the method prescribed by the Senate for its own guidance. A single instance as indicated, might prove the forerunner of untold evils.
>
> > " 'Twill be recorded for a precedent,
> > And many an error by the same example
> > Will rush into the State.'

"It must not be forgotten that the rules governing this body are founded deep in human experience; that they are the result of centuries of tireless effort in legislative halls, to conserve, to render stable and secure, the rights and liberties which have been achieved by conflict. By its rules, the Senate wisely fixes the limits to its own power. Of those who clamor against the Senate and its mode of procedure it may be truly said, 'They know not what they do.' In this Chamber alone are preserved, without restraint, two essentials of wise legislation and of good government—the right of amendment and of debate. Great evils often result from hasty legislation, rarely from the delay which follows full discussion and deliberation. In my humble judgment, the historic Senate, preserving the unrestricted right of amendment and of debate, maintaining intact the time-honored parliamentary methods and amenities which unfailingly secure action after deliberation, possesses in our scheme of government a value which can not be measured by words. The Senate is a perpetual body. In the terse words of an eminent Senator now present: 'The men who framed the Constitution had studied thoroughly all former attempts at republican government. History was strewn with the wrecks of unsuccessful democracies. Sometimes the usurpation of the executive power, sometimes the fickleness and unbridled license of the people, had brought popular governments to destruction. To guard against these dangers, they placed their chief hope in the Senate. The Senate which was organized in 1789, at the inauguration of the Government, abides and will continue to abide, one and the same body, until the Republic itself shall be overthrown, or time shall be no more.' "

At the conclusion of his speech Stevenson had said: "For the able and distinguished gentleman (Garrett A. Hobart) who succeeds me as your presiding officer, I earnestly invoke the same coöperation and courtesy which you have so generously accorded me." But the Senate received its new President with aloofness. His inaugural address excited alarm. What would be his attitude toward those laws of the Medes and Persians, the sacred rules? An attack on them would command strong support outside the Chamber, and not that of the *hoi polloi* alone. The *Nation,* special representative of the social and intellectual aristocracy of the country, had suggested a speech in which Hobart should tell the Senate that it had disgraced itself by its failure to transact business and do its duty.

Hobart, of course, used no such violent language. He spoke of the honor he felt in being Vice-President, of the delicacy of his position because he was imposed on the Senate, not chosen by it, and of his need and anticipation of the indulgent aid always given to his predecessors. He even announced his intention of enforcing the rules and conserving time-honored precedents. But he also said: "It will be my constant effort to aid you, so far as I may, in all reasonable expedition of the business of the Senate and I may be permitted to express the belief that such expedition is the hope of the country. All the interests of good government and the advancement toward a higher and better condition of things call for prompt and positive legislation at your hands. To obstruct the regular course of wise and prudent legislative action after the fullest and freest discussion is neither consistent with true Senatorial courtesy, conducive to the welfare of the people, nor in compliance with their just expectations."

It is probable that both the Senate and the public regarded the admonition as a forerunner of an attempt to change the rules. The New York *Tribune,* perhaps hoping to soften the hard heart of the Senate, made the soothing comment: "No member of the deliberative branch who is not suffering from an extreme case of supersensitiveness will discover in or between the lines . . . . anything more than a reasonable and becoming wish that the Senate shall perform its duty and that its presiding officer may prove equal to the opportunities of his position."

But the Senate *is* sensitive, perhaps supersensitive. It resents any appearance of dictation. It is inclined to regard even quick movement as unworthy of its dignity. Senator Cullom says: "It is quite important that the President of the Senate should be a pleasant natured gentleman, and the gentleman in the Senate will almost always respond to the gentleman in the chair. Senators do not submit easily to any exercise of authority. . . . . Vice-Presidents Wheeler, Morton and Stevenson asserted their authority with as little show of force as if they were presiding over a company of guests at their own table. But the order and dignity of the body have been preserved. Hobart came in with the decision and aplomb of a busy and experienced administrator. I never saw anything like Hobart's easy despatch from the time he began swearing in the new Senators. They say he presided over both Houses of the New Jersey Legislature and some think he considers the Senate about the same. He gives a commercial touch to the body it has not had in my time."

Like other Vice-Presidents, Mr. Hobart failed to really hurry the Senate, and he freely acknowledged his failure. Later, in referring to his inaugural address, he quoted in substance his condemnation of mere obstruction and said: "That remark was made in all innocence, but I soon discovered that the Senate's definition of reasonable expedition differed very much from my own conception of the meaning of that phrase. The 'expediency' (expedition) which was heralded as the hope of the country has finally come, but it has come through no effort of mine, and through no improvement of the rules of the Senate."

But Mr. Hobart, like the dyer's hand, soon became subdued to what he worked in. In replying to a toast to the Senate he said: "The Senate goes on forever, a permanent, fixed quantity, and in its permanency, solidity and conservatism a striking evidence of the wisdom of the great men who made our Constitution." This judgment expressed the Senate's firm opinion of itself; it cordially accepted the submission of its chief, and he ruled by obeying. His capacity of persuasion and of making friends caused Senators to feel that he was one of themselves, and gave him an influence with them probably greater than any other Vice-President has enjoyed.

CHAPTER VII.

The Vice-Presidents and the Senate Rules: Roosevelt to Dawes

A SEVERE critic of Oliver Cromwell has said that he rose to supreme power because he could direct a cavalry charge better than any other man in England. Theodore Roosevelt became Vice-President partly because of his career as a "Rough Rider," and when he took the chair of the Senate, the feelings of that body probably resembled those of the Macedonian phalanx on the approach of the Persian cavalry. Doubtless some who cared little for politics looked forward with zest to so fierce a combat. Even men who regarded the war of parties and factions more seriously could not refrain from treating the situation with some degree of levity. The Philadelphia *Times* said that "the Speaker of the House of Commons summoned police and threw out men who had refused his command to vote. The timeliness of this suggestion for the Senate is obvious. The Vice-President would not need to call the police. All that would be necessary when a Senator had occupied the floor a reasonable time and refused to leave off, would be for the Terrible Teddy to descend from his dais and with his own strenuous arm fire the recalcitrant into the lobby. The Senate rules should be so amended as to give the Vice-President the needed authority."

There was reason for apprehension, but of a different kind. Colonel Roosevelt proved not so much a dictator as a *roi fainéant*. The biographers of Vice-President Hendricks say that "he had never sought or aspired to the position he held and its quiet and negative functions were far from suitable to his active genius." This was even more true of Roosevelt, who was years younger than Hendricks, and had no previous service in the Senate to accustom him to its modes of action. David S. Barry, in his *Forty Years in Washington,* states that Roosevelt himself said that he was the poorest presiding officer that the Senate ever had. He explains that Roosevelt's "active mind would be rambling off continually from the particular business on hand, and when called back to it, the presiding officer would make frantic efforts to get on the track again, but generally with poor success. It was a happy day for him when the session adjourned *sine die.*"

Roosevelt's immediate successors were delightful contrasts to him. Cullom, who, it must be remembered, was writing of fellow-Republicans and men with whom he would have much personal intercourse, said of Fairbanks, "I do not know of a Vice-President who so strictly observed the obligation adherent to his office as did Mr. Fairbanks." Of the "reigning" Vice-President, Mr. Sherman, Cullom said that he was "an accomplished Parliamentarian, a fact which taken in connection with his genial disposition, his kindness of heart and above all his love of justice, renders him one of the most acceptable presiding officers that the Senate ever has had."

Yet Mr. Fairbanks took extraordinary measures which subjected him to severe criticism. The dignified, elderly Senator Bacon of Georgia accused him of wilfully cutting off debate by putting the question before gentlemen, whose age and dignity prevented them from leaping to their feet like members of a backwoods debating society, could address the chair. Senators are called in alphabetical order. The first name on the roll was that of Senator Aldrich of Rhode Island, and Bacon intimated that by pre-arrangement Aldrich was ready to answer without an instant's delay, and then, voting having begun, no further debate was in order.

Vice-President Marshall was given to witticisms which, though striking in form and sensible in substance, may not have always been consonant with his very dignified position. But he was a most pleasant, likeable man and won the favor of the Senate.

Mr. Coolidge came to the Vice-Presidency, a firm believer in the much maligned rules. On taking the chair he said:

> "To the House, close to the heart of the Nation, renewing its whole membership by frequent elections, representing directly the people, reflecting their common purpose, has been granted a full measure of the power of legislation and exclusive authority to originate taxation. To the Senate, renewing its membership by degrees, representing in part the sovereign states, has been granted not only a full measure of the powers of legislation but, if possible, far more important functions. To it is intrusted the duty of review; that to negotiation there may be added ratification, and to appointment, approval. But its greatest function of all, too little mentioned and too little understood, whether exercised in legislating or reviewing, is the preservation of liberty; not merely the rights of the majority, they little need protection, but the rights of the minority, from whatever source they may be assailed. The great object for us to seek here, for the Constitution identifies the Vice-Presidency with the Senate, is to continue to make this Chamber, as it was intended by the fathers, the citadel of liberty. And enormous powers here conferred, capable of much good or ill, open it may be to abuse, but necessary, wholly and absolutely necessary, to secure the required result.

"Whatever its faults, whatever its human imperfections, there is no legislative body in all history that has used its powers with more wisdom and discretion, more uniformly for the execution of the public will, or more in harmony with the spirit of the authority of the people which has created it, than the United States Senate. I take up the duties the people have assigned me under the Constitution, which we can neither enlarge nor diminish, of presiding over this Senate agreeably to its rules and regulations, deeply conscious that it will continue to function in harmony with its high traditions as a great deliberative body, without passion and without fear, unmoved by clamor, but most sensitive to the right, the stronghold of government according to law, that the vision of past generations may be more and more the reality of generations yet to come."

Some years later when, as Vice-President, he had watched the Senate at its daily work and, as President, had been anxious for the passage of legislation, he wrote in his *Autobiography*: "Presiding over the Senate was fascinating to me. That branch of the Congress has its own methods and traditions which may strike the outsiders as peculiar, but more familiarity with them would disclose that they are only what long experience has demonstrated to be the best methods of conducting its business. It may seem that debate is endless, but there is scarcely a time when it is not informing, and after all, the power to compel due consideration is the distinguishing mark of a deliberative body. If the Senate is anything it is a great deliberative body."

In consonance with his nature, Vice-President Coolidge was slow to exercise even his clearest powers. It is said that once when Senators were shouting at one another, and one of the officers of the Senate whose real, though extra-legal, duty it is to prompt the Vice-President, called earnestly to him to use his gavel and restore order, Coolidge calmly replied: "I will if they become really excited."

The inauguration of Vice-President Dawes brought that open, determined struggle between the Senate and its President which many had expected when Roosevelt became Vice-President, and which perhaps was only prevented by the death of President McKinley before the regular session of Congress. Mr. Dawes, however, did not wait for this, but openly threw down the glove in his inaugural speech. In a high-pitched voice at first nervous then rasping as he became cooler, he flung out his arguments, emphasizing them by jerking and once by waving his arms. Shaking his finger in the faces of the Senators, he declared:

"What I say upon entering this office should relate to its administration and the conditions under which it is administered. Unlike the vast majority of deliberative and legislative bodies, the Senate does not elect its Presiding Officer. He is designated for his duty by the Constitution of the United States.

"In the administration of this office his duty is to be concerned with methods of effective procedure as distinguished from any legislative policy of the body over which he presides. It is not for the Vice-President to be personally concerned with the interests of political parties or with the policies or projects involved in legislative action, save in that unusual contingency where, under the Constitution, it becomes necessary for him to cast the deciding vote in case of a tie. Nor should he, in view of that unusual contingency, assume any attitude toward prospective legislation until the contingency occurs. Any other course would inevitably lessen the weight of his influence in those impartial and non-partisan matters with which it is his duty, under the Constitution of the United States, to be concerned.

"In my conduct I trust I may yield to no Senator in fairness, courtesy, and kindliness and in deference to those unwritten laws which always govern any association of gentlemen, whether official or private. It shall be my purpose not to transgress in any way those limits to my official activity, determined by the Constitution of the United States and by proper parliamentary procedure. But the Vice-President, in part because he is not elected by the Members of this body, nor by a State, but by the people of the United States, and his constitutional and official relations are to the Senate as a whole, should always express himself upon the relation of its methods of transacting public business to the welfare of the Nation.

"For him, therefore, to officially call to the attention of the Senate any collective duty such as an improvement in the method under which its business is carried on, so far from being an irrelevant and uncalled-for action on his part, is a supreme duty.

"In past years, because the Members of this body have cherished most commendable feelings of fairness, courtesy, and consideration for each other as individuals, certain customs have been evolved. These have crystallized into fixed and written rules of procedure for the transaction of public business which, in their present form, place power in the hands of individuals to an extent, at times, subversive of the fundamental principles of free representative government. Whatever may be said about the misuse of this power under the present rules of the Senate, the fact remains that its existence, inimical as it is to the principles of our constitutional government, can not properly be charged against any party, nor against any individual or group of individuals. It has evolved as a natural consequence of the mutual confidence of high-minded men, determined that in their official association as Members of the Senate, full and fair opportunity to be heard on all public questions shall be enjoyed by each and every Senator, irrespective of whether or not they are in the minority, either of opinion or of party.

"But however natural has been the evolution of the present rules, however commendable that existing desire on the part of all that the rights of each individual Senator should be observed, the fact remains that under them the rights of the Nation and of the American people have been overlooked—and this, notwithstanding that their full recognition of the rights of the nation is in no wise inconsistent with the recognition of every essential right of any individual Senator.

"What would be the attitude of the American people and of the individual Senators themselves toward a proposed system of rules if this was the first session of the Senate of the United States instead of the first session of the Senate in the Sixty-ninth Congress? What individual Senator would then have the audacity to propose the adoption of the present Rule XXII without modification when it would be pointed out that during the last days of a session the right that is granted every Senator to be heard for one hour after two-thirds of the Senate had agreed to bring a measure to a vote, gave a minority of even one Senator, at times, power to defeat the measure and render impotent the Senate itself? That rule, which at times enables Senators to consume in oratory those last precious minutes of a session needed for momentous decisions, places in the hands of one or of a minority of Senators a greater power than the veto power exercised under the Constitution by the President of the United States, which is limited in its effectiveness by the necessity of an affirmative two-thirds vote. Who would dare to contend that under the spirit of democratic government the power to kill legislation providing the revenues to pay the expenses of government should, during the last few days of a session, ever be in the hands of a minority or perhaps one Senator? Why should they ever be able to compel the President of the United States to call an extra session of Congress to keep in functioning activity the machinery of the Government itself? Who would dare oppose any changes in the rules necessary to insure that the business of the United States should always be conducted in the interests of the Nation and never be in danger of encountering a situation where one man or a minority of men might demand unreasonable concessions under threat of blocking the business of the Government? Who would dare maintain that in the last analysis the right of the Senate itself to act should ever be subordinated to the right of one Senator to make a speech?

"The rules can be found, as is the custom in other deliberative and legislative assemblies, to fully protect a Senator in his right to be heard without forfeiting at any time the greater right of the Senate to act. The Constitution of the United States gives the Senate and the House of Representatives the right to adopt their own rules for the conduct of business, but this does not excuse customs and rules which, under certain conditions, might put the power of the Senate itself in the hands of individuals to be used in legislative barter. Proper rules will protect the rights of minorities without surrendering the rights of a majority to legislate.

"Under the inexorable laws of human nature and human reaction, this system of rules, if unchanged, can not but lessen the effectiveness, prestige, and dignity of the United States Senate. Were this the first session of the Senate and its present system of rules, unchanged, should be presented seriously for adoption, the impact of outraged public opinion, reflected in the attitude of the Senators themselves, would crush the proposal like an egg shell. Reform in the present rules of the Senate is demanded not only by American public opinion, but I venture to say in the individual consciences of a majority of the Members of the Senate itself.

"As it is the duty on the part of the Presiding Officer of the Senate to call attention to defective methods in the conduct of business by the body over which he presides, so, under their constitutional power, it is the duty of the Members of this body to correct them. To evade or ignore an issue between right and wrong methods is in itself a wrong. To the performance of this duty, a duty which is nonpartisan, a duty which is nonsectional, a duty which is alone in the interest of the Nation we have sworn to faithfully serve, I ask the consideration of the Senate, appealing to the conscience and to the patriotism of the individual Members."

The new Vice-President instantly followed theory with practice. It was his duty to swear in the new Senators, on this occasion, thirty-two in number. It was customary for the Senators to be conducted to the Vice-Presidential desk in groups of four, and there be sworn in and sign the roll. Two quartettes were inducted in the usual form, then the patience of the energetic, practical Dawes gave way and he cried out: "Bring them all up. This is too slow. Bring them on together!"[1] The Vice-President then hurriedly administered the oath, and directed the Sergeant-at-Arms to clear the Chamber that the inaugural procession might form, making a motion with his hand as if he were shooing hens out of a barn-yard.

The Representatives, who were accustomed to limiting debate and perhaps also to being quietly looked down upon by members of the "Upper Chamber" for being obliged to do so, enjoyed the Vice-Presidential lecture,

---

[1]These are the words as given in Paul R. Leach's *That Man Dawes*. The Congressional Record reports him as saying, "Call the names of all the Senators who are to take the oath," which is probably at once a more "correct" and a less accurate version.

but President Coolidge appeared to disapprove and the majority of the Senators were angry. Many did not follow the President to the reviewing stand to hear his inaugural, but remained behind exchanging denunciatory and alarmed comments on the address of Mr. Dawes. Their opinions were quickly spread over the country. The chair of the Senate had for once proved an unequalled rostrum; the roaring of the "March lion," as Dawes was called, and its echoes in that "Cave of the Winds," the Senate Chamber, drowned out the inaugural of the President; and Mr. Coolidge found the speech he had carefully prepared for the great occasion of his life relegated to the second page of the newspapers to make room for the ordinarily unnoticed words of an understudy.

Of course the President said nothing for publication, but it was generally believed in Washington that he was by no means pleased at the way in which Mr. Dawes had "stolen the inauguration." Even while he was speaking, reporters had rushed away to interview the Senators.[1] There is really little for reporters to do at an inauguration; a set plan is followed and even if a President should swear at the heat and the crowd, the story, unless perhaps the oath was unusually picturesque, would probably be "killed" in the newspaper offices. The inaugural address itself is sent in advance to the press, to be held in absolute confidence until it is delivered. The New York *Times* correspondent made the following report:

> "Senator Caraway (Democrat) of Arkansas: The best example of what a speech should not be is that of the Vice-President. He disclosed that he was almost as lacking in knowledge of the rules of the Senate and the Constitution of the United States as he was in good taste; almost but not quite.
>
> "Senator Bruce (Democrat) of Maryland: I am heartily in sympathy with the idea of revising the Senate rules in such manner as to accelerate the transaction of the public business. But I shall have to see a little more of Vice-President Dawes before I express an opinion as to whether he has the skill and address to induce the Senate to break with its past. The only statement that I can hazard about him at this time is that he is evidently 'a character.'
>
> "Senator Reed (Democrat) Missouri: His melody of voice, grace of gesture and majesty of presence were only excelled by his modesty.
>
> "Senator Swanson (Democrat) of Virginia: This is one of the great and dignified occasions in the history of America. I regret that such an occasion was perverted into a farce.
>
> "Senator Norris (Republican) of Nebraska: I have an opinion and a strong one, but I do not care to express it.

---

[1]This desertion was not in reality as disrespectful as it might appear to be.

"Senator Robinson (Democratic leader) of Arkansas: The ceremonies are necessarily formal. It is regrettable that they were made ridiculous.

"Senator Smoot (Republican) of Utah: It would be better if he had made it in some other place than the Senate. If there was hope before for changing the rules, that hope has departed now.

"Senator Fletcher (Democrat) of Florida: Dawes undertakes to upset the rules of the Senate in a way that may be spectacular but not desirable or wise.

"Senator Ashurst (Democrat) of Arizona: It was the most acrobatic gymnastic speech I have ever heard in the Senate.

"Senator George (Democrat) of Georgia: The Vice-President defeated any likelihood of a change in the rules. There are some features of the rules, no doubt, that should be changed, but he defeated any change by the brutal and clownish way in which he went about it. With all its faults, the Senate is the greatest deliberative body in the world, and the only body in which gag rule has not been applied. Dawes comes in here from the business world, where there is impatience of restraint. Here deliberation is necessary as a check against hasty and ill-considered action, and to prevent the complete domination of executive authority.

"Senator Oddie (Republican) of Nevada: It was a virile speech and shows that he is full of fight, something that the Senate needs.

"Senator Edwards (Democrat) of New Jersey: Hell and Maria, and not much Maria."

"The Republican floor leader, Senator Curtis, prudently made no statement."

There was a wide-spread feeling that the fight had just begun. On March 5, the correspondent of the New York *Times* wrote that many Senators pointed out that it was a difficult matter for a Vice-President to ride rough-shod over a Senate which numbered among its members experts in Parliamentary law, and that it was reported that two of the best in the Democratic ranks, Messrs. Reed of Missouri and Harrison of Mississippi, were "gunning" for their official chief. The Cleveland *Plain Dealer* said of Senators: "What these hard boiled statesmen will do to the gentleman from Marietta and Chicago belongs to a future chapter." Washington believed that Senators would fling back Dawes' gauntlet as vigorously as he had thrown it down, and packed the Senate galleries to enjoy the fight. But though there were some return thrusts, the buttons were on the foils, and no blood was drawn.

The explanation was that a truce had been arranged which leaders on both sides of the Chamber hoped could be turned into a permanent peace. When the first indignation aroused by Dawes' speech had cooled, reporters found

Senators who had expressed themselves very freely, unwilling to extend their remarks for quotation. Republicans realized that a violent and spectacular quarrel between a Senate in which they had a majority, although a small and uncertain one, and a Republican Vice-President would be very bad politics. Old Senators, Democratic as well as Republican, saw that in such a contest the cherished dignity of their body must suffer[1] Senator Curtis acted as the dove of peace and his olive branch was accepted, but some of the Democrats received the offering unwillingly and made it an absolute condition of forbearance that Dawes should refrain from arm waving and "torrid remarks," without as well as within the Senate.

Curtis' task was the more difficult, as Dawes, just after lecturing the Senate, had twice failed to perform his own duties and had thereby raised some embarrassing legal questions. The rules require that Senators take the oath of office and sign the roll in the presence of the Senate. But when Dawes hurried the Senate and its guests to the Portico for the inauguration of the President, he left the incoming Senators to sign, and, therefore, the oath was not subscribed in the presence of the Senate. Furthermore, the Senate is in session at the inauguration and formally adjourns after it. When, however, the Senate had returned to its Chamber, there was no Vice-President to be found; the President *pro tem,* George H. Moses, was absent, and apparently there was no official present who was authorized to call the Senate to order. The Republican Floor Leader, Senator Curtis, had gone to the White House with the President. The Senators sat looking at each other in perplexity. Some of the chief Republicans conferred, and Senator Watson of Indiana, the Assistant Leader, took the chair and called the Senate to order. The Senate voted that it would meet the next day at noon, and on motion of Senator Wesley Jones of Washington, adjourned, the motion being withheld by request until Senator Ashurst of Arizona, who had refused to subscribe the roll in the absence of the Senate, had signed it.

The Senate met at the appointed hour and the vitriolic Senator Reed of Missouri, who it was reported would assail Dawes for his absence of the day before, addressed the chair. But Senator Hale of Maine, a most influential Old Guard Senator, did the same and obtained the floor. Briefly, but clearly and fully, he exonerated Dawes. He told the Senate that he had seen criticism of the Vice-President in the papers; that he thought that it was his duty as it was his pleasure to explain that, after the inauguration, Mr. Dawes had said that he must return to the Senate; but that he himself had told him that he was to go to the reviewing stand. "The Vice-President," said Senator Hale, "was in the hands of the Committee on Arrangements and he had to

---

[1]Dawes' manner, which was, indeed, unsuitable to the occasion, gave more offense than his language or even his proposal itself. The *Independent* made the rather harsh comment, "It was not so much their (the Senate's) devotion to the solemn fooleries of filibuster that was injured as it was their vanity; they suffered particularly from the indignity of being sworn in *en masse* like a herd of immigrants taking out their first papers."

follow out their instructions. If any blame of any kind attaches, it rests entirely upon my shoulders." This took the wind out of Reed's sails and the subject was allowed to drop.

There remained the matter of the subscription to the roll. Reed stated that without wishing to blame any one, he must say that the rules required a signing in the presence of the Senate; a failure to do so might at a critical moment raise a question of the right of a Senator to his seat; and he offered a resolution that the signing and the presidency of Watson be confirmed owing to the special circumstances of the cases, but that they were not to be regarded as precedents. The matter had all been previously arranged. When Dawes suggested that the Senators could sign then, he was told that this would take longer, and the resolution was passed without objection. On this day Dawes nearly violated another rule of the Senate, for he reached for his famous underslung pipe, but fortunately remembered in time that smoking in the Senate Chamber was forbidden.

Dawes' absence on March 4 was of only technical importance; a few days later he was again out of the chair, and this time his presence was most needful and his excuse, though similar, was less perfect. President Coolidge had nominated Charles B. Warren, of Michigan, as Attorney-General. Democrats and Insurgents united to oppose confirmation, on the ground that the nominee's professional relations with the Sugar Trust made him an unsuitable person to enforce the laws against combinations in restraint of trade. The fight was long and fierce. Dawes was accustomed to take an afternoon nap. On the afternoon of March 9 he inquired of Senators Robinson and Curtis, the Democratic and Republican leaders, if there would be a vote that day. He was assured that there would not and so deemed it safe to seek rest and sleep at his hotel, the New Willard.

But he is a wise man who follows the counsel of the poet, "Trust no future howe'er pleasant." The brilliant oratory of Senators Reed of Missouri and Walsh of Montana staggered the Republicans.[1] It was not a question of the coming of Bluecher *or* night. Another day would surely bring absent Democratic Senators to Washington and give victory to their party. But if the Administration chief dared to play the part of Montrose and instantly "put it to the touch and win or lose it all," the battle might yet be won.

The trumpet sounded. Leader Curtis marshalled his forces for the fray, and gave the word for a vote. As the roll-call progressed, it soon appeared there was great danger of the loss of the motion. The Vice-President's secretary rushed to a telephone with an S. O. S. and got his message through. Then he and Senator Cameron of Arizona took their stand on the outer balcony that not a second might be lost. The chief clerk called the names of Senators with a dignity and deliberation, particularly a deliberation, which

---

[1]The majority included a group that, while remaining under the old standard, regarded the insurgents not as traitors, but as honorable men whose zeal for righteousness had lead them a little astray.

would have delighted Senator Bacon himself, unless the partisan Hyde in his soul had overcome the Senatorial Jekyll.

But all seemed vain. Tallying Senators saw that the vote stood 40 to 40. A tie defeats a motion. Senator Moses, the President *pro tem,* had voted as a Senator and could not vote again, but the Vice-President was known to be on the way and might arrive at any moment. To the eager Democrats, President Moses seemed as slow in declaring the vote as the chief clerk had been in taking it, and there were attempts to hurry him. The announcement came. But in the Senate, as in the ring, one may be down yet not out. There is a possibility of recovery. A member who has voted with the majority may move to reconsider the vote, and a Senator, before the vote is announced, can change his vote for this very purpose. To gain time, Senator Reed of Pennsylvania had done so.

Senator Walsh of Montana, as keen to defeat Parliamentary trickery as to expose graft at Teapot Dome, instantly moved to table the motion. The roll was called. The hearts of the Republicans were throbbing with the silent cry, "Sister Anne! Sister Anne! Is there any one coming?" And lo, the straining eyes of the watchers on the wall were gladdened by the sight of a taxi approaching with a speed of which neither Paul Revere nor the elder Dawes had ever dreamed; and from it leaped the Vice-President. Secretary and Senator each grasped an arm and rushed the new champion to the Senate Chamber. Flinging off coat and hat Mr. Dawes would have charged over the floor to the chair; but he was induced to go to his private room and assume his post in the usual way.

Alas, all he could do was to watch the rout of his friends. A single Democrat, Senator Overman of North Carolina, had voted with the Republicans, perhaps because he believed that the President should be allowed to choose his own Cabinet, and perhaps because he thought that the appointment of Warren would hurt the Republicans. But after voting against Senator Walsh's motion to table the motion to reconsider, Mr. Overman announced that in order to settle the matter, and because his party did not seem to want Warren for Attorney-General, he should change his vote. Reed's motion was accordingly tabled, and Warren lost his seat in the Cabinet.[1]

Dawes found himself in a situation like that when he failed to preside over the Senate after President Coolidge's inauguration. The managers of the Vice-President and even Mr. Dawes himself are said to have been much alarmed. After lecturing the Senate on its failure to do its duty, he had not performed his own. To make matters worse, he had subjected himself not only to blame but to ridicule, which is sometimes the more dangerous politi-

---

[1] It is possible that even Dawes' arrival might not have saved the day. The question has been raised and ably argued, but never definitely passed on, whether the Vice-President's right to vote is not limited to legislative business. There was a report that the Democrats planned to raise the point and prolong debate on it until next day, when the arrival of more Democrats would defeat the confirmation of Warren.

cally. Dawes had founded a society named the "Minutemen of the Constitution," and his delay elicited the gibe that the Minuteman of Chicago was two minutes late. The *New Republic* was very severe, saying, "It will of course be a long while before the Capital stops laughing at the dashing Dawes, his afternoon snooze at the Willard, the wild taxi ride up the Avenue, the trusty secretary in the balcony of the Capitol, and the arrival of the Vice-President just in time to see the body cut down but too late to save the prisoner. It is extremely doubtful whether he will again be able to get himself taken seriously in political circles."

Senator Norris read in debate a poem which he said had been handed him by a friend. It was a parody on "Sheridan's Ride," and described Dawes in his taxi speeding to the Capitol now ten, now two, blocks away, and ended with the lines:

> Hurrah, hurrah for Dawes!
> Hurrah, hurrah for this highminded man!
> And when his statue is placed on high,
> Under the dome of the Capitol sky,
> The great Senatorial temple of fame,
> There with the glorious General's name,
> Be it said, in letters both bold and bright:
> O, Hell and Maria, he has lost us the fight!

Dawes' biographer states that he sat grinning at the fun and when Norris ended, said, "The Chair cannot refrain from expressing his appreciation of the delicate tribute of the Senator from Nebraska." The last laugh was on Norris.

There were some who heartily condemned Dawes, but did not express their opinion in public. It is not strange that among them was not Attorney-General Warren. An unfortunate circumstance strengthened his feeling. At the Republican National Convention he had been the only delegate from Michigan who voted against the nomination of Dawes, and it was said that, while life lasted, he would believe that the absence of the Vice-President was a deliberate retaliation. Mr. Coolidge again, as propriety required, played the rôle of "Silent Cal," but it was reported that he was much displeased. Dawes, however, had a reasonably good defense, for he had been assured that there would be no vote that day.

Perhaps the fairest comment on the unfortunate affair was that of Senator Royal Copeland, made just after Norris had read his poem: "Mr. President, I assume that the Vice-President now presiding over the Senate has been here long enough to realize that Senators are, in the language of the street, 'hard boiled eggs'; I have no doubt that what the Vice-President said about revising the rules is a thing which the country approves and which many Senators approve, but I would remind him, if I may, that one of the unwritten rules of the Senate is that the President of the Senate is supposed to be in the chair. So it is not Senators alone who are disagreeable or fail to live up to the traditions of the Senate. However, unfortunate things happen both on the floor and in the chair."

But probably the country did not much care about a bit of accidental absenteeism. The great question was, what did the press and the people think of Dawes' attack on the Senate rules? Many of the leading newspapers of the country gave it their approval; among them were the Boston *Herald* and *Post*, the Springfield *Republican*, the New York *Times*, and *Herald-Tribune*, the *Independent*, the *Literary Digest*, the Pittsburgh *Post*, the Rochester *Herald*, the Cleveland *Plain Dealer*, the Washington *Star*, the Atlanta *Constitution*, the New Orleans *Picayune*, the Louisville *Courier Journal*, the Cincinnati *Enquirer*, the Indianapolis *News*, the Chicago *Tribune*, the Detroit *Free Press*, the St. Louis *Globe Democrat* and *Star*, the Kansas City *Star*, the Omaha *World Herald*.

In some cases, the approval was unqualified and was accompanied by bitter censure of the Senate. The New York *Times* said: "For such a deliverance, appalling in its frankness, the Senate has unwillingly been preparing the stage for the last few days. Before a weary and disgusted country, it had exhibited Senate procedure at its worst. Dawdling and deadlock, filibustering and obstruction, had throttled bill after bill and left the Senate majority a pitiful spectacle of helplessness before obstinate Senators. Repeatedly the Senate has shown that its obsolete methods had become subversive of representative government. Of the intolerable Circumlocution Office which the Senate has become under its petrified rules General Dawes spoke with the utmost bluntness and earnestness. The Senate found that the *enfant terrible* had arrived." The Springfield *Republican* remarked that "the latitudinarian speech-making propensities of the Senate's most celebrated morons have caused the country some amusement."

On the other hand, there were papers which unqualifiedly opposed Dawes. Some were mere fossils blindly dreading change; others, situated in the South, probably feared that a partisan majority might pass another Force Bill; and a third group, strange as it may seem, represented the New Liberalism. The Richmond *Times Despatch* said that "the Senate rules are sometimes abused of course, but they have served also to prevent great abuses more than once." W. D. Cochrane, of the Washington *News*, wrote: "Mr. Dawes is leading a fight to fool the people of the United States into making the Senate surrender its constitutional power into the hands of a political party machine.

"An organized campaign is on to discredit the United States, with Vice-President Dawes as its spokesman.

"My belief is that the purpose is to strengthen the executive branch of the government at the expense of the legislative.

"If the Dawes scheme works and the Senate ceases to be a check on Presidential power, future Presidents will be dictators."

The *Nation* which, twenty-eight years before, had advised Hobart to tell the Senate that it had disgraced itself by its delays and inefficiency, now said of Dawes' speech: "General Dawes' attack on the Senate rules of procedure was marked by his usual lack of tact and eccentric mannerisms. His method and tone have probably ended any possibility of the reforms he championed. In some degree his criticisms were justified; the Senate does on occasion need to speed up its proceedings. But the best way to accomplish that would be to create within the Senate a public opinion to compress debate into briefer limits. If it comes to a question of legislative action to restrict debate in the Senate, we are opposed to it. . . . . The most amusing part of the whole campaign is that it comes from men who were bitterly outraged last summer at the so-called attack upon the sanctity of the Supreme Court embodied in the La Follette platform. Now they are joining in an attack upon the Senate which might easily deprive it of the very privileges which make it the kind of public body which the founders wanted it to be."

The *Plain Dealer* and other papers endorsed the substance of Dawes' speech, yet so far agreed with the *Nation* as to disapprove his manner and his choice of time and place. The Pittsburgh *Post* stated that "the severest comment appears to be that the inauguration was not the proper occasion for the outburst. The ceremony was supposed to pass off smoothly, in an atmosphere of sweetness and light." But to such objections the St. Louis *Star* replied: "George Bernard Shaw is fond of saying: 'If you do not say a thing in an irritating way you may as well not say it at all, because people will not trouble themselves about anything that does not trouble them.'"

Senators might, as Senator Caraway is reported to have done, compare their President to an ass in a lion's skin. The press was more formidable, but it was not omnipotent and now it spoke in slightly uncertain tones. But there was another power which even Senators must fear—the people. As the Indianapolis *News* pointed out: "It is quite possible that the issue between the Vice-President and the Senate may become one between the Senate and the people." The New Orleans *Times Picayune* said: "The Senate may not care a hoot about the personal opinions of Vice-President Dawes. But most of the members do care what the country thinks of them and of the Senate as an institution."

Prudence itself bade Dawes, now that he had drawn the sword, throw away the scabbard. Some Senators were desirous of changing the rules, but Dawes had alienated them by his violence. The Vice-President could not debate, make a motion, or even vote except in case of a tie. To quote the *Picayune* once more: "The General has antagonized the strict formalities in the House of Elders. These defenders of the rules will fight back to the last ditch and the last moment. They fight on their own ground with weapons of their own choosing and practice. Whereas the Vice-President, after seizing his golden opportunity to dramatize the conflict, now is bound to silence, unless he elect to carry the fight outside the Senate Chamber."

There were special circumstances favorable to such action. Various Senators were coming up for reëlection that year and they were, therefore, peculiarly sensitive to public feeling. For rousing the people it seemed that "both the hour and the man were come." The Boston *Globe* said: "No one before, not even Colonel Roosevelt in his best fighting days, ever made a dent in that fine old encrusted Senatorial tradition, buttressed by antique rules and practices and solemnity defended by conservative and radical Senators alike." In another issue, the *Post* said that the average man would stand in line for hours to watch a parade but would leave it for a fight or a fire, and that it was now an off season for the sport-loving part of the public, since the baseball season was not in full swing. Even the New York *Independent,* an organ of the mass of the religious and the educated, so far succumbed to the barnstorming spirit as to say: "On March 4, 1929, the Vice-President will have another chance to make a speech to or at the Senate. A patient country awaits that purple morn, praying that the event will not find General Dawes suffering either from a sprained wrist or a bad cold."

It is a little strange that there should have been any doubt as to the Vice-President's intentions, since he had already proclaimed them. On the afternoon of the famous fourth of March, newshawks, with papers containing reports of vigorous interviews with horrified Senators, descended on the New Willard. Less important than a roll-call, they were obliged to wait for the completion of the Vice-Presidential nap. When Dawes appeared it was only to make a short statement. "I have had my say; let them have theirs," was all the reporters could get out of him in response to the columns of Senatorial sarcasm in the Washington afternoon newspapers. Senator Frank B. Willis, Ohio Republican, was standing there in a group of Ohio American Legion members. "Of course, what you Senators think does not make any real difference," he shot at Willis. "I am going over the heads of the Senators anyway on the issue of changing the rules. This thing is important and I am absolutely right. Unless this issue goes to the people the fundamental institutions of the country will suffer."

Some newspapers saw clearly that the Washington truce was merely a local one. The Philadelphia *North American* said: "The lanterns are lit in the steeples and the General is off on his ride." The allusion proved particularly appropriate as Dawes fired the first gun in his nation-wide campaign, at a Chamber of Commerce luncheon in Boston to celebrate the hundred and fiftieth anniversary of the Revere-Dawes alarm. The Vice-President had not expected to speak on the subject of the rules until the twenty-first, at an Associated Press luncheon in New York, before six hundred newspaper publishers and their guests. But Senator Butler was present at the Boston banquet. It was part of Dawes' plan to sick constituents on lagging Senators, and with characteristic frankness he announced that he had modified his speech and why. After outlining his position in regard to majority closure, he smiled at his audience.

"The reason I am going to talk on Senate rules is because Senator Butler is here," he said. "I appeal to you, his constituents, to express your attitude on reform of the Senate rules. That reform concerns principles for which your fathers fought 150 years ago. If you are for it, stand up and say so."

His words were greeted by a yell, and 1,000 men leaped to their feet. The congenitally silent Mr. Butler had been smoked out.

The Senator rose, condemned the rules, and stated that he would devote time to their improvement. But later, Senator Harrison of Mississippi pointed out on the floor of the Senate that Butler's chief grievance seemed to be that he, a freshman, was not given the important committee places which had been held by his predecessor, Henry Cabot Lodge, a veteran of years' service.

Dawes went to New York as he had planned, and before the opening of Congress in December, visited New England, the Middle West, the South and the Pacific Coast, proclaiming his gospel. He replied to a speech by Senator Moses in New Hampshire, and wrote a brief article for the *Forum* as part of a symposium to which Senators Norris and Pepper also contributed. Senator Norris said that the great size of the House rendered closure necessary, but that the result was that a few "leaders" in the secrecy of committee rooms decided both what the House should consider and when it should consider it. Hence public discussion was confined to the Senate.

Mr. Norris admitted that there was a great deal of reason in Dawes' attack on the filibuster, but said that "his remedy would put us out of the frying pan into the fire." Filibusters were not wholly bad; one had just defeated a ship subsidy bill which the influence of the executive would have otherwise driven through a "lame duck" Congress against the wishes of the people and of Congress itself. Senator Norris argued that the true cure for the evils of filibustering was the adoption of an amendment to the Constitution which had already been twice passed by the Senate, making a new President and Congress take office in January, and so getting rid of short sessions.

Dawes' speech at New York had been received by the press with only mild approval, but on his stumping tour he was applauded by enthusiastic crowds, and he returned to Washington convinced that there was a tremendous popular demand for a change in the rules, which Senators would neglect at their peril. He was wrong. But the issue was not one to stir intense public feeling unless some bill of great and wide-spread popularity had been defeated by filibustering, and such was not the case. The ovations which Dawes received were better explained in an insulting speech addressed to him in the Senate by Senator Harrison of Mississippi. Mr. Harrison said:

"Mr. President, do not forget in your enthusiasm that a Vice-President is liable to get attention, no matter where he goes. If a curio is placed in a window here on F Street, crowds will gather to look at it. A lot of people go out to see a man who occupies the first page of the press of the country, as a curiosity. But I may say to the distinguished Presiding Officer, do not mistake the great crowd and the acceptance of the invitation to rise at these banquets as the sentiments of the American people.

"In conclusion, let me commend to the Vice-President a fable. It was about some specimen of mule, an unruly, unmanageable, intractable mule. Such a kind that would break out of enclosures and promptly run away. So the owner yoked him, and one day this unruly specimen of a mule broke down the fence and away he went in high spirits to the city; up and down the streets he paraded, swinging his yoke, and ringing his bell. Out of amusement and curiosity crowds gathered. This poor deluded, misguided specimen of a mule mistook the laughter as the plaudits of the crowd."

But if the attendance of crowds at Dawes' speeches and even their applause was imperfect evidence of the feeling of the people, Harrison's insolence did not wholly reflect that of the Senate. It will be remembered that in the interviews after Dawes' attack on the rules, a few Senators had approved a change, and on May 17, 1926, Senator Underwood of Alabama had introduced a resolution permitting majority closure. Harrison himself had attacked Dawes for claiming as his a policy which had been previously advocated at various times by different Senators.

There was a serious filibuster defeating much legislation in the winter of 1926 and another in that of 1928. With this object lesson before the Senate, it was thought that something might be accomplished for rules reform, and Senator Underwood called up his resolution June 4. Every Senator knew that under the existing rules it was probable that he could carry or defeat a measure by threatening to turn himself into a permanent phonograph. Reed of Missouri made a most powerful speech on the evils which majority rules had caused, including in his list the crucifixion of the Savior; and it is probable that he and others would have continued speaking indefinitely if the Underwood motion had been seriously pushed.

The filibusters won the day. Dawes' great Crusade had failed; the infidels held not only Jerusalem but all outlying posts, and it might have been expected that the new Coeur de Lion would have won nothing but hate for his attack and scorn for failure. But this was not so. He became, on a lesser scale, a second Hobart. The Senate likes to have the public business done, provided that there is preserved to each member the right to stop it when he pleases. There was no change in the rules but, through Dawes' influence, little by little, customs were modified or, rather, suspended. The reading of the Journal of the previous day would be dispensed with, uncontested bills would be passed at a stroke, in each case by unanimous consent. The fact that these conserved minutes might be consumed later in the day in long droning speeches to which nobody listened, is another story.

The attitude of the Senate toward its President was entirely altered. He had proved an excellent presiding officer, and Senators had found that the desire of the practical business man to get things done could be attractive and useful as well as shocking. The *Outlook* of May 2, 1928, said: "In fairness let it be added here that the Senate, in three years of association with Dawes, has grown not only to like him, and not only to recognize the uniform fairness of his rulings, but actually to respond to his influence in matters of legislation —a circumstance which has not occurred for more than a generation.[1] Politicians generally like him because he speaks their language and because they know he will 'play ball.' In contrast is Mr. Hoover who can not or will not do either."

When the Presidential campaign of 1928 was over, and there was less temptation to act for partisan reasons, the Senate on March 2, 1929, took a recess and then presented to the Vice-President a silver tray with an inscription stating that it was a token of esteem from his associates in the United States Senate. To this were appended the engraved signature of every Senator, even those of Senators Harrison and Reed, who had so bitterly denounced and ridiculed him. The presentation was made by Senator Robinson, the Democratic leader in the Senate, and defeated candidate for the Vice-Presidency.

---

[1] The Vice-President had arranged a combination which passed the McNary-Haugen Bill and the McFadden Branch Banking Act.

CHAPTER VIII.

The Vice-President's Casting Vote

THE Constitution makes the Vice-President President of the Senate but it defines his powers in only one respect, that of voting. It says that he shall have the right in case of a tie and not otherwise. This high prerogative has been exercised 191 times by 24 Vice-Presidents. Their names, down to March 4, 1929, with the number of votes given by each, follow: Adams, 29; Jefferson, 3; Burr, 3; Clinton, 11; Gerry, 8; Tompkins, 5; Calhoun, 28; Van Buren, 4; R. M. Johnson, 14; Dallas, 19; Fillmore, 5; Breckinridge, 10; Hamlin, 7; Colfax, 13; Wilson, 1; Wheeler, 5; Arthur, 3; Morton, 4; Stevenson, 2; Hobart, 1; Sherman, 4; Marshall, 10; Dawes, 2.

Fairbanks, Coolidge, and all the Vice-Presidents who succeeded to the Presidency before the regular meeting of Congress, except Chester A. Arthur, gave no casting votes.[1]

It will be observed that the first Vice-President, John Adams, gave more casting votes than did any of his successors and far more than did any of them except Calhoun, who almost equalled his record. His votes were also the most important, and it is a curious fact that the first in the long list of casting votes of Vice-President acting as President of the Senate,[2] extending over a period of nearly a century and a half, had the greatest influence on the governmental and political history of the Nation. A bill before the Senate for establishing the Department of State contained a phrase which recognized the right of the President to remove the head of the department and hence all similar officers. Senator Maclay moved to strike out the clause; the vote stood ten to ten; Adams voted against the amendment; and the power of removal remained with the President. It was questioned when Jackson

---

[1]For these statistics I am indebted to a very thorough study published in the *American Historical Review* for April, 1915 (Vol. XX, p. 571), and to a supplemental list prepared for me by a senior student at Barnard College.

[2]The above statement must be understood in a strictly technical sense. Adams assumed the right to act as chairman of the committee of the whole and as such had previously given two casting votes on a tariff bill before his vote on the power of removal. The first was in favor of lowering a proposed duty on loaf sugar, the second against increasing one on salt.

removed Secretary of the Treasury Duane; limited by the Tenure-of-Office Act; and in 1926 was decided by the Supreme Court to have been conferred on the President by the Constitution, the opinion being written by an ex-President, Chief Justice Taft. The Senate had obtained great power by its right to concur in nominations; could it block removals also, the President might have become its servant.

Adams had carefully considered the question and prepared for his own use a memorandum, now lost, of the reasons for his decision; but in the Senate his vote was given without hesitation and, indeed, if Senator Maclay may be relied on, in a hurried and undignified manner. Mr. Maclay notes in his diary that "the Vice-President with joy cried out 'it is not a vote,' without giving himself time to declare the division of the House and give his vote in order." Maclay says that there had been much private discussion of the bill, or, as he calls it, "caballing"; that Adams was very active in this; and that it was generally believed that he was responsible for the conversion of Senators Dalton of Massachusetts and Bassett of Delaware, who announced that they had changed their opinions. Maclay also credits, or discredits, Adams with weakening the support of the amendment by his old friend, Lee of Virginia.

Another very important vote of Vice-President Adams given on April 28, 1794, defeated a bill for suspending imports from Great Britain. Its passage might have prevented the mission of John Jay and led to war with England, or at least caused a collapse of public credit, which might in turn have brought down our newly established government.

Of minor importance but still of interest were Adams' votes on the salaries of judges and the pension of Baron Steuben. A bill was before the Senate giving the Chief Justice of the Supreme Court four thousand dollars a year and the Associate Justices three thousand each. It was moved to raise the latter sum to three thousand five hundred and the motion was carried by the vote of the Vice-President. Adams also voted twice in favor of a bill giving a pension to Baron Steuben, a Prussian officer who had rendered most valuable service as Inspector-General of the Continental Army, and who could claim that he had received a semi-promise that the government would provide for him. Adams' votes were usually strongly Federalist, but he occasionally won the praise of that unterrified Democrat, Senator William Maclay of Pennsylvania.

During Adams' administration the Federalists had a good working majority in the Senate and Vice-President Jefferson's often expressed desire to escape from the burden of public cares was gratified, at least, in the matter of giving the casting vote. He was obliged to perform this duty on only three occasions, and one of them must have given him great pleasure; for he was able to save an amendment to the famous Alien bill, which provided that nothing in it should be construed in a manner to contravene existing treaties.

Burr, like Jefferson, gave only three casting votes. Two of them were on the same bill, which was one of considerable importance. At the close of

Adams' administration, the defeated Federalists had established new circuit courts and filled them with their own partisans, to the great wrath of Jefferson who, in a letter to a friend, made the famous declaration that "they have retired into the Judiciary as a stronghold and from that battery all the works of Republicanism are to be battered down and erased." The judges could not be removed but the law creating the courts could be repealed; "You could not take the Judge from the office but you could take the office from the Judge."

In January, 1802, the Senate passed a bill repealing the Judiciary Act of 1801; but the Federalists proclaimed with great energy and eloquence that the repeal was unconstitutional and nearly succeeded in defeating it. When the vote on the third reading was taken, two Republican Senators were absent and the bill was only saved by the casting vote of the Vice-President. The next day Senator Jonathan Dayton of New Jersey, a moderate Federalist who had once inclined to the Republicans,[1] moved that the bill be referred to a select committee with instructions "to consider and report the alterations which may be proper in the judiciary system of the United States." Dayton said that he had learned that one gentleman who voted for the third reading had not perfectly heard and understood the question and that he, himself, only asked that the two parties might agree on a modification of the whole judicial system.

This gave Burr the opportunity of playing the part of the ideal presiding officer, the impartial moderator. He said that "he felt disposed to accommodate the gentlemen in the expression of their wishes, the sincerity of which he had no reason to question, to ameliorate the provisions of the bill that it might be rendered more acceptable to the Senate. He did this under the impression that their object was sincere. He should, however, discountenance by his vote any attempt, if any such should be made, that might in an indirect way go to defeat the bill." Burr, however, was given no opportunity to do this. A few days later when a Republican Senator had returned and a Federalist Senator was absent, the bill was taken from the committee and passed. Burr's vote had no effect on the bill but much on his political position.

Burr's view of the matter was certainly defensible. Senator Beveridge in his *Life of John Marshall* says that Burr's action was perfectly correct, that as an impartial presiding officer he could not well have done anything else. Alexander J. Dallas, the Republican Attorney-General of Pennsylvania, wrote the Vice-President approving his action. Nathaniel Niles, a rampant Republican, sent Burr a letter thanking him for his vote. As a Republican, he wanted his party to be fair, he said.

But President Jefferson and most of the party leaders severely blamed Burr for disloyalty, and there is this to be said for their view. Burr had been elected by the Republicans; the impartiality expected in a presiding officer

---

[1] Jefferson believed that his change of mind was due to a hope of becoming Secretary of War under Adams.

varies widely. There is a great contrast between the Speaker of the House of Representatives and his venerable brother of the House of Commons. Moreover it might be urged that Burr was not deciding a question of order where non-partisanship is a solemn duty, but voting on a question of making a law where a certain consideration may rightly be paid to party policy. It was Senator rather than Chairman Burr who delayed the decision of the Senate. As in the Presidential election, Burr alienated his allies yet failed to conciliate his opponents. The former condemned him as a traitor who had failed in his duty, the latter as a coward for not defeating Jefferson and for not killing the Circuit Court bill; and both sides believed that he was trying to form a party of his own.

Vice-President Clinton gave three casting votes, one of which defeated a bill whose loss caused great embarrassment to the country. The charter of the United States Bank was to expire in 1811. When it was founded in 1791 the Jeffersonians had vehemently opposed its creation as contrary to the Constitution and to Republican principles. But in 1810 the Republican Secretary of the Treasury, Albert Gallatin, believed that a bank was "necessary and proper" for executing the lawful powers of the government, and was most anxious that the Bank of the United States should be rechartered. A bill for this purpose was indefinitely postponed in the House of Representatives by a single vote. In the Senate the vote on the passage of a like bill was a tie.

Clinton was both in theory and in feeling a strong States' Rights and strict construction man. He was bitterly opposed to President Madison and to Gallatin and he voted against the bill, doubtless with the joy of one to whom his duty is both plain and pleasant. Clinton accompanied his vote with a brief statement of his reasons for giving it. He said that the means for carrying out the enumerated powers must be appropriate. The power to create corporations is not expressly granted. It is a high attribute of sovereignty and in its nature not "accessorial or derivative by implication, but primary and independent." Clinton expressed the opinion that his interpretation of the Constitution would not in any way defeat its purpose, while the opposite construction would have an inevitable tendency to consolidation. He said that in the course of a long life he had found that government was not strengthened by the assumption of doubtful powers and reminded the Senate that the Constitution could be amended if the powers granted by it were found to be insufficient.

The address resembled part of an elaborate argument against recharter which had been delivered by that future stalwart champion of a bank, Senator Henry Clay. It also differed markedly in its style from that of the uncultivated and sometimes headlong Clinton. The most probable explanation is that Clinton had accepted the help of the brilliant Kentuckian. John Quincy Adams noted in his diary for November 26, 1825, that Clay said that he wrote the speech, "which was perhaps the thing which had gained the old man more credit than anything else that he ever did." But Clay added that he had written it "under Mr. Clinton's dictation and he should never think of claiming it as his own composition."

The right of the Vice-President to give a casting vote when the Senate is equally divided may seem the one great substantial power of a rather unsubstantial functionary; yet two Vice-Presidents, Gerry and Dallas, in their inaugural addresses expressed the hope, the first indirectly, the second by implication, that they would have no occasion to use this right. Gerry and Dallas were courtly gentlemen and it possibly may be that their apparent humility was due more to what they considered the demands of etiquette than to real modesty. But the political careers of both men had shown that they were "born of the willow, not of the oak," and probably they were honestly and prudently anxious to escape responsibility.

Mr. Blaine says in his *Twenty Years in Congress* that the right of a Vice-President to vote in case of a tie "is a contingency, more apt to embarrass than promote his political fortunes." This was recognized from the first. After John Adams, very readily and gladly it would seem, had broken a tie by voting for an amendment giving higher salaries to the Associate Justices of the Supreme Court, there was another tie on the question of increasing the salary of the Attorney-General. Maclay wrote in his journal that Adams looked pitiful and said that he would be made the scape-goat for everything. However, a Senator changed his vote and the victim was freed. On another occasion Maclay gleefully noted that Adams had the yeas and nays called on him.

These ties were the result of a nice balance in a small Senate of representatives of two schools of political thought. Later, ties were sometimes deliberately contrived to injure the Vice-President. In 1811 it was reported truly or falsely that the Administration had arranged a tie to throw the onus of defeating the bank bill on the Vice-President, Mr. Clinton. The story was that Senator Worthington of Ohio was opposed to the bank and would have voted against the recharter if this had been necessary to defeat it; but his name was the last on the roll and when he saw that his vote, if given in the affirmative, would make a tie, he voted for the bill because he knew that the Vice-President would vote no, and so offend the Federalists who were friends of the bank and whose help the anti-Virginia Republicans of New York, now led by Clinton, were anxious to obtain.

In the "Middle Period" of national history two Vice-Presidents, past or future, Van Buren the Little Magician, and Calhoun the austere master of logic, plotted to drive each other into traps, and probably the "godlike" Webster lent his aid. In 1827 a bill which actually, though not formally, greatly increased the tariff on woolen goods was before the Senate. The bill had aroused intense feeling on both sides and either support or opposition was dangerous for possible candidates for the Presidency. Senator Van Buren of New York voted on several occasions for the bill but when Senator Hayne of South Carolina moved to lay it on the table he remained silent. A tie resulted; Vice-President Calhoun gave a casting vote in favor of the motion and became responsible for the loss of the bill. As a matter of fact, there was not time to pass it before adjournment, but this might not have been generally realized. Calhoun had formerly been considered a moderate protectionist and his action, while popular in the South, might offend voters in the North whose support he would soon need.

A little later Calhoun had an opportunity for revenge which he used to the full. When the question of consenting to the nomination of Van Buren as Minister to England was before the Senate, Calhoun gave three casting votes against the appointment, two on preliminary questions and one on that of concurrence; although as Van Buren was accused of deliberately causing a breach between the two chief officers of the Nation, Calhoun was acting as judge in his own cause. Ben Perley Poore, not indeed a wholly reliable authority, says that the last tie was a contrived one, Webster leaving the Senate Chamber for that of the Supreme Court in order to throw the burden of decision on Calhoun.

In 1836 an opportunity came for Calhoun to strike again at his old rival. A bill was before the Senate excluding from the mails matter intended to excite slaves to insurrection. It was very extreme, giving great powers of decision to local postmasters and it had no chance of passing, as even some Southern Senators were opposed to it. But a tie was arranged on the question of the engrossment of the bill. If Vice-President Van Buren should vote against it, he would seriously offend the South, where he was regarded as an intriguing politician and a foe to States' Rights, and was even accused of being an abolitionist. But should he vote for the bill, he would displease many of his New York constituents. Accordingly, Clay and Calhoun arranged several ties. On one Van Buren did not vote, but when the Senate divided equally on the engrossment of the bill, he could not escape and he bravely faced his foes who, for a moment, believed that they had frightened him from the field.

An often quoted description of the incident by Benton is thus summarized by Denis Tilden Lynch in his life of Van Buren, *An Epoch and a Man*: "When the vote was taken Van Buren was out of the chair. Calhoun loudly demanded the presence of the Vice-President, calling upon the sergeant-at-arms to produce him. Van Buren was pacing up and down behind the colonnade back of his desk. He let Calhoun enjoy a momentary thought that he had deliberately absented himself and then took his seat, rising a moment later to given the casting vote for the engrossment." The bill was finally defeated by a vote of 25 to 19.

In 1846 Vice-President Dallas of Pennsylvania was called on to decide what was probably the longest remembered and the most personally embarrassing question ever submitted to a holder of his office. Should he save or slay the tariff law of 1846? The Democrats were pushing through a bill substituting for the Whig and Protectionist tariff act of 1842 one which was founded on Free Trade principles and which made a very heavy reduction of duties. Though the proposed law had aroused the bitterest opposition in Pennsylvania, Dallas was ready to follow the President and the mass of the party rather than the people of his own State; but he was naturally anxious to avoid offending either. His situation was especially difficult because in the Presidential campaign of 1844 he and the Democrats generally had been busy assuring the protectionists of Pennsylvania that Polk was sounder in the faith than Clay, and that they might safely vote for him.

Desperate efforts were being made to defeat or at least to modify the bill; the Senate was almost equally divided and there was great doubt as to what the final result would be. Senator Haywood of North Carolina, a Democrat who had been in college with the President, believed that the change in duties, if made immediately before business was given a brief time to prepare for the reversal of policy, would be bad for the country. Senator Jarnagin of Tennessee, a Whig, was thoroughly opposed to the bill, but he had been instructed to vote for it by the Legislature of his state and felt it his duty to vote yea on the direct question of its passage. His conscience, however, might allow him to kill the bill indirectly.

The Administration was willing to compromise if this was necessary to save the bill, but was very reluctant to do so. The Democrats did not rely on Jarnagin, but even if he should vote against the bill, if Haywood voted for it, there would be a tie; and Dallas was expected to vote yea. On July 22 Polk had an interview with Haywood and begged him for the sake of the party, the country, and his own political future, to vote for the bill. Haywood withdrew, much impressed by these adjurations. Two days later the President, the Vice-President, and the Secretary of the Treasury discussed a compromise proposed by a leading manufacturer, namely, to enact the reductions in the bill but make them gradual instead of immediate, postponing one-half for ten years. Polk says in his *Diary*: "Mr. Dallas was in favor of the proposition. I did not encourage it, fearing it might produce confusion and be the means of losing the Bill. Mr. Dallas said if the Democrats did not agree to it he would let them know, if it came to his casting vote, they might loose (lose) the Bill as it was."

Next day Senator Haywood resigned his seat in the Senate and Senator Jarnagin, in the presence of the President and the Cabinet, stated that he would vote for the bill. But clever politicians are often "juggling fiends," who keep the word of promise to the ear and break it in the spirit. That staunch protectionist, Senator Clayton of Delaware, with the avowed intention of killing the bill, moved its reference with certain instructions to the Committee on Finance and the motion passed, thanks to Mr. Jarnagin's vote in its favor. The committee, however, which was controlled by friends of the bill, reported next day that the instructions were incapable of execution. Then, three ballots secured the passage of the bill; on two of them Mr. Jarnagin did not vote and the bill was saved by the casting vote of the Vice-President. On the final passage Mr. Jarnagin, in accordance with his instructions and his statement of intentions, voted yea, and there being no tie, Mr. Dallas was relieved from voting.

But all knew that he could have killed the bill had he chosen, nor did Dallas himself make any attempt to conceal the fact. As the roll-call on engrossment showed an even division of the Senate, he rose and gave his reasons for the vote he was about to give in a brief but dignified speech. He said that he believed that the people had declared against protection; that the friends of the system had said that they only asked for help until the industries assisted could get a fair start; that most of those affected by the bill had been established for a considerable time; and that they should now take their chances with others. He admitted that he thought that the bill went too far, but said that he believed that he should not assume a qualified veto power by defeating it.[1]

The defense had little effect on Pennsylvania, for which state it was chiefly intended. The Whigs, indeed, paid scant attention to Dallas. They were after bigger game and trained their guns on the Democratic party, savagely reminding the people of a mildly protectionist letter which Polk had written to a prominent Pennsylvania politician, and how Democratic processions had displayed transparencies and banners with such inscriptions as "Polk, Dallas, and the Tariff of 1842," sometimes having the audacity to add, "We dare the Whigs to repeal it." The Pennsylvania Democrats, however, felt that they had been stabbed by a friend and brother and they turned on the traitor with fury.

In Philadelphia, which was the chief seat of the Dallas faction, and in other places, the Vice-President was burned in effigy. The *American Sentinel,* formerly a supporter of Dallas, said: "Should Mr. Dallas live to the age of Mathuzalah *(sic),* he will never be able to make ample atonement for his severe onslaught upon the home industry of Pennsylvania. Farewell to all Vice-Presidents for the future from Pennsylvania. We have had enough of one to last us while all who live now shall continue to breathe the breath of existence in our fair land." For a sensitive, rather timid man like Dallas, such assaults must have been hard to bear; but he did not flinch. In his farewell address to the Senate he pleaded, not without a certain dignity and pathos, that he had sought the welfare of the whole. He said that he had voted about thirty times.[2]

---

[1]The last argument was weak. The President by his veto defeats the will of a majority, perhaps a large majority. Dallas, by voting, would merely enable the Senate to have a will.

[2]Really only nineteen times; possibly he included votes given when the Senate was in committee of the whole.

PART TWO

*Vice-Presidential Nominations
and Elections*

CHAPTER IX.

The First Election Under the New Constitution

A T THE first election of President and Vice-President, that of 1788, there was no contest for the chief office. All the electors wrote the name of George Washington upon their ballots. On the Vice-Presidency there was not such ready and full agreement. Although there had been no opposition to Washington, the choice of the electors themselves had been a partisan one. The "Federalists," as the friends of the Constitution were called, endeavored to send men of their own way of thinking to the House of Representatives, the Senate, and the Electoral College; their opponents, the "Anti-Federalists," did the same. The result was a victory for the Federalists, which, in the choice of electors, was overwhelming. There was a kind of understanding that the Anti-Federalists would support Governor George Clinton of New York for Vice-President, and the only attempt to turn the electors into what they soon came to be, mere registering automata, was made in his behalf. His followers in New York assumed the name of Federal Republicans. The title was not inappropriate. The anti-Constitutionalists were much more federal than their opponents and somewhat more republican. With still better reason they might have called themselves democrats or radicals. Like their chief, they were of the masses rather than the classes.

Clinton's father was an Irish emigrant, who won an honorable place for himself in his new home. When Clinton was first elected Governor of New York, a competitor, the aristocratic Schuyler, made the comment that his family and connections did not entitle him to so distinguished a predominance. But Schuyler nobly added, "He is virtuous and loves his country, he has ability and is brave, and I hope he will experience from every patriot, support, countenance and comfort."

George Clinton was born in Ulster County, New York, on July 26, 1739. He served with credit in the French and Indian War and was an early, active, and constant supporter of the rights of the Colonists. In 1777 he became the first Governor of the state of New York and held that office continuously for six terms of three years each. As a war Governor, though brave and energetic, he was less successful than might have been expected from his early military record; but he showed skill in the difficult duties of managing the Indians and the finances. Clinton loved New York, he understood the great advantages which her position gave her, and both from local patriotism and personal pride and ambition he had no wish to see the State of which he was the head absorbed in a larger whole. He therefore fought the establishment of the more perfect union with all his strength.

De Alva S. Alexander, in his *Political History of the State of New York,* says of Clinton: "It has been given to few men in New York to inspire more passionate personal attachment than George Clinton. He was . . . . intolerant, often domineering, sometimes petulant, and occasionally too quick to take offense, but he was magnetic and generous, easily putting himself in touch with those about him, and ready without hesitation to help the poorest and carry the weakest."

The faction which attempted to make Clinton Vice-President was composed mainly of old "Liberty Boys" who had led in riotous attacks upon the royal government in the times of the Stamp Act and the tea duty, and of younger men who had joined them in opposing the return of the Loyalists, in favoring paper money, and in fighting the ratification of the Constitution. A committee acting in their name issued a circular letter saying that it was necessary that there should be some one in the new government who wished to amend the Constitution; that George Clinton was such a man; that there was some reason to believe that New York would support him; that some gentlemen in Virginia had been consulted and had replied that the people of their state would favor him; and that it was therefore hoped that the voters in every state would instruct their electors to cast their ballots for Clinton. But this first attempt of a New York organization to carry the country for its candidate proved a total failure. Three districts in Virginia elected Clinton men and that was all. In New York the Legislature chose the electors, the two Houses could not agree on how the choice should be made, and the vote of the State was lost.

It remained for the Federalist electors to name the Vice-President, but they were unpledged. There was nobody who could speak for the party, and the electors must vote as their individual judgments, the opinion of the Federalist leaders, and their own understanding of the wishes of their constituents, should guide them. As in later elections, regard to geography played a great part in the choice. Washington was a Southerner; therefore the Vice-President must come from the Middle States or New England. Large states were felt to have special claims. Of the leading men of Pennsylvania, Franklin was old and infirm, and Robert Morris was busy with banking and investments in wild land, practices which were held in much suspicion by the majorty of the people. Other prominent Pennsylvanians, like James Wilson, were regarded by the masses, though not by the chiefs of the Federalists, as too aristocratic.

New York could offer a statesman and patriot in John Jay, who had distinguished himself by his courage and independence of France in the negotiation of the treaty that closed the war with England, and who was now Secretary for Foreign Affairs. But many believed that his experience specially qualified him for his present position, and that there was unfinished business before his department which made a change at this time particularly unwise. Moreover, he had proposed to Congress that in return for an advantageous commercial treaty with Spain, the United States should waive for twenty-five or thirty years its claim to navigate the Mississippi to the sea, and this concession had made him very unpopular in the South and West. In Pennsylvania, too, where Jay had been highly regarded, he had recently given offense by supporting certain changes in her constitution, taking part, though not a citizen of Pennsylvania, in the discussion of a proposed new Constitution. To make matters worse, the new Constitution which was favored by Jay was less directly democratic than the old.

There remained Massachusetts, the number of whose electoral votes, though inferior to that of Virginia, equalled that of Pennsylvania and excelled that of every other State. Virginia and Massachusetts had been co-leaders in the Revolution and their preëminence had been acknowledged by their associates. The first President of the Continental Congress came from Virginia and the second from Massachusetts. Virginia furnished the commander-in-chief of the army, and Massachusetts the next in rank. In Congress the Lees of Virginia and the Adamses of Massachusetts usually stood together and often their action determined that of their colleagues. There was, therefore, strong precedent for placing beside Washington a citizen of Massachusetts. Two were seriously considered, Governor Hancock and John Adams, who had lately returned from diplomatic service.

The first might well be known in history as Hancock the Magnificent. He was a wealthy Boston merchant, touchy, ambitious, and vain. Hancock early joined the Whigs where, although he possessed no great ability, his wealth and social eminence made him very welcome. He was used as an impressive figurehead while others planned and executed policies. In spite of his lack of statesmanship, Hancock grew to be the Boss of Massachusetts. Circumstances gave him a reputation for preëminent patriotism, his wealth furnished the means of binding others to him by financial favors, and he possessed a personal charm which in a single interview could transform an opponent into a follower.

Moreover, Hancock was surrounded by a band of clever politicians who managed and stage-managed him with great skill. Hancock himself was most wary when his popularity was endangered, a convenient fit of the gout often preventing him from taking the field when both victory and defeat were dangerous.

In 1776, as President of the Second Continental Congress, he immortalized himself by writing his name in a large, bold hand at the bottom of the Declaration of Independence. In 1780 he became the first Governor of the State of Massachusetts and held that office until his death in 1793, except for two years in the period of Shays' rebellion. At this critical time he stood aside, leaving the dangerous responsibilities of the executive chair to his rival, James Bowdoin. During the greater part of the struggle in Massachusetts for the ratification of the United States Constitution, Hancock was confined to his house by gout, but at last his health permitted him to be taken to the hall where the State convention sat and to read a speech advising the ratification of the Constitution, but proposing at the same time various amendments guarding the rights of the states and of the people. It is probable that the paper was writen by Theophilus Parsons, the future Chief Justice of Massachusetts, after careful consultation with two other eminent Federalists, Theodore Sedgwick and Rufus King, and that Hancock's assent was secured by a promise that Bowdoin's friends would not oppose him at the next election for Governor. Hancock was also told that he was considered the natural person for President if, as was by no means unlikely, Virginia should refuse to ratify the Constitution. Perhaps the Vice-Presidency was also mentioned.

John Adams in some respects resembled Hancock; in others was a great contrast to him. Late in life, in defending Hancock's memory against the attacks of men who had also become his own opponents, Adams wrote: "I can say, with truth, that I profoundly admired him, and more profoundly loved him. If he had vanity and caprice, so had I. And if his vanity and caprice made me sometimes sputter, as you know they often did, mine, I well know, had often a similar effect upon him. But these little flickerings of passion determine nothing concerning essential characters. I knew Mr. Hancock from his cradle to his grave. He was radically generous and benevolent. Nor were his talents or attainments inconsiderable. They were far superior to many who have been much more celebrated. He had a great deal of political sagacity and penetration into men. . . . . If statues, obelisks, pyramids, or divine honors were ever merited by men, of cities or nations, James Otis, Samuel Adams, and John Hancock deserved these from the town of Boston and the United States." But Adams was a far abler and stronger man than Hancock and at critical moments in the history of the country his action was both brave and wise.

Adams was a lawyer and had been Hancock's adviser professionally and, in a measure, politically. He was an early favorer of independence; before and in the Revolution he was a member of the Continental Congress, where he obtained great influence, partly because of his patriotism and industry, but also on account of his excessive fear of a strong central government and of the army influence. Adams was one of the commission to negotiate peace, and served as Minister at the Hague and at London. After the ratification of the Constitution by the required number of states, the current set strongly in favor of Adams for Vice-President. An article in a Philadelphia paper of October 8, 1788, said, "of the several respected candidates in nomination[1] for Vice-President, circumstances seem most in favor of John Adams, Esq. While the conciliating talents of Governor Hancock, and the attachment to him that prevails in Massachusetts, render him necessary to the peace of New England, Mr. Adams is perfectly at leisure . . . . "

The reasons for the selection of Adams were well summed up in a letter to Madison by Tench Coxe of Philadelphia, "a mousing politician" fond of corresponding on public affairs with leading men. "Mr. Adams is esteemed by the people, has high ideals of government (that is, he believed in a strong government), is a friend to property, will take the feelings of New England with him, has been used to the forms of legislation and diplomatic business; he is a man of pure private character." But during the Revolutionary War Adams had often failed to "think Continentally" and had been foolishly jealous of Washington. These old errors now returned to plague him. Some feared that if introduced into the new government, he would use his influence to weaken rather than to strengthen it, and that his election would be personally disagreeable to Washington. Adams' friends endeavored to remove these prejudices, as they regarded them, against their candidate. General Lincoln of Massachusetts, one of the most distinguished officers from that state in the army of the Revolution and a valued correspondent of Washington, wrote to his old commander praising Adams: "I was altogether disposed to acquiesce in the prevailing sentiments of the electors without giving any unbecoming preference or incurring any unnecessary ill-will." To Knox, Washington wrote that Adams would doubtless make a very good Vice-President and that he himself would be entirely satisfied with such an arrangement.

But George Washington, though he did not remember old quarrels with rancor, was not a no-party man. He believed it most important that the new government should be placed in the hands of its friends and, therefore, he allowed certain electors in Maryland and Virginia to be informed that the election of Adams would be entirely agreeable to him, and that he considered it the only certain way to prevent the choice of an Anti-Federalist.

Next to Washington himself, the most important Federalist for a candidate to win over was Alexander Hamilton. Unlike Washington, he had not held a high public position and there were no considerations of propriety to restrain him from mingling in the fight over the Vice-Presidency; but he was a little doubtful under whose banner he would enlist or, perhaps he would have said, to whom he would assure the prize. Adams' supporters were not unmindful of Hamilton's influence and Theodore Sedgwick wrote to Hamilton in his behalf. Hamilton replied: "The only hesitation in my mind in

---

[1]The nominations referred to, except that of Clinton, were merely informal suggestions.

regard to Mr. Adams has arisen within a day or two from a suggestion by a particular gentleman that he is unfriendly in his sentiments to General Washington. Richard H. Lee, who will probably come from Virginia, is also in this style. The Lees and Adamses have been in the habit of uniting, and hence may spring up a cabal very embarrassing to the Executive, and of course to the administration of the government. Consider this, sound the reality of it and let me hear from you. What think you of Lincoln or Knox? This is a flying thought."[1]

Lincoln appears to have been dropped without further consideration. Of his fellow general, then occupying the almost sinecure position of Secretary of War, Hamilton wrote to Madison: "As to Knox I cannot persuade myself that he will incline to the appointment. He must sacrifice emolument by it, which must be of necessity a primary object with him." A month later Hamilton wrote to the same correspondent: "On the question between Mr. H(ancock) and Mr. A(dams), Mr. King [Rufus King, a leading Federalist of Massachusetts and New York] will probably have informed you that I have, upon the whole, concluded that the latter ought to be supported. My measures will be taken accordingly. I had but one scruple, but after mature consideration I have relinquished it. Mr. Adams, to a strong understanding, has always appeared to me to add an ardent love for the public good; and, as his further knowledge of the world seems to have corrected those jealousies which he is represented to have been once influenced by, I trust nothing of the kind suggested in my former letter will disturb the harmony of administration."

Yet, in spite of Hamilton's recognition of Adams' excellent qualities, he favored him less for these than for reasons of practical politics. Two weeks after the letter to Sedgwick, Hamilton wrote Madison that he had decided to support Adams, though "not without apprehensions on the score we have conversed about." Adams wished to wait before amending the Constitution until time should show the need, and Hamilton believed that was better than amending it at once as so many were demanding, though, in his own opinion, amendments such as were sought would be unwise at any time. Moreover, Adams was very popular in the East and if he were not chosen Vice-President, one of two worse things would be likely to happen. "Either he must be nominated to some important office for which he is less proper or he will become a malcontent and give additional weight to the opposition to the government."

Had Adams read this letter of his supporter, he might well have exclaimed: "Deliver me from my friends." Hamilton's acts matched his words; his chief effort seems to have been to reduce the vote for his candidate. The reason he usually gave was that some electors might vote against Washington

---

[1]Probably there would have been some objection to both these gentlemen because their chief services had been military.

and that if all his friends voted for Adams, the latter might have the most votes and so, as the ballots were cast with no distinction of office, Adams might be President and Washington Vice-President. Hamilton's effort was certainly successful. When the ballots were counted, it was found that Adams had obtained thirty-four votes and that thirty-five had been scattered among ten gentlemen who received from one to nine votes each. Adams, was, therefore, elected but had the great mortification of being a minority Vice-President when, if the electors had voted according to their wishes, he would have been chosen by a large majority. John Trumbull, a son of Jonathan Trumbull, the war Governor of Connecticut, wrote angrily to Adams: "In the choice of V. P. you had certainly no rival. All that could be done by your enemies was to deprive you of a certain number of votes. Many of your friends were duped on that occasion. I will inform you how it was managed in Connecticut. On the day before the election, Colonel Webb (an officer who had a fine record in the Revolutionary War) came on express to Hartford, sent, as he said, by Colonel Hamilton, etc, who, he assured us, had made an exact calculation on the subject, and found that New Jersey were to throw away three votes, I think,[1] and all would be well. I exclaimed against the measure, and insisted that it was all a deception; but what could my single opinion avail against an expression armed with intelligence and calculations? So our electors threw away two votes where they were sure they would do no harm."

Elbridge Gerry, an old companion of Adams in pre-Revolutionary struggles and in the Continental Congress, wrote him: "Maryland threw away their votes on Colonel Harrison, and South Carolina on Governor Rutledge, being, with some other states which were not unanimous for you, apprehensive that this was a necessary step to prevent your election to the (Presidential) chair." Gerry believed that all the votes against Adams were given for the purpose of making Washington's success certain, but this is not wholly true. A letter of Peter Carr to Madison shows that in Virginia three Anti-Federalist electors voted for Clinton. It is probable that the scattering farther South was largely due to Hamilton's influence, but it must be remembered that personal and local loyalty always played a large part in Southern politics, and that the scattering votes went almost wholly to favorite sons.

The reasons for Hamilton's conduct have been much debated. Adams' friends have agreed with Trumbull that his doubt of Washington's success was a "deception," and it has been charged that Hamilton's real motive was a malignant desire to weaken Adams' influence by cutting down the vote which, had no trickery been used, he would have obtained. Today it seems impossible to believe that Hamilton feared that Adams would outrun Washington. But Mr. Stanwood is of the opinion that there was a plan in New York to

---

[1] As a matter of fact, New Jersey threw away five of her six votes, giving them to John Jay.

cut Washington and throw the vote of the State to Clinton and to Adams, or some other than the great Virginian, and that it was no more than common prudence for Hamilton to make Washington's election sure by reducing Adams' vote. In the Madison manuscripts there are some contemporary expressions of opinion resembling that of Mr. Stanwood. Tench Coxe wrote Madison that he thought that Adams would lose a few votes north of Maryland from a fear that he would outrun Washington or endanger his election. "This," said Coxe, "tho in my mind a very small hazard indeed, I am pleased to observe is foreseen and will be attended to." Carrington of Virginia wrote Madison that he believed that it had been proper to scatter some votes in order to assure General Washington's being foremost. Probably Hamilton acted from two motives, extreme care for Washington's election, and a wish to diminish the prestige of the heir apparent. In the letter to Madison already quoted, he said that it was inadvisable to unite on a single candidate for the Vice-Presidency, that he was not unmindful of the possibility of a tie from the circumstance that the Constitution had not provided the means of discriminating between the votes intended for President and those for Vice-President.[1] But Hamilton also expressed the opinion that "it would be disagreeable to have a man treading close upon the heels of the person we wish to be President. May not the malignity of the opposition be, in some instances, exhibited even against him (Washington)? Of all this we shall best judge when we know who are our Electors, and we must in our circles take our measures accordingly."

---

[1] This actually happened twelve years later.

CHAPTER X.

The Re-election of Adams and the Election of Jefferson and Burr

WASHINGTON'S first administration was chiefly devoted to organizing and maintaining a national government. Alexander Hamilton, the Secretary of the Treasury, took the lead in devising and executing measures for this purpose. The Secretary of State, Thomas Jefferson, frequently objected to them and was regarded by the opposition as their leader, but he remained in the Cabinet at the urgent request of the President, who was most anxious to avoid an open breach among his advisers. The last year of the administration saw the overthrow of the monarchy in France and the execution of the king, our "august" and most useful ally during the war for independence. Already two parties were forming in the United States, the friends of the Administration who kept the old name of Federalists, and its opponents who called themselves Republicans or sometimes Democrats, a word frequently applied to them by the Federalists as a term of reproach, as Socialist is often used today.

With the deposition and execution of Louis XVI and the violent measures which followed, the chasm between parties in the United States became wider. The Federalists were certain that the vile "Democrats" were communists, anarchists, and atheists. The Republicans pointed to the consolidating and capitalistic measures of Hamilton, and to the ceremony surrounding the President, and declared that their opponents wished to establish a monarchy, and that they themselves were the champions of the people in the age-long conflict between liberty and despotism now reaching its crisis in the struggle of republican France against the allied monarchs of Europe.

The more rabid Republicans assailed Washington in most insulting terms, but his hold on the people was too strong to be broken. His influence was potent in preserving the Union. "North and South will hang together," said Jefferson, "so long as they have you to hang on." Both Hamilton and Jefferson begged their chief to serve a second term, and when it was known that he would consent to do so, there was no longer a Presidential question. But there still remained a Vice-Presidential one. The reëlection of Washington made that of Adams natural. As president of the Senate he had given casting votes for important Federalist measures, and the leaders of the party, including Hamilton, decided again to support him for Vice-President.

He was to meet, however, a solidified and dangerous opposition. The Republicans were unwilling or afraid to present a candidate against Washington, but they decided to make the choice of Vice-President a means of expressing disapproval of the "doctrines of the monocrats," and their enemy had delivered himself into their hands by writing two books on government with special reference to the state and national governments in America. Adams was no believer in universal suffrage or in unchecked popular rule, and his books were ransacked in a thorough but unfair manner for unfortunate phrases to prove him an aristocrat and a monarchist. Adams' stiff, reserved manners and his coach and liveried servants, which he displayed at Philadelphia, also gave offense.

The Republicans, however, had some difficulty in deciding whom they would oppose to Adams. Jefferson and Madison were excluded because they came from the same State as the President. The party then turned to New York, but hesitated between Governor George Clinton and Senator Aaron Burr. Clinton was a much older man than Burr, with far more experience in public affairs. He was a radical and a strong particularist and was, therefore, a natural candidate for a Democratic and States' Rights party. Burr's public life, though short, had been very active and he was allied with the powerful Livingstons who had only recently joined the Republicans. Burr himself had avoided taking a prominent part in various contests. He still had a foot in the Federalist camp, and his nomination might win some doubters.

Burr also had a certain strength outside New York. His father, who died young, had been a learned and pious president of Princeton; his mother was a daughter of Jonathan Edwards, the American Calvin; and this holy ancestry drew Puritans toward the New York politician and profligate. Virginia would probably vote against Adams, and attempts were made to divert her strength from Clinton by the allegation that he had opposed locating the capital on the Potomac. Clinton was fortunate in having a supporter more powerful in the Old Dominion than any of his opponents—Patrick Henry. Like Clinton, Henry had fought the ratification of the Constitution and had favored amending it after its adoption; he now wished to see Clinton Vice-President. At a conference between three representatives of New York, Pennsylvania, and Virginia, respectively, it was decided to drop Burr[1] and work for the election of Clinton. It was hoped that Henry's influence would carry North Caro-

---

[1]The Federalists had endeavored to divide their opponents by a futile attempt to induce that staunch Republican Governor, Mifflin of Pennsylvania, to try for the Vice-Presidency.

lina, which frequently followed the lead of Virginia, and it was believed that a few votes could be won in Adams' own section, New England.

The campaign between the two parties was bitter and personal. The Federalists declared that Clinton had opposed the Constitution with the utmost violence and would have resorted to civil war had not his followers shrunk from him, and that he had stolen the New York governorship at the last election.[1] The Republicans accused Adams of being a monarchist.

When the electoral ballots were counted, it was found that, as the Republicans had hoped, New York, Virginia, and North Carolina were for Clinton. He also won in Georgia, which was largely settled by Virginians, and he picked up a stray vote in Pennsylvania, but met with complete defeat in New England. Kentucky showed her admiration of the Republican Democratic leader by casting her four votes for Thomas Jefferson. South Carolina, where the opposition party was poorly organized and Clinton was little known, gave seven votes for Adams and one for Burr. The total vote stood, Adams 77, Clinton 50, Jefferson 4, Burr 1. Adams could rejoice in receiving the full support of his party (even Hamilton had worked hard against Clinton), and in the fact that he was no longer a minority Vice-President.

The second administration of President Washington was concerned chiefly with foreign affairs. War was raging in Europe, and both England and France gave the United States the most serious cause of complaint; but the Federalists justified or excused the one nation, and the Republicans the other. Hamilton and Jefferson had resigned from the Cabinet but, though officially in private life, each guided and inspired his followers. In the summer of 1796 it was known to many, though not yet publicly announced, that Washington had decided to refuse another term, and the members of Congress of each party met privately and unofficially to agree on candidates for the succession and for the Vice-Presidency. The outstanding Federalists were Hamilton, Jay, and Adams. Hamilton was devotedly followed by most of the intellectual aristocracy of the party, although Jay and Marshall maintained their independence. But Hamilton's measures had aroused so much opposition, and he was considered so extreme a Federalist, that it would have been unwise to nominate him for President. Jay had recently given offense by negotiating a treaty with England which, though advantageous in certain respects, failed to protect American commerce.

There remained John Adams. His position as Vice-President seemed to give him a certain claim to the succession.[2] He was popular with the rank

---

[1] It was true that Clinton's title was doubtful and at best technical rather than moral. Mr. Alexander says: ". . . . the people gave Jay a majority of their votes; but at the count a majority of the State canvassers gave Clinton the governorship."

[2] Congressman Goodrich of Connecticut wrote: "By instituting the office of Vice-President, the constitution contemplates a succession; it means to provide a candidate on probation for the Presidency; it means to avoid (both) the evils of hereditary succession and the turbulence of the public mind being entirely left afloat."

and file of the Federalists, and to throw him aside would offend New England. He was an able man and had done good service for the party. Hamilton and his friends, therefore, came to his support, although Hamilton afterward admitted that he would not have been displeased had the system of double election brought in Adams' second. This was Major Thomas Pinckney of South Carolina.

The choice was made for politico-geographical reasons. A little before the selection, Jefferson wrote Madison of the crafty management of the wily Federalists. He said: "Most assiduous court has been paid to Patrick Henry. He has been offered everything which they knew he would not accept. Some impression has been made, but we do not believe it is radical. If they thought they could prevail upon him they would run him for their Vice-President, their first object being to produce a schism in this state (Virginia). As it is, they will run Mr. Pinckney, in which they regard his southern position rather than his principles."

Indeed, Jefferson, who had a keen eye for possible converts and who was skilled in making them, had hoped to bring Pinckney into the Republican camp. On August 25, 1791, he wrote to Edward Rutledge: "Would to God, you yourself, General Pinckney (Charles Cotesworth Pinckney, brother of the candidate) and Major Pinckney would come forward and aid us with your efforts. You are all known, respected, wished for; but you refuse yourself to everything. What is to become of us, my dear friend, if the vine and the fig tree withdraw and leave us to the bramble and the thorn?" As late as June 30, 1792, Jefferson, in a letter to a political friend, called Thomas Pinckney a good Republican. Jefferson's readiness to see things as he wished them led him too far; but Professor U. B. Phillips in his careful study describes Pinckney as "an ornament to, rather than a working member of, the Federalist party."

Thomas Pinckney was born in South Carolina in 1750. In 1753 he was taken to England by his father, who had been appointed agent of the Colony, and remained abroad for nineteen years. He was educated at Westminster Public School and at Oxford, and studied law at the Inner Temple. He also spent a year in France, in military study. He served with credit in the Revolutionary War and as Governor of his State in 1787 and 1788. In 1792 he went as Minister to Great Britain, where he did the routine work of the post carefully and well, while the important matters were handled by Hamilton in Philadelphia or by Jay, the special United States envoy, in London. In 1795 Pinckney himself became a special Minister, going to Spain to obtain recognition of the right of the United States to navigate the Mississippi, and was so fortunate as to conclude a treaty giving them this right, the boundaries they claimed, and permission to land and store goods for export; though whether the last concession was permanent or temporary was not made perfectly clear.

Pinckney obtained credit for this treaty which he did not deserve. Professor S. F. Bemis in the introduction to his careful and thorough monograph, *Pinckney's Treaty—A Study of America's Advantage from Europe's Distress,* says that he calls it Pinckney's Treaty only because Pinckney signed it; that the Spanish Minister, Godoy, reversed his country's policy because of the critical condition of her foreign affairs, not on account of the diplomatic ability of Mr. Pinckney. Yet, it must be remembered that Pinckney acted with intelligence and courage, and that Godoy only yielded the right of deposit when Pinckney asked for his passports.

Like many Vice-Presidents and nominees for the office, Pinckney, though no genius, was a worthy, competent, and agreeable man. He was an able and clear reasoner, at home in the classics, and of polished manner and elegant appearance. With him politics was not a career, but one of the occupations of a gentleman. He did his part therein with the same care that he looked after the interests of his clients and developed his large plantation.

The Republicans, like the Federalists, had some difficulty in determining who should be their second candidate. Four men had been considered, Butler of South Carolina, Langdon of New Hampshire, and Burr and Livingston of New York. Butler was ruled out because it would be unwise to run another southerner with Jefferson, and Langdon because he had "no influence." There remained the New Yorkers. Livingston had strong support in Virginia because of articles which he had written against Jay's treaty, while Burr's loyalty to the party was distrusted there and perhaps in other states as well. But Burr was more powerful in New York than Livingston, and when the Congressional caucus balloted, it was found that a majority of the members favored Burr.

The dates of the nominating caucuses are not known, but probably they were held a little before or immediately after the adjournment of Congress, which took place in June. No announcements of the nominations were made in the newspapers, and men of both parties in close touch with public affairs appear to have remained ignorant for months of what action had been taken. In September Oliver Wolcott, the Secretary of the Treasury, asked Jonathan Dayton, the Speaker of the House, whom their opponents would support for Vice-President, and Dayton replied that Chancellor Livingston had been talked of but·that the Democrats would probably change when they found that his nomination would not strengthen their interest. Early in October a prominent Maryland Federalist wrote: "No vice is yet mentioned here," and just before the choice of electors he asked: "Who is thought of for Vice-President (by the Federalists)?"

The Federalist leaders had unanimously put the name of Adams on the party ticket with the understanding that he should be considered its candidate for President, but this did not mean that they considered his election rather than Pinckney's as the primary object. It was quite probable that the electors of South Carolina and perhaps some from other states would vote for Jefferson and Pinckney; and if all the Federalist electors voted for both their candidates, though Adams should be defeated, a Federalist might still be President. William Vans Murray, later appointed by Adams Minister to Holland and Special Commissioner to France, wrote to his friend, Mr. McHenry, the Secretary of War, suggesting that letters be sent to all the State capitals urging the electors to run Pinckney for Vice-President, "that we may have two strings." Oliver Wolcott, the Secretary of the Treasury, at first proposed that enough votes be diverted from Pinckney to ensure the election of Adams as President, care being taken not to scatter so many as to allow Jefferson to be either President or Vice-President. Wolcott recommended also that Pinckney be cut in the Middle States only, since if this were done in New England, where the particular friends of Adams were most numerous, "distrust may be excited which both now and hereafter may be very prejudicial . . . . It is possible that the event may be different from our wishes, but it will be the fault of the Constitution if such be the case."

Later, however, when Jefferson's election appeared extremely probable, Wolcott decided, though with great reluctance, that Adams and Pinckney ought to be supported equally, in order to prevent Jefferson being either President or Vice-President. Wolcott came from plain-living, staid Connecticut, and he shuddered at the thought of Jefferson's intrigues and dinners. He wrote to his father that if Jefferson were Vice-President, he would become the rallying point of faction and French influence; he would probably reside at the seat of government, where, without any responsibility, he would by epicurean and other devices divide, undermine, and finally subvert the rival administration. "It is my sincere opinion," he said, "that as Vice-President, Mr. Jefferson would at present be more dangerous than as President."

Some Federalists would have been pleased to see Pinckney win. Alexander Hamilton made great exertions to secure an equal vote for Adams and Pinckney in the Eastern states. To many he used the two-string to the bow argument, urging that "the exclusion of Mr. Jefferson is far more important than any difference between Mr. Adams and Mr. Pinckney"; but he told his confidential friends that Pinckney would probably be the better President, "since he, to every essential qualification for the office, added a temper far more discreet and conciliatory than that of Mr. Adams."

But Adams' friends regarded his election as of first-rate importance. Unless a fair number of Federalist electors deliberately cut Pinckney, it was nearly certain that he would outrun Adams. He was almost sure to carry his own state of South Carolina, where he was very popular with the Federalists, and was on excellent terms with the powerful Rutledge family, which, like the Livingstons of New York, had recently joined the Republicans as much from pique as from principle. Pinckney's chances were the greater because in the South local pride and individual feelings were often stronger than

THOMAS JEFFERSON, VIRGINIA, THE SECOND VICE-
PRESIDENT OF THE UNITED STATES, 1797-1801.

partisanship. In this very election William Vans Murray, in announcing the victory of an unpopular Federalist candidate, said that the word was, "our choice is a party question, not a personal matter," and Murray added, "this for a Southern election is a pleasing proof of the people's goodness."

Pinckney could hope for Republican support outside his own State. There were members of the party who were extremely anxious to exclude Adams from the Vice-Presidency, and to accomplish this they were ready to vote for Pinckney rather than Burr. They were the more willing to desert their candidate as Pinckney had never been an offensive partisan, and many of his associates had been Republicans, a circumstance which Governor Wolcott of Connecticut, the father of the Secretary of the Treasury, considered a reason against his being President. Some Northern Federalists were cool toward Pinckney as too moderate and a Southerner, and many Republicans distrusted Burr as unreliable politically and ambitious to head a Northern party.

Secretary Wolcott left a memorandum, written, however, many years later, stating that "in a convivial moment, a prime agent of the Virginia party said, in effect: 'I have watched the movements of Mr. Burr with attention and have discovered traits of character which sooner or later will give us much trouble. He has an unequaled talent for attracting men to his views, and forming combinations of which he is always the center. He is determined to play a first part; he acts strenuously with us in public, but it is remarkable that in private consultations he more frequently agrees with us in principles than in the mode of giving them effect. Mr. Burr's habits of thinking are of a military cast. His manners create him no personal enemies, and we all know that mere political animosities cease with the causes which produce them. I shall not be surprised if Mr. Burr is found, in a few years, the leader of a popular party in the Northern States; and if this event ever happens, this party will subvert the influence of the Southern States. Notwithstanding all the scoffing and reproaches against us as slave-holders, the cause of republicanism in this country is connected with the political ascendancy of the Southern States. Freemen cannot be employed generally in laborious and servile occupations without debasing their minds.'"

There is an interesting description of the situation in a letter from Representative Harper of South Carolina to ex-Senator Izard of the same State. Harper tells his correspondent that the great point is to prevail on Pinckney to stand. "Every effort will be used by his pretended friends, and by Ned Rutledge among the rest, to persuade him not to let his name be run. They will tell him that he ought not to act as Vice-President, that he is intended to be made a tool of by people who will deceive him. That he is brought forward to divide the votes of the Southern States, and that the Eastern people when it comes to the test will not support him. If he should not arrive before election, Ned Rutledge will give out that his friend Major Pinckney, in whose most intimate confidence he will declare himself to be, will not consent to serve as Vice-President. By these means it is possible, under the mask of friendship, they will prevent him being voted for. But Major Pinckney may be assured, I speak from the most certain knowledge, that the intention of bringing him forward was to make him President. I do not say that the Eastern people would prefer him to Mr. Adams, but they infinitely prefer him to Jefferson, and they support him because it gives them a chance to exclude Jefferson, and to get a man whom they can trust. With the very same views against Adams is Pinckney supported by many of Jefferson's warmest friends; and there are not wanting many who prefer him to either. Upon the whole I have no doubt of his being elected if it should not be prevented by himself or those who call themselves his friends, ..."

New England, New Hampshire, and Rhode Island threw away their votes on Oliver Ellsworth of Connecticut, recently appointed Chief Justice of the United States. Connecticut gave five of her nine votes to John Jay, and Massachusetts scattered three of her sixteen votes. Vermont and Rhode Island voted solidly for Adams and Pinckney. Some electors who thus diverted their votes were uncertain until the last moment what to do. Governor Wolcott of Connecticut wrote his son that when he went to the meeting of the State electors, he expected that all would vote for Adams and Pinckney. But Ellsworth and others were extremely desirous of securing the election of Adams to the Presidency. The voting was postponed until evening to wait for the mails. But they brought nothing new, the majority of the electors determined that considerable risk should be run to ensure the election of Adams, and it was decided that four or five votes should be taken from Pinckney.

In Pennsylvania the Republicans won. Yet, though the electors were chosen by general ticket, the failure of some lazy Republicans to completely mark their ballots, or personal preference, gave the two highest men on the Federalist ticket a majority over the lowest on the Republican. But Secretary Wolcott described one of the "Federalists" as of "somewhat doubtful principles." The result was that Adams received one vote, and Pinckney two. One elector, a Mr. Miles, probably the man referred to by Wolcott, voted for Jefferson and Pinckney. Mr. Stanwood says that this is the only instance of a Presidential elector betraying the trust reposed in him, and Mr. Miles was sharply attacked in a public letter. It may be, however, that he did not consider himself, as his critic did, chosen "to act, not to think." In the same election a candidate for elector in Virginia (who was not chosen) refused to state for whom he would vote, claiming that a pledge would be improper.

In Maryland, Mr. Plater voted for the two ablest candidates without regard to their political views and cast his ballot for Adams and Jefferson, and two Federalist electors threw away their votes on John Henry, a Senator of their state.

Burr was even less successful than Pinckney in obtaining a full party support. From Virginia he received but one electoral vote, Samuel Adams of Massachusetts being complimented with fifteen, Clinton with three, and George Washington with one. North Carolina also gave Washington one, a second complimentary vote went to C. C. Pinckney, Thomas Pinckney's brother, and three to a distinguished fellow-citizen, Judge Iredell of the United States Supreme Court. The other five Republican votes were given to Burr. Georgia voted solidly for Jefferson and Clinton. The votes against Burr showed a serious lack of party organization and harmony, and the New Yorker was angry and hurt. A Federalist Congressman wrote to Governor Wolcott: "There is no real friendship among the (Republican) leaders. Virginia has treated Burr scurvily in the election, and North Carolina not much better. Langdon is simple enough to say he might have known they would lurch him."

It is said that some Democratic electors wished for the choice of Adams as Vice-President, though they dared not vote for him for fear of excluding Jefferson. Their support, however, was that of Greeks bearing gifts. They thought that Adams would decline to serve under Jefferson, and that this refusal to accept what the people had given would enable the Republicans to accuse him of ambition and pride.

When the electoral ballots were counted, it was found that Adams had received seventy-one votes, Jefferson sixty-eight, Pinckney fifty-nine, and Burr thirty. There were nineteen scattering. Adams and Jefferson were, therefore, chosen President and Vice-President.

During President Adams' administration the difficulties with France came to a head. France withdrew her Minister, refused to receive a new Minister from the United States, Charles Cotesworth Pinckney,[1] and ordered him to leave the country. Adams now made a last attempt at reconciliation by sending to Paris a special commission consisting of Pinckney, John Marshall, and Elbridge Gerry. The French government, the "Executive Directory," declined to receive them, and the Foreign Minister, Talleyrand, gave them a personal interview only after months of delay. There was, however, an exchange of letters.

Meanwhile agents of Talleyrand were insisting that the United States should buy an arrangement by what, in effect, would be a large payment to the French Treasury, and a *douceur* of over two hundred thousand dollars to the Directory, Talleyrand, and other officials. Gerry, who was a vain and vacillating man, was ready to yield. Talleyrand offered to negotiate with him if his colleagues would go home and, in effect, sent Marshall and Pinckney out of France. Gerry had declared that he would not be separated from his associates, but finally remained in Paris "to prevent war." He held informal

---

[1]Washington had recalled James Monroe on the grounds of neglecting to carry out his instructions, and of acting with partiality to France

discussions with Talleyrand and his agents, but at last, disillusioned by the Frenchman's trickery and browbeating,[1] left France over two months after receiving orders to return.

When the people of the United States learned what had happened, there was an outburst of anti-French feeling. A provisional army was raised and armed French vessels in West Indian waters, whether national or merchant, were captured by American frigates and privateers. The notorious Alien and Sedition Laws for the expulsion of aliens and the punishment of "seditious" writing and speaking were enacted by Congress. But preparation for war was expensive. In 1798 the Virginia and Kentucky Legislatures passed some famous resolutions denouncing the Alien and Sedition Acts and enunciating extreme States' Rights doctrines. Popular enthusiasm for war cooled. France sent an assurance that a Minister from the United States would be received and treated with proper respect, and Adams wisely despatched a second commission to Paris. It found Napoleon in power and negotiated a convention which, after some modifications, was ratified by both countries. France was released from liability for previous depredations on our commerce, the United States was freed from the entangling alliance of 1778, and obtained the acceptance of certain demands in regard to the treatment of its vessels.

At the beginning of the Presidential year of 1800, the political situation closely resembled that of the previous campaign. The Republicans were united on Jefferson. The bulk of the Federalists favored Adams. Most of their chiefs were opposed to him, but deemed it imprudent to say so publicly.

The fight between the parties grew hot, but no leaders were named by either side. Then May Day brought bright blooms of hope for the Republicans, and dark clouds for their opponents. The Presidential electors of the State of New York were chosen by the Legislature, which was itself chosen on the last two days of April and the first of May. The city of New York elected the whole Republican legislative ticket, thereby making the State Republican and giving the party an excellent prospect of carrying the country. The victory was largely due to the cleverness and assiduity of Aaron Burr, and his friends were quick to claim the credit for him. One, at least, had done so by anticipation. On March 29, his zealous lieutenant and future biographer, Matthew L. Davis, wrote to Albert Gallatin, the leader of the Republicans in Congress: "If we carry this election it may be ascribed principally to Colonel Burr's management and perseverance. We shall open the campaign under the most favorable impressions and headed by a man whose intrigue and management is most astonishing." At midnight of May 1, Davis dashed off a brief report to Gallatin giving the great news, which he headed *Republicanism Triumphant* and ended with a certificate of service: "To Colonel Burr we are indebted for everything. This day has he remained at

---

[1]Gerry had the manliness to disregard hints that he might be arrested.

the polls of the Seventh Ward ten hours without intermission. Pardon this hasty scrawl; I have not ate for fifteen hours."

On May 5 Davis wrote again. He said that it was generally expected that the Vice-President would be taken from New York and that only three men could be thought of, Clinton, Livingston, and Burr. Davis described Clinton as desirous of retirement and as growing old and infirm, and Livingston as timid at critical moments and of an unpopular family and connections; "Colonel Burr is therefore the most eligible character, and on him the eyes of our friends in this State are fixed." Davis said that he could judge of the effect in New York only, that Burr's election as Vice-President would assure a Republican Governor, and that "if he is not nominated, many of us will experience much chagrin and disappointment." But Davis professed complete ignorance as to Burr's willingness to accept the office.

Gallatin received another enthusiastic letter from his father-in-law, Commodore Nicholson, formerly a gallant officer in the navy of the Revolution, now a zealous warrior in the political battles of New York City. The Commodore wrote: "This business has been conducted and brought to issue in so miraculous a manner that I cannot account for it, but from the intervention of a Supreme Power and our friend Burr, the agent.[1] His generalship, perseverance, industry, and execution exceeds all description, so that I think I can say he deserves anything and everything of his country; but he has done it at the risk of his life. I shall conclude by recommending him as a general far superior to your Hamiletons (Hamiltons) as much so as a man is to a boy; and I have but little doubt this State through his means and planning will be as Republican in the appointment of electors as the State of Virginia."

But theie was another powerful Democrat who had been somewhat superseded by Burr yet who was still mighty in the land, ex-Governor Clinton. Nicholson did not forget this. He told Gallatin: "I have not been able since my being here before today to visit my friend and neighbor Governor Clinton. I understand his health and spirits are both returning. His name at the head of our ticket[2] had a most powerful effect. I cannot inform you what either Burr's or his expectations are, but will write you more particularly about the Governor after my visit."

The Republicans at the capital had fully determined to give the second place on the ticket to New York's favorite. But they were uncertain whether his name was Burr or Clinton, and as Congress was about to adjourn, they deputed Gallatin to find an answer to the question at once. That gentleman passed the inquiry on to his wife who, as Gallatin doubtless intended, made her father the oracle. Commodore Nicholson saw Clinton, who refused to run; but being told that his presence on the ticket was important for the suc-

---

[1] As Nicholson was Burr's friend we need not be surprised that he failed to add: "God moves in a mysterious way his wonders to perform."

[2] Burr had put Clinton's name at the top of the Republican legislative ticket. The ex-Governor had refused his assent, but was induced to promise not to decline publicly.

cess of the party, agreed to accept a nomination if it were understood that he would be at liberty to resign the office if he so desired. Nicholson drew up a report of the interview which he showed to Burr, who said that he did not want the nomination and gave his reasons. He then left the room. Two Republicans who were present told Nicholson that duty to the party required Burr to run. They then brought him back, he reluctantly agreed to accept, and Nicholson revised his report, making Clinton's refusal absolute. Nicholson afterward prepared a statement in which he said that he told Clinton what he had done and that Clinton manifested no displeasure, and Clinton in a private letter said that this account was correct.

Nicholson's letter to Gallatin in its final form announced that Clinton declined, that "his age, his infirmities, his habits and attachments to retired life, in his opinion, exempt him from active life. He thinks Colonel Burr is the most suitable person and perhaps the only man. Such is also the opinions of all the Republicans in this quarter; their confidence in A. B. is universal and unbounded. Mr. Burr, however, appeared averse to being the candidate. He seemed to think that no arrangement could be made which would be observed to the Southward; alluding, as I understood, to the last election, in which he was certainly ill-used by Virginia and North Carolina. I believe he may be induced to stand if assurances can be given that the Southern States will act fairly.[1]

"Colonel Burr may certainly be Governor of this State at the next election if he pleases, and a number of his friends are very unwilling that he should be taken off for Vice-President, thinking the other the most important office. Upon the whole, however, we think he ought to be the man for V. P. *(sic)*, if there is a moral certainty of success. But his name must not be played the fool with. I confidently hope you will be able to smooth over the business of the last election, and if Colonel Burr is properly applied to, I think he will be induced to stand. At any rate we, the Republicans, will make him."

Nicholson's letter put an end to hesitation and on May 12, Gallatin wrote his wife: "We had last night a very large meeting of Republicans (Senators and Representatives) in which it was unanimously agreed to support Burr for Vice-President."

About a week earlier the Federalists had held a similar conclave, where it was agreed that their candidates should be Adams and Charles Cotesworth Pinckney. Many of the Hamiltonians had thought seriously of supporting Ellsworth or Jay as President and C. C. Pinckney, or perhaps his brother, the candidate in the last campaign, as Vice-President. Such action, however, would have fatally divided the party and so they accepted Adams, but with a clear understanding on both sides that Adams and Pinckney should be sup-

---

[1] Another account of this affair which, however, is probably erroneous, states that a majority of the Republicans who were consulted favored Clinton and that Nicholson drew up a report to this effect, but that Burr induced him to falsify it.

ported equally. C. C. and Thomas Pinckney were not only brothers in blood, but in character and way of life. Mr. Phillips says that they were "similarly devoid of records as party men, but similarly distinguished for integrity, public spirit and high social standing, and they were similarly passive when they themselves were candidates."

Both brothers were well above the average; neither was a great man. When C. C. Pinckney was appointed Minister to France, Speaker Dayton said of him: "Possessing great frankness, candour, and integrity, he unites with a nice sense of honour, talents, which though not the most brilliant, are nevertheless good and may be equally useful." Each at the time of his nomination for Vice-President had some personal éclat which was not wholly deserved. Thomas Pinckney was unduly praised for his treaty with Spain, and C. C. Pinckney was wrongly credited with giving to the plundering demands of Talleyrand the ringing reply, "Millions for defense, but not one cent for tribute." As a matter of fact, the words were a toast at a banquet to Marshall on his return. But Pinckney had firmly resisted the French attempts at extortion and on one occasion, to a call for an "answer" after a clear refusal, he replied: "No, no, we will not give you a sixpence."

Pinckney made a strong appeal to the local pride of South Carolina by his residence and to the wider patriotism of the whole country by his conduct in France, real and supposed; but he was vulnerable in the land of the Puritans. The Congregationalist clergy had much to say of Jefferson's Deism and falsely asserted that in his household he had substituted the observance of the French "decade" for that of the week and Sunday. The Republicans retorted by quoting the opinion of an eminent clergyman that Pinckney was an atheist, and pointing to the fact that he was so devoted to horse-racing that he was president of a club organized for that purpose. It would seem that the Federalists might have retaliated with pungent and truthful comments on the habits of Aaron Burr, but apparently this was not done, at least in New England, where, as has been noted above, the name of Burr suggested learning and piety. His father had been President of Princeton, and his mother was a daughter of the great theologian, Jonathan Edwards. Moreover, Burr himself had coquetted with the Federalists.

Even more than in 1796 the campaign was marked by manœuvre and intrigue among the Federalists. Gallatin wrote that the party caucus had intended to make Pinckney President, though Adams was formally made the candidate for the first place in order to carry New England. There had been a definite agreement that Adams should be considered as the nominee for President, but many hoped that, without effort on their part, local feeling would give Pinckney the vote of South Carolina and so place him ahead of Adams.

Immediately after the New York election Adams called for the resignations of Secretaries Pickering and McHenry. Pickering refused to resign and was removed.[1]   Adams' action roused the ire of Alexander Hamilton, whose close political friends the dismissed Secretaries were.   Added to this was his resentment at a remark attributed to Adams, to the effect that Hamilton was under British influence.   After two letters regarding the alleged remark had brought no reply, he wrote an essay on "The Public Conduct and Character of John Adams, Esq., President of the United States."   In this, after arguing at much length to show Adams' great unfitness for the Presidency, he advised everyone to vote for him but to vote for Pinckney also, a course which, as all knew, would mean the election of Pinckney or Jefferson.

Robert G. Harper carried treachery so far as to propose that Adams be supported publicly until after the choice of electors, and that then such of them as considered him unfit to be President should quietly vote for some one else.   Offers were made to Pinckney to give the vote of South Carolina to him and Jefferson, but he refused to sell out his colleague and by the efforts and management of his cousin, Charles Pinckney, "blackguard Charlie," as the Federalists called him to prevent confounding the two, a small majority of the South Carolina Legislature voted for the Jefferson and Burr ticket. Friends of Adams on their part manifested a strong inclination to disregard the agreement at Philadelphia, and to cut Pinckney.   There were rumors of a new Adams party of moderates to be called the Constitutional party.

There were reports of plots in the Republican camp also, and whether Burr was as honorable as Pinckney may be doubted.   It is said that one New York elector was urged to drop Jefferson.   Burr himself traveled in New England, and Hamilton alleged that he was intriguing with all his might in New Jersey, Rhode Island, and Vermont, with some prospects of success. "He counts positively on the unanimous support of the anti-Federalists and that by some adventitious aid from our quarter he will overstep his friend, Jefferson."   Theodore Sedgwick wrote to Rufus King that Burr was for sale.   Some Federalist leaders may have been inclined to bargain.   Fisher Ames wrote to Wolcott: "It seems as if Burr would have little chance unless by forcing a (an equal?) vote from the Jacobins (Republicans), that would put Jefferson too much at risk.   Foreseeing this, will he not wish to join some other candidate who may need him and whose friends could make him stand a better chance of being second?   He is like Lord Stanley at the battle of Bosworth, ready to act according to circumstances."

All these plots had no result except to stain the character of those engaged in them.   Every Republican elector voted for Jefferson and Burr, and every Federalist but one for Adams and Pinckney; in Rhode Island a single vote was cast for Adams and Jay.

With Jefferson and Burr tied for first place, the final determination went to the House of Representatives voting by states.   There were enough Fed-

---

[1]This is one of the few instances of a cabinet officer compelling a President formally to remove him.   The others are Duane under Jackson, and Stanton under Johnson.

eralist states to prevent an election, but after thirty-five ballots some Federalists refrained from voting, and Jefferson was chosen.   Burr automatically became Vice-President.   Full accounts of this election can be found in various histories and biographies, but the exact truth of the affair may never be known.   It is probable that Jefferson gave a statement of his intentions regarding the offices and certain public matters to an inquiring Democrat to be passed on to the Federalists, and that Burr, from prudence, perhaps, refused actively to play false, but hoped and quietly endeavored to wrongly win.

President Jefferson's first term was an extremely successful one.   Before the election by the House of Representatives, Hamilton had advised his friends to choose Jefferson, saying: "To my mind a true estimate of Mr. Jefferson's character warrants the expectation of a temporizing rather than a violent system."   Time proved Hamilton right.   Jefferson shocked the Federalists by removing many of them from office, by getting rid of judges, by approving the abolition of courts, and by cutting down the navy.   But there were circumstances which justified or at least palliated all these acts, and the Republicans refrained from seizing the property of the "wise and good," as the Federalists called themselves, and spared the "sacred ties of marriage," which Rev. Dr. Dwight, the President of Yale, declared were dissolved by Jefferson's election.   Finally circumstances enabled Jefferson to buy from Napoleon the great province of Louisiana, thus settling all questions of the right to navigate the Mississippi and securing what seemed limitless possibilities for expansion.   The people, already angry at the hauteur and exclusiveness of the Federalists, now found that the much abused "Democrats" had brought not ruin but prosperity and peace, and they flocked to the standard of Jefferson.

In 1804 the Federalists felt it useless to make a real contest for the Presidency, and they took the advice of Gouverneur Morris to wait for their triumphant and numerous enemies to fall out among themselves.   But they were ready to fight hard for the control of the states which they still held and deemed it advisable to have a national ticket.   Some wished to nominate C. C. Pinckney and Rufus King of New York, leaving the electors to determine precedence.   On February 22, 1804, at a Federalist dinner at the capital, it was decided to support these gentlemen.   Later it was agreed that Pinckney should be the candidate for the first place, and King for the second.

Rufus King was born at Scarborough, Maine, then a part of Massachusetts, on March 24, 1755.   His father, Richard King, was a wealthy merchant and landowner, and was said to be the chief exporter of lumber in Maine.   Rufus was fitted for college at the Byfield Academy and graduated from Harvard in 1777, "with some distinction for his classical and literary attainments, and for his oratorical powers, which he had studiously cultivated."   Mr. King kept his interest in the classics throughout his life, regarding them as the essential part of education.

In 1820 he wrote to his friend and sympathizer, Christopher Gore:

> "The truth is we have no scholars, or so few that the value of the ancient authors is neither understood nor properly estimated; the young men are to study Chemistry, and Philosophy, and Eloquence; and are to depend on Blair, instead of Longinus, and on modern Poetry and History in preference to the fine models of both Greek and Roman masters.
>
> "I discard the pretension that we are all to become Chemists; few, very few of the great statesmen of old or modern times were even Mathematicians; in saying this I do not depreciate the Sciences. I honor and w'd prove my veneration for learned Chemists, tho' I believe while we have smatterers in abundance, we have no man who deserves to be called Learned in this branch.
>
> "We have our Bowditch and Adrian who are almost the only Mathematicians who can read la Place.
>
> "It is with Mathematics, as with music: unless there be a natural propensity, neither is worth pursuit, and the former only so far as the ordinary calls of life require the same."

After graduating from Harvard, King studied law in the office of Theophilus Parsons, and in 1780 was admitted to the bar. But he soon abandoned active practice to become a professional politician in the older and better sense of the term. He resolved to devote himself to the higher business of the state, and read and thought on the science of government to fit himself for this occupation. To carry out his plans, office was necessary. In 1783 he was sent to the Massachusetts legislature and in 1784 to the Congress of the Confederation, then seriously fallen in prestige. Here Mr. King showed the earnest desire to prevent the spread of slavery into new territory which was a characteristic of his whole political life. In the struggle between what may be termed the national and the States' Rights parties, he at first aided the latter and went so far, in coöperation with his colleagues, Elbridge Gerry and Samuel Holton, as to assume the responsibility of suspending the execution of an order from the Massachusetts Legislature to present resolutions in favor of calling a convention to revise the Articles of Confederation.

When at last such a convention assembled, King was sent as a delegate from Massachusetts. By this time the weakness of the government both at home and abroad had wrought a change in his views,[1] and he was now an advocate of the creation of a strong central authority. Farrand in his book, *The Framing of the Constitution,* places King among the dozen members of

[1] It is fair to remember that one of King's arguments for delay had been that time should be given to test the Articles of Confederation.

the convention who exerted the most influence. He says of him: "Rufus King, somewhat over medium height, was an unusually handsome man and with great personal charm. Of marked ability and an eloquent speaker with a sweet clear voice, it is no wonder that . . . . he should be regarded as one of the coming men of the new nation."

A member of the convention, William Pierce of Georgia, has left us a careful description of his colleagues. He says of King's oratory, for which he was much distinguished: "In his public speaking there is something peculiarly strong and rich in his expression, clear and convincing in his arguments, rapid and irresistible at times in his eloquence, but swimming and graceful; but there is a rudeness of manner sometimes accompanying it. But take him *tout en semble* he may with propriety be ranked among the luminaries of the present age." It sounds strange to hear a man of King's culture and temperament accused of rawness. Probably there was such a defect, but time removed it. John A. Dix, in giving his recollections of the Missouri debate of 1820, where King led the free state men, described his oratory as "calm, dignified, argumentative, forcible and at times fervid . . . . Rufus King responded in all respects to my conception of the old Roman Senator, maintaining in his manner the quiet dignity appropriate to the undisputed masters of the greatest empire in the world."

King was also a member of the Massachusetts state convention for considering the Constitution; where he aided, both by argument and by management, in procuring its ratification. King had devoted himself with conscientious care to public affairs; he had rendered good service; and he not unreasonably hoped for a United States senatorship; but the Massachusetts legislature chose two lesser men, Dalton and Strong. One reason for King's failure was a belief that he had ceased to be a resident of Massachusetts.

For several years he had lived, for most of the time, in New York. His absence was partly due to the fact that Congress was sitting in that city and partly to his marriage to the daughter of a prominent New York merchant, John Alsop. Mr. Alsop was old and in feeble health and needed King's assistance in carrying on his business. But these circumstances were not fully appreciated in Boston.

The New York Federalists had a high opinion of King and wished to draw him to themselves. They held out hopes of political preferment should he become a citizen of New York; and King, who was considerably mortified by his failure in Massachusetts, accepted the invitation. He was rewarded with a Senatorship and had the good fortune to draw the six-year term. When it expired, he was reëlected. But almost immediately afterward there came a lull in politics. King found absence from his family, and the petty duties of his office, trying; he had helped to organize and launch the government of the nation, and he now felt a desire to try his hand in diplomatic work. At his request, Hamilton, of whom he was a loyal political ally and personal admirer and friend, recommended him to the President as Minister to England to succeed Thomas Pinckney, transferred to Spain.

Washington had no doubt of King's fitness, but thought that the appointment might be unwise as King was widely accused of holding opinions in favor of monarchy. Hamilton replied that this was a general charge of the opposition and could not be regarded without depriving the government of the services of the best men. Of the candidate actually under consideration, Hamilton said: "Mr. King is a remarkably well informed man, a very judicious one, a man of address, a man of fortune and economy, whose situation affords just ground of confidence; a man of unimpeached probity where he is known, a firm friend to the government, a supporter of the measures of the President—a man who cannot but feel that he has strong pretensions to confidence and trust."

The appointment was made. King served for seven years and justified Hamilton's recommendation. He handled affairs carefully and well, though his point of view was that of a Federalist. King made himself agreeable to the English government,[1] to the opposition, and to literary men, but he did not forget nor allow others to forget that the United States was a wholly independent nation, not a satellite of any European power.

King had a high sense of what was due to himself as well as to his country. Though genial and entertaining with intimate friends, and, in his old age, willing to share with younger men the lessons which a long public life had taught him and an excellent memory enabled him to retain, yet King was proud and sensitive and his general bearing was reserved if not haughty. Although a convinced Federalist, he remained as Minister during a part of Jefferson's administration, by the desire of the President. Then, certain negotiations with which he was charged having been completed, and the government not seeming inclined to place in his hands the forming of a new commercial treaty with Great Britain, King sent in his resignation and returned to the United States. This step had the full approval of Hamilton, who thought that if a good man continued in a kind of political association with the Republicans, he might both strengthen the influence of those undesirable citizens, and injure his own reputation.

---

[1] A striking instance of this and of the lack of the "Imperial" spirit of a later day is the attitude of the English ministry on the question of the Maine-Canadian boundary. They felt that it was of little practical importance to England, that fifty years hence Canada would be independent; and King was informed unofficially that they had full confidence in his fairness, and that any line which he personally would decide on as just would be accepted by them. But the matter was not concluded until after King had ceased to be Minister, and the treaty in which it was incorporated was rejected by the Senate.

CHAPTER XI.

Vice-Presidential Elections to the Era of Good Feeling

ON February 25, 1804, the Republican Senators and Representatives met in caucus, for the first time without any attempt at concealment. There was no doubt that the President would be renominated, and that the Vice-President would not. Immediately after the election of Jefferson by the House of Representatives, the Federalists were angry that Burr had not definitely joined them, and the Republicans were grateful or at least well disposed to him for the same reason. In the first distribution of offices, Burr was not forgotten. His friend Swartwout was made United States Marshal of New York, and Osgood wrote to Madison, Jefferson's Secretary of State, that he had felt a certain mortification at Burr's being taken up after some not very creditable manœuvres at Philadelphia. Osgood said that he had strong evidence that the three gentlemen appointed to important offices in New York City were devoted to Burr, and he believed that if it had been in Burr's power, Jefferson would not have been President. Osgood then recommended that in the distribution of the patronage of New York, the President should consult Clinton. The mass of the party, when looking back at the late election, appear to have adopted Osgood's view of Burr, and Jefferson coldly refrained from granting him further recognition.

Matthew L. Davis had a reasonable expectation that he would displace an ex-Tory who was naval officer of the Port of New York, and when no change was made, he obtained something like a recommendation from Gallatin, now Secretary of the Treasury, and went to Monticello to plead his own cause. Jefferson's conduct suggests the formula by which the kings of England vetoed bills; he took the matter into consideration. Burr begged Gallatin that he might be granted the only request he had ever made, a decision of the question, but Jefferson continued his policy of watchful waiting until

May, 1803, and then appointed Osgood Naval Officer. DeWitt Clinton[1] and the Livingstons combined against Burr, and ruthlessly proscribed not only his friends, but all who would not join them in the war. Burr and his followers struck back. W. P. Van Ness, later his second in the duel with Hamilton, defended Burr and lampooned his opponents in one of the ablest, bitterest, and most effective pamphlets in the history of New York politics. Burr himself accepted an invitation to a Federalist banquet, which had been given in the secret hope of embroiling him with his party, and proposed the toast, "The union of all honest men."

Yet at the last he flinched. Of renomination for the Vice-Presidency there was no hope. A month before the Congressional caucus, Burr stooped to call on Jefferson and say that he believed it better that he should not stand for the nomination, but that he desired some mark of favor (an office) that he might not seem to fear to meet his enemies. According to Jefferson's memoranda (the *Anas*), Burr even said that he accepted the Vice-Presidency "with a view to promote my fame and advancement and from a desire to be with men whose company and conversation had always been fascinating to him." One is reminded of Raleigh's pitiful plea to King James that he had not been discontented because, among other reasons, his meetings with the king gave him constant opportunities of profiting by His Majesty's learning and wisdom.

It had been arranged that Burr was to be cast into outer darkness, and his friends did not attend the caucus. But if Burr was thrown aside, the old Virginia-New York combination was not. Two Virginia members had written to DeWitt Clinton, who obtained the consent of his uncle, the Governor, to accept the Vice-Presidential nomination. A letter to that effect from the elder Clinton was read to the caucus. The New England Republicans had not been consulted; surprised and angered by such treatment, they tried to adjourn the meeting. But the motion was defeated, and Clinton was nominated by a vote of 67 to 41 for five other gentlemen. The runner-up was John Breckinridge of Kentucky with twenty votes; an equal number was given to three New Englanders, and Samuel Maclay, brother of the diarist, received a single vote. In the election the Republicans swept the country, carrying even Massachusetts. Only Connecticut and Delaware and two electors from Maryland remained loyal to Federalism.

President Jefferson found his second term a sad contrast to his first. Everywhere was perplexity, confusion, and division; the United States saw its commerce plundered by both England and France and its seamen impressed by England. When it placed an embargo on external trade, it not only failed to coerce foreign powers, but nearly caused civil war at home. The President probably wished his friend and Secretary of State, James Madison, to

---

[1]DeWitt Clinton, the Governor's nephew, was now the real chief of the Clinton faction, his uncle playing the part of king to DeWitt's Richelieu. It should be said to the credit of the old Governor that he opposed DeWitt's wholesale removals; but he was outvoted in the Council of Appointment.

be his successor; but in public at least he maintained neutrality, and the Secretary of State found what later was called the "easy succession" a difficult and dangerous path. Northern Democrats had been chafing under Virginia rule; they had defeated the reëlection of Speaker Macon of North Carolina, the dutiful follower of Virginia, and replaced him by Varnum of Massachusetts, and now they were hoping for the Presidency itself. DeWitt Clinton was demanding that New York have her turn and that his uncle, the Vice-President, known for his long public service and his sturdy democracy, succeed Jefferson, as Jefferson had succeeded Adams, and Adams, Washington. In Virginia, too, there was much disaffection. Many felt that the President had become a little unsound in the Republican faith, and Madison much more so. John Randolph was bitterly assailing both.

Ths usual Republican Congressional caucus was held, and renominated Madison and Clinton by overwhelming majorities. But a considerable minority of Republicans did not attend the caucus, and seventeen issued a formal protest against its assuming to nominate. Clinton repudiated its authority and stood forth as a candidate for President. Yet there was no attempt to read him out of the party, or even to declare his nomination as Vice-President forfeited. The caucus itself had claimed no right to bind the party, the administration had little prestige, and "the public was treated to a curious spectacle. The regular party candidate for the Vice-Presidency became the open rival of the regular candidate for the Presidency. Clinton's newspapers attacked Madison without mercy, while Madison's friends were electing Clinton Vice-President." The experience, however, though certainly "curious," was not wholly new to Clinton. In 1777, he had been elected both governor and lieutenant-governor of New York.[1]

Could all Madison's opponents have united on Clinton, it is quite possible that he would have been elected. But the Virginia dissenters were still loyal to the Old Dominion and rallied around James Monroe, whom they regarded as ill-used by the President, and a true champion of the principles of 1798. Clinton could only win by Federalist aid; all chance of that was lost by the division among the insurgents, and in October the Federalists decided to support their old ticket of Pinckney and King. A serious quarrel of long standing among the Pennsylvania Republicans was compromised and the vote of that state saved for Madison; the Virginia Legislature declared in his favor, and, at Jefferson's request, Monroe withdrew. But DeWitt Clinton, always dictatorial and stubborn, refused to yield. The New York electors were chosen by the Legislature, and he demanded that it select those who would vote for New York's candidate. The members of the Legislature might have paid this empty compliment to an old man whom they sincerely honored but

---

[1]Conservatives, like Jay, had hoped to save Schuyler by providing an honorable place for Clinton, and the followers of a second radical candidate, John M. Scott, were glad to vote for Clinton for his own sake. Clinton did not attempt to hold both his offices, and the President of the Senate acted as Lieutenant-Governor.

for the strenuous objections of Governor Tompkins. "Without being of the slightest use to George Clinton, he contended, such a course would exhibit an unhappy division in Republican ranks, excite the jealousy of Madison's friends, impair the influence of New York Republicans with the Administration, and make them appear ridiculous to their brethren in other states." DeWitt Clinton, however, was insistent and an understanding was reached that the electors might vote as they pleased.

The election was a triumph for the Republicans, though not so great as that of 1804. For President, Madison received 122 votes, Pinckney 47, and Clinton 6. For Vice-President, King ran evenly with Pinckney. Clinton received 113 votes for Vice-President; the six New York electors who supported him for President divided their Vice-Presidential votes equally between Madison and Monroe. Ohio bolted Clinton and gave her three votes to John Langdon of New Hampshire for Vice-President.

President Madison succeeded to the perplexities as well as to the office of President Jefferson. England and Napoleon, locked in a life and death struggle, continued to trample on the rights of neutrals, and the people of the United States remained intensely interested in the contest but divided in their sympathies, the Federalists supporting England, the Republicans denouncing her and excusing, if not justifying, Napoleon. In 1812, there appeared in the House of Representatives a group of comparatively young Republicans who in theory held the doctrines of the party, but were ardently national in feeling. Two of them, John C. Calhoun and Henry Clay, have won a foremost place among American statesmen, and others like Richard M. Johnson, though half-forgotten now,[1] had a country-wide fame in their day. The "war hawks," as these men were called, held the cautious Madison firm in the resolution to which his reason already had led him, to appeal to the sword; and on June 18, 1812, on the recommendation of the President, Congress declared war against Great Britain.

The Presidential campaign of 1812 had already opened. The situation was not unlike that of 1808. There was a faction in New York ready to make a deal with the Federalists, or with any one who could command voting strength, to put a Clinton in the Presidential chair. But the Clinton was not the same in 1812 as in 1808. The Vice-President had died in April and DeWitt Clinton was now both the real and the formal head of the clan. On May 12, the Republican Congressional caucus met, but about one-third of those eligible stayed away, New York having only a single representative. Madison was renominated unanimously, but the old, established practice of allowing a New Yorker to play the second string to Virginia's first was abandoned. Clinton would not have accepted the Vice-Presidency even with a promise of the succession, and other New Yorkers who might have received it did not wish, by taking the place, to seem to sell out the favorite of their

---

[1] Johnson, however, has eleven counties named after him.

state. The caucus, therefore, turned to New England and nominated John Langdon of New Hampshire by a vote of 64 to 16 for Elbridge Gerry, and 2 scattering. It may be that this was an appeal to the vanity of New England rather than a compliance with her wishes. It is said that the New England Republicans preferred Gerry, but were defeated by Southern votes and those of docile Pennsylvania.

John Langdon was born in Portsmouth, New Hampshire, June 25, 1741. He was an early and active supporter of the Colonial cause, performed some military service in the Revolution, and when it was instantly and vitally important to check Burgoyne, he lent a large part of his fortune to the cause. Langdon's service in Congress was slight, but business and politics soon drew him home. He was a member of the Constitutional Convention at Philadelphia, and his speeches there seem most inappropriate for a future leader of the Jeffersonian, Democratic, and States' Rights party. But Langdon was active in business and commerce, and therefore favored a strong central government. He led one faction in New Hampshire; General Sullivan, the other. Both were zealous Whigs, but the French Minister, Otto, informed his government that Sullivan was the man of the people, Langdon the protégé of the gentlemen, that Sullivan was supported by the country people, and Langdon by the merchants. In the convention, Langdon was careful of the interests of foreign commerce and he vehemently opposed allowing Congress to emit bills of credit, saying that he would rather reject the whole Constitution. He favored allowing Congress on its own initiative to suppress rebellion against state authority, and of giving it power by a two-thirds vote of both Houses "to negative all laws passed by the several states, interfering, in the opinion of the legislature, with the general interests and harmony of the Union."

Mr. Langdon said that the power conferred by the Constitution should be judge-determined nationally rather than by the state governments—a truly Hamiltonian opinion. Indeed, Langdon held the nobly national sentiments expressed by Patrick Henry in 1774: "All distinctions are thrown down. All America is thrown into one mass. I am not a Virginian, but an American." In debates on the control of the militia, Langdon said that there was more danger from disputes between the central and the state governments concerning their respective rights than there was of oppression by either. Mr. Langdon also said that "he could not understand the jealousy expressed by some gentlemen. The general and state governments were not enemies to each other, but different institutions for the good of the people of America. As one of the people, he could say: 'The national government is mine, the state government is mine, in transferring power from one to the other, I only take out of my left hand what it cannot so well use, and put it into my right hand, where it can be better used."

Under the government, established by the new Constitution, Mr. Langdon was elected to the Senate and had the honor to be its first president, being chosen to the office "for the sole purpose of opening and counting the votes for President of the United States." To Langdon also fell the privilege of writing to Washington the official notice of his election.

Although Langdon entered the Senate as a Federalist, he soon joined the opposition. He and Senator Robinson of Vermont were the only New England Senators to vote against the ratification of Jay's treaty, which Langdon is said to have described as "a damned thing made to plague the French." Langdon served two terms in the Senate and then declined a reëlection; he also refused the position of Secretary of the Navy offered him by President Jefferson, assigning as reasons, duty to his family, age, and ill health. It may well be that thoughts of home played their part in his decision. Mrs. Cutts, a sister-in-law of Mrs. Madison, wrote that Langdon had a beautiful wife and a superb and elegant residence. The French minister reported that "they say that he (Langdon) is jealous of his wife, a very unusual thing in America. Several French officers have found to their mortification that this jealousy was not well founded."[1]

Langdon had made a fortune in business and was known as the Robert Morris of the East. He lived expensively and, like Hancock, used his wealth to increase his political strength. He was much attached to France, was well acquainted with her ways, and imported beautiful manufactures from Paris, for the purpose, according to the French Minister, of spreading a taste for them among the Americans. It was more agreeable to live in a large, richly furnished mansion in comfortable and aristocratic Portsmouth than in the new, crude, inconvenient village of Washington. It is probable, too, that Langdon could do better financially by attending to his business at home, than by making his main residence in distant Washington and drawing his official salary. But whether he was physically equal to Cabinet work or not, he was neither too old nor too feeble to take an active part in the politics of his state, where he had been a pioneer in preaching the doctrines of Republicanism.

Isaac Hill of New Hampshire, writing more than twenty years later, stated that in 1798, "with the exception of Langdon and a few sterling patriots, there could not be said to be in this state a party favorable to the principles of Thomas Jefferson." In 1799, came the first break in the hitherto solid phalanx of New Hampshire Federalism. Banks were then rare; their charters were usually granted for partisan reasons, and politics even entered into their loans. In 1799, the only bank in New Hampshire was located in Portsmouth and managed chiefly for the benefit of its wealthy traders and ship owners. Most of the stock was owned by Federalists. Langdon founded a new bank with numerous stockholders in the country districts, and a policy of lending these outlanders small sums of money for long terms. The Fed-

---

[1]On prétend qu'il est jaloux de sa femme chose assez rare en Amerique. Plusieurs officiers français ont vu avec chagrin que cette jalousie n'etait guères fondée.

eralist legislature refused to grant a charter and passed a law restricting the powers of unincorporated institutions. Great was the indignation. Some Federalists who had petitioned for the new bank now joined the Democrats in supporting a very moderate Federalist for governor; and in 1800, the state saw its first vigorously contested gubernatorial campaign.

Coalition failed, but in 1802 the Republicans nominated Langdon and continued to do so until 1805, when they elected him. With the exception of two years when the embargo had weakened the Republicans, he was rechosen until 1812. In this year he declined further service because of age. When a public man rejects an opportunity to run for office on the ground of poor health, the real weakness is often political rather than physical; but Langdon's *nolo episcopari* was probably a truthful one, for on receiving notice of his nomination as Vice-President, he declined for a like reason, being the first of four men to refuse a nomination for the office by an important party after it had been formally and fully made.[1] Langdon was an old man who had played his part faithfully, and now, as he passed from the stage, he was offered a box where, with little to do, he could in comfort and honor watch the play awhile before he left the theatre. His public work had not been brilliant. George Cabot, when irritated at his success in inducing some "respectable" people to condemn Jay's treaty, declared that it had been supposed that he would have no influence in Boston because of his want of sense. A New Hampshire historian says: "Governor John Langdon was never a man of severe study. In literary, scientific and legal acquirements or oratorical powers he was not a great man. He was a good business man; ever judicious, he looked danger calmly in the face, and generally overcame it." Personally Langdon was honorable and reliable. John Randolph said of him: "If Nature ever formed an honest man, he is one"; and that he was the only man of the "universal Yankee nation" whom he had ever found true as steel under all circumstances.

When Langdon declined to be a candidate for the Vice-Presidency, the caucus reconvened and by a practically unanimous vote nominated his competitor at the earlier meeting, Elbridge Gerry. Like Langdon, Gerry was a patriot of Revolutionary days. He was of a good, though by no means a leading, family, had engaged in foreign trade and by his business ability had won a fortune, and high place among the merchants of his state. He had had much greater experience in national and international affairs than Langdon, but like him, his most recent work in political life had been done as official leader of Republicanism at home and as Governor of his State. Elbridge Gerry may be described as the Marquis of Halifax, the champion "Trimmer" of his day.[2] Yet the comparison may be unjust to Halifax. The Englishman urged that all good things trimmed between opposite extremes, and that his trimming

[1]The others are Silas Wright, Benjamin Fitzpatrick, and Frank Lowden.
[2]See Macaulay's *History of England*, Chapter II.

was of this nature. There was much truth in the plea. The views of Halifax on the bitterly fought questions of his day were nearer than those of any other public man of the time to the calm judgment of history.

Gerry has been less fortunate. If history has not forgotten him, she has remembered him chiefly as one who showed reprehensible vacillation in important positions; by the people he is known, if at all, as the man who was responsible for a grossly partisan redistricting of Massachusetts, which was called after him a "Gerrymander" and so linked his name with a trick which was to prove only too common in American politics. But it should always be remembered in Gerry's favor that he did not, like John Hancock, evade issues; his opinions were given promptly and frankly and his course was not influenced by thoughts of place or profit. He was broad-minded enough to see dangers on either side, and to endeavor to plot out a course which would take the good and avoid the evils of each. But unhappily Gerry was vain, suspicious, and irritable; in nature as in person, a little man. John Adams, his warm friend and usually his companion, once accused him of "an obstinacy that will risk grave things to secure small ones."

In 1787, the French Minister to the United States described Gerry as *"rempli des petites finesses";* and a colleague in the Constitutional Convention accused him of opposing everything which he did not himself propose. Moreover, if Gerry was always changing sides, it was not because of a logical, ultra-subtle mind like those of two later Vice-Presidents, Calhoun and Tyler, but on account of an inability to seize and hold fast what was vital. It may be said further that Gerry was inconsistent because there were really two "Gerrys" in a single person and that now one and now another took control.

S. E. Morison has discussed the matter in a thorough and interesting article in the January number of the *New England Quarterly* for 1928. He calls his essay, *Elbridge Gerry, Gentleman-Democrat,* and says that nature and circumstances united to make Gerry both. His mother's granduncle, for whom he was named, a wealthy merchant of Bristol, England, had been much interested in the settlement of Maine and left a great fortune, part of which came to Gerry. He spent his boyhood in a fine colonial house at Marblehead, which is still a show place, and graduated from Harvard College. After he had acquired a fortune he bought the estate of Elmwood in aristocratic Cambridge. He traveled in a "chariot" and wore fashionable and expensive clothes. He mingled in and enjoyed the pleasures of society and though a faithful and affectionate husband, was very attentive to the ladies, who were not unappreciative. On Gerry's death, a Republican clergyman of Salem wrote in his diary that "he was in his manners the nearest to the gentleman of any northern patriot (non-Federalist?), Governor Hancock being the only person in competition with him." The gentleman appeared in other things than manners. Gerry sometimes refused to adopt means which Sam Adams believed to be justified by the cause in which they were employed. When he came home from France, he was treated with insulting neglect by the Federalists, but bore it calmly. Yet the "democrat" was as strongly ingrained as the "gentleman."

Gerry grew up in the rude, "stinking" fishery town of Marblehead, noted for the rude vigor of its inhabitants, female as well as male. Little is known of his childhood. Whether Marblehead filled the lad with love of liberty, or shocked him into personal refinement, or both, we can not say. Colonel John Glover, whose regiment of Marbleheaders with other fishermen soldiers rowed Washington's army to temporary safety after the disaster of Long Island and through cold and storm to victory at Trenton, and Colonel Orne, a third patriot of the town, erected a smallpox hospital on the not distant Cat Island. But the management was bad, patients died, the disease spread to the town, many believed inoculation disrespectful to the Almighty, and the hospital was closed. This, however, was not enough, and a band of Marbleheaders burned down "Castle Pox." Gerry, always sensitive, withdrew from public affairs, called on the red-coated "tyrants" in Boston for protection, and described his "patriotic" fellow-citizens as a "savage mobility."

Yet Gerry was a Democrat by conviction if not feeling. He early came under the influence of Samuel Adams and with a few characteristic vacillations, he was a defender of the masses and of limited government for the rest of his life. When the Port Act cut off the trade of Boston and great quantities of goods for her relief came pouring into Marblehead, Gerry became one of a committee for handling them, and his mercantile knowledge and business ability proved extremely valuable. After war broke out, he rendered a like service for the army besieging Boston, finding and buying as well as organizing. In 1776, Gerry entered the Continental Congress, where he had much to do with matters of finance and supply. On army questions he had the narrow views of a Democrat and a civilian, modified by the practical sense of a man of affairs. On February 19, 1780, he was not allowed to move to reconsider a certain motion, and was refused the yeas and nays on an appeal from the decision of the chair. Thereupon he declared the rights of his state infringed, and resigned. Three years later he was induced to return to Congress, his course having been rather mildly endorsed by the state Legislature.

Gerry was a member of the Constitutional Convention, and of the Congress from 1789 to 1793. During this period, his conduct in regard to a strong central government suggests that of poor Zekiel in Lowell's "Courtin'."

> He stood a spell on one foot fust,
> Then stood a spell on t'other,
> An' on which one he felt the wust,
> He couldn't ha' told ye nuther.

Zekiel at last cut the Gordian knot by proposing marriage, and Gerry did so by temporarily abandoning public for domestic life.

In 1797, he went as Special Commissioner to France. His conduct there has been noticed already. The President attempted to protect him from criticism, but Adams could not control the Federalist party and Gerry was treated as an outcast. While still in France, Federalist roughs had "milled" round his home, hung him in effigy, and shouted indecent explanations of his remaining in France, for his wife's benefit. On his return the Federalist gentlemen cut him on the street and excluded him from their homes. Only about half a dozen families in "good society" would receive him. Gerry, while defending his own conduct, refused to justify that of France or to desert Adams. But the Massachusetts Federalists maintained their ostracism. Gerry had been an Independent. The Jeffersonians were eager to adopt him and he acquiesced. On several occasions the Republicans made Gerry their candidate for Governor and in 1810 and 1811 they elected him.

As Chief Magistrate, from the Federalist point of view, Gerry played to perfection the part of Jekyll-Hyde. His first term was one of virtue; there was no radical legislation; even Federalist office holders were left undisturbed. "The Democrats began to tell each other that all gentlemen were Federalists under the skin." At the beginning of the second year there was a sudden and violent change. A Federalist caucus had adopted some extreme resolutions. The Governor in his inaugural address retaliated in kind and a violent controversy began in which Gerry forgot dignity, moderation, and even the care which a "Republican" should have maintained for freedom of speech.

The quarrel did not stop with words. Federalist office holders were removed in a manner and to an extent that anticipated the rule of Andrew Jackson. The Governor and the Legislature remodelled the land laws, the suffrage law, the Senatorial districts, the courts, the charter of Harvard College, and cut down the privileges and powers of the Congregationalist Church. Many of these changes were wise, but they horrified conservatives and were long cited with effect as proofs that the masses were unfit for government. At the election of 1812 Gerry was defeated, but by a small majority. Mr. Morison says: "Gerry was soon consoled with the Vice-Presidency; it was Massachusetts who suffered, as she has often suffered from those loudly professing their love. Had Gerry managed to keep the old Adam in him suppressed for another year, and prolong the gentlemanly phase, he would undoubtedly have been reëlected. In that event Massachusetts would have coöperated as a State in the war of 1812, and there would have been no Hartford Convention to live down and explain."

Gerry accepted his nomination as Vice-President, but it may be that there was an understanding that he should withdraw in favor of DeWitt Clinton if the New Yorker would consent to inherit his uncle's office. But Clinton was inflexible. He hoped for Federalist support, and made private advances and promises of concluding peace with England. The chief Federalists arranged for a selection of delegates by leaders of the party, to consider whether Clinton should be supported. The meeting would probably have decided to do so but for the vigorous opposition of Rufus King, who felt that it was more important that the Federalists should preserve their reputation and principles than that they should replace Madison by an unscrupulous and unreliable politician such as King considered DeWitt Clinton to be. The "convention" made no nomination, passed some ambiguous resolutions, and adjourned.[1]

But Clintonians and Federalists united in the choice of a single Peace ticket of electors. A convention of seventeen counties in Virginia nominated Rufus King for President and William R. Davie of North Carolina for Vice-President, but there was a general understanding that Peace men should support Clinton for President, and Jared Ingersoll of Pennsylvania for Vice-President. The latter gentleman was a Federalist of a somewhat mild type and he served as a bait for his party and his State. The ticket is noteworthy because both candidates were taken from the same section of the country. Mr. Ingersoll was a transplanted Connecticut Yankee, the son of a Tory father who, before the Revolution, had been chief stamp distributor in New England and admiralty judge in Pennsylvania. Young Ingersoll graduated from Yale in 1766, studied abroad for over six years, and then settled in Philadelphia, where he at once won high distinction at the bar. In 1811, he was appointed Attorney-General of Pennsylvania and served until 1816. In 1820, he became chief judge of the district court for the county and city of Philadelphia, and held the place until his death in 1822.

Scharf and Westcott, in their history of Philadelphia, say that Mr. Ingersoll, though of keen mind, was courteous, had great powers of persuasion, and avoided violence and exaggeration. He saw with extraordinary quickness whatever points in his adversaries' cases were weak, and when he saw them, he used just the force that was necessary, and no more, to overcome them. It has been said of him that in this respect and in that of defending weak points in his own cases, he was the first man of his time at the bar.

The election attracted less interest than might have been expected, being overshadowed by the war. All the states east of Pennsylvania, except Vermont, went for the Peace ticket; all west and south of Pennsylvania supported Madison. The Keystone state was Republican as usual, and saved the party. Gerry ran slightly ahead of his chief, one Clinton elector in New Hampshire and two in Massachusetts voting for him.

When the year of the next Presidential election, that of 1816, dawned, it was manifest that the contest would be only a sham battle and hardly even that. The Hartford convention, Jackson's overwhelming victory at New Orleans, and the conclusion of peace "with," as the Republicans joyfully proclaimed, "not an inch of territory ceded or lost," had damned the Federalists in the public mind as faint-hearted and disloyal. The Republicans were in

---

[1]For an excellent account of this prototype of the nominating convention of today, see Morison, *Otis,* I : 309-12.

the situation of the triumphant Parliamentarians of England after they had defeated King Charles. "Now," said a leader of an abortive Royalist rising whom they were about to execute, "now, gentlemen, you may go play unless you choose to fall out among yourselves." The American Republicans disagreed in the sharing of the spoils, but party loyalty and the old Virginia cement for a time held them together.

The leading candidates for the Presidential nomination in 1816 were James Monroe of Virginia and William H. Crawford of Georgia, both members of the Cabinet. Monroe had been won over from his affiliation with the extreme Republicans of the John Randolph school, was now Secretary of State, and had the good wishes of the President. William H. Crawford, a thorough politician but also a statesman of force and ability, was Secretary of the Treasury. Crawford was driven from public life by ill health, which not improbably cost him the Presidency and a chance to stand higher in history and to win, shall we say, a place in the *American Statesman Series*. He had the misfortune to be a colleague of the scrupulous, censorious diarist, John Quincy Adams; various biographers used him as a foil to bring out the virtues of their own heroes, and Mr. Phillips, in his sketch of Crawford in the *Dictionary of American Biography,* says that he is so nearly forgotten that he has only "the reputation of a reputation" remaining.

The Treasury Department has recently revived for a moment the memory of Crawford by placing his picture on the new one hundred thousand dollar bills; but it is a doubtful honor, for in the matter of portraiture the Department seems usually to have gone on the principle, the greater the denomination the smaller the man. Crawford in his time was considered both able and handsome, but few of us today know much of his financial principles, and it is to be feared that still fewer will have an opportunity to pass judgment on his personal appearance by examining the bills.

There was a third candidate. In February, 1816, the New York Legislature desired the New York Representatives to support in the Congressional Caucus for nominating a President, the Governor of that State, Daniel D. Tompkins, who had acquired much reputation by the manner in which he performed the duties of his office during the war. In the early fall of 1814, Madison had offered Tompkins the State Department, but he had declined it, pleading a desire to finish the work in which he was engaged. It is probable, however, that his real reason was a belief that the Governorship was a better ladder to the Presidency. Alexander pronounces this a serious error of judgment. He thinks that the pleasing, diplomatic Tompkins would have harmonized with the sensitive President, something which Monroe did not always do; and he points out that Tompkins was personally unknown beyond his state, that his manners were charming, and he would have met many influential men in Washington. But the latter circumstance might have hurt more than it helped. Tompkins lacked iron in the blood and won good-will rather than admiration from men who were acquainted with him.

As the critical moment approached, Madison remembered that both he and Monroe were sons of the Old Dominion. He threw his influence in favor of his compatriot, and followed the rule of the Virginia Dynasty to weaken an upstanding New Yorker by helping his rivals. Accordingly, he appointed opponents of Tompkins in New York to Federal offices. At this evidence of disfavor various former adherents of Tompkins, obeying the political law of gravitation, fell away from the Governor. At Washington, Tompkins was injured by the circumstance that his work had been wholly local.

The usual Congressional Caucus met on March 17, 1816, and nominated Monroe by a vote of 64 to 54 for Crawford.[1] It was recognized by all that Tompkins' nomination was hopeless, and no one threw away a vote on him. But after he was cut down, the usual poultice was applied, and he was nominated for Vice-President by a vote of 85 to 30 for Governor Snyder of Pennsylvania. Crawford would not have accepted the Vice-Presidency; moreover he was from the same section of the country as Monroe.

Daniel D. Tompkins was born at Scarsdale, New York, on June 24, 1774, and was the son of a farmer, a circumstance which he and his friends turned to good use in his political battles. His rise had been rapid. He graduated from Columbia at twenty-one, became a lawyer, and took an active part in politics as a Burrite. In 1801, he was honored by a seat in the state constitutional convention. The main object of calling it was to hobble the Governor and lay a foundation for the spoils system. The New York Constitution provided for a Council of Appointment consisting of the Governor, who, however, had only a casting vote, and four Senators, one chosen from each of the four "Great Districts" of the State. Disputes arose as to the right of the Council to nominate as well as confirm and in 1800, when the Republicans gained control of the state affairs, a constitutional convention was summoned to consider the appointment question. Tompkins' old leader, Burr, was made President; and the convention, with about a dozen dissenting votes, gave to the Council and to each individual member the right to make a nomination. Among the little minority who dared to proclaim their useless opposition to the popular will, was Daniel D. Tompkins.

His courage, however, seems to have done him no harm. Three years later he was elected a Representative in Congress, a position which he almost immediately exchanged for a judgeship of the state Supreme Court. There he modified the customary judicial severity by human sympathy, and Alexander says that only the shortness of his service prevented his winning high distinction as a judge. But in 1810 he was drawn back to political life. In 1804, Clinton and the Livingstons had joined in making Chief Justice Lewis, Governor. But the union was a mere marriage of convenience. Alexander says: "The Livingstons, already jealous of DeWitt Clinton's growing influ-

---

[1]It was subsequently said by Crawford and his friends that he had withdrawn before the nomination, but apparently the declination was not regarded as absolute or was not generally known.

ence, secretly nourished the hope that Lewis might develop sufficient independence to check the young man's ambition. On the other hand, DeWitt Clinton, equally jealous of the power wielded by the Livingstons, thought the Chief Justice a kind, amiable man of sixty, without any particular force of character, sufficiently plastic to mould to his liking."

Time showed that the Livingstons were right. Lewis was a brother-in-law of Chancellor Livingston, the head of the clan, and he waged war against Clinton in the most bitter and personal way. In 1807, Clinton was seeking a candidate with whom he could defeat the Governor, and he tried his old experiment of taking an amiable, popular judge from the Supreme bench. A part of the Legislature nominated Tompkins, a smaller number Lewis, and at the election Tompkins won by a good majority. But, as in 1804, Clinton's success proved only a nominal one. Clinton was a man of great force and he may have trusted to that to beat down any independence of mild men like Lewis and Tompkins. But his judgment proved utterly wrong. Though a practical politician, Clinton seems to have felt that he had a right to the gratitude of the men whom he had raised. But in public life gratitude is often "a lively sense of favors to come"; and in this case the receipt of favor in the past might have been denied by the supposed beneficiaries.

Clinton had not dared to nominate a man who would be recognized as a mere tool; moreover both Lewis and Tompkins had strength independent of Clinton, and could oppose the claims of family ties to those of political aid. Lewis was a brother-in-law of Chancellor Livingston, the able dean of that influential family. Tompkins was a son-in-law of Mangle Minthorne, the wealthy leader of the Martling Men, a powerful organization, later to absorb Tammany, which was anti-Clintonian. Clinton's hoped-for lieutenant became his steady opponent and rival. Alexander says: "What the struggle between Stalwarts and Half-Breeds was to our own time, the struggle between Clinton and Tompkins was to our ancestors of two or three generations ago." When Jefferson put the Embargo through Congress, Tompkins vigorously defended it. Clinton had at first opposed, and then made an undignified jump back to the side of the national administration, deserting his chief newspaper supporter, the notorious editor, Cheetham, and his uncle, the Vice-President.

In the Presidential election of 1808, Clinton insisted that New York throw away her electoral votes on George Clinton. Tompkins wisely pointed out that this would result only in injuring the party and weakening the influence of the state at Washington.

In 1810, Tompkins was reëlected Governor and was similarly favored in 1813 and 1816. In 1812, there was a great legislative scandal with charges of attempted bribery to gain support for a charter incorporating an enormous bank. Tompkins, seeing the coming storm, sent a thundering anti-bank message to the Legislature. DeWitt Clinton kept silent probably because he needed bank support in his plan to get a Presidential nomination from the

Legislature. A few months later came the war with England. Clinton ran for President on an independent ticket, tried to make a secret alliance with the Federalists, and in general behaved in an unworthy, deceitful manner.

To Tompkins, the war brought the opportunity of his life. In times of the greatest discouragement he never seemed to flinch. The war had been going badly; Washington had been captured and burned; and there was much talk of disunion. In the face of this, Tompkins set about to rouse the people. In 1814, when an unexpected wave of feeling gave the Republicans full control of the Legislature, the Governor led in most vigorous measures of public defense. When the war ended, New England was in disgrace for her luke-warmness; New York was honored for her energy and loyalty, and the chief credit for this was given to Tompkins.

Alexander says of Tompkins' position at this time: "For the moment every one seemed to be carried away by the fascination of the man. His friends asserted that he was always right and always successful; that patriotism had guided him through the long discouraging war, and that . . . . in every step he took and in every measure he recommended, he was actuated by the most unselfish purpose." In reality, while Tompkins had shown courage and ability, he was not in essence a hero or a statesman. A patriot he undoubt-edly was, but even here his nature was by no means free from the alloy of selfishness. In December, 1813, Senator Jeremiah Mason, the eminent New Hampshire lawyer, wrote of "a silly story to gull the good Democrats of New York," that Tompkins would be a candidate for President, and said that he was "reported to be a good tempered, inoffensive man of moderate talents."

Alexander thinks also that the praise for good nature was only partially deserved. He says that though Tompkins was extremely sympathetic and affable, "his capacity for friendship depended upon whether the success of his own career was endangered by the association." Since his first nomina-tion for Governor, Tompkins had kept his eye fixed on the Presidency and he had clung to or cast aside men as they helped or hindered his progress to that goal. DeWitt Clinton stood in his way, and accordingly was well buf-fetted by the man to whom he had once been so useful. The New York Constitution gave the Governor the prerogative of adjourning the Legislature for sixty days. The privilege had been exercised but once between 1777 and 1812, but in the latter year Tompkins availed himself of it nominally to defeat the charter of a mammoth bank, the Bank of North America, but really, it is to be feared, to prevent the New York Legislature from endorsing Clinton for President before the meeting of the Congressional Caucus. Whatever Clin-ton's errors at the outbreak of the war, in 1814 when mayor of New York, he was the life of a movement for the defense and fortification of the city, lent $300,000 to the State in his official capacity, and was most active in pro-curing a desperately needed loan to the national government. But when

Clinton, who was a major-general of militia, asked for assignment to active service, Tompkins refused it because Clinton did not approve the war.

Alexander says of Tompkins and the sources of his strength:

"He was one of those men not infrequently observed in public life, who, without conspicuous ability, have a certain knack for the management of men, and are able to acquire influence and even a certain degree of fame by personal skill in manipulating patronage, smoothing away difficulties and making things easy. Nature had not only endowed him with a genius for political diplomacy, but good fortune had favored his march to popularity by disassociating him from any circumstances of birth or environment calculated to excite jealousy or arouse the suspicions of the people. He was neither rich nor highly connected. The people knew him by the favorite title of the 'farmer's boy' and he never appeared to forget his humble beginnings. He had the faculty, says James Renwick, formerly of Columbia College, who knew him personally, of never forgetting the name or face of any one with whom he had once conversed, of becoming acquainted and appearing to take an interest in the concerns of their families; and securing, by his affability and amiable address, the good opinion of the female sex who, although possessed of no vote, often exercise a powerful indirect influence."

The election of Monroe and Tompkins was a foregone conclusion, and the Federalists made no real effort even to cut down their majority. Federalist Legislatures in Massachusetts and Connecticut and Delaware chose Federalist electors. Rufus King was the leading Northern Federalist and received the support of the electors of his party for President. Whether this was from arrangement or was due to fellow feeling merely, is uncertain. On the Vice-Presidency there was no union. The Massachusetts electors agreed, probably at the last moment, to support John E. Howard of Maryland, a gallant soldier of the Revolution. He was a staunch Federalist, but had been a leader in preventing a surrender of Baltimore in 1814. The Connecticut electors would seem to have been composed half of moderates, half of die-hards. Five of them voted for Chief Justice Marshall and five for James Ross, formerly a very intransigeant Senator from Pennsylvania. Delaware voted for her neighbor, Robert G. Harper, who had moved from South Carolina to Maryland.

The year 1820 is remarkable for being the only one where there was no opposition ticket. The disappearance of the Federalist organization may be said to have been long overdue. Even in 1802, Alexander Hamilton had foreseen the end of the Federalist party as then organized,[1] and the election of

---

[1] He wrote Bayard of Delaware in April, 1802, prophesying the demise of the Federalist party, since "men are rather reasoning than reasonable animals, for the most part governed by the impulse of passion"; and outlined the plan of a new political organization to take its place.

1804 showed that there was no place in the United States for an openly aristocratic party. Its revival was caused by the non-intercourse policy, which expired with the war. Though the stimulant restored the patient for a time, it could not renew the old vigor; and this was fatal. A party which is continually defeated soon ceases to exist unless there is felt to be some pressing, vital danger to be met where it is strong, like that of negro domination in the South. As early as 1812, Rufus King wrote to Christopher Gore of "the difficulty which daily increases of confining the young men of the Country to a political Creed which is sure to prevent them in sharing in public distinctions." Apparently matters were even worse in New England, for Gore replied: "Many of the middle-aged and ardent politicians of our section of the Country have been tired of waiting for Peace and Distinction. They sigh to represent the U. *(sic)* States at some foreign court, or to enjoy Power and Influence at home." The disappearance of the Federalist party was hastened by the rout of 1816. On December 13, 1816, the eminent New Hampshire lawyer, Jeremiah Mason, then a Federalist member of Congress, wrote to Gore: "The Federalists having lost all hope, and having no bond of union, cease to act with any degree of concert. I see nothing which will again unite them."

Many of the wisest Federalists became willing that their army should dissolve, but it was instinct that led them to what might seem a counsel of despair. The field was lost, but not the war. Conservatism, like radicalism, may change its form but the thing remains. As early as Jefferson's first term there were signs of a cleavage between the moderate and the ultra-Republicans. And now the distinction was becoming very marked. Some of the old Federalists, while "too honest or too proud" to change, themselves, believed it best for the country that their young followers, instead of hopelessly excluding themselves from political influence, should enlist under the enemy's flag and when the forces of the wicked should divide, go with the least unrighteous part and make much of what Federalism had stood for, triumphant under another name. By 1820 the Republicans had chartered a bank, increased the navy, and passed a protective tariff law.

There was also a special local reason why Federalists should endeavor to maintain the "era of good feelings."[1] Massachusetts had a large claim against the national government for expenses incurred in the war of 1812. A Republican Congress refused to pay it because Massachusetts had on certain occasions refused to comply with the President's calls for militia. The action of Congress was due both to anger and to policy. Massachusetts had not been forgiven for her unpatriotic conduct; moreover, refusal of the money enabled

---

[1]The phrase was first used in a debate in the House of Representatives in reference to the absence of partisan rancor, and modified by a change of the last word from the plural to the singular. It spread through the country and was long in use. But if party distinctions nearly disappeared, personal factions did not, and never was there more manœuvering and intriguing to obtain the Presidency than in that period which came to be viewed in retrospect as a golden age of patriotism and moderation.

the Massachusetts Republicans to declare that the traitorous Federalists had deprived the State of a million dollars. The eloquent and agreeable Harrison Gray Otis had been elected Senator from Massachusetts in the hope that he could get the desired appropriation. In 1816, he had been urgent with his brother Federalists to please the Republicans by refraining from opposition to Monroe. He had failed, but the spirit of conciliation had strengthened in the last four years, and now though Federalist electors were nominated in Massachusetts, it was understood that those who might be chosen[1] would vote for Monroe.

Other states followed the lead of Massachusetts. The Republicans as a national party also made no nominations. A call was issued for a Congressional caucus not of Republicans only, but of all who wished to attend. Only about forty members accepted the invitation and on the motion of R. M. Johnson of Kentucky they decided to make no recommendations. Everybody was agreed on the renominations of President Monroe. It is said that the plan of those favoring a caucus was to nominate Henry Clay for Vice-President. If so, it might seem surprising that the motion to take no action was made by Johnson, a fellow-Kentuckian; but there was considerable rivalry between the two men.

Possibly the caucus would have recommended the old ticket had there not been doubt both of Tompkins's acceptance and of the advisability of his renomination. The last four years had seen a change for the worse in the Vice-President's fortune, reputation, and character. As war Governor of New York, Mr. Tompkins had been obliged to do in great haste an immense amount of work, more of a business than a political character. He had spent his own money in the public service and pledged his own credit by endorsing the notes of the United States as Governor without legal authority. Unfortunately Mr. Tompkins was a poor accountant, he had worked at high pressure, and he could produce no vouchers for large amounts of money drawn by him from the treasury.[2]

In 1819, the Legislature had allowed Tompkins a commission on loans obtained by him which was believed would enable him to balance his accounts. It would have done so and a little more, but he put in a claim for a larger commission, making the State his debtor for some hundred and thirty thousand dollars. Alexander says: "It was a strange mixup and the more committees examined it the worse appeared the muddle." Stung by charges that he was an embezzler, Tompkins, who was not a strong man, sought relief from anxiety and wounded feelings in drink and acquired habits of intemperance which he was never able to throw off permanently. But in spite of the unfor-

---

[1] The election was by districts.
[2] His own cash and that of the State were not banked in separate accounts, and it is probable that without realizing it he had at times used public money for family expenses.

tunate condition of his accounts, most people believed that he was guilty only of carelessness and a legislative caucus attended by 64 members almost unanimously nominated him for Governor. Martin Van Buren and Rufus King, who had obtained a seat in the Senate chiefly because of Van Buren's aid, believed that Tompkins should not run for Governor until his accounts were settled, and Van Buren tried to get others to persuade him to decline the nomination. But this Tompkins would not do, thereby confirming the opinions of many close acquaintances. Joseph C. Yates, an experienced politician then on the Supreme bench and ordinarily very mild and gentle, said that Tompkins never refused an offer of any sort in his life.

The New York Federalist party had dissolved. Forty-eight of their leaders were about to join in a public announcement of the fact; the Republicans or Democrats, as they were now being called, were divided into two factions so strongly opposed to each other that they were almost separate parties, the followers and the opponents of DeWitt Clinton. The latter, or Bucktails, included Tammany, were the better organized, and although they received the support of the exclusive Federalist remnant, probably had the best claim to "regularity." They were recognized by the government at Washington and liberally nourished with offices. As the Clintonians were weak in the Legislature, they made no contest there but nominated their chief for Governor at a meeting in Albany. The fight was hot. The Bucktails carried the Legislature, but Clinton by a small majority defeated Tompkins, to the latter's bitter mortification. There was nothing now to interfere with Tompkins' holding the Vice-Presidency, to which, indeed, the Congressional caucus would probably have nominated him had the result of the New York election been known when it met; and by a general understanding the Republicans supported him.

Though there was in effect but one candidate for President,[1] there were a number of Federalists among the Electors chosen. All joined in supporting Monroe, but a convert to Republicanism refused to do so. This was William Plumer of New Hampshire, an ex-Senator and ex-Governor who had voluntarily withdrawn from public life. He had been complimented by being placed without his knowledge at the head of the electors of his State. To the general surprise of the country he voted against Monroe, casting his ballot for John Quincy Adams. It was currently reported that Plumer's motive in preventing a unanimous election was to confine that honor to Washington alone. But such was not the case. Mr. Plumer believed that Monroe had not the high ability which should be made an absolute condition of holding the office of President and that his administration had been grossly extravagant. Tompkins was less fortunate than his chief. In New Hampshire an

---

[1]An anti-Monroe ticket was put up in Pennsylvania and was voted for by some men who believed that he had been too favorable to slavery.

elector refused to vote for him and complimented Richard Rush of Pennsylvania with his support. Whether the recalcitrant in this case was Plumer is not known.

Daniel Webster wrote to Jeremiah Mason: " . . . . there will be a number of us, of course, in this State (Massachusetts), who will not vote for Mr. Tompkins, and we must therefore look up somebody to vote for." He asked Mason to try to find out how votes for John Quincy Adams would be regarded at Washington. In the end the eight Massachusetts Federalists voted for Richard Stockton of New Jersey. Little Delaware, faithful to Federalism to the death, cast her four votes for one of her own sons, Daniel Rodney. Maryland gave one vote to Robert G. Harper. The other electors voted for Tompkins.

The second administration of President Monroe was described as an "era of good feelings." The term was applicable as far as parties were concerned. The Federalist party was at the point of death and most of its members were accepting the fact very calmly. Old issues were settled, new ones had not become clear, and the Republicans had adopted many of the measures of their opponents. But if there was little partisan contest since one side was too weak to fight, there was much and bitter strife between personal factions of the victors. The Republican party swelled to an unwieldy size, and deprived by the accession of most of its opponents of the need of discipline and harmony, was split into groups partly representing principles or at least tendencies, but mainly devoted to desperate struggles to secure the Presidency for their several leaders. Eliminating minor aspirants, there were six candidates for the succession to Mr. Monroe. They were John Quincy Adams of Massachusetts, the Secretary of State, whose office had served as the "easy succession" to the Presidency since 1808, William H. Crawford of Georgia, Secretary of the Treasury, John C. Calhoun of South Carolina, Secretary of War, Henry Clay of Kentucky, Speaker of the House, with brief intervals, from 1811, DeWitt Clinton of New York, and Andrew Jackson of Tennessee.

Adams was a former Federalist and represented the men who had come into the Republican party during the administration of Jefferson, and believed in taking a *via media* in solving the questions, that authority in government should be given to the Nation rather than the states, and to men of education and property rather than to the masses. Calhoun and Clay had been "war hawks" of 1812, and were supported by young Republicans who favored a protective tariff, internal improvements, and a national bank. Crawford was the favorite of Republicans of the old school and probably had the good wishes of the President, who, however, took no open part in the Presidential contest. Clinton was a strong States' Rights man devoted to his own interests and those of New York.

Jackson was a thorough believer in the fitness of the masses to rule, and was enthusiastically supported by them. He combined a theoretic adherence to States' Rights principles with intense national feeling. Jackson was coached more carefully than he knew by some of the cleverest politicians in the country. He was also supported by some aristocratic Southerners who indulged the delusive hope that they might use the popular frontiersman as a tool to repair or raise bulwarks against the impending flood of democracy and nationalism.

But though the candidates represented divisions and subdivisions of the Republican party, none could hope to succeed without help from other factions than his own and therefore all avoided taking a definite stand which might alienate possible recruits. Nor did their Republicanism prevent their angling for the votes of such Federalists as were willing to enlist in the Republican ranks, but were uncertain what regiment to join. Calhoun and his supporters appear to have been very active in this work. At a public dinner at his home at Edgefield he toasted the memory of Fisher Ames, the Federalist leader and orator of Massachusetts, and Calhoun newspapers were set up in that State.

Friends of Jackson also busied themselves in enticing Federalists into their camp. In 1816, the General had written letters to Monroe in favor of the appointment of William Drayton of South Carolina as Secretary of War. Drayton had been a Federalist, but Jackson said that there was a difference between truly American Federalists like Drayton and the monarchical wing of the party. He also urged Monroe to "crush the monster called party spirit"[1] by making the appointment. At the same time, Jackson, as became a dyed-in-the-wool American of the frontier, said that had he been in command at Hartford when the notorious convention met there, he would have court-martialed its three leaders for traitorous communication with the enemy. The correspondence was made public by Jackson's friends and though the praise of Federalists and disregard of party lines alienated some stiff Republicans, it gained more of their opponents.

Of course there was much negotiating with promises of recognition and office if some candidate would consent to stand aside. A frequent bait was the Vice-Presidency. On January 29, 1822, General Peter B. Porter, an able and worthy volunteer soldier of the War of 1812 and a political leader in western New York, wrote to Clay that there was a rumor that they were to run together and that, considering the feeling in New York, such an alliance would be absolutely fatal. But on August 31 of the same year, Patrick Henry of Virginia, a son of the great orator, wrote Clay praising Clinton in the highest degree, saying that Clay could and must make Clinton, President;

---

[1] William B. Lewis, of Tennessee, revised the letter and was the true author of this phrase, which came to be quoted throughout the country.

that Clinton would be grateful; that Clay would have the succession and meanwhile could be Vice-President or Secretary of State.

The friends of Crawford were very anxious to help their candidate by buying off an opponent. One of Crawford's cleverest and most active supporters was Martin Van Buren of New York, the leader of the "Albany Regency," a group of skillful politicians of the better sort which was beginning a long domination of the party in the Empire State. Van Buren, though a wholehearted champion of Crawford, was well disposed to Clay personally and some of his closest friends held the Kentuckian in even higher regard. The New York leader decided that Crawford's election could be secured and a split in the party averted if Clay would accept the Vice-Presidency on the Crawford ticket. Van Buren had just taken his seat in the United States Senate, and he turned for help to a colleague only slightly his senior in service, Thomas H. Benton of Missouri. The choice of Mr. Benton as emissary was an appropriate one, for he was a friend and admirer of Clay and their wives were cousins. Van Buren held several interviews with him in which he urged the advantage to the party and to Clay himself of the union he proposed, one of his arguments being that Crawford would serve but a single term and that Clay would doubtless succeed him. Benton approved the plan and laid it before Clay, but without avail.

Senator Thomas of Illinois applied to a friend of Adams, Representative and ex-Speaker Taylor of New York, in terms most complimentary to the Secretary, urging that he run with Crawford. Thomas not only used arguments like those often employed in similar circumstances, that Adams' acceptance of the second place would win the favor of the friends of the candidate to whom he yielded precedence and would doubtless secure his own election to the higher office at a later date, but went so far as to say, "that from the state of Mr. Crawford's health it was highly probable that the duties of the Presidency would devolve upon the Vice-President, which made it necessary to select with peculiar anxiety a person qualified for the contingency which was to be apprehended." Thomas' proposal was, however, declined by Taylor, who knew from Adams himself that he would not accept a nomination by a Congressional caucus.

Somewhat later Governor King of Maine, a brother of Rufus King and one of Crawford's most devoted adherents, was urgent with Representative Crowninshield of Massachusetts that Adams would accept the Vice-Presidency with Crawford. King soon made an unqualified statement that Adams' friends had agreed to this proposal. Adams says in his *Diary* that when this was told him, "I applied an epithet to King for saying this, which I will not commit to paper . . . . adding that it was impossible that any friend of mine should have undertaken thus to dispose of me without my consent." A few days later Adams entered in his diary a statement that King might have misunderstood something which he had said, so perhaps it was as well that Adams had exercised the unwonted self-restraint of not writing down his full opinion.

Another combination proposed was that of Adams and Jackson. Many tickets bearing their names were printed and a newspaper called for the support of

> John Quincy Adams
> Who can write
> And Andrew Jackson
> Who can fight.

The union of the Harvard graduate, scholar, and minister at European courts, with the uncultivated frontiersman seems a strange one, but it had the persistent and cordial approval of Adams himself. Adams was a thorough American and a hard fighter, and he admired these qualities in Jackson. When in 1818, Jackson followed raiding Seminoles into the then Spanish province of Florida and seized the Spanish fort at Pensacola, Adams had been his sole defender in the Cabinet, saying that "if the question was dubious it was better to err on the side of vigor than of weakness, on the side of our own officer who had rendered the most eminent service than on the side of our bitterest enemies and against him."

Adams was now firm in maintaining the great propriety of electing Jackson Vice-President. Secretary of the Navy Southard expressed the fear that if Adams' friends supported Jackson for the Vice-Presidency, they would thereby increase his chances of becoming President. Adams replied: "I had no doubt it would. But what then? My friends would vote for him on correct principle . . . . his fitness for the place, the fitness of the place for him, and the peculiar advantage of the geographical association. If by voting for him as Vice-President my friends should induce others to vote for him as President, they and I must abide by the issue. It is upon the whole the best course to be taken and besides the impulse to the course in the popular feeling is given. It is too late to withstand or to control it."

Jackson's Drayton letters, though winning some Federalists particularly in the Middle States and the South, were alienating others in New England. Congressman Livermore of New Hampshire came to Adams to say that he feared that an alliance with Jackson would hurt him more than it would help because of Jackson's statement that he would have hung the leaders of the Hartford Convention. Adams replied that "it was hardly fair to hold Jackson responsible for an undigested remark in a confidential letter and that it was offset by his noble sentiments regarding party spirit." Livermore was still unconvinced, but Adams told him that " . . . . the Vice-Presidency was a station in which Jackson could hang no one, and in which he would need to quarrel with no one. His name and character would serve to restore the forgotten dignity of the place and it would afford an easy and dignified retirement for Jackson's old age."

As the time for a Congressional Caucus approached, there was a general recognition of the fact that Crawford would probably be the nominee, and his opponents set themselves busily to work to contrive a combination which would defeat him. A leader in the movement, Colonel Richard M. Johnson, asked Adams if he would agree to an amalgamation of forces for this desirable purpose. Adams replied that he would, that he had already told his friends to disregard his interests entirely, " . . . . and to concur in any arrangement necessary for the union of the Republican party and the public interests." Two days later Johnson, speaking, he said, for Calhoun, proposed the formation of an alliance to make Adams President, Jackson Vice-President, Clay Secretary of State, and Calhoun Secretary of the Treasury. Adams, true to a resolve to refrain from promises regarding Cabinet places, did not answer. Some months later, it was suggested that he agree to appoint Clinton Secretary of State, and Calhoun Secretary of the Treasury. Adams says in his diary that he replied, "that I was not disposed to sell the skin before the animal was taken, and while my own election was a bare possibility, I should not even deliberate in my own mind, much less would I announce to others, how my cabinet might be composed if I should be chosen."

Calhoun had relied chiefly on Pennsylvania. His advocacy of the tariff of 1816 and of internal improvements had pleased that state; he probably was the choice of the business interests there, and the politicians had moved to his support. But in all this there was little enthusiasm. Calhoun had no real hold on the people and when the candidacy of Jackson was announced, the masses swept resistlessly to his standard. One of Calhoun's supporters, George M. Dallas, who twenty years later was to be Vice-President himself, wrote Calhoun that probably it would be necessary to give way when the state convention met. But Dallas found that delays were dangerous and declared at an important meeting in Philadelphia that the public interest imperatively required all patriots to forego their personal wishes and unite on Jackson. He offered resolutions to this effect which were passed without opposition.

A fortnight later, the state convention nominated Jackson for President with only two dissenting votes, and Calhoun for Vice-President by a majority of two to one. Calhoun's supporters went with the tide, the Jackson men telling them that the Vice-President would not only stand next to the throne officially, but would be recognized as heir apparent, and that Jackson would serve but one term. The action of Pennsylvania was a disappointment to Calhoun. He greatly desired to be President. Many of his acquaintances and friends thought that the Vice-Presidency was no place for him and he himself seems to have been uncertain what to do. In the planning of a union against Crawford under the Adams banner, he asked for the Treasury Department, not the Vice-Presidency.[1] Postmaster-General McLean told

---

[1] It should be remembered, however, that Jackson, if he came in, must be Vice-President, since the only cabinet post for which he was fit was the Secretaryship of War, and that was considered an office of second rank.

Adams that he thought that the Vice-Presidency was not a sufficiently active station for Calhoun and Southard, the Secretary of the Navy, seems to have held the same opinion. General Jacob Brown, who, as commander-in-chief of the army, had been brought into close contact with Secretary of War Calhoun, informed Adams that Calhoun's friends wished him to be in the Cabinet in a more active situation than the Vice-Presidency, but that he inclined to the latter office probably for the sake of a certainty of not being thrown out of place.

After the Harrisburg convention Adams saw that a Calhoun alliance would be proposed, but he had no liking for the plan. On March 31, he wrote in his diary: "Calhoun's game now is to unite Jackson's supporters and mine on him for Vice-President. Look out for breakers." Adams had formerly thought highly of Calhoun, but he had been angered by the organized attempt to capture his own State of Massachusetts for Calhoun and by what he considered grossly unfair treatment by Calhoun newspapers, and he now expressed the wish that his friends would support Jackson for Vice-President until their aid was definitely refused. Adams said that in such a case he would be satisfied personally by the choice of Nathaniel Macon of North Carolina.

But Adams' friends preferred Calhoun. Though a Southerner and a former war-hawk, he was strong in New England and with the Federalists. There were Calhoun papers in Massachusetts and the "lords of the loom" and the "Southern Bashaws" were drawn together by a common interest in cotton. Adams' men in Massachusetts were anxious to conciliate Calhoun because he was reported to be growing cold toward the Massachusetts' claim for militia expenses in the War of 1812. The greatest of the ex-Federalists and Calhoun's future rival, Daniel Webster, would not have been unwilling to see him President and had strongly favored him for the Vice-Presidency. On March 14, 1824, he wrote his brother Ezekiel: "I hope all New England will support Mr. Calhoun for the Vice-Presidency. If so he will probably be chosen and that will be a great thing. He is a true man and will do good to the country in that situation." On January 18, 1825, when the election had gone to the House and the result was very doubtful, he submitted several questions to the oracle in the old home and among them were the startling queries: "Is it advisable under any circumstances, to hold out (that is inflexibly adhere to Adams and so prevent an election) and leave the chair to Mr. Calhoun?

"Would or would not New England prefer a man of the power of Calhoun to a choice of Genl. Jackson?"

Calhoun, after the defection of Pennsylvania, at first awaited events in dignified silence, but later formally withdrew as a Presidential candidate and was supported for Vice-President both by the Jackson and by the Adams men.   Adams, however, gave the action of his followers a bare and reluctant acquiescence.   On September 19, 1824, he told Peleg Sprague of Maine that "the Pennsylvania nomination (of Jackson and Calhoun) was an absolute proscription of New England and that my friends here should think twice before they lend their aid to any part of this inveterate exclusion of themselves."

There was talk also of a Clay-Adams ticket.   Adams made the comment that he did not believe Clay wished his friends to vote for him (Adams) for Vice-President, but some of them might wish his own to do so and "thus pledge themselves to an exterminating hostility against Crawford's interest," and that he did not think such a course would be "either just or expedient."

Clay's friends, at the suggestion of their leader, decided to support Nathan Sanford of New York for the place now held by his fellow New Yorker, Daniel D. Tompkins.   Tompkins would have been glad to once more succeed himself and had even indulged in some quite unwarranted hopes of the Presidency.   But though his health, fortune, and habits had all improved, and his financial difficulties with the state and Federal governments had been settled, there was no reason for giving him a third term as Vice-President.

The then Governor of New York, Joseph C. Yates, ardently desired to imitate Tompkins and step from the Governorship to the Vice-Presidency. The leaders of the Crawford faction were most anxious to defeat a plan to transfer the choice of the New York electors from the Legislature to the people, and the Governor, who had not heretofore been closely bound to the regency, lent them public and most efficient aid.   When Rufus King in Washington heard the news, he told Van Buren that Crawford's friends ought to send Yates a picture of the Vice-Presidential chair, which they had doubtless promised him.   Van Buren denied the offer, but as a matter of fact, unknown to him, the State Treasurer, a member of the Regency, had won Yates over by giving strong hopes that help in the matter of postponing a change in the electoral law would bring the satisfaction of his ambitions.   But the people were furious at being tricked out of their desires, the Regency made Yates their scapegoat, and not only failed to get him the Vice-Presidency, but denied him a renomination as Governor.

William H. Crawford, as everyone expected, won the caucus nomination. His opponents, realizing his strength there, refused to attend and Crawford was nominated by a vote of 64 to 4.   For Vice-President, the caucus nominated that veteran Republican and able statesman, Albert Gallatin, the vote standing Gallatin 57, Erastus Root of New York 2, and one each for John Quincy Adams and William Eustis of Massachusetts, Samuel Smith of Maryland, William King of Maine, Richard Rush, John Tod, and Walter Lowrie of Pennsylvania.

Albert Gallatin was born at Geneva, Switzerland, on January 29, 1761. Finding the political atmosphere of his native city too close for one of his free spirit, he determined to emigrate to America, and landed at Boston in October, 1781. After a short stay at that place, he bought some land in the frontier part of Pennsylvania—on the Monongahela in the southwestern part of the State—and built a home there. A natural inclination toward politics soon asserted itself. In September, 1788, he was a member of a convention which had assembled at Harrisburg to consider ways and means of revising the newly made United States Constitution. His future place in the American political scene was here foreshadowed by his avowed opposition to even the mild degree of centralization embodied in that instrument. Now followed a long, varied, and distinguished career in American statecraft. Beginning in 1790, he served three terms in the Pennsylvania Legislature, where he became a leader in both the initiation and the drafting of legislation, among which were bills for the reform of the penal code, the abolition of slavery, and for a system of state-wide education. An able report, which he drafted for the Ways and Means Committee, gave him financial leadership in the Legislature. Elected to the United States Senate early in 1793, he was denied a seat by the Federalists on the grounds that he had not been a citizen of the United States for the required nine years (a strained interpretation of the Constitution). But his temporary admission, pending the decision of his claim, had been of sufficient duration to permit him to introduce a resolution calling for an annual, detailed, statement of the finances of the government.

In 1794, Gallatin was elected to the United States House of Representatives and served there three terms. By 1797 he had won recognition as the Democratic-Republican leader in that body. His persistent interest in the field of finance led to the creation of the Ways and Means Committee, and finally the fixed accountability of the Treasury to Congress. When Jefferson became President in 1801, there were abundant reasons why he should have turned to Gallatin for the Treasury portfolio, not the least of which were personal fitness because of his financial ability and experience, his political philosophy, truly Jeffersonian in type, and lastly, his political availability. Gallatin remained at the head of the Treasury Department until February, 1814, a period rivaled in length only by that in recent years of Andrew Mellon. His work was distinguished not only by a technical excellence in the administration of the funds—to him fell the problems of war finance—but by the broad social objectives which accompanied it. His work at the Treasury was terminated by an appointment to a diplomatic mission to Russia, and this was the beginning of ten continuous years of such service abroad. He was one of the commissioners who drafted and signed the Treaty of Ghent ending the War of 1812, and he held the post of Minister to France for seven years. Upon his return to the United States, he was urged by the friends of Crawford to allow his name to be put forward as a candidate for the Vice-Presidency, and to this he finally reluctantly gave his consent.

Of his nomination as Vice-President Gallatin wrote a frank account to a friend of his youth, Jean Badollet, who had also settled in the United States. Gallatin said: "During the twelve years I was in the Treasury, I was anxiously looking for some man who could fill my place there and in the general direction of the national concerns, for one indeed that could replace Mr. Jefferson, Mr. Madison and myself. Breckinridge of Kentucky[1] only appeared and died; the eccentricities and temper of J. Randolph soon destroyed his usefulness, and only one man at last appeared who filled my expectations. This was Mr. Crawford, who united to a powerful mind a most correct judgment and an inflexible integrity; which last quality, not sufficiently tempered by indulgence and civility, has prevented his acquiring general popularity; but notwithstanding this defect (for it is one), I know so well his great superiority over the other candidates for the office of President, that I was anxious for his election and openly expressed my opinion. Almost all the old Republicans (Mr. Jefferson and Mr. Madison amongst them) think as I do; but they were aware that Mr. Crawford was not very popular, and that the bond of party, which had with many the effect of patriotism and knowledge, being nearly dissolved, neither of the other candidates would withdraw, and they were at a loss whom to unite to him as Vice-President. I advised to nominate nobody for that office, or, if anybody, some person from New York or New England. The last was attached to Adams; there were contentions in New York. The friends of Mr. Crawford thought the persons proposed there too obscure, and that my name would serve as a banner and show their nomination to be that of the old Republican party. I thought and still think that they were mistaken; that as a foreigner, as residuary legatee of the Federal hatred, and as one whose old services were forgotten, and more recent ones (as Minister to France) though more useful were but little known, my name could be of no service to the cause." But Gallatin's friends insisted, and he did not feel justified in declining.

The smallness of the attendance at the Congressional caucus weakened its already diminished authority. Webster said that it had "injured no one but its friends" and this became the general verdict. But such was not the first impression. Those groups of powerful political managers popularly known as the "Richmond Junto," and the "Albany Regency," strongly favored Crawford. It was feared that they would swing Virginia and New York to the Georgian, and with them the party which had been accustomed to follow the lead of these two great states. The hasty endorsement of Jackson at the Philadelphia meeting was perhaps in a measure due to fear lest if the State convention should meet divided between Calhoun and Jackson, the Crawfordites, by appealing to the authority given by custom to the nomina-

---

[1]Breckinridge is now chiefly known as the sponsor of the famous Kentucky resolutions of 1798. He was, however, a "constructive reformer." The penal code of Kentucky was largely his work and he had a powerful influence in the forming of the second Constitution of his State.

tion of a Congressional Caucus, and by urging the adoption of a third candidate as a compromise, might carry an endorsement of Crawford.

But the Crawford managers had their troubles also. They had relied on the divisions in the enemies' ranks. They were much alarmed by the elimination of Calhoun; and they now resolved on a similar move themselves. The nomination of Gallatin had been made with a hope of winning Pennsylvania, but it proved of little use in that respect for, as one candidate himself said, the State was "Jackson-mad." Moreover, though the selection of Gallatin pleased the alien-born, it offended nativists and he was bitterly attacked as a foreigner.[1]

The powerful Richmond Junto decided that Gallatin ought to be replaced by Clay in much the same manner as Calhoun had been by Jackson. But first it was necessary to induce Gallatin to withdraw. Van Buren saw Senator Lowrie of Pennsylvania and Lowrie, in a respectful and sympathetic manner, wrote Gallatin that his friends despaired of his success, that under existing conditions Calhoun would almost certainly be elected Vice-President, either by the electors or the Senate, and that Gallatin's withdrawal so that Clay might take his place would help Crawford. The situation must have been deeply mortifying to Gallatin. When asked to run for Vice-President, he had replied that he did not desire the office but that he would dislike to be proposed and not elected. Gallatin had spent his life in faithful and important public service, and now the American people refused him the gratitude which was his due. He had a scruple, too, about deserting those who had nominated him.[2] He also felt it would be cowardly to withdraw from fear of defeat.

But Gallatin had a high sense of duty, and he believed that withdrawal would be proper if it would help Crawford or prevent the election of an "unsuitable person" as Vice-President. Friends who were well qualified to judge told him that his leaving the field would aid Crawford greatly and afford the only reasonable chance of defeating Calhoun. To Gallatin, these arguments were potent. His opinion of Crawford has been quoted above. Of Calhoun his judgment was extremely severe. In the confidential letter to Badollet he called him "a smart fellow, one of the first among second rate men, but of lax political principles and a disordinate ambition not over delicate in the means of satisfying itself." But of Clay he said: "Mr. Clay has his faults, but splendid talents and a generous mind."

Under these circumstances Gallatin decided to send a simple note of withdrawal to be published at the discretion of the Virginia Central Committee, which Gallatin regarded as the representative of the Virginia Legislature by

---

[1] There was, indeed, a doubt if Gallatin was a citizen of the United States at the time of the adoption of the Constitution, and if he was not, he was ineligible for the Vice-Presidency.

[2] In reality it was he who was deserted. The politicians had taken him up as bait and threw him away when it was found that the Pennsylvania fish was on the Jackson hook.

whom he had been nominated. The discretion was promptly exercised, but Clay was not to be enticed or bullied into giving up his chance for the Presidency, although had the offer been made earlier, it is possible that it might have been accepted.

The union of the Jackson and Adams men in Calhoun's favor gave him 182 electoral votes to 30 for Sanford, 24 for Macon, 9 for Van Buren, 13 for Jackson, and 2 for Clay. Virginia voted solidly for Macon, and Georgia for Van Buren. There were some curious combinations. Connecticut cast her eight votes for Adams and Jackson, and one New Hampshire elector did the same. Missouri voted for Jackson and Clay. For President there was no choice by the electors, and from the three leaders, Jackson, Adams, and Crawford, the House chose Adams, Clay having thrown his influence in his favor. There were furious but unjust charges of "bargain and corruption" which were strengthened in the popular opinion by Adams' making Clay Secretary of State. In truth there had been no definite agreement. In response to inquiries Adams assured Clay's friends of his good-will toward him, and that in considering the claims of the West to office, he could not overlook Mr. Clay. On the other side, Jackson's friends courted those of Clay; and Samuel Houston and James Buchanan said—the one directly, the other by clear implication—that Clay's support of Jackson would be rewarded by the "first" place in the Cabinet.

CHAPTER XII.

1828-1832-1836: *Calhoun, Van Buren and Richard M. Johnson*

THE period of Mr. Adams' presidency saw the formation of two factions, the "Administration" and the "Opposition," which developed into real parties, the National Republican, later the Whig, and the Democratic Republican or Democratic. Crawford's health was broken and most of his followers joined the Democrats. Calhoun and his supporters did the same, though as a rather distinct wing whose differences with the main body became more and more marked. In 1828, the Jackson men and their allies united on the old ticket of Jackson and Calhoun. The National Republicans joined in supporting the President for reëlection. But there was much doubt concerning the Vice-Presidency.

In 1826 some of Clay's friends in different parts of the country expressed the wish that he should be the next Vice-President. Clay mentioned the matter to Adams, but said that he thought that it should be decided solely with reference to the effect which his nomination would have on the election of the latter. Clay was then much troubled by ill health and Adams replied that if the work of Secretary of State was beyond Clay's strength, he would be satisfied that Clay should be Vice-President, but that otherwise he thought that it would be for the advantage both of himself and of the public that Clay should continue in the far more arduous and important office of Secretary of State. A little later Richard Rush of Pennsylvania, then Secretary of the Treasury, expressed the opinion that it might be necessary to nominate Clay in order to hold Illinois and Missouri.

Some men who had been followers of Crawford but now supported the Administration, such as Lewis Williams of North Carolina, a patriarch of the Democratic party, proposed the nomination of Crawford; Nathaniel Macon, who would be pleasing to old States Rights Democrats, was also suggested. But Adams disapproved of both. Two prominent Virginians,

John Hampden Pleasants, who was to become the chief Whig editor in the state, and ex-Governor and Senator James Barbour were considered. Barbour was a man of remarkable simplicity and purity of character, but he was objectionable to Pennsylvania because, when Governor, he had denied the power of Congress to protect manufacturers and to make internal improvements.

General William Henry Harrison was strongly supported by the Ohio and by other western Congressmen, but neither the legislature of Virginia, his native state, nor that of Ohio where he lived, and which he represented in the Senate, would put him in nomination.[1] The Administration was unfavorable also. Clay may have been offended by a failure of Harrison to reply to an attack upon him in the Senate in connection with the bargain and corruption charge; and Adams, while crediting Harrison with a certain ability, believed him to be bombastic and overrated and an indefatigable office seeker.

On January 4, 1828, a convention at Harrisburg, Pennsylvania, presented the name of the Governor of the State, John Andrew Shulze, for Vice-President, and on his declining nominated another fellow-citizen, Secretary Richard Rush, who had already been considered for the place. Four days later, an assembly of anti-Jackson men endorsed the nomination. Rush asked Adams what he had better do. Adams says in his diary: "I told him candidly that so far as I had been consulted by the friends of the Administration I had advised that the selection should be made of a citizen residing south of the Potomac. This had been fully considered and judged not indispensable. The Harrisburg convention having made the nomination, I hoped it would be universally acceptable and supported and I assured him that no nomination could have been made more pleasing to me." Rush had been Minister to Great Britain, and had a desire to return to the diplomatic service, giving as a reason that his health would not permit him to bear the burdens of the Treasury Department. But the President suspected that the real reason was "a preference of the harbor to the tempest." Adams told Rush that he believed that the interests of the nation and of Rush himself would be best served by his remaining at the Treasury; Rush consented to do so and also to stand for the Vice-Presidency.

The nomination of Rush was regarded by the National Republicans as a strategic move, since it would serve to bring them strength in what they regarded as the "doubtful" state of Pennsylvania. As the campaign progressed, however, it became apparent that the "uprising of the people," which the Jacksonian party had confidently proclaimed, was actually in progress. Pennsylvania returned a popular vote of almost two to one in favor of the Jackson-Calhoun ticket, and the opposition received not one electoral vote

---

[1]It must be remembered that in the campaign of 1828 "nominating" was done exclusively by local bodies, the Congressional caucus was dead, and the National Convention not yet born.

south of the Potomac and west of Pennsylvania. Their total was only eighty-three, while the "Old Hero" received one hundred seventy-eight and his running-mate, Calhoun, fell short of that amount only by the seven of Georgia, which were cast for William Smith of South Carolina.

Of the memorable events of the first Jackson administration, the Peggy Eaton affair was the most important in determining the Democratic Vice-Presidential nomination in 1832. When the various cabinet wives refused to call on the wife of Eaton, the Secretary of War, Martin Van Buren, the Secretary of State, won the heart of Jackson by championing her cause. Calhoun, an aspirant for the favor of the Administration and the succession in 1832, had been conspicuously unsuccessful, and his leadership in the Nullification movement in South Carolina completed the breach between him and Jackson. A cabinet so torn by dissension was a liability to the President. Van Buren, firmly established in his confidence, saw that a dissolution of the cabinet would not only serve the President well, but save himself from certain political embarrassments. After four days of persuasion, Jackson consented to the resignation of Van Buren, regarding the offer as further proof of his unselfishness. The logic of the situation was not lost on Eaton and he agreed to resign at the same time. The complete break-up of the cabinet soon followed.

By withdrawing from the cabinet, Van Buren had weakened the force of the widely circulated argument of the Calhoun faction and the opposition party that he was the shrewd manipulator of the President. The mission to England, which Jackson had offered him at the time he broached the question of resignation, would remove him from the scene of the cabinet squabbles and still further weaken that argument. Some of Van Buren's friends, however, doubted the wisdom of both moves. At the first news of his resignation they feared that it would be taken by the public as an indication that he had lost the President's favor. Furthermore, they feared that his absence in England would cause him to lose control of the situation at home. There were ample evidences, particularly in the South, that powerful sections of his own party did not share the enthusiasm which General Jackson felt for his favorite.

But if Van Buren's friends had unwittingly led him astray, his enemies equally blindly brought him back to the right path. The appointment of Van Buren came before the Senate at its meeting in December, 1831. Presidential nominations to high diplomatic positions are usually confirmed without regard to politics. There seemed to be no non-political reason for rejection in this case, but the opposition was determined to find or make one. The Committee on Foreign Relations, by its chairman, Senator Tazewell of Virginia, reported in favor of confirmation, but the Senate considered charges that Van Buren as Secretary of State has issued instructions to Minister McLane at London which were humiliating to the country, and which introduced party questions into a discussion with a foreign government. The Clay and the Calhoun men joined forces; the former expatiated on the alleged impropriety of the instructions; the latter accused Van Buren of having, by his intrigues, caused the breach between the President and the Vice-President. By the casting vote of Calhoun himself, the nomination was defeated.

Members of the opposition rejoiced, believing they had ruined Van Buren and injured Jackson. Benton says in his *Thirty Years View* that when someone expressed a fear to Calhoun that the result of this assault on Van Buren might be beneficial to him, Calhoun replied: "It will kill him, Sir, kill him dead. He will never kick, sir, never kick." John J. Crittenden of Kentucky, afterward Senator from that state and a devoted follower of Clay, wrote him: "The intelligence of Mr. Van Buren's nomination being rejected was rec'd with general satisfaction by your political friends in the West and seems to produce but little feeling among the Jackson men. The truth is he has no popularity here."

Though such was the general feeling of the Whigs, one of the shrewdest of them, Thurlow Weed, had written in his paper, the Albany *Evening Journal,* that a rejection would give Van Buren an opportunity to pose as a martyr and secure him a nomination as Vice-President. The New York Democrats viewed the matter as Weed did. Several of their leaders had wished for a rejection. Weed, in the letter quoted above, said that he both expected and ardently desired such action. Cambreleng and Jackson himself, agreed with Weed that rejection would help Van Buren, but they believed that the opposition was too timid, though not too magnanimous, to venture it.

Once the blow was struck, other friends of Van Buren saw the advantage which he might derive from it. The day after the vote, the Secretary of the Senate, Walter Lowrie of Pennsylvania, wrote Van Buren: "At first your friends were rather vexed at the result. No party wishes a defeat even if that defeat may be supposed to lead to results which they much desire. Now however, altho but one day has passed, some of your friends I know, and among them myself, would not change the result if they had the power." In London, a member of the cabinet, Lord Auckland, congratulated Van Buren, saying: "In all my experience I have seldom known the career of a young man[1] in your position crowned with marked success who had not been made in the course of it the subject of outrage."

At home, instant steps were taken to "vindicate" Van Buren. Some friends, including Jackson himself, at first thought of meeting the insult of the Senate by renominating Van Buren as Minister. Editor Ritchie demanded that this be done, but the plan was quickly dropped. The President felt that he could not with propriety take an active and public part on a purely Senatorial question. Success, too, was doubtful. Possibly some opponents of Van Buren could be won over, but former supporters might be lost. A

---

[1]Van Buren was then in his fiftieth year and Auckland about a year younger.

renomination could be represented as a practical denial of the right of the Senate to confirm appointments, and it was probable that on such a question the Virginia senators, Tyler and Tazewell, and other strict constructionists would vote against the Administration. Finally, even a victory would simply leave things as they were before.

Jackson wrote to Van Buren, February 12, 1832: "The people will properly resent the insult offered the Executive and the wound inflicted in our national character, and the injury intended to our foreign relations, in your rejection, by placing you in the chair of the very man whose casting vote rejected you." Lowrie told Van Buren that "the question most likely to have produced division and embarrassment in the Republican party, was the Vice-Presidency. The Kentucky candidate, R(ichard) M. J(ohnson), seemed in a fair way to unite the whole of the West. At the South were Crawford and Smith & Penna. had two (George M. Dallas and William Wilkins). Many prominent men would hear of no name but yours, & others, much more numerous, would not agree that your name should be mentioned. The vote of the Senate has brought these two classes together. I have not heard nor heard of, any opinion but one, & that is, that you are to be the candidate on the ticket with the old Chief & all his friends believe that he and you will be elected. This, too, is the opinion of many of the friends of Mr. Clay."

Jesse Hoyt, a well-known and very "practical" New York politician, whose defalcation as collector of customs was later to give the Whigs great cause for triumph, wrote Van Buren: "Personal pretensions are rapidly yielding to the voice of public opinion and many pretenders to the Vice-Presidency have voluntarily given up all hopes or claims and declared for you and it is no longer a matter of doubt that you are to be very unanimously nominated—and subsequently elected by a great vote, probably with the same unanimity as will attend the election of the President," and many meetings up state passed appropriate resolutions. Andrew Stevenson of Virginia, then Speaker of the House of Representatives, wrote Ritchie that the Whigs were making the opposition to Van Buren the basis of a plot to win the Vice-Presidency, and that the welfare of the party and the triumph of its principles required every member, whatever his former views, to work heartily for the nomination of Van Buren. Stevenson did not forget to add that the President was earnestly in favor of such a course.

This statement was fully warranted. Before the rejection, though Jackson would have been much pleased by Van Buren's nomination, he was not prepared to force him on the party, but the action of the Senate was a trumpet call which aroused the old warrior to battle. At first he was infuriated, but soon relapsed into a Jacksonian coolness which suggests "the most perfect calm, French calm," described by Mark Twain, the aggrieved person being engaged in tearing out his hair. Lowrie said in his letter to Van Buren: "The President bears the vote of the Senate, just as you who know him,

would expect. He *was* angry, and when he is angry he speaks freely. I
took up the return of the vote yesterday; I was also there this morning. He
now talks over the matter with perfect coolness, but with much emphasis, &
his remarks are often pointed & severe."

Jackson did not confine the expression of his feelings to conversation.
He caused Major Lewis, one of his personal lieutenants and managers, to
write numerous letters favoring the nomination of Van Buren and making
use of the President's name. But these efforts were only partially successful.
Ritchie, who had a keen sense for popular feeling in Virginia and a great
respect for it, refused to change his position. Although Calhoun's conduct
had hurt him in Virginia, and Ritchie's brother-in-law, a member of the leading Junto and an editor of a very influential paper in the Shenandoah Valley,
came out for Van Buren, yet the Democratic state convention would not
endorse him and the most his friends could do was to prevent the recommendation of anyone for the Vice-Presidency.

Two weeks later, the Democrats of the legislature held a caucus which,
following the advice of Ritchie, left the matter to the people to decide by
electing Van Buren or other delegates to the National Convention, it being
understood that all the delegates should accept the decision of the majority
and vote as a unit. Van Buren made an excellent showing, but a Virginian,
Philip P. Barbour, obtained more of the delegates and, according to the
preëlectoral understanding as well as a later rule of the National Convention,
all Virginia's votes for a Vice-Presidential nominee were counted for Barbour.

Pennsylvania was equally recalcitrant. Van Buren, never popular there,
was further injured by the circumstance that the Legislature of his state,
New York, had declared against the recharter of the United States Bank,
which was located in Philadelphia. The Whigs had nominated a Pennsylvanian, John Sergeant, for Vice-President, and the Democrats of the state
were resolved that their party should pay her a like compliment. In March
a state convention met, told how faithful to the party Pennsylvania had been,
said that she now presented a beloved son in whom she was well pleased, and
demanded that the party recognize her services by supporting him for Vice-
President.

But it took the convention ten ballots to decide who should play the part
of "beloved son." The struggle was between William Wilkins and George
M. Dallas, whose votes were nearly balanced throughout the contest; but for
nine ballots, from 17 to 10 delegates kept the banner of James Buchanan
flying, despite the fact that he had written a letter declining the nomination.
From 4 to 1 devoted Jacksonians voted for Martin Van Buren. On the
tenth ballot the vote stood Wilkins 67, Dallas 63, Van Buren 1. The one
was George Kremer, famous for his leopard coat and his bringing the bargain and corruption charge against Clay in 1825, and then failing to main-

tain it. So much was the convention opposed to Van Buren that it not only refused to nominate him, but took special pains to prevent his obtaining the support of Pennsylvania. A formal vote was passed that if the nomination of Wilkins should fail by death or "otherwise" (that is, should Wilkins withdraw), the electors were to vote for Dallas as he had received the second largest number of votes in the convention; and the state committee was directed to obtain a promise from each Democratic Pennsylvania candidate for elector, to vote for Jackson and Wilkins, and to replace him if he refused or neglected to give the pledge.

In other states, opposition to the hand-picked candidates, Van Buren and Richard M. Johnson, appeared. The friends of Judge White of Tennessee had placed him in nomination for the Presidency, and announced themselves as opposed in general to the New York school of politicians, who placed too much emphasis on the spoils of office. Down in Mississippi, a popular convention named Thomas H. Benton for the Vice-Presidency.

In April Senator Tyler wrote to a friend that "Richard M. Johnson is daily rising, and if all rivals are slain in the contest for the Vice-Presidency, the *Hero of the Thames* may quietly walk into the Presidency; for the day is rapidly approaching when an *ounce of lead* will, in truth, be worth more than a pound of sense."

Van Buren's friends were divided as to whether he should return to the United States and mingle in the fray, or remain abroad until after the convention. There was even some doubt at first if it would be wise for him to seek the Vice-Presidency. Many Jackson men in New York and Albany wished him to be Governor. Some advised that he go to the Senate. But Marcy wrote him that few Jackson men out of New York wanted him to take the governorship, and that in the Senate Calhoun and Clay were desperate and would have tools to whom Van Buren could not abase himself. A somewhat startling statement was made, "to the victor belong the spoils," to "the little magician." Marcy's opinion was that the Vice-Presidency was the key position and the present the critical moment, and that danger or no danger, Van Buren should come home and fight.

Van Buren received many other letters urging his prompt return, but Cambreleng and Lewis recommended his remaining abroad modestly awaiting the action of the people. Cambreleng combined an earnest desire for Van Buren's success with a readiness to sacrifice him for the good of Jackson and the party. He said: "What you will do when you come home, leave to circumstances; if things go right, you must go for the V. P. (*sic*), you must not quit the national course. If things do not go as we think they will, and if our friends in Virginia have difficulty and it is found it will aid the opposition in that quarter, you can at any time go into the Senate, but the national course for the V. P. with Old Hickory is the true plan. Your rejection has blown up many great schemes here. We had many cabinet (secret?) candidates for the Presidency, but we will talk that matter over when I see you." Lewis' support of Van Buren was unconditional and he made skillful use of the President's name to win over the delegates to the national convention. Eaton, formerly Jackson's Secretary of War and a skillful politician, went to the convention prepared to work against Van Buren, but was brought to heel by a letter from Lewis bidding him support the New Yorker unless he wished to quarrel with Jackson. Eaton, though yielding, replied that he believed Van Buren's nomination would injure Jackson and even Van Buren himself.[1]

Van Buren doubtless weighed with care the various arguments he received; and he decided to remain away until after the nomination, thus, as he said, giving the lie to assertions of intrigue, and leaving his fate to the unbiased decision of the party. Such virtue was good politics. Van Buren's standing apart looked well and with Jackson, Lewis, and other clever managers active in his behalf, there was no need for the "magician" to cast any personal spells.

Nevertheless, though victory at Baltimore was substantially certain, Van Buren was not to obtain the almost unanimous nomination which had been predicted. Immediately after his rejection as Minister, Francis P. Blair wrote to him that the opposition, seeing that it was impossible to defeat Jackson, would concentrate on the Vice-Presidency, so that if Jackson died in his second term, they would have the Presidency; if not, with the Vice-President and the Senate, they could hold the Executive in check. He said that the Calhoun faction would declare that nullification would be necessary unless the South could have the security of a States' Rights Vice-President. The man selected for this position was Judge Philip P. Barbour of Virginia. Both as a matter of expediency and a matter of principle, the choice was an excellent one. It would appeal to the state pride of Virginia; it would please the Calhounites, most of whose principles Barbour firmly held; yet it would not affront the Jackson men, for Barbour had not broken with the Administration. Barbour was a watchful defender of States' Rights and of strict construction; Van Buren, in his autobiography, calls him "that pure and inflexible sentinel on the ramparts of the Constitution." John Quincy Adams, with the sweetness and fairness which he usually showed to opponents, describes him as "a shallow pated wild cat . . . . fit for nothing but to tear the Union to pieces."

Mr. Barbour, however, was a man of ability and public experience. He was born May 25, 1783, and was a younger brother of James Barbour, Secretary of War under Adams, who had declined to make the race for Vice-President with his chief in 1828. Both brothers served several terms in Congress, but while James was noted for his flowery and abundant rhetoric,

---

[1]Lewis asked Eaton to destroy his letter, but apparently he did not do so, for Parton says in his life of Jackson that he had seen it.

Philip was a close, subtle, and pertinent reasoner who appealed to the intellect rather than to the emotions. John Randolph said of the brothers that "Phil could split a hair but that Jim could not hit a barn door." Some one wrote on the walls of the chamber of the House of Representatives:

> Two Barbours to shave our Congress long did try.
> One shaves with froth; the other shaves dry.

Philip Barbour had also some experience as a presiding officer. He had been Speaker of the National House for one term, President of the important and stormy Virginia constitutional convention of 1830-31, where he showed impartiality and skill in dispatching business, and President of a national anti-tariff convention in 1831. He had been a state judge and in 1830 was appointed a United States district judge. His political career had prevented his acquiring great legal lore, but he was able, conscientious, and very industrious, and his knowledge and judicial capacity, particularly after an appointment to the United States Supreme Court in 1836, increased rapidly and continuously until his death in 1841.

The Democratic Convention met at Baltimore on May 20. A committee to prepare rules by which the convention should act was appointed, and reported through its chairman, William R. King of Alabama, that two-thirds of the votes in the convention should be necessary to nominate a candidate for the Vice-Presidency.[1] In a brief speech Mr. King said that the committee believed that such a majority would give the nomination of the convention greater weight, and that the requirement of two-thirds would prevent the choice being determined by votes of states which it was certain that the party could not carry in the election.[2]

But one ballot was taken. Van Buren received 208 votes, Barbour 49, and Johnson 26. Pennsylvania, notwithstanding the direction of the state convention that her electors support Wilkins, voted for Van Buren. Little attention had been paid to that newfangled contrivance, a national convention; small groups had chosen the delegates, and they followed Andrew Jackson with the docility for which Pennsylvania was famous. Wilkins had considerable strength in the country, but as the delegates of his own state would not support him, those from other states would not. Virginia and South Carolina voted for Barbour as did six delegates from North Carolina, six from Alabama, and three from Maryland.[3] Johnson polled the full vote of Kentucky and Indiana and received two votes from Maryland. Van Buren was declared the nominee, a short recess was taken, and then delegations of

---

[1] The convention, by the terms of its call, was one of Jackson's supporters and the members cordially endorsed various nominations which he had received, but did not formally nominate him themselves.

[2] In 1860, President Buchanan, in a speech urging the right of Breckinridge rather than Douglas to the support of Democrats, gave the second argument as the reason for the adoption of the two-thirds rule in 1832.

[3] The convention had enacted a "unit rule," but it was not strictly enforced.

Virginia, Kentucky, Indiana, and Alabama announced their concurrence in the nomination, and a resolution was passed that the convention concur unanimously. But the question remained—would the party recognize the right of the convention to represent it?

Johnson's conduct had been dubious. When Van Buren was rejected as minister, Johnson loudly advocated his nomination for Vice-President, but apparently his friends did not lay down their arms. In April John Tyler believed that Johnson's prospects were increasing and many years later Lewis told Van Buren that Johnson only consented to withdraw a few days before the convention met, and that he did so very unwillingly. Even then forty-six delegates voted for him, but this may have been a mere complimentary gesture or obedience to instructions. At least after the convention, Johnson and his followers seem to have supported Van Buren loyally during the campaign.

The leaders resolved not to risk a revolt in Pennsylvania and there the only Democratic ticket was a Jackson-Wilkins one. In Virginia Ritchie slowly and reluctantly decided to support Van Buren, his hesitation being due not to any personal dislike, but because he believed the nomination bad for the party in Virginia. The majority of the Virginia Democrats finally accepted the New Yorker. But many States' Righters remained unconverted. They proposed that the Jackson-Van Buren electors promise to vote for Barbour if a majority of the Virginia Democrats should declare in his favor, and when their compromise was not accepted, they nominated a straight out Jackson-Barbour ticket.

A convention in North Carolina took like action, but South Carolina was too busy with Nullification to attend to other matters. In Alabama a Barbour movement failed completely, although in the convention six of her seven delegates had voted for him. Barbour's own attitude was uncertain; his answer to the North Carolina convention was appreciative but ambiguous. Earnest efforts were made to induce him to refuse to run. Indeed, they had begun months before his nomination.

Andrew Stevenson in the letter to Ritchie cited above, said of the opposition: "They do not wish P. P. Barbour or any one of our true men to be selected V. Prest. but are willing and anxious they should run and divide the vote of Virginia and N. Carolina and so bring the election of V. P. to the Senate. They would then be able to carry their man whoever he may be, and sacrifice V. B. and the administration. . . . .

"Will it not be possible to advise P. P. B. of the true state of things and induce him to write to his friends at Richmond not to use his name in caucus, or in fact to say at once he will not consent to receive a nomination if made? That his friends here (Washington) expect it of him and he should be apprised that they will not be satisfied if he does less."

The Richmond Junto put much pressure on Barbour to withdraw, but found him very unwilling to do so. However, late in the canvass, Van Buren, in response to a letter from certain gentlemen at Shocco Springs, gave a statement of his political views. On the tariff he was rather vague or "Van Burenish," as his opponents were apt to describe his declarations, but in general the letter was Southern in point of view, and many conservatives in that quarter had come to feel that since the Erie canal had been completed by New York, Van Buren would no longer urge national assistance for internal improvements, and they desired his "presence at court as a sort of balance wheel." This could not be without its influence on Barbour, and there was also a strong personal reason for his remaining on good terms with Jackson. Another judge was advanced in age, and Barbour was most desirous of a seat on the Supreme Bench. He had not directly accepted his nomination, and on October 24 he wrote a letter indirectly declining it. He said that the opposition exulted over the split in the Democratic party, and already were "exultingly anticipating a triumph from that cause." If, in consequence of the divided ticket, the vote of Virginia should be lost to the present Chief Magistrate, it would be a source to him of the deepest regret. He would not presume to dictate, but asked that his friends throughout Virginia should vote for the Jackson-Van Buren ticket.

Many of them, indeed, condemned both, believing that he had been swayed by hope of a judgeship. It was too late to substitute another name, but not a few States' Righters proclaimed their loyalty to principle by voting for a man whom they regarded as a deserter. Western Virginia, however, though uneasy under the rule of the Junto, heartily admired Jackson, and in the Shenandoah Valley there were thousands of settlers of German descent who considered Van Buren as a fellow-countryman. In the West, too, were moderate Democrats of the Madison school who believed protection and internal improvements to be constitutional but inexpedient. Such men were influenced by a charge that Barbour was a Nullifier. These causes, particularly the withdrawal of Barbour, saved the state for Van Buren.

There may have been a plan to get Wilkins to withdraw also. In September, a Pennsylvania elector, Samuel McKean, wrote an angry public letter in which he stated that there was a plot for little groups of men to meet after the choice of electors and pass resolutions praising Wilkins, regretting that there was so little prospect of his election, and requesting him to withdraw for the sake of harmony. McKean declared that a belief that part of the electors would vote for Van Buren would turn thousands of votes from Jackson, and that if persisted in, it might lose him the state. McKean announced that he had informed the central committee that he would never vote for Van Buren, in order that if there was any latent understanding, his own name might be struck off the electoral ticket. McKean also said that he lived near the New York line and had had an opportunity to observe Van Buren's course for twenty years; that he was a selfish political chameleon; that if Wilkins withdrew, he himself would, as the State convention had directed, vote for

Dallas; and that if he were compelled to vote for a man outside the state, it would be Barbour.

The National Republicans were free from doubt either as to their principles or their candidate. They were in favor of internal improvements, protection, and a United States Bank, and all these had been championed with ability and much eloquence by Henry Clay. A convention of National Republicans held a convention at Baltimore on December 12, 1831, and nominated Clay unanimously. So eager were the delegates for Clay, that they seem to have assembled without a thought of the Vice-Presidency, but it is probable that the leaders held a conference, and John Sergeant of Philadelphia was unanimously nominated for the second office.

Mr. Sergeant was born at Philadelphia on December 5, 1779. He graduated from Princeton in the middle of his sixteenth year, entered the law office of Jared Ingersoll at seventeen, was admitted to practice before he was twenty, and in a comparatively short time became a leader of the Philadelphia bar. The city attracted eminent lawyers from all parts of the state but produced few itself, and Philadelphians were accustomed to speak with great pride of *our* John Sergeant. Sergeant was much interested in politics as well as law. He had served several terms in Congress and had been one of Adams' commissioners to the abortive Congress of American Republics at Panama. Unlike many nominees for Vice-President, his views on public matters were in close harmony with those of his leader. He believed in protection; when in the state Legislature, he introduced the first bill giving the aid of the state to internal improvements; in Congress, he had favored from the first the establishment of the (Second) United States Bank, and he was now one of its standing counsel, an intimate friend of President Biddle and an ardent champion of recharter.

But in person, temperament, and manner of life, there was little resemblance between the two candidates. Clay was tall, quick, very emotional, a most brilliant orator, a man of the world in tastes and habits. Sergeant was a little man with a weak voice and, in court, at least, "his forte was solid terseness, direct to the truth but didactically dry." In private circles he was more pleasing, but he did not try to dominate his company as perhaps Clay did. Nathan Sargent says of him: "In the recollection of his unassuming deportment, pleasant conversation, the overflow of kindly feeling, and a well-stored mind, spiced not infrequently with kindly humor, it is pleasant to linger over his name, a green tree in the desert of politics." As a legislator Mr. Sergeant paid careful attention to public morals. He introduced an act into the Pennsylvania Legislature forbidding masquerades, which were supposed often to lead to wrong-doing, and in Congress his efforts defeated a bill for a lottery. He favored a bankruptcy bill partly, doubtless, because it was desired by the mercantile community, but probably also from sympathy with the unfortunate. His life corresponded with his theory. He gave freely to charity and aided in the management of many benevolent institutions.

The campaign was fierce and was mainly waged over the character and records of the leaders, Jackson and Clay. But the National Republicans did not let the people forget how much Van Buren owed to Jackson, and also that the latter had been greatly helped by the New York politician. Caricatures poorly designed and worse executed were published in great numbers. A favorite idea was to depict Mr. Van Buren as an infant in the arms of General Jackson, receiving sustenance from a spoon in his hands. But one popular cartoon represented the President as taking a crown from Van Buren and a sceptre from the devil.

Virginia was doubtful, although Van Buren profited by the Shocco Springs letter. In the eastern part of the state many threw the blame for the breach between Jackson and Calhoun on him; in the West, Clay's advocacy of internal improvement was popular and there was discontent from local causes. But, during the campaign, came Jackson's vote of the recharter of the United States Bank which diverted attention from Van Buren personally, and Ritchie raised the cry that the fight was one "of Clay, Calhoun and Webster."

Clay and Sergeant ran evenly, receiving 49 votes each. Vermont cast her 7 votes for Wirt and Ellmaker. South Carolina was in the midst of the Nullification struggle, and the Legislature, which then chose the electors, declared that it was inexpedient to vote for either Jackson or Clay, and that "in testimony of our high esteem and consideration for the patriotic devotion of John Floyd of Virginia (then Governor, and the father of Buchanan's Secretary of War) and Henry Lee of Massachusetts (who had published an elaborate treatise against protection) to the principles of States' Rights, and the great cause of Free Trade, we will give to them the vote of the state for President and Vice-President." But the Middle Atlantic, the Southern, and the Western States, as a whole, stood faithfully behind the "Old Hero," and he and his running-mate received the handsome majority of 219 out of the total of 279 electoral votes.

The political situation in the Democratic party during what may be called the nomination campaign for the election of 1836 was not unlike that of 1832. Jackson was determined to make Van Buren President as he had made him Vice-President, and he had behind him a great popularity and an efficient machine, but had to encounter a coolness toward his candidate in the party in general, and definite opposition in the Southern section. This latter obstacle was much more serious in 1836 than in four years before. The President could not control his own state. His lieutenants, Eaton and Lewis, though, like himself, Tennesseans, were very unpopular there, as indeed they were in other parts of the country. In revolt against back-stairs influence, Tennessee called on one of its Senators, Judge Hugh L. White, a strict construction Democrat, a man who, though not brilliant, was justly esteemed for his high character, to consent to be a candidate for the Presidency. But in Virginia, Ritchie and the Junto came out for Van Buren, carried the Assembly over their opponents now known as Whigs, and gave the state to Van Buren. The

Junto victory in Virginia assured his nomination, but the question of the Vice-Presidency remained to divide the party.

The feeling in Pennsylvania, that her long proved Democracy worked against her, had not died out in the state. On February 3, 1834, S. Pleasanton wrote from Washington to James Buchanan: "I am strongly of the opinion that Pennsa. will obtain no considerable office during the residue of Genl J's term. She has been so steadfast a friend, under all circumstances, and likely to remain so, that they have no motive, for assigning to her offices, which may be important in making friends, in other quarters of the union." Some of Buchanan's followers were desirous that Pennsylvania should seek her reward in his nomination for Vice-President. Buchanan had spoken at a Jackson celebration on January 8 at Harrisburg, and A. B. Chansey wrote him that he had conversed with persons who were present, that they were very much pleased with his speech, and that they said there was a pretty general feeling manifested in favor of Buchanan for Vice-President. Buchanan, like other politicians, had been moving round among his constituents and A. J. Pleasanton wrote him that he was pleased to read of the cordial reception he had met, that he should travel through the state more, "with you making acquaintances is making friends."[1]

But neither all of Buchanan's friends nor Buchanan himself were sure that the Vice-Presidency would be of real advantage to him. In January, 1832, George M. Dallas, then a Senator from Pennsylvania, unexpectedly declined a reëlection and Samuel McKean, whose very unfavorable opinion of Van Buren has been quoted above, slipped in and seized the prize. Another vacancy was looked for, as Senator Wilkins was expected to be rewarded for his vigorous support of the administration[2] with the Secretaryship of the Navy.

James Page wrote Buchanan that he should have been Senator, and that it was expected if Wilkins went to the Cabinet, Buchanan would succeed him in the Senate. Page thought that the question of the Vice-Presidency was a a difficult one, and that the safety of the party and its principles must be cared for. Another friend wrote that Wilkins' expected and deserved appointment would leave a three years' vacancy in the Senate, for which all Wilkins' friends would support Buchanan. For political reasons the new Cabinet appointment was not made until May, and then the prize was given to Senator Dickerson of New Jersey. But Mr. Wilkins' services were not forgotten. He was

---

[1] Pennsylvania voters seem to have been much influenced by meeting candidates personally. At the same time that Pleasanton wrote to Buchanan, G. H. Goundrie wrote Van Buren highly approving of a projected tour and urging him to include the counties of York and Lancaster. Goundric said: "This is the thickest settled part of our State, and the inhabitants generally Germans; you could not pass through a finer and richer country and better Democrats and kinder hearts you would find nowhere. A visit would work wonders."

[2] Wilkins had now turned against his old friend the Bank, and assailed what Prof. Catterall pronounces as perfectly legal conduct with "maudlin pathos."

appointed to the Russian Mission recently held by Mr. Buchanan, and in December the Pennsylvania Legislature sent that gentleman to replace Mr. Wilkins in the Senate.

Mr. Buchanan, however, still had thoughts of the Vice-Presidency and on January 25, 1835, sought the advice of his friend W. B. Mitchell. Mr. Mitchell was rather against Buchanan's taking the office, and recommended that he remain silent until the state convention on the fourth of March. But Buchanan decided to withdraw from the contest and on February 5 he did so in a public letter, giving as his reason that he believed that he would thus promote the harmony and success of the Democracy throughout the Union. It is probable Buchanan believed what he said, and also he realized that patience was good policy. The West and Virginia each had a candidate whose success they earnestly desired; Buchanan would hardly make a strong appeal; his strength was mainly local outside of Pennsylvania; and, moreover, as one of his friends wrote him, it would be bad policy to nominate a Vice-President from a state adjacent to New York, which would probably furnish the candidate for President. The latter consideration did not prevent the friends of Mr. Dallas in Philadelphia and elsewhere from pressing his nomination and appealing to state pride, but they developed little strength. There had also been talk of Wilkins, but the movement for him never became formidable.

There was also discussion of the claims of out-of-state men. Thomas H. Benton had distinguished himself in the fight against the bank, and as an unflinching champion of President Jackson; moreover, he had introduced and pressed a bill for distribution among the states of the proceeds of the sale of the public lands. With this revenue lost to the central government, there would be less reason for reducing the tariff. Moreover, Pennsylvania wanted money to carry out her own plans of internal improvements, and a rather promising Benton boom was started. It was soon killed by Benton's declining to run, but not before it had seriously interfered with the movement for Buchanan. There was some talk of another Jackson warrior, Roger B. Taney, who, as recess Secretary of the Treasury, had removed the public money from the United States Bank, and then achieved the reputation of a martyr by having his nomination non-concurred in by the Senate. But Taney was not strong in Pennsylvania. Some Pennsylvanians wished for Rives, the Virginian candidate, but far more favored Johnson of Kentucky. Some, while not approving of him personally, were willing to accept him for reasons of policy. A friend wrote Buchanan, for instance, that he had little confidence in Johnson's fitness, but that if he would answer the purpose better than another, "so be it."

By Jackson's desire, a national nominating convention was held, which met at Baltimore on May 20, 1835. There were now only two candidates for the second place, apart from dark horses who found themselves obliged to remain in the darkness. The open entries were Johnson of Kentucky, hero of Tippecanoe and favorite of the West, and William C. Rives of Virginia, on whom high hopes were based. Editor Ritchie and other members of the Richmond Junto, exhilarated by their success in carrying the Virginia Assembly, were full of great plans for the future. Virginia had lost her leadership of the Democratic party, the West[1] was wielding the sceptre, and Calhoun and South Carolina had seized the position of special champion of States' Rights. Ritchie had been on the best of terms with Van Buren, and he had hoped that Virginia, assisted by New York, would control the elderly, uneducated Jackson. The plan failed. The King, not Warwick, reigned. But now there was a new hope. Van Buren, who had been making advances to the South, should be recognized as heir with a Virginian beside him who, in due time, should succeed him as he had Jackson, and in accordance with the eternal fitness of things, Virginia would once more rule the Nation.

A beautiful dream, but the dreamers were too ready to believe that it would of itself become reality. A few days before the convention met, Ritchie wrote to Senator Rives: "You know I have carefully forborne touching upon the Vice-Presidency. Not a word, line or syllable has been exchanged between us on the subject. But I think it high time to tell you (P. P. Barbour being out of the question, who in my opinion has superior claims to any one in the Union on account of his long service) that my heart is now set upon your elevation from the Floor to the Chair of the Senate. I had hoped that the thing was fixed; and I had given myself less concern than I ought to about it, but I am informed since Friday that some of our strongest friends at Washington think that Richard M. Johnson ought to have the nomination, great as they admit your claims to be." Ritchie mentioned various steps taken to obtain support for Rives and concluded: "What the result may be it is utterly impossible to guess. I shall be most deeply disappointed if we do not prevail. I have freely told and written my friends that with your name associated on the ticket, I think Virginia and the South will be safe; with Col. Johnson less than safe. . . . . But be content if you receive the nomination to accept it in a way which you so well know how to express, and if the Cup be unfortunately passed to another lip, to bear your disappointment as becomes you."

The cup passed. The convention chose ex-Speaker Andrew Stevenson as chairman, and by a vote of 231 to 210 refused to accept the report of the committee on rules that two-thirds should be necessary for a choice. It was urged with much force that it was "unrepublican" thus to frustrate the will of a majority. The chairman of the committee, Romulus M. Saunders of North Carolina, declared that no one had the remotest desire to do this, though it was strongly suspected that the rule had been brought in for the especial purpose of defeating Johnson. But on the succeeding day, the vote

------

[1]The slavery issue had not yet become paramount and most of the newly settled states west of the Old Thirteen, whether slave or free, had a strong community of feeling and interest.

was rescinded and the rule adopted. On the request of the delegations of Virginia and of New York, a recess was taken. It is probable that a messenger had been sent to Washington to ask for instructions, and that the New York delegation wished to wait his return. The Virginians, who, in asking for the recess, explained that they had been engaged in an important and unfinished discussion, may have wished for time to decide what they would do if Johnson should be nominated. Before the convention reassembled, it was said on the streets that word had come from Washington to nominate Johnson.

There was a great excitement. "The Virginians foamed and threatened to withdraw if Rives were not taken." The church where the convention met was packed with eager spectators. A Virginia delegate announced that he and his associates would not deem themselves bound to support the nominee unless he was of Democratic principles. Van Buren was unanimously nominated, as per schedule. Then came the nomination of a Vice-President. Maine, ten of the fourteen Massachusetts delegates, New Jersey, and Maryland, Virginia, North Carolina, and Georgia voted for Rives; the other states that were represented, for Johnson. The Kentuckian had received four more than the necessary two-thirds and was declared the nominee of the convention.

Some attempts were made to change the record. An Ohio delegate said that seven members from that State had voted for Johnson because they had supposed that the delegates were obliged to go together; it was demanded that such a rule be followed in the case of Massachusetts, a majority of whose delegates had voted for Rives. There was much disorder, many delegates talking at once, but probably there was unwillingness to throw all into confusion by annulling the nomination, and the disturbing motions were withdrawn.

All the states except Virginia politely came forward and pledged themselves to Johnson. But the Virginians would not even inferentially assent by silence. Her delegates had hissed when New York decided the battle by casting her forty-two votes for Johnson, and now they announced that they did not believe that they could be assured that Johnson would support Virginia doctrines, and therefore they could not recommend him to their constituents. They had gone as far as they possibly could in voting for Van Buren and would go no further. A Kentucky delegate praised Johnson in high-flown terms. A Virginian, stung, perhaps, by a hint that Virginia delegates refused to play because disappointed in a hope of spoils, retorted that they thought of principles, not of men; that they had fought and fought to put successfully out of office an able and worthy United States Senator, because he might in some circumstances favor a United States Bank; and he asked triumphantly how, after doing this, her delegates could go back to their constituents and request them to support Johnson, "a bank man, an internal improvement man, a tariff man."

It was a strong argument. Silas Wright, a leading Democratic manager of New York, but personally a thoroughly honorable man, wrote Van Buren that the Virginians were too "astute as to their principles and too little practical in their political course," and that they were "wild," though he refrained from saying that they were asses. It was good, perhaps necessary, strategy to put a Westerner on the ticket, but at times one feels that it is nobler to fail with doctrinaire principles than run with a magician. However, worthy or not, the "slayer of Tecumseh was now the regular Democratic candidate for Vice-President."

Richard Mentor Johnson was the son of Colonel Robert Johnson, one of the early settlers of Kentucky, and was born near Louisville on October 17, 1780. He attended Transylvania University, and at nineteen began the practice of law. In 1807, he was elected to the House of Representatives and was a member until 1819, except for two years of military service in the war with Great Britain. In 1819, he entered the Senate, remained there for ten years, then, having failed of reëlection, returned to the House, of which he was a member at the time of his nomination as Vice-President.

In the War of 1812, Johnson commanded with much distinction a Kentucky regiment of mounted riflemen which he had raised himself. His friends declared that he was the real victor of the battle of the Thames, that Harrison held the command, but Johnson both planned and led the fight. Certainly his regiment did much to win the victory. Johnson himself was severely wounded, his horse was killed under him, and an Indian warrior rushed forward with his tomahawk to give a fatal blow, but Johnson, still entangled with his dead horse, drew a pistol and shot the savage dead. Tecumseh, the chief of the Shawnees, perhaps the greatest man his race has produced, was killed in the battle and Johnson, on examining his body, believed he recognized the Indian whom he killed. L. W. Meyer, in his recent book, *The Life and Times of Colonel Richard M. Johnson,* brings forward pretty substantial proof in support of Johnson's claim, but not enough to remove all doubt. At least, there was no doubt of his gallantry in the battle, and this was proclaimed by his political followers from the housetops.

As a soldier Colonel Johnson was a fierce fighter, but in civil life he played a very different part. There he was found repeatedly running about trying to harmonize people and to smooth over difficulties. True it is that the peacemakers are blessed, but sometimes they are moved by a fussy timidity rather than by deep feeling, and Johnson has been regarded by historians as a tool rather than a force, like Lepidus,

> A slight unmeritable man
> Meet to be sent on errands.

In Congress he clearly showed his kind and facile disposition. He took an active part in securing pensions by a general and by special acts, and requested to be discharged from the committee on claims because of the harshness to individuals which he said it was obliged to exercise. He was one of the fore-most in abolishing imprisonment for debt under United States law.[1] He was chairman of a committee of the House sent to investigate the United States Bank and his vote carried an unfavorable report, but it is said that he acted to oblige his colleagues and did not look at a single document while he was in Philadelphia. But the bank escaped more easily than was pleasing to the Jacksonians, and Benton, a rank partisan it is true, attributed it to Johnson's kindness of heart, which rendered him unfit for the investigation of crimes.

The civil work for which Colonel Johnson was probably most widely known was the official authorship of the report of a special committee to whom had been referred numerous petitions against the carrying of the mails on Sunday. It is probable that the report was really written by the Rev. O. B. Brown of the Post Office Department, "who later became for the time a very distinguished man on account of relations with mail contractors, which if innocent, were very improper." But Johnson signed the report and received great honor.

Stopping the mails on Sunday was extreme Sabbatarianism and amounted to an entering wedge for a state establishment of religion, since it threw the weight of the government's approval in favor of one faith or sect, as against those which claimed Saturday as the divinely ordained holy day. It was to be remembered that "the proper object of government is to protect all persons in the enjoyment of their religious as well as their civil rights; and not to deter-mine for any, whether they shall esteem one day above another or esteem all days alike holy." The speeding of the mails was itself not without spiritual significance; the report went on to say quite in the Johnson style: "The mail bears, from one section of the Union to the other, letters of relatives and friends, preserving a communion of heart between those far separated, and increasing the most pure and refined pleasures of our existence. The mail is the chief means by which intellectual light irradiates to the extremes of the republic."

Johnson's report brought him praise from the liberal-minded in widely separated parts of the Union, and he was referred to as "breaking the darts of bigotry." An admiring neighborhood at Baton Rouge, Louisiana, sent him a silver goblet as a tribute. G. H. Goundrie wrote Van Buren from Bethle-hem, Pennsylvania: "Everybody has heard of Col. Johnson and at every tavern in the country you will find his Sunday mail report hung up."

Johnson was the nominal leader in another matter which stirred the whole country, and threatened to drive him from Congress as it did drive many of his less fortunate colleagues. This was the compensation bill of 1818. Con-gressmen were then receiving wages of six dollars a day while in attendance at

---

[1] This subject may have appealed to him with special force, for he and his brother had failed in business, and in 1824 the United States Bank cancelled his obligations, a favor it was accustomed to extend to such of its debtors as were hopelessly insolvent.

the sessions. The members felt, and probably truly, that the pay was inadequate, but to many of their constituents it appeared ample and it was a dangerous matter to increase it, especially dangerous to be the proposer of this plutocratic change. It is said that Johnson, on account of his great popularity, was chosen to bell the cat. He moved that the question of the compensation of Senators and Representatives be referred to a special committee, at the same time repudiating any intention of increasing salaries. Johnson was made chairman of the committee and reported a bill, which duly became a law, giving a fixed annual salary of fifteen hundred dollars and making it retroactive to the beginning of the Congress then sitting.

There was an outburst of wrath throughout the country. The increase itself, for such the fixed salary was thought to be, was unpopular, but that men who had impliedly agreed to serve at a known rate should assume to vote themselves more was considered outrageous. Many members who supported the bill were defeated for reëlection. In Kentucky, Johnson and Clay were spared, but they came back with reduced majorities and on a pledge to follow the will of the people by favoring a repeal of the law. Johnson had promised to atone for his sin by himself introducing a repealing bill, and he kept his word. But some little relief was given to straitened Congressmen by raising their *per diem* to eight dollars.

As a party man Johnson usually showed a fondness for moderation.[1] His success in political life was due in no small measure, according to R. Thomas in his book, *The Glory of America,* to a habit of distinguishing measures from men, and of "proffering the hand of friendship to the noble-minded of both parties."

Johnson joined the war hawks of 1811, thus exemplifying the spirit of the West, but he showed also an interior provincialism from which Clay was free. Johnson proclaimed that as a general principle he was opposed to the extension of the national boundaries by force, but that since Great Britain was proving herself our deadly enemy and in effect waging continued hostilities against us, he would never die contented until he saw her expulsion from North America, and her territories incorporated with the United States. But Johnson, like many Western and Southern men, violently opposed a large navy. He told the House that history showed the evils it had wrought. "I will refer to Tyre and Sidon, Crete and Rhodes, to Athens and to Carthage. Navies have been and always will be engines of power, employed in projects of ambition and war."

Johnson vigorously defended Jackson's conduct in Florida, and he was so much of a States' Rights man as to propose a constitutional amendment providing that when the Supreme Court should decide a state law to be unconstitutional, there should be a right of appeal to the Senate. But the West

---

[1] A striking exception, however, if the tale is true, was his declaration concerning John Quincy Adams' administration: "By the eternal, if they act as pure as the angels that stand at the right hand of the throne of God, we will put them down."

wanted protection for its products, and roads and canals to get them to market, and Johnson's course on tariff and internal improvement questions much displeased the States' Rights wing of the Democratic party. He had acted as spokesman for a number of Western members of Congress in a vain attempt to prevent Jackson's disapproving a bill giving government assistance for the construction of the once famous Maysville Road. The interview was a colorful one. Johnson, bringing fist on palm, told Jackson that a veto would crush his friends in Kentucky (where the road was located) like a sledge-hammer striking a fly. Jackson sprang to his feet; Johnson did the same, and there was quick thrust and parry over the condition of the Treasury. Then, at a hint from Van Buren, who was present, Jackson assumed the attitude of one who was pleased to receive advice and who had taken no final decision, and Johnson resumed what Van Buren terms his "accustomed urbanity." But the colonel was not deceived, and told his friends that "his private opinion decidedly was that nothing less than a voice from Heaven would prevent the old man from vetoing the bill, and he doubted whether that would!"

Johnson had many of the virtues and the deficiencies of the man of the farm and the frontier. Mrs. Bayard Smith says that he was of domestic habits and disposition, preferred his home to parties, and was plain in dress and manners. "His eloquence is not that of imagination but of the heart. His mind is not highly cultivated, or rather, I should say, his taste. He has always been too much a man of business to have much time for reading." Van Buren says that Johnson was grandiloquent both in public and in private speech.

Though the Democrats were so divided that Tennessee, the state of the President, repudiated his favorite, the nominee of the party convention, and the delegates of Virginia, the state of all the former Democratic Presidents, instantly bolted the nomination for Vice-President; yet the opposition was in a worse situation—they dared not hold a convention at all. It had been said with some justice that the Democratic "argument" had been "Hurrah for Jackson!" But the opposition—it was too compound a creature to deserve any other name—now adopted the principle of "anything to beat Jackson." It feared to meet in convention for it would certainly quarrel and fall apart, unable to agree on either policies or candidates. Accordingly, it was decided that two or three tickets should be run against Van Buren in the hope that the election would be thrown into the House for the result to be determined by luck and intrigue. Webster was put forward to hold New England; it was hoped that White would carry the Southwest; and an Anti-Whig convention in Pennsylvania nominated General William Henry Harrison. Webster later withdrew, and Harrison was understood to be the candidate of the Whigs.

There was much division about the Vice-Presidency. The Harrison men tried to tempt Webster, and the Webster men to tempt Harrison to come over to them and accept the second place; but each refused. Finally, the Anti-

Masons and the Clay Whigs united on Francis Granger of New York. Granger came of good old Democratic blood. His father had for twelve years been Postmaster-General under Jefferson and Madison, and had then lost his office because of his support of DeWitt Clinton for President in 1812. But this sin against regularity, a term not so easily defined then as now, was probably easily forgiven in Clinton's own State. The younger Granger, like his father, was a graduate of Yale. From his youth he had been in politics, enjoyed the game, and played it coolly and well, but was desirous of money as well as office. He had good memory, so useful to a politician, good judgment, and the happy faculty of obtaining credit for every bit of ability that he possessed. Like a later and more successful New York politician, Chester A. Arthur, Mr. Granger was tall and handsome, dignified yet affable, fond of the good things of life, and one of the best dressers in the metropolis.

The White men adopted John Tyler of Virginia as their candidate for Vice-President, and many of the States' Rights, pro-Southern Harrison men in Ohio wished to do the same. A friend of Tyler wrote him that he was the real choice both of the people and of the nominating convention, but that word came from Washington that if the convention did not nominate Granger, the failure to do so would offend the Anti-Masons and react severely on Harrison, and the Granger nomination was put through. Tyler's son, in his *Letters and Times of the Tylers,* alleges that Clay did not wish the Whigs to unite on a candidate for Vice-President lest he should be elected over Johnson, and the prestige thus acquired make him President four years later.

The Virginia Democrats were determined not to vote for Johnson; neither did they wish to desert to some other party or faction. Accordingly, they pledged their electors to throw away their votes on Judge William Smith, then of Alabama. Mr. Smith was by birth a South Carolinian, who had served in the United States Senate and had distinguished himself at the bar. He had strongly opposed Nullification and had been appointed by a union convention to write to and visit the union men of Alabama, with a view to assembling a convention of citizens to determine what action should be taken.

It has often been said that Jackson put down Nullification, but in South Carolina the Nullifiers boasted of victory. Jackson's proclamation and Force Bill they treated as mere words; they had declared Nullification a legal peaceful remedy; they had tried it; there had been no civil war; and Congress had passed an act reducing the tariff, by degrees it is true, to a revenue standard. The anti-Nullification party almost collapsed. The event had proved their opponents right, and many of their leaders left the state. Among them was Judge Smith, who moved with most of his property to Alabama.

But the strategy of the variegated opposition to the Jacksonian party did not avail to defeat its ticket, although Van Buren went in with a majority below that of 1832, and Johnson failed to receive a majority of the electoral votes. Ohio, New Jersey, and Indiana now went over to the Whig side, which was only meagerly compensated for by the accession of Connecticut and Rhode Island. The Virginia Democratic electors remained true to their instructions, voted for William Smith for Vice-President, and so for the first and last time in our history threw the election into the Senate. That body in one ballot, with the aid of the "lame duck" Senators from Indiana, gave the "Hero of the Thames" that place of victory alongside his running-mate, Van Buren, which the electoral college had denied him.

CHAPTER XIII.

Slavery and Sectionalism: the Elections of 1840, 1844 *and* 1848

THOUGH there had been much unfavorable criticism of Van Buren among the Democrats, the opposition was not strong enough seriously to endanger his renomination. Johnson was less fortunate. There was much objection to him in the South, and a general absence of enthusiasm for him in other parts of the country. The rival candidate for the nomination was James K. Polk of Tennessee. He was a loyal supporter of Jackson, and had served fourteen years in the House of Representatives, where he had been chairman of the Committee on Ways and Means, and Speaker. Polk had just been elected Governor of Tennessee, and it was alleged that he had been transferred from the national to the state service that his popularity might redeem Tennessee from the Whigs, and that the prestige thus won might help him to the Vice-Presidency.

The Democrats throughout the country were much divided on the question of who should be Vice-President. Conservatives, wishing to keep things as they were, favored Johnson. But the young men supported the middle-aged Polk, stiff and Puritanic as he was, rather than the genial but elderly Johnson, ex-cavalry leader and Indian killer, because they believed that Polk's nomination would be a triumph over old-fogeyism. William Allen of Ohio, a radical Democrat of some ability who felt and went with the crowd, and whose flamboyant and jingoistic rhetoric made him a popular speaker and a power in the politics of his state for forty years, wrote Polk that many supposed that the Vice-President would of course be renominated, that in this belief was Johnson's only strength, and that if it was decided to hold a national convention, some means must be found to induce him to accept another situation. Allen said that Johnson would be a dead weight on the party, that while he himself would cheerfully support him if nominated, he knew a large body of Democrats in Ohio who could not be induced to do so. As in 1836, many States'

Rights men had accepted Van Buren reluctantly; they felt that they should at least be given the Vice-Presidency, and many politicians wished to replace Johnson by Polk in order to strengthen the ticket in the South.

The President, in public at least, was neutral. But Andrew Jackson strongly favored Polk on the ground of expediency. He wrote Van Buren that he respected Johnson as a brave soldier and a patriot, but that with Polk, Van Buren would carry Tennessee by twenty thousand majority; with Johnson there was danger of the Whigs carrying it and perhaps Alabama, Louisiana, and Mississippi also. Kendall, Blair, Buchanan, and Benton agreed with their leader that Polk should be the candidate. Calhoun was abandoning his attitude of independence and returning to the Democratic party, and Aaron V. Brown, an influential politician of Tennessee, sent Polk the glad tidings that the South Carolinian preferred him on account of "your *position,* your *abilities,* and your *principles.*" (Italics in the orginal.) A convention in Virginia, probably acting under the influence of friends of Calhoun, whose power in the state was increasing, nominated Polk for Vice-President.

The Democratic National Convention met on May 4 at Baltimore. Polk's friends were on the ground several days in advance. They decided that the convention would not nominate Polk, and that it would not nominate Johnson unless New York supported him. It appeared to them that Polk would have the best chance for election in a free-for-all race and the "astute" Felix Grundy of Tennessee entered into negotiations with Silas Wright of New York, with a view to having the convention make no nomination. A lieutenant of Polk wrote in his diary that Buchanan feared that Polk's election as Vice-President might make him President, that accordingly Buchanan's friends were urging the choice of Senator William R. King of Alabama as a compromise candidate, but that if this plan failed, the supporters of both King and of Buchanan would unite on Johnson.

The Johnson men at first demanded that the convention make a nomination, but when it appeared that even a two-thirds vote would not unite the party, they agreed to a policy of non-action; and the convention accepted a resolution, offered by the committee on nominations, stating that several gentlemen had been nominated for Vice-President; that the states presenting some of them were not represented in the convention; that all those gentlemen had proved their worthiness to be Vice-President; that it was inexpedient at the present time to choose between them; and that the members of the convention left the selection to their Republican fellow-citizens[1] in the several states, trusting that before the election should take place, their opinions would become so concentrated as to secure the choice of a Vice-President by the electoral college.

The Whig convention had already met at Harrisburg in the preceding December and, acting by a rather complicated method specially contrived by

---

[1]The "Democrats" still clung to their old party name, and the Whigs also claimed it as their own.

men who wished to defeat Clay, nominated William Henry Harrison for President.

The Clay men were filled with grief and anger at the defeat of their leader, the more so as he had been beaten through intrigue and by an inferior man whose chief claim was military success. But their active aid was absolutely necessary if the party were to win. Accordingly, the Harrison supporters praised Clay in the highest terms and asked the Kentucky delegation to name the Vice-President, but this it refused to do. Clayton of Delaware, a typical Clay Whig, Benjamin Watkins, one of the increasing body of Virginians who, alarmed for state power and the ascendency of the old aristocracy and slavery, were swinging away from Jeffersonian theories as to the divine right and the wisdom of a numerical majority, Governor Dudley of North Carolina, and Samuel L. Southard of New Jersey, all of whom had been nominated for the Vice-Presidency, were withdrawn by themselves or their friends. Finally the committee on nominations recommended John Tyler for Vice-President, and he was unanimously nominated.

The future proved the choice extremely important and, as the great majority of the Whigs believed, extremely unfortunate also; and many stories in ridicule of Tyler became current. Among them was one that he had wept himself into office. It was said that the convention wished to conciliate the Clay men by naming one of his devoted followers for Vice-President, that Tyler had felt so badly over Clay's defeat that he cried, and that because of this proof of attachment to the Kentuckian, he was nominated. Tyler himself denied that he cried, and his relations with Clay had not been so intimate as to render such emotion natural. Clay had favored the election of Rives over Tyler as Senator from Virginia in order to strengthen the Whigs, and it is probable that his friends told the friends of Tyler that if they would throw their votes to Rives, as some of them did, Tyler should have the nomination for the Vice-Presidency in 1840. But there was an excellent reason for the convention's taking up Tyler. He was strongly States' Rights and anti-Bank, and would therefore help reconcile the South to voting for Harrison. Contradictory statements on the matter were made many years later in memoirs. Nathan Sargent denies that Tyler was nominated to conciliate the anti-Bank wing, and Thurlow Weed says that after the declinations, Tyler was taken as the only man left; but Henry A. Wise declares that previous to the meeting of the convention, there had been a full understanding that it should choose Tyler. It is probable that the last statement is nearest the truth, but it may be that in the North the understanding was one of the Clay leaders and not of the mass of the party.

The Whigs had dared to hold a convention and nominate candidates, but they showed the better part of their valor by adopting no platform. "The convention adjourned without having given expression in any form to the principles of the party which it represented. Even in the many speeches made during the four days session, there was hardly a positive assertion of a principle made by any delegate. It was all hatred and opposition to Van Buren and the 'Loco-Focos.' "

Although the Democrats might be accused of offering the people a double-tail or no-tail ticket, there was a general feeling that they were presenting Van Buren and Johnson. The party organ published by Kendall and Blair practically, though not formally, supported Johnson, and in August Polk withdrew his name for the sake of harmony.

The Presidential contest of 1840 was the famous log cabin and hard cider campaign and the Whigs roared, sang, and hard-cidered the "hero of Tippecanoe" into the White House. His *nom de guerre* and that of his associate proved almost ideal, musically speaking. The chief campaign song had for a refrain:

> With Tippecanoe and Tyler too.

All over the country the Whigs proclaimed:

> With Tip and Tyler
> We'll bust Van's biler.

In one lay the Whigs called attention to the union of old foes by singing:

> National Republicans in Tippecanoe
> Democratic Republicans in Tyler too.

But in general, the Whigs kept disputed principles as much out of sight as possible and the Democrats, after a vain attempt to draw them into a discussion of public questions, resorted to the practices of their opponents.

Both sides stooped to personal ridicule and abuse, but Johnson did himself honor by publicly defending Harrison when accused of displaying incompetency at the battle of the Thames. This is the more creditable as in 1834, Harrison had declined to attend a celebration of the victory on the ground that it was planned to put Johnson's services on a level with his own, and had published a long argument to prove that he himself was the true victor of the Thames. The Democrats attempted to claim the glory of the Thames for Johnson or, as Jackson expressed it in a letter to Van Buren: "The Democrats in order to thwart the Wigs *(sic)* in their game of Mock Enthusiasm for Mock Harrison[1] invited the Vice-President as a real Hero . . . . to visit Michigan." But neither argument, abuse, nor publicity stunts availed the unhappy Democrats. Harrison received 234 votes in the electoral college and Van Buren but 60. Tyler ran evenly with Harrison, but South Carolina and one elector in Virginia, while accepting Van Buren, found Johnson too bitter a pill. South Carolina threw away her votes on that steadfast friend of

---

[1]Jackson had written a letter, which was published, expressing a poor opinion of Harrison's military ability.

States' Rights, ex-Governor Tazewell of Virginia; the Virginia elector voted for Polk.

President Harrison died a month after his inauguration. Whether he could have held his heterogeneous party together is doubtful, but Tyler wholly failed to do so. Clay was domineering and wished to treat Harrison's election as an endorsement of measures which the Whigs during the campaign had declared not to be at issue; Tyler, on his part, though anxious to be conciliatory, was somewhat finical and vacillating. He vetoed two bank bills, one of which had been drawn with especial care to meet his wishes. The Whig Senators and Representatives, with Clay at their head, thereupon read him out of the party, and the great bulk of the Whigs said Amen. All the Cabinet except Webster promptly resigned in a body and he did so later, attempting to explain his dallying with Tyler by the necessity of completing the Ashburton treaty with England, which he then had in hand. Some of the States' Rights Whigs adhered to Tyler; the quarrel between Congress and the President drove others to unite more firmly with the Nationals; and when the Whig convention met in May, 1844, it registered the will of a united party by promptly and unanimously nominating Henry Clay for President. On the Vice-Presidency there was no such agreement.

There had been plans for a Clay-Webster ticket. In October, 1843, a friend of Webster approached General Peter B. Porter, a Whig leader in western New York, and friend of Clay, with an assurance of Webster's intention of reuniting himself with the Whig party in Massachusetts, of his high opinion of Clay, and of his intentions to support him for the Presidency. He also seems to have expressed a hope that Clay would favor making Webster his associate. Clay replied with dignity: "I have done him (Webster) no wrong, and have therefore no reconciliation to seek. His course since Mr. Tyler's accession, but especially since the extra session [of Congress] has greatly surprised me. Should I be a candidate for the Presidency, I shall be glad to receive his support or that of any other American citizen; but I can enter into no arrangements, make no promises, offer no pledges to obtain it. It is impossible that I can be a party to any arrangement by which Mr. Webster, or anybody else, is to be run as the candidate for Vice-President with me. I have declined all interference on behalf of Davis, Sergeant, or Clayton, or anybody else, and must continue to. My duty is to remain perfectly passive until the nomination is made, and after that to give to the nomination, of whoever may be proposed, such support as I can consistently with honor, delicacy or propriety." The letter suggests a cold douche but General Porter wrote Clay that the latter's friends were delighted with his answer and that "even Webster's were forced to acknowledge that it was perfectly correct and proper."

On January 9, 1844, Nicholas Biddle wrote Gales, the editor of the *National Intelligencer,* urging the importance of a full and public union of

Clay and Webster because he believed "that the thing most desirable now would be the nomination of Mr. Clay for President and Mr. Webster for Vice-President and this rather because it would show both in this country and in Europe the cordial union of these two American statesmen, in whom the most confidence is placed in Europe, than because of any adaptation of Mr. Webster for the Station, which is one of mere pageant." Webster probably agreed with Biddle that the station was not worthy of his acceptance; it would have been extremely mortifying to him to follow in the wake of Clay, and he declined to be a candidate.

General Scott's military services had won him considerable popularity. He was very ready to listen to men who told him that the people called for him to act in a civil capacity also, and he wrote Clay that he would go on his ticket if it would win for him a single state. But probably Scott never had any chance of the nomination.

The convention met and firmly resolved to run no risk of another Tyler, but to select a Henry Clay Whig to run with Henry Clay. Clayton of Delaware and Evans of Maine, who had been mentioned as candidates, sent letters withdrawing for the sake of harmony, which probably meant that the first did not wish to uselessly interfere with the chances of another New Jersey, and the second with those of another New England candidate. The convention politely passed a resolution expressing its high estimation of their characters because of the services of both these gentlemen to the Whig party, and as high approbation of their pure and disinterested course. A letter of declination from that perpetual candidate, active or receptive, Judge McLean of Ohio, was then read; but he obtained no resolve that he was a good and useful fellow and had acted magnanimously in getting off the track. The convention then decided that the delegates should vote not by states, but as individuals.

The first ballot stood Theodore Frelinghuysen of New Jersey 101, John Davis of Massachusetts 83, Millard Fillmore of New York 53, John Sergeant of Pennsylvania 38. On the third ballot Frelinghuysen was nominated by a vote of 155 to 76 for Davis, and 40 for Fillmore, Sergeant's name having been withdrawn. The contest was one of persons and localities rather than of principles or even types. All the candidates were men of excellent character, able but not brilliant. It is said that once in the British Parliament when a small group of eminent Peelites, which included Mr. Gladstone, decided to take an independent position, they had considerable difficulty in deciding whether they should call themselves Conservative-Liberals or Liberal-Conservatives. A like difficulty might be felt in describing the candidates for the nomination for Vice-President. Sergeant has already been noticed; his support was chiefly from his own state; on the second ballot his vote fell, and his name was then withdrawn.

Millard Fillmore was the New York candidate and had the active or passive support of the powerful political firm, Seward, Weed, and Greeley. But yet it is probable that the partners were not equally zealous. Greeley had picked Fillmore because, as chairman of the Ways and Means Committee of the National House, he had led in the passage of the Tariff of 1842, a law much approved by the Protectionists. But some of the friends of Seward wished him to try for the Vice-Presidency. The relations of the two men were, outwardly at least, courteous and friendly. In the preceding September, Seward and Fillmore had what the former described as "a pleasant interview," and each politely prophesied that the other would be nominated for Vice-President. Seward, however, for personal and political reasons, declined to try for the prize and Weed, ever a watchful defender of his rights, accepted the decision, though with some doubt as to its wisdom.

But the Fillmore men were not satisfied. One of them told Seward that Fillmore and therefore New York would lose the Vice-Presidency, and that he and Weed were to blame. Seward wrote Weed that he replied that "I had signed off everything, put my political estate to liquidation for the satisfaction of all my creditors, and now had endorsed Mr. F—— as fully as anybody, and that he would be nominated if it was best, and if not that it was no fault of mine." Perhaps Seward in his heart of hearts[1] felt that it was not "best." After the convention, Fillmore was induced to run for Governor. At the preceding election, the Democrats had won by a great majority, and Fillmore's friends told him that Weed and Seward wished to weaken him by defeat.

Another candidacy which had been launched by a mass meeting of Whigs in Dayton, Ohio, was that of the junior Senator from Massachusetts. "Honest John" Davis, as he was called, was a man of high character and of considerable legislative experience. Like his rivals for the nomination, he was not brilliant. A careful, friendly notice of him in the proceedings of the American Antiquarian Society says that he was deficient in imagination, but excelled in clearness and logical arrangement of thought. Yet he was a scholar and a thinker. Although he had a wide knowledge of public law, in court he relied more on his knowledge of the various legal principles and deductions from them, than on a citation of a mass of authorities and cases. He was also very well informed in matters of finance. A speech delivered in the United States Senate in 1840, during a debate on the Independent Treasury Bill, was circulated as a pamphlet and is said probably to have had more influence with the masses than any other document issued from the press that year.

Davis had been defeated for the Senate two years before, John Quincy Adams said, by a Webster movement for the formation of a new party to be led by Webster, Tyler, and Calhoun. Davis was strongly opposed to slavery and respected the motives of the bulk of the Massachusetts Abolitionists, but he regarded them as utterly impracticable men of one idea, who should neither

---

[1]Seward, provoked by what he regarded as Fillmore's unreasonable conduct, made the sharp comment: "He wants promotion and can not bide his time."

be abused nor courted, but quietly let alone.   He was an earnest protectionist and had a special interest in the welfare of the factory laborers, which might be of use in the campaign, since the labor question was beginning to be important politically.   Moreover, Davis was from New England, and that section had contributed many votes and many able men to the Whig cause, but had never been allowed a place on the Presidential ticket.

Unfortunately, however, Davis had not the solid support of his own section.   The Rhode Island delegates worked hard against him. A correspondent of the Boston *Atlas* reported that he had deeply offended that state in an important and delicate matter; that refuted slanders against Davis reappeared in attractive dresses; that delegates from a distance who came to Baltimore from districts well disposed to Davis and who were themselves inclined to him were affected by the stories; that several Massachusetts gentlemen strove hard to reconvert those who had fallen away, but that there was not time. The correspondent said that the slanders came from Washington, and that he believed if the convention had met at Harrisburg or some other place remote from the capital, Davis would have been nominated.

Mr. Frelinghuysen and his supporters appear to have taken no part in these personal attacks; and Davis' friends, though much disappointed, had no bitterness against the nominee who, indeed, must have been acceptable to them in his character and in his political views.

Another candidate, Theodore Frelinghuysen, was born at Millstone, New Jersey, on March 25, 1787.   He was a member of an old Dutch family whose founder was the Rev. Theodorus Frelinghuysen, despatched from Holland by the Dutch Reformed Church in 1719, in response to a call for a pastor from the church at Camden.   He played an active part in the Great Awakening and other religious movements of the day and his descendants furnished faithful and useful leaders in the fight for an independent American church, and later for an American Nation.   They were also devoted champions of the cause of education.

Theodore Frelinghuysen followed in the footsteps of his forefathers.   In the course of his life he held the Presidency of the American Bible Society, the American Tract Society, and the American Board of Foreign Missions. "It may be fairly said perhaps that he was the leading layman of the country in Christian movements of his time."   In 1844, he had been for several years Chancellor of New York University.   Like others of his race and family, he had maintained the closest connection with the Dutch Reformed College of Rutgers, and he was later to become its president, serving from 1850 to his death in 1862.

But for all his churchly work and churchly feeling, Mr. Frelinghuysen was no stranger to the wickedness of the world and to politics.   He had been Attorney-General of New Jersey from 1817 to 1829, and Senator from 1829 to 1835.   In the Senate, as befitted his humane disposition, he earnestly opposed the removal of the Cherokees from Georgia, and favored more liberal pension laws; he also advocated stopping the Sunday mails. He went with his party in voting against the confirmation of Van Buren as Minister to England, and was a staunch protectionist. The correspondent of the Boston *Atlas* declared that there was not a more consistent Whig in the United States. Perhaps he might have added, or a more typical one. Courteous in manner, kind of heart, well-inclined to reform as he was, Mr. Frelinghuysen could not forget that he was a lawyer and a man of property. He shrank from illegality and even from great changes. He was a member of the Colonization Society and opposed the repeal of the Missouri Compromise, but he did not follow the majority of his party into the Republican fold, and in 1860 he joined other well-meaning Laodiceans, who voted for Bell and Everett.

Unlike many candidates for the Vice-Presidency, Mr. Frelinghuysen was an ardent admirer of his chief. After his nomination he wrote to Clay: "I have been rather impatiently waiting for my lame arm to (improve) to write a few lines to my honored friend that I might express to you the heartfelt gratification that I feel at the recent association of my humble name with yours, a distinction as honorable as it has been to me surprising. And should the results of the fall elections confirm the nomination, of which there now seems very strong indications, it will, I assure you, be among my richest practical privileges to contribute any mite of influence in my power to render prosperous and lasting in benefits the administration of a patriot whose election I have long desired. Our names have been brought together here by the names of our fellowmen. My prayer for you and my own soul shall be fervent, that, through the rich grace of our Savior they may be found written in the Book of Life of the Lamb that was slain for our sins. My good wife, who has never ceased to cherish the hope of your election to the Chief Magistracy, unites with me in kind respects to Mrs. Clay and yourself."

That Clay should be equally pleased with his associate was not to be expected; that he even preferred him to the other three candidates may be doubted. Clay was no contemner of religion and, indeed, received baptism a few years later, but his life and conversation had never been that of a member of the church. Like most Southern gentlemen he played cards for money, and drank; and he is said to have been full of wrath and profanity when he lost the nomination in 1840 under circumstances, it must be admitted, fit to try the temper of a saint. Shortly before the date of Frelinghuysen's letter, Clay wrote to Thurlow Weed: "The nomination of Mr. Frelinghuysen was no doubt unexpected by you as it was by me. I think, nevertheless, that it is a most judicious selection, and if he does not add any strength, which however, I think he will do, he will take away none from the ticket. The only regret about it is that so many able and good men should have been disappointed in regard to the selection of their favorite."

The Democratic convention met at Baltimore on May 27, and distinguished itself by nominating the first dark horse, James K. Polk, who, publicly at least, had been groomed only for the second place. Calhoun, Cass, and Buchanan had all been brought forward for the Presidency. Levi Woodbury of New Hampshire had been mentioned. The ever ready Johnson was also active. He was nominated by the Democratic Convention of his state of Kentucky for the third time and wore on this, as he had on the previous occasions, a certain red vest, an act which he appears to have regarded as the equivalent of unfurling his banner. He had the support of the Anti-Bentons in Missouri, and of earnest followers in Pennsylvania. Among the Johnson leaders in the state was Simon Cameron. Johnson cultivated the Eastern harvest in person, visiting Pennsylvania, New York, Vermont, and Massachusetts. John Davis wrote Clay from Worcester: "Colonel Johnson has been here and called to see me. What he hopes for, or what he anticipates is difficult to say, though he seems in good spirits. He wears his red jacket, and the papers say and the people think that he cares nothing about dress. . . . ."

But in December, 1843, Marcy wrote Van Buren that Johnson's popularity was decreasing, and in January Johnson announced that, having been nominated for the Presidency by his own State and by various bodies in other states, he could not then withdraw; but should the national convention see fit to nominate him for either the Presidency or the Vice-Presidency, he would accept, and in any case would support the nominee—a statement generally regarded as announcing his own candidacy for the second office. Calhoun disapproved of national conventions, especially when the delegates were chosen by state conventions, which he regarded as representing the politicians, not the people; and in January, 1843, he announced that he would not accept a nomination by the national convention.

Buchanan had withdrawn after a majority of the Pennsylvania delegates had pledged themselves to or been instructed for Van Buren, and stated that he felt in honor bound to adhere to his resolution so long as Van Buren remained in the field, and his friends considered his success possible. Van Buren's nomination seemed assured, when he wrote an open letter opposing the annexation of Texas, for which a treaty had just been sent to the Senate by President Tyler. Instantly the South was in arms. Some delegates who had been instructed for Van Buren resigned, others announced that they should disregard their instructions because they knew that by doing so, they would carry out the present will of their constituents. Still others believed that they would obey their instructions if they gave useless votes for Van Buren for a few ballots.

On the first vote of the convention, Van Buren had a majority of twenty-six votes,[1] but the convention had already made his nomination impossible

---

[1] It is possible, however, that more of his Southern delegates would have deserted him if that had been necessary to defeat him.

by readopting the requirement of a two-thirds majority for a choice. In the following ballots, Van Buren's vote fell steadily and that of Cass increased with but one slight break, passing Van Buren's on the fifth ballot. On the eighth ballot forty-four votes were given for James K. Polk. He was an excellent compromise candidate; he had taken particular pains to avoid offending Van Buren; had always been regular and Jacksonian; and was strongly in favor of annexation. During the ninth ballot, the New York delegation retired for consultation and on its return Van Buren's manager, that skillful politician, Benjamin F. Butler, who must not be confused with Benjamin F. Butler of Massachusetts, read a letter from Van Buren, directing his withdrawal when necessary for the sake of harmony, and then withdrew his name. The vote of the state was cast for Polk. At once there was a rush of delegates to the Tennessean, and the dark horse had won the race.

Having rejected Van Buren, the convention now attempted to soothe his followers by nominationg for Vice-President his trusted ally, Senator Silas Wright of New York. It was an excellent choice for other reasons than to placate the runner-up in the race for the nomination for President. One of Polk's managers wrote him enthusiastically: "What a *ticket*. How *pure* and *elevated* and Herculian *(sic)* in intellects." It was true that Polk and Wright were appropriate companions. Both were clean men, simple in their tastes,[1] hard working and able, but solid rather than brilliant, and especially fitted to deal with financial questions.

Wright was notified of his nomination by a new contrivance of Professor Morse, known as the electro-magnetic telegraph. By the same means he declined. He was asked to reconsider and replied that his mind was made up. Word was then sent him that the convention had adjourned for the day, and that a committee of five had been appointed to confer with him, and would be in Washington in the morning. The convention reconvened at seven-thirty a. m., that early hour having been chosen to allow delegates to catch the afternoon train for home. After some business had been transacted, Mr. Butler of New York read a letter from Mr. Wright, requesting him to thank the convention profoundly for the "unmerited honor" conferred upon him and "to say for me that circumstances, which I do not think it necessary to detail to it, but which I very briefly hint at to you (in another private letter to Mr. B.) render it impossible that I should, consistently with my sense of public duty and private obligations, accept this nomination."

The message was a trifle cryptic, but the main point was sufficiently clear; the convention had extended the olive branch and it had been returned with formal courtesy, but yet in a manner which must have aroused great alarm for the success of the campaign. Wright's refusal, however, was in strict accord-

---

[1]It is said, however, that while Polk was president, no liquor was served at the White House, and that Wright failed of nomination to the Presidency because of intemperate habits.

ance with a long formed and consistently maintained determination not to abandon or even seem to abandon his leader. In 1842, Poinsett of South Carolina, an active and not over honorable politician, wrote that Silas Wright had been taken to a high place where he could behold our fair land and offered dominion over it, if he would fall down and worship John Calhoun, but that Silas said "Avaunt, Satan"![1]

Just before the convention, it was suggested to Wright that the two-thirds rule might be adopted, and Van Buren's success thereby rendered impossible; and he was asked if under such circumstances he would accept the nomination himself. Wright positively refused and wrote Butler to this effect, and the letter was read to the New York delegation in their conference which preceded the withdrawal of Van Buren's name. The public duty mentioned by Wright probably referred to his opposition to slavery and the annexation of Texas. He is reported to have said that he did not choose to ride behind the black pony.

Wright's refusal left the convention, like a ship on a heavy sea, without pilot or compass. There had been, it is true, a vigorous struggle for the Vice-Presidency, with the situation much resembling that of four years before. The leading candidates were Polk and R. M. Johnson, with the choice of William R. King urged as a compromise. Andrew Stevenson of Virginia was also mentioned. Johnson was thought to have a presumptive right to his old office, and was supported by conservatives. Probably most of Van Buren's friends favored Johnson, but in private letters to Van Buren, Kendall and Butler expressed the strongest opposition because of charges which they believed to be true against Johnson's private character. Johnson's pilgrimage in a red vest in search of votes has been mentioned above. Polk did not travel but he plied his pen, writing to friends to get the support of party leaders in different states. In one letter he expressed the wish that politicians and papers would declare themselves for him, before Johnson, seeing that his hopes for the Presidency were vain, should become a candidate for the second place.

Early in January, 1844, Laughlin (a Polk lieutenant and later editor of his "organ") and others procured from General Jackson letters to political leaders in various states, which were used to induce state conventions to declare a preference for Polk. A letter by "Amicus" that appeared in the *Globe* and advocated the nomination of William R. King, gave Johnson and A. V. Brown of Tennessee an opportunity to sound Polk's praises and urge his nomination. In an article signed, "A Tennessee Democrat," they pointed out that King voluntarily, and Van Buren under instructions, had voted for the charter of the United States Bank, and that it would never do to have two candidates who had endorsed that institution. "But," they asked, "who

---

[1]According to Poinsett, a like offer was then made with the same ill success to Levi Woodbury of New Hampshire.

does not remember in Jackson's battle against the Bank 'the unterrified ability displayed by Governor Polk on these trying occasions?' "

There were, of course, alliances and rumors of alliances between candidates for the Presidency and for the Vice-Presidency. Buchanan was said to be supporting Johnson; and Cass, Stevenson of Virginia. Polk believed Van Buren would win and was therefore insistent that his friends should hang on to the New York chariot, at the same time conveying a strong hint that it was expected that this loyalty would be reciprocated; Jackson, as has been seen, supported Polk, but Benton favored King; Blair, as always, was cool toward Polk, who believed that he treated him unfairly in the *Globe*. The younger and even the middle-aged men of the party were warmly in favor of Polk as against Johnson. The old leaders, like the chiefs in Homer, received the best portions of the political feast and men who, if not elderly, were yet of mature years and had done long service for the party, complained that they were treated as mere boys. After the nomination, Buchanan, who was not usually considered a junior, wrote Polk: "The old office holders generally have had their day and should be content. Had Mr. Van Buren been our candidate, worthy as he is, this feeling which everywhere pervades the Democratic ranks would have made his defeat as signal as it was in 1840." Even Polk, he added, would have run better in Philadelphia had it not been rumored that he would distribute the patronage among the "old hunkers."

Geographically Polk was well placed. In the fall of 1843, Polk had stated one of the strongest arguments for his selection for Vice-President, namely, that Van Buren would probably be nominated and that therefore "the candidate for the Vice-Presidency must come from the West, and from a slave-holding State."[1] But the unexpected nomination of a Southern candidate had rendered useless previous combinations and calculations. Now it was clear that the Vice-President must come from the East and from a free State. The convention seemed turning to the extreme Northeast for a man to balance the Southwestern candidate. It might have been willing to recognize a defeated candidate for the Presidency, but when Buchanan's name was mentioned, it was promptly withdrawn by his friends. Governor Morton of Massachusetts, who was present as a delegate, was proposed and received some votes, but he immediately withdrew his name. The first ballot stood, Senator and ex-Governor Fairfield of Maine 107, Woodbury 44, Cass 39, Johnson 26, Commodore Stewart 23, Dallas 13, Marcy 5. Messrs. Johnson, Stewart, and Marcy received the solid votes of Pennsylvania, Ohio, and Michigan respectively, and no support from any other state, even their own. Probably these three states intentionally threw away their votes, waiting until the fog over the battlefield should lift a little.

---

[1]This classing of Tennessee as a western State is noteworthy. The slavery question had not yet entirely obliterated the distinction of East and West, new and old states, in that of South and North.

Apparently the Southerners, irritated by Wright's refusal, had determined to defy the Van Burenites. Cass and Woodbury were especially disliked by the ex-President, and every vote for them came from the South, except those of Woodbury's state of New Hampshire. The Southerners continued to urge their claims, but finding strong opposition in various quarters, began to consider Fairfield. It would have made an excellent combination of captain and mate. If Polk was a dark horse, Fairfield was even darker. He had served creditably as Governor of Maine and in Congress, and was a type of the best class in the towns of rural New England. John Fairfield was intelligent, industrious, and conscientious. He was loyal to the church, supported education, and believed that intemperance and slave-holding were sinful. His condemnation of slavery led him to do an act which was a powerful factor in depriving him of the Vice-Presidency, but which gave him his little niche in the temple of history. While Governor of Maine, he had refused to honor a warrant from the Governor of Georgia for the extradition of the captain and the mate of a ship for "slave-stealing," carrying away negroes on their vessels, and the refusal had caused great feeling against him in that state.

Before the second vote of the convention was taken, there had been discussion of the views of Fairfield and of Dallas on the Texas treaty and the bank respectively. Their friends did their best to make satisfactory statements. Nathan Clifford of Maine, later a Justice of the United States Supreme Court, said that he could not speak by authority for Mr. Fairfield, but that he believed that the Maine Democrats were in favor of annexing Texas and taking possession of Oregon, and that Mr. Fairfield, as a good Democrat, approved both measures. General Romulus M. Saunders of North Carolina assured the convention that Mr. Fairfield favored annexation. But this was not satisfactory to the Southerners; the matter of the refusal of extradition was recalled; and an agreement was made with the Pennsylvanians to support Dallas. The alliance proved irresistible.

Some interesting information on the inside forces of the convention is found in the letters of Delegate Whitman of Ohio to William Allen of the same State. Whitman wrote that he himself had favored the nomination of Allen for the Vice-Presidency, but that from prudential considerations of the future, he had refrained from pressing it, since "to have a man defeated is to kill him.". Cass was a native of Ohio, a portion of the delegation favored him, and Whitman was of the opinion that had Ohio swung to him on the second vote, he would ultimately have succeeded; but Whitman protested most earnestly against the state's supporting its son.[1] Cass was withdrawn and the delegation was about to go to Fairfield when word was received of the South-Pennsylvania union on Dallas; and Ohio, finding that Dallas would

---

[1] Whitman considered Cass an opponent of the Jackson-Van Buren policies, and an ally of Calhoun and a favorer of the undemocratic two-thirds rule.

be nominated, resolved to get on the winning side to preserve her influence. It is a rule with politicians as in Heaven, "to him that hath, shall be given," and on the second ballot Dallas polled 220 votes out of 256, only Maine, Vermont, Rhode Island, and part of Massachusetts remaining loyal to Fairfield, and New Hampshire to Woodbury.

Mr. Fairfield took his defeat very calmly. He wrote the causes of it to his wife, and added: "With the result I am entirely satisfied. It is honor enough for me to have been a candidate for nomination." Three days later he told Mrs. Fairfield that there had been a rumor that Dallas had declined, "whereupon a few had begun to rejoice and to talk of my immediate nomination by a Congressional Convention. The rumor, however, turns out to be untrue, and I am glad of it. I would prefer a much humbler situation, one better suited to my talents and taste. 'Ain't I modest?' I don't care whether I am believed or not, I speak the truth."

A delegation was sent to inform Mr. Dallas of his nomination and it was reported that Mr. Fairfield was at the head of it; that the nominee was called out of bed and appeared in *déshabillé,* much alarmed lest he had been summoned to hear bad news of a sick daughter. The account appeared in contemporary newspapers and would seem to be worthy of credence, yet Mr. Fairfield's correspondence shows that in part at least, it was false. Fairfield wrote his wife: "You will perceive that the papers insist upon it, that I went to Philadelphia and in the dead of night and to the alarm of everybody announced to Mr. Dallas his nomination to the Vice-Presidency; while in fact I was snugly ensconced in my bed at Washington, dreaming of far more agreeable matters than politics, to wit of wife and children and all the dear delights of home. I don't know how the mistake originated, but I have not deemed it of sufficient consequence to make a public correction."

George Mifflin Dallas was born at Philadelphia on July 10, 1792. He was the son of Alexander James Dallas, an ardent Republican and Secretary of the Treasury under Madison. Notwithstanding this membership of the strict construction party, he recommended and supervised the establishment of the second Bank of the United States. Young Dallas graduated from Princeton in 1810. In 1813 he accompanied the Peace Commission to Europe as Gallatin's secretary, returned in 1814 with an important dispatch, worked with his father in the Treasury, and soon took up law and politics. Originally a supporter of Calhoun for President, he went with the Jackson tide and is said to have written the nominating address of the State Convention. In 1831 he was sent to fill a vacancy in the United States Senate, but declined the nomination for a full term, some said because he feared defeat. Later it was thought he had changed his mind and was intriguing and looking for non-Democratic support; but if this were true, the plan totally failed, the two leading Democratic contestants killed each other off, and the prize went to James Buchanan.

Early in 1837 President Van Buren appointed Dallas Minister to Russia. He took an active part in the social life of St. Petersburg, for which he was probably fully as well qualified, as for diplomacy and law.   In person he was of the middle height with prematurely white hair which increased rather than diminished the favorable impression which he made on those he was accustomed to meet.   Of the elder Dallas, it was said that he excelled in everything, and his son inherited much of this quality.

He resigned his post in October, 1839, having creditably performed the little work he had to do, and returned to the United States.   After his return he devoted much attention to his profession, and though not a great lawyer, built up a good practice.   He did not, however, forget politics.   On January 1, 1844, he wrote a letter to be read at a New Orleans celebration of Jackson's victory, in which he declared that the establishment of the English there would have prevented the annexation of Texas, which would be advantageous commercially and was "a just and necessary consequence upon (*sic*) the genius and maxims of our confederated system."   On February 4 he wrote to Robert J. Walker of Mississippi, who had published a pamphlet in favor of annexation: "Nothing can remove or resist your facts, and I defy ingenuity to assail the justice and integrity of your deductions, ... your admirable *brochure* comes to me like manna in the way of starved people.   I cannot tell you without using words which you might consider extravagant, how highly I appreciated your labors, and how sincerely, as an American, I thank you."

This letter was published with the author's consent, in a Richmond paper. Dallas had made his opinions clear on what was to be the chief issue of the campaign; but the Democrats had pronounced most definitely and vigorously on another matter where Dallas had been obliged to turn a sudden somersault to Jackson's side, like that which he executed when he deserted Calhoun. This was the recharter of the United States Bank.   In 1831 President Biddle was anxiously considering the advisability of applying immediately for a recharter.   The most conservative and cultured Jacksonians, including the majority of the Cabinet, believed that they could persuade the President to sign such a bill if he were not irritated by pressure.   They also feared that should he veto it, he would lose Pennsylvania and therefore the Presidency, in the ensuing election.   Accordingly, they urged the postponement of the application for a recharter.

The bank was located in Philadelphia; it was strong in Pennsylvania, and leading Democrats in the state were well disposed to it, although the mass of the party in the country and the President were not.   Under these circumstances the Pennsylvania Senators, Dallas and Wilkins, both favored postponement.   Yet if a recharter were to be asked, Dallas was very anxious to present the petition, himself, because of the part his father had taken in establishing the bank.   Biddle decided in favor of an immediate application, but passing over Webster and other National Republicans, friends of the bank, sent the memorial to Dallas in order to avoid irritating the President and the Democrats by selecting one of their political opponents.

However, when Dallas presented the petition, he disappointed the advocates of the bank by stating frankly that he disapproved applying at that time, because the charter had still some years to run and because recharter had not been made an issue when the present Congress was elected. Yet Biddle, who was most unwilling to abandon all hope of winning Jackson, attempted to use Dallas as a missionary to the White House. Dallas refused; but as chairman of the select committee, to whom the subject of a recharter had been referred, he reported a bill for that purpose with such changes from the old charter as the bank was willing to accept; and, with certain amendments, the bill was passed. It was vetoed by Jackson, and Dallas voted to override the veto. But "the first evidences of Jackson's wrath filled him with dismay, and before the end of the session he was talking to his intimates about repudiating the bank. On his return home he saw a town meeting condemning the veto and got up another approving the veto." He defended his change on the ground that the bank was mixing in politics, that while he approved a bank, he did not regard it as of immense and essential importance, and that "the institution as an useful agent of government is one thing, its directors, or managers or partizans are quite another thing—both united are not worth the cause which depends on the reëlection of Jackson. I was always for the sentiment which is now lifted most high—Jackson, bank or no bank!"

The dreaded breach in the Democratic party was postponed four years. Silas Wright consented to take the nomination for Governor, though election would mean a giving up of his seat in the United States Senate, and Van Buren wrote a letter to a ratification meeting endorsing and praising both nominees. Polk made his acknowledgments, and Dallas gave thanks in a most fulsome style.

In the campaign, both parties had much to say about the candidates for the Vice-Presidency. Each, however, had names sadly unsuitable for songs or alliterative war cries. The *Whig Minstrel,* a lively and full collection of songs of the Tippecanoe order for rallies, and parades, does not once mention the name or, indeed, refer to the second string of the party fiddle. Each laid stress upon the ancestry of its man. The Whigs declared that the Democrats made a practice of calling their candidates J. *Knox* Polk and G. *Mifflin* Dallas. Polk's mother was said to be a descendant of a brother of John Knox, and Dallas' mother was a daughter of Thomas Mifflin, a leading Pennsylvania Democrat in the early days of the Republic. On the other hand, the closing paragraph of the Whig platform said that Frelinghuysen inherited "the principles as well as the name of a father who, with Washington on the fields of Trenton and of Monmouth, perilled life in the contest for liberty, and afterward, as a Senator of the United States, acted with Washington in establishing and perpetuating that liberty." The Boston *Atlas,* in a long sketch of Frelinghuysen, referred to his honorable, noble-hearted, patriotic ancestry.

Attempts were made by each party to show that the union of the opposition candidates was most incongruous. A Democratic paper said of Frelinghuysen: "He is of an irreproachable moral character and in this respect there is a very strong contrast between him and Mr. Clay . . . . He is an enemy to *gambling, lasciviousness, horse racing,* and duelling." All of which were charged against Clay. The Whigs on their part gleefully pointed out that Dallas had differed from Polk on the tariff, internal improvements, the bank, and the distribution of the surplus revenue. They published long lists of votes by Dallas favorable to the bank, and attempted to show that the Democrats, by nominating Dallas, had proved the dishonesty of their opposition to a bank. The *Forum* of Philadelphia contrasted Dallas' conduct with the explicit statement of the Democratic Convention that Congress had no power to charter a bank. The Democrats had foreseen the danger. On June 11, 1844, J. W. Forney of Pennsylvania, a follower of Buchanan, wrote his chief that the Democrats were worried by the nomination of Dallas, "that his course on the bank question is very questionable, to say the least, and improperly handled may operate vastly to our injury. Nothing can save him but the union and enthusiasm which now pervade the party."

Curiously enough, however, Dallas' dubious conduct in regard to the bank proved an advantage to the Democrats. Pennsylvania was a high tariff state; Clay and the Whigs, the Northern ones at least, were high tariff men, and the Pennsylvania Democrats eagerly welcomed a discussion of Dallas' attitude toward a United States Bank in order to divert attention from the protection issue. Dallas met the attacks on him by condemning certain actions of Biddle, and declaring that he would never consent to the chartering of another national bank. The Democrats asserted that Dallas had acted under instructions from the Pennsylvania Legislature. According to the Democratic and Southern theory, a Senator was an ambassador of his state bound to obey the orders of its Legislature, or resign, as Tyler did when bidden to vote for Benton's resolution expunging from the records of the Senate its vote censuring President Jackson for "removing the deposits" from the Bank of the United States.

The Whigs replied that the vote of the Pennsylvania Legislature was an expression of opinion, not a formal instruction, and asked why, if the bank was as bad as the Democrats said, Dallas did not resign like Tyler. They also pointed to a statement of Dallas in 1836 that Congress had the constitutional right to charter a bank, and that it would be possible to devise a beneficial one. Other Whig papers admitted that Dallas was an appropriate companion for Polk, but described him as an insignificant man, a sycophant, and a traitor to the interests of his State. Particularly was this the case in New England. A Portland paper said: "Three-fifths of the Democratic voters of this State will ask in perfect ignorance: 'Who is this Mr. Polk?' and five-sixths of them, if not more, will demand: 'Who is this Mr. Dallas'?"

The Boston *Atlas,* a leading Whig paper, in giving an account of its opponent, began by stressing the need of one. It said:

"George M. Dallas, the loco foco[1] candidate for the Vice-Presidency has been so much in the background, for some reason or other during the last ten years, that very many of both parties are heard to ask, 'Who is George M. Dallas'? To all such that come to our knowledge we do not hesitate to answer: the very person best fitted to run on a ticket with James K. Polk at its head, and with Texas and free trade for its motto and rallying cry.

"In 1831 Mr. Dallas was elected a Senator in Congress from Pennsylvania to fill a vacancy. He was sent there from the city of Philadelphia, the pledged friend of the U. S. Bank. At first, he redeemed the pledge of those who sent him. He voted for the rechartering of the bank. It was vetoed by Jackson, and Mr. Dallas knelt at the footstool of usurpation and outrage. He basely surrendered up the rights and wishes of his constituents and sustained the President in his dangerous inroads upon the Constitution and liberties of the country. He confessed his own sins in voting for the renewal of the charter, by sustaining General Jackson in his veto, and the war he afterwards waged upon the bank and the currency of the Nation. Of all the instances of abject and slavish submission to the dictator, there was none so disgracefully servile as (that of) George M. Dallas.

"It was not only on the bank question, however, that Dallas was false and treacherous to the interests and wishes of his constituents. On the tariff question—the question of all questions to the people of Pennsylvania—he meanly truckled to nullification. All his speeches, during the brief period he was in the U. S. Senate, are marked with a subserviency to the enemies of protection, eminently disgraceful to the representative in the Senate of the strongest tariff state in the Union."

---

[1]A nickname given opprobriously to the Democrats by their opponents. Some years before, one faction of the party in New York held radical socialistic views. On one occasion their rivals, being in a minority in a meeting, attempted to break up the meeting by extinguishing the lights. But the majority, anticipating the manœuver, had brought the new illuminators known as loco foco matches and the hall was re-illuminated. From this circumstance the extremists became known as loco focos and the Whigs, who believed thoroughly in the rights of property, joyously applied the term to the whole Democratic party.

Dallas was also a member of the committee to which Clay's compromise bill was referred, and joined Webster in what the latter described as "unrelenting hostility" to it.

But if Dallas was in certain respects a somewhat embarrassing candidate, Frelinghuysen proved an absolutely dangerous one. There were two movements that were sure to be very troublesome to politicians, whichever side they took—Abolitionism, so-called, and Anti-Catholic Nativism. In 1840 the more moderate "Abolitionists" decided to seek political remedies for the evil of slavery, formed the "Liberty party," and nominated James G. Birney of New York and Thomas Earle of Pennsylvania for President and Vice-President. They polled only a trifle over 7000 votes in the whole country. But they were not discouraged, and in 1844 renominated Birney, associating with him Thomas Morris of Ohio. Anti-slavery sentiment was growing, particularly in Western New York, where the Whigs were strong. On February 22, 1841, Thurlow Weed had written to Francis Granger, who was to be a member of Harrison's Cabinet, begging that care be used in the preparation of the inaugural. "There is," he said, "a world of anti-slavery feeling to be aroused by gratuitous provocation. For God's sake don't incense such an element." Now, Fillmore wrote Weed that in the matter of public questions there was only one thing to fear, the Abolition vote, and he suggested that Cassius Marcellus Clay of Kentucky, who was working for emancipation there, might be of use in New York.

Frelinghuysen was a strong friend of the Colonization Society, whose object was to settle free negroes in Africa. It had been founded by men who believed slavery an evil, yet who shrank from the other evils that would arise from the presence of a vast number of ignorant blacks, allowed to work or not as they chose, and free from close personal supervision. Many Southerners abhorred the society as essentially abolitionist, while the Abolitionists themselves considered it a flattering unction which would merely scab over the sore of slavery. A Mississippian wrote Frelinghuysen asking his views on slavery. Frelinghuysen answered: "I cheerfully respond that I am not an Abolitionist and never have been. I have been an ardent friend of the Colonization Society and still am. Slavery in the states is a domestic concern that Congress has not the right or power to interfere with." The tone of the letter offended William Jay, a son of John Jay, and a highly respected philanthropist and anti-slavery leader, and he published a reply which not only hurt Frelinghuysen's feelings, but injured him with anti-slavery men. An old and unflinching abolitionist even accused him of being a slave-holder because, when slavery was abolished in New Jersey in 1846, an aged slave had preferred to remain in the family. But the anger of the Abolitionists could not save Frelinghuysen from the wrath of the defenders of the "peculiar institution."

The Whigs also suffered from their connection with the Native Americans, and the supposed anti-Catholic feeling of their candidate for Vice-President. From the first, the immigrants had usually voted with the Jeffersonians; they had been scorned and lashed by the Federalists; and they in turn hated Federalism as a class organization resembling the despotisms from which they had fled. The Whigs were successors of the Federalists, and some of them retained the old prejudices and antipathies. Washington Hunt, a Whig Congressman from New York, wrote to Clay: "We shall carry the state but I assure you we have no strength to spare, especially since Charles King (President of Columbia and a son of Rufus King) will not permit the Irish or the Dutch to vote the Whig ticket. I am exceedingly indignant at this Native American movement, and the folly of our people in giving their aid and countenance to disorganizers." It would seem that placing Frelinghuysen on the ticket must have pleased the Dutch, but it repelled the Catholics and therefore the powerful Irish. It is said that the Catholic Archbishop of New York, who was born in Kentucky, stated that he would vote for Clay but not for Frelinghuysen; but on being told that this would be impossible, replied that then he would not vote for Clay. One cause of this antipathy was Frelinghuysen's prominence in the Bible Society, which gave much effort to the conversion of Catholics. There were Protestants also who were repelled by Frelinghuysen, disliking his Puritanism. If Johnson had been popular in Pennsylvania because of his defense of transporting the mails on Sunday, Frelinghuysen must have been the reverse. Indeed, many attacks were made on him in the state because of his Presidency of the Bible Society.

At the election, the Democrats carried New York by a small margin and thereby elected Polk. The defeat of the Whigs is usually attributed to the refusal of the Liberty men to support Clay, but he might have slipped through but for Frelinghuysen. Fillmore wrote to Clay: "The Abolitionists and the foreign Catholics defeated us in this state. . . . . Our opponents by pointing to the Native Americans and Mr. Frelinghuysen, drove the foreign Catholics from us—." There was no scattering of electoral votes. Polk and Dallas each received 170, and Clay and Frelinghuysen 105.

President Polk's administration was a remarkably successful one. It settled the dangerous question of the Oregon boundary peacefully, and in a manner not unfavorable to the rights of the United States. It waged a successful war with Mexico by which, at a small cost both of blood and money, the Nation acquired a vast amount of valuable territory. Yet, as the time of the next Presidential campaign approached, the Democrats found themselves in an embarrassing position. The technical reasons alleged for the war with Mexico and the manner of bringing it on, gave opportunity for attack; the question of slavery in the new territories was pressing and threatened to split the party; and though the war was a Democratic war, the glory went to the opposition, for the chief heroes, Scott and Taylor, were both classed as Whigs. Taylor's Whigism indeed was vague and uncertain; but he had a popular appeal which was wanting in the brave and able, but vain and quarrelsome Scott.[1]

Moreover, the country was weary of parties and politicians. Scott had been closely connected with them while Taylor had not, and the difference helped Taylor. There were several independent nominations of Taylor which the General accepted, but he was said to have promised at the last moment to withdraw should the Whig convention nominate another. But the convention, influenced by what Daniel Webster was to call the great, far-seeing doctrine of availability, cast aside Webster, Clay, and all the minor statesmen, and took Taylor for its candidate.

Clay, indeed, obtained a good vote, but it was felt that already he had had a full chance, that the questions on which he had led were no longer at issue, and that he should not be given a mortgage on the Whig party. Yet the majority respected the grief of the Clay followers in what must be the final defeat of their leader. It also wished to conciliate New York. But that state seemed to have no candidate for the Vice-Presidency. In 1839 Thurlow Weed had urged Webster in vain to accept the second place. In 1848 he made a similar appeal and if his *Memoir* may be trusted, Webster was much impressed and might have consented to yield precedence to the man whom he described as an "illiterate frontier colonel," but just at the wrong moment Fletcher Webster entered the room with a glowing description of the increasing strength of the movement to make his father President, and Weed's labor was lost.

Seward's friends wished him to enter the race and he might have agreed had the Whigs of New York been united, but there were various other influential aspirants. The Governor attempted to make an alliance with Taylor, but failed. He had been lacking in tact, and had offended the property owning and conservative classes, and he sank into obscurity. Nathaniel Tallmadge, the leader of the New York Conservatives of Van Buren's day, had been rewarded with a Senatorship, and probably had received definite encouragement to hope for the Vice-Presidency. But the managers felt that his nomination would be unwise, and saw no reason for sacrificing expediency to "delicacy," although they realized the great importance of placating Tallmadge's followers.

When the convention met, Abbott Lawrence of Massachusetts, the great cotton manufacturer, an unflinching conservative Whig, was slated for the Vice-Presidency. His nomination would be very pleasing to the Webster men, but highly offensive to the "conscience Whigs" of the state. Henry Wilson, who was reckoned one of their number, although his conduct as a politician gave no evidence of any peculiarly sensitive moral view, told the convention that Massachusetts spurned the bribe of the Vice-Presidency. It was later alleged that this gesture lost Lawrence the vote of Virginia, which

---

[1]Taylor's nickname was "Rough and Ready," and Scott's "Fuss and Feathers."

might have given him the nomination. Taylor owned a large cotton plantation in Louisiana, and his nomination had greatly angered the "conscience
men" delegates from Massachusetts, as the anti-slavery wing of the party
was called, who declared that they would not have cotton on both ends of the
ticket.

John A. Collier of New York, who had been temporary chairman of the
convention, took the platform and "in a stirring speech in which he eloquently
pictured the sorrow and bitterness of Clay's friends, he presented as a peace
offering the name of Millard Fillmore as one that would in a measure reconcile all the defeated candidates, and described Fillmore's loyalty and services
as a Whig and his strength at the polls." At first it seemed that this appeal
would bring a unanimous nomination of Fillmore, but the friends of Lawrence and other candidates threw off the spell and the first ballot stood Fillmore 115, Lawrence 109, scattering among ten also-rans, 51. There was a
break to the leader, and on the second ballot Fillmore received 173 votes and
Lawrence 87, with 6 scattering.

Millard Fillmore was born on January 7, 1800, in a village in the forests
of Western New York. His father was a pioneer with little furniture, and a
sap trough served as a cradle for the child. Young Fillmore went to school,
worked in the mills, taught school a little, studied law, and was admitted to
the bar. In 1830 he settled in Buffalo and lived there, a devoted and public-
spirited citizen until his death in 1874. In 1828 he was elected to the Legislature and was reëlected in 1832. He proved himself active and efficient
and took a leading part in repealing the statutes which permitted imprisonment for debt, and which denied persons without religious belief the right of
testifying in court. He assisted Chief Justice Spencer in drawing the bill for
the first reform, and himself drew and introduced that for the second. He
also wrote a pamphlet defending the proposed change and showing the evil
effects of the existing law. In 1830 Fillmore was elected to Congress, declined a renomination in 1832, but was again chosen in 1834, 1836, and 1840.

In 1841 he stood second in the Whig caucus for nominating a Speaker
and, as was customary, was therefore given the chairmanship of the Committee on Ways and Means. He devoted himself to the duties of the position
with his usual industry, and was regarded as the father of the protective
tariff of 1842. Mr. Fillmore was also a thorough Whig in the matter of the
improvement of harbors, paying special attention to the Great Lakes; but he
was not anxious to establish a National Bank and he proposed, instead, that
state banks be allowed to issue currency based on United States bonds, thus
anticipating the measure adopted in the Civil War.

After Fillmore's failure to secure the Whig nomination for Vice-President in 1844, partly because it was feared that his opposition to slavery would
offend the South, he was induced to become the party's candidate for Governor, as it was thought that these very views would strengthen the national

ticket among anti-slavery and church people in sections where it was specially weak. George W. Patterson, a former anti-Mason and a man who combined high ideals with caution and political shrewdness, wrote Thurlow Weed, of Fillmore: "You may rest assured that he will help Mr. Clay to a large number of good men's votes. Mr. Clay's slaves and his old duel would have hurt him with some men who will now vote the ticket, as Fillmore is a favorite everywhere, and among the Methodists, where old Father Fillmore is almost worshipped, they will go for him with a rush."[1] The Democrats induced Silas Wright to resign from the Senate and run for Governor and he was elected, but Fillmore gave him a hard fight. In 1846 Fillmore was chosen Comptroller of New York, and was serving with much efficiency when he was nominated for the Vice-Presidency.

In appearance Mr. Fillmore was attractive and impressive. Alexander H. Stephens wrote to his wife: "His countenance is open and bland, his chest full. His eye is bright, blue, and intelligent; his hair thick and slightly gray;[2] no man can look at him without feeling that he is a man far above the average." Appearances are frequently deceptive, however. Paul R. Frothingham, the author of a full and careful life of Edward Everett, says of Fillmore: "He was safe and suave and neither aggressive nor domineering. His large stature lent him the look of an autocratic ruler, but his habitual attitude was one of courtesy and deference." He "believed in moderation as a principle, and disliked not only extreme positions, but extreme statements in support of them."

Fillmore worked hard and steadily, had a grasp of detail, and understood finance. Though not an orator, he was clear and forcible in discussion, could make his cause seem the cause of justice, and impressed an audience with his earnestness and honesty. But, like Silas Wright, he spoke with more advantage to a board or a Legislature than to a public meeting. Like Wright, too, he was pure, temperate, and rigidly honest. He had early determined to eschew not merely evil, but temptation. On December 6, 1838, he wrote to Weed refusing to accept a nomination for the office of Comptroller, saying: "I made up my mind when I entered political life never to go so far as to feel for a moment that I depend upon any office or popular favor for a livelihood. That moment I should lose my independence, I fear my integrity. He is miserable whose happiness hangs on princes' favors. But he is not only wretched but infinitely degraded whose means of support depend upon the wild caprice of the ever changing multitude. I can not become a slave to such a master."[3]

Yet in spite of his scruples, Mr. Fillmore, as might be expected of a man of his administrative ability, was a good campaign manager. In 1844 he

[1]The "old father" was but forty-four years of age, and the darling of the Methodists was a Unitarian.
[2]Perhaps it was the silvering hair that gave Fillmore the appellation of Father.
[3]One sees that Fillmore was a Whig of the old school.

wrote to Weed of the serious danger "that our friends will mistake great meetings for the election, and omit to take the requisite steps to canvass every town by school districts, and furnish proper information to doubtful men, and make necessary arrangements to bring every Whig to the polls." Nor was Fillmore's skill confined to the mere running of a machine. He called Weed's attention to the evils which might follow if Seward should take a political trip with two of the principal landowners in the Whig stronghold of Western New York, where there was imminent danger of an outbreak of disorder because of difficulties concerning the payment of quit-rents by the actual holders and improvers to descendants of original grantees. When, in 1839, Whig politicians were either sincerely or as a means of weakening Clay, encouraging the candidacy of General Scott, but were attempting to make it appear that it was the Democrats that were coming out for him, Fillmore was honest or shrewd enough to write Weed: "There is nothing gained by any *false pretence* that this is a loco foco movement for Scott."

The Democratic Convention had already met at Baltimore on May 22. Lewis Cass of Michigan led on the first three ballots and received the necessary two-thirds vote on the fourth. For Vice-President the first vote stood 115 for William O. Butler of Kentucky, 74 for John A. Quitman of Mississippi, 25 for William R. King of Alabama, 24 for John Y. Mason of Virginia, 13 for John J. McKay of North Carolina, and 1 for Jefferson Davis of Mississippi. On the second ballot Butler was nominated, receiving 162 votes to 62 for Quitman, with 22 scattering.

Both Quitman and Butler had excellent war records, the one in the war with Mexico, the other in this war, and in that of 1812 as well. Quitman was a fire eater, a violent pro-Southern, pro-slavery man who was soon to be deeply involved in filibustering expeditions for the liberation of Cuba. Butler was more moderate and though a slave-holding Southerner, came from the northern edge of the South. T. R. R. Cobb wrote to his brother Howell: "I am not a great admirer of Cass, although I think it a generous act on the part of Northern Democrats to nominate both anti-Wilmot Proviso[1] men. I think a more *judicious* (italics in original) ticket could have been selected. Michigan and Kentucky are too close together to have been selected. I do not see what strength Butler carried to Cass that any Southern man would not have carried, and more especially Quitman. And on the score of military glory, Scott or Taylor if nominated will overshadow that of either. King of Alabama would have been a much more *judicious* (italics in original) nomination although I would vote for no man sooner than General Butler." Cobb added that these were his "first impressions," and while his comments were shrewd, it is probable that he did not do justice to the advantages of having Butler, who was a power in the doubtful state of Kentucky,

---

[1] The Proviso introduced by David Wilmot forbidding the existence of slavery in any territory acquired from Mexico.

on the ticket. He was a leader of the Kentucky bar, had run for Governor of the State in 1844 when Henry Clay was the candidate for President, and though defeated had cut the Whig gubernatorial majority of 20,000 at the preceding election to 5,000.

In 1848, as in 1844, there was an "anti" party in the field with no hope of success, but with power to determine the results of the election. And, to add to the uncertainties, the Democratic party of New York, as often before and since, was split into two factions. In 1848 one was known as the Hunkers, so-called because of their alleged hankering after office. They had no wish to meddle with slavery and were extremely regular. The men of the second division were nicknamed Barnburners by their opponents, who compared their policy, which they regarded as extreme and one-sided, to the acts of a Dutch farmer who burned his barn for the sake of getting rid of the rats.

Each division sent a full delegation to Baltimore. The convention, unwilling to favor either faction, offered to divide the vote of New York between them; but both rejected the compromise, the Hunkers were seated, and the Barnburners went home declaring that, if Cass were nominated, they would defeat the ticket. Cass was particularly hated by Van Buren men because it was believed that his underground work had lost their leader the nomination in 1844.

The Barnburners now held a convention at Utica, New York, which delegates from other states attended, and nominated Van Buren for President and Henry Dodge of Wisconsin for Vice-President; but that gentleman not long afterwards withdrew and announced that he would support the Democratic nominees.

In June a Free Territory Convention met at Columbus, Ohio, and called for a national convention for the purpose of nominating candidates, pledged to the principles of the Wilmot Proviso. Accordingly, a "Free Soil" Convention met at Buffalo, New York, August 9, and drew up a platform demanding "Free Soil, Free Speech, Free Labor, and Free Men." With a regard for politics most unusual in reformers, they nominated Van Buren. For Vice-President they nominated Charles Francis Adams, a son of John Quincy Adams, whose war against the slave power had that year been ended by death. The younger Adams had been leading the Conscience Whigs of Massachusetts in a struggle with their "Cotton" brethren, and Thurlow Weed says that it was believed that he would attract a large Whig vote, particularly in New England.

Fillmore had been nominated to reconcile the Clay men and to win antislavery votes. In both he was successful. At a ratification meeting his principal rival, Abbott Lawrence, after assuring the audience that Taylor was as good a Whig as he himself was, added, "and as regards Mr. Fillmore, I will speak as of a friend warm and intimate. There is not a man in this wide

Union more worthy of support by the people of this country than Mr. Fillmore." Robert C. Winthrop, writing to a New York ratification meeting, said, after praising Taylor: "And if any accident should befall him (which Heaven avert) your own Mr. Fillmore will carry out such an administration to its legitimate completion."

Clay himself, while refusing to endorse Taylor, said of the Whig candidate for Vice-President: "I have great pleasure in bearing my humble testimony in favor of Mr. Fillmore. I believe him to be able, indefatigable, industrious and patriotic. He served in the extra session of 1841 as chairman of the committees of the two houses of Congress and I had many opportunities of witnessing his rare merits."

The two Whig candidates expressed themselves as much pleased with each other. Fillmore, in his brief letter of acceptance, endorsed Taylor for the benefit of a doubting party, and expressed full confidence that he would always find him a "warm and consistent Whig, a safe guide, and an honest man"; Taylor, in a letter which was supposed to define his rather uncertain position, said, "and I may add that these emotions were increased by associating my name with that of the distinguished citizen of New York whose acknowledged abilities and sound conservative opinions might have justly entitled him to the first place on the ticket." This was one of several letters carefully prepared for Taylor, and Thurlow Weed says in his *Autobiography* that he himself wrote it, and presented it to Fillmore for suggestions before he sent it on to Taylor.

Many Whigs were displeased by the nomination of "an ignorant frontier colonel" whose opinions were unknown, and hesitated long before they would pledge their support to the ticket. Newspapers usually decide at once, but now several waited for some time. Among them were the New York *Tribune,* and an old Whig champion, the Poughkeepsie *Journal.* Both finally came into line and both were influenced by the presence of Fillmore on the ticket. Greeley announced that one reason for his supporting Taylor was that the fates of Fillmore and of Patterson (the Whig candidate for Governor, a worthy and able man) were linked with his. The *Journal,* the last of the doubtful papers to rally to the colors, said that it rejoiced at the opportunity of supporting Fillmore.

Robert C. Schenck of Ohio, who had strongly opposed the nomination of Taylor but who at last decided to support him, after giving a long explanation of his reasons for doing so, said: "I will make no remark upon the very excellent nomination of Vice-President. There is not perhaps one Whig in Ohio that takes exception to Mr. Fillmore." The Boston *Atlas* urged Fillmore to bring both anti-slavery men and old Whigs to the support of Taylor. It said that Fillmore, without being furious or sectional, had always abhorred slavery, that his nomination would be the salvation of the ticket in New York, Michigan, Ohio, Indiana, Northern Illinois, Wisconsin, and Vermont, that only Fillmore could guarantee that the election of Taylor would sanction neither slavery nor loco focoism, and that the casting vote in the Senate might be of more value than the veto power.   The *Atlas* probably meant that the one might secure legislation, the other could only defeat it.   In earlier campaigns, the Whigs had had much to say in praise of "internal improvements." The coming of the railroads had made rivers and highways of less importance, but the old war cry could still rouse the veterans of the party, and harbor development was a living issue.   The *Atlas* said: "Mr. Fillmore's geographical affinities with the lake region are also a sufficient definition of the relations of the ticket to the harbor question."   The Cleveland *Herald* proclaimed that "the interests of the great Northwest have no abler and more deserving champion than Millard Fillmore."

Appeals were made in Fillmore's name both to the wealthy classes and to the masses.   The *Atlas*, the organ of the business men of Boston, said: "From the great financial leader of the illustrious and patriotic Twenty-seventh Congress, no pledges of devotion to measures promotive of the interests of the country and of a severe economy, ever need be exacted."   A meeting at Philadelphia resolved to support Fillmore "because he has risen from poverty and obscurity to honor and distinction by merit alone, by toil, integrity, and perseverance, and we regard it as a glorious illustration of the happy theory and form of our republican system, that enables the humblest in the land to aspire to, and attain the highest stations."

But if Fillmore was an asset in the North, he threatened to be a heavy liability in the South.   The Whig party was, on the whole, the propertied party of the country.   The Southern wing has been described as "a club of gentlemen, politically inclined;" it included most of the great planters of the rich bottoms, and also many rigid States' Righters who cared more for their allies in the South than for the welfare of the national party.   These men were carrying on a second "Tippecanoe campaign," hurrahing for "Old Zach" and his horse "Old Whitey."   The disgusted Democrats declared that their opponents should have nominated "Old Whitey" for President; and they had much to say of what the actual candidate for that office really stood for.   An ex-Congressman from North Carolina wrote to Howell Cobb that he considered the ticket of the Whigs as a proof that they were afraid of their principles.   "They put up 'Old Zac' and surround him with a blaze of military glory, and just behind them is Fillmore lurking, holding ready to fasten upon the country all the odious and rejected measures of the Whig party.   Can they succeed?"   The Boston *Post* declared that in 1841 the Whig cormorants killed off General Harrison by their unceasing importunities for office.   "Many of them now think, no doubt, that if Gen. Taylor is elected they will be able to get rid of him in the same way, leaving Mr. Fillmore, who is an ultra Whig,[1] for President.   The Democrats will save old Rough and Ready from your murderous hands, Messrs. Office-holders."

---

[1]Taylor had described himself as a convinced but not an ultra Whig.

The Southern Whigs were dropping former issues in the hope of winning Democrats who had favored Taylor as their own party candidate and were proclaiming their devotion to slavery and Southern Rights. Cass, on account of his Nicholson letter anticipating Douglas's Squatter Sovereignty and because of other concessions to the South, was regarded by anti-slavery Whigs, and has been represented by anti-slavery historians, as a dough-face, a "northern man with southern principles." But many in the South claimed an absolute right to enter the territories with their slaves, and therefore found the Nicholson letter unsatisfactory. Southern Whigs declared that no Northern man could be trusted, pointed to the apostasy of Van Buren, and called on all Southerners to vote for the Southern planter and slave-holder, Zachary Taylor.

But what of Fillmore? He had been one of the most advanced of the anti-slavery Whigs of New York and when in Congress had given several votes offensive to the South, though his regard for the party and his respect for law had kept him from anything "furious." But in 1836 he had been questioned by an Anti-Slavery Society as to what position he would take on certain questions. He refused, as he always did in like circumstances, to give a definite pledge and thereby become a machine, but he stated that he believed that petitions concerning slavery and the slave trade should be respectfully considered, that he was opposed to the annexation of Texas under any circumstances so long as slaves were held there, that slavery should be abolished immediately in the District of Columbia, and that Congress should exert all its constitutional power to abolish the slave trade between the states. The last answer touched the South in a peculiarly sensitive place, for if Congress under its authority to regulate inter-state commerce could forbid a certain kind of commerce and should prohibit inter-state trade in slaves, a terrible blow would be given to the "peculiar institution."

Fillmore's letter was now republished and was at once seized on by the Democrats. Toombs of Georgia wrote to Senator Crittenden of Kentucky that the Democrats "refrain from opposing Taylor but furiously denounce Fillmore all the time. We were turning the tide very well on to him, when that infernal letter of 1838 to the abolitionists was dug up. That has fallen upon us like a wet blanket and has very much injured us in the state. It gave an excuse for all Democrats who wished to go back to their party to abandon Taylor."

The Whigs did their best to parry the blow. In Louisiana, S. S. Prentiss, the great Whig orator, stumped the state, speaking with an ardor and earnestness that was most impressive, and breaking down his health by his exertions. He wrote in the following year: "With regard to Fillmore, I did more than any man in this region. I had served with him in Congress, and my opinion therefore had greater weight. I denounced the various slanders both oral and written, that were circulated in this state against him in a manner which while it tended to destroy their effect, threatened daily to involve me in dangerous political difficulties." The Augusta (Georgia) *Chronicle* defied the Democrats to give a single instance of Fillmore's attending an abolition meeting of any kind, or of any such meeting or journal speaking of him in any but a hostile manner. Fillmore himself came to the aid of his friends by replying to inquiries, that he was not an Abolitionist. He frankly acknowledged that he believed that petitions relating to slavery should be respectfully treated, but he announced a change of view in respect to the inter-state slave trade. In the case of *Prigg vs. Pennsylvania,* the Supreme Court had ruled that the Federal Government alone had the power to regulate inter-state slave transportation, and Fillmore said that he thought the opinion carried conviction to every unprejudiced mind.

In the end, the Southern Whigs were able to laugh the charges off as trifles. What hurt in one section might help in another, and a Democratic pamphlet published in the South to prove that Fillmore was an abolitionist was reprinted in Pennsylvania to win Free Soil votes. Caleb Cushing of Massachusetts said that, even when Congress and the President were opposed to each other, bills were prepared by the heads of departments, and that though Fillmore reported the Tariff Act of 1842, it was the work of Walter Forward of Pennsylvania, Tyler's Secretary of the Treasury.[1] But at least Secretary Forward did not pilot the bill through the House. On the other hand, a Cass paper said that the Democrats had taxed tea and coffee temporarily as a war measure, but that Fillmore and the Whigs had made the tax permanent.

The determining factor in this election, as in so many after the Civil War, was the electoral vote of New York State. Thanks to Van Buren and his Free Soil party, the Whig ticket received a plurality of the popular and consequently the entire electoral vote of that state. Its success in Massachusetts, Ohio, and Pennsylvania might well be attributed to the same cause. The Free Soil ticket won a total of nearly three hundred thousand popular votes, but none in the electoral college. Taylor and Fillmore triumphed in that body by a vote of 163 to 127 for Cass and Butler.

---

[1] A like statement is made by Mr. Stanwood in his *American Tariff Controversies in the Nineteenth Century.*

CHAPTER XIV.

The End of the Old Régime and the Beginning of the New: King, Breckinridge and Hamlin

THE Whigs won in 1848 because of the Van Buren bolt in New York, and because their own candidate could be featured as a hero rather than a Whig. In 1852 conditions had changed: the Barnburners had returned to the Democratic fold; Taylor had died in office; and the Whig party was split wide open by the passage of the Compromise of 1850 with its Fugitive Slave Law. The Whig national convention took fifty-two ballots without result. On the fifty-third ballot it rejected the Whig President and the great Whig orator, and, passing by Fillmore and Webster, took for its candidate another hero, General Winfield Scott.

Scott was the choice of the wing of the party which had opposed the Compromise, though there was a convenient doubt as to what his own attitude had been; and true to the political doctrine of balance and trade, the South was given a platform which promised the maintenance of the Compromise, including the Fugitive Slave Law. General Scott, though born in Virginia, was, in the eyes of the public, more identified with the North than with the South, because his military career had early taken him from his native state, given him Northern associations, and as a part of his official duty during the Jackson administration, thrown him into sharp conflict with the Nullificationists of South Carolina. According to custom, the Vice-President must come from the South; and, according to custom also, the selection was made in great haste.

Mr. Graham, though a somewhat young man for the office of Vice-President, being only forty-eight years old, was yet a father of the Whig party. Under Adams he had been a faithful follower of Clay, and with another North Carolinian, George E. Badger, had led the National Republicans into the new Whig party. Their endeavors to keep its Southern and Northern wings united, greatly strengthened their own national feeling, though when the breach finally came they went with their state and their section. Graham had served as Governor of his state for four years, had filled a vacancy in the United States Senate for two years, and had been Secretary of the Navy for a like period. As a Senator, in response to Southern sentiment he had voted against the Whig tariff of 1842; but it is said that he would have supported it had his vote been necessary to secure its passage. As Secretary of the Navy, Mr. Graham proved himself a good administrator, a man who wished to open up new fields, and who loved science. He reorganized both the personnel of the navy, and the coast survey; proposed and planned the expedition of Perry to Japan, and another which explored the Amazon.

Mr. Graham's influence and the work accomplished by him were greater than might be inferred from the offices which he held. He was ambitious, but perhaps not wise in his choice of means if he wished to attain high public distinction. He sought the Governorship rather than a seat in the United States Senate, in spite of the remonstrances of his political ally, W. P. Mangum, who urged that the Senate was his true place. He also declined diplomatic posts for which he was well fitted. It must be remembered, however, that the position of Minister, unless perhaps to Great Britain, was hardly a rung in the ladder of political progress. The preference for the Governorship may have been due to Graham's strong local patriotism. A son of an active Whig of the Revolution, he loved his state intensely, and much of his best work was done in and for her.

When he was a young man, North Carolina was retrograding. Her people were poor, ignorant and apathetic. Mr. Graham began a successful struggle which ceased only with his life to raise the "tar-heels" to a higher level. He endeavored to improve their material condition by fostering better roads and other means of communication, that the farmers might move their crops. He gave even more care to the cause of education, paying much attention to history, for he believed that the sons of North Carolina would be inspired by a knowledge of her past[1]. Himself a graduate of the University of North Carolina, he regarded it as one of the greatest ornaments of the state, and watched over it constantly and wisely.

Like most of the former Vice-Presidents and candidates for the place, Graham had had little experience as a presiding officer, but for the ornamental and social duties of the Vice-Presidency, he possessed special qualifications. He was fully six feet tall, with clear-cut classical features, which were sometimes stern, but always calm. He has been described as the handsomest man in public life in North Carolina, and the handsomest man in the Cabinet. Fillmore's enthusiastic biographer, William E. Griffis, in speaking

---

[1]Just before his death, he delivered a careful address intended to prove the substantial truth of the tradition that a Declaration of Independence was adopted by Mecklenburg County in May, 1775.

of Graham says: "Of commanding figure, elegant manners and most agreeable address, his presence at the levees and receptions was eagerly courted."

As president of the Senate, Graham would have maintained the dignity of the position, for his manners, while elegant, were genial only with intimate friends and he usually maintained a certain reserve. But though somewhat formal in society, Graham was not so before a jury, a Legislature, or a general audience. It was said of him that he knew the danger of "the logical short cut" in dealing with public questions and that his addresses, though always well ordered, were never closely reasoned. "His style was that which finds so much favor among eminent English statesmen, the style in which the results of thought and research are given with the warmth and ease of animated and unpremeditated conversation." Graham's voice was pleasing and well-modulated, his action was easy and graceful, but sometimes forcible when occasion demanded. This change was characteristic of the man. Like the great French generals, such as Vendôme, Masséna and Foch, Graham was at his best when the enemy was winning. "As difficulties thickened around him, his courage seemed to rise and his resources to develop. No man ever fought a losing cause with more courage and constancy." But the hard fighter maintained his self-control and dignity. However vigorous his argument, his face did not change and he never stooped to cajolery, browbeating or personalities.

The Democratic Convention had already met at Baltimore, on June 1. The Barnburners were mostly back in the ranks and there was no difficulty in adopting a platform pledging support to the Compromise, including the Fugitive Slave Law, as a final settlement of the slavery question. But agreement on a candidate was a more difficult matter. The friends of General Cass, notwithstanding his defeat in the last campaign, thought that he should be given another chance. James Buchanan, an old party war horse who had succeeded in supporting legislation favorable to slavery, but who opposed certain of its most indefensible demands which were not of great practical importance, had good prospects.

Stephen A. Douglas of Illinois represented young America. His followers claimed that they ought to replace the Old Fogies who had managed affairs qute long enough. William L. Marcy of New York was a formidable compromise candidate. There were several seekers of the Vice-Presidency whose fortunes were linked with those of aspirants for the first place. In the South, the passage of the Compromise had been followed by a fight over its acceptance. Its friends formed a Union party composed of Whigs and Democrats; its opponents, a States' Rights party which was chiefly made up of Democrats and favored secession. The Union party won victories in various states, and the great majority of the States Rights men acquiesced in the result, abandoned secession and proclaimed themselves Democrats once more. In Mississippi, the Union men had elected a Democrat, H. S. Foote,

Governor, though by a small majority. Foote was reported to be very desirous of the Democratic nomination for Vice-President and willing to return to his old party to obtain it, a reason which could not be publicly announced.

Daniel S. Dickinson, a leading Democratic Hunker of New York, who also supported Cass, hinted that Foote had ulterior ambitions in desiring to run on the same ticket with the elderly Michigander. In Tennessee, the Douglas men brought out Pillow, the state's hero in the Mexican War, for Vice-President; the Buchanan men countered by proposing the popular Governor Trousdale for that office, but were obliged to consent to split even with their opponents. Both Pillow and Trousdale were endorsed by the State Convention and six Buchanan and six Douglas delegates were sent to Baltimore. There was talk of combinations of Cass and Stevenson and of Buchanan and King.

The convention of 1852 closely resembled that of 1844. None of the leading candidates was able to win the nomination, and after a long, confused struggle, the convention on the forty-ninth ballot chose a dark horse, Franklin Pierce of New Hampshire. The hall was hot, the delegates exhausted and little time was given to the selection of a Vice-President. On the first ballot, William R. King was nominated unanimously. While he was generally well regarded, the choice was in part a sop for a defeated candidate and his friends. Cass had had his chance in 1848, and it might be held that he and his followers should ask for nothing more. There would be several opportunities for "young" Mr. Douglas to try again, but it was not unlikely that Buchanan's defeat would be final.[1] The Keystone state might be bitterly offended by the rejection of her son for a man whose experience in public life was so much less than his.

To Buchanan no nomination could have been more agreeable than that of King, with whom he had had the closest relations both politically and personally. King had supported Buchanan's motion to refer the question of excluding anti-slavery documents from the mails in such states as might forbid them, to the committee on the post office instead of a special committee, because the latter course would increase agitation. King, Buchanan and Silas Wright were the only prominent Senators who opposed Clay's bill for the repeal of the law limiting the terms of Federal officers to four years and requiring the President to state his reasons for removals. In March, 1850, Buchanan found himself perturbed by the question which so often embitters the life of a politician: "How wide a straddle should I make?"

Clay's committee of thirteen was considering a compromise but had not yet reported. Buchanan was about to write a public letter on the slavery question. For personal, political, and also for patriotic reasons he wished

---

[1]Buchanan himself wrote to Marcy: "We are now both shelved"; and to a supporter he wrote: "After a long and stormy public life, I shall go into retirement without regret. . . ."

to placate the South. But there was a North to be offended and a strong feeling in Pennsylvania against the extension of slavery; it would be embarrassing indeed, if he should declare that prudence and justice required certain concessions to the South and then a committee of conciliation should propose less! In this dilemma, Buchanan appealed to King, saying: "I wish you to be my mentor, and I now write to you for advice." This call for help was doubtless due in part to the circumstance that King was a member of the committee but there were other reasons that accounted for the fact that he had written him such a letter as he had never written to any other friend. Both gentlemen were bachelors, and at Washington they shared the same apartments. King was the only correspondent who took the liberty of beginning his letters to the formal Pennsylvanian, "Dear Buchanan," and in them he expressed an affection which suggests a sentimental school girl rather than a Senator of the United States.

King had opposed the Compromise of 1850, but when it passed he promptly accepted it for the sake of the Union, and his nomination was a bid for the support of the numerous Democrats in Alabama and elsewhere who had taken a similar course. It might attract many of the Henry Clay Whigs, who, angry at the nomination of Scott and, fearing the anti-slavery wing of their own party, were uncertain what to do. Geographical considerations played but a minor part in the selection of King; a Southerner must be chosen to run with Pierce, but Alabama could not be regarded as a doubtful state. There was also a special personal reason for nominating King for the Vice-Presidency. He was exceptionally well informed on Parliamentary law, had frequently been President *pro tempore* of the Senate and was then holding that office, to which he had been chosen unanimously on the accession of Vice-President Fillmore to the Presidency.

William Rufus King, like his competitor, William Alexander Graham, was a North Carolinian by nativity, education and early political experience. He was born in Sampson County, North Carolina, April 7, 1786, attended the state university, from which he graduated shortly after completing his seventeenth year, became a lawyer and held various state offices. In 1810 he was elected to the national House of Representatives and served until 1816, when he became Secretary of Legation at Naples. Two years later he returned home and immediately removed to Alabama, which was about to be admitted to the Union. He was made president of its constitutional convention, chosen United States Senator and held that position until 1844, when he was appointed Minister to France.

As would be expected in the Senator of a "new" state, King warmly favored a very liberal policy in the disposition of the national domain. As chairman of the Senate Committee on Public Lands, he presented a voluminous report May 18, 1832, which was said to have been written by Thomas Hart Benton, condemning the use of the public lands as a source of governmental revenue and favoring a reduction in the price to fifty cents per acre in order to accelerate sales to the actual settlers. In 1841 he opposed sacrificing a land bill in order to save one for distributing the surplus revenue. In regard to internal improvements King was an orthodox Jacksonian Democrat, and at the close of the session of 1850-51, filibustered to defeat a river and harbor improvement bill. On the bank question, his position was not unlike that of Dallas. Personally he was inclined to a recharter but was not ready to go against Jackson, the party and the feeling of his constituents. King's early nationalism did not modify his partisanship. In 1844 he wrote that he "should view the election of Clay as a death blow to our national prosperity if not to the government itself."

As Minister to France, King's dignified but courteous manners and ample fortune ensured success in the performance of the ceremonial and social duties of his post. His chief public duty was to prevent the government, to which he was accredited, from taking active steps to prevent annexation of Texas, a task which the caution of Louis Philippe and the state of public feeling in France made comparatively easy. But in its execution, King had a dispute with the French Foreign Minister, the historian Guizot.

The French were pressed from two sides. Their *entente* with Britain made necessary a show of friendliness towards a joint protest against the proposed annexation of Texas by the United States; while the relatively small damage such a consummation would do to French interests in the Western hemisphere rendered such a joint protest, with the resultant hostility of the United States, poor policy. Guizot, therefore, while contending in the Chamber of Deputies that the interest of France demanded that the balance of power in the Western hemisphere should not be upset through the annexation of Texas by the United States, was quietly informing King that it would not lead to hostile action on the part of France. Then came the publication of the correspondence between Secretary of State Calhoun and King, in which Guizot was so quoted; editorials in the London newspapers accusing the French of duplicity; and finally a solemn assurance in the London *Times* that King's version of Guizot's statement was "utterly false;" that France actually had joined with Great Britain in a protest against American annexation of Texas.

This statement was immediately copied in the *Journal des Debats,* the ministerial organ. Thus placed in a position where his veracity was questioned, King demanded an explanation of Guizot, reminding him that he had explicitly said that there would be no concerted action with Great Britain. "Impossible! Your Excellency must have misunderstood me. The error arose from my bad English," Guizot exclaimed. "But you speak English perfectly and I jotted down the conversation at the time," King retorted. Guizot went on to assure King that, while France would not acquiesce in the annexation of Texas, she would not take hostile action. He then sent King a letter in his capacity as a private citizen explaining the reasons for his official conduct.

King returned to the United States in 1846 and in 1848 was appointed to a vacancy in the Senate and later elected and reëlected. In the House, King had belonged to the new school Republicans. He strongly supported the declaration of war against Great Britain, and had he remained in North Carolina it is possible that he might have accompanied many of its able political leaders into the Whig party. But like other frontier states, Alabama was strongly Democratic, and environment and personal interest checked King's early latitudinarianism. Nor should he be condemned as acting from consciously selfish reasons. Many men had drawn away from the old States' Rights Republicans and then been frightened back by President Adams' Federalist broad-construction views and the danger to the South and slavery. It is said that the influence of John Randolph had a powerful part in the conversion of King, as it did of others.

King's dignity and moderation kept him during the greater part of his career from a close junction with the fire eaters, but he remained a consistent orthodox Democrat, one of a group of Southern Senators of ability and long service who swayed the Senate and watched carefully over the interests of their section and of slavery. In 1841 King opposed the nomination of Edward Everett as Minister to England, saying that if any man holding his opinions in regard to slavery were confirmed, the Union itself would be dissolved. This provoked from Henry Clay the retort: "And I tell you, Mr. President, that if a gentleman so preëminently qualified for the position of Minister should be rejected by this Senate, and for the reason given by the Senator from Alabama, the Union is dissolved already." He denounced the signers of certain anti-slavery petitions as "weak women and fanatics" who could be easily wrought upon; and said that if the North should persist in its hostile course, he would favor separation. In the struggle over the disposition of the territory acquired from Mexico, King at first joined the extremists of his party, but accepted the Compromise of 1850.

Perhaps the qualities most characteristic of Mr. King were his dignity and regard for order and propriety. A tall, large man of distinguished appearance, he was fitted to hold an unruly Senate in awe. Although conservative in dress as in other matters, he exposed himself to ridicule by retaining the wig of older days, long after it had been discarded by his colleagues. At the memorial meeting of the Senate after King's death, Caleb Cushing said of him: "He stands to the memory, in sharp outline, as it were against the sky, like some chiselled column of antique art, or some consular statue of the imperial republic wrapped in its marble robes, grandly beautiful in the simple dignity and unity of a faultless proportion."

This is from what may be described as a funeral oration by a political ally; opponents when engaged in a heated conflict or even when giving their recollection of it long after, described manifestations of the same qualities in a less friendly manner. When President Tyler vetoed for a second time a bill rechartering the United States Bank, a number of the Democratic Senators called at the White House to express approval of this act of their one-time brother.

A few days later, Henry Clay delighted the Senate with an imaginary description of the gathering. Of King, he said: "Then there was the Senator from Alabama standing upright and gracefully as if he were ready to settle in the most authoritative manner any question of rule or etiquette." Nathan Sargent, a thorough-going Whig describing the speech in his memoirs,[1] says that King was "a nice, precise, natty gentleman very tenacious of the observance of etiquette, who prided himself on his knowledge of the rules of the Senate, and who was ever ready to state his opinion. He was so exactly limned by Mr. Clay in the few words he devoted to him that all who knew him could not but cry out 'How lifelike.' Still there was just enough of caricature in it to add greatly to the merriment, much to the Colonel's[2] chagrin, who was always as serious as an undertaker at a funeral and deemed this sort of thing 'quite out of order' and derogatory to the dignity of the Senate."

Of such a man it is not surprising to learn that "conceding to all men the full measure of what was their due, he was punctilious in the exaction of what was due to himself." But the same authority (Senator Clayton of Delaware, a Henry Clay Whig) said that the manners of Mr. King were "unobtrusive, retiring, gentle," and that the urbanity for which he was noted was that which marks "not so much the man of conventional breeding as the true gentleman at heart." R. M. T. Hunter of Virginia said: "Nor was his one of those cold and impassive characters which shed their light without heat, but its kindly influence fell, with genial and friendly warmth, within whatever circle he might move."

No one would assert that King was one of the great men of his day or even place him in the second rank, but if standards are high, it is creditable to reach the third. Some would deny him even that place. Professor Nichols, in his thorough and interesting monograph, *The Democratic Machine, 1850-1854,* bluntly calls King "a wig-topped mediocrity." His eulogists often admit the absence of brilliant qualities and describe him in language suited to men who miss the reputation which they deserve because their work is not spectacular, but which may also be used to hide the utterly commonplace.

Senator Clayton said of his late colleague, "He was remarkable for his quiet, unobtrusive, but active, practical usefulness as a legislator. He was

---

[1]*Public Men and Events, from the Commencement of Mr. Monroe's Administration in 1817, to the Close of Mr. Fillmore's Administration in 1853.*

[2]Like many men of the day, particularly in the South, Mr. King bore the title of Colonel.

emphatically a *business member* (italics in the original) of the Senate, and, without ostentation, originated and perfected more useful measures than many who filled the public eye by great display. He never sought with some of his contemporaries to earn a brilliant reputation by the exhibition of splendid powers of oratory; and to his honor be it spoken, he never vexed the ear of the Senate with ill-timed, tedious or unnecessary debate." Though not eloquent, King was a clear, pleasing and well informed speaker, and if not brilliant he had that quick perception of the point at issue and that readiness to decide, which are so important in a presiding officer. These qualities, together with his knowledge of the rules of Congressional procedure and his unfailing courtesy, not only secured his election as President *pro tempore* of the Senate when Vice-Presidents Tyler and Fillmore became President, but caused him to be given that position during temporary absences. It was said that he was in the chair of the Senate during the greater part of the terms of five Vice-Presidents.

There were several minor parties that went through the form of putting tickets in the field. None received any electoral votes and none appeared in later campaigns. The only one which showed any popular strength was the "Free Soil Democrats," who nominated John P. Hale of New Hampshire and George W. Julian of Indiana for President and Vice-President respectively.

It is probable that both the Vice-Presidential candidates of the chief political parties strengthened their tickets, certainly Mr. Graham did. The news of his nomination was favorably received in Washington and by the New York papers. The Boston *Journal* approved it and described Graham as able, modest, practical and pure. In the campaign Graham gave testimony to Scott's approval of the Compromise, which was very important in the South. His name was also useful as a party war cry, a matter to which much attention was paid in the forties and fifties. The Democrats ridiculed Scott because of an expression in one of his letters, "a hasty plate of soup." The Whigs refused to be ashamed of the slip and declared that they would give the Democrats Scott soup and Graham bread.

Mr. King's health was poor and he was unable to take an active part in the campaign.[1] Indeed the Democratic leaders feared that he might die on their hands, leaving the party without a candidate for Vice-President, or with one nominated in an irregular manner. But they said little or nothing publicly about this and King was praised for his fidelity to the Constitution and the laws, his knowledge of parliamentary procedure, and his long experience in public affairs. The *Pennsylvanian,* a strongly Buchanan newspaper, said of its hero's friend: "Indeed he seems to be one of the few remaining polished

---

[1]King, however, replied to a serenade at Washington, in which he praised Pierce and made a promise, which was doubtless most pleasing to his hearers, that if elected he would do his best to further the prosperity of Washington.

links now in political life between the great statesmen of the past and the present generation." The Whig organ, the *National Intelligencer,* paid King a somewhat embarrassing compliment, such as has more than once been given to the enemy's second choice, saying that it would have thought it more fit and more politic if the Democrats had reversed the places of their candidates for President and Vice-President.

When election day came, the Whigs were routed. They had pussy-footed, had tried to please both sections and had lost both, carrying only four states, Massachusetts, Vermont, Kentucky and Tennessee. Their candidate for Vice-President could not save his own home state, North Carolina going for Pierce by a small majority. Graham had worked hard, and Scott was stronger at the close of the campaign than at the beginning, but a leading States' Rights and pro-slavery Whig, Thomas L. Clingman, bolted to Pierce. His influence in his own part of the state swung a block of five counties and gave North Carolina to the Democrats, Pierce and King.

King was an ambitious man. After his return from France, he was accused of an almost childish desire to return to the Senate. He had special qualifications for the Vice-Presidency, had been repeatedly supported for it in Democratic conventions, and it was probably the aspiration of his life. He received it, but it came to him in a foreign land as an empty honor bringing no opportunity of service, and under circumstances that often make worldly honors seem poor indeed. King's health, which had improved somewhat in the autumn, became much worse in the winter; as a last resort he tried the mild climate of Cuba and a special act permitted the Vice-Presdential oath to be administered outside the United States. But King's case was hopeless, his last desire was to die at home among his friends. He was brought back to the United States and he barely lived to reach his house, expiring on the day after his arrival.

For Graham, life held much of active and honorable and sometimes successful work. He remained true to Whig principles and to conservatism when many of his allies became Democrats and secessionists. After the disaster of 1852 he made earnest efforts to keep the Whig party alive; when it proved impossible to save it under that name, he supported Fillmore in 1856 and Bell in 1860. After Lincoln's election he, in conjunction with Badger, his ally since the old National Republican days, denied the constitutional right of secession and urged that the time for revolution had not yet come, that North Carolina, having gone into the election, should not revolt because she had been out-voted.

In May, 1861, Graham, Badger and their sympathizers at last admitted that the moment for revolution had arrived, but still urged that the North Carolina Convention rebel, not secede; and presented a declaration setting forth the alleged injuries and the danger of the South and accusing Lincoln of breach of faith. But Jefferson Davis and the other managers of the secession movement were determined that the states should all express the States' Rights constitutional view and simply "resume their sovereignty." They were probably wise. Much depended on the attitude of the Northern Democrats and of Europe, and sovereign states fighting for independence would win much more sympathy than would a rebellion in behalf of slavery. The "Revolutionists" could muster only about forty votes; the fatal ordinance drawn in accordance with the Calhoun view was passed and its opponents, unwilling to weaken the State by division, appended their signatures.

The political situation after the campaign of 1852 was not unlike that which followed the election of Monroe. The minority party had been overwhelmingly defeated, and old issues were dead or excited but little interest. The Democrats, having absorbed many of their opponents, were themselves yielding to their influence. There were prospects of a second era of good feelings. But such hopes were destroyed by the action of Stephen A. Douglas, who forced through Congress a bill which repealed the Missouri Compromise by allowing the settlers in the newly organized territories of Kansas and Nebraska to admit slavery if they so desired it. Part of the Southern Whigs opposed the bill and in the North there was a mighty surge against it. Anti-Slavery men united to fight repeal and in 1854 formed a new party with the time-honored name of Republican, partly chosen to show that their attitude toward slavery was the same as that of Jefferson and Madison, and partly because the members wished to proclaim that they were not revolutionists or abolitionists, but disciples of the patriot's golden age.

There was another new party, the Native American or Know-Nothing, which opposed allowing the foreign-born, and especially the Catholics, to vote or hold office, and favored requiring at least a long preliminary residence, perhaps one of twenty-five years. A nativist movement had been in existence for many years but until recently the men concerned in it had usually opposed or supported the candidates of the regular parties according to their views on the alien question, instead of nominating candidates of their own. But in the early fifties, however, circumstances caused an outbreak of feeling against foreigners and Catholics which led to the formation of a separate party, and conditions were especially favorable for its acquiring temporary strength.

Many Whigs were asking as Webster is said to have done when Tyler's Cabinet resigned, "Where shall I go?" Their old home was merely a mortuary. They considered the Democrats demagogues and architects of ruin. Here was a third party which might afford them a comfortable shelter and with whose principles they had much sympathy. Immigrants had usually been Democrats. In the early days they had supported the "Jacobin" and "Atheist," Thomas Jefferson; in 1844 they, with anti-slavery help, it was true, had defeated Henry Clay. Naturally Federalists and Whigs had considered them undesirable citizens.

The "American" convention was the first to meet, assembling on February 22, 1856. Like the country it was sorely divided by the slavery question.

Early votes showed that the conservatives had a two-thirds majority; and about a fourth of the members, led by Henry Wilson of Massachusetts, a clever politician who had hoped to make the Americans the anti-slavery party of the country, withdrew. The convention then nominated Fillmore for President and Andrew Jackson Donelson for Vice-President. In September, a Whig convention, without accepting nativism, ratified these nominations, but on the sole ground of Mr. Fillmore's character, fitness, and ability to unite the country.

The Democratic convention met on June 2. The Kansas-Nebraska act was a heavy load to carry, particularly as "border ruffians" from Missouri had invaded Kansas and helped the pro-slavery men with their votes and their guns. The convention, however, endorsed the law, and the administration of Pierce. It might seem that logic required that the author or the executor of the law, Douglas or Pierce, be the nominee; but after a long struggle the convention on the seventeenth ballot chose James Buchanan. As in the convention of 1852, Buchanan had the able services of John Slidell as manager and the good fortune to please the pro-slavery South without specially irritating the Democrats of the North. In 1852 President Pierce had appointed him Minister to Great Britain and, while Buchanan fully endorsed non-intervention in the territories, his absence from the United States had prevented him from being personally engaged in the struggle over Kansas.

On the first ballot for Vice-President, Justman of Mississippi received 59 votes, Breckinridge of Kentucky 55, and eight other gentlemen a total of 155. With such division and the leaders so close there seemed promise of further contest. But Douglas' manager, Richardson of Illinois, asked Slidell to support Breckinridge, in other words to permit the friends of the closest contestant for the first place to name the candidate for Vice-President.[1] The Douglas men had been courteous to their opponents and Slidell willingly assented to Richardson's request; most of the other candidates were formally withdrawn and on the second ballot Breckinridge was nominated unanimously.

Slidell's support was not, however, the only reason for his victory. Justman had been deeply concerned in filibustering in Cuba, and many felt that such conduct rendered him an unfit person to be Vice-President. Breckinridge was very popular in his own state, which was doubtful. Though a political opponent of Henry Clay, he was a personal friend and admirer, and on his death had delivered an eloquent eulogy which might make the path to the Democratic camp easier for hesitating Whigs. Breckinridge, himself, was only thirty-five years of age, and if elected would be the youngest of the Vice-Presidents by nearly ten years, a circumstance which could scarcely fail to appeal to the Douglas men, who had been shouting for Young America.

---

[1] In the voting for President, Pierce had grown weaker and weaker, on the fourteenth ballot he was withdrawn and the final battle was between Buchanan and Douglas.

John Cabell Breckinridge came of one of the oldest and most distinguished families of Kentucky.   His grandfather was accredited with the authorship of the famous Kentucky resolutions of 1798.   He himself was born on January 21, 1821, at "Cabell's Dale" near Lexington, Kentucky.   He graduated from Transylvania University, practiced law, served as major in the latter part of the Mexican War and represented Clay's district in the National House for two terms, where he displayed brilliant eloquence.   He refused a third election and an appointment as Minister to Spain and returned to his law practice.   His fellow-Kentuckians, without distinction of party, were proud of Breckinridge and he was loyal to the state and all her institutions, including her famous beverage which he used moderately but regularly and which was to him a faithful friend.[1]

After the nomination, the Cincinnati *Commercial* thus described the personal appearance of the candidate: "He is a tall and gracefully formed young man, with delicate features and would be strikingly handsome if his profile line were more prominent.   Looking at him sidewise his forehead, nose and chin are nearly in a line.   But his eye beams with intelligence, his nose is handsome in outline and the habitual compression of his lips indicates resolute will. On the whole there is a poetic glamour about him. His manner in speaking is proud, defiant, and full of passion, tempered by discretion."

The Republican convention met at Philadelphia.   The members were full of idealistic enthusiasm but the leaders, at least, had some of the wisdom of the serpent.   Both Seward and Chase refused to be candidates, probably because they believed that they could not be elected.   There remained John C. Frémont and John McLean; the latter withdrew but, it being represented that Frémont could not carry Pennsylvania, whose support was necessary for success, he again consented to stand.   The two men represented different sections of the imperfectly amalgamated party.   McLean was the candidate of the old Whigs who had been driven by the passage of the Kansas and Nebraska bill and by the outrages in Kansas to enlist under a new banner, but who, though they were levying war against slavery, would not make it a war to the knife, and like true Whigs shrank from extreme action.

John C. Frémont, young, ardent and romantic, the Pathfinder who had explored and then helped to conquer California, was classed as an ex-Democrat.   His wife, the charming and devoted Jessie, was a daughter of that old Jacksonian, Thomas H. Benton, who, after thirty years of service, had been defeated for reëlection to the Senate by the Southern wing of his party. Such leadership might be proof to the former Democrats that the Republicans were not Whigs in disguise.   An informal ballot was taken.   Frémont received 359

---

[1]Breckinridge was one of the officers who negotiated for the surrender of Johnston's army.   It is said that Sherman was so rash as to offer whiskey to the parched Confederates, and that thereupon Breckinridge, who had been dull and apathetic, blazed forth into a learned and brilliant legal argument which Sherman found most difficult to answer.

votes to 196 for McLean, and scattering 3, and Frémont was then nominated unanimously.

When the convention assembled there appeared to be no decisive preference for any individual for Vice-President but there was a strong belief, probably because of the expected nomination of Frémont, that an old conservative Whig would be chosen. The names of Banks and Wilson of Massachusetts, Dayton of New Jersey and "Proviso" Wilmot of Pennsylvania were freely discussed. On June 18, the day of nomination, James S. Pike, the correspondent of the New York *Tribune,* wrote to his paper that the Vice-Presidency was engrossing all minds, that everybody was discussing candidates, possible and impossible, and that there was much feeling between the East and the West. Massachusetts, which had claims for recognition, begged the convention to let her alone, saying that the nomination of Governor Banks, Senator Wilson or Senator Sumner would make a vacancy whose filling would "throw fire brands amongst us."

Ohio was divided between two candidates and so presented neither. Pennsylvania was in a similar situation. Johnson, the nominee for Vice-President of the seceding "Americans," was a citizen of that state and the "Americans" doubtless hoped that their refraining from nominating a President would bring from the Republicans an acceptance of him for the second place on their ticket. But they believed that the choice of Johnson would awaken old quarrels in Pennsylvania and lose the state. Wilmot was proposed as one who would be a tower of strength in Pennsylvania and make success there sure. But William Jay rose to say that "while he entertained the highest respect for Judge Wilmot, he did not think it would be wise to nominate a second Democrat." Wilmot himself, though strongly supported in Pennsylvania and New York, had declined to run and Thaddeus Stevens withdrew his name.

The Indiana delegation worked hard for the state's favorite son, Colonel Henry S. Lane, the chairman of the convention. But the most interesting candidature today is that of Abraham Lincoln of Illinois. Unfortunately for his success, he was not brought forward with any earnestness until after the convention had begun its work. But late on June 17, his friend, W. S. Archer, discussed his nomination with the members of the Illinois delegation and from eight o'clock till midnight they worked earnestly in Lincoln's behalf. Ohio and Pennsylvania, whose support was much desired, proved rather irresponsive, but Allison of Pennsylvania consented to nominate Lincoln. Judge Spalding of Ohio, asked half in jest: "Will Mr. Lincoln fight?" Whereat, says the New York *Times,* "Archer leaped a full foot and a half in the air, waved his long arms and shouted, 'Yes, sir, he is a son of Kentucky!' " John M. Palmer of Illinois, who seconded the nomination, said that, like Jay, he admired Wilmot, and that he was going to name his next boy after him, but that he believed that they could lick Buchanan a little easier if they had Lincoln on the ticket with John C. Frémont.

As in the nomination for the Presidency, an informal ballot was first taken. Dayton received 159, Lincoln 110,[1] Banks 46, and twelve others a few votes each. Lincoln accepted the result very cheerfully. It is said that when told of the vote given him he replied that there must be a mistake, that there was a great man named Lincoln in Massachusetts. This may be one of the many aprocryphal stories told of Lincoln, but it is certain that he wrote to a friend: "When you meet Judge Dayton, present my respects and tell him that I think him a far better man than I for the position he is in, and that I shall support him and Col. Frémont most cordially."

Dayton's nomination was a sop to conservatives and former Whigs, men whom it was most important to conciliate. Lincoln, in a personal letter, had urged the nomination of McLean on the ground that many would vote for him who could stand the nomination of Blair or Frémont for Vice-President, but would go no further. The Newark *Daily Advertiser* approvingly quoted the Trenton *State Gazette,* which said that the nomination of Dayton would "secure the earnest support of all the substantial class of Jerseymen, even if they were disposed to be lukewarm on other grounds. His name will add great strength to the ticket, his past career as a Whig of the old school furnishing a sufficient guarantee that an administration with which he is connected will be restrained from any extreme measures which would tend to impair the domestic peace or unity of the states. Those who preferred Judge McLean and who doubted J. C. Frémont's ability to carry this state are perfectly reconciled by the nomination of Judge Dayton."

The Boston *Chronicle* said: "His position, as far as we are aware, has always been perpendicular and firm against making any new concessions to the slave power, but in favor of fulfilling all settled compromises to the letter." Minor reasons for the nomination of Dayton were his residence in a doubtful state and the fact that he had held relations with both Pennsylvanians and "Americans." His connection with Pennsylvania, due to his residence on the border at Trenton, was a powerful factor in giving him the victory over Lincoln; his being earlier in the field was also a great advantage.

William Lewis Dayton was born at Basking Ridge, New Jersey, on February 17, 1807, of an influential New Jersey family. His grand-uncle, Elias Dayton and Elias' son, Jonathan, both served in the army of the Revolution, the former attaining the rank of brigadier-general. The latter was prominent in political life, became Speaker of the National House and United States Senator, and had dubious relations with Aaron Burr. William L. Dayton was graduated from Princeton in 1825, became a lawyer, served as justice of the state Supreme Court from 1838 to 1842 when he was appointed to a vacancy in the United States Senate, and remained there until 1851. He disapproved of the

---

[1] These votes were widely scattered, no state contributing many except Illinois and Indiana; Illinois naturally voted for her own son, and probably Indiana felt that Lane's chances were hopeless and that the second best thing was to help her next door neighbor.

extension of slavery and lost a reëlection because of his opposition to the Compromise of 1850.

It was said of Mr. Dayton after his death that he was always a conciliator and harmonizer, and it was added also that he was a man of large appetite and fond of the pleasures of the table.[1] These qualities are suitable for a Vice-President since it is his duty to maintain order and expedite business in the Senate, and he is expected to attend and to give many official dinners.

The convention sent the New Jersey delegation to Trenton to inform Mr. Dayton of his nomination. In reply, the candidate made a brief speech condemning the repeal of the Missouri Compromise, favoring the admission of Kansas as a state, approving river and harbor improvements and the building of a railroad to the Pacific, and expressing the hope that the people would give and demand freedom of conscience and of speech. Mr. Dayton praised Frémont but did not attack Buchanan, saying that he wished the contest to be one of principles, not men. The speech evidently was meant to please opponents of slavery, Old Line Whigs, and those who believed religious discrimination to be contrary to the spirit of our government, and it doubtless did so; but Dayton's compliment to Frémont had little effect on that gentleman. He said after the election that the nomination of Dayton was the great mistake of the convention; that if the party had taken Cameron and had paid more attention to Pennsylvania, the result would have been different.

But Cameron would have been a strange head of a moral movement. In his own state he was the head of a powerful faction of the Republicans, but not the leader of the party; and the nomination of a former very active Democratic politician to run with Frémont, who had been a Democrat, would have angered the ex-Whigs. It may be, however, that the Republicans, after promising all the speakers, men and money needed to carry Pennsylvania, neglected her.[2]

Breckinridge took an active part in the campaign, stumping Illinois and Indiana. The Boston *Journal* alleged that leading Democrats at Washington had written him that unless he did so, both states were lost. Whether from Breckinridge's eloquence and Republican mismanagement or from conservatism and fear that Republican success would mean disunion, Illinois, Indiana, and Pennsylvania all went Democratic, as did Dayton's own state of New Jersey. Kentucky, as was expected, stood by her brilliant son. Buchanan was elected by 174 electoral votes to 114 for Frémont and 8 (Maryland) for Fillmore. The latter, however, had a large but unconcentrated popular vote.

In the administration of President Buchanan, the schism over slavery widened greatly. The decision of the Supreme Court in the case of Dred Scott, that Congress had no power to exclude slavery from a territory, shocked the North and strengthened the Republicans. The attempt to force

---

[1]He died suddenly, a few hours after a heavy dinner, which included an ample quantity of pumpkin pie.
[2]See Going, *David Wilmot, Free Soiler*, pp. 492-93.

on Kansas a state constitution which would allow citizens to keep slaves owned by them in the territory at the time of admission, caused a definite breach between Douglas and the administration. On the other hand, the raid of John Brown and the honors paid to his memory in many parts of the North, greatly inflamed the South.

The Democratic convention for the nomination of a President and Vice-President, met at Charleston on April 23, 1860. When it refused to adopt a platform pledging support of the decisions of the Supreme Court, a number of Southern delegates withdrew; and after repeated failures to obtain for any candidate a two-thirds majority of the number of delegates entitled to seats, the convention adjourned to meet at Baltimore on June 18. At Baltimore there were further secessions, and finally the convention chose Douglas by a vote of two-thirds of those present and declared him the nominee of the party. A resolution was added to the platform stating that, with respect to any existing constitutional restriction on the territorial legislatures in regard to their domestic institutions, it ought to be enforced by the National Government, if it had been or whenever it should be, passed upon by the Supreme Court. The resolve avoided the question whether a part of the Dred Scott decision was of no force because not required by the case under determination; but it might be interpreted to give countenance to a national slave code for the territories.

Benjamin Fitzpatrick was born in Georgia but moved to Alabama about 1818. His wife was a member of the influential Elmore family of South Carolina; her sister married Dixon H. Lewis, a political leader and United States Senator from Alabama; and these connections were very useful in advancing Mr. Fitzpatrick's fortunes. Soon after his marriage, ill-health compelled him to cease legal practice and retire to his plantation. In 1840, he became Governor of Alabama and served for five years. In 1848 he was appointed to fill the vacancy in the United States Senate caused by the death of his brother-in-law, Dixon H. Lewis. In 1853 he was designated in like manner to succeed King and was elected in 1855. He also succeeded King as President *pro tempore* and served four sessions, thus being heir apparent throughout Pierce's administration.

Like King, too, he had opposed the Compromise of 1850, but accepted it after its passage. Mr. Fitzpatrick was courteous but honest and frank. He scrupulously performed all his duties as a public officer and required those under him to do the same.

His nomination as a companion of Douglas by a thoroughly Douglas convention was somewhat of a surprise, but the Douglas men were more than willing to follow the custom of giving the second place to the faction they had defeated. Du Bose, in his *Life of William L. Yancey* of Alabama, an early and strenuous advocate of secession, has this version of the nomination. The friends of Douglas invited Yancey to the room of one of them, G. E. Pugh, of Ohio, and there G. N. Saunders, a prominent South Carolinian, divulged that in 1856 Douglas had demanded the right to name the candidate for the Vice-Presidency. Saunders then proceeded to offer the place to Yancey, with the succession in 1864, and even referred to Douglas' poor health (Douglas died the next year) as a pledge that Yancey would receive the promotion before the four years were up. But Yancey was not to be tempted.

The nomination of Fitzpatrick was well received at Washington, where it was regarded as a judicious selection of a good compromise candidate. As was the custom, on receipt of the news, the fortunate one was promptly serenaded; but he had gone to bed, and requested a friend to return thanks for the political and musical compliment. The failure to appear and the careful limitation of the reply to simple thanks was significant. Fitzpatrick was thought to desire the Vice-Presidency, because he believed that his reëlection to the Senate was very doubtful, and it was rumored that he had been allied with Douglas for over a year; but after a delay of two days he wrote to the notification committee, declining the nomination.

He placed his refusal of the honor on the grounds that it came from a divided Democracy. The Black Republicans and the Constitutional Union parties had met harmoniously and put forward candidates for President and Vice-President. But the Democrats presented a divided camp. "What a melancholy spectacle; it is calculated to cause every Democratic citizen, who cherishes the Constitution of his country, to despond if not to despair, of the durability of the Union." With a view to the "restoration of the peace, harmony, and perfect concord" of the party, no alternative was left him but to decline the nomination.

Should the old convention be summoned from its grave or should a new one be assembled? It was doubtful if there was any power to take the first course, and the second would mean great trouble and perhaps more quarrels. In these circumstances the executive committee determined to assume authority to fill the vacancy, and after consulting with Mr. Douglas, nominated for Vice-President, Herschel Vespasian Johnson of Georgia. When men are born at the edge of an advancing tide of settlement it is sometimes difficult to give a name to the place where the event occurred, and Mr. Johnson tells us in his *Autobiography,* that he was born on September 18, 1812, "within about three miles of Farmers Bridge, across Brier Creek, in the piney wood of Burke County, state of Georgia." At the age of twenty-two he graduated from Franklin College, later the University of Georgia, having Howell Cobb for a classmate and Alexander H. Stephens, two years his senior in grade, for an intimate friend. After graduation, Mr. Johnson was admitted to the bar and took an important part in the legal and political life of the state. He served four years as judge of the Superior Court and four as Governor. He sat in the United States Senate one year.

Mr. Johnson took great interest in educational and literary matters and wrote well. His public speeches, which he preserved with great care, were admired by his hearers, but have too much of the florid rhetoric which was then popular. In religion Johnson was a Swedenborgian; he was credited with a belief in "spiritualism," and a faction which he headed was nick-named "the spirit rappers."

On the slavery question, Mr. Johnson was a firm advocate of Southern claims. In speaking on the California and New Mexico Government Bill of 1849, he denied that either Congress or a local Legislature could exclude slavery from the territories and said that strict construction was the only hope of the South. In July, 1849, he wrote Calhoun that he did not see how it was possible to refuse admission to California but that, "it seems to me that before the South consents we ought to demand a just compromise as to New Mexico, and a total abandonment on the part of the North of their aggression in respect to the District (of Columbia) and slavery in the states. Now is the time for a settlement in full. If we yield now we are gone. Concession will invite further insult and we shall utterly lose our self-respect and become worthy our degraded fate! How dark the future looks! If you have time, drop me a word on these points. I want light and I desire to know the views of our sage statesmen."

When the "Georgia Platform," endorsing the Compromise of 1850 but advocating secession in case of various specified "aggressions," was adopted, Johnson became its staunch supporter. In 1856 Robert Toombs wrote to a friend: "I am strongly inclined to the opinion that you are right in your estimate of Johnson. I firmly believe that he is sincere and reliable upon the Georgia platform and would risk himself in defense of great public principles —and that is a rare virtue."

When the Democratic convention at Charleston split, the question arose as to what the Georgia Democrats would do. Johnson says in his *Autobiography,* "I had seen for years, that the only hope of the Union was in the integrity and ascendancy of the National Democracy. After the surrender of California, I saw there was nothing worth struggling for, so far as slavery was concerned, and I have become satisfied that slavery was safer in, than out of, the Union. In addition to all this, I knew that Douglas was our true friend; that he was honest, bold and wise. He had my sympathy in the war raised against him by unprincipled Democrats and Presidential aspirants. Therefore I could not sanction and approve the conduct of that portion of the Georgia delegates who had withdrawn from the Convention at Charleston. I knew that the overthrow of the National Democracy was the prelude to disunion and that disunion promised nothing but unmixed evil to the South."

A special Democratic State Convention discussed the matter at great length and with ability and earnestness. Johnson set forth his views with much eloquence; both friends and opponents told him that he had made the best speech of his life. But the convention approved the action of the bolters and sent the old delegation with its former instructions, to the conventions of both wings. About fifty protested, formed a separate convention and sent a delegation to Baltimore. There Johnson was frequently approached on the subject of the nomination for the Vice-Presidency, but he resolutely declined it. He says in his *Autobiography* that he had no wish for the honor which, because of the rupture of the party, he knew to be an empty one.

After Fitzpatrick's resignation, however, he accepted. He told the executive committee that he had persistently refused to countenance his own nomination "but invariably urged that if Georgia were to be thus honored, it was due to another of her sons, distinguished for his talents and great public services. This was my earnest desire and the desire of the delegation of which I was a member. But the convention in its wisdom deemed it best to nominate a statesman of Alabama. This was entirely satisfactory. Alabama is the child of Georgia, and the mother cordially responds to any compliment bestowed upon her daughter." Mr. Johnson criticized the action of the seceding delegates as precipitate and unwarranted and declared that the safety of the country depended on the maintenance of the principles of non-intervention.

The seceders at Baltimore met with certain seceders from Charleston and delegates who had been refused seats by the Douglas convention, and nominated Vice-President Breckinridge for President and Joseph Lane of Oregon for Vice-President. A convention at Richmond ratified these nominations.

Joseph Lane was born on December 14, 1801, in Buncombe County, North Carolina. He moved with his family to Vanderburg County, Indiana, and was active in the building up of the state. He served in the Mexican War, where he met with both good and ill fortune. His regiment broke at Buena Vista and was exhorted by the commander of a Mississippi regiment, Colonel Jefferson Davis, to rally behind the "wall" of his own men. Indiana was long taunted with the conduct of her troops. As late as 1883, in a debate on a bill giving a service pension to soldiers of the Mexican War, when Senator Voorhees of Indiana reproached Massachusetts with sending but one regiment to the war, Senator Hoar asked if it did not behave as well as an Indiana regiment. The Hoosiers maintained that their brethren were greatly outnumbered and placed in a position which no troops could have maintained, and that what misconduct there was, was the fault of officers appointed for political reasons.

In 1849, he moved to Oregon and in 1859 was elected Senator from the new state. His nomination for Vice-President was clearly a bid for local support. His popularity in Indiana might save that state for the Democrats and his residence in Oregon would perform the same service there. The latter state with its three electoral votes would ordinarily be of little importance but in 1860 it might be decisive. But it was by no means impossible that the election would be thrown into the House and the vote of Oregon would be as valuable as that of New York.

The Republican convention met at Chicago on May 16. The members were very hopeful of victory and somewhat more ready to use political strategy to obtain it than they had been in 1856. Lincoln and Seward were the leading candidates and the former was nominated on the third ballot chiefly because it was thought he would be more likely to carry certain important states and because he was supposed to be less radical than Seward, who could at times use language which was, or at least appeared to be, startlingly extreme. Seward was also injured by his connection with politicians and business concerns of unsavory reputation and by his unpopularity with the "Americans."

There had been much scheming for the Vice-Presidency. Lincoln's friends had brought him forward originally, less with an expectation of success than with a hope of getting the Vice-Presidency for him. Seward thought well of Senator William Pitt Fessenden of Maine as a compromise candidate if he himself should fail of the nomination. In such a case it was intended to give the nomination for Vice-President to Lincoln. But though this would combine the East and the West, yet it would make the ticket wholly ex-Whig, a very unwise step. If Seward should be nominated, his friends planned to conciliate Illinois by nominating one of her Senators, the ex-Democrat, Lyman Trumbull, for Vice-President.

The followers of Simon Cameron, the Pennsylvania boss, were ready to support a Cameron-Lincoln ticket and the Illinois delegates were willing to accept it reversed. Cameron, however, declined the Vice-Presidency. Lincoln appears to have consented to take the second place, according to one account, if his friends thought this wise; according to another, if his acceptance were necessary to keep the party together. Cameron had no chance for the Presidency but it was believed at Washington that Pennsylvania would be given the Vice-Presidency as a bait. In such a case the candidate would probably be John Hickman who had the support of the Blair influence and of the friends of "bluff Ben Wade" of Ohio, who hoped to make their leader President. The latter combination was an appropriate one, for both men were of the same type. There was also talk of Lincoln and Banks. Kentucky presented one of her sons, Cassius M. Clay, who had been fighting slavery for twenty years and who, ten years before, had led a strong movement for emancipation in his state.

The nomination of Lincoln, of course, greatly affected that for Vice-President. His friends told the New York delegates that any one whom they might name would be nominated by acclamation. But they felt that a great man had been sacrificed to a small one and refused the trivial atonement offered. They, however, let it be known that their preference was for Hannibal Hamlin of Maine. The Cameron men were said to have abandoned Hickman for an assurance that their leader would be given the Treasury.[1] Clay was weak with the politicians because, although a nomination from a slave state could be used to meet the charge that the Republican was a sectional party, yet Clay could carry no doubtful state.

As in 1856, there was a new major party in the field. This was known as the Constitutional Union party. It was chiefly composed of old line Whigs

---

[1]There is good evidence that, after having asked this, they turned to Lincoln on a promise by his manager, given against Lincoln's direction to make no binding contracts, of an unnamed place in the Cabinet.

but it hoped also to draw in Americans, dissatisfied Democrats, moderate Republicans and even the more radical Republicans, when they found that they could not succeed by themselves, into a great conservative party such as the Whig had been. It was even proposed to adopt the old name, but it was feared that this would offend the "Americans" and the party received the honorable title of Constitutional Union. Its national convention was held at Baltimore on May 9, 1860. It anticipated the Christian Scientists of a later day, decided to cure the diseases of the country by ignoring them, and offered as its platform a brief declaration in favor of the Constitution, the Union and the enforcement of the laws.

On the question of candidates, there was a serious division. The Whig and Northern section wished for John Bell of Tennessee, a reasonably able orthodox Whig. The "American" Southern section supported Samuel Houston, the hero of the Texas war for independence, a wild Jackson Democrat, who was very popular in the South and West. Eight other gentlemen received votes, the four leaders being John J. Crittenden, Edward Everett, John McLean and William A. Graham. On the second ballot, Bell was nominated by a good majority over Houston, most of the supporters of the minor candidates turning to him. Edward Everett was unanimously nominated for Vice-President.

A Bell-Everett ticket must have seemed a very appropriate one. The candidates were elderly, cultured, conservative gentlemen and had been political allies for years. Yet the Constitutional Union party narrowly escaped the mortification of having its candidate for Vice-President refuse to run. Everett had received 25 votes for President but he had taken little interest in the matter; he was only the second choice of the delegates of his own State, Crittenden being the first; and when it appeared probable that the convention would choose Houston and Bell he telegraphed his friend, George S. Hillard, to withdraw his name. Hillard did so, but without stating that he acted by Everett's direction. Everett had never thought of the Vice-Presidency. His biographer tells us that a second place was never to his taste; and he now frankly expressed this feeling in his private correspondence. He wrote to a friend: "It looks like favoring an officer with the command of a sloop-of-war after he had magnanimously waived his claim to the command of the Mediterranean squadron in favor of a Junior officer." Everett explained that he was "nominated with a kind of *furore* which precluded explanations; otherwise, Mr. Hillard would then no doubt have stated that, having declined being a candidate for the first office, he could not think the second ought to be offered me."

Everett wished formally to refuse what had been thrust upon him, but he was entreated not to do so. He was assured that his correspondence would be cared for, and that he would merely be asked for advice on weighty matters; and he finally sent an acceptance. In the conventional manner, he expressed his gratitude for an "honor" which he really considered almost an insult and explained, as far as it was fitting to do publicly, his hesitation to receive it. Mr. Everett quoted from a speech made five years previously on leaving the Senate, in which he gave failing strength as a reason for resigning. He said that he had since then avoided engaging in politics, partly because of his health, which was now in a measure restored, and partly because he was engaged "in a more congenial and, as I venture to think, more useful occupation, that of rallying North and South on the memory of Washington." This consisted of delivering in many cities an oration on Washington for the benefit of a Ladies Association which had bought and was now raising a fund to preserve Mount Vernon.

Mr. Everett feared that it would be impossible for him to do this while before the people as a candidate for office. He admitted that third parties were usually objectionable, but argued that now one was necessary. He urged that the Union must be preserved by harmony, not by military force, and justified the failure of his party to define what it meant by "The Union, the Constitution and the Enforcement of the Laws" on the ground that if men differed on the interpretation of a law they would also differ in expounding any gloss or commentary. Everett ended by highly praising Bell and regretting that the convention had not put it in his power "to pay an equally cordial and emphatic tribute to some worthy candidate for the Vice-Presidency."

The laudation of Bell, while perhaps technically sincere, like Everett's thanks for the nomination, was in essence hypocritical. Everett wrote to Crittenden: "I must add, with all frankness and with entire regard for Mr. Bell, that if it were necessary my name should be used, I should have preferred it that it had been *under your lead,* as the acknowledged *head* of the Constitutional party."

Edward Everett was born at Dorchester, Massachusetts, on April 11, 1794. He graduated from Harvard at the age of seventeen and was chosen pastor of the Brattle Street Church at nineteen. He was elected professor of Greek at Harvard, and after extensive travel in Europe, began his duties as professor. He edited the *North American Review* and delivered many public lectures on a variety of subjects. He served in the United States House of Representatives for ten years, as Governor of Massachusetts for four years, and was defeated for a fifth term by a single vote. He was Minister to England for two years, President of Harvard for three, Secretary of State for a few months after the death of Webster, and served a short term in the Senate.

The nominations for the Vice-Presidency in the campaign of 1860 seem to have drawn more fire from opponents than is usual. Mr. Hamlin had a dark complexion; "Parson" Brownlow of Tennessee, who was campaigning with his usual coarse violence for those refined and cultured gentlemen, Bell and Everett, declared that Hamlin was in mind, manners and appearance so like a negro that if dressed up indifferently he could be sold in the South for a field hand. Rhett, the South Carolina fire-eater, made the direct charge that Hamlin was a mulatto, and the falsehood was widely believed in the South. In the North, Democratic papers praised Hamlin but did so in a way embarrassing to both the candidate and his party. They said that he was more widely known and more experienced than Lincoln and that he was better fitted to be President. The Republican newspapers could hardly meet this attack directly without reflecting on Hamlin, but they praised both candidates, and took pains to answer other possible criticisms on their Vice-President by frank admission, denial, or intimation that the matter was unimportant.

The Boston *Journal* openly referred to Lincoln's and Hamlin's vote-getting abilities. It said: "The ticket is fortunate in the personal character of both its members, in their diverse political training (that is, one had been a Whig and the other a Democrat), in their representative capacities as Republicans, in their local sources of strength as well as in the sections from which their nominations have been secured, and in the absence of all those repellent qualities which might have made impossible the nearly certain combination of all the anti-Democratic elements of the *country* to work for one common and glorious victory."

Senator Hamlin had not formally left the Democratic party until 1856, when its national convention approved the Kansas-Nebraska act. In anticipation of a complaint like that of the laborers, in the parable of the vineyard, who remonstrated because very long and very short service received the same reward, the Detroit *Daily Advertiser* said that Hamlin had been among the first in Congress to resist the attempt to force slavery on the territories. "He is not a late recruit but a veteran in the service, and there is nothing more just than that he should share the honors of the coming victory." The Boston *Journal* said: "As Mr. Lincoln stayed by the old Whig party till it was no more, so Mr. Hamlin remained with the Democracy till it received its mortal wound through the Kansas-Nebraska bill."

One reason for the selection of Hamlin was the obtaining of a balance for the ex-Whig, Lincoln. Shortly after his nomination, Salmon P. Chase said of him: "He has been a life-long Democrat, not of the modern type, but of the school of Jefferson and Franklin. His Democracy is not of the kind which consists in subserviency to the dictates of a slave-holding class, and whose highest manifestation is the alacrity with which its devotees chase a nigger, but that Democracy on which our institutions are based, the expressed will of an intelligent people."

Mr. Hamlin was no Prince Rupert of debate, nor of statesmanship. His early speeches in Congress were of the rhetorical school and he might have attained a fair success in this style, but he soon deliberately abandoned it, partly because no one could hope to rival Clay and Webster and partly because the country, and especially the North, was beginning to weary of long, artificial orations. Moreover, Mr. Hamlin was better fitted by nature to do the work than blow the horn, and he was already noted for his self-control and practical ability.

The Newark *Daily Advertiser,* after calling attention to the candidate's splendid exterior,[1] said: "His character is marked by solid judgment, prudence, caution and conservatism." The old Whig organ, the *National Intelligencer,* spoke highly of Hamlin, calling him a worthy gentleman of well-known fidelity and industry. The *Boston Traveller,* a neutral paper, said: "Mr. Hamlin has always held a high place in the Senate, and probably there is no man in the country who has a better acquaintance with its great interests or who had labored more industriously or intelligently for their advancements."

The Republicans attacked Lane with much vigor. Hickman of Pennsylvania, who had been supported in the Republican convention for Vice-President, though he had been acting with the Know-Nothings, now announced his support of the Republicans. In his speech, he said that the only practical question before the people was whether they should choose Lincoln or throw the election into the House; that the House would fail to elect; that the two leading candidates for Vice-President would be Hamlin and Lane (the latter forecast proved correct); and that the Senate would choose Lane, "who, possessing neither education, experience nor executive ability,[2] has been selected to enable the Senate to make the most of an accident, if it shall occur. To out-Lane Lane in apostasy to the North, in crouching, fawning subserviency to the South, need not be attempted by the most ambitious in that line, not even by a federal office-holder."

Professor E. D. Fite in his history of the campaign of 1860 says: "Henry J. Raymond frequently spoke on this subject; David Dudley Field devoted an entire speech to it in Philadelphia. Almost every Republican speaker sounded the alarm, Lincoln or Lane." The New York *Tribune* asserted that after the Charleston convention voted down the establishment of a Congressional slave code for the territories, Lane three times telegraphed the Indiana delegation to bolt.

The Republicans poured hot shot on Johnson also. Attempts were made to alienate old Whigs from the Douglas ticket by alleging that Johnson had shown disrespect for all their principles. He was accused of saying that owners of slaves in the territories should be protected as were other property owners. John Sherman declared that the Democrats were playing their old game of deception. "They have on the same ticket squatter-sovereignty and a slave code for the territories, unfriendly legislation and the Dred Scott case, non-intervention and the African slave-trade, Douglas and Johnson."

It might have been expected that Everett's moderate and gentle course in the past would have saved him from personal attacks, but such was not the

---

[1]Hamlin was a large man of imposing presence, though friendly and uncondescending in manners, as a good politician should be.

[2]Might not the same objection have been made against Lincoln with even more truth?

case. His refinement had led him to shrink from violent contest and his moderation seemed to many cowardly trimming. An article in the New York *Tribune* reminded the voters that he had failed to attend the indignation meeting at Boston, held after the attack on Sumner, and that the Connecticut Senate had therefore reconsidered and defeated a resolution inviting him to deliver his lecture on Washington before the Legislature. The *Tribune* said: "He would willingly be on the right side if it were quite sure that it were going to be the winning side as well and he would be oftener than he is where he ought always to be, were it not that he lacks that instantaneous apperception and quickness of determination which is essential to a genuine success in public life. He has missed many opportunities, when he might not only have done virtuously but have done wisely in his generation too, when he would have found the right to be great gain into the bargain. And when he dies after his long course of outward success and inward disappointment, what will he leave behind him? An example for the warning of ambitious selfishness in his life, and in his works a few truly admirable passages for the declamation of school-boys."

Everett was an instance of the gentleman and scholar in politics; but the more forward looking of his own kind, like James Russell Lowell and Charles Eliot Norton, condemned him. Lowell told a friend that his letter of acceptance was a convincing statement of the reasons against accepting. More serious, practically, was the repercussion of two of the bravest things Everett ever did. Perley,[1] the correspondent of the Boston *Journal,* wrote to his paper: "Bell is gaining ground in Virginia (he carried the state by a few hundred majority over Breckinridge); but the F. F. V.'s find it hard to swallow Everett, even with the *Saltonstall Amendment* (Italics in the original). They say that he must publicly retract his abolition heresies of 1839, and the Democratic papers assailed him unmercifully." Perley also said that the Know-Nothing papers declared that they never would vote for Everett, "who so denounced and sneered at Sam."[2]

The Democratic candidate for Vice-President took an active part in the campaign. As soon as Johnson reached home he began a series of speeches defending his own course and that of the Douglas wing of the Democracy. He was soon asked to make a tour in New York, the West and Northwest. He accepted and traveled four thousand miles, addressing immense meetings. Mr. Johnson says in his *Autobiography:* "A thing that impressed me was the enthusiasm of the people. I found them as warm-blooded as those of the sunny South. It was remarkable what immense gatherings could be had on three or four days notice. Less than ten thousand was considered a small meeting and deplored as a failure. Their devotion to the Union was almost idolatry and I came to the conclusion that peaceable secession was out of the

---

[1] "Perley" was the pen-name of Benjamin Perley Poore.
[2] Sam was the nickname for the Know-Nothings, one of whose pass-words was said to be the question: "Have you seen Sam?"

question and that war with such a people should be avoided as long as possible."

Johnson denounced Breckinridge and Lane as enemies to the Constitution and seemed to think that they were as dangerous to the Union as were the Republicans. On another occasion he spoke contemptuously of Bell. Johnson stated that he was treated with great courtesy in the North, but once at least he was interrupted and contradicted. The Southerners were fond of asserting that Northern factory workers were really slaves. At one factory town Johnson said: "Look at the slaves in your own workshops. They are driven to the polls at the behest of their masters, under penalty of being discharged." At this came shouts of, "Not so," "No sir," "No sir."

Lane took the stump and called on the people to save the Union by supporting his wing of the party; but to the crucial question of what ought to be done if Lincoln should be elected, he replied that four years would quickly pass and that the candidates of the Breckinridge party would then prevail.

Everett took no part in the campaign but his record was brought forward as an issue. It was said that the Constitutional party was one thing in the North, and something else in the South. Bell, himself, had at various times been on both sides of the slavery question; now he was pictured in the Southern states as a friend of slavery, and in Everett's own state of Massachusetts, as its foe. Politicians of the opposition parties reminded the public that Everett had once said that "slavery was a social, political, and moral evil" and that he had openly approved Sumner's course in the Senate with respect to the Kansas question. In view of the state of public sentiment, it was difficult for any party which refused to commit itself on the slavery question, to stand the gaff of a political campaign. And, as the outcome showed, it was not of great moment as to what the exact sentiments of Bell and Everett on that vexing question were.

Hamlin made one speech in Boston and marched in the ranks of the Wide Awakes, a Republican club of a semi-military nature, which spread throughout the North. But he did not, as had been his former custom, take the stump in Maine, for there it was held proper for nominees for the chief national offices to await calmly the judgment of the people. Mr. Hamlin did, however, do important work in organizing the state at the request of Lincoln, himself. The last names of all the Vice-Presidential candidates were not by themselves suited for songs and war cries, but that of Hamlin, like Breckinridge's four years before, combined well with his chief's. Many Republican banners bore the inscription, Abra*Ham Lin*coln, and the combination was the source of many jokes and puns. The Christian names of the candidates were also stirring. Schuyler Colfax, later Vice-President with Grant, wrote that it it had been well said that "with the faith of Abraham and the courage of Hannibal we shall surely conquer wrong and maintain the right." Herschel V. Johnson's Christian name gave a jeer to the Republicans, one paper saying that it was rumored that he had been nominated because the Democrats expected to see stars after the election.

Confidence of the Republicans in victory was well warranted. They were in a minority in the country, but their opponents were divided. In the North they could not concentrate their strength, and the Republican ticket received 180 electoral votes to 123 for all other candidates.

CHAPTER XV.

Vice-Presidential Elections of the War and Reconstruction Periods

AFTER the Republican victory, the more Southern states began to carry out their threats of secession, and when Lincoln and Hamlin were inaugurated, South Carolina, Alabama, Mississippi, Louisiana and Texas had passed ordinances of secession, formed a new union, styled the Confederate States of America, and established a provisional government. Within their boundaries, the United States held only the island forts, Sumter and Pickens. When President Lincoln attempted to provision Fort Sumter, it was bombarded and taken, and when he called for troops to aid him to enforce the laws and maintain the authority of the United States, Virginia, North Carolina, Tennessee and Arkansas joined the Confederacy. Civil war was accepted and staunchly waged by North and South alike.

Parties were divided as well as the country. Stephen A. Douglas came vigorously to the support of the President in his policy of coercion. "There are now," he said, "only two parties, patriots and traitors." Unfortunately, he died on June 3, 1861. After the passing of the first enthusiasm, the defeat of Bull Run, and the rigorous measures taken by the government against opponents of the war, a large section of the Democrats stood forth against "making the war an abolition war," demanded the preservation of "the Union as it was, and the Constitution as it is," and negotiated with the Confederacy. What this faction would do, if the South refused all terms, was not certain. Perhaps a majority of those who belonged to it did not know themselves. But many of their former political allies, now called "War Democrats," remained staunchly in favor of the suppression of the rebellion.

The Republicans were also divided. Some probably were ready to buy the return of the South almost on its own terms. A larger "Radical" section wished to wage the war with slight regard for the legal rights of men who differed from the government, and to seize what they regarded as a God-given opportunity to emancipate the slave. The President and the mass of the

Republicans made the salvation of the Union their great objective to which both the preservation and the abolition of slavery must give way.

Other serious questions were: When the rebellion should be subdued, what ought to be the treatment of the conquered states? And should the President or Congress decide the question? Mr. Lincoln had a plan which he was partly putting into effect for recognizing new state governments, provided that certain conditions were met. Congress had another, which gave practically all power to the law-making body, and it passed a bill for this purpose. The President killed it by a pocket veto because, unlike his own, it refused to recognize what had been done and to accept anything which might be done in the future unless it conformed exactly with the Congressional plan. Two members of Congress, Henry Winter Davis, a Representative from Maryland, and Benjamin F. Wade, a Senator from Ohio, published a furious attack on Lincoln because of his action, accusing him of usurping power. The Radicals of the party were inclined to sympathize with them, partly because the President's plan would allow the new states to exercise a temporary guardianship of the freedmen.

The first political party or faction to meet in convention in 1864 for the nomination of a President and Vice-President was that of the Radicals. About three hundred fifty of their leaders assembled in mass convention at Cleveland, Ohio, on May 31. For President, they unanimously nominated John C. Frémont, then of New York. Frémont had been removed from command in Missouri by Lincoln, had later suffered a like fate in the Shenandoah Valley, and was left without employment. In Missouri, he had issued an Emancipation Proclamation which Lincoln believed untimely and annulled. He had proven disappointing from a military point of view and had given offense to conservative Unionists by his high-handed methods. For Vice-President, the convention nominated, with only a few dissenting votes, its president, John Cochrane of New York, although it had been supposed that the honor would go to B. Gratz Brown of Missouri. John Cochrane was a grandson of Dr. John Cochran (the final *e* was added to the name by the father of the second John) the devoted and efficient chief physician of Washington's army. He was born at Palatine, New York, on August 27, 1813, and attended Union and Hamilton colleges, receiving his Bachelor of Arts from the latter. He became a lawyer and was successful in his profession but was better known as a clever leader in Democratic politics. In 1848, he was an active "Barnburner," but he belonged to the wing which cared more for revenging on Cass the defeat of Van Buren than for preventing the extension of slavery.

Like most of the Barnburners, he soon returned to the Democratic fold. He campaigned for Pierce in 1852 and was rewarded by being made surveyor of the Port of New York. But the old division of the Democratic party remained, former Hunkers and Barnburners being now known as Hards and Softs. After the passage of the Kansas-Nebraska Bill, the two factions held separate conventions and Cochrane's skillful management induced the Softs, who were divided much as the Barnburners had been, to accept the law and declare it beneficial to the territories, while at the same time describing it as inexpedient and unnecessary.   Truly, Delegate Cochrane was a spiritual brother of Bird-of-Freedom Sawin, with his desire of facing South by North.

Cochrane served two terms in Congress, from 1857 to 1861, where he sided with the South on the questions that divided the country.   He was a delegate to the Democratic Charleston-Baltimore Convention in 1860, and his appearance and political position at the time were thus described by Murat Halstead:

> "Cochrane is a large but not a big man, full in the region of the vest, wears all his beard, which is coarse and sandy, trimmed short; and is bald—a blemish which he attempts to conceal by combing the hair that remains at the side over the barren region.   His countenance is bold, but not amiable, and there are assurances in his complexion that he is what is known as a generous liver, in fact, he looks as though it would require a very strong cup of coffee to bring him into condition in the morning.   He is a fair type of the fast man of intellect and culture, of the city of New York, whose ambition is to figure in politics.   He is in Congress, as most of our readers know, and can command the ear of the House at any time. His great trouble is his Free Soil record.   He had a very violent attack of Free Soil opinions some years ago.   He took Free Soilism like a distemper, and mounted the Buffalo platform.   He is well over it now, however, with the exception of a single heresy, that of the Homestead Law.   He is for giving homesteads to the actual settlers upon the public land."

Cochrane opposed the nomination of Douglas, yet loyally supported him as the party candidate.   He, however, seemed to retain his sympathy for the South, and in a speech at Richmond, Virginia, on March 14, 1861, he declared that if the state would notify New York of her utimatum, New York would support it.

But the attack on Sumter transformed Cochrane into a Unionist and a Coercionist.   In describing a monster meeting in New York City on April 20, Alexander says:

> "Of the fifty or more speeches delivered from the several platforms, perhaps the address of John Cochrane, whose ridiculous Richmond oration was scarcely a month old, proved the most impressive.   Cochrane had a good presence, a clear penetrating voice, and spoke in round rhetorical periods.   If he sometimes illustrated the passionate and often extravagant declaimer, his style was finished, and his fervid appeals deeply stirred the emotions if they did not

always guide the reason. It was evident that he now spoke with the sincere emotion of one whose mind and heart were filled with the cause for which he pleaded. In his peroration, pointing to the torn flag of Sumter, he raised the vast audience to such a pitch of excitement, that when he dramatically proclaimed his motto to be, 'Our Country, our whole Country,—in any event, a united Country,' the continued cheering was with great difficulty sufficiently suppressed to allow the introduction of another speaker."

Soon after, the convert proved that his new loyalty was not that of a mere politician or talker, by entering the Union Army at the head of a regiment which he had raised himself. He became a brigadier-general but early in 1864 was obliged to leave the service because of ill health. On returning to civil life he acted with the Union Republican party and was elected Attorney-General; but he became dissatisfied with the Administration and entered what President Lincoln described as the Cave of Adullam, at Cleveland. The platform of the dwellers in the Cave stated that the confiscation of the lands of the rebels would be a measure of justice; but both candidates in their letters of acceptance declared themselves opposed to such a measure. Each letter attacked the Administration; Frémont's was violent and extreme, Cochrane's milder and fairer.

The next convention was that called by the Republican National Committee. But the committee disregarded party lines and addressed itself to all "who desire the unconditional maintenance of the Union, the supremacy of the Constitution, and the complete suppression of the existing rebellion with the cause thereof, by vigorous war, and all apt and efficient means." Democrats sat in this "Union" convention and during the election the party took the name of National Union. The convention adopted a platform which called for the prosecution of the war and the unconditional restoration of the Union, and renominated President Lincoln by a roll-call of the states, every delegation but that of Missouri, which was instructed for General Grant, voting in the affirmative.

For Vice-President, the first ballot stood: Andrew Johnson of Tennessee, the vigorous and staunchly Unionist Military-Governor of his State, 200 votes; Hannibal Hamlin of Maine, who was concluding a faithful and satisfactory term as Vice-President, 150; Daniel S. Dickinson of New York, a leading War Democrat, 108; Benjamin Butler of Massachusetts, 28 (20 of these being from Missouri, 2 from Massachusetts, 2 from Rhode Island, 2 from New Hampshire, and 2 from Vermont); L. H. Rousseau of Kentucky, 21 (the solid vote of his state); Schuyler Colfax of Indiana, 6 (Oregon); Ambrose E. Burnside of Rhode Island, 2; Joseph Holt of Kentucky, 2; and David Tod of Ohio, and Preston King of New York, one each.

Immediately, Kentucky swung to Johnson and was followed by Kansas and Oregon. These changes might have been enough to start the usual rush to get in behind the leader, yet Kansas' vote had been much scattered, and Kentucky and Oregon had been grooming dark horses whose heads had just barely peeped out on the track and of whose success their backers themselves must have had little hope. But now the astute Simon Cameron, speaking for powerful and politic Pennsylvania, threw the fifty votes of the state for Johnson and a roar of applause came from the galleries. New Jersey, which had given twelve of her fourteen votes for her neighbor, Dickinson, now plumped for Johnson; and Maine, seeing the day was lost, did the same. Other states bowed to the will of the convention, and the vote as announced stood Johnson 494, Dickinson 17, and Hamlin 9.

Two reasons of public policy were potent in determining Johnson's nomination. It was extremely important to obtain the support of as many War Democrats as possible and Johnson had been one before the war began. In the winter after Lincoln's election, when the North was unnerved, anxious to win back the South by liberal concessions and almost ready to adopt Horace Greeley's advice and "let the erring sisters depart in peace" rather than resort to civil war, Johnson had made a ringing speech in the Senate denouncing secession as treason and clearly implying that it should be suppressed by force. The selection of a Southerner was not all policy. Horace Maynard of Tennessee gave a most powerful description of the sufferings of the Southern Unionist, which moved the convention deeply and is said to have won votes for his candidate, which oratory seldom does! Second, it was thought that the nomination of a Southerner would show Europe that the South itself was divided and help prevent the recognition of the Confederacy by European powers. Such a nomination could also be used to prevent a charge of sectionalism, because of taking both candidates from the North, which had been brought against the Republicans in the last campaign.

The Democrats themselves now did what they had condemned, nominating a President from New Jersey and a Vice-President from Ohio. James Russell Lowell made stinging reference to the inconsistency by declaring with cat-like moderation: "We shall say nothing of the sectional aspect of the nomination, for we do not believe that what we deemed a pitiful electioneering clamor, when raised against our own candidates four years ago, becomes reasonable argument in opposing those of our adversaries now."

To some, however, the "argument from geography" appeared to be against Johnson. The radical and virulent Thaddeus Stevens asked in disgust: "Can't you get a candidate for Vice-President without going down into a damned rebel province for one?" Cameron, with what now seems an intuitive perception of the future, wrote William Pitt Fessenden: "Johnson will be a strong candidate for (before?) the people, but in the contingency of death, I should greatly prefer a man reared and educated in the North." Senator Morrill of Maine, Hamlin's manager, wrote him: "I wish I could feel that we have not made a *bad* (italics in the original) mistake. We have two Western men

(New England was still thinking in terms of East and West as well as North and South) for candidates and one of them in an insurrectionary state."

As a candidate, Johnson had certain advantages over Hamlin. His courage and energy as Military Governor of Tennessee had caused him to be known and admired throughout the North, while his rise from the humblest position and his constant, thoroughgoing championship of the common man, in language often more fit for the stump than the parlor, strongly appealed to the masses. Hamlin had been a Democrat from early youth, even formally remaining one after the passage of the Kansas-Nebraska bill and leaving his party only when, in 1856, its national convention approved the law. In principles, feelings and ways he was democratic and he knew the political value of such a reputation. But his family had been one of means and local prominence; his father was a doctor who had studied at the Harvard Medical School; and in politics he had been first a Federalist and then a Whig. Hannibal's brother was a graduate of Brown. He, himself, when a youth, had enjoyed the friendship of his townsman, Governor Enoch Lincoln, a man of culture, a graduate of Harvard, the son of one Governor of Massachusetts and brother of another. True, Hamlin had grown up on a farm and helped to work it, and he would stand well with "the people"; but he would not make the same appeal as Johnson, while his plainness might repel the rich and scholarly.

The nomination of Johnson was due not only to his own strength but to the effect which the election of either of his chief opponents would have on the filling of other important offices. Charles Sumner had frequently been worsted in encounters with his colleague, William Pitt Fessenden of Maine, who was perhaps the best debater in the Senate, although a less polished rhetorician than Sumner. Both men were able and patriotic but one was an orator, the other a thinker. Sumner often used the Senate as a sounding board for the proclamation of principles. Fessenden treated it as a council for the formulation of definite legislation.

Sumner never had any doubt that he was entirely right and his opponents totally wrong and, from what he regarded as patriotic motives, he set to work to get Mr. Fessenden out of the Senate. The latter's term would expire on March 4, 1865. Should Mr. Hamlin lose the Vice-Presidency, he would probably contest Mr. Fessenden's renomination and, as he was very popular in Maine and a most skillful politician, he would have a good chance of success. Accordingly, Sumner did his best to turn Massachusetts away from Hamlin, and so great was his influence that, notwithstanding the opposition of his colleague, Senator Wilson, and of Governor Andrew, only three delegates from the state voted for the New England candidate. A contributory reason for his triumph was the aid of Governor Tod of Ohio, who hoped to be a compromise choice for Vice-President, if the leaders lost. Another cause was the wish to recognize the War Democrats, and the personal regard in which Dickinson was held.

But Sumner's plot against Fessenden failed. Hamlin, indeed, sought the nomination for Senator but he withdrew at the last moment because, thanks perhaps to the inertness or treachery of his manager, Fessenden was the stronger; and a fight in the Legislative caucus would hurt the party without helping the man who caused it.

But the ejection of Fessenden from public life was not the only reason for the action of the Sumner Radicals. They would have been glad to defeat Lincoln but, as this was impossible, concentrated their energies on getting Secretary Seward, who was regarded as the chief of the Conservative Republicans, out of the Cabinet. Seward was from New York; even the Empire State could not expect to have both the Secretaryship of State and the Vice-Presidency. Give her the latter office and there would surely be a new Secretary. There were two War Democrats in New York who would make strong candidates for the Vice-Presidency: Daniel S. Dickinson and John A. Dix, one, a representative of the "Hard," the other of the "Soft" wing of the party. Dix declined to be a candidate, but Dickinson was willing and his friends urgent. Certain Massachusetts delegates promised help, but though they brought him seventeen votes and thereby defeated Hamlin, they could not give him the victory, for his own state was divided.

Seward's close allies and other Conservatives knew what Dickinson s nomination would mean and spared no effort to prevent it, though they were obliged to conceal their real motive. The night before the convention met, the New York delegation held a conference and took an informal vote to ascertain individual preferences. Hamlin led, but Dickinson was a close second. The exact vote is uncertain. Hamlin's manager, Senator Lot M. Morrill of Maine, reported to his chief that he had received twenty-eight votes, the remainder being divided between Dickinson and Johnson. But John Savage in a life of Johnson written in 1866 states that the vote stood, Hamlin 20, Dickinson 16, Tremaine, Dickinson's manager, 6, and Johnson 8. Savage adds that all the Tremaine, and some of the Johnson voters, really favored Dickinson.[1]

Much canvassing followed the adjournment. Morrill, who seems to have been over-ready to believe agreeable things which were told him, went to bed happy, thinking victory sure. The Dickinson leaders were also much pleased with what they had accomplished. But Massachusetts struck a blow against Hamlin which was fatal to him, and, as it proved, to Dickinson as well. Morrill had been suavely assured that Massachusetts wished to pause a little, but would do Hamlin no harm, and he believed that Rhode Island, Connecticut and New York were waiting to follow Massachusetts. But suddenly Massachusetts announced that she would vote against Hamlin; and New England was with her. Maine, of course, was solid for the Vice-President but in no other New England delegation did he have even a majority, while Massachu-

---

[1] The delegates then adjourned till next morning, which would leave ample time for further conference, as the convention did not meet till ten A. M. the next day.

setts gave him only three out of twenty-six votes, and Connecticut, the state of Secretary Welles, with whom he was not on speaking terms, none. Connecticut's course did not greatly matter for she often acted as a satellite of New York rather than as a part of New England; but the defection of Massachusetts, accompanied by that of New Hampshire, Vermont and Rhode Island, was of tremendous importance.

Great use was made of it to turn Middle Atlantic and Mid-West states from Hamlin. In New York it proved decisive. When her delegation met according to adjournment, Tremaine made a powerful speech of half an hour setting forth the claims of the War Democrats in general and of Dickinson in particular. He urged his hearers as loyal New Yorkers to vote for Dickinson unanimously, and ended with a motion that New York present a New Yorker to the convention as her candidate for the Vice-Presidency. While Tremaine was talking the Seward leaders were making a careful estimate of votes. They decided that they had a majority, though a small one, and Raymond was about to move that New York endorse the old ticket when a report came that Massachusetts had declared against Hamlin. Instant inquiry brought word that she would not support him under any circumstances. The news was astounding; some delegates thought that there must be a grave objection to Hamlin personally. Tremaine saw that the foe was in disorder and like a wise general launched an attack. He called for an informal vote; it was taken and Dickinson led.

But Tremaine was facing a Nestor in war who knew when to make an instantaneous change of front. Thurlow Weed whispered to Raymond: "Take Johnson." The quick-witted Raymond stopped a possible rush to Dickinson by making the point of order that Tremaine's motion to present a New York candidate was before the delegation. Speaking to it, he praised Dickinson highly and expressed deep appreciation of the noble conduct of the War Democrats but said that New York should not confine her recognition of their merits to her own citizens; and lauded the men of the Border States who had remained true though assailed by every temptation; said that the country was more indebted for the victory over the rebellion to Andrew Johnson than to any other man not in the government or the army; and moved that New York make him her choice for Vice-President.

A sharp discussion followed. George William Curtis, who stood by the President but was somewhat Radical in his principles, remarked bitterly that he thought that it ought to be understood that the true reason for the opposition to Dickinson was a wish to keep Seward in the Cabinet. The Seward men were delighted; the effect of the relation of the nomination of Dickinson to the retention of Seward had been publicly mentioned but not by them. Raymond retorted that Curtis had revealed that the true cause of the support of Dickinson was opposition to Seward, and that while he, himself, was willing to assent to any change in the Cabinet which might be for the good of the country, he protested against using Dickinson as an instrument to degrade

Seward. The Dickinson men denied any such intention but Raymond's stroke told, and Tremaine's motion was defeated by a small majority. Raymond then moved that the New York delegates vote not as a unit but as individuals. His motion was carried and a poll stood: Johnson 30, Dickinson 28, Hamlin 7, and Holt 1. Before the result was announced, the Holt delegate and one Hamlin man changed to Johnson, and the vote thus modified was declared to be that of New York.

The most interesting of all the questions connected with Johnson's nomination and perhaps the hardest to solve is: Did President Lincoln plan it? There is no doubt that publicly his position was one of strict neutrality. The President's private secretary, John G. Nicolay, went to the convention, not as a member but merely as an interested spectator. He found the Illinois delegation and its chairman, B. C. Cook, puzzled and worried. They had supposed that the old ticket would be renominated, but a few of their number personally desired Lincoln's defeat, and Leonard Swett of Illinois, a very intimate friend of the President, had telegraphed the delegation urging it to support Holt of Kentucky for Vice-President. This seemed suspicious but if Holt were really Lincoln's choice for Vice-President, the delegation was ready to do his will in this as in other matters. Accordingly Nicolay wrote to his fellow secretary, John Hay: "Cook wants to know confidentially whether Swett is all right; whether in urging Holt for Vice-President he reflects the President's wishes; whether the President has any preference, either personally or on the score of policy, or whether he wished not even to interfere by a confidential indication." The President himself endorsed the letter: "Swett is unquestionably all right. Mr. Holt is a good man but I had not heard or thought of him for V. P. Wish not to interfere about V. P. Cannot interfere about platform. Convention must judge for itself." This would seem to show that Lincoln remained firm in a policy of neutrality; but in after years, statements were made that he did not.

Two days after Mr. Hamlin's death, the Philadelphia *Times* contained an editorial stating that the writer (A. K. McClure) had been invited by Lincoln to a conference just before the Baltimore convention; that Lincoln urged the nomination of Johnson because of the effect which the nomination of a Southerner would have abroad; and that he, himself, returned to Baltimore to work and vote for Johnson's nomination. John G. Nicolay, who was Lincoln's private secretary from his nomination in 1860, until his death, at once telegraphed Mrs. Hamlin that the editorial was "entirely erroneous." The telegram was widely published in the newspapers and a bitter personal controversy followed between Messrs. Nicolay and McClure.

The evidence adduced by each may be briefly summarized as follows: In favor of the theory that Lincoln worked for Johnson's nomination, there is, first, some direct testimony that he wished for the nomination of a War Democrat. General Benjamin F. Butler stated repeatedly that Senator Cameron of Pennsylvania came to him from Lincoln to propose that he should

ANDREW JOHNSON, TENNESSEE, SIXTEENTH VICE-
PRESIDENT OF THE UNITED STATES, 1865.

be a candidate for the nomination as Vice-President, with Lincoln's support, but that he preferred to remain in the army. Cameron at various times gave interviews confirming this statement. On the question directly at issue, Mc-Clure stated that Lincoln asked him to support Johnson. Lamon, an intimate friend of Lincoln, corroborated him. Henry J. Raymond, the editor of the New York *Times,* was a Lincoln leader in the convention. He died before the McClure-Nicolay controversy, but George Jones, the principal owner of the paper, said that he had frequently discussed Johnson's nomination with Raymond, and that McClure was absolutely right. Benjamin C. Truman, Johnson's secretary, declared that he knew that Lincoln favored Johnson's nomination. Judge Pettis of Pennsylvania stated that when he called on Lincoln and asked him whom he favored for Vice-President, he replied in an earnest whisper: "Governor Johnson of Tennessee."

On the other side there is Lincoln's endorsement on Nicolay's letter, Nicolay's statement, and a similar opinion by his colleague, John Hay. Secretary Welles wrote in his diary that Lincoln was inclined to the policy of renominating Hamlin, though personally, his choice was Johnson. Nicolay says that Lincoln told him that as the leading candidates for the Vice-Presidency were all his friends he thought that it would be unbecoming in him to advocate the nomination of any of them, but that privately and personally he would prefer that the old ticket should be renominated. Cook stated years after that, not being satisfied by Lincoln's endorsement on Nicolay's letter, he went to Washington to see the President and became satisfied that he desired the renomination of Hamlin. The telegraphers in the War Department united in testifying from direct or immediately indirect knowledge, that Lincoln showed not pleasure but anxiety on hearing of Johnson's nomination.

In endeavoring to estimate the value of these very contradictory pieces of evidence, it must be remembered that recollections given long after the event are untrustworthy; that in the flight of years imagination often takes the place of memory and that in reminiscences as in nature "great oaks from little acorns grow."

Let us first consider the evidence of Lincoln's favoring Johnson. Mc-Clure's stories are not wholly consistent and he had a very high opinion of his own importance. It is said that when he was about to publish a book some one remarked that it would be another volume in his series, "How I Saved the Union." Butler and Cameron were unscrupulous politicians and their statements must be received with caution. Nevertheless Lincoln's anxiety to win the War Democrats was such that the story of the offer to Butler is by no means improbable. McClure states that Cameron and he had an understanding and that Cameron's apparent support of Hamlin was an intentional deception. Just after the convention Cameron wrote to Senator Fessenden: "I strove hard to renominate Hamlin both for his sake and for yours, but failed only because New England, especially Massachusetts, did not adhere to him."

Of course the letter may have been a mere bit of camouflage to keep the writer on good terms with the Maine statesmen.

Jones' account of his conversations with Raymond is very important, but there is to be set against it a statement of Noah Brooks that Raymond asked him the day before the convention: "Do you know who is Lincoln's choice for Vice-President? I cannot find out." The value of Truman's stories is weakened by the fact that they do not entirely square. Pettis' statement was at first accepted by Mr. Hamlin, but he later came to believe that Pettis had misunderstood the President. It seems strange that Lincoln should thus confide in a comparative stranger. Moreover, Pettis wrote to Johnson congratulating him on his nomination, but dropped no hint that Lincoln desired it.

In regard to the testimony on the other side, it may be said that Lincoln's endorsement on Nicolay's letter is less conclusive than has been asserted. He says that he cannot interfere about the platform; but only that he does not *wish* to interfere about the Vice-Presidency. Undoubtedly he did not *wish* to. The statements of Nicolay, Hay, and Cook are of much importance. Still it must be remembered that it was Lincoln's policy to avoid committing himself and to speak well of all the candidates, and this attitude might easily be misunderstood. The testimony that Lincoln appeared disturbed by the news of Johnson's nomination was given by men of unusual intelligence, who rose to the highest positions in the telegraphic world. An attempt, however, has been made to weaken its force by urging that it was given after they had joined Johnson's political enemies.

Historians disagree on the question. Rhodes accepts the offer to Butler but says nothing about the McClure-Nicolay controversy, and Stanwood also makes no reference to the matter. Dr. Brummer, in his *History of New York During the Civil War,* appears to disbelieve McClure's story. Alexander says: "The reason for Raymond's ardent support of Johnson will probably never be known. In his long and bitter controversy with Nicolay, however, McClure furnished testimony indicating that Lincoln whispered his choice and that Raymond understood it." Morse, in his life of Lincoln, in the *American Statesmen Series,* sides with McClure. Several recent writers on the Reconstruction period, who show a strong admiration for Johnson, have no doubt of Lincoln's intervention in his favor.[1]

The Democratic convention met at Chicago on August 29. It adopted a platform demanding that "after four years of failure to restore the Union by the experiment of war, ... immediate efforts be made for a cessation of hostilities, ... that at the earliest practicable moment, peace may be restored on the basis of the federal Union of the States." Then, by an overwhelming majority it nominated for President, General George B. McClellan, the candidate of those Democrats who, while opposing any interference

---

[1]Lloyd Paul Stryker, in his *Andrew Johnson,* thinks it "incredible" if Lincoln did not have a hand in the nomination of Johnson. George Fort Milton, in *The Age of Hate,* completely accepts McClure's version of the matter.

with slavery or the liberty of public discussion, yet were ready to continue the war rather than dissolve the Union. According to custom the defeated faction was given the Vice-Presidency. On the first ballot the vote for that office stood: Guthrie of Kentucky 65½, Pendleton of Ohio 55½, other candidates 104½, Mr. Nobody (a blank vote) ½. The leader, Mr. Guthrie, had received a comparatively small vote. He had been run close by Mr. Pendleton and he was of the same wing of the party as General McClellan. Accordingly his name was now withdrawn as were those of the other candidates except Mr. Pendleton, and that gentleman was nominated unanimously.

George Hunt Pendleton was of a good family, and a leader in society and in politics. His grandfather, Nathaniel Pendleton, was a nephew of Edmund Pendleton of Virginia, famous as a Whig of the Revolution, though a conservative one, and as a jurist. Following the war, Nathaniel removed to New York, became a friend and follower of Alexander Hamilton and acted as his second in the fatal duel with Burr. Nathaniel's son moved to Ohio in 1818 where he held an honorable position. Both father and son were good lawyers and both were members of Congress.

The grandson, George Hunt, was born at Cincinnati on July 19, 1825. He received "a good academic education" and continued to be a resident of Cincinnati, living in a quarter of the city distinguished for the culture and refinement of those who dwelt there. A "handsome and dashing" young man, he was well fitted to shine in society. Oberholtzer says of him: "Fastidious in his dress and polite and chivalrous in his bearing, he was known as Gentleman George." Though active in politics and able in argument, he avoided personalities. Garfield, when about to meet him in public discussion, wrote: "On some accounts I dislike such a scramble. I hate to be a spectacle, that people go to see as a dog fight. But Pendleton is a gentleman. We shall have a courteous debate." When nominated for Vice-President, Pendleton was completing his fourth consecutive term in Congress. Later he became a United States Senator and died in 1889 as Minister to Germany.

In public life, Pendleton was chiefly known as a Peace Man during the Civil War, an Inflationist after it, and as the godfather of the first civil service reform law, the so-called Pendleton Act of 1883. The last role was the most creditable one, but, though he was rightly honored as the reporter and defender of the law, it was mainly drawn and much of the work creating a public sentiment demanding its passage was performed by that early and steady champion of civil service reform, Dorman B. Eaton.

In 1868, Pendleton sought and nearly obtained the Democratic nomination for President as the representative of the "Ohio Idea," that is, the payment of the principal of the United States bonds in Greenbacks, which would mean the issue of a great quantity of paper money. Pendleton's course subjected him to harsh criticism, because when the Legal Tender Act was before Congress he had opposed it most vigorously saying: "I firmly believe that it (the Government) cannot maintain itself against the shock of the accumulated and manifold dangers which follow inevitably, closely in the wake of an illegal, unsound and depreciated paper currency." He denounced the paying of debts already incurred in paper because, "every promissory note, every bill of exchange, every lease reserving rent, every loan of money reserving interest, every bond issued by the Government, is a contract to which the faith of the obligor is paid in the gold and silver coin of the country." He referred to the evils caused by the paper money of the French Revolution and the suspension of specie payment by England, and followed with the quotation above concerning an illegal, unsound and depreciated paper currency.

After such a definite, uncompromising declaration in favor of specie payment, Pendleton's espousal of inflation seemed to many, rank demagoguism, a manifest barter of truth and right for a chance of being President. Yet, it should be remembered that John Sherman and other Middle West Republicans wavered in their allegiance to hard money; that the bonds themselves promised the interest in coin but the principal only in "dollars"; and that whatever the ultimate general advantage of payment in specie, its first result would be an enormous profit for great capitalists and heavy taxation for the masses.

But in 1864, neither Pendleton's opinions on civil service reform nor on the currency were of much importance, what mattered then was his attitude toward the war. In the winter of 1861, although he had been a supporter of Douglas, he was openly and completely a non-coercionist. He delivered in the House of Representatives and printed and circulated a speech in which he said: "If these Southern states cannot be conciliated, if you gentlemen cannot find it in your hearts to grant their demands, if they must leave the family mansion, I would signalize their departure by tokens of love; I would bid them farewell so tenderly that they would be forever touched by the recollection of it; and if, in the vicissitudes of their separate existence, they should desire to come together with us again in one common government, there should be no pride to be humiliated, there should be no wound inflicted by my hand to be healed. They should come and be welcome to the place they now occupy."

The outbreak of war modified Pendleton's views or, at least, the expression of them. Six Ohio Democratic Congressmen, among whom were Pendleton, William Allen. the jingo of the forties, and the soon to be notorious Vallandigham, issued a public letter declaring that the charge that the Democratic party opposed the Government or favored disbanding the armies was a slander, that what it opposed was waging war in a spirit of oppression or interfering with the rights of a state. Such language could have been used by the mass of the Republicans and by President Lincoln himself, although there might have been a difference as to the meaning of the terms; but the general effect of the address was to encourage the Peace Democrats. As the war progressed, some Democratic papers became so violent in opposition to the Government and the war that soldiers and others of the Union wrecked their offices. Individuals were also attacked. This conduct drew from Pendleton the threat that though he favored opposing the Administration only by peaceful means, if these should be taken away and mob violence imposed, retaliation would follow.

In the House of Representatives, Pendleton was the leader of the Democrats. Though a hard hitter, he was tactful, he had a logical mind and a keen eye for the weakness of an opponent's position, and his speeches were both polished and forceful. His ability was recognized by such Republicans as Thaddeus Stevens and James G. Blaine, the first on the floor of the House, the second in his history.

Pendleton vehemently opposed all legislation which gave rights to the negro or denied them to the states. He fought the arming of the colored men, declaring that if this were done it would be impossible to obtain more money or men. In the debate on the Wade-Davis bill which was based on the theory that the seceded states had by their own act forfeited their rights and might be reconstructed at the pleasure of Congress, Pendleton said: "If this be the alternative of secession I should prefer that secession should succeed. I should prefer to have the Union dissolved, the Confederate States recognized; aye more, I should prefer that secession should go on, if need be, until each state resumes its complete independence. I should prefer thirty-four republics to one despotism . . . . I would rather live a free citizen of a republic no larger than my native county of Hamilton than be the subject of a more splendid empire than a Caesar in his proudest triumphs ever ruled, or a Napoleon in his loftiest flights ever conceived."

Pendleton denounced the Thirteenth Amendment to the Constitution abolishing slavery and said that if it passed, the South would free and arm its slaves, obtain at least the moral support of Europe, and establish its independence. "If," he said, "you propose that amendment on the dissenting states by force, it will be their right to resist you by force and call to their aid all the powers which God and nature have given them to make that force effective. If you propose to establish over them, by force, a constitution which you have just amended by force, I warn you that you will destroy the last lingering hope, faint and small as it now is, that you will ever be able to restore this Union or even to maintain the jurisdiction of the federal Government over those states."

The choice of each convention for Vice-President was well received by its party and of course criticised by its opponents. Mr. Johnson, like Mr. Lincoln, was of humble origin and this was recognized by friends and foes alike and by the candidate himself. When he heard the news of his nomination, he asked: "What will the aristocracy do with a railsplitter for President and a tailor for Vice-President?"

At the North the ticket of Lincoln and Johnson was a drawing card. In primitive cartoons, "Abe" would be exhibited splitting rails to mend the Union. "Andy" would be seen sewing up the torn garment of the Constitution. One cartoon was very effective. It was called "The Rail Splitter and Tailor repairing the Union." On a table there was a large covered globe with the cover, a map of the Union, rent and torn. Andy was sitting on top of the globe busy with his needle and shears, while Abe was prying the rent together. "Take it quietly, Uncle Abe," Andy was saying, "I will draw it closer than ever and the good old Union will be mended."

But the Democratic New York *World* expressed the opinion that: "The age of statesmen is gone; the age of rail splitters and tailors, of buffoons and fanatics has succeeded; . . . . in a crisis of the most appalling magnitude requiring statesmanship of the highest order, the country is asked to consider their claims for the highest stations in the Government. Such nominations in such a conjuncture, are an insult to the common sense of the people. God save the Republic!"

Such, of course, was not the view of the "Union" papers. The New York *Tribune* and the New York *Times* praised Johnson highly. The Union papers of Maine and even of Bangor, Mr. Hamlin's state and city, received Johnson's nomination cordially saying that it was due to reasons which implied no reflection on the Vice-President. The *Jeffersonian,* Mr. Hamlin's special organ, said that the choice of Johnson was made "not from any lack of confidence in the true patriotism, integrity, ability, or statesmanship of the distinguished gentleman who now holds that office, but solely from the desire of making another and more signal recognition of the patriotic services of those few Democrats in seceded or border states who, without waiting to hear the roar of the rebel cannon against Fort Sumter, declared to the country that, live or die, armed secessionists and defiant traitors should be, and must be, coerced into subjection to the Federal laws by the national forces."

The Bangor *Whig* said: "The people of Maine felt a strong interest in the renomination of Hannibal Hamlin, but nevertheless, will cheerfully and cordially support Mr. Johnson. It is peculiarly fitting at this time that the Vice-President should be taken from the Border States, and it is also peculiarly fitting that Mr. Johnson should be the nominee. A man of marked ability, a patriot in the highest sense of the term, thoroughly devoted to freedom, his name will add strength to the ticket and his nomination will be received with unusual favor."

An enthusiastic ratification meeting was held in Bangor, and was addressed by Mr. Hamlin in a magnanimous speech in which he eulogized *both* the nominees. His praise of Johnson was in striking contrast to the subsequent opinions of both himself and of the majority of his auditors. A year later, the *Jeffersonian,* in its report of the meeting stated that Mr. Hamlin said that "from an intimate acquaintance of Andrew Johnson of over a quarter of a century, he knew him to be an honest and incorruptible patriot, a statesman of large experience, and eminently qualified not only for the duties of Vice-President, but for the Presidency, should he, in the providence of God, be called to that post."

The Democratic candidates, like those of the Republicans, were men of similar type. Each was honest, cultured, and belonged distinctly to the "upper classes." The selection of Pendleton was doubtless popular. The War wing of the party had received the nomination for the Presidency, and could hardly object to the opposite faction being given that for Vice-Presidency. Moreover, Pendleton was not so extreme as his fellow Ohioan, Vallandigham.[1]

The New York *Daily News* said that it would have chosen Pendleton for Vice-President in preference to all others and that his nomination was "a tribute worthily offered to the peace sentiment of which he is a worthy champion." The "Unionists" agreed to the description though not to the praise. The *Tribune* called Pendleton "an anti-war Copperhead of the intensest shade."

James Russell Lowell, in an article in the *North American Review,* poured indignant scorn on the Democrats for their inconsistency in placing McClellan and Pendleton on the same ticket. He said: "Meanwhile, the time is getting short and the public impatience peremptory.

'Under *which* king, bezonian? Speak, or die!'

The party found it alike inconvenient to do the one or the other, and ended by a compromise which might serve to keep them alive till after election, but which was as far from any distinct utterance as if their mouths were already full of that official pudding which they hope for as the reward of their amphibological patriotism. Since it was not safe to be either for peace or war, they resolved to satisfy every reasonable expectation by being at the same time both and neither. If you are warlike, there is General McClellan; if pacific, surely you must be suited with Mr. Pendleton; if neither, the combination of the two makes a *tertium quid,* that is neither one nor the other . . . . The nomination is a kind of political *What-is-it?* and voters are expected without asking impertinent questions, to pay their money and make their own choice as to the natural history of the animal. Looked at from the Northern side, it is a raven, the bird of carnage, to be sure, but looking as decorously dove-like as it can; from the Southern, it is a dove, blackened over for the nonce, but letting the olive branch peep from under its wing."

Johnson was ever ready to proclaim and fight for his principles and he answered the call to battle without waiting for its official transmission. When the news of his nomination reached Nashville, a mass meeting was promptly held to serenade and congratulate him. He replied in a characteristic speech showing both the weakness and nobility of the man. With the "inferiority

---

[1]When head of a committee to ask President Lincoln to revoke the order of General Burnside sending Vallandigham into the Confederate lines, his language was more moderate than that of his colleagues.

complex" which was ever with him, he referred to his personal treatment and feelings and proclaimed his scorn of the "exclusive aristocracy about Nashville which affects to condemn all who are not within its little circle." He boasted that he had always defied it and therefore had always compelled its respect.

But he stood with Jefferson and Lincoln in his faith in the people, and one of his sentences recalls the Gettysburg Address and anticipates Woodrow Wilson's by fifty-four years. "I am for putting down this rebellion because it is a war against democracy." Like Webster, he pleaded for Liberty and Union, but he used the former term in a broader sense than did the Massachusetts statesman. "Let us," he said, "fix the foundation of the Government on principles of eternal justice which will endure for all time. . . . I am for emancipation . . . . because it is right . . . . and because in the emancipation of the slaves we break down an odious and dangerous aristocracy. I think that we are freeing more whites than blacks in Tennessee." The speaker called on all to forget differences, unite and save the country and free government in foreign lands. "For myself," he ended, "I mean to stand by the Government until the flag of the Union shall wave over every city, town, hilltop and crossroads in its full power and majesty."

As befitted one who had introduced a Homestead bill in the United States Senate, and who had been a leading champion of such legislation, he said: "I want to see slavery broken up, and when its barriers are thrown down, I want to see industrious, thrifty immigrants pouring in from all parts of the country." But Johnson's love for the people was not accompanied by that fairness and Christian charity for opponents which was the glory of Abraham Lincoln. The lands for the thrifty immigrants were to be obtained by confiscating those of the wealthier rebels, and all who had taken part against the Government were to undergo a long period of probation before being admitted to political power.

Johnson considered this speech an acceptance of the nomination, but as the committee of notification desired a special reply, he wrote a brief letter referring to and summarizing his address, dwelling on the wickedness of slavery and expanding a brief appeal to his former political brethren. "In accepting the nomination," he told them, "I cannot forego the opportunity of saying to my old friends of the Democratic party proper, with whom I have so long and pleasantly been associated, that the hour has now come when that great party can justly vindicate its devotion to true democratic policy . . . . Minor questions of policy should give way to the higher duty of first preserving the Government . . . . This is not the hour for strife and division among ourselves."

Late in October, Johnson delivered another speech at Nashville. There had been much disorder in the State, and his conduct as Governor had been fiercely assailed. His friends countered by a procession in his honor made up chiefly of white mechanics and of negroes, and to them Johnson made a vehement and bitter address. He spoke of the insults he had met because he had risen from and championed the rights of the masses; defended what had been termed "brandishing a club to frighten the people into submission" as necessary to put down the rebellion; referred most bitterly to the immoralities of slavery; of his own authority proclaimed universal freedom in Tennessee; and in response to the enthusiastic calls of the negroes promised if no worthier should arise, to be their Moses and to lead them "through the Red Sea of war and bondage to a fairer state of liberty and peace."

But Johnson was no visionary who believed that a mere declaration of right would work miracles or transform the just-freed slaves into worthy citizens. In his earlier speech he had warned them that "liberty means liberty to work and enjoy the fruits of your labor." Now he demanded of them: "If the law shields those whom you hold dear from the unlawful grasp of lust, ... will you endeavor to be true to yourself, and shun the path of lewdness, crime and vice?"

Johnson did not confine his efforts to words or to the limits of the state. He arranged for an election to be held, and devised a system of registration and required an oath so strict, before a citizen could vote, that the McClellan electors, after appealing in vain to Lincoln to overrule his Military Governor, withdrew their candidacy. Under these circumstances, Lincoln and Johnson carried Tennessee without difficulty, but Congress passed a joint resolution rejecting the votes of seceded states.

Johnson's early and vigorous denunciation of secession and his courage and energy as Military Governor of Tennessee had endeared him to the North. He was a powerful debater, terrible in attack, and he was earnestly entreated by party leaders and managers to take the stump. The chairman of the Illinois State Committee told him that Illinois would be close and begged him to come. Robert G. Ingersoll asked for a speech at Peoria, saying: "Your name would secure an additional attendance of at least 20,000. The name of Johnson has become a household word over the Great West." The Ohio Executive Committee invited him. The chairman of the National Committee, Henry J. Raymond, wished to know if he could not visit the Northeast, saying: "Your position, reputation, and ability give great weight and influence to your words." But the most urgent calls were from Indiana. "I do believe," wrote John B. DeFrees (of Indiana), Superintendent of Public Printing at Washington, "you can do more good in Indiana than any other dozen men."

Speaker Colfax urged that the October elections would settle the Presidential election as they had done in '56 and '60, and that Indiana was by far the hardest of the three states to carry. "No one man living can do us more good than you," he said, offering to pay Johnson's expenses on the trip. J. W. Wright, the Indiana Union Committee chairman, kept up a constant stream of telegraphic appeals. Johnson was unwilling to leave his work at home and attempted to compromise by writing letters for publication, in which he stressed an argument then much and effectively used in the Middle West, that "peace" would bring not peace but the sword, for the separation of North and South would be followed by others and would mean continual war.

But at last Johnson yielded to the call for his personal presence and made a tour of Indiana[1] in company with John Sherman, who states in his *Recollections* that Johnson addressed great audiences, and that his arraignment of the autocracy of slave-holders in the South was very effective.

The probability of "National Union" success varied greatly from time to time. The outcome of the political campaign depended on the military one. In June the prospects of both were good and Lincoln, with that easy optimism which in him was mingled with strong feeling and deep melancholy, could laugh at the Radical convention at Cleveland. But when Sherman failed to reach Atlanta and Grant only succeeded, with ghastly loss and by flank marches rather than fighting, in arriving at what the Confederates called McClellan's graveyard, and Early nearly captured Washington, the North almost despaired. Lincoln and Raymond believed that the chances were greatly in favor of Democratic success. Everything possible must be done to unite their opponents. Earnest appeals were made to Frémont and Cochrane to withdraw and they consented. Frémont did an honorable thing in an ungracious way. He refused the handsome offers made him personally, but in his letter of withdrawal reiterated his heavy censures on the Administration. But Cochrane waived all censure on errors past, and urged his followers to support the Lincoln ticket.

By early November, however, the military situation had become decidedly more favorable to the Union cause. Although McClellan had committed his party to a vigorous prosecution of the war, the defeatist declarations of the Chicago platform could not be entirely neutralized. More and more it became plain that to repudiate the Lincoln administration would be tantamount to a willingness to compromise with the South on the basis of something less than a complete restoration of the Union. Prominent War Democrats supported the Lincoln ticket. The result was its sweeping success in the Electoral College by a vote of 219 to 21, and a popular plurality of almost a half million. Edward Everett wrote exultantly to Charles Francis Adams at London that one of the most agreeable incidents of the election was the "good-humored acquiescence of a large number of Democrats in the result."

On May 20, 1868, the Republican convention met in Chicago to nominate candidates for President and Vice-President, but in performing the first duty the members had merely to sign on the dotted line by casting their ballots for Ulysses S. Grant. General Grant had never voted for a Republican as President. Before the war he was a Democrat; in 1864 he favored Lincoln but

---

[1]Not of Ohio, as is said in a recent life of Johnson.

important engagements prevented his going home to vote. Shortly after the war, he had travelled through the South and had made a report on the situation there which must have been very pleasing to the Democrats. He had had no experience in civil life and many Republican chieftains felt that the Presidency should go to political heroes.

On the other hand, a difference with President Johnson had driven Grant to the side of the Radicals and his support had been of the greatest service to them. A number of the Republican leaders had examined Grant's public statements and had discussed political affairs with him personally, and they were satisfied that his Republicanism could be relied on. But, in fact, they had no choice unless they were prepared to suffer martyrdom for the principle of civil offices for civilians. The situation was not unlike that which brought about the nomination of Tyler in 1848. The people were weary of politicians and ready to turn to an unassuming victorious soldier. The Democrats would have been delighted to welcome back their former brother and the "Republicans had to nominate Grant or else the Democrats would."

But on the selection of a Vice-President, there was no unanimity either in the ranks or among the officers; and the members of the convention, deprived of what might be regarded as their right to a fight over the nomination for the Presidency, turned with zest to the contest for the second honor. There was, however, little ill-feeling. Men fought for the pleasure of the game rather than because they believed that their favorite had super-eminent claims. The day before the meeting of the convention, the correspondent of the New York *Tribune* reported that there was great excitement and that the question, "Who shall the party offer for Vice-President?" had swallowed up all others, including that of the platform.

There were four outstanding candidates: Benjamin F. Wade of Ohio, Reuben Fenton of New York, Henry Wilson of Massachusetts, and Schuyler Colfax of Indiana. There were also minor candidates of whom the chief were: Andrew G. Curtin, the War Governor of Pennsylvania, and ex-Vice-President Hannibal Hamlin. A few other gentlemen received complimentary votes, but they dropped out after the first ballot.

Benjamin F. Wade was born in 1800 at Springfield, Massachusetts. In 1828 he moved to Ohio and settled on the "Western Reserve." In 1851 he was elected to the United States Senate and had served continuously. During Johnson's term he had been President *pro tempore,* and therefore acting Vice-President. As befitted a representative of the Reserve, Wade was intensely opposed to slavery. He was a sincere, frank man, a hard fighter and was popularly known as Bluff Ben Wade and Honest Ben Wade. Wade was sometimes more vigorous than wise. He had been a member of the Congressional Joint Committee on the Conduct of the War, which, in its ignorance of military affairs, often hampered more than it helped. He considered Lincoln far too cautious and conservative, and in 1864 joined Henry Winter

Davis of Maryland in a manifesto opposing the renomination of the President. On questions of reconstruction, Wade was extremely radical, heartily approving the Stevens-Sumner policy of Thorough.

Henry Wilson resembled Wade in many respects, though not in all. He was a self-made man and had from his first entrance into politics opposed slavery and the Southern aristocracy. While a man of strong feelings, perhaps one should say prejudices, he was of a much more flexible nature than Wade.

Reuben Fenton was but forty-nine years of age and therefore a much younger man than either Wade or Wilson, but he had had considerable experience in public life. He had sat for ten years in the House of Representatives and was now serving a second term as Governor of New York. Alexander describes him at the time of his nomination for Governor as ". . . . a well-to-do business man, without oratorical gifts, or statesmanlike qualities, but with a surprising genius for public life. He quickly discerned the drift of popular sentiment and had seldom made a glaring mistake." Fenton was a superb organizer. His chief accomplishment in Congress was the forming of a combination that made Galusha A. Grow, Speaker of the House. He saw that his constituents were duly cared for, and made many friends and but few enemies. "He was suave in address, so suave, indeed, that his enemies often charged him with insincerity and even duplicity, but his gracious manner, exhibited to the plainest woman and most trifling man, won the hearts of the people as quickly as his political favors recruited the large and devoted following that remained steadfast to the end."

The fourth candidate was Schuyler Colfax. He was born in New York City on March 23, 1823, but had lived in Indiana since he was thirteen years old. He first distinguished himself as the editor of the newspaper of a country town, was a zealous Whig, and a strong anti-slavery man.

In 1854 he was elected to Congress and had held his seat for fourteen years. In 1863 he was chosen Speaker and was reëlected in 1865 and 1867. In certain respects Colfax resembled Fenton, but their supporters were men of widely different types. Blaine in his *Twenty Years in Congress* says of Colfax that he was ". . . . always instinctively quick to discern the current of popular thought" and that, "genial and cordial with unfailing tact and aptitude, skillful in cultivating friendships and never provoking enmities, he had in a rare degree the elements that insure popularity. The absence of the more rugged and combative qualities which diminished his force in the stormy struggle of the House served now (in the convention) to bring him fewer antagonisms as a candidate."

The last sentence shows that Blaine believed the amiable and affable Speaker to be deficient in vigor. Others were of the same opinion. His enemies nicknamed him "Smiler" Colfax. The vitriolic Gideon Welles, when angered by Colfax's course as Speaker, wrote of his "heartless everlasting smile and slender abilities." He also said that Montgomery Blair told him that Lincoln favored E. B. Washburne for Speaker rather than Colfax because, though he had no high opinion of Washburne, he considered Colfax "a little intriguer, plausible, aspiring beyond his capacity and not trustworthy."

Some of Colfax's friends took an entirely opposite view. His biographer and brother-in-law, O. J. Hollister, maintains that "this weak man stood firm when others bent"; and a brother Odd Fellow made the assertion that Colfax was "a man of convictions who did not ask 'Is it policy?' but 'Is it right?' That settled, his position was irrevocably taken." It is certain that Colfax was not a great man, few are. But he was well read though not profound, a pleasing writer and speaker, careful, industrious, with a quick mind and a sound judgment, who rose to the occasion. Whitelaw Reid, after speaking with scorn of a proposal to make Colfax editor of the New York *Tribune,* after Greeley's death, added: "There is then to be said about Colfax, that he has always surprised people in every position he has obtained by doing better than they expected."

If Fenton had the support of experienced politicians, Colfax had the earnest good-will of a class quite as respectable and when roused as powerful, the men and women of the country towns, who loved their church and strove to cultivate their minds, though neither their theology nor their knowledge was that of the metropolis and the university. Mr. Colfax was himself an extremely popular lecturer, receiving the then large remuneration of one hundred and fifty dollars a night. But if many of Colfax's supporters had something of the dove, others had their share of the wisdom of the serpent. For nearly twenty years Mr. Colfax was owner and editor of an Indiana country paper. The correspondents at Washington were most cordially disposed to their pleasant and obliging brother and their frequent and friendly notices did much to increase his popularity and influence.

The convention met formally on May 20, but by May 18 the delegates had gathered and an earnest canvass for the Vice-Presidency had begun. All the team work was good but that of the Fentonites was best. Every member of the New York delegation had been carefully considered and his election approved by Fenton himself. The correspondent of the *Tribune* made the sweeping declaration that his interests were in charge of "the best organized delegation that has ever attended a political convention." But though the New York delegation was unanimous for Fenton the Republicans of the state were not. Fenton's friends showed a letter in his favor from Horace Greeley, but the retired Boss, Thurlow Weed, differed *toto caelo* from his erstwhile partner and a number of Weedites came to Chicago with the intention of playing the same part against Fenton that Greeley had against Seward, eight years before. But Weed had no *Tribune* behind him, and Fenton, though a very different man from Grover Cleveland, was, like him, helped by the enemies that he had made. Delegates voted for Fenton because they were disgusted by the persistent attacks on him by men whom they regarded as intrusive bolters.

Next to Fenton, Wade had the most industrious and best organized supporters, but he had some very injudicious friends at Washington. Many telegrams came from the capital stating that Grant and various Senators desired Wade's nomination. They were said to have come from men who believed that the choice of Wade, a violent advocate of the unsuccessful impeachment of President Johnson, would be a rebuke to the seven Republican Senators who had voted for acquittal. But though the convention was highly displeased by the conduct of these men, the manœuvre did not bring a single vote to Wade. Wade led on the first ballot, but he was seriously injured by the circumstance that some of the Ohio delegation only voted for him because they were instructed to do so.

Wilson was weakened for a similar reason. Massachusetts was solid for him, but New England was not. The Maine delegates were firm for Hannibal Hamlin, believing that he was the second choice of the majority of the convention, and that when the leaders had killed each other off, he would be nominated.

Colfax's friends were the least thoroughly organized. They were also the least active in soliciting support. This, however, was not from lack of zeal, but from prudence. They hoped that when the Wade and the Fenton men found that success was hopeless, both, if not irritated by earlier clashes, would turn to Colfax. But while the Colfax delegates played a waiting game, his friends outside were very active. Colfax, though a member of the Reformed Church, was highly estemed by the Methodists; a convention of Methodist clergymen was in session at Chicago; the leaders were unanimous for Colfax, and they took care to drop a word in season to the right persons. Colfax said afterward, that the meeting of the two conventions at the same place and time was one of the pieces of good fortune with which his whole life was filled.

The candidates were evenly matched; now one, now the other seemed the strongest. Many thought that some wholly new man must be taken as a compromise. Senator Williams of Oregon, a rigid Republican who was skillful in making long and rhetorical speeches, and Galusha A. Grow of Pennsylvania, a father of the Republican party and an originator and persistent champion of the first Homestead Law, were considered. The first day the convention devoted itself to organization and minor matters. On the second, it adopted a platform, nominated Grant unanimously on a roll-call of the states, and then somewhat wearily turned to the selection of a candidate for Vice-President.

Mr. Hassaurek of Ohio, a prominent German-American, who had already addressed the convention in a long speech, nominated "that champion of human rights, Benjamin F. Wade, the child of the people and a self-made man, one of such incorruptible virtue that the people know him as Honest Ben Wade." Jones of North Carolina seconded this nomination of "the old Roman veteran" and declared that his state was ready to "Wade in." Judge Tremaine of New York nominated Fenton. He sketched Fenton's public work and praised him as a great political organizer and the soldiers' friend. He made great claims in regard to Fenton's strength, and called for his nomination in order to make the victory in New York secure.

But Fenton suffered from the over-zeal of his friends. In seconding his nomination, an Illinois delegate encountered John A. Logan, who coolly remarked that Fenton would get three votes and no more from his state. To meet this blow, Daniel E. Sickles in a brief speech deftly included Fenton with Morton of Indiana, Curtin of Pennsylvania, Andrew of Massachusetts, and other great war governors. In such company, however, Fenton, who had served less than four months during the war, and this at the close, seemed out of place and Sickles received no applause except that of three hundred enthusiastic supporters who had come from New York to work and bellow for their chief.[1] Pierce of Virginia nominated Henry Wilson, offering the somewhat startling argument that were he nominated there would be no reason to assassinate Grant. He also said that the nomination of a Massachusetts man by a delegate from Virginia showed that that state was reconstructed.

Senator Lane of Indiana nominated Colfax, and was seconded by delegates from New Jersey and Michigan. Lane said of Colfax: "He is from Indiana, near to our homes, near to our hearts. We know him, we love him, the people are united for him, there is but one voice. Although his residence is in Indiana, his fame is co-extensive with the whole country. He is a young man, representing the religious and moral sentiment of the commonwealth, and to a great extent a tried and true leader,—no doubtful man." The seconders spoke of Colfax as "the candidate of the young men" and "as true to principle as the needle to the pole."

Four ballots were taken without any decisive result. Wade and Colfax gained considerably. Wilson had lost. Fenton showed little change. The minor candidates dropped out except Hamlin. The delegates were weary, and anxious to leave for home that day. The general feeling was: nominate someone, no particular matter whom, but nominate. The *Tribune* correspondent thus describes the longed for "break." "At the end of the fifth ballot it was known that Wade and Colfax were close but that Ohio was not solid for her son. The friends of Colfax had been importuning Iowa, and

---

[1]The day before, the *Tribune* correspondent had telegraphed: "The Fenton men have secured tickets for admission for a host of outsiders, and his friends will be in the convention tomorrow, in full force." Machinery, however, could not match the power of locality, especially when combined with wide popularity, and Colfax was strongest with the spectators.

just as the result of the ballot was to be announced, the chairman of the Iowa delegation, General G. M. Dodge, asked leave to change its vote, while the delegates held their breath in expectation. He cast the solid vote of Iowa for Colfax.[1]

"That was enough. Two-thirds of the audience rose and cheered and swung their hats several minutes, while Mr. Wade's friends saw that a flood was coming on, which would soon engulf all other candidates but Indiana's favorite son. The effect of Iowa's action was electric. Pennsylvania, whose politicians are always on the winning side, announced through Mr. McClure that the Keystone State would also vote solid for Mr. Colfax. Then it was evident that no human power could keep the nomination from Colfax, and the different delegations began a scramble to see who would be first in line and on the winning side. Ohio and New York chose to sink with colors flying, but before the result of the fifth ballot was announced officially, all the other delegations had joined the victor."

The convention had shown an astonishing disregard for geographical considerations. Never before and never since has a party nominated its candidates from contiguous states. The friends of Colfax believed that his greatest danger was a combination of the East against the West, and it is not improbable that had New England acted as a unit, Wilson or Hamlin would have been the nominee. The Republican candidates were neighbors in time as well as space, and had also certain physical resemblances. The *Tribune* said: "There is but the difference of a year in the age of Grant and Colfax. They are about the same stature and weight and not unlike in personal appearance, though it would be easy to tell from their faces which is the soldier and which is the civilian. Grant's face is fixed and intense in its open firmness and reserve, while Colfax has an amiable countenance, and is a constant and rapid talker."

In temperament, however, the two men were opposite, as was well illustrated by their bearing after the action of the convention was known. The *Tribune* correspondent reported that "Grant takes his nomination quietly, and is apparently the coolest man in Washington. Colfax is radiant and joyous, and makes no secret of his satisfaction at the result."

Colfax's nomination was received most cordially both by those who knew him and those who did not. "With his friends around him Colfax received dispatches in the Speaker's room in the Capitol. When his selection was finally announced, he was overwhelmed with congratulations, Republicans and Democrats, Wilson and Wade men, joining, and the room rang with cheers again and again. He immediately sent the dispatch to his mother on Lafayette Square. As he left the room, the employees in the building gathered around him, and in the most affectionate manner tendered their felicitations. In the Capitol grounds people who knew his sunny face, but who had never

---

[1] A few votes had been given for Fenton.

spoken to him before, stopped him for a hand-shake and the privilege of telling him how glad they were. His progress up Pennsylvania Avenue was an ovation participated in by everybody." Colfax's rivals and their followers, the press and the public joined in praising him. Wade's comment was that of a man bravely accepting disaster. He said: "I guess it will be all right; he deserves it and he is a good presiding officer." Circumstances rendered Wade's defeat peculiarly hard for him. He had just lost his reëlection to the Senate, and he was a poor man. Thaddeus Stevens, then in his last illness, wrote Colfax: "I must congratulate you in *writing* (italics in original) if congratulations are needed between us. I was for Wade, as he will be left in the cold, and not for any personal preference. You must take care of him when I am dead and gone, which I doubt not the party will do."

The Republicans gave Wade no office—perhaps it might have been difficult to find a sufficiently dignified one for which the old veteran was suited; but two years later, on Colfax's recommendation, Wade was appointed agent, that is, lobbyist, for the Northern Pacific at Washington, at a good salary, and subsequently obtained valuable contracts for building a portion of the road. Meanwhile Colfax had, in a sense, personally taken care of Wade by espousing his niece; and since the Republican ticket won, Wade, though he could not be Vice-President, became the uncle of one by marriage.

Fenton, on hearing of Colfax's nomination, telegraphed him: "I congratulate you upon your nomination, and General Grant on having an associate so worthy to share with him the cordial support of the people." The New York *Tribune* said that the nomination was well received in New York: "It was also remembered that he was born in this city, and that, in the estimation of many, entitled him to distinction, and he was accordingly acclaimed as the representative of New York. Governor Fenton's friends announced a hearty determination to support the affable speaker of the House of Representatives." But others were not so ready to bury the hatchet. The *Tribune* declared that Wade or Fenton, particularly the first, would have been a dead weight, but that the choice of Colfax was "the most universally satisfactory that could be made. Notwithstanding the desire to avoid taking both our candidates from the West or rather from the Center, as we must soon come to regard Illinois and Indiana, it was wisely felt that no geographical reasons should weigh against the imperative wisdom of putting forward our two best men, both for availability before the people and for capacity and integrity in office."

To these general arguments for the nomination of Colfax the *Tribune* added another which must have appealed particularly to his brethren of the press. "He has had the valuable training of a newspaper editor, a vocation which in this country is the best of schools for an aspiring politician. It teaches him all the ins and outs of the profession, and how to avoid those shoals and bars upon which so many of our greatest statesmen have foundered. The rail splitter and the tailor (Lincoln and Johnson) were a powerful team, but the tanner (Grant had been one) and the editor will match them. There is nothing like leather, and the newspaper is the Third Estate of the Nineteenth Century." The New York *Herald* said: "Speaker Colfax, for one of his age, is a man of great experience and superior abilities and sagacity." Much stress was laid on the excellence of Mr. Colfax's personal character. Hannibal Hamlin, at a ratification meeting in Bangor, shortly following the Chicago convention, told his hearers that while he had been deceived in Andrew Johnson, he was sure of Colfax, "for all his past record and blameless life were guarantees of his future"; and, at a similar meeting in Portland, that Colfax was "a man to be trusted unreservedly."

The Bangor *Daily Whig and Courier,* the Republican paper of Mr. Hamlin's home, had, after praising Colfax as a man of ability and the son of his own works, said: "There is no stain upon his character or habits, and no enemy can point the finger of contempt or scorn at him." The *Putnam's Monthly* said that Colfax was pure and moral, that he sympathized with every good reform and had the warm and enthusiastic confidence of Christians and temperance reformers.

The Democratic National Convention was the direct opposite of the Republican. The latter had been unanimous on the question of the Presidency but much divided on the subject of the second office; the Democrats cast twenty-two ballots before nominating a President, but chose their Vice-President on the first ballot and unanimously.

The principal candidates for the Presidential nomination were George H. Pendleton of Ohio, Winfield Scott Hancock of Pennsylvania, and Thomas A. Hendricks of Indiana. When the choice seemed to lie between Hancock and Hendricks, a sudden burst of enthusiasm, probably prepared with much skill by Samuel J. Tilden, carried the convention for its chairman, Horatio Seymour, the Governor of New York. Seymour had held the same position in 1863, and, though he performed his constitutional duties when called on to do so by the President of the United States, he had shown himself a strong political opponent of the Administration.

The nominee for Vice-President was Francis P. Blair, Jr. The choice of Seymour was pleasing to the liberal Democrats, yet not displeasing to the old "Hard Shells;" the selection of Blair must have thrilled the latter faction with joy, not because of his record as a whole, parts of which were doubtless extremely offensive to them, but on account of his present position. Francis P. Blair, Jr., was a member of the famous Blair family. His father, who was still living, had begun life as editor of a newspaper in Kentucky, and had fought Andrew Jackson when he ran for President in 1824 and 1828. But Blair was strenuously opposed to a National Bank and to Nullification. After Jackson's breach with Calhoun, he was summoned to Washington and

made owner and editor of the new Administration organ, the *Globe*. He became a devoted friend and counsellor of the President and remained a kind
of official spokesman for the Democratic party until the nomination and election of Polk.

In 1848, Blair left the Democratic organization and joined the Free Soilers,
who had nominated Jackson's friend, Van Buren. His son, Montgomery
Blair, was made Postmaster-General by Lincoln. The Blairs were at first
friendly to Frémont, but became bitterly opposed to him. They were largely
responsible for his removal from command in Missouri, and in 1864 Blair
was asked to resign from the Cabinet as the price of Frémont and the Radical
Republicans withdrawing their opposition to the election of Lincoln.

Francis P. Blair, the younger, left the family home in Maryland, and
took up his residence in St. Louis. Like his father, he was a Republican
from the earliest days of the party. On the outbreak of the Civil War he
took an active and important part in keeping Missouri in the Union. He
enlisted in the army, served with credit, and became a corps commander. He
mixed politics with war, entered the House of Representatives, where he had
already sat for one term, and in 1861, unsuccessfully contested the Speakership with his fellow Republican, Galusha A. Grow.[1] He became involved in
bitter disputes with Secretary Chase and the Treasury officials, attacked them
in a scathing speech, resigned his seat in the House and resumed his place
in the army.

Father and son favored a conciliatory policy in dealing with the rebellion
and slavery and when, after the close of the war, the questions of reconstruction arose, and a breach came between Congress and President Johnson, they
adhered to the latter. Frank, as was natural for an old Democrat and one
of the Blair clan, took a similar position. The reorganization of "sovereign
states" and the changing of their suffrage laws by Federal power was to him
anathema. Just before the convention met, he wrote a letter to Colonel J. O.
Broadhead of Missouri, declaring, with characteristic vehemence, that the
President should forcibly undo what he by force had done; allow the Southern states to elect state officers and Congressmen according to their old laws;
and recognize such men, and those who should meet with them, as the lawful
Congress. Mr. Stanwood is of the opinion that it was this letter which gave
Blair the Democratic nomination for Vice-President.

Both Colfax and Blair took an active part in the campaign. The former
proved a great help to his party; the latter, a heavy burden. Mr. Oberholtzer
credits Colfax with stumping the West as far as Denver "with the affable
fluency which had influenced the leaders of the convention to give him the
nomination." But Mr. Hollister, who at the time was the editor of the *Rocky
Mountain News,* a Denver paper, states that the trip was one of recreation
and romance. His presence makes him a valuable witness. Moreover, as

---

[1]The Democrats made no nomination and scattered their votes.

Colfax proposed to Miss Wade on Mt. Lincoln, Hollister himself to Miss Carrie Matthews, the Speaker's half-sister, and the Secretary of the Territory, to Miss Sue Matthews, there are plenty of facts to support the romance.

Colfax carried his affability so far as to state in a speech on his return home that he considered it improper for a candidate to indulge in personal criticisms of his opponent. But he had felt no such compulsion of courtesy toward the President of the United States, for in replying to the notice of his nomination he had said: "On the fourth day of March next, the people's champion will be borne by the people's votes to yonder White House, that I regret to say is now dishonored by its unworthy occupant." Yet Colfax's sense of propriety did not allow him to take the stump until shortly before the state elections in October, when danger to the Republicans caused him to violate his principles of exaggerated delicacy. "Everywhere he was received with enthusiasm. Acres upon acres of people assembled in town after town over Indiana, Ohio, and indeed all the states to listen to the Speaker and many capable and distinguished party leaders. Speaking at Detroit and going next day to Niles, Michigan, Mr. Colfax was called out at stations and spoke twenty-one times." He told of the glorious work of the Republican party in preserving the Union, freeing the negro and raising him from degradation. Other Republicans praised Colfax and lauded him as a constant and efficient laborer at these noble tasks.

Blair had none of the scruples of Colfax in advocating his own election. At the opening of the campaign he threw himself into the fight and made speech after speech on the lines of the letter to Broadhead. It was a grave tactical error. Many Republicans were beginning to be shocked at the vulgarity and corruption of the negro and carpet-bag governments which had been forced on the South, and the North was weary of strife and longed for rest. General Grant had shown great generosity at Appomattox and he had closed his letter of acceptance with the words, "Let us have peace." Blair was yelling for action which might bring civil war in every State in the Union. Moreover, there was a recrudescence of Democratic outrages in the South; they were exaggerated by Republican politicians and used most effectively to prove that the ex-slave-holders and rebels were unreconstructed at heart, and could not safely be trusted with power in State and Nation.

Thirty years later, it might have been argued that the Vice-President had little power and that his opinions were unimportant, but in 1868, memories of Tyler and Fillmore were still vivid; Andrew Johnson was in the White House; and it was not possible to regard the Vice-President as a mere superfluous Excellency. Alexander says: "The issue finally resolved itself into Blair and Revolution, or Grant and Peace." Blair's earlier political course had made him many enemies, and the Republicans did their best to revive old feuds. The Germans had been devoted to Frémont, and they were not allowed to forget, which indeed there was little danger they would do, that

SCHUYLER COLFAX, INDIANA, SEVENTEENTH VICE-
PRESIDENT OF THE UNITED STATES, 1869-1873.

Blair had been his bitter enemy.   In Missouri the war had been largely a guerrilla struggle and the Southern sympathizers were reminded of Blair's vigorous efforts to stamp it out.

"Petroleum V. Nasby," the leading American humorist of the day, whose epistles during the rebellion from "Confederit X Roads" had held the "Dimmikrats" up to scorn by seeming to set forth their views, had continued his efforts in behalf of the Republicans after the war.   For the campaign, he wrote a series of letters.   In one, he described a Democratic Seymour and Blair ratification meeting at the Cross Roads, at which some one called for three cheers for Blair.   " 'Three cheers for Blair,' yelled Punt, 'an Abolishinist and Linkin hirelin which shot my unkle in Missoury, and burnt my grandmother's house near Vixburg.'

" 'He aint no abolishinist,' exclaimed Issaker, 'reed his letters.'

" 'It's difficult to say what he is today, but I'll swear to it that he wuz three years ago; but it makes no difference.   I swore four years ago to lick any man who hurrahed for any of the Blare family'."

It would seem that such attacks might prove a boomerang; that they would remind readers of Blair's support of the Union and help bring War Democrats back to their old party.   But Blair played into the enemy's hands by at least half-repudiating what Unionists considered best in his own past. He publicly said that he had opposed secession because he believed that it would lead to military despotism.   "That, however, was but an opinion; if radicalism be maintained, we shall have the continuance of an existing despotism, which will be intensified by success.   In that event, many who like myself, opposed secession and rebellion for the sake of constitutional government, and fancied ourselves wiser than the rebels if not more patriotic, will have to confess our mistake.   In the present aspect of affairs, I have to confess that it is yet to be decided whether those who fought for the Union and in doing so, saddled the country with a great debt and founded great mercenary interests and corrupting influences, hostile to every form of freedom, have not blundered."

The Blairs held loyally together and the Republicans treated the shortcomings of each as the ill-doing of all.   A Republican said: "If ever there was a race of 'carpet-baggers' on the face of the earth, the Blair family belongs to it.   Does anyone know where the Senior Blair belongs?   The pestilent Montgomery of that ilk, carpet-bag in hand, hailing from half a dozen different states in the Union, has been a persistent office beggar at Washington ever since he was of age.   He claimed a residence in Virginia and Missouri, and ran for the United States Senate in Maryland, and lived on the line of the District of Columbia.   Frank Blair was born in Kentucky, elected to Congress from Missouri, appointed to the army from the District of Columbia, and is the owner of estates and franchises in Tennessee, where he will run for Congress after he has been defeated for Vice-President."

Colfax's reputation was at that time absolutely untarnished, but Blair was accused of intemperance. Nasby described him as becoming conservative and increasing his ration of liquor three pints a day. A Republican paper asserted that the Democrats were alarmed by his violent speeches, that they recalled those made by Johnson at his inauguration as Vice-President, and when "swinging round the circle."[1] Reverend Theodore L. Cuyler, a clergyman of national repute, wrote to the *Independent*: "With the partisan politics of Messrs. Seymour and Blair, we have nothing to do, but while one of these gentlemen (Seymour) has an unhappy tendency to insanity in his family, and the other is addicted to strong drink, we submit whether Christian patriots should be called on to commit the mighty interests of the Republic to their hands."

The Democrats made a hard fight in Maine and Vermont, but with poor results. The October states went Republican. On October 15, the New York *World* called for a new ticket and the chief question for the Democrats was: "How shall we be saved from our Vice-President?" The Providence *Journal,* a Republican paper, asserted that Frank had offered to withdraw in favor of some one who thought as he did, but talked less. His father, however, was very angry with the *World,* and said very reasonably that its action would hurt the Democrats in November. Montgomery, Jr., who had a deep admiration and affection for his brother, was willing to make a change provided that Frank were put at the head of the ticket, and a civilian of equal ability associated with him. No change was made, but the frightened Democrats sent Blair to the rear, and Seymour, who had written a very mild letter of acceptance, traversed Western New York, Ohio, Indiana, and Illinois, repeating the argument which he had made in his letter—that a Democratic victory could have no bad effects since the Senate would still be Republican, while a Democratic President and House would hold the Senate in check. But all was vain. The Republican candidates were elected by a large electoral and a moderate popular majority. Probably no man in the country could have defeated Grant, but his victory was made the surer and greater by Blair's wild talk.

---

[1] Johnson was intoxicated, probably because of what may be described as an accident, when he was sworn in as Vice-President; and his abusive and undignified language on his trip about the country in 1868 was wrongly thought by many to be that of a drunken man.

CHAPTER XVI.

The Heirs Apparent of the Civil War Soldier-Presidents: Wilson, Wheeler, and Arthur

T HE administration of President Grant proved very unsatisfactory to some of the best Republicans in the country. In the South a considerable portion of the whites remained disfranchised, and ignorant negroes and political adventurers from the North controlled the government. The whites resorted to intimidation and violence, and Congress answered by suspending the writ of *habeas corpus,* and passing various laws which the Supreme Court later pronounced unconstitutional. In the North, too, the situation, if not so bad, was yet becoming intolerable to many to whom democracy meant a triumph of righteousness, not equal access to a feeding-trough. The spoils system had produced in almost every state a "boss," whose endorsement was a necessary condition of appointment to public office. The men who felt these evils most deeply usually held the view that another great abuse was the high tariff, which they believed benefited special interests rather than the people as a whole. It seemed impossible, however, to secure reforms within the party. The "organization" controlled the patronage, it was led by strong men of real ability, and it had the support of President Grant.

From Missouri came an appeal for independent action. There the Civil War had been one within as well as without the state; the fighting by the Confederates had been largely of a guerrilla nature; it had been met with the severities usual in such a struggle; and after victory was won, the triumphant Unionists had imposed severe disabilities on sympathizers with the South. But many Republicans soon came to feel that, with peace established, a different policy should prevail. In 1869, the party was divided into two factions, the "liberals" and the "eternal haters," and the former sent Carl Schurz to the United States Senate. In 1870, the breach widened. Each wing presented a full ticket for state offices and the liberals, aided by the D· .nocrats, who had made no nominations, elected Benjamin Gratz Brown, Governor.

In January, 1872, a mass meeting of Liberal Republicans held a State convention and proclaimed themselves in favor of universal suffrage and universal amnesty throughout the Nation. The suffrage clause was understood to apply to men only; women were not then regarded as universals. Tariff reform and civil service reform were also endorsed and, what was much more important than any merely state declaration, a call was issued for the meeting of a national convention of Liberals at Cincinnati, on the first of May. Some of the best men and best newspapers in the Republican party at once joined the movement; other papers like the New York *Evening Post* and the *Tribune,* while not definitely pledging their support, expressed sympathy with its aims. Horace White of the Chicago *Tribune,* one of the journalists who was heart and hand in favor of the attempt at reform, and who was a prominent delegate at Cincinnati, has left us an interesting account of what happened there, that is probably reliable, though it was written many years after the events described.

First, the assembly, which was a kind of mass meeting, was changed into a regular convention with due representation allotted to the several states. Then, a platform was constructed. There were three main questions, amnesty, civil service reform, and the tariff. On the first two, there was no difficulty, but so great was the division on the third that the convention frankly acknowledged its inability to come to a decision on the matter, and referred the subject to the people in their Congressional districts. All this and the organization of the convention took three days.

Meanwhile there had been much discussion of candidates. The gentlemen most frequently mentioned were Charles Francis Adams of Massachusetts, who had rendered very valuable service as Minister to Great Britain during the Civil War and who had just sailed for Europe to act as one of the arbitrators of the Alabama Claims, Lyman Trumbull of Illinois, who had been a Senator for seventeen years and had shown himself well worthy of his place, David Davis also of Illinois, a close friend of Lincoln and then a judge of the United States Supreme Court, Horace Greeley, and Governor Brown.

The last-named, while he was not to receive the crown, was to play or at least appear to play the part of King-Maker. On the night before the voting, though not a delegate, he appeared at Cincinnati accompanied by Frank Blair. Probably their purpose was to help any one who could defeat Adams, because they feared that if Adams became President, Schurz would dominate Missouri politics. After the first ballot, Brown, who had received 95 votes, was allowed to address the convention; he declined the honor of the nomination and advised that of Horace Greeley. On the second ballot Greeley gained nearly a hundred votes, but only a third of the Missouri delegates joined his army. On the sixth ballot he made a heavy gain, Adams only a small one. "This was a signal to all who wished to be on the winning side to take shelter under the old white hat." Votes were changed, Greeley was nominated by a great majority, and Brown was made the party candidate for the Vice-Presidency on the first ballot and with practically no opposition.

The Democratic convention met on July 9. Not all the members of the party were read to follow humbly in the wake of the Republican seceders, especially when the latter had nominated a man with the long anti-Democratic record of Horace Greeley. There were rumors of a compromise alliance by the nomination of a straight-out Democrat and Brown. It was said that the Blair family cared only for Brown, and that the Brown managers were bent on his nomination by the Democrats at any sacrifice of Greeley's interests. But the convention decided to swallow the whole dose, adopted the Liberal platform, and nominated Greeley and Brown.

The Republican convention met at Philadelphia on June 5. Both the masses and the machine were in favor of Grant for President, and his unanimous renomination was a foregone conclusion. The question was: Would the convention renominate the old ticket or only the head of it? A very large minority were heartily in favor of the first course. But Colfax had special obstacles to encounter. In 1868, the opposition to him had been much divided. Now it was substantially united. No new candidate strong enough to be seriously dangerous had entered the field. James G. Blaine had thought of doing so, but had decided to remain in his present position, that of Speaker of the House. Wade was old and definitely out of politics. Hamlin had returned to the Senate and was well satisfied to remain there. Fenton had gone over to the Liberals, being one of the comparatively few professional politicians who joined them. Curtin, who had been a minor candidate for the Republican nomination four years before, was also with the reformers.

There remained Henry Wilson. He could claim that Colfax, of all men, should not run against him. In 1870, the Vice-President had announced that he should retire from public life at the end of his term. There was great remonstrance. He was told that his party needed him, and in 1871 he stated that he would make no effort for the nomination, but that should the convention choose him, he would not be so ungrateful as to decline. Thereupon his friends set to work with a will. But the Wilson men declared that Wilson had entered the race on the assurance that Colfax was out of it, and that he had no right to reverse his position so late in the day.

In 1868, there had been little or no personal feeling against Colfax; in 1872, he found old opponents embittered and old friends changed to foes. When Speaker, Colfax had been actively concerned in the distribution of offices, particularly those in his own district. Custom gave no patronage to the Vice-President. Yet in a sense the whole country was his district, and Colfax was beset with letters begging his support of applications for office. But, while willing to join Senators and Representatives in recommending suitable men, he did not believe that the Vice-President should be an office-monger and firmly refused to become one.

Doubtless the Roman poet was right in saying that "Hell hath no fury like a woman scorned," but she is run close by a politician who feels that he has lost a place because a luckier fellow-politician has churlishly refused him a little help which he might easily have given. Such men rejoiced in the opportunity to aid in defeating Colfax. Furthermore, the members of the organization preferred Wilson. Their choice was a natural one. Wilson had been more active in practical politics than Colfax, and the latter was a strong temperance man who was not only a total abstainer himself, but did not serve liquor to his guests. Moreover, though Colfax was a good party man, he had had intimate relations with Liberals and half-Liberals.

The organization was very close to Grant and it is probable that in opposing Colfax it had the private assistance of the President, in spite of the fact that the two men had written to each other in the most friendly terms. In August, 1871, Grant, in the language of one requesting a favor, had asked Colfax to accept the post of Secretary of State for the latter part of his own term, and after the adjournment of the convention Grant praised Colfax highly. But the Independent wing of the party had a great esteem for Colfax, and much effort had been made to induce him to contest the nomination with Grant. The President had come to desire a renomination as a vindication from the gross charges which had been made against him, and it is probable that he included Colfax among his opponents.

Hollister says that there is no evidence that Grant was ever jealous, but that "he never hesitated to set aside a man who displeased him, if it was in his power, and he did it with the impassiveness of fate." He thinks that Grant did no more than maintain a strict neutrality when a word would have given the prize to Colfax, but it is probable that the President went further, playing the same part against Colfax that Colonel McClure alleges that Lincoln did against Hamlin in 1864. Horace White says in his life of Trumbull that General G. M. Dodge stated to him in writing that Grant had no liking for Colfax, and that before the convention met he had informed Dodge that he desired the nomination of Wilson.

Extremely important also was the opposition to Colfax of the Washington newspaper correspondents. As Representative and Speaker he had been on the most friendly and familiar terms with them; as Vice-President he stood apart from his old cronies; "he would not look at a newspaper man" they said, and they eagerly grasped the chance of taking revenge.[1] It may be that they did not make allowance for an alteration of circumstances. Colfax's new position entailed social obligations which consumed much time. Moreover, he was no longer a widower living in a flat, but a married man with a house and family. Yet it would seem that Colfax must have deliberately turned his back on the ladder by which he rose, to have incurred the bitter enmity which he did. Not all, indeed, united in assailing him.

---

[1]Taft injured himself by a somewhat similar change of attitude when he became President.

A lady correspondent of the New York *Independent,* a high class weekly with which Colfax had close connections, thus described the situation:

"He is the very Schuyler Colfax that he was when his name gave such magnetism to the ticket of 1868. The Vice-Presidency was the flood-tide of his favor. The popular Representative, the lionized Speaker, once ensconced in a place without patronage, irrevocably possessed by a wife, secure in his own castle, suddenly ceased to be in the public thought, the happy hail-fellow-well-met, the fêted, followed, lauded lion of the hour. In that hour of supreme success, did he forget his fellows, the men and women who had pushed his triumphal car, with steadfast, untiring, unselfish hands to its final goal? I know not, I only know that of the sin of ingratitude he is loudly accused and remains today unforgiven. My own belief is that what seemed ingratitude to many was the result of new conditions, and not of deliberate will. No less from that hour he has been pursued and punished by the power of the press.

"We hear so much about the power of the press! Well it is a fiendish power so far as it represents personal enmity and private spite. It is terrible to contemplate that a man's character may be filched away from him in type because Jackanapes, who penned it, is enraged that he was not invited to his victim's house to dinner. He missed the dinner but not the revenge; not he! Honest Job and Jemima read the paragraph in their isolated home. They ponder over it in sorrow. Their newspaper says it. Meanwhile Jackanapes crows to his cronies in newspaperdom: 'He didn't invite me to dinner but I can write him down. We'll bring the gentleman to his level. He'll feel the power of the press to his sorrow.' "

When the Republican delegates gathered at Chicago there were, as Hollister expresses it, two real candidates and several complimentary ones. The real were Colfax and Wilson; the complimentary included ex-Governor Dennison of Ohio, William D. Kelley of Pennsylvania, and a John F. Lewis of Virginia. On the day before the opening of the convention, the correspondent of the New York *Tribune* wrote his paper that it was reported that Colfax had more delegates instructed for him than had any other candidate, but that he could not make gains. Pennsylvania was instructed for her true son, that dyed-in-the-wool Republican and staunch protectionist, William D. Kelley, known as Pig Iron Kelley from his constant championship of a high tariff on that basic product of his state. The Pennsylvania delegates urged that a Vice-President should be nominated who could carry a doubtful state, that neither Colfax nor Wilson could do this, but that the choice of Kelley would make Pennsylvania safe.

It seems strange to hear Pennsylvania called doubtful, and in the election she was to go Republican by a tremendous majority; but she had given only a moderate majority for Grant in 1868, and it is said that she might have been allowed the second place had not all her candidates been inferior men. It was generally understood that the endorsement of Kelley was not to be taken seriously, but had been made for trading purposes, and it was reported that on the second ballot his supporters would go to Dennison. As between Colfax and Wilson, the Pennsylvanias were said to be divided. "The Colfax delegates were extremely active; arguing with their fellows and bringing them to the Colfax headquarters for further pressure." The Wilson men, on the other hand, were advanced in years, deficient in push, and apparently not practical politicians. The chief thing they did was to get out a circular in praise of Wilson, which was so long that few read it.

But the deficiencies of the special friends of Wilson were made up by the energy and shrewdness of those enemies of Colfax, the newspaper correspondents. They threw themselves into the fray and worked early and late, buttonholing delegates and men who could influence them. They brought their special abilities into play by preparing and having printed a slip containing the refusal of Colfax to run, and a few pithy arguments in favor of Wilson. The Colfax supporters were almost ready to yield when they were heartened by a fierce diatribe on the motives of the anti-Colfax journalists sent to the New York *Times* by L. L. Crounse, one of Colfax's few friends among the correspondents. The delighted Colfax men thought of circulating the letter. A *Tribune* correspondent angrily informed his paper that "they did not appear to realize the fact that to give publicity to Crounse's shallow attempt to throw dirt upon his fellow-journalists for differing with him as to candidates, would injure instead of helping the cause of Colfax." Possibly it would. It doubtless further embittered the feeling against Colfax, but reporters as well as public men may be influenced by unworthy motives, and there is no good reason for treating them as sacrosanct.

The first day of the convention was devoted to organizing, and listening to numerous orators until a committee was ready to report. Next day there was more speaking while waiting to hear from the platform committee. Finally the convention suspended the rules, passed to the nomination of a President, and, by a roll-call of states and territories, unanimously nominated Grant. The convention then became a musical one, and various songs were played and sung, but still no platform appeared.

The convention suspended the rules again and proceeded to nominate a Vice-President. The delegates were weary and anxious to leave, but were obliged to sit with what patience they could while seven nominators praised Wilson; four, Colfax; and others lauded Davis of Texas, Lewis of Virginia, and Maynard of Tennessee. Wilson's chief sponsor was Morton McMichael, of Pennsylvania, who had been temporary chairman of the convention. He made a long speech withholding Wilson's name till he had reached a grand climax, and bored delegates called to him to tell them whom he was advocating. Colfax was more fortunate. The *Tribune* correspondent wrote that

"Lane of Indiana nominated him in one of the shortest and crispest speeches heard in the convention. When he had concluded there was another shout heard from the Colfax men. The friends of Henry Wilson saw that their opponent had gained by being presented in such good taste." But the Wilson men were encouraged by a short seconding speech from a colored man who said that his delegation and the South generally were for Wilson.

It is possible that the speeches may have affected some votes, but probably the nomination had been determined already by the powers that sit in darkness and, often, rule. Blaine says that before the opening of the convention two or three of the largest delegations met and decided in favor of Wilson. The chairman of the Indiana State Committee wrote Colfax that he had abandoned hope when, on the day before the convention, Cameron refused to support Colfax. It was said that many of the Pennsylvania delegation favored him but that their boss, autocratic as an old chief of his clan, forbade them to vote as they wished. Kelley was not given even a complimentary support; the name of Dennison of Ohio, who was reported to be the real candidate of Pennsylvania, was withdrawn; and most of her delegates ranged themselves under Wilson's banner. The Southern members had held a caucus of their own, but it broke up without taking action, it being thought that it would be better for the states to act independently. Yet despite the odds against him, Colfax nearly reached the goal. The first vote stood Wilson 364½, Colfax 321½, scattering 66.

Then management and enmity to Colfax secured Wilson's triumph. It had been foreseen that the weary convention would not take the time needed for a second ballot, but would break to one of the leaders. The situation in Virginia was peculiar. The delegates cherished a grudge against the Administration. They said that Grant had done nothing for them, and that Colfax had treated them with coldness and indifference, and they would gladly have seen the old ticket scrapped. Nevertheless they had voted for Grant because, as one of them frankly admitted, he was sure to be nominated, and opposition would merely put them outside the patronage pasture. Colfax had no such protection; the Virginia vote for Lewis was merely complimentary. In fact the delegates favored Wilson or anybody else who could displace the Vice-President.

On the instant the result of the first ballot was announced, members of the convention sprang up to change their votes. The organization had put a Wilson man in the chair for this very occasion. His properly directed eyes recognized Mr. Walker of Virginia, who transferred the vote of that state from Lewis to Wilson. Other changes followed. It was seen that Wilson had received a majority, the convention cheered wildly, and chairmen of delegations fought for recognition that they might put themselves in the "Me too, class." The chairman recognized Lane of Indiana, who, yielding to the inevitable, moved to make Wilson's nomination unanimous, and the motion was carried by a rising vote.

The correspondents were as happy as an Indian brave who has scalped his foe. Some in the gallery were seen shaking hands and saying: "There is one for Smiler." Others on the floor who had received the nomination of Grant with great calmness and decorum, now jumped on tables and roared their delight. They had reason for joy; it was their pens which had given a deep, possibly the fatal, wound. Stanwood and Blaine both express the belief that in the closely balanced contest the opposition of the correspondents turned the scale against Colfax. White thinks that Grant's message by Dodge was the deciding factor. Probably the convention, in any case, would have refused to give Grant a colleague to whom he definitely objected; but had it not been for Colfax's previous refusal to run and the work of the correspondents in diminishing his popularity, it is not unlikely that the organization and the President might have acquiesced in his renomination.

It must be remembered, however, that Wilson had strength of his own. He was an old anti-slavery man, and therefore could appeal to the original Republicans and those who honored them. Labor was making itself felt in politics, and Wilson had been a poor boy with scarcely any schooling, who began life at the cobbler's bench. He never was ashamed of the class from which he came, was mindful of its interests, and had recently been very active in putting an eight-hour bill through Congress. A few days before the convention met, Charles Sumner had assailed Grant in a characteristically long, carefully wrought, and one-sided oration; and, as in 1868, Radicals wished to nominate Wade as a rebuke to the Senators who voted to acquit President Johnson, so in 1872, men felt that it would be proper to express their disapproval of Sumner's conduct by nominating his colleague for the Vice-Presidency.

Yet, curiously enough, Wilson was not a Grantite, or to use a later term, a "Stalwart." He had opposed the President in the San Domingo matter, and the deposition of Sumner from the chairmanship of the Committee on Foreign Affairs, and he favored a Southern policy more liberal than that of the Administration. Later, he even went so far as to tell Garfield that the President "is more unpopular than Andrew Johnson was in his darkest days, that he is struggling for a third term, in short that he is the millstone round the neck of our party that would sink it."

Wilson is one of many men of whom it may be said that he was so good and able a man that it is a pity he was not a little better and greater. Senator Hoar pictures him as an ardent and not over-scrupulous politician, but one who, though he was in many fights, never bore malice. "There was not a drop of bigotry or intolerance or personal hatred in him.[1] He was a popular stump orator. He never made speeches that were quoted as models of eloquence or wisdom. But he knew what the farmer, the mechanic, and the workmen at his bench were thinking of, and he addressed himself to their

---

[1] Presumably his Know-Nothingism was purely political.

best and highest thought. He was a great vote making speaker. He had a remarkable gift for gathering and uttering popular sentiment. He would seem to hesitate and vacillate and have no will of his own, yet at last a swift and resistless bolt flashed out, and the righteous judgment of Massachusetts came from his lips."

There were several minor parties in the field. Dissatisfied Democrats, unwilling to be transferred to Horace Greeley, nominated Charles O'Conor of New York, and John Quincy Adams, second, of Massachusetts. Both gentlemen declined to accept, but O'Conor was run, nevertheless, and obtained about thirty thousand votes. The Labor Reformers nominated Judge Davis of Illinois, and Judge Parker of New Jersey. After waiting from February to June both definitely declined, and the party nominated O'Conor without a Vice-President to fall at his side. The Prohibition party appeared in the national field for the first time, and nominated James Black of Pennsylvania, and John Russell of Michigan. It will be noted that no party took a candidate from the ex-Confederate states, and that, with the exception of the seceding Democrats, all balanced the East against the West, and made the Alleghanies the dividing line.

All the candidates for the Vice-Presidency and the holder of the office, took the stump. Mr. Colfax had promptly congratulated his successful rival, and pledged his own support to the ticket. Further, he did not desire to go. He felt that his loyalty to Grant had not been recognized, and he did not wish to be brought into personal conflict with his old friend, Horace Greeley. Moreover, his mother was dying of cancer, and his own health was poor.[1]

But the Vice-President was too good a Republican to desert his party in its hour of need, and from all sides came calls for help. Blaine begged him to come to Maine, and Cornell to New York. A committee from the latter state sent word: "The cry goes up from Lake County, 'Oh, that Colfax would come. One speech from him would work our deliverance.'" Zachariah Chandler, the chairman of the Congressional Committee, wrote: "It is deemed of the highest importance, and as, in fact, an essential element of the campaign in its present aspects, that you should make a speech at the earliest moment possible, at any place and under any circumstances that you choose, so that the same may be published and scattered broadcast. Your present silence is working great harm. A timely speech will do us great good. Please telegraph a reply."

Two days after the letter was written, Colfax delivered a speech which was circulated in tens of thousands of copies as a campaign document. On August 10, at the earnest wish of his dying mother, Colfax left her bedside to introduce and praise Henry Wilson, who was speaking in his home town. Later he took a more active part in the campaign, addressing great mass meetings with the highest success. He was, however, obliged to defend not only

---

[1] About a year before he had been prostrated while presiding over the Senate, and had not fully recovered.

the Republican party, but his own character.   The Credit Mobilier scandal was beginning, and Senator Cullom says in his *Recollections* that it was well that the Vice-President was not renominated, as his name would have hurt the ticket.   But Colfax had thousands upon thousands of friends, and it has been pointed out that the Mobilier affair reached its most serious stage after the campaign.   Moreover, Wilson, also, was involved.

As in 1868, the Democratic candidate was accused of intemperance.   The leading Republican paper in Missouri expressed the hope that after the state convention was held, Governor "Boozy Gratz Brown" would find time to attend to the duties of his office.   The Republicans alleged specific instances of drunkenness, and the Democrats published affidavits in reply.   At the Yale Commencement, Brown attended a dinner of his class, took too much, and made a speech which was very uncomplimentary to the East.   But Brown's earlier record was a Democratic asset in the North, and ex-Governor Fenton wrote a letter in which he said that Brown, "though reared in the midst of slavery . . . . was one of the first to urge emancipation, and after the war he was one of the first to urge amnesty."

The Democrats expressed much sympathy for the rejected Colfax, and declared that his defeat in the convention would be avenged at the polls.   The facts, however, did not warrant such optimism.   Both Liberal nominations had been shocking to the originators of the movement.   Greeley was an extreme protectionist; and what was more serious, he was excitable and erratic, and though personally honest, he was easily influenced, and was surrounded by a clique of grafters as unscrupulous as those who misled Grant.   Brown's nomination seemed the result of a deal in the virtuous convention, which had drawn its skirts aside from the dirty ways of the wicked politicians.   Carl Schurz was bitterly grieved, and declared that the German vote was lost by what appeared to be "a brazen political swap."   Ardent free traders, angry at the nomination of Greeley and the failure to take a stand on the tariff question, went back to Grant.   William Cullen Bryant of the *Evening Post,* and Godkin of the *Nation* did the same, because of their distrust of Greeley.

Other Liberals made the best of what had happened.   Schurz unwillingly gave a qualified support to Greeley.   He wished to smash what he regarded as a corrupt organization dominating the Republican party and the country, and he said that it was physically impossible for Greeley to have participated in a Greeley-Brown arrangement at Cincinnati.   Frank Bird, an idealist, who had been an extremely radical anti-slavery man, wrote to Charles Sumner: "Don't believe a word about the trade, in any discreditable sense, between Blair and Brown on the one part and the Greeley men on the other.   Undoubtedly Blair wanted to head off Schurz and, equally true, an arrangement was made or an understanding reached on Thursday night, in a certain contingency, to unite a portion of the Brown and Greeley forces; but except, perhaps, in the motives of the leading negotiators on one side, nothing that is not usually, indeed, almost necessarily, done in such conventions; nothing that was not contemplated and even proposed by the Adams men." Probably this was an exact statement of the case and a needed reminder that compromise, if made with honorable motives and kept within due limits, is not disgraceful and is usually necessary for success.

As the campaign advanced, the Republican cause brightened. Greeley's political errors during the Civil War were ruthlessly pointed out by his opponents. Grant was still strong with the people, and there was a wide feeling that the results of the war would be endangered by putting the Democrats and the South in power. The Republicans won by a great majority, both popular and electoral. A few days after the election, Greeley died, and the Democratic electors voted for whom they pleased with no serious attempt at union. Hendricks of Indiana received 42 votes for President, and Brown 18. Brown received 39 for Vice-President.

The second administration of President Grant was marked by gross corruption, by a total failure of most stringent measures to quiet disorder in the South, and by an increasing feeling in the North that the attempt to put political power in the South into negro and Republican hands had failed both from the political and the moral standpoint. The panic of 1873 had brought the problem of the currency to the front, and Greenbackism and the resumption of specie payments were practical questions of the first importance. Congress had fixed January 1, 1879, as the date of resumption, and had given the Secretary of the Treasury large powers to ensure its maintenance; but a great majority of the Democrats and a considerable minority of the Republicans would have been glad to see the law repealed.

Some effort had been made to bring General Grant forward for a third term, but public opinion was so clearly unfavorable that the attempt was soon abandoned. The organization was greatly weakened by the loss of the President as a candidate, for he was highly regarded by many and was considered a better man than his supporters. Moreover, though he probably favored Roscoe Conkling of New York as his successor, he had made no definite statement to that effect, and the machine men and thick-and-thin Grantites were divided between Conkling and Senator Oliver P. Morton, the War-Governor of Indiana. The reform wing favored Benjamin H. Bristow of Kentucky. The strongest candidate was James G. Blaine of Maine, the brilliant and popular Speaker of the House. Two minor candidates who had solid support were Governors Rutherford B. Hayes of Ohio, and J. F. Hartranft of Pennsylvania.

The Republican convention met at Cincinnati on June 14. Six ballots were taken without result. On the seventh, compromise triumphed, and the nomination went to Hayes, who has been termed a "poultice." Stanwood says: "As he was entirely unobjectionable to the friends of all other candidates, it was less difficult to concentrate votes upon him than upon any other person in the list. H. J. Eckenrode in his recent life of Hayes says that Hayes' managers had so shrewdly represented him as all things to all men, that everyone saw in the candidate what he wished to see, whether that was a better government or jobs and contracts. Hayes was a man of stainless private life, a church member, and a teetotaler. During his Presidency, wine appeared only once on the White House table, at a state dinner to the Russian Grand Duke, Alexis.

He had served with credit in the Civil War, where he obtained the ranks of Brigadier and Brevet Major General. He was twice sent to Congress, retiring during his second term to become the Republican candidate for Governor of Ohio. He was elected to this office for three successive terms, defeating Allen G. Thurman, perhaps the ablest Democrat in the United States, George H. Pendleton, the Democratic candidate for Vice-President in 1864 and the leading champion of "soft money" in the country, and the old ex-Governor "Fog Horn" William Allen, whose oratory had delighted the masses in the 'thirties and 'forties. Hayes was chiefly known for his able arguments in defense of "sound money," but he was also a firm believer in civil service reform. He came from the West, and his nomination was more pleasing to the reformers than to the organization. Therefore, it might have been supposed that the convention would give him for a companion a New Yorker, approved by the machine.

The New York leaders had such a candidate ready, and one of whom any faction might be proud, Stewart L. Woodford. Mr. Woodford had served honorably through the Civil War, resigning a good office to enter the army. He had presented Conkling's name to the convention with an oratorical power that won admiration, and delegates from Ohio, Indiana, and other western states where his voice had been heard against Greenbackism, had not forgotten the brilliant rhetoric which clothed his powerful arguments. But the Blaine states manifested great enthusiasm for another New Yorker, William A. Wheeler.[1]

Mr. Wheeler was a man of pure life, ripe culture, and sincere and practical principles, who had won the esteem of his associates in Congress. He had a good presence, was a pleasing and sensible speaker, and had established a deserved reputation for ability by his service in the State Legislature, in Congress, and as President of the New York Constitutional Convention of 1866-1867. Although the New York politicians favored Woodford, Wheeler was well managed. Two Massachusetts delegates steadily voted for him for President, in order to keep his name before the convention.

His nominators for the Vice-Presidency were carefully selected. The first was Luke P. Poland of Vermont, a Republican Representative of long

---

[1]Wheeler had deserved well of Blaine's friends. There had been a movement which seemed to have good prospects of success to make him Speaker in the next Congress instead of Blaine. But sometime before, Wheeler had told Blaine that he would not be a candidate. Blaine now said to Wheeler that he understood that he was to run. Wheeler answered: "No, I have given you my word once to the contrary and that is enough"; and no urging could make him change his ground.

service known for his independence and honesty. Colleagues of Wheeler at Washington did much missionary work. Hoar was active with the Southern delegates, but did not neglect men of a different type, from his own state. An appeal to James Russell Lowell was met by the objection that he knew nothing about Wheeler. Hoar assured him that the stranger was a sensible man and read the *Biglow Papers*. Lowell declined to pledge himself; but later Hoar heard him say to another delegate that he understood that Wheeler was a very sensible man, without mentioning the special proof that Hoar had offered! Before the first roll-call was finished, it was seen that Wheeler had a strong lead. Woodford and other candidates were withdrawn, and Wheeler was nominated unanimously.

Hayes and Wheeler, unlike most candidates for President and Vice-President, were a well-matched pair. Their selection had been forecast as early as the preceding January, General Sherman having written to Mrs. Hayes late in the month a letter, which had been made public, and which correctly prophesied the ticket. Curiously enough, there was some likelihood of the General's being proved right as to the candidates, but wrong in his order. There was a strong feeling in favor of giving the minor candidate from Ohio the nomination for the second place, should he fail of the first. Hayes was willing to accept, but not to run with Blaine.[1]

Just before the convention, Congressman Farwell of Illinois had expressed an opinion that when the friends of Conkling and those of Blaine found that they could not carry their own man, they would go to Wheeler, whom both liked. This, however, seems a little improbable, as Wheeler highly disapproved of the New York manager and dictator. Hoar says that Wheeler very much disliked Roscoe Conkling and all his ways, that Conkling once said to him: "If you will join us, and act with us, there is nothing in the gift of the state of New York to which you may not reasonably aspire." To which Wheeler replied: Mr. Conkling, there is nothing in the gift of the state of New York which will compensate me for the loss of my own self-respect."

---

[1]Hayes' attitude toward Blaine was peculiar. Three days before the convention met, the Maine statesman suffered an attack of the nature of a sunstroke which at first seemed likely to affect him permanently. Hayes wrote Blaine that his own eyes were almost blinded with tears, that he was affected as he had been by the death of Lincoln. But at the same time, he wrote to a friend that the nomination of Blaine on an early ballot seemed probable and that while he had the greatest sympathy for him, ". . . I feel that his nomination would be fatal to the cause. I do not see how we can get through in Ohio with him at the head of the ticket. It is proposed to put me in the second place. This will not help the case. It is the man at the head who makes the canvass. I have the greatest aversion to being a candidate on the ticket with a man whose record as an upright public man is to be in question, to be defended from the beginning to the end. I do not care about defeat with such men as Fish, Morgan, Washburne, etc. etc." Hayes also wrote to his representative at the convention, E. F. Noyes, to withdraw his name for the Vice-President, should Blaine be nominated. But he told Noyes to treat the letter as strictly confidential, as he would not wish to injure Blaine or lessen the chances of the party by one disparaging word. It may be that Hayes weakened a little the next day, for he instructed Noyes by telegraph: "You know my views about the Vice-Presidency. Do what you think best."

The Liberal Republicans were no longer in the field. Disheartened by the Greeley fiasco, and soothed by the nomination of Hayes and of Wheeler, men who were very "Liberal" in spirit, most of the seceders returned to the party fold and were cordially received.

The Democrats had no desire again to follow in the wake of bolting Republicans, but they wished to attract as many of the Liberals as possible, and fortune gave them a man well qualified to do this, Governor Samuel J. Tilden of New York. Mr. Tilden was now sixty-two years of age, and for most of his life had taken an active part in Democratic politics. But he had opposed Vallandigham and the peace men in the convention of 1864, and for some years thereafter gave his chief attention to his private affairs. He had a lucrative law practice, and a wonderful business instinct which enabled him to accumulate a great fortune by judicious buying and selling of United States bonds and railroad stocks. Mr. Tilden had won a national reputation by his successful war against corrupt men of his own party, especially the notorious Boss Tweed; and his position in the financial world was proof of his economic orthodoxy.

The Democratic convention met at St. Louis on June 18. On the first ballot Mr. Tilden received a majority, leading his nearest competitor, Governor Hendricks of Indiana, by 277 votes; on the second ballot he obtained the necessary two-thirds, and was then nominated unanimously and enthusiastically.

But there was fear in the hearts of the victors. Tammany was bitterly opposed to Tilden and carrying New York was most important, if not absolutely necessary, for Democratic success. Tilden represented the hard money wing of the party, and a platform satisfactory to it had been adopted, in spite of the efforts of the soft money faction. The October state of Indiana held a key position, and the convention had rejected her favorite son, the most popular Democrat in the state, who was a moderate soft money man and on very friendly terms with Tammany. Tilden's supporters wished to heal up all by inducing Hendricks to accept the second place. But the Hendricks men were in a most unconciliatory mood. During the discussion over the nomination for President, Tilden's followers had been careful to avoid giving offence to those of Hendricks; but this consideration had not been reciprocated.

Even in the public speeches nominating Hendricks, thrusts were made at Tilden because of his lack of support at home. One delegate said of Hendricks: "There is no fire in his rear here"; another said: "We find that his own people come up here in solid phalanx for him, like the Macedonian phalanx, with its lances all pointed outward, and none towards their friends." Immediately after the nomination of Tilden, it became evident that Westerners felt bitterly the rejection of their candidate, and that the Indiana delegation would spurn the offer of the Vice-Presidency, and in Hendricks' name decline the nomination if he were chosen.   The Tilden men, therefore, carried an adjournment to the next day to allow time for passion to cool, and, according to the correspondent of the Chicago *Tribune,* to give opportunity for selecting a candidate who was personally and geographically fitted to strengthen the ticket in Ohio and Indiana.

It was found that the delegates from the South and Southwest and a great majority of those from the West desired Hendricks, but that Ohio was unanimous for her son, Henry B. Payne.   He also had some support in Pennsylvania, though the majority from that state were for General Hancock.   Illinois, too, had a favorite son, Colonel William R. Morrison, a worthy and able man.   New York and New England were alarmed by the views of Hendricks and his followers on the financial question, but they were told that he himself was sound, and that the convention had shown itself firm for principle in its platform.

The next day Hendricks was unanimously nominated on a roll-call, eight Ohio delegates not voting.   The Indiana delegation, though voting for Hendricks, announced that it was not authorized to say that he would or would not accept the nomination.   But the convention promptly adjourned, leaving Hendricks to play the part of Fitzpatrick, if he chose, but giving him no opportunity to follow in the steps of Silas Wright.   Hendricks' neighbors immediately serenaded him; his reply indicated that on being officially notified of his nomination, he would accept; and he did so.

Thomas Andrews Hendricks was born in Ohio on September 7, 1819, but while still a young child was taken by his parents to Indiana.   His uncle was the second Governor of the state, and served two terms in Congress.   His father was active in developing the district where he lived, but never entered politics.   Thomas was educated at Hanover College (Indiana), and studied in a law school of which a maternal uncle was the head. He soon distinguished himself at the bar, served in the Legislature, and was a fairly prominent member of a state constitutional convention.

In 1851, he went to Congress for two terms, and was shortly afterward appointed by President Pierce, it is said, without his own solicitation, Commissioner of the General Land Office.   He served with much efficiency until 1859 when he resigned, partly because of the interference of President Buchanan with the management of the office, and partly because of his loyalty to Stephen A. Douglas, between whom and Mr. Buchanan there was now open war.   In 1860, Hendricks was nominated by the Democrats for Governor of Indiana, but was defeated.   In 1863, his party having carried the Legislature, he was elected United States Senator.   While holding this position he was a minor candidate for the Democratic Presidential nomination in 1868, and in the same year was nominated by his party for Governor, but was again defeated.   In 1872, he was once more elected to the United States Senate.

During his public career, Hendricks had been obliged to deal with two groups of questions of great difficulty, one related to the Civil War and the negroes, the other to the currency. His stand on the first was Democratic and conservative, on the second, such as appealed to Greenbackers and radicals. Yet it is to be noted that he did not go with the extremists of these factions, and that the reasons which he gave for his positions often seemed consonant with the principles of the other side. In the constitutional convention of 1850, he objected to allowing free negroes to enter Indiana on the ground that the South, instead of bearing her own burden, was sending her aged and diseased negroes North in order to strengthen slavery.

During the war, Hendricks objected to enlisting negroes for the reason that it would be extremely offensive to the white troops, and therefore weaken the Union. He objected to the abolition of slavery, because changes in organic law should not be made in times of great excitement and strife, and because Southern states that were to live under the Constitution would have no part in the adoption of the amendment. To the Republican policy of Reconstruction, Hendricks offered unflinching opposition. In all this there was nothing inconsistent with a firm determination to preserve the Union. On April 24, 1861, he had publicly denied a story that he had refused to attend a Union meeting, and added: "Since the war commenced, I have uniformly said that the authority of the Government of the United States is not questioned in Indiana, and that I regarded it as the duty of the citizens of Indiana to respect and maintain that authority and to give the government an honest and earnest support in the prosecution of the war, until in the providence of God, it may be brought to an honorable conclusion, and the blessing of peace restored to our country, postponing until that time all controversies in relation to the causes and responsibilities of that war."

But Hendricks did not always maintain this loyal position. On Jackson Day (January 8), 1862, a Democratic State Convention met and elected him chairman. He made a long speech, charging the Republicans with frequent and gross violations of the Constitution, attacking Lincoln's plan for compensated emancipation in the loyal slave states by their own consent, because it would lead to the overrunning of neighboring states by negroes and thus depressing the wages of labor. He accused Pennsylvania and New England of grossly oppressing the West by means of the tariff. He declared that if "we are now not to become 'the hewers of wood and drawers of water' for the capitalists of New England and Pennsylvania, we must look to the interests of our section; and for the first time in my life I intend to speak as a sectional man. We are not a manufacturing people, and can not well become such; our wealth must come from the cultivation of the soil, and of those heavy and bulky articles that require a convenient market and cheapness of transportation."

The speaker prophesied that the regions near the seacoast would be enriched by a foreign demand for their products, but not the West, "for railroad transportation can not become cheap." New England was never so prosperous, but:

"For the want of the Southern market, the men of Indiana lose nearly half the rewards of their labor. Why that market is of such value to us, is apparent from a moment's reflection; the transportation of our heavy and bulky products is easy and cheap; it is the interest of the South mainly to employ her labor in the production of rice, sugar, hemp, tobacco, and cotton, articles which we do not produce, and to depend upon and buy from us the productions of our land and labor. To encourage and stimulate the people of the South in the production of their peculiar commodities, that they may be large buyers from us, has been and, so long as grass grows and water runs, will be the true interest of the Northwest, and that political party that would destroy that market is our greatest foe. . . . .

"The first and highest interest of the Northwest in the restoration and preservation of the Union upon the basis of the Constitution, and the deep devotion of her Democracy to the cause of the Union, is shown by its fidelity in the past; but if the failure and folly and wickedness of the party in power render a union impossible, then the mighty Northwest must take care of herself and her own interests. She must not allow the arts and finesse of New England to despoil her of her richest commerce and trade, and to render her labor wholly subservient to an Eastern, sectional, and selfish policy, Eastern lust of power, commerce, and gain."

In 1863 the Democratic Legislature passed resolutions violently condemning various acts of the national government, including arbitrary arrests, trial by military commissions, and the Emancipation Proclamation.

Hendricks, from his first entry into public life, had been specially interested in financial questions. In the Indiana Constitutional Convention he sharply attacked paper currency and banks, but said that Indiana should neither depend on other states for paper money, nor do without it altogether, and so suffer all the miseries of a gigantic contraction of the currency. As between a state bank and a free banking system, he preferred the former, because the state would then make a profit. On the question of the resumption of specie payment by the United States, Hendricks declared himself in favor of it, but wished the repeal of the law directing it to commence on January 1, 1879, because he believed that the country was not yet prepared for the change.

Hendricks' theories and his acts often seemed to disagree, and one is reminded of Jefferson's complaint that in the discussions in Washington's cabinet his fellow-Republican, Attorney-General Randolph, gave the shell to him and the oyster to Hamilton. But Hendricks usually, though not always, fed the oyster to his own party. Many judged Hendricks severely, accusing him of lack of backbone and of principle. Oliver P. Morton called him "The Artful Dodger." Oberholtzer says in his history that Hendricks personally was a man of good character, but essentially a politician without any object in view.

But like Colfax, Hendricks had friends who declared that the accusation of weakness, though superficially plausible, was fundamentally unjust. After Hendricks' death, the St. Louis *Republican,* which was a Democratic paper as the *Globe Democrat* was a Republican one, made the rather surprising statement that Hendricks "never swam with the current." Senator Voorhees said:

> "Sometimes on the eve of a political battle he paused and weighed the issues at stake with such a care and prudence that those who knew but little of the quality of his mind thought he hesitated to go to the front. Nothing could be more incorrect than such a conclusion. While others were at times more aggressive and more rapid in their decisions at the beginning, yet none led more boldly or further in advance. . . . . Governor Hendricks was never so strong, so magnetic, and so irresistible as when under assault or crowded in discussion by an able antagonist. In joint debate before the people from day to day, and from week to week, he had no superior in the history of the country. His qualities for such an ordeal were of the highest order. A self-possession never for a moment disturbed, a mental concentration no excitement could shake, a memory of facts never losing its grasp, a will which never faltered, and a courage which rose in the presence of danger like the mercury in the tube."

A similar judgment of his work at the bar was given by an excellent authority, Judge Walter Q. Gresham: "As a trial lawyer he was self-reliant and courageous, and when a case took a sudden and unexpected turn, and defeat seemed almost inevitable, he exhibited rare skill and great reserve power. It was on such occasions that he appeared to best advantage."

Such evidence is not to be disregarded, but it was given at a memorial meeting at the time of his death, when not only are a man's faults passed over, but his virtues somewhat exaggerated. It is difficult to avoid a belief that in the fight for the life of the Nation and in the confused struggle over the currency Hendricks displayed too much of the willow, too little of the oak.

As a speaker, Hendricks though "earnest, at times vehement, was always graceful and dignified, and therefore pleasing and persuasive." Judge and Senator Turpie of Indiana, a popular and rather flowery orator, said of Hendricks:

"In illustration he was sparing; in diction, choice, accurate; upon occasion, ornate and elegant; fluent without superfluity. In pronunciation a purist, clear, precise, with an ear of most delicate fancy. In the collocation, or arrangement of words in the clause or sentence, not so capable; as apt to close an important sentence with one of the smallest of English prepositions as with a term whose quantities might give both to the voice and ear the cadence of repose. For mere humor he found not often a place, though happy when so used; for invective or denunciation very seldom. The most malignant miscreant in the record was treated by him usually as one who had but fallen into some mistake or error.

"His deportment toward his brethren of the bar, the jury, his auditors, and especially toward the officer presiding, was the model of courtesy and complaisance. As an advocate he must take high rank in the first class, a class not numerous. He was especially able in adaptation. Fact was closely fitted to fact and the whole structure of circumstance dovetailed into the law of the case. The parts matched like mosaics in the most highly finished mechanism. To this was united a suave plausibility and a subtle economy which made much of little, when little fell to his side. He had a copious command of familiar terms and expressions even upon abstruse topics, which became his interpreters to the jury, and this kind of interpretation had for itself the choicest medium, a voice which persuasion had herself attuned to the very touch.

"His imagination was strong, active, vivid; not lawless but sedulously tempered to the theme he dealt with. None knew better than he when to use it, when to forbear."[1]

Hendricks carried his consideration for men whom he fought in court into political life. He was courteous in debate, seldom resorted to personalities, and gave even the Radical Republicans credit for honest motives. His biographer states that he had an affectionate reverence for Lincoln, and that the President said: "We have differed in politics, but you have uniformly treated my administration with fairness." On the floor of the Senate, Hendricks spoke highly of Sumner. In 1880, he praised George W. Julian's courage and admitted that he himself had been mistaken in opposing abolition. He told a leading newspaper correspondent: "I have always stood up for Hayes. We have no business to abuse him for abiding the issue of a trial we proposed."

Personally, Hendricks was thoroughly honest, a man of culture but without hauteur, fond of mixing with his fellows, agreeable and conciliating.

Hendricks had been nominated by the efforts of his opponents in order to placate the soft money men and get Western votes, and the attempt

---

[1] *The Indianapolis Journal,* December 1, 1885, p. 2.

appeared likely to succeed. A Washington correspondent of the St. Louis *Republican* wrote: "The Western men did not generally believe that Hendricks would accept the second place with Tilden, and his nomination has much encouraged them." The New Haven *Register* said that Indiana seemed assured to the Democracy by the nomination of Hendricks. Yet Hendricks was a serious hindrance as well as a help. Before the convention met, the New York *Evening Post* said that "the nomination of Hendricks would be a contradiction of the whole political theory upon which Gov. Tilden commands the respect and confidence of honest and independent voters. A hard money candidate would be handicapped by an inflationist trickster. A man who represents the new and better ideas of politics would be associated with a politician of the old and vicious school. Such a ticket could not carry New York or any other doubtful state. If this scandalous nomination is seriously proposed, it ought to be promptly rejected by Governor Tilden."

The facing-both-ways ticket was adopted and it seemed that the Democrats dared not straighten it. The Cincinnati *Commercial* said that if Tilden softened, the Democrats could not carry New York, and that if Hendricks hardened, they could not carry Indiana. The platform also was rather flexible and the Republicans jeered fiercely. Nasby was still writing, and he reported that a prominent citizen of Confederate X Roads had asked the Democratic candidates to explain what the platform meant; that Tilden replied: "Hard money, of course, but soften it a good deal in the West"; and that Hendricks answered: "Soft money, of course, but harden it a good deal in the East." Hendricks' soft money views were the subject of constant attack and gave the Liberals of four years before a reason for rejoining their old party.

No sooner was Hendricks nominated, than Carl Schurz assailed him as a soft money man with no views of his own on the financial question, and announced that he would support Hayes. The *Staats Zeitung* took a similar position. Whitelaw Reid, who had succeeded Greeley as editor of the New York *Tribune,* made Hendricks' nomination his justification for accepting Hayes' promises of reform and aligning himself with Conkling and Morton.

The Republicans dwelt on the danger of having a man of Hendricks' financial theories President, and hinted and even openly declared that Tilden, if elected, would not live out his term. One Republican speaker, using the forms of perfect respect, always referred to the Democratic candidate as the venerable Mr. Tilden. Some Republican papers pictured Tilden as a broken-down old man. The Cincinnati *Gazette* having described him as feeble, Henry Watterson replied that Tilden was "a gentleman seen every day taking the most arduous exercise (horse-back riding) and who is known to perform the most arduous daily toil." Parke Godwin argued that it was not likely that Hendricks would ever have any legislative function since "Mr. Tilden is of a long-lived family, has never had any organic disease, is in good health, of temperate and active habits, and likely to live out the ordinary span of life."

In addition to blame for financial heresies, came accusations of weakness
of character. The Boston *Journal* said: "Mr. Hendricks has been mainly
spoken of by the Republican press as an amiable politician of the shilly-shally-
ing order on the financial and other leading questions." It is possible that
many Eastern Democrats thought the same, although, of course, they did not
say so publicly. John Bigelow, who was a close ally of Mr. Tilden and
after his death wrote the official biography of that gentleman, said of Hendricks: "He was a man of considerable talent, he had made a creditable record
as a political leader in Indiana, and he might have been a statesman if he had
been less of a demagogue. He was more or less infected with the political
heresies of the section in which he resided. Instead of leading his people,
he was ready to yield to any clamor and foster any delusion that promised
him votes." In his letter of acceptance Tilden devoted much space to a discussion of the currency question, making plain his stand in favor of a resumption of specie payments and "sound" money. Hendricks, in his letter of
acceptance, tried to ride both horses. He stated that he was in favor of
making the national currency convertible into gold and silver, but was opposed
to all artificial measures for the contraction of the currency. He ended un-
convincingly by saying: "It will be seen . . . . that I am in accord with
the platform of the Convention" and by giving the highest praise to the head
of the ticket.

There was some attempt by Hendricks' friends to represent him to the
East as more of a hard money man than had been supposed; but the candidate himself maintained his old position. In a speech at Indianapolis shortly
after his nomination he opposed fixing a definite day, even one in the future,
for redemption, and dwelt on the evils of contraction. The New York
Nation sharply replied: "We must take the liberty of warning the Democrats
that Mr. Hendricks, already a heavy load to carry, may readily become heavier
by making speeches. He is in some respects a ridiculous nomination and
would be worse than ridiculous if he were to have any political duties. But
such as he is, his speech at Indianapolis, denunciatory of the Resumption
Act, is calculated to make him still more objectionable." The *Nation* declared
that resumption would of necessity contract, and that a date for it must be
fixed and resolutely maintained. Senator Morton made bitter attacks on
Hendricks, assailing him as a pro-slavery man and one who had favored a
Northwestern confederacy unless slavery were given equal rights in the territories. Morton also said that no man who had been in public life for thirty
years had a record so barren of achievement as did Hendricks. Others
appear to have made a similar criticism; and Hendricks' biographers were
seemingly a little disturbed by the charge and replied that Hendricks was a
minority Senator; that the majority seldom allow a member of the minority
to originate or mould legislation; and that the Reconstruction Republicans
were particularly rigid in this particular.

The Republicans professed themselves much shocked by the tone of Hendricks' letter of acceptance. The *Tribune* called it "a very bitter, narrow, partisan document, by all odds the weakest political document of the present campaign," and said that "Hendricks rattles off the reasons for his political beliefs, so far as he gives them, in the manner of a backwoods stump orator without cohesion, logic, or sense, while throughout it all runs such a strain of denunciation of political opponents as would hardly be deemed decent in the loose courtesies of oral debate." But political papers are not usually characterized by sweet reasonableness, and the Republicans had done much that deserved severe censure.

At the close of the campaign the Secretary of the Treasury, Lot M. Morrill, went to New York and called for the defeat of the Democrats in order to secure a sound currency. Speaking from the steps of the subtreasury building in Wall Street, he put sharp questions to which, of course, he gave Republican answers. He told his audience: "It is said the head of the Democratic ticket is a hard money man, but will he stick, will he adhere? That depends on the hands into which he falls. Look at the other end of the ticket. Is he hard or soft? Decidedly soft. In which end of the ticket is the strength? (A voice, "In the tail"). Very well then, he will wag it. On this great financial question, financial men, Wall Street men, laboring men, be sure how you vote next Tuesday."

Mr. Wheeler played a decidedly less prominent part in the campaign than did Mr. Hendricks. The Democrats were worried by much that needed defense or explanation in their candidate's record; the Republicans were embarrassed by what seemed to be the lack of any record at all. The sketch of Wheeler bound in with the official campaign life of Hayes began: "It is doubtful if there can be found a man in public life anywhere whose biography is more difficult to write than that of William A. Wheeler . . . . He has a power to attract close attention to what he is saying or doing and to keep himself in the background." The Boston *Journal* spoke of him as one who, "whatever the quantity of his reputation, has a quality that can not be excelled." The *Journal* truly said that men of the greatest weight and influence in a Legislature were often overshadowed by the popularity of others less deserving; and that information concerning William A. Wheeler should be sought from his colleagues. It may be that among those who needed information was Hayes himself. In January, when his wife reported General Sherman's prophecy that the ticket would be Hayes and Wheeler, Hayes had replied: "I am ashamed to say, 'Who is Wheeler?'"

The nomination of Wheeler was cordially received by all factions in New York and doubtless helped swell the Republican vote, but this was of no practical importance as Tilden carried the state. Wheeler went to Vermont and there made his most important campaign speech in which he declared that the South was trying to control the Government by the election of Tilden, and that "no such proposition, for audacity, has its parallel in the history of the country. We confront the old issue. Let your ballots protect the work so effectively done by your bayonets at Gettysburg, and on many a field of strife."

Election day passed; the votes were counted. In some of the states there were multiple returns, and the result remained uncertain. Into the history of this dangerous dispute, it is not necessary to go. The matter was ultimately referred to an extra-constitutional Electoral Commission, which by a strictly party vote decided every disputed case in favor of the Republicans. This gave the election to Hayes and Wheeler by the uncomfortably close margin of 185 to 184.

In 1880 President Hayes was not a candidate for renomination, thereby keeping a pledge which he had made four years before. It may be that he would have adhered to his promise even under great temptation to violate it, but the actual conditions made a candidacy ridiculous. Mr. Hayes had withdrawn military support of the few carpet-bag governments which were left in the South, although they were counted in by the same boards that he was himself; and the Democratic candidates installed themselves in office. Moreover, Mr. Hayes had introduced civil service reform to such an extent as to greatly offend men of the old school, yet had made enough exceptions to enable them to charge him with hypocrisy. Consequently, a majority of those who were active in politics and, perhaps, of the whole party, were hostile to him.

The two leading candidates before the convention were General Grant, who had just returned from a trip around the world on which he had received high honors, and James G. Blaine. Minor aspirants were John Sherman, George F. Edmunds, and William Windom. The delegates showed remarkable persistency in adhering to their candidates, and it was not until the thirty-sixth ballot that a decision was received. The choice fell on a dark horse, General Garfield of Ohio, who was a member of the convention, where he had shown much sagacity and tact. The nominee was a man of high culture and ideals, "a scholar in politics," not exactly a "Liberal," but a near one, and highly regarded by the reform wing of the party.

Four years before, Mr. Hayes had been given a companion of similar type, and agreeable to the same faction as himself; but in 1880, the active support of the Grant men, the Stalwarts as they were called, was absolutely necessary to carry New York and the election, and the convention threw itself at their feet. Garfield, indeed, preserved some feeling of propriety, although, as his letter of acceptance was soon to show, he was ready to conciliate the Conkling wing. After the usual formalities of making the nomination unanimous with speeches that contained more courtesy than truth, the convention recessed to give an opportunity for negotiations over the Vice-Presidency. Garfield had already sent ex-Governor Dennison of Ohio to Levi P. Morton of New York to ask him to accept the Vice-Presidency.

Mr. Morton was a wealthy banker who had taken much interest in politics. He was allied with the Grant wing and had been "prominently mentioned" as the candidate for Vice-President if Grant should be nominated. Morton told Dennison that he must consult his friends and promptly saw Conkling, but Conkling bitterly resented Garfield's nomination,[1] predicted his defeat at the polls, and did not hesitate to dissuade Morton from accepting the nomination for Vice-President. He told Morton: "If you think the ticket will be elected, if you think you will be happy in the association, accept." To this Morton answered: "I have more confidence in your judgment than in my own." Conkling then added: "Governor Boutwell of Massachusetts is a great friend of yours. Why don't you talk with him?" Acting upon this suggestion Morton sought Boutwell, who advised against it. Morton acquiesced, and refused the use of his name.

After returning to their headquarters at the hotel, the Stalwarts, upon the suggestion and insistence of George H. Sharpe, quickly agreed upon Chester A. Arthur, who gave an affirmative response to their appeal. Conkling was not present at the time, but subsequently in Arthur's room, where Howard Carroll and several other delegates lingered, he bitterly opposed putting a Stalwart on the ticket, and expressed in unmeasured terms his disapprobation of Arthur's acceptance. On their way to the convention, Sharpe told Woodford of the pungent flavor of Conkling's invective, and of Arthur's calm assertion of the propriety of his action. At the Wigwam, Conkling refused Sharpe's request to put Arthur in nomination.

Upon the reassembling of the convention, California presented Elihu B. Washburne for Vice-President, a nomination which Dennis McCarthy of New York, amidst cordial and hearty applause from the galleries, seconded in a forceful speech. This indicated that Arthur was *persona non grata* to the anti-Grant delegates of the Empire State. Jewell of Connecticut, Ferry of Michigan, Settle of North Carolina, and Maynard of Tennessee, were likewise presented. As the call of states proceeded, New York made no response in its turn; but when Woodford subsequently proposed the name of Arthur, Dennison responded with a spirited second, various delegates followed, and the convention nominated him by a vote of 468, to 193 for Washburne and 90 scattering.

Chester Alan Arthur was born in Fairfield, Vermont, on October 5, 1830. His father was a Baptist clergyman, respected by his brethren for his strict orthodoxy and his knowledge of theology. Arthur's campaign biographer thought that much credit was due him for escaping the debauchery and crime into which many ministers' sons have fallen. He says that "the very worst and the most disagreeable situation in which a child can be placed, is to be a son of a preacher of the gospel, since the parishioners flatter him and the father, wishing he should set a good example, tries to make his young chil-

---

[1] Conkling disliked and distrusted Garfield personally.

dren into staid and sensible old people." / As a boy, Arthur was fond of an active, outdoor life, but his father so well instructed him that when only fourteen, he entered Union College. His work there was respectable, but not brilliant. After graduation, he taught school in Vermont for two winters, studied law, and finally opened an office in New York City, where he quickly won an honorable position.

He was a special advocate of the claims of the colored people. In 1856 a respectable negress was violently ejected from a street car in New York. Arthur took her case, obtained damages, and established the right of negroes to use the public conveyances. In 1852, Jonathan Lemmon of Virginia determined to take eight of his wife's slaves to Texas. They went by steamer from Norfolk to New York City and were there to have been reshipped to Texas. However, upon the initiative of local New York people, Judge Elijah Paine of the Superior Court of the city, issued a writ of *habeas corpus* in their behalf. The case was argued by distinguished counsel on both sides, with the result that on the 13th of November the court ordered the release of the negroes on the ground that, having been brought to a free state by their master, they had been made free.

The decision created great excitement in the South, and the Legislature of Virginia ordered the Attorney-General of the state to appeal. When the matter came before the Supreme Court of New York, the Attorney-General of Virginia, and the eminent New York lawyer, Charles O'Conor, represented the master. The New York Legislature requested the Governor to appoint counsel for the negroes, and the position was finally given to Chester A. Arthur and William M. Evarts. The court sustained Judge Paine and an appeal was taken to the United States Supreme Court; but when it came to trial, the Civil War had broken out and the state of Virginia did not appear.

Arthur had taken much interest in the militia and had been chief engineer and inspector-general. In 1861 Governor Morgan appointed him Quartermaster-General and he served two years, performing the many and complicated duties of that office with great ability and rigid honesty. The election of a Democrat as Governor prevented Arthur's reappointment, and he resumed the practice of law. He gave great attention to the collection of claims on the Government and to the drafting of bills, and thus obtained a handsome income. As a boy he had always attended political parades and jubilees. As a man he retained his interest, showing it in more mature ways, and proved a most useful lieutenant, first of Fenton, and then of Conkling. Kindly, tactful, and persuasive, he won the confidence of the district leaders, and in 1871 was given the key position of Collector of the Port of New York.

\ Alexander says of him: "In party initiative, Arthur's judgment and modesty aided him in avoiding the repellent methods of his predecessors. He did not wait for emergencies to arise, but considering them in advance as possible contingencies, he exercised an unobtrusive but masterful authority when the necessity for action came. He played an honest game of diplomacy. What others did with Machiavellian intrigue or a cynical indifference to ways and means he accomplished with the cards on the table in plain view, and with motives and objects frankly disclosed. No one ever thought his straightforward methods, clumsy, or unbusinesslike, or deficient in cleverness."/ He recommended reforms but he was hampered by a vicious system "upon which every political boss from DeWitt Clinton to Roscoe Conkling had relied for advantage." He would not declare war on it, and President Hayes became convinced that there could be no change in the members while the head remained, and removed him from the Collectorship.

Garfield was the scholar in politics, Arthur the Beau Brummel. "The skill of an artist tailor exhibited his tall graceful figure at its best, and his shapely hands were immaculately gloved. His hat advertised the latest fashion, just as his exquisite necktie indicated the proper color.[1] He was equally particular about his conduct. Whatever his environment, he observed the details of court etiquette." Yet he was not glacial. His stately elegance of manner easily unbent without loss of dignity, and although his volatile spirits and manner of living gave him the appearance of a *bon vivant*, lively and jocose, with less devotion to work than to society, it was noticeable that he attracted men of severe mould as easily as those vivacious and light-hearted associates who called him "Chet." Probably they saw both the surface and beneath it. Congressman O'Ferrall of Virginia says in his *Recollections*: "President Arthur impressed me with his amiability, courtesy, laborious habits, and strict attention to business. In the social circle, he was delightful."

In the early part of Hayes' Presidency, many Democrats had declared that he was no rightful President, termed him, "His Accidency," and demanded the nomination and election of the "old ticket" as a vindication of the right. But time calms political excitement, and the discovery and translation of the "cipher despatches," showing a conspiracy by various Democrats, including the editor of the New York *World* and the nephew and housemate of Mr. Tilden, to bribe, did much to mitigate the scandal of the "counting in" of Hayes by returning boards in the South.

Tilden's health was somewhat feeble, and the political situation in New York was unfavorable to him. He wrote a letter declining a renomination; but it was couched in such terms that his friends argued that he would not refuse one if offered him. A correspondent at the convention wrote that an intimate friend of Tilden said that he was a man of gigantic intellect, and that the character of his mental organization was such that it was utterly

---

[1] Senator Cullom, however, says in his *Memoirs* that Arthur, though always well dressed, was not as exquisitely so as was popularly supposed; that Arthur's leadership in New York City politics had caused many men of refinement outside the state to think of him as a "rough neck"; and that, to correct this mistake, stories of his elaborate ultra-fashionable attire were deliberately circulated.

impossible for him to bring any matter to a decisive conclusion. But just before the opening of the convention, another letter arrived making his refusal more definite, and nearly all of his followers joined other groups. There were several candidates but, except Hendricks, none inspired much zeal in their supporters. On the first ballot, General Winfield Scott Hancock had a slight lead. On the second, the delegates broke to him and he was nominated unanimously.

One of the minor candidates was William R. Morrison. The delegates of his own state of Illinois had stood staunchly by him for a while and then swung to Hancock. It is said that they expected he would receive the Vice-Presidency as a reward; but the leaders of the convention decided on William H. English of Indiana, and when the voting began, he found but one opponent, Richard Bishop of Ohio. Bishop was a man whose chief qualification was a superficial popularity. A correspondent wrote: "He hand-shook himself into the Governor's chair and now he is at it again in a wild hope of the Vice-Presidency." His nominator made a flat failure to stir the convention by exhorting it to choose "your Uncle Dick," and before the first ballot was completed, English was so clearly the favorite that Bishop was withdrawn and English nominated unanimously.

English might be described as an almost forgotten fossil whose memory was not sweet. He had served from 1852 to 1860 in the House of Representatives, where his chief accomplishment was the passage of the "English bill" admitting Kansas as a free state should she so desire, but forbidding her to emancipate the slaves then in her borders or their issue. A liberal grant of public lands was to be made if she accepted this limitation of a power held in full by other states; but Kansas was reasonably sure of generous treatment in the matter of land whether she came in slave or free, and refused the bribe. Since 1860, English had held no public office, but had become president of a large bank, speculated in mortgages, and made a handsome fortune. The last circumstance was probably an important reason for his nomination. Mr. English was the first of the "angels," men who have been nominated for the Vice-Presidency because of their ability and willingness to fill the party war chest.[1]

There was need of such help, for other plans had failed. Tilden's supporters had hoped to nominate as his colleague, the Ohio Oil King, Henry B. Payne, and it was reported that between them they would give half a million. Thomas F. Bayard of Delaware, a leading candidate for the Presidency, was also wealthy and had rich friends. But General Hancock was a man of modest means, with no special allies in the world of high finance.

---

[1] Financial considerations may have played a part in the nomination by the Whigs in 1844 of Mr. Frelinghuysen. In 1848, there was a story that Abbott Lawrence had offered a hundred thousand dollar contribution to the Whig campaign fund in return for the Vice-Presidential nomination.

Geography, as usual, played an important part in the nomination for Vice-President. In the last campaign the Democrats had selected a citizen of Indiana for Vice-President and had carried the state, and they hoped that history would repeat itself. Why, then, did they not renominate Hendricks? Perhaps because Tilden and his supporters did not like his former associate. Before the definite withdrawal of Tilden, the Indiana delegation informed that of New York that a conference was necessary. The New Yorkers merely sent their secretary. The Indiana men denied a story that Hendricks had said that he would not run with Tilden, and stated that Hendricks was a candidate for the Presidency, but that no one had authority to say that he would or would not run on the old ticket.[1] The olive branch had no effect on the Tilden men. The Cincinnati *Commercial,* a Republican paper, it is true, asserted that they nominated English with the special purpose of annoying Hendricks. Certainly the two were old foes. Hendricks had been a close ally of Douglas; English, an adherent of Buchanan and a lieutenant of Senator Jesse D. Bright, who cherished a personal grudge against Douglas.

Each party went into battle hampered as well as helped by its Vice-Presidential candidate. Arthur, not wholly justly, was identified in the minds of many with the spoils system, and all that was worst in Republican politics. Some of the Republican papers in New York took no notice of him whatever; others were very cool in their comments. The writer of a Democratic campaign sketch of English quoted criticisms of Arthur by President Hayes and Secretary of the Treasury Sherman. But the nomination of the scholarly and idealistic Garfield reconciled reformers to the Republican ticket; and the biographer of Arthur stated that the latter was removed from the Collectorship because of a conscientious difference of opinion between him and the President as to the means of carrying out reforms which they both desired.

The Republicans took much pleasure in making frequent and loud assertions that their opponents had deceived themselves both in their hope of votes and in that of cash in return for taking up English. The Cincinnati *Gazette* said: "The ticket is obviously weak where it should be strong. It is weak in the doubtful October state, Indiana. The nomination of English is not only not strong in itself, it is a blow at Hendricks . . . . There is wailing on the Wabash." The New York *Tribune* sarcastically remarked: "The whole Democratic party in Indiana ought to be united now. Its candidate for Governor is a soft money ranter of the worst type, while its candidate for Vice-President is a hard money man, and a banker. The party must attempt to carry the state on the soft money issue in October and on the hard money issue in November. It must denounce national banks and bankers one day and vote for a national banker on the next."

---

[1]Hendricks' biographers state that he had definitely refused the Vice-Presidential nomination, but perhaps may have felt at liberty to suppress a private letter.

The *Tribune* also asserted that English was one of the most unpopular Democrats in Indiana. Attacks were made on him both politically and personally. His famous bill was denounced as a truckling to the slave power. The Indianapolis *Journal* alleged that, in 1860, Stephen A. Douglas told a party of friends that English was his bitterest enemy; the *Journal* also stated that Douglas called English the "man Friday" of Senator Bright (who was expelled from the Senate for disloyal conduct), and said that he had done more than any other man in Indiana, except Bright and his brother, to plunge the country into civil war.[1]

English was described as timid and miserly, a man who slept in an ironbound bedroom, dealt in mortgages, and was harsh to the occupants of houses he bought in. It was charged that he promised fifty thousand dollars for his nomination and gave five. A story was told that when he was asked to contribute to the relief of the sufferers by the Chicago fire, he generously handed over a dollar, but that on being warned that he was hurting himself politically, he sent a hundred dollars with an explanation that he had misunderstood the request made of him.

In October came the all-important state election in Indiana, awaited everywhere as an indication of how the country would go in November; and the Republican candidate for Governor was elected by a majority of eight thousand. The Republicans were jubilant, the Democrats sore and angry. Many of the latter laid the blame for their defeat on what they termed the mismanagement of English, and on his bad relations with the leading Democrats of the state. But the Republican victory revived the feeling of lovers of clean politics against Arthur. Indiana was a corrupt state where buying of "floaters" was the regular custom. After the election, Democrats and Republicans charged each other with extensive bribery, and probably both told the truth. Shortly before voting day, the Republicans "knew" that in response to urgent demands Eastern Democrats had sent a large sum of money to Indiana. But it is probable that Republicanism in the state was also quickened by a golden shower. The biographers of Hendricks say that the Republicans used the tariff question effectively, and that the Democrats failed to meet them squarely; but that the real cause of Republican success was a visit of their national chairman, Senator Dorsey, later of Star Route fame, and his able assistant, United States Marshal W. W. Dudley, destined to become known for his advice given in the campaign of 1888: "Let the floaters be divided into blocks of five, each group being placed in charge of one man who shall be responsible for results." Holcombe and Skinner say that Dorsey came to Indiana armed with $400,000, took full charge, and bought his way to victory. On Dorsey's return to New York, grateful Republicans gave a banquet to the man who carried Indiana.

---

[1] If Douglas meant to accuse English of anything worse than errors of judgment, he was unfair. English opposed secession, and believed in maintaining the authority of the government.

But if Arthur scandalized and possibly injured the Republicans, he helped them too, for he had charge of the campaign in New York, and his abilities as a manager proved of great service.

Again there were two minor parties in the field, the Greenback and the Prohibitionist. The former nominated James B. Weaver of Iowa, and B. J. Chambers of Texas. The Prohibitionists nominated Neal Dow of Maine, and A. M. Thompson of Ohio. The Greenbackers nearly quadrupled their popular vote of four years before; the Prohibitionists made a gain of less than a thousand; but neither obtained any electoral votes. The Republicans won by carrying New York. Had that state gone Democratic, Hancock and English, like Hayes and Wheeler, would have been elected by a single electoral vote.

CHAPTER XVII.

The Democracy Wins, Loses, and Wins Again: 1884-1888-1892

PRESIDENT Garfield was shot by an assassin on July 2, 1881; he died on the nineteenth of the following September; and the rest of his term was served by the Vice-President. President Arthur proved himself worthy and capable, and he not unreasonably desired the honor of a second term. But the friends of James G. Blaine were determined to put their favorite in the presidential chair. The Republican convention met at Chicago on June 3. Mr. Blaine was nominated on the fourth ballot at a morning session, and the convention then adjourned until evening when, with only a few dissenting votes, it nominated General John A. Logan of Illinois for Vice-President. General Logan had been a minority candidate for President, but when the delegates of a majority of the states which must be relied on for Republican votes cast their ballots for Blaine, Logan, who felt that their wishes should be decisive and who desired to give the crown if he could not wear it, sent a telegram asking his friends to vote for Blaine.

Logan's nomination as Vice-President was, therefore, an acknowledgment of timely service; it was also a conciliation of the minority faction of the party, for Logan had been a thorough-going follower of Grant. Furthermore, he was very popular with the Union veterans, and this was an important consideration because for the first time since the war the Republicans had failed to put a Union soldier at the head of their ticket. The choice of Logan as second to Blaine was not unexpected, for their headquarters were side by side and their managers had frequently consulted during the convention. But the alliance was a recent one. Logan was a Grantite. Blaine had come to a personal breach with the General. Logan was an ally of Conkling. Conkling and Blaine had not been on speaking terms for years. A squib aimed at Logan's lack of education, but also referring to the coolness between him and the man who was now his chief, represents him as saying:

> "We never speak as we pass by
> Me to Jim Blaine nor him to I
> We merely nod and drop our eye."

John A. Logan was born in an Illinois village on February 9, 1826. He was educated at an academy at Shiloh, Illinois, served in the Mexican War, studied law, and began practice in 1851. He early entered politics as a Democrat and proved himself an eloquent, vigorous, and effective stump-speaker. In 1856 he was an elector on the Buchanan ticket, was chosen a Representative in Congress, and was reëlected in 1858 and 1860. In 1861 he resigned to enter the army as colonel of an Illinois regiment, served with great distinction, and retired at the close of the war with the rank of major-general. He was probably the best known and the most popular of the volunteer generals. Logan was again elected to Congress in 1866, and with a break of two years served as Representative or Senator until his nomination.

In person Logan was tall and commanding, with an enormous moutache, raven hair, and a complexion so swarthy that the soldiers named him "Black Jack," and political opponents falsely alleged that he was part Indian. At least he was Indian in temperament, intense in his loves and hates, sensitive, and apt to take too personal a point of view of public affairs. A Blaine paper rejoicing in the defeat of the Grant wing at the convention of 1880 described him as "Logan the volcanic."

The cultured East looked with disdain on this son of the West. The *Nation* in its issue of April 3, 1884, had said: "In point of education training, solidity of parts, mental grasp, and the general equipment so desirable in a Presidential candidate, General Logan is so seriously deficient that his nomination (for President) would be looked upon in the Eastern states as something altogether outré."[1] Even in the West a critic said of Logan: "Nature made him a soldier and a politician, but neither nature nor art ever designed him for a statesman." Yet there may be an excessive regard for polish. Logan could see the weak places in an opponent's argument and strike there with shattering force. The cultured Senator Hoar told an audience that he wished that those who laughed at Logan's English could meet him in debate on the floor of the Senate.

The Democrats found themselves in a dilemma not unlike that of 1876. In their own party there was a demand for reform; many Republicans were ready to join them if a satisfactory candidate were nominated; and they had one at hand in Governor Grover Cleveland of New York. Mr. Cleveland had been swept into the Governorship by a great anti-boss wave. He was a hard money man, a courageous reformer, and strengthened in the nation, if weakened in his own state, by the opposition of Tammany. The Democratic convention met at Chicago on July 8, and seizing its opportunity, cast a majority of votes for Mr. Cleveland on the first ballot, and nominated him on the second.

But then came fear. What of Tammany, of the soft money men, and the old hard shells? The situation was in some ways worse than in 1876. Tilden

---

[1] Quoted in Arthur C. Cole's *The Era of the Civil War*, 146, r.

was a veteran in the Democratic ranks. Cleveland was a much younger man who cared little, and his followers less, for the old issues. As in 1876, the Democrats sought safety in a contrast and once more nominated Thomas A. Hendricks for Vice-President.

During the campaign the personalities and records of both the leading candidates came under heavy fire from their opponents. Strange as it seems today, the Republican cartoonists pictured the Democratic ticket as a kangaroo with a very small head and a large tail, edged with teeth. This conception of relative importance appeared in various forms. Many cultured and high principled Republicans who had announced that they would support Cleveland were vigorously reminded of their inconsistency in voting for Hendricks. One of the leading "Mugwumps," as the Republican bolters were called, George William Curtis, had said in 1876 that the nomination of Hendricks showed the insincerity of the Democratic cry for reform, and the power in the party of the Repudiationists. The New York *Times,* which had come out for Cleveland, had called Hendricks a rebel sympathizer, a salary and land grabber, and a political jobber. These opinions were carefully reprinted in Republican papers. Carl Schurz had again allied himself with the Democrats and a Republican paper, the St. Louis *Globe Democrat,* represented Hendricks as urging Schurz to emphasize the fraud issue of 1876, and Schurz as much embarrassed at the recollection that he himself had been a member of the Cabinet of President Hayes. Hendricks had stressed "vindication" in his reply to the notification of his nomination, and the Philadelphia *Press* made the comment: ". . . . It is unfortunate for his party that Mr. Hendricks is not gifted like Mr. Tilden with a nice sense of the ridiculous, or he would see the absurdity of trying to vindicate the tail of the 'old ticket' only."

Not all the Republican papers took up the cry of "Kangaroo." The Providence *Journal* alleged that hardly a man had been mentioned for the Vice-Presidency who would not have done more to strengthen the ticket than Hendricks, "even if no account is made of that silent and secret animosity which makes its lair in the breast of Samuel J. Tilden, and which has punished many who have stood in the way of his ambition or thwarted his schemes."

Both the Vice-Presidential candidates were charged with sympathy for slavery and with disloyalty. It seems strange indeed for such an accusation to be brought against Logan, an early volunteer and a "bloody shirt" Republican. But Logan had been a Democrat before the war, and whenever he fought he fought fiercely. He lived in Southern Illinois, popularly known as "Egypt" because of its sympathy with the South, and it is not strange that in act and speech he had been violently opposed to the anti-slavery movement. In 1853 he introduced in the lower house of the Illinois Legislature the famous or infamous black laws.

When Stephen A. Douglas broke with Buchanan on the question of slavery in Kansas, Logan stood with the President. In the Presidential campaign of 1860, the Republican wave swept into Logan's own stronghold, but Black Jack was undaunted. Arthur C. Cole says in the *Era of the Civil War,* a volume in the Centennial History of the State of Illinois: "John A. Logan, the champion of Egyptian Democracy, contested every inch of ground that was lost, sometimes by methods hardly scrupulous in character. It was by such tactics that the determined Congressman acquired the cognomen of 'Dirty Work' Logan." Dr. Cole states that he compared the secessionists to the Revolutionary fathers struggling for liberty. He was accused of having encouraged enlistment in the Confederate army, of intending to join it himself, and of planning a secession of Egypt from both Illinois and the United States. But Logan, with all his daring, was not without a crafty prudence.

He made no public pronouncement of his position till neutrality was no longer possible, and then he stepped forth as the champion of the Union. Mrs. Logan in her *Reminiscences of a Soldier's Wife* says that it was the sight of the wounded soldiers of Bull Run that finally decided her husband, and it must be remembered that many Democrats who were not disturbed by slavery in other states and were full of Calhoun notions of state sovereignty, suddenly found themselves devoted Americans of the Jackson type when the unity of the country was at stake. After the war, Logan made vigorous speeches, calling for the punishment of the secession leaders; but like such Republicans as John Sherman and Governors Morton and Andrew, he at first favored Johnson's policy of reconstruction, though here again he did not publicly commit himself. But in 1866 the party, by a small majority, decided against Johnson, largely because he seemed to represent ex-rebels and Copperheads, and Logan, with other Moderates, joined the Radical wing. Once there, he showed himself an unflinching advocate of its most extreme policies.

Logan's unobtrusively neutral attitude in the Johnson-Congress contest, immediately after the war, was not likely to hurt him, but the alleged sympathy with the Confederacy in 1861 was a more serious matter, and an official campaign biographer of the Republican candidates thought it well to anticipate a renewal of the charge by a strong though not a complete refutation. The guilt of anti-Republicanism was treated as purged by time and repentance. Old anti-slavery men were to be found supporting Cleveland and bringing Logan's earlier views against him. To this it was replied: "They say they were abolitionists when John A. Logan was a Democrat. The first shot fired at Sumter blew out of John A. Logan every drop of Democratic blood in his body. It is not so much the question when you began to do right, but have you held on? Judas was an apostle before Paul was."

The Republicans twitted the Democrats with turning down a soldier like Rosecrans and nominating Hendricks. General Grosvenor of Ohio said: "The soldiers have not forgotten that he (Hendricks) was what we called in our state a copperhead. The young men now have an opportunity to strike at the man who struck at their fathers on the battlefield."

Both Logan and Hendricks took an active part in the campaign. Logan spoke in the East and the West, and attended the Grand Army annual reunion, where he was most enthusiastically received. He also accompanied Mr. Blaine in a speech-making tour in the October state of Ohio. Five hundred Confederate veterans of Virginia requested him to address them on political issues of the day. He replied that his engagements would not permit him to accept, but advised his correspondents to adopt the policy of protection, and invite Northern capitalists to invest in manufacturing in their state, and to assist in the development of the industries to which Virginia was well adapted.

Mr. Hendricks wielded for the Democrats a blade which, like that of Fitz-James, was both sword and shield. In a speech at Indianapolis he asserted that a proper examination of the public accounts would show numerous defalcations, and instanced one recently discovered in the Navy Department. There followed a discussion by letter between Mr. Hendricks and Secretary Chandler as to whether there had been negligence in management. Hendricks made many speeches in Indiana and in the neighboring states, and when Blaine visited the West, he took the stump in reply and spoke with much effect. The Democratic candidate for Vice-President, the old school politician, also came to the help of his chief, the darling of the reformers, when attacked for moral weakness. Mr. Cleveland, though a bachelor, was also a father. The Republicans discovered his slip and proclaimed it loudly and joyously. Suggestions were made that Cleveland withdraw. Hendricks, who was correct in his personal conduct, wrote a letter in which he stated that the circumstances of the affair did not require it, and that it was now too late to change the ticket.

But probably Mr. Hendricks' greatest service to the Democrats was given not publicly, but privately. The Tammany chief, John Kelly, was much opposed to Cleveland, and was inclined to sulk in his tent. Hendricks had been on excellent terms with Tammany and was a personal friend of Kelly, who had tried to stampede the nominating convention to him for President. Hendricks now went to New York and by his personal influence induced Kelly to lead his braves into the fray.

An anti-Monopoly party which "had no prior or subsequent history" nominated Benjamin F. Butler of Massachusetts for President, and left the nomination of a Vice-President to the National Committee, who took the Greenback candidate. The Greenbackers nominated Butler for President and put beside him A. M. West of Mississippi. The prohibitionists offered John P. St John of Kansas and William Daniel of Maryland. None of the minor parties carried a single state. The Greenback vote fell from 308,578 in the preceding campaign to 175,370; the Prohibitionist vote rose from 10,305 to 150,369. Between the Democrats and Republicans the contest was very close and the result was for a few days in doubt, but the Democrats carried New York by 1,149 votes, and therefore the election.[1]

In 1888 the Democratic convention unanimously renominated President Cleveland without the formality of a roll-call. There could be no question of the old ticket, as Mr. Hendricks had died early in his term. For the second place there were two leading candidates, Governor Gray of Indiana, and Senator Thurman of Ohio. The contest in the convention was brief but picturesque. Mr. Stanwood thus describes the meeting of the two hosts: "During Judge Thurman's long service in the Senate the country had been accustomed to hear much about the 'red bandanna' of which he was in the habit of making use after taking a pinch of snuff. The friends of Governor Gray were present in strong force, all waving high white hats as badges.[2] But the advocates of Judge Thurman had provided themselves with a great quantity of red pocket handkerchiefs and these articles proved to be far more popular badges than did the white hats. When the voting for a candidate was about to begin, the California delegation displayed the bandanna at the top of a long pole, and the appearance of the emblem was received with the wildest cheering.

"The Indiana delegation strove in vain to offset the demonstration by elevating a white hat on another pole. The red bandanna fluttered in all parts of the immense hall, and the delegates and spectators cheered until they were hoarse. . . . ." But the popular enthusiasm only endorsed what had been decided on by the throne. Congressman Scott brought word from the White House that the President desired the nomination of Thurman; and though many of Mr. Cleveland's special friends were not well pleased by his intervention, which they thought too much resembled machine methods; and though before the convention Gray seemed to have an excellent chance of success, the President's wish, together with the loyalty to party and the good character and ability of Mr. Thurman, prevailed, and he was nominated on the first ballot by an overwhelming majority.[3]

Allen G. Thurman was born in Lynchburg, Virginia, on November 13, 1813. His family removed to Chillicothe, Ohio, in 1819. He studied law, was admitted to the bar, and entered upon the profession of the law. He served a term in the House of Representatives from 1845 to 1847, and was from 1851 to 1854 an Associate Judge of the Supreme Court of Ohio, and from 1854 to 1860 Chief Justice. During the war he was a steadfast Democrat, but usually free from Copperheadism. In 1869 he was elected to the United States Senate, in which body he soon attained the leadership of his

---

[1] A cartoon in *Puck* represented Miss Columbia's school, and the teacher saying, "Miss New York, your answer is correct, but please to speak a little louder in the future."

[2] The phrase, "high hat," is of comparatively recent origin, and in 1888 it was not dangerous for a man to be called the high hat candidate.

[3] A minor cause of Gray's defeat was the publication of a letter from a former friend to whom he had refused a favor.

party. He was for a long time the chairman of the powerful Judiciary Committee and, during the Forty-sixth Congress, President *pro tempore* of the Senate.

Blaine says of Thurman: "His rank in the Senate was established from the day he took his seat and was never lowered during the period of his service. He was an admirably disciplined debater, was fair in his method of statement, logical in his arguments, honest in his conclusions. He had no tricks in discussion, no catch phrases to secure attention, but was always direct and manly." Like most Western men in public life, his conduct on the currency question was thought by sound money men to be a little truckling. In general, however, Thurman held a steadfast course, and his party loyalty caused his fellow Democrats to speak of him as "the old Roman."

But he did not carry his partisanship into social intercourse. Griffin says in his *People and Politics Observed by a Massachusetts Editor:* "George F. Edmunds was his intimate. They crossed swords in debate but loved one another like brothers." Another Republican Senator with whom Thurman was on most friendly terms was Hannibal Hamlin. It was a matter of comment how often "the old Roman" and "the old Carthaginian" were seen together at the Capitol. These intimacies were doubtless in part due to the fact that both Edmunds and Hamlin were about Thurman's age and all had reached, or at least were approaching, that time of life when, as was said by Talleyrand's niece in explaining her uncle's emotion at the death of La-Fayette, "all our contemporaries are our friends."

The Republican convention met in much uncertainty. Mr. Blaine had twice declined the nomination, and though some followers were resolved to force it on him, the great body of the delegates turned their attention to others. Many Blaine men, however, consulted with a view to uniting on a candidate, and they may have hoped for a spontaneous and irresistible rush to their beloved chief. While the convention was in apparent deadlock, a prominent Republican received this telegram from Andrew Carnegie, with whom Blaine was touring Scotland: "Victor immovable. Take Trump and Star;" which, according to a cipher previously agreed on, meant that Blaine was unshakable in his resolution, and advised that the convention nominate Benjamin Harrison of Indiana, and William Walter Phelps of New Jersey. Harrison had been a general in the Union army and a United States Senator, and had won credit in both positions. Had Blaine been nominated, it is not improbable that the Vice-Presidency would have gone to Harrison.

Phelps was a journalist of ability and culture, a forceful and brilliant writer. Unlike many of his associates, he was not a Mugwump, but a close friend and staunch defender of Mr. Blaine. The Blaine faction went for Harrison and he was nominated; but Phelps' name, though forcefully presented, aroused little enthusiasm, perhaps because his own friends knew that he had no chance of success; for when the great states united on Harrison, they also determined to give the second place to New York. Her different factions had united on Levi P. Morton, and the convention, as expected, replied Amen, but not in full chorus. The vote stood: Walter F. Thomas of Texas 1, Blanche K. Bruce of Mississippi 11, William O. Bradley of Kentucky 103, William W. Phelps of New Jersey 119, and Levi P. Morton of New York 591. Blanche Bruce was neither a Scotchman, a lady, nor even white, but a gentleman of color, who had served a term in the United States Senate without discredit. Bradley was a worthy and able man and a zealous Republican, who, time after time, stood up to be knocked down in his Bourbon State. It is pleasant to know that this faithful, much enduring warrior finally obtained the Governorship, thanks to a division in the enemy's ranks.

Levi Parsons Morton was of the purest and oldest New England stock. His father was descended in an unbroken male line from George Morton, an exile at Leyden, the compiler and nominal author of *Mourt's Relation,* who came to Plymouth in the ship *Ann* in 1623. His son assisted in the foundation of Middleboro, Massachusetts where " . . . . he built the old Morton house which was handed down from father to son in the Morton family for two hundred years and long remained the oldest house in Plymouth County." Levi P. Morton's father spent eighteen years of his life as a faithful and beloved minister in Shoreham, Vermont, where he had gone in 1814, a missionary in spirit though not in form, to fight the intemperance and disorder common in frontier towns, and the infidelity caught by many soldiers of the Revolution from their French comrades. Morton's mother, Lucretia Parsons, was a descendant of Joseph Parsons, who came to New England in 1630, and helped to found Springfield and Northampton. Lucretia's brother, Levi Parsons, was the first American missionary to Palestine.

His namesake, the future Vice-President, was born at Shoreham on May 16, 1824. Levi was a younger son; his father was not able to give him much education; and at fourteen he went to work in a store for board, lodging, and fifty dollars a year. As he grew up he developed marked ability, and was soon doing business on a scale which made his father feel that he was taking unnecessary risks, and his maternal grandfather, the Reverend Justin Parsons, anxious lest his worldly success might endanger his soul. But though Morton was a true Yankee in devising new means to get trade, and continually extended his operations, his boldness was the result of careful thought and observation, and neither then nor in after years, when his reputation and power were national and international, did he employ harsh or unfair means, or forget the claims of higher things in the pursuit of wealth.

At the age of twenty-five, he took a position in the great Boston cotton house of J. M. Beebe & Company, and when only twenty-seven, became a junior partner. At the same time the firm admitted as a principal partner, Junius Spencer Morgan, a most able financier, but now chiefly known as the father of J. Pierpont Morgan, then a lad of thirteen. This was the beginning of a Morton-Morgan friendship which lasted over half a century. In 1854 Morgan became a partner in the banking firm of George Peabody & Company of London, and Morton was sent to New York as manager of a branch of the Beebe Company. But almost immediately he set up for himself, as the head of Morton, Grinnell & Company, wholesale dry goods commission.

The business was chiefly with the South, and the outbreak of the Civil War drove the firm into bankruptcy; but Morton reorganized it, and in 1868 himself paid the old creditors with interest, though not under any legal obligation to do so. This was the more honorable as he was no longer identified with the company. The same shrewdness and courage that led him to expand his country business in a manner which alarmed his cautious father, now induced him to go into banking where, because of the fluctuations of the currency, though the risks were great, so also were the rewards. Mr. Morton knew not only the money market but men. One of the chief causes of his success was his skill in choosing associates and subordinates. He set high standards of integrity and industry, but to those who maintained them he showed a courtesy which made no distinction between a junior clerk and a millionaire client, and an absolute loyalty. Mr. Morton was also fortunate in combining the sometimes inconsistent qualities of power of quick decision and grasp of detail.

Morton on entering banking allied himself with his old friend, J. S. Morgan, and Morton's London house finally displaced Jay Cooke & Company as agent for the United States in the world's financial capital. During the dispute between the United States and Great Britain over the Alabama Claims, Morton took an active though unofficial part in bringing the two countries together. From international, Morton passed to home politics, and in 1876 was nominated for Representative in Congress for the Eleventh Congressional District of New York, the dwelling place of the wealth and fashion of the city. But many of the voters were neither rich nor in society. Morton was attacked as "a plutocrat . . . . seeking to protect the citadel of plutocracy" and the sitting member, a Democrat, was reëlected, though by a greatly reduced majority.

Morton was renominated in 1878, took a frank and courageous stand for the resumption of specie payments, and was elected by a majority of over seven thousand. His victory was partly due, however, to a Greenback split in the Democratic party. In Congress, Morton's high position in the financial world freed him from the duty of effacement usually imposed on new members. His speeches were not orations, but very brief, clear, and forcible statements of the points at issue. He gave his chief attention to questions of the currency, winning a high reputation as an advocate of sound money; but he also spoke in favor of the regulation of immigration, the encouragement of the fisheries, and the building of a canal across Nicaragua. He was a convinced Protectionist, believing that the policy would develop American trade and increase the wages and standard of living of the

American working man; but he was not a blind stand-patter, and introduced bills for abolishing the duty on steel rails and reducing those on salt, type, and print paper. His chief work, however, was done on committees, where he was highly esteemed as a wise and cautious adviser. Though only in his first term, he sat on the important Committee on Foreign Affairs, and many of its reports were written by him.

In 1880 Mr. Morton was thought of for the Vice-Presidency by the Grant men because it was understood that he would be agreeable to the Blaine faction, and he was offered the same position by Garfield in order to conciliate the Stalwarts. But Morton declined the honor and adhered to his decision, although urged to accept by William Walter Phelps and Whitelaw Reid. By Garfield's desire, he became chairman of the party committee on finance and of a special committee to raise and expend funds in New York. The victory won, there came the question of the division of the spoils. Morton maintained that he had been selected for the Secretaryship of the Treasury should he desire it, and he had determined to accept, although his chief political ambition was a seat in the United States Senate. Garfield, however, decided that the feeling in the West forbade putting a Wall Street banker at the head of the Treasury, and denied making any pledge.

There was an election for Senator from New York the ensuing winter, and the Conkling men favored Thomas C. Platt. Morton believed that his refusal of the Vice-Presidency gave him a right to Conkling's support, and he demanded that he call Platt off. But Conkling, one of the most despotic bosses who ever ruled New York, professed that he had no right to do so, and Platt was sent to join his leader in the Senate. Morton now appealed to Garfield to give him the Treasury saying that the belief that he would receive it had cost him the Senatorship, but the conciliatory President was as obdurate as the autocratic Senator had been, though he said that he would gladly make Morton Secretary of the Navy.

But this did not satisfy the Stalwart. The patronage of the Treasury was not to be lightly relinquished. Their enemy, Blaine, was to be Secretary of State; at least a trusty member of their clan must have some one of the other great departments, Treasury, Interior, Post Office. Better New York should have nothing than the insignificant Navy! Probably they had honestly mistaken friendly remarks of Garfield and a promise to "consult" them, for definite pledges, and they became bitter at what they regarded as treachery. Reid told Mrs. Garfield, who was stopping at his house in New York for pre-inauguration shopping, that Morton had said of her husband: "This Ohio man can not be relied upon to stand by his pledges." On the other hand, Reid and his friends declared that the Conkling men would never be loyal to Garfield unless he allowed them to rule him absolutely, and that a Stalwart in the Cabinet would be a spy of Conkling's. Blaine made the surprising declaration that Morton was unfit for the Treasury, and protested against admitting any New

York machine man to the Cabinet. On February 26, Garfield wrote Morton, politely requesting an immediate decision on his offer of the Navy Department. Morton accepted, then declined,[1] then consented to accept, but stated that as he had been a hard-working business man, he would prefer to go as Minister to England or France, and the President gave him the latter post.

Mr. Morton's wealth enabled him to lease a house in Paris not unworthy of being the seat of the American embassy, and to indulge in a liberal hospitality which, coupled with his own social qualities and the tact and charm of his wife, increased the popularity and influence both of the United States and of her Minister. The questions with which Mr. Morton had to deal, though difficult, were not of the first importance; some he had inherited from his predecessors and bequeathed to those who followed him. He was able to obtain for American corporations a right to sue in French courts, a privilege which, though enjoyed by many nations, had been denied to the United States, chiefly because France had not been satisfied that she had a like right in all the states of the Union.

In other matters Mr. Morton was less successful. He failed to obtain recognition of the purity of the American hog. Stories of trichinosis in American pork had created alarm in France and had been made an official reason for forbidding its importation. Probably, however, the chief cause was the demand of French pig-breeders and others for protection for their business. Mr. Morton devoted much attention to this matter, employing both persuasion and gently worded threats of retaliation on French wines, some of which he said even French scientists declared unhealthful because of adulteration, though they made no such charge against American meat. Mr. Morton was on excellent personal terms with the French ministers, and he finally induced them to withdraw the ban, but it was once more imposed by the Chamber of Deputies.

Mr. Morton, like other ministers, also failed to induce France to recognize as American citizens, sons of Frenchmen born in the United States before the naturalization of their fathers. The Minister was embarrassed by obduracy and narrowness at Washington as well as at Paris. Congress laid a heavy duty on works of art. This created much irritation in France, not only because it interfered with an important branch of trade, but as an ungrateful return for the valuable privileges given in France to American students of art and music. Mr. Morton wrote to the Secretary of State that probably these special favors would be withdrawn unless the new tariff were repealed or greatly modified. Congress took no action, but Mr. Morton, thanks to the friendliness which he had shown to and his cordial relations with the French press, artists, and ministers, was able to prevent retaliation.

---

[1]Garfield says in his journal that remonstrating Stalwarts got him out of bed at four o'clock in the morning.

His influence was due not only to his agreeable manners and dinners, but to the fact that he never forgot that France was America's oldest ally, had been the first to recognize her independence, and had maintained it with the sword. He drove the first rivet in the Bartholdi Statue of Liberty, given through a popular subscription, by France to America, and he postponed a visit to the United States, where he had pressing business, to formally accept the completed work. Mr. Morton's action was not merely formal and official. He had watched with interest the progress of the new colossus and did much to lighten the by no means inconsiderable difficulties caused by art's delays. Moreover, his last official act before delivering his letter of recall, was to preside and speak at a banquet on the occasion of the presentation of a smaller bronze copy of the statue to the City of Paris by the Americans residing there.

But though Mr. Morton appreciated the charms of Paris and the claims of France, he never neglected his own countrymen, whether Republican or Democrat, Union or ex-Confederate. At the close of his mission, the Americans residing in Paris, and some of his French friends invited him to a banquet. The *British Morning News* said of the occasion: "The honors paid Mr. Morton yesterday were a fitting conclusion to perhaps the most successful reign (*sic*) ever enjoyed by an American Minister to France. It must not be supposed that the tribute offered to the departing Minister last night was the consequence of a precedent. It was in fact a novelty. Mr. Morton has endeared himself to the Americans in Paris as few ministers have. His relations with the French people and with French ministers have been undoubtedly most cordial, but it is his services to his countrymen, his encouragement to every American interest, charitable, diplomatic, and commercial, which aroused the outburst of feeling last night."

Mr. Morton's term of office had been both creditable and agreeable, but it ended with, as it was preceded by, a great disappointment. There was an election for Senator in New York in January, 1885. Morton was again a candidate, and he now had the vigorous support of his old opponent, Mr. Platt, who was rapidly becoming the commander of the Republican party in the state. But he was not yet undisputed wielder of the baton, and his approval was a source of weakness as well as of strength. Morton realized this, and probably had no desire to call public attention to their alliance. Platt, however, benefited by association with a banker and diplomat of Morton's high position. It was also good copy for reporters, and the union became generally known. As a result the Arthur faction and others who had no love for Platt concentrated their fire on Morton. They shrewdly chose for the opposition candidate, William M. Evarts, a man of ability and character, cultured, scholarly, the leader of the New York Bar, with considerable experience in political life, where he had been careful, some thought too careful, to avoid disagreements. Evarts had no machine, but this commended him

LEVI PARSONS MORTON, NEW YORK, TWENTY-SECOND
VICE-PRESIDENT OF THE UNITED STATES, 1889-1893.

to "eager young reformers like Theodore Roosevelt, who were weary of Albany methods." The combination was too strong for Platt to overcome, and Evarts was elected by 61 votes to 28 for Morton, and 3 for Depew.

Mr. Morton returned to the United States in the spring of 1885. His business did not require a great deal of his time, and he devoted himself to home-making and politics. He sold his country estate at Newport, Rhode Island, and purchased a tract of a thousand acres near Poughkeepsie. On it he erected an Elizabethan house designed by Richard Hunt, and established a scientific farm stocked with choice Guernseys. There was the usual result of "gentleman farming," a success in every way save the financial. Mr. Morton is reported to have said that he served milk and champagne alternately; one cost him as much as the other.[1] Farmer Morton met with delays which could not have been foreseen in getting his country estate in full running order, and he found politics as difficult a road as agriculture. In 1887 he was again a candidate for the Senate, but the Legislature was deadlocked, and after sixteen ballots Morton withdrew in the interest of harmony. It was a great sacrifice, but it was not unappreciated and this regard for the party welfare helped to give him the nomination for the Vice-Presidency in the following year.

The choice of Harrison and Morton was well received by the Republicans. Leading papers praised the convention for selecting good men, and for paying careful attention to their vote-getting qualifications. The Bangor *Whig,* a strong Blaine paper, said of Morton: "A clean, sound business man, and experienced in national affairs, he will command the hearty support of a united party in New York, and this means that the Empire State will be in the Republican column this fall." The New York *Tribune* said that Morton's nomination "will give special satisfaction to business men of this state, who well know his merits. True to the policy, which has led it to select candidates with peculiar regard to their strength in doubtful states, the convention was not able to concede the first place to the choice of New York (Chauncey M. Depew) but accepted for the second place the candidate named by this state, remembering how creditably he had acquitted himself in public service at home and abroad, in Congress, and as Minister to France." The Philadelphia *Press* congratulated the country on the ticket, saying: "There is politics in it and of the best. There is principle in it and of the highest. It means enthusiasm in the ranks and support from the leaders. It will poll the soldiers' last vote and call out all the support organized industry can give. It will summon labor and capital to the support of protection and unite both in the advocacy of a ticket of self-made leaders of men."

---

[1] Possibly the story was only "well invented"; a like tale is told of Daniel Webster and his beloved Marshfield.

As usual there were several minor parties in the field, of which the most important were the Union Labor and the Prohibitionists. The first nominated Alson J. Streeter of Illinois, and Samuel Evans of Texas; the second offered Clinton B. Fisk of New Jersey, and John A. Brooks of Missouri.

In the campaign, some effort was made to call attention to Morton's ancestry as well as his personal record. The very conservative Boston *Journal,* in its praise of Morton, added pride of family and honor to true principles of sound finance. It said that Morton "is a sound business man of comprehensive and progressive views. Like General Harrison's, his ancestry goes back to colonial days, and Mr. Morton's successful career as a banker and public man has afforded admirable illustrations of the solid and sturdy quality of the stock from which he springs. Mr. Morton possesses in an unusual degree the confidence of the business community and he has fairly won it by his uprightness and sagacity, while the great mass of our citizens hold his name in gratitude for the part he took in making a resumption of specie payment in the United States a possibility."

In the matter of mud-slinging the campaign was in refreshing contrast to that of four years before, and the candidates for Vice-President met with little personal attack. Morton's chief weakness was the fact that he was a wealthy Wall Street banker. In a hope to moderate criticism on this account, he resigned official connection with the banking and other business concerns in which he had been the moving spirit.

General Fairchild, a leader in the Republican party and in the Grand Army, described Morton as " . . . . a man who is rich but rich honestly, a man who always has an open hand and an open pocket, a just and an upright man." In 1880 the crops had failed in Ireland, and Americans subscribed to send a great shipload of grain and potatoes for her relief. Morton had paid for a quarter of the cargo, and the Republicans did not forget to remind the voters of this generosity.[1] The Democrats charged Morton with much less honorable exportations, alleging that during the Civil War he had traded to Bermuda for the benefit of the Confederates, but they were unable to bring proof to offset Morton's solemn denial.

The chief objection made to Thurman was his advanced age. Even in the Democratic convention a delegate who nominated Black of Illinois referred to the danger that Thurman would die in office and the Senate be cursed with another Ingalls,[2] and the thrust was received with cheers from the floor, though with hisses from the gallery. The *Nation,* which supported Cleveland, said that Thurman was a fine man personally, but that a candidate for the Vice-Presidency should be qualified to discharge the duties of the Presidency, and that all would admit that a man in his seventy-fifth year was not equal to this task.

----

[1]He was ready, if necessary, to pay for the whole cargo.

[2]A very partisan Senator whom the Republicans had made president *pro tempore* of the Senate after Hendricks' death.

Republican papers were ready to pronounce Thurman a has-been, and his nomination a blunder. The Philadelphia *Press* said: "Mr. Thurman touches the straight Democratic heart and is popular with the old-line Democrats. But they were sure, anyway, and he brings no strength from any other quarter. He can not begin to make Ohio doubtful and his nomination over Governor Gray lets down the bars for Indiana and opens that state to the Republicans." The Chicago *Inter Ocean* said of Thurman: "He has been for thirty years a Bourbon of Bourbons. There was a time when he was immensely popular in Ohio but that was before the war." Ex-Senator Riddleberger of Virginia declared that the Democrats had simply nominated a pocket handkerchief.

But the Democrats had not shrunk from the bandanna; indeed, they waved it high. Red pocket handkerchiefs bearing the portraits of Cleveland and Thurman were produced in large quantities. A campaign book in which fifty-seven prominent men gave their reasons for being Democrats, was issued under the title, *Our Bandanna*. Five copies were printed on satin and sold for $250 a piece; three hundred were printed on Japanese paper and could be obtained for only $25; while to the rank and file who were not used to such luxury, copies were sold for a dime. But though some were attracted by the "old bandanna," others were repelled. The use of pocket handkerchiefs was not disagreeable to the American people in general or to Republicans in particular. Indeed, as late as 1880, the Republicans themselves got out campaign handkerchiefs. The Democrats may have thought that Thurman would be helped by his bandanna as "Tippecanoe" Harrison was by his imaginary log cabin, and Lincoln by his rails. But the cabin and the rails suggested simplicity and hard work. The Americans were a tobacco-using people and might have resented, as aristocratic, an attack on the habit; but snuff-taking had nearly passed away, and was coming to be regarded as disgusting.

Senator Thurman was far from being out of place in refined society. Mr. Blaine says of him: "He was a discriminating reader, and enjoyed not only serious books, but inclined also to the lighter indulgences of romance and poetry. He was especially fond of the best French writers. He loved Molière and Racine, and could quote with rare enjoyment the humorous scenes depicted in Balzac. He took pleasure in the drama and was devoted to music. In Washington he could usually be found in the best seat of the theatre when a good play was to be presented or an opera was to be given." But Solomon B. Griffin thinks it well to explain that Thurman in his distant youth had acquired from a French refugee the *then* polite habit of snuff-taking.[1] The Republicans, therefore, felt no need of treating the bandanna with respect.

---

[1] Solomon Bulkley Griffin, *People and Politics Observed by a Massachusetts Editor,* pp. 302, 303.

The campaign was fought chiefly on the issue of high or low tariff; the Republicans asserted that they were patriotically defending the Nation and one of their minstrels sang:

> "When free trade, from a lofty craig,
> Would spread her banner to the air
> She tears aside the old time flag
> And sticks a big bandanna there."

There were also criticisms of Mr. Thurman's opinions. Mr. Cleveland, like other Presidents, had found it extremely difficult to thoroughly carry out his principles in regard to civil service reform. Many "deserving Democrats" were given post offices and Henry C. Lea of Philadelphia, the eminent church historian, wrote: "The mails have been rendered insecure and the business of great communities like New York and Philadelphia obstructed in order, to use the language of the Democratic Vice-Presidential candidate, that the boys might be taken in to warm their toes while working for Mr. Cleveland's renomination." At New York, Mr. Blaine said that he would speak of Thurman only as a friend of many years and his personal admirer, but that however amiable and agreeable he was, the greater would be his influence with the American people; and he reminded his audience that the vote of Vice-President Dallas had destroyed the tariff of 1842, and that the next Vice-President might have a similar power.

In the election the Republicans were in a minority of the popular vote, but had a majority of the electoral, and therefore won.

In 1892 the Republican convention gave President Harrison a renomination on the first ballot by a vote of 535 1-6 to 369 5-6, but chose a new candidate for Vice-President.[1] Mr. Morton would have liked the honor of a renomination. President Harrison and many leaders favored it but Boss Platt did not, and he withdrew Morton's name without consulting him. The cause is uncertain. Partly for good and partly for bad reasons, Harrison had offended many Republican chiefs and chieflets. His manners were reserved and cold, he had not the qualities which stir enthusiasm in the masses, and his support for renomination came mainly from office-holders and from Southern states which were sure to go Democratic on election day. Mr. Platt said in private that the President had no chance of success, and that he withdrew Morton rather than see him sacrificed in November. Some thought, however, that what Platt really wished was to see Harrison sacrificed, and that he hoped to bring it about by taking Morton off the ticket and so weakening it in New York.

Circumstances and the action, or rather the non-action, of Mr. Morton and his friends helped in his elimination. In the winter of 1891-92, an effort was made to pass a law for the national supervision of national elections.

---

[1] The fractions were caused by the division of the votes of North Carolina and Mississippi among rival delegations.

The intention was to protect the negro in his legal right to vote, and thereby greatly strengthen the Republican party. As this might result in a return of negro rule in Southern states, the Democrats, especially those of the South, resorted to every possible parliamentary trick to prevent a vote on the bill in the Senate. Vice-President Morton declined, without a rule of the Senate to justify him, to imitate the example of Speaker Reed in refusing to put dilatory motions, or even to give any opportunity for a President *pro tempore* to do this; and the bill was killed by filibustering. While Morton's action may not have caused the special friends of the bill to lay plans for his defeat, it probably made them not unwilling to see him replaced by another. Rumors were circulated, either innocently or as a political trick, that his health was poor, and that he did not desire a renomination. Such reports gained credence from the dignified silence of the Vice-President.

When a candidate for office, Mr. Morton had not refused to work in his own behalf. He had applied to Vanderbilt, to Conkling, to Garfield, and had repeatedly advised Platt about the conduct of his campaign, but now he took the position that the Vice-President of the United States should quietly await the decision of the convention. He did, however, write to Cornelius N. Bliss, a wealthy New York banker who was interested in politics as well as finance, asking about the Vice-Presidential situation. Mr. Bliss replied that matters had been very uncertain and that he had heard little on the subject, but that the sky was beginning to clear and he believed that if Harrison were renominated, there was little doubt that New York would unanimously support Morton for Vice-President. But Mr. Bliss gave no hint that Morton's friends should organize and act. This was the more strange as he reported that Mr. Milholland of the *Tribune,* apparently supported by its publisher and city editor, had made a "raid" upon "the hitherto harmonious and sure 11th Assembly district," and that some believed that this was part of an attempt to get the nomination for Whitelaw Reid. Bliss, however, was of the opinion that Reid himself had nothing to do with it. But if Bliss did not sound the bugle to gather the Morton legions, he at least called upon the keeper of the guillotine, the Secretary of the Treasury, to see that Milholland was removed from a Government position enjoyed by him.

The national convention met at Minneapolis on June 7, 1892. On June 10, in the middle of the afternoon, Harrison was nominated, and the convention then adjourned until 8 p. m. to allow the New York delegation to select the candidate for Vice-President. At seven, about sixty of the seventy-two members met. The chairman, Warner Miller, and some ten or a dozen others, feeling the call of home and business, or disgusted with the nomination of Harrison, had taken the evening train for New York. Morton was sweetly slaughtered. Many praised, but no one voted for him. The whole current, perhaps directed by dams previously arranged, set toward Reid. A number of the leaders spoke briefly in his favor. The *Tribune* had had serious trouble with its printers, and no party wishes for a candidate who is objectionable to labor; but the energetic Mr. Milholland brought in the president of the Typographical Union, who stated in writing that the difficulties had been satisfactorily adjusted, and that the Union was now very friendly to Reid. One delegate said that Morton did not wish a renomination. It was urged, not quite correctly, that there was no precedent for renominating both a President and Vice-President.

Finally, when the hour fixed for the reassembling of the convention had nearly arrived, the meeting voted unanimously to present Reid's name. Senator Spooner of Wisconsin wrote Morton: "The motives and policy of the New York delegation you doubtless understand. I confess that I do not." Spooner told Morton that he had tried to influence such New York delegates as he could reach, but that "I was informed that the Platt contingent was for Reid and that it must go that way. It is due to Hiscock that I should say that he seemed to agree with me that you ought to be renominated, but said he was powerless."

Yet Reid had never been a special friend of Platt. He had attacked him in the *Tribune;* two years later they became bitter enemies; and Platt says in his *Autobiography* that "Harrison's renomination caused a chattering of the teeth among the warm-blooded Republicans of the East. When there was added to it the choice of Whitelaw Reid, a persistent assailant of the New York organization, many of the New York delegates, including myself, wrapped ourselves in overcoats and ear-muffs, hurried from the convention hall and took the first train to New York." Alexander is of the opinion that Depew and Hiscock were early inclined to Reid, and neither of them was closely allied with Platt. Perhaps, in after years, Platt unconsciously antedated his intense antagonism to Reid, and at the time the "Easy Boss," as Platt was called, thought it well to let his followers take their own course. Reid had been United States Minister to France for several years and therefore had not been concerned in the most recent quarrels; he had returned from Paris for the express purpose of harmonizing the New York factions, and the bulk of the politicians may have felt that the best chance for reconciliation lay in the nomination of the reconciler.

In the convention itself no name was heard but that of Reid or Reed. A Tennessee delegate nominated Thomas B. Reed of Maine, but withdrew his name when a delegate from that state stated that he would not accept. The convention listened to three speeches urging it to do what everyone knew that it would do, and without wasting more time nominated Reid by acclamation.

Whitelaw Reid was born in Xenia, Ohio, on October 27, 1837. He graduated with distinction from Miami University in 1856, taught school for two years to earn money to pay his father the cost of his education, and at twenty-one became editor and proprietor of the Xenia *News,* taking the New York *Tribune* for his model. He was an ardent Republican, and supported Frémont both in his editorial columns and on the stump. In 1860, notwithstanding his admiration for Salmon P. Chase, he favored the nomination of Lincoln, the *News* being the first Western paper outside of Illinois to do so. He secured the election of a Lincoln delegate to the national convention from the Xenia district, and thereby increased the break in the Ohio column which Chase so bitterly resented.

But Mr. Reid's talents soon carried him beyond his native state. In 1869 he became managing editor of the New York *Tribune,* and after 1872, its editor-in-chief. He was appointed by President Harrison, in 1889, Minister to France, which post he held until 1892. Of his work as minister, Blowitz, the influential correspondent of the London *Times,* wrote: "He added to the cleverness of the Americans the urbanity of the French." His chief task was to persuade France to withdraw the ban which, in common with other European countries, she had laid on American pork. Mr. Reid told the French Minister that France was sure to lift the ban sooner or later, that Germany was about to do so, that France was not accustomed to follow Germany, and that it was characteristic of her when she made a concession to do it gracefully. The Frenchman saw the point and the prohibition was withdrawn. Reid also induced France to be the first nation to promise to take part in the Columbian Exposition, or World's Fair of 1893.

Reid, like Arthur, might be described as peculiarly a "gentleman," though in a slightly different sense of that word of various meanings. He knew and obeyed the rules of etiquette and dress, but the story was never told of him as of Arthur that in one January he ordered twenty coats from his tailor. Reid was, however, a man of much culture, intelligence, and *esprit,* who would have been at home in a French salon. He enjoyed the Society which spells itself with a capital S, and appreciated the privilege of sitting next to a Duchess at dinner.

The Democratic convention met shortly after the Republican, and, obeying the will of the party rather than that of the managers, nominated Mr. Cleveland. Then, true to precedent, they gave the New York reformer for a colleague, a machine politician from the Middle West, Adlai E. Stevenson of Illinois. But one ballot was taken. Stevenson led, with Governor Gray of Indiana second; and the delegates, who probably were eager to get home, then unanimously nominated the gentleman from Illinois.

Mr. Stevenson was born in Christian County, Kentucky, October 23, 1835, and received his higher education at Centre College. His family removed to Bloomington, Illinois, where he studied law, and was admitted to the bar in 1858. His entrance into politics on a major scale was as a member of the House of Representatives of the Forty-fourth and Forty-sixth

Congresses. He received further recognition through his appointment by President Cleveland as First Assistant Postmaster-General. The sweeping removals which he made in this capacity did not particularly commend him to the civil service reformers.

Champ Clark, in his *Memoirs,* gives a full and interesting description of Stevenson. He says: "General Stevenson was a most resourceful lawyer. Like most country lawyers he practiced politics about as much as he practiced his profession; his profession, for profit, politics, for sheer joy. He was one of the most popular campaigners in the land, and was the delight of the multitude. Stevenson always spoke right out in meeting and did not mince his words. One thing that commended him to his audiences was his handsome presence. Tall, slender, well-knit, lean of flank, he always reminded me of a race horse. His information was wide and varied; his voice musical and far carrying; his elocution good; and he was not afraid. He had the nose, eye and chin of a fighter, which he was. He had been First Assistant Postmaster-General and in that office, he flung Republicans out and put Democrats in with such expedition that those who loved him not dubbed him the Headsman or the Axeman."

In accordance with custom, the candidates for the Vice-Presidency took the stump. Each made effective speeches and had an enthusiastic following. Each, too, had special weaknesses. Friends of Morton were bitterly angered by the failure to renominate him. Reid had supported Greeley in 1872, and probably those Republicans who worshipped regularity did not forget it. It is probable, too, that Labor remembered Reid's trouble with his printers.

If Adlai and his Axe enthused the Democratic "boys," he shocked the reformers; but they were too happy over the nomination of Cleveland to greatly care. Moreover, they may have thought that the Headsman would do less harm presiding over the Senate than swinging his axe in a department.

The unpopularity of the McKinley tariff, labor troubles, approaching private war, and a general dissatisfaction with conditions gave the victory to the Democrats, who obtained 277 electoral votes and the Republicans 145. But, for the first time since 1860, a third party was represented in the electoral college, where the twenty-two votes of seven trans-Mississippi states were cast for James B. Weaver of Iowa and James G. Field of Virginia, nominees of the Populist party. A Socialist-Labor convention had nominated Simon Wing of Massachusetts, and Charles H. Matchett of New York, but they received but a trifling popular vote. The Prohibitionists nominated John Bidwell of California, and J. B. Cranfill of Texas. They polled nearly a quarter of million votes, but were too scattered to carry any state.

Doubtless "Uncle Adlai" was delighted with the result of the battle, and saw beatific visions of Republican heads falling beneath the guillotine. His opponent bore defeat very philosophically, writing to his chief that he had enjoyed making the campaign and that he considered it an honor to have been on the ticket with him.

CHAPTER XVIII.

Vice-Presidential Elections, 1896-1916

PRESIDENT Cleveland, during his second administration, made an earnest effort to carry out what seemed to be the mandate of the people by securing the passage of a low tariff bill, but he was obliged to acquiesce in the enactment of a law with higher duties than he approved. At the close of his term, the tariff question was thrust aside by that of the currency. The radicals obtained control of the Democratic National Convention, and that body declared for the free and unlimited coinage of silver at the ratio of sixteen to one, and nominated an eloquent champion of free silver, William Jennings Bryan of Nebraska. Five ballots had been necessary to choose a candidate for President, and an equal number were needed to select one for Vice-President. On the fourth ballot, the leader was John R. McLean of Ohio. Politicians favored him because of his wealth and his ownership of an influential paper, the Cincinnati *Enquirer.* But Bryan announced that McLean represented the dangerous money interests which he was fighting and that if McLean were nominated, he would withdraw. The convention then took the second on the preceding ballot, Arthur Sewall of Bath, Maine.

Mr. Sewall was a member of a prominent Massachusetts and Maine family. His yard for the building of wooden ships was said to be the largest in the United States, and his ships were among the largest built. But he had become convinced that conditions of commerce required ships of such a size that wooden ones could not withstand the strain, and in 1893 he began the construction of iron vessels. Mr. Sewall was part owner of the Bath Iron Works and was interested in banks and railroads. He might seem a strange companion for William J. Bryan, but he was a firm believer in the free coinage of silver. Moreover, he was able to make large financial contributions to the cause, and this circumstance is said to have had weight.

In 1892 a new political organization, the People's party or Populists, had developed great strength, and in eight states the Democrats and Populists had fused in whole or in part. When radicalism triumphed in the Democratic convention of 1896, the advanced members hoped that the Populists would make no nominations of their own, but would endorse those of the Democrats. There was, however, a serious obstacle. Though Bryan was satisfactory to Populists, Sewall was the reverse. Mr. Arnett in his *History of the Populist Movement in Georgia* says that Sewall's "selection was doubtless inspired by a desire to counteract the charge of sectionalism (West against East) and to save as much as possible of the moderate Democratic vote." But to many it seemed a compromise with Satan to nominate a national banker on a platform which called for the abolition of the system that he represented, and a railroad president as the candidate of a party which demanded a stricter control of railroads to "protect the people from robbery and oppression." The Populists were quick to see the inconsistency. It strengthened the hands of the most radical element in the party and made complete fusion impossible. The Populist National Convention decided to nominate their candidate for Vice-President first. Thomas E. Watson of Georgia received 539¾ votes, Arthur Sewall 257⅛, four other candidates a total of 540 10-16. Many votes were then changed and Watson was declared nominated. Bryan was then nominated for President.

The question immediately rose: Would the candidates accept and be half loaves in the political bread pan? They were obliged to consider the feelings of their followers and the public effect of union and of disunion. The Democratic National Chairman, Jones, telegraphed Bryan that he had better refuse unless Sewall were nominated also, and Bryan agreed. Watson accepted, but later in a signed editorial stated that he would not have done so had he understood the situation; that he preferred that the Populists should present two independent candidates; but that to prevent a split in the party on the one hand, or an entire swallowing by the Democrats on the other, he accepted the nomination. He called Sewall a corporation plutocrat, said that no one who voted for Sewall ought to vote for him, and demanded, but without success, that Sewall withdraw or be taken down.

The Republican convention, acting as the mouthpiece of Mark Hanna, proclaimed William McKinley of Ohio its choice for President. McKinley was a kindly, popular man, known chiefly as the champion of Protection. Hanna was a successful banker and business man of Cleveland, Ohio, who believed that big business created the prosperity of the country, and that leaders in politics should be closely allied with, if not controlled by, those in the financial world. Under any circumstances, McKinley would have been a formidable candidate for the Republican nomination; aided by the organizing and influencing power of Hanna, he was irresistible. When the convention met, his nomination was assured and it came on the first ballot by a great majority.

Mr. Hanna and his friends had also picked the candidate for Vice-President. This was Garret A. Hobart, a leading business man and politician of

New Jersey. His reputation was mainly local, but he had done much to strengthen the party in his state, and had also been of great service on the national committee. Like Hanna, he was active both in business and politics, and he was even more genial, tactful, and skillful in making adjustments. He also was rich enough to contribute handsomely to the campaign fund. True, he was not from New York, but Hanna and Platt had no love for each other, and the New York Republicans were so torn by factions that a nomination from that state might be positively hurtful. Moreover, the Republicans had definitely declared for the gold standard, and thus were believed to have secured New York. Platt tried to save his face by offering ex-Vice-President Morton, but he telegraphed a refusal. When Platt persisted, the McKinley League of New York resolved that the nomination of Morton would weaken the party in the state; the McKinley delegates refused to take a candidate from a state where the Republicans were so divided; and Hobart was nominated on the first ballot by a good though not an overwhelming majority. The opposition to Hobart was scattered, but the bulk of its votes went to Henry Clay Evans of Tennessee.

Garret Augustus Hobart was born on June 3, 1844, at Long Branch, New Jersey. "Three strains of blood from the most vigorous nations which have made modern history mingled in his veins; and to a remarkable degree, he possessed the most characteristic qualities of each one. His father was of English stock, and from him he inherited a sturdy spirit, strength of purpose, and practical judgment. His mother was of mingled Dutch and French-Huguenot stock, and from her he inherited the industry and perseverance of the Dutch and the affectionate nature, the buoyancy of heart, and the religious tendency of the Huguenots."[1]

The first American Hobart came to Massachusetts from Hingham, England, in 1633. Two years later he was followed by his son, the Reverend Peter Hobart, and they with others of their family settled at Bear Cove, whose name, probably through their influence, was changed to that of Hingham. There the younger Hobart lived as minister until his death forty-four years later, at the age of seventy-four.

The oldest son, Joshua, removed to Southold, Long Island. One of his grandchildren was active in the Revolutionary movement in New York, and sat for three months in the United States Senate. Another became the Episcopal bishop of New York, and one of the founders of the General Theological Seminary and of Hobart College. Mr. Hobart's grandfather moved from Massachusetts to New Hampshire, and his father to New Jersey. There he became a successful school teacher, a storekeeper, farmer, and co-founder of the Reformed Church of Long Branch.

Usually, however, the Hobarts were humble though worthy folk. It was said of them that "successive generations furnished numerous teachers, and

---

[1]David Magie, *Life of Garret Augustus Hobart,* p. 2.

occasionally, a preacher; but for the most part, they were plain, honest farmers, who served God and their country in their generation, and left behind them good names, large families, and small estates."

Mr. Hobart's mother was descended in a direct male line from a Dutch immigrant to New York, then New Amsterdam, in 1659. Her mother was the daughter of Reverend Benjamin Du Bois, the descendant of a Huguenot refugee. He was one of the founders of Queen's College, later Rutgers College, and University; and was a trustee from 1783 to 1827. Here the young Hobart had passed from the Congregational to the kindred Dutch Reformed Church, and had been sent to Rutgers for his college education. He graduated when barely nineteen, receiving his diploma from the hands of President Theodore Frelinghuysen, the candidate for Vice-President on the Whig ticket in 1844. In college, Hobart showed himself a close and conscientious student of unusual ability, winning the mathematical prize and delivering the English salutatory at commencement.

After graduation, he entered the office of a prominent New Jersey lawyer, Socrates Tuttle of Paterson, and in due time was admitted to the bar. Mr. Tuttle was a mentor to his pupil in love and politics, as well as law. He had been a childhood chum of the elder Hobart, and later, half in jest, they agreed that their children should marry. Apparently Hobart, Jr., as befitted a lawyer, had a firm belief in the sanctity even of semi-contracts. Miss Jennie Tuttle seems to have been of a like opinion. In this particular case they found duty a primrose path and on July 21, 1869, the two began a very happy wedded life.

The Hobarts had been Democrats; Mr. Tuttle was a zealous Republican. Rutgers had turned Garret toward Republicanism; Mr. Tuttle's influence confirmed his decision, and he soon became active in party contests. Men are often engaged in both law and politics, but seldom do they give the two professions equal attention, and usually it is the latter which obtains the better part of their time and thought. With Mr. Hobart, the reverse was the case. He said of himself, truly: "I am a business man, engaged in politics for recreation." But the recreation was far from that of a dilettante. He was Speaker of the House and President of the Senate of his state, being the first man in its history to hold both positions. Moreover, he did the very professional work of serving on important party committees. From 1880 to 1891 he was chairman of the Republican State Committee. In 1884 he became a member of the National Committee, on which he was serving at the time of his nomination for Vice-President. Nor was his activity, like that of many members, chiefly occasional or local, for he served during several campaigns as the vice-chairman of the State Republican Committee.

Mr. Hobart, in speaking (as above) of politics and of his participation therein, described himself not as a lawyer, but as a business man. In truth, he was both. Criminal law did not appeal to him; he was not versed in technicalities; and though his mind passed easily from one subject to another and he was very quick and usually correct in making a decision, he was not fluent or self-confident when on his feet. But he knew the principles of the law, and how to apply them in order to produce the results which his clients desired. Accordingly, Mr. Hobart was seldom seen in court, but became an office lawyer, an organizer and adviser of great corporations, whose shrewd counsel enabled big business to work its will yet keep within the letter of the statute. His principal client was the Jersey Midland Railroad, which divided rule over New Jersey with the Pennsylvania Railroad, the former dominating the northern part of the state, and the latter the southern. Mr. Hobart was a shrewd judge both of business and of character, and could give wise advice on such questions as, "Is it best to buy control of the 'X' Railroad?" or "How will the Legislature regard a proposal to enlarge its franchises?"

Both in law and in politics Hobart gave little attention to detail, refusing to do what he termed "boys' work." Personally he was a man of strict integrity and great industry, but probably his distinguishing characteristic was his kindly, genial nature. In college his fellow-students went to him for help in their lessons; in after life men in difficulties or with friends in difficulties appealed to Hobart for assistance; and to both he gave aid, willingly and unostentatiously. His cordial ways were the subject of frequent remark. He was a prudent manager and a skillful conciliator, and this quality was one reason for his success in organizing campaigns and trusts.

In the Presidential contest of 1896, there was a wise division of labor between the Republican candidates, McKinley doing most of the speaking, and Hobart retaining his position on the National Committee and attending carefully to the duties of that office. But he did not consider himself a mere junior and silent partner of the head of the ticket. McKinley was the bearer of the gold banner, and today he is often thought of as the gallant leader of the "sound money" host. But in Congress he had manifested a certain friendliness to silver, and in the nomination campaign Hanna had avoided using the word "gold," knowing that should he do so, he would hurt McKinley in the West. The Republican convention had declared that the currency should be based on gold, but its candidate for President avoided the word in his letter of acceptance.

Mr. Hobart was franker and bolder, and characteristically took his stand at once. The convention sent a delegation headed by a future Vice-President, Senator Charles W. Fairbanks of Indiana, to formally notify Mr. Hobart of his nomination. Mr. Fairbanks' speech was very brief. He gave as one reason for Mr. Hobart's selection, his "intelligent and patriotic devotion . . . . to a currency whose soundness and integrity none can challenge," but did not commit himself as to what that currency should be. Mr. Hobart was less cautious. His reply was a defiance of the Bryanites and a trumpet call to battle. He said that gold was the "final standard of all enlightened nations."

All financial transactions of whatever character, all business enterprises, all individual or corporate investments, were adjusted to it. An honest dolla: worth 100 cents everywhere, could not be coined out of 53 cents of silver, plus a legislative fiat. Such a debasement of our currency would inevitably produce incalculable loss, appalling disaster, and national dishonor. The question admitted of no compromise. It was of vital consequence that this question should be settled now in such a way as to restore public confidence here and everywhere in the integrity of our purpose. A doubt of that integrity among other great commercial countries of the world would not only cost us millions of money, but that, which as patriots, we should treasure still more highly—our industrial and commercial supremacy.

Mr. Hobart was equally unflinching in a few speeches which he made and in his formal letter of acceptance. In replying to the notification committee, Mr. Hobart had said that he appreciated the honor of his nomination "the more because it associates me in a contest which involves the very gravest issues, with one who represents in his private character and public career, the highest intelligence and best spirit of his party, and with whom my personal relations are such as to afford a guarantee of perfect accord in the campaign which is before us."

Further acquaintance with Mr. McKinley strengthened Mr. Hobart's regard for him as a man, but it by no means produced "perfect accord." As is often the case, the candidate for Vice-President gave an advance copy of his letter of acceptance to his chief. Messrs. McKinley and Hanna advised a softening of the remarks on the currency, but Mr. Hobart replied: "I think I know the sentiments of Eastern men better than you can, and with this knowledge and my convictions, I must retain the statements as I have written them." The newspapers of New York highly praised Hobart's downright language, and some contrasted it with that of McKinley in a manner not flattering to the Ohio politician. But in another important respect, the two candidates were in full agreement; both were thorough-going believers in protection and had no hesitation in proclaiming their faith.

Hobart's speeches, though able, were few; but his faculty of conciliation proved useful. Sewall also did not appear much on the stump. Watson, like Bryan, made a whirlwind campaign, but it is said that the latter rather avoided his associate.

There was an unusual number of minor parties in the field, whose expenses were chiefly met by a secret contribution from the Republican war chest. The Prohibitionists split in two on the silver question; old Democrats nominated a "National Democratic" ticket; there was a tiny Socialist-Labor party.

The result was great confusion followed by a sweeping Republican victory. McKinley and Hobart received a great popular majority and 271 electoral votes to 176 for Bryan. For Vice-President, Sewall received 149 votes and Watson 27. It is probable that had Bryan been elected, there would have been no choice for Vice-President, and in that case the Republican Senate would have chosen Sewall.

In 1900 the Republican convention met at Philadelphia on June 19, and gave President McKinley the customary renomination. He was popular with the party and the country. His interests were well cared for by Hanna, and his nomination on the first ballot was assured before the convention met. But concerning the Vice-Presidency, there was uncertainty. Vice-President Hobart had died in office, and the old ticket was therefore impossible. The Administration had no candidate. Hanna was inclined to Cornelius N. Bliss of New York, who had been Secretary of the Interior; McKinley, to Senator Allison of Iowa. But neither would run. Bliss was not on the best of terms with Platt; *his* boss seems to have been his wife who was averse to his holding public office. Hanna was a close friend of Bliss and had persuaded Mrs. Bliss to agree to her husband's entering the Cabinet, but the Ohio magician did not choose to exert his powers a second time. Allison preferred to remain a leader of the Senate, not its ornamental chairman.

There were many active or receptive candidates; among them were Secretary of the Navy Long of Massachusetts, Senators Dolliver of Iowa, Fairbanks of Indiana, Elkins of West Virginia, and Lieutenant-Governor Timothy Woodruff of New York. It is said that Hanna was opposed to Dolliver because he charged a hundred dollars a speech when campaigning against Bryan in 1896. Fairbanks, while ready to accept the position, was not anxious to obtain it. In striking contrast was the sharp eagerness of Woodruff, an eagerness shared by few others. "Tim" Woodruff, as he was usually called, was a clever and successful local politician, known chiefly for his obliging disposition and his brilliant, many-colored waistcoats. The New York machine gave Woodruff a formal support for the Vice-Presidency, but they rightly held him to be lacking in the force of character needed to be Governor of New York. Hanna barred his way to Washington for a like reason. When Woodruff begged Hanna's support, the latter asked him if he considered himself fit to be President and Woodruff frankly acknowledged that he did not. Herbert Croly says that he might have replied that the nomination of politicians for the Vice-Presidency, who were not fit for the office, was one of the most ancient and best established of American political traditions, and that from any such point of view his qualifications were unimpeachable.

But Hanna had determined to break that precedent. "It was characteristic of him," says his biographer, "to provide against the inconvenient contingency of having his Harrison succeeded by a Tyler." Probably Hanna thought that all contingencies apart, the nomination of Woodruff would be a mistake. He is said to have declared that "we are not going through this campaign with a highly colored vest as the tail of the ticket."

But while Woodruff knew that he was not fit to be President, his modesty stopped there. Before the convention, he had been most active and most confident in his canvass for the second place. On January 30, 1900, Theodore Roosevelt wrote to his close friend, Henry Cabot Lodge: "Woodruff is a most good humored, friendly fellow, wild to have me nominate him for Vice-President, which I suppose for my sins I might have to do (not if I can help it) and he is amusingly and absolutely certain that nothing can prevent his nomination." To this Lodge replied: "If New York offers Woodruff as the Vice-President, the Vice-Presidency will go elsewhere and New York does not want to lose it, and if I am not much mistaken, they will insist on your taking it."

Lodge was right in feeling that his correspondent might be made a candidate against his will. His qualities and his supporters made a combination as striking and as varicolored as Tim Woodruff's vests. Theodore Roosevelt was a descendant of an old Dutch family of some prominence, was a graduate of Harvard, a man of wide information, and the author of several valuable books on American history. He had also been a rancher, police commissioner of New York and, in the Spanish War, the commander of a volunteer cavalry regiment raised largely among the plainsmen of the West, which was popularly known as the Rough Riders. By nature Roosevelt was a mixture of the conservative and the radical. He was highly disapproved of by the *Nation* school of reformers. Yet he was followed by men of great culture and of lofty ideals, and was a thorn in the flesh of the Republican organization of New York. He was picturesque in any position and had a genius for the limelight. In the West, his breezy dash, up-to-date ways, and spectacular contests with criminals, politicians, and Spaniards had made him immensely popular.

Two of the chief politicians of the country, Boss Quay and Boss Platt, insisted on supporting him for the Vice-Presidency whether he would or no. Their motives were in full accordance with their past careers. Quay had been overshadowed by Hanna, the new national boss, and was glad to annoy him by nominating a man whom he did not want. Platt asserts in his memoirs that he had no feeling against Roosevelt, that he wished to nominate him in order to strengthen the party ticket; but he admits that he told Roosevelt at the time of the convention that he could not be renominated for Governor of New York; and there was a general belief that Platt wished to bow the popular and unruly Governor out of political life by the Vice-Presidential gate.

Why, when bosses of great states and great masses of the rank and file wished the usually unimportant office of Vice-President to be given to Colonel Roosevelt, did not Hanna and McKinley assent with at least outward cordiality? Partly because of the Spanish War. Hanna had long opposed it, and when he consented, he did so largely for business reasons. Roosevelt favored it early because he wished to clean up a mess at America's front door, free the Cubans from oppression, and strengthen the United States in the Caribbean. Hanna was a financier, Roosevelt a crusader. Moreover, Roosevelt had criticised the Administration in private for the way it managed the war. But far more important was the fact that Hanna thoroughly distrusted Roosevelt, and did not consider the Vice-Presidency unimportant. It is said on good authority that during the convention, Hanna came from a telephone in his private room very angry, declaring that he would have nothing more to do with the campaign, and on being asked what was the matter, replied: "Matter? Why everybody has gone crazy. What is the matter with all of you? Here is this convention going headlong for Roosevelt for Vice-President. Don't any of you realize that there is only one life between that madman and the Presidency? Platt and Quay are no better than idiots! What can he do as Governor of New York compared to the damage he will do as President if McKinley should die?"

Another strenuous objector to Roosevelt's nomination was Roosevelt himself. He was far too clever a politician not to see that the Vice-Presidency might be for him a blind alley. He had discussed the matter most carefully with Senator Lodge. At one time it was thought that Secretary Root might accept the Vice-Presidency, and Lodge and Roosevelt agreed that the latter ought to have a seat in the Cabinet. Root refused to leave his position, and Roosevelt thought that he himself should also hold his place and remain Governor of New York. Lodge advised him to accept the Vice-Presidency with the intention of resigning to become the first Governor-General of the Philippines. Mrs. Roosevelt was at first opposed to her husband's being Vice-President, but as the time of the convention approached, inclined to favor his accepting the office.

Many of Roosevelt's Western friends were wild for him to go on the ticket to strengthen it, but others said that his support was merely a scheme to shelve him. Friends in New York felt that acceptance would be a desertion of the fight for good government there, and could not understand why he should even consider leaving them. On the other hand, the Westerners at Washington did not realize what the local conditions in New York were, and would consider a declination of the Vice-Presidency a sign of weakness. Yet strong as the call for Roosevelt was in the West, he received many letters from that section urging him not to run. But Lodge told him that he believed that these men were opposed to the nomination of McKinley, and did not wish to see a man on the ticket whom they would be compelled to support enthusiastically. Lodge and Roosevelt discussed the precedent of Silas Wright. Roosevelt said that he had refused the nomination for the Vice-Presidency, had run for Governor of New York, and had polled more votes than the Democratic candidate for President, James K. Polk. Lodge answered: "I have forgotten the incident of Silas Wright, but let me call your attention to the fact that he was never President while Vice-President."

Roosevelt's conduct in relation to the Vice-Presidency was uncertain and extremely vacillating. This is clearly shown by his attitude in his correspondence with Lodge. To Kohlsaat, the editor of the Chicago *Times-Herald,* he wrote that the Vice-Presidency was the very last office which he should want or care for, but there was a certain implication in the letter that he would not refuse it. In June, 1899, he made a trip to New Mexico to attend a reunion of the Rough Riders, and his reception on the way proved his great popularity; but he gave a written statement to the reporters, "Under no circumstances could I or would I accept the Vice-Presidency," and he added, "I am happy to state that Senator Platt cordially acquiesces in my views on this matter." Later, Roosevelt wrote Lodge that the railroad, insurance, and other interests, which were very important to Platt, were urging him to get rid of the Governor, and that the boss was beginning to yield.

Roosevelt came to Washington "with a frown on his strenuous brow," as Secretary of State Hay wrote to Whitelaw Reid, to declare that he would not accept the nomination, and was promptly told by Hanna: "Of course, you're not fitted for it." Roosevelt is reported to have been a trifle dashed by the annunciation of this simple truth; yet his feeling, if unreasonable, was quite human. One may honestly believe in his own unworthiness and yet not relish other people's having full faith in it. President McKinley was perhaps not quite frank. There had been some attempt to bring Roosevelt forward for the Presidency, but after his Western tour he wrote the President that he favored his renomination and that the West did also. In March, 1900, Lodge wrote Roosevelt that McKinley was perfectly content to have him as his companion on the ticket. On April 16 Lodge wrote that the President said that he had talked with Roosevelt in New York; that much as he would like to have Roosevelt on the ticket, he was inclined to think that the Governor could help it most by standing for reëlection.

When the convention met, McKinley would not let Hanna exert his authority. After Hanna's outburst against Roosevelt, Payne of Wisconsin replied: "You control the convention, why don't you nominate another man?" "I am not in control," shouted Hanna. "McKinley won't let me use the power of the Administration to defeat Roosevelt. He is blind or afraid or something." Dunn, who tells the story, is of the opinion that McKinley was by nature a little timid, and did not wish to do anything that would prevent his unanimous nomination or endanger his election.

Probably Roosevelt did not want the Vice-Presidency, and he certainly said so definitely and loudly, but his actions did not always square with his words. It was the custom for a Republican Governor of New York to go to the national convention as one of the four delegates-at-large, and Roosevelt did what his predecessors had done. But under the circumstances his attend-

THEODORE ROOSEVELT, NEW YORK, TWENTY-FIFTH
VICE-PRESIDENT OF THE UNITED STATES, 1901.

ance could not fail to rouse his friends to renewed efforts, for Roosevelt was a man whose presence set the prairies on fire. Lodge had written him that if he attended the convention, he would be nominated; that a refusal of the nomination would seriously injure him; and that unless the question of the Vice-Presidency were settled before the convention met, he would find himself unable to go. But Roosevelt not only went, but went in a manner which seemed as significant to many as the white toga of the Roman *candidatus*. The ex-colonel of the Rough Riders was seen everywhere wearing his sombrero. Wayne McVeagh, a business lawyer of Philadelphia, who had been active in politics, when told of the headgear, said: "Gentlemen, that is an acceptance hat." The Roosevelt wave rose higher and higher, and the unhappy Administration delegates had not even a recognized candidate to play the part of life preserver.

The convention did not formally meet until Thursday, June 19, but there was a gathering of the clans on the 16th. On June 17, Charles Dick of Ohio, the secretary of the national committee, told McKinley: "I have made a canvass of our friends so far as they are able to control our delegates, but it is very difficult to rally them to nothing; we have no candidate. We don't want to say we are opposing this man. 'Don't be in a hurry, be deliberate and wise,' we say to them, but that is not going to do very long." There was a general desire to get on the band wagon before it started. Dick asked precise instructions whether he and his associates should join the Roosevelt movement or take strong measures to stop it. But he advised the former course for the very practical reason that "we can not afford to have it said that something was done in spite of ourselves. The judgment of our friends is that it was inevitable. Most of our friends think there is only one thing to do, that is to make it appear that it is in entire harmony with our desires." The President, however, refused to give advice on a matter which belonged to the convention to decide.

On Tuesday there was a conference of Administration men. One of them, Charles G. Dawes, later himself Vice-President, wrote an account of the meeting in his *Diary*. Hanna was very angry, declared that the Western stampede for Roosevelt[1] was being engineered by Quay and Platt, and wished to line up the Administration delegates for Secretary Long; but Dawes insisted that this would start a Western stampede for Roosevelt. A proposal to throw the Long men to Dolliver was met with the objection that one could not transfer a bunch of New England delegates to Iowa without dropping a good many of them in New York.

To pacify Hanna, Dawes held a telephone conversation with the White House. Private Secretary Cortelyou was at the telephone, but the President was beside him with a second receiver. Dawes reported that the friends of

---

[1]Western delegates had been promenading the corridor before Hanna's room chanting, "We want Teddy."

other candidates, considering Roosevelt's declination as final, were rallying to their favorites, but that if the Administration should advise that Long be taken, the West would regard this as dictation and go for Roosevelt. Dawes said that if nothing came from the White House before about ten o'clock, word would go out that the Administration wanted Long. Dawes had been talking with Private Secretary Cortelyou with McKinley listening in. But the latter now took the telephone himself and said that the President's friends should not dictate. Hanna was a little perplexed, but agreed. A further conference was held without result.

At about the same moment, Roosevelt surrendered. He had been pressed very hard and his sense of party loyalty had been appealed to by being told that his popularity was needed to defeat Bryan. At the request of Senator Platt, he went to his room for a conference with Platt and other New Yorkers. When he returned, "his tail feathers were down." His emphatic and oft-repeated declarations that he did not want the nomination, that, if necessary, he would rise on the floor of the convention and refuse it, now gave way to: "I cannot disappoint my Western friends, if they insist, etc"; "I cannot seem to be bigger than the party." According to Platt's version of the conference, he told Roosevelt that he would not be renominated for Governor, but that he could be Vice-President; that Roosevelt agreed not to refuse the Vice-Presidency, if nominated, although he asserted that he would ask the New York delegation to endorse some one else from that state for the place; and that he therefore remained silent when friends told him to announce a refusal.

According to Roosevelt's story, more probable than the account in Platt's generally unreliable *Autobiography*, the former retorted that he would make a straight-out fight for the Governorship, and that he would tell the assembled delegates of Platt's threat. This brought Senator Platt to terms at once, the effort to instruct the New York delegation for Roosevelt was hastily dropped, and the name of Lieutenant-Governor Woodruff presented in his place.

At any rate, Roosevelt refrained from speaking the absolutely decisive word. Hanna, too, gave way. It was not, however, a popular rush, but the management of another boss, that finally brought Hanna down. Senator Quay of Pennsylvania, who had paired with Platt in the move to nominate Roosevelt, was threatening to raise the troublesome question of the right of the Southern states to full representation in the convention. Since all these delegations were Administration-controlled, such a move was a threat to Mr. Hanna's leadership and loaded with at least enough dynamite to disrupt the harmony of the convention. The upshot was that Hanna issued a statement denying that the Administration had a candidate for the Vice-Presidency or was opposing any candidate; and Senator Quay's threatened revolt did not develop.

The call of the roll gave Roosevelt the nomination by an unanimous vote.

The Democratic nomination for the Presidency was as predetermined a matter as that of the Republicans. Mr. Bryan was now at the height of his powers and his popularity. While the conservative Eastern elements of the party were not enthusiastic for him, he had a following in the West and in parts of the South, which was almost fanatical in its devotion. To have put him aside for another candidate would have been party suicide. Many politicians of the conservative ranks supported his renomination because they believed his magnetic leadership might bring party success.

The Democratic convention met at Kansas City, Missouri, July 4, in a spacious hall specially erected for the purpose. After two days of contest over the platform, resulting in a clean-cut victory for Mr. Bryan, he was unanimously nominated on the first ballot.

With respect to the second place on the ticket, there was considerable more uncertainty. Once again it was determined by the exigencies of local New York State politics. There existed a bitter rivalry between ex-Governor David B. Hill, the state leader, and "Boss" Croker, of Tammany Hall. While Hill had retained his place in the late Democratic convention of the state and had prevented the adoption of a resolution endorsing the Chicago platform of 1896 with its 16-to-1 plank, his hold had been seriously threatened. Mr. Hill had stopped off at Lincoln, Nebraska, on his way to the Kansas City convention in an effort to dissuade Bryan from bringing forward the silver plank again, but without success. When the New York delegation caucused at Kansas City, there was a struggle between the forces of the two leaders. "I accuse you," exclaimed Hill, facing Croker in the caucus, "of trying to make me a Vice-Presidential candidate against my will, and I now tell you that I will not have it. You cannot humiliate me on one proposition and feed me a sop on another."[1] Croker, it seems, had not been unobservant of Platt's technique three weeks earlier in disposing of Roosevelt. The caucus then proceeded to choose Robert Van Wyck over Hill as the New York member of the committee on resolutions, and to name Norman E. Mack for the national committee. This was the setting when the time came for Vice-Presidential nominations.

There were aspirants enough for the honor, and eight names were formally presented to the convention. The Populist-Silver wing of the party had high hopes for one of their own, Charles A. Towne of Minnesota, but the Bourbons of the convention would not permit both places on the ticket to be held by men of that stamp. Croker, meanwhile, had not foregone his intention of placing Hill on the Vice-Presidential toboggan. Thomas F. Grady, one of his lieutenants, proceeded in a fulsome speech to place him in nomination. The demonstration which started at the mention of Hill's name was second only to that which had been accorded Mr. Bryan. Hill, in great agitation, made his way to the platform and there, after a time, made a wildly

[1] D. S. Alexander, *Four Famous New Yorkers*, 343.

enthusiastic audience understand that he could and would not accept the honor. Nevertheless, when the votes of the first ballot were totaled, it was found that Hill had received over two hundred, Towne but eighty-nine, and Adlai E. Stevenson 565. The names of all other candidates were then withdrawn and Stevenson given the nomination unanimously. New York thus lost the nomination through the play of petty local politics.

There were no strong reasons for the choosing of Mr. Stevenson other than that he was agreeable to Mr. Bryan and had given offense to no faction. While a Bourbon delegate was extolling him in a seconding speech, someone in the gallery yelled: "What good is he?" "I'll tell you," the delegate replied. "We are a solid Democracy. We don't care so much for platform and candidate, but we know that when he was in the Postmaster-General's office, Adlai Stevenson didn't leave a Republican standing. He is a good old-time Simon-pure Democrat." An Iowa delegate expressed a similar sentiment to the staff correspondent of the New York *Outlook:* "We've got Bryan to look after the principles and we've got Uncle Adlai to look after the offices."

Mr. Stevenson's nomination gave offense to no considerable party faction. It was of little moment that he was of a colorless, forceless personality. The ticket was headed by a candidate who could supply all in the campaign that was lacking in his running-mate. Non-partisan intellectuals interested in civil service and other reforms, found in Mr. Stevenson a target for their darts. The New York *Nation* remarked: "One might almost say of Mr. Stevenson's nomination for the Vice-Presidency that he was a candidate for this office eight years ago without any particular reason, and that he was taken up at Kansas City because he had run once before. His first selection was due to the fact that he seemed the most available man when the friends of Mr. Cleveland wanted to escape having Governor Gray of Indiana upon the ticket, while his second success came from the natural reaction against the truckling to Populists which had characterized the previous action at Kansas City. In truth, the Illinoisan is one of those colorless men who find it equally easy to support a Cleveland on a sound-money platform, and a Bryan on a 16-to-1 plank. The sole distinction which he ever achieved was as a thorough-going spoilsman under the first Cleveland Administration, when, as First Assistant Postmaster-General, he cut off the heads of fourth-class Republican postmasters at a rate which causes him still to be remembered with affection by 'former Dimmycrats,' and which was used as a strong argument in his behalf last week. Mr. Stevenson would stand on any platform, but it is highly appropriate that there should not be even so much as a line in favor of civil service reform in the one on which he tries his luck this time."

An unusually large number of minor parties presented candidates for the two offices: The Social Democrats, Eugene V. Debs of Illinois, and Job Harriman of California; the United Christian party, J. F. R. Leonard of Iowa, and David H. Martin of Pennsylvania; the Middle-of-the-Road Populists, Wharton Barker of Pennsylvania, and Ignatius Donnelly of Minnesota; the National Prohibition party, John G. Woolley of Illinois, and Henry B. Metcalf of Rhode Island; the Union Reform party, Seth H. Ellis of Ohio, and Samuel T. Nicholson of Pennsylvania. The Fusionist Populists had met at Sioux Falls, South Dakota, the first week in May and nominated Bryan for President and Charles A. Towne of Minnesota for Vice-President. About a month following the Democratic convention, Mr. Towne withdrew his candidacy and thereafter his party supported both Democratic candidates. The convention of the Silver Republican party was in session at Kansas City at the same time as the Democratic. They, too, nominated Bryan for the Presidency and there was a determined effort to name Mr. Towne for the second place, but on the earnest solicitation of himself and other leaders, this was not done and the matter was referred to a committee with power to act, which soon voted to accept Mr. Stevenson.

The two leading Vice-Presidential candidates participated in the campaign, but the activities of Mr. Bryan completely overshadowed those of Mr. Stevenson. The situation was just reversed with the Republicans, however. Both the dignity and the personal inclinations of Mr. McKinley forebade his active participation; but the vigorous Roosevelt set a new mark for Vice-Presidential campaigning. He appeared in over a half of the states of the Union and is said to have made over six hundred speeches. McKinley's administration had coincided with the upward curve of an economic cycle. Rising prices brought a prosperity both to the farms and the factories more general than had been known in a generation. This was an argument vastly more convincing to the millions of voters than all of Mr. Bryan's statements, however sound and ably stated, against American imperialism and the unequal distribution of wealth. Added to this was something of the glamour that comes from the winning of a war, and the great admiration of the millions of Westerners for the Vice-Presidential candidate, a hero of that war. The result was a substantial popular majority for the Republican ticket and their winning of the Electoral College by a vote of 292 to 155.

On September 6, 1901, President McKinley was shot by an assassin and died on the 14th following. Mr. Roosevelt duly succeeded him and though feeling bound in a measure to carry out the policy of his predecessor, yet he took vigorous action against what would be called the Trusts and Wall Street, or the business interests and economic safety of the country, according to the speaker's personal point of view. The President's conduct brought him enthusiastic support. The conservatives received another blow in the death of Mark Hanna, and they abandoned any attempt to prevent the nomination of Roosevelt in 1904.

They were, however, determined to name the Vice-President and there may have been a tacit understanding that this price should be paid by the Roosevelt men for the unanimous nomination of their leader. Senator Elkins of West Virginia, an old Republican politician and a very successful business man, was urged to accept the Vice-Presidency. He consulted Whitelaw Reid, who replied advising him to remain in the Senate, and Elkins accepted the advice. Reid favored Secretary Root, but he, too, declined. Probably Roosevelt wished for the nomination of Speaker Cannon, not that either "Teddy" or "Uncle Joe" had any love for the other, but the President found the Speaker rather independent and was reviving the drama of four years before and playing Platt to Cannon's Roosevelt.

Cannon, however, had no desire to step up in form and down in fact, and the conservatives agreed to support Senator Charles W. Fairbanks of Indiana. That gentleman was anxious for the place. Senator Lodge wrote to the President, May 27, 1904, that Fairbanks had called on him and had expressed a desire to be of service in any possible way, and that "though he did not mention the Vice-Presidency he made it perfectly evident to me that he did want it and is after it, and means to get it. If he pushes for it he will get it. So you must tread warily and say nothing." Which was what McKinley did when Roosevelt was being thrust upon him!

By the time the convention met, it was fully understood that Fairbanks was to be given the second place. Messrs. Dolliver, Depew, Foraker, and Pennypacker, of Pennsylvania, nominated Fairbanks in laudatory speeches. Pennypacker also praised Pennsylvania for her fidelity to Republicanism, saying: "She is unselfish in her devotion. During the period of half a century that is gone no (Republican) son of hers has been either President or Vice-President. She has been satisfied . . . to have been the Maker of Kings. She has been content that you should have regard to the success of the party and the welfare of the country rather than to the personal interests of her citizens." Favorite sons who had been nominated for form's sake were withdrawn, and Fairbanks was nominated unanimously on the first ballot.

In most respects, Charles Warren Fairbanks was a typical Hoosier, although he had been born in the neighboring state of Ohio and had received his education at one of her institutions, Ohio Wesleyan University. In person, he was of the beanpole order and because of this characteristic obliged to endure many witticisms. In temperament, he might seem less typical. He was no Lincoln, full of witty stories and friendly with everyone. Yet, like Lincoln, the pioneers had a deep vein of melancholy in their nature, and this cropped out in Fairbanks in a very noticeable tendency to funereal speech. Once in Indianapolis while delivering a political address, Mr. Fairbanks referred to the great leaders of the party "sleeping in yonder cemetery" and was surprised to have his touching words received with a burst of laughter.

At the time of his nomination, Mr. Fairbanks was fifty-two years old, and experienced both in party politics and in public life. He was a man of ability, one of careful and considerate manners, a certain marked reticence, a seeming lack of confidence in those whom he met, and a general aloofness, which gained for him the reputation of being a cold, austere sort of personage, which was ever damaging to his political prospects. That this was a misconception concerning him made no difference. He was the victim of his mannerisms, which his enemies were always anxious to exaggerate and use to his disadvantage.

The Democrats were somewhat discouraged by the two defeats of their "peerless leader." Mr. Bryan announced that he would not be a candidate; and the gold Democrats succeeded in carrying a platform which stated in a way pleasing to the silver men that the silver question was not now an issue, and in nominating Judge Alton B. Parker of New York, a gold man concerning whose views there was a certain doubt until after the nomination had been made.

The Parker men had not given much attention to the Vice-Presidency. A large majority of them seemed to favor Senator Turner of Washington state. He had served on the joint international commission for determining the Alaska boundary, and had represented the Government in the Northern Securities case. He was strong in Washington and the neighboring states and their few votes might be important. But it was urged that he lived too far West, that he was too much of a Populist; and that to bracket him with a conservative like Judge Parker would be manifestly a political dodge. Judson Harmon of Ohio and John C. Black of Illinois were ruled out as being closely connected with Grover Cleveland, and, therefore, extremely obnoxious to the followers of Mr. Bryan. Senator Kern of Indiana was considered, but was said not to be popular in his own state. J. R. Williams of Illinois was the first candidate on the ground. The local papers published interviews with him and printed his picture. He was advocated as a representative of the Middle West and a supporter of Parker. But his boom sprouted early and it soon withered away.

The convention finally passed by all these candidates and nominated Henry Gassaway Davis of West Virginia, a wealthy gentleman of advanced age, who was a cousin and business and political ally of Senator Gorman, the Democratic leader of Maryland, and father-in-law and former business partner of Senator Elkins, an experienced Republican politician who had been chairman of the Republican National Committee in 1884.

Henry Gassaway Davis was born at Woodstock, Maryland, on November 16, 1823. His parents were farmers, but he himself began life as a brakeman on a railroad. Later he acquired interests in lumber and coal and in a savings bank. He formed a partnership with Stephen B. Elkins, and they constructed railroads to haul their coke to the sea and towns to house their employees; and so built up the southwestern part of West Virginia. In politics Mr. Davis was a Henry Clay Whig before the war, and a conservative, frankly protectionist Democrat after it. He was the first Democratic Senator from West Virginia, served two terms, and then declined to be a candidate for reëlection. He had been chairman of the Committee on Appropriations, and had secured valuable improvements in the manner of keeping the books of the Treasury Department.

In leaving office, Mr. Davis did not abandon his interest in politics. He had been a delegate to every Democratic convention from that of 1868 up to and including that of 1904. In the Senate Mr. Davis had inclined to soft money and had voted to override Grant's veto of the inflation bill of 1874. He had twice voted for Bryan for President. But he was believed to have become "harder" than he was in the seventies, and to stand for what Mr. Bryan opposed. He had advised the election as delegates to the national convention of men who were conservative, representative Democrats without regard to former differences of opinion. Davis was chosen because it was thought his nomination might sweeten the Parker pill for the Bryanites, while his financial interests and his conservatism would make him acceptable to the East. Davis was decidedly *persona grata* to the friends of Senator Gorman, who had been a candidate for the first place, and if any Democrat could carry West Virginia, he could. Finally, he was able to make a handsome contribution to the campaign fund.

In religion Mr. Davis was a convinced Presbyterian and his manner of life befitted a member of that conscientious, logical, and austere denomination. For many years he kept the Sabbath in Puritan fashion, and at the time of his nomination, it was said that probably he had never read a novel because, as he explained, "the people in the stories are not real." Davis' speeches were carefully worked out. "He was always sure of his facts and his statistics were carefully verified." He loved details. He did not seek larger fields for his abilities, because he did not wish to be responsible for things to which it would not be possible for him to give his personal superintendence. John Sharp Williams of Mississippi, in notifying Davis of his nomination, described him as "one of the best products of American institutions in a period of freedom, freedom to develop as his own master and not merely as the well trained and well managed industrial servant of another." But either the Presbyterian doctrine of "total depravity" or experience in a long life kept Davis from glorying in his own works. Williams told him that the American people "see in you what Oliver Wendell Holmes said is a rare thing, a self-made man who yet is not proud of his maker."

During the campaign the Republicans endeavored to make capital of Mr. Davis' age. Postmaster-General Payne said: "The unprecedented preference in the selection of a candidate for the second place on the Democratic ticket, of a man who has passed fourscore was dictated by political expediency. Ex-Senator Davis is an estimable, old gentleman, but it would seem rather unkind to lure him from his self-sought retirement after twenty years and to impose the exactions of the campaign, to say nothing of the responsibilities that success would bring to him." The New York *Tribune* said: "Happily there is no prospect of his being called on, at the end of his long life, to preside over the Senate and hold himself in readiness to assume responsibilities which would overwhelm him in an instant."

The Democrats replied that Mr. Davis was old in years only, and told how strong he was. Mayor McClellan of New York, on being asked if he did not think Davis a little old, replied: "A man's only as old as he feels. Any man who can sit through two night sessions of the convention as he did is not an old man." A telegram to the New York *Tribune* from the town of Elkins, West Virginia, stated: "The look of weariness which the convention left on Mr. Davis' features had disappeared yesterday when he rose at 5 o'clock, after a sound night's rest, and took a horseback ride over the country roads back of his home. This is a favorite diversion of his."

The Boston *Globe* said that Mr. Davis was the youngest old man of the decade. "The accounts of his physical endurance would read like stories if we did not know that Gladstone felled trees when 80, and that Leo XIII performed the arduous duties of the papacy when 90. Cicero, in his dissertation on old age, has immortalized that young old Cato, who at 85 was the dominant figure in the Roman Senate, and who at 80 began to study Greek. It was the period of Rome's political and commercial supremacy, a period not unlike the present, when the counsel or the services of a patriarch may be beneficial to a young and giant republic."

The Democrats had much to say concerning the relations between the Republican candidates. They had a story that Mr. Roosevelt had described his running-mate as "a woolly horse from Indiana." Mr. Fairbanks paid a visit to his leader's home, and the Democrats made themselves merry over it. A despatch to the Boston *Globe* from Indianapolis announced that Fairbanks had drafted his speech and letter of acceptance, but that he would take them to Oyster Bay before giving them final form. The *Globe* made the comment: "Here's hoping that he will be able to recognize them after their revision by the President." After Fairbanks' return home, the *Globe* stated that "Senator Fairbanks is rewriting his letter of acceptance. He must wish now that he hadn't wasted any time on the first draft."[1] Mr. Fairbanks' visit was rather brief, and it was said that it had been shortened by a disagreement with his host.

All these stories were, of course, branded as false by the Republicans. From Washington came a denial "on the highest authority" of the tale of the woolly horse. The New York *Tribune* informed the world that there was no ground whatever for the friction rumor, that Mr. Fairbanks did not leave Oyster Bay a moment earlier than he had planned. It was explained that the visit was short because there was not much to be done, and Private

---

[1] Such taunts were hardly suitable when a despatch from Elkins to the *Tribune* had announced that Davis would say nothing on the money question until Judge Parker had spoken.

Secretary Cortelyou expressed the opinion that the newspaper correspondents, in despair at finding so little real news, had turned to romancing.

The campaign was one of the least interesting since the Civil War. The nomination of Judge Parker, a conservative, by the party which had had radical leadership for eight years and which had swallowed the radical Populists, was a deep disappointment to many of its members. The issues, which had enlivened the campaigns of 1896 and 1900, were dead, thanks to the vigorous and liberal legislative leadership of the Republican President. While he had alienated a considerable number of the "stand pat" politicians of his own party, their voting following was not formidable. The upshot was that Roosevelt held the greater part of the regulars of his own party and attracted large numbers of Democrats and independents. The Republican popular vote increased almost 400,000 over four years ago, while the Democratic vote decreased more than a million and a quarter. This gave the former party 336 votes in the electoral college, to 140 for its major opponent. The Socialist ticket, headed by Eugene V. Debs, of Indiana, and Benjamin Hanford, of New York, astonished the country by gathering in more than 400,000 votes; while the Prohibitionists, with Silas C. Swallow, of Pennsylvania, and George W. Carroll, of Texas, and the revamped Populists, with Thomas E. Watson, of Georgia, and Thomas H. Tibbles, of Nebraska, together rolled up only a slightly smaller total.

Mr. Roosevelt closed his second term with a record of many achievements and some failures, and received much praise and much blame. The old leaders of the party were cool toward him; the bulk of the rank and file enthusiastic in their approval. He had picked Secretary of War Taft to succeed him and carry on his policies. The "Old Guard" were hoping for someone outside the Roosevelt circle, little matter who. In 1907 Senator Lodge wrote the President that Senator Penrose and his allies were planning to control the convention, but that they would not nominate either Fairbanks or Foraker, since they believed that this would mean defeat at the polls.

On June 16, 1908, the Republican convention met at Chicago with Taft's nomination almost assured, but with various favorite sons such as Speaker Joseph G. Cannon of Illinois, Charles W. Fairbanks of Indiana, Charles Evans Hughes of New York, Joseph B. Foraker of Ohio, Philander C. Knox of Pennsylvania, and Robert M. LaFollette of Wisconsin, scheduled for a complimentary vote, which might lead to a nomination for Vice-President. There were three other active candidates in the field, ex-Governor Franklin Murphy of New Jersey, Governor Curtis Guild of Massachusetts, and Representative James S. Sherman, a Congressman of long service from New York. Roosevelt telegraphed Lodge that the Administration would not attempt to influence the convention in its choice of the nominee for Vice-President,[1] but

---

[1]Delegates wish sometimes to be, or at least to think that they are a determining power, and like Monsieur Beaucaire they crave the privilege of having "one leetle fight."

that protests had been made to Taft against the nomination of Sherman because he could be held partly responsible for the failure of the House to pass the Postal Savings bill, and because he did not believe in modifying the power of courts to issue injunctions, a policy to which Taft was committed.

Lodge telegraphed back that Senator Crane thought there would be no trouble about the passage of the Postal Savings bill; that he himself would oppose such an injunction plank as would satisfy Samuel Gompers, the head of the Federation of Labor; and that he saw no use in a "colorless one." Lodge concluded his telegram: "Think you are absolutely right in your position as to Vice-President. Result will probably be Fairbanks. Probably best under not very good conditions."

Mr. Lodge's opinion of his colleague was fully endorsed by both the retiring President and the gentleman whom he had picked for his successor. There was always a coolness between "Icebanks" and the "Rough Rider" and in the letter already quoted, and after the President had been run away with, Taft told him that if the latter meant to ride any more fractious horses, he wished he would take Fairbanks with him. Newspapers had just carried interviews purporting to come from Fairbanks, stating that the Administration wished him to be on the ticket, and Taft's joke convinced his aide, Major Archibald W. Butt, that he wished Fairbanks anywhere else. Butt made the comment in one of a series of letters intended as a diary, "Certainly he (Fairbanks) will be a misfit with Taft, for one seems to be as crafty and shrewd as the other is open and genial."

Taft desired the nomination of a man from the Middle West as an offset to the certain Bryan candidacy; Senator Dolliver of Iowa was his first choice. Iowa Republicans had long been divided into two factions; the Conservatives headed by Senator Allison, Lafayette Young, and George D. Perkins, and the Progressives, with Governor Cummins as leader. The breach had temporarily been closed, but a vacancy in the Senate would probably cause the old feud to break out with fury. If Dolliver were removed from the Senate, through a Vice-Presidential nomination, Governor Cummins or one of his faction would be appointed to his place. This the Conservatives were determined to prevent at all costs. Taft and Roosevelt would have been willing to take either Dolliver or Cummins or any other Iowan within reason, whom that state delegation might agree upon. The Boston *Globe* correspondent stated that, if local considerations were disregarded, there were good reasons for the nomination of Cummins. He said: "Cummins is a strong tariff revisionist and, as the platform is to declare for revision, he would be able to render great assistance in the campaign, as he is one of the best vote-getters in the West."

But the Conservatives played the part of the dog in the manger. There were thinly veiled threats of a bolt if Dolliver should be selected and Perkins, in the name of twenty members of the Iowa delegation, wired Private Secretary Loeb, demanding to know if the Administration was favoring Dolliver. Mr. Loeb replied that it was not and did not intend to. But, as he quickly pointed out, the Administration "did not mean Mr. Taft."

Mr. Sherman, likewise, was hampered by a division in the delegation from his state, and this was the more important as he had little strength outside New York. A large majority of the New York delegates had been instructed to support Governor Hughes for President. His case was hopeless but the written rule remained. Chauncey M. Depew recalled how in 1896 New York had adhered steadily to its instructions to vote for Levi P. Morton for the Presidency despite all the blandishments of Hanna, who offered the Vice-Presidency, and he said that now no member of the New York delegation could give a thought to the Vice-Presidency until the fate of Hughes had been settled by the convention itself, and that any delegate who did so would be politically damned.[1]

Such loyalty to instructions could not save Hughes, but might lose New York the Vice-Presidency by preventing the friends of Sherman from canvassing for him. The suggestion was made to Hughes that he should release his delegates; he replied that he had not asked them to vote for him and that they must continue or withdraw their support as they judged proper. This was in accordance with the famous pronouncement of Lowndes that the Presidency should neither be shunned nor sought; but one is reminded of the just comment of the French general when he saw the charge of the Light Brigade, "It is magnificent, but it is not war." Hughes' dignified conduct was not politics; neither was it required by ethics. There are many circumstances in which the most scrupulous man may honorably decline a candidature. In the old days mere citizenship of the Empire State might have given the Vice-Presidential nomination to Sherman, but Bryan was certain to be the Democratic candidate for President; and most Republicans, including Mr. Taft, believed that this would remove New York from the doubtful column. Therefore her sceptre was falling from her hand.

Sherman's personal appearance hurt him. He wore "perceptible though not aggressive" side whiskers and looked like an Englishman. Some Western delegates said that he must make speeches and therefore would be seen; that even should he shave, the change would not be sufficient; and that his face would repel those Irishmen whom Roosevelt had corralled. Vice-President Fairbanks had been a candidate for the first place and had renounced the second; but Taft's nomination had become a certainty and many conservatives centered their hopes on again obtaining the second place for Fairbanks. It is most important that a President should be in vigorous health, and this was now being demanded of the possible successor. The correspondent of the Boston *Globe* reported that the qualifications of one candidate for the

---

[1]Mr. Platt, however, neglected to state that he himself controlled the New York delegation in 1896, and that he was glad to annoy Hanna by reducing McKinley's majority.

Vice-Presidency of the United States were mainly measured by a lung-tester, and that another's unfortunate gall-bladder was cited for his disqualification for that office. "At present," he continued, "the office of Vice-President is seeking Mr. Fairbanks. He has put in no physician's certificate but it is well known that he is now a man of steady habits who never more looks upon the wine when there is a cherry in it. In the absence of any discouragement from him, the ticket is most likely to be Taft and Fairbanks. The general opinion is that he will not decline. The Vice-Presidency is the only thing in sight for him. He can not return to his old seat in the Senate. He is rich, out of business, and fond of Washington and public life."

But Mr. Fairbanks did resolutely decline. He came to the convention with less love than ever for Mr. Roosevelt and his friend Taft. Alone of all the candidates for President, he had made a Nation-wide campaign; he had received considerable response; and he believed that he would have won had not the President thrown all his influence to the help of Secretary Taft. Fairbanks' treatment in the convention must have accentuated this feeling. Defying the American dislike of being bored and of wasting time, Governor Hanly of Indiana, who went through the form of nominating Fairbanks, inflicted a long speech on his impatient audience. Disorder broke out in the galleries; there were insulting cries of "chilblains," "cocktails," and "Get the hook!"

Mayor Bookwalter of Indianapolis, who followed Hanly, retorted: "It dawns upon me that the slow movements of the road-roller no longer satisfy the gentlemen in charge of the convention (hisses). In Indiana we have only two things that hiss, snakes and geese." After this unfortunate outburst, Bookwalter made the soothing announcement: "I am going to nominate the longest candidate in the shortest speech."

Taft men, on their part, were irritated by the attacks on their methods. James E. Watson of Indiana had made a strong speech in favor of a resolution cutting down representation in Republican National Conventions of districts which gave few Republican votes. The Indiana delegation supported the proposal and the Southern delegates were therefore very bitter against Fairbanks. The Vice-President sent a second letter re-affirming his declination and this greatly encouraged the friends of Mr. Murphy. There had been a kind of understanding that when Murphy's nomination for President proved to be impossible, his men would go to Fairbanks, and they hoped that the Fairbanks followers would now reciprocate by helping Murphy.

Mr. Murphy's claims were eloquently presented by Thomas M. McCarter, who told the convention that Murphy had entered the Union army at sixteen, and that this might be the last opportunity of the Republicans to give a place on their ticket to one of the boys in blue. Mr. McCarter praised Mr. Murphy as a manufacturer who had helped develop his state, but who had never had any trouble with his employees, and as a man who had proved his kindness by his treatment of the negroes. The friends of Governor Guild were obliged to play a waiting game. As the correspondent of the Boston *Globe* pointed out, a candidate from the staunch Republican State of Massachusetts must at first be receptive. Later there were charges that Senator Lodge and other Massachusetts men had been treacherous to Guild. But probably this was not true, at least as far as Lodge was concerned. Shortly before the ballots were cast, some Massachusetts delegates were threatening to vote against their fellow-citizens, but Lodge read the riot act to them so vigorously that they all submitted.

Dark horses were of course thought of. A Taft Senator proposed Seth Low, a wealthy man who had been a reform Mayor of New York and was now president of Columbia University; but the leaders refused to consider him. There was talk of another New Yorker, Stewart L. Woodford. He was to nominate Hughes, and it was suggested that he might be so eloquent that there would be a stampede to him. Perhaps with an intention of preparing this "spontaneous" outburst, the matter was mentioned to Woodford. He very sensibly replied that no man of his age should aspire to the office of Vice-President with its possibilities of succession to another, which required in its holder the greatest powers of endurance.

To many there was an unreality about the whole contest. The Boston *Globe* correspondent wrote his paper that it was merely a sham fight which would be decided when Washington said the word. The New York *Tribune* correspondent stated that Roosevelt could nominate the Vice-President by letting his preference be known, and that Taft could turn the convention to Dolliver (whose stock had been falling) by saying that he still favored him. On June 17 the *Tribune* correspondent reported that Fairbanks was sure of a renomination unless Washington endorsed some other candidate, but that the motto of the Administration was one fight at a time. As the last part of the sentence shows, a boss is often less powerful than he seems; his strength ultimately depends on the support of his followers; and if he persists in ruling in disregard of their wishes, he is likely to win battles but lose campaigns and see his power pass to another. The President had no wish to injure Taft, for whom there was no enthusiasm to spare, by seeming to dictate also the selection of the Vice-President.

But the Taft men carried an adjournment against the wishes of the "allies,"[1] who believed that the purpose was to get the steam roller working. In the evening the leaders gathered at the rooms of Mr. Hitchcock, the chairman of the national committee, and sat up till four or five in the morning discussing the Vice-Presidency. There was much telephoning to Washington concerning the Iowa candidates. Taft would have been pleased with Dolliver, but was told that Iowa demanded that Dolliver remain in the Senate, and that Taft's own supporters believed that Cummins was too much of a

---

[1] A name applied to the men who disliked Roosevelt and his ways and deeds.

low tariff man to be nominated for Vice-President. Taft was nevertheless willing to take him, but after further conversation Cummins shared the fate of Dolliver.

The New York *Tribune* thus described the manœuvers by which the nomination of Sherman was brought about: "Mr. Taft and the President were advised that Michigan had practically endorsed Sherman. Then they said that they had no objection to Sherman, but thought a Western man would add greater strength to the ticket. Fairbanks and Beveridge were then suggested. Either would be agreeable to the Secretary (Taft), came the word from Washington.

"Then 'Joe' Kealing was sent for. He said emphatically that Mr. Fairbanks would not accept it and that the Indiana delegation was instructed to withdraw his name if presented. With regard to Beveridge, Mr. Kealing stated that Indiana would not offer him, and it must be made obvious that he was a Taft selection. If he was nominated under these conditions, the Indiana delegation would vote for him. This was communicated to Mr. Taft, who replied that he could not accept Beveridge on those conditions. Meanwhile Senator Long of Kansas had been suggested, and had absolutely declined the nomination. Finally the word came from Washington that Sherman had better be chosen if the convention so wished. This got out, and the Shermanites, who had already three hundred votes for their candidate, did some very lively work."

Mr. Hitchcock also was busy till the convention met, pleading for harmony and urging that all should line up behind Sherman, who had shown greater strength than any other candidate. The missionaries waked up the leaders, who arranged for some early informal meetings of the several delegations who were agreeable to Sherman. The President and Mr. Taft took no further part in the negotiations.

When the convention met, everything went harmoniously or, as one correspondent expressed it, with a bang. The states are called for nominations in alphabetical order. Delaware withdrew in favor of New York. Timothy Woodruff, the head of the delegation, was busy telling someone how many votes he had for Sherman "when the chair recognized Governor Woodruff of New York, caught the state chairman's ear at last and before he knew it, people were shoving him to the platform."

Woodruff praised Sherman personally, but like the practical politician he was, also laid much stress on his availability. He declared that New York would not be sure for the ticket with both Hughes and Sherman turned down. No Republican ticket, he said, had ever been defeated with a New York Republican upon it "except once [1888] when our opponents were wise enough to select a New York Democrat to head the Democratic ticket."

The old warrior, ex-Speaker Cannon of Illinois, followed Woodruff. The representative of the Boston *Globe* wrote: "Here were a figure and a voice of the pre-Rooseveltian period. His wildly flying arm clove the enervating air. His head bobbed up and down and around like a cork in the surf, while he pranced and jumped about the stage and seconded Sherman's nomination in a shouting, fervid, camp meeting exhortation"; and Sherman was chosen.

A young man who had distinguished himself as a cheer-leader at the convention four years before was rushed to the platform with a megaphone, but this was more than the dignified chairman, Senator Henry Cabot Lodge, could endure, and grasping the intruder by the nape of the neck, he projected him to the floor. But there was no need of assisted cheering. The "allies" were glad that the nomination had not been made by the President or his friends. Congressmen rejoiced at the recognition of a coördinate branch of the Government; and Stevenson of Illinois said that it would mean that "every member of Congress will get out in his district and work like a whitehead." Illinois delegates were happy at the success of the candidate of their choice, in whose victory they or, more strictly speaking, their leader, Mr. Cannon, had had so large a share. The New York delegates were gratified by the recognition of their state and, according to the *Tribune* correspondent, everybody went home happy.

But it may be that this happiness was neither deep nor appropriate. On June 24 Roosevelt wrote to Lodge: "Sherman's nomination, I think, helps us in New York by interesting the organization, but in the upper Mississippi Valley he is considered identified with Cannon and I have been disturbed by the extent of the hostility to and the revolt against Cannon."[1] A correspondent wrote: "The Sherman nomination is regarded as a mere filler. It is generally admitted here that he brings no element of strength to the ticket. The New York delegation united upon him tardily and reluctantly. There is nothing in his known record in Congress or in the prevailing estimate of his mental equipment which promises any contribution to the party's success."

James S. Sherman was born on October 24, 1855, at Utica, New York. He graduated from Hamilton College in 1878, the same year that Taft did at Yale. In 1884 he became mayor of Utica. In 1887 he entered the Congress, and with the exception of a single term, served until his nomination for the Vice-Presidency. In 1899 he was a candidate for the Republican nomination for Speaker, but was defeated by David B. Henderson of Iowa. For many years he had been chairman of the Committee on Indian Affairs, and had saved millions of dollars for the Indians. He also reached the important place of second on the Committee on Finance. He was frequently made chairman when the House was in Committee of the Whole, where his popularity and pleasant ways and his wide knowledge of parliamentary law made him an admirable presiding officer. He presided over the debate on the

---

[1] Sherman, however, had had the support of Senator Curtis of Kansas.

Dingley bill for many weeks, and also over that on the Cuban War Revenue bill.

In 1899 President McKinley offered him the position of Appraiser of the Port of New York, but a mass meeting at Utica protested against his leaving his seat in Congress, and he declined the appointment. In 1906 Mr. Sherman was chairman of the Republican Congressional Committee and originated a plan for every Republican to contribute a dollar, which earned him the nickname of "Dollar Jim." But in his attention to *hoi polloi* Mr. Sherman did forget the rich and the great, and went into Wall Street as a "fat fryer," where he met with but moderate success. His rebuff by Harriman, who resented Roosevelt's attack on the railroads and on himself personally, was the occasion of the President's letter to Harriman beginning, "You and I are practical men." In 1908 Sherman was considered both for Governor and Senator, but the New York delegation, while on the train to Chicago, got together, decided that he was New York's strongest candidate for Vice-President, and agreed to support him unitedly.

In person Mr. Sherman was short and stout, but vigorous and active. Allowance being made for difference in age, he much resembled Senator Hoar, of whom he was a distant cousin. Four years later the *Tribune* correspondent said of Sherman: "He tips the scales at about 225 pounds, and looks as jolly as his somewhat heavier running-mate Mr. Taft. Generally he wears a square-topped derby hat, an English walking coat, maybe a green or purple waistcoat, and conspicuous spectacles. His face is round and his smile is rarely missing."

Mr. Sherman was a forcible and able speaker. He was open and honest for a politician, and he made friends everywhere. He was never discouraged when things went wrong, and his sobriquet was "Sunny Jim." He received the announcement of his success with refreshing simplicity and frankness. Declining to make a speech, he expressed his gratitude to the New York delegation, and said that the nomination was "an honor which I wanted but had little thought of securing."

The Democratic convention met at Denver on July 7, 1908, ready to nominate Bryan and whomsoever he should sponsor for Vice-President. As the delegates gathered, there was talk of John Mitchell, the labor leader. It was said that he was not extreme in his views, yet would make a fine contrast to the capitalistic Sherman; but Mr. Mitchell absolutely declined to be considered. The correspondent of the Boston *Globe* pronounced the refusal wise because the choice of Mitchell would have been a forced selection made with the obvious desire of catching the labor vote; and Vice-Presidential nominations of that kind never fail to react; the very gudgeons that smart politicians seek to catch run away from the hook. Several other names were considered, but there was no great interest in the second place, and the matter was left in abeyance until the wishes of the "Peerless Leader" should become known. Bryan's known preference for Judge George Gray of Delaware, caused his name to be prominently considered throughout the state delegations, but a telegram from him absolutely declining to allow his name to go before the convention ended that discussion. Champ Clark approached "Boss" Charles Murphy of New York in the interest of Francis B. Harrison, but Murphy let it be known that New York would back no candidate nor take any other active part in the proceedings of the convention.

One correspondent wrote: "Vice-Presidents are usually picked up around the breakfast table, and so it was in the present instance." Early in the morning of the 10th, the last day of the convention, a few leaders met in the room of Mr. Charles W. Bryan. Mr. Bryan stated that his brother would prefer a New Yorker. Lewis Nixon, of that state, was proposed. Daniel F. Cohalan, a delegate, doubtless acting under instructions from Murphy, replied: "Gentlemen, New York will not present a candidate for the Vice-Presidency." It was then agreed that Senator John W. Kern of Indiana should be named.

The usual sham battle was planned and it was made to look real by sending champions to the lists. When the time came for the Convention to "decide" who should be nominated for Vice-President, as one correspondent described it, "the Indiana delegation moved up to the front, and brought the band from the gallery to sit with them and play 'On the Banks of the Wabash' on every opportunity. Thomas R. Marshall, the Democratic Governor of Indiana, a lean and malarial Hoosier, presented the name of Kern as a citizen of a state where everyone was either a statesman or an author."

Governor Folk of Missouri, famous as a prosecutor of bribery cases, seconded the nomination, though Kern would have nominated Mitchell had he not declined. Heflin of Alabama turned for a moment from leveling his spear at his dearest foe at Rome and brandished it in behalf of Kern. Ollie James from the Blue Grass, devoted servant at once of his party and of the card table, proclaimed Kern one of the knightliest Democrats in the world.

There can be no tournament, even a fictitious one, if the champions all wear the same colors. Accordingly, Archibald McNeil of Bridgeport, Connecticut, couched lance in behalf of K. J. Walsh of Connecticut. Sir Archibald must have had every confidence in the beauty of his "ladie faire," for when the delegates reached Denver they found the walls of the convention hall plastered with Walsh portraits. Mr. McNeil, who from his residence and name would appear to be a Connecticut Yankee of Scotch extraction, described his candidate as a Christian coal dealer. With memories of the great coal strike still painfully fresh, he doubtless thought that so extraordinary a combination would make a powerful appeal.

Ex-Governor Thomas of Colorado put up Charles Towne. Mr. Towne was an able man who had been a Senator from Minnesota and was a delegate from New York, but as a Vice-Presidential candidate he was a waif; neither

Minnesota nor New York would father his boom and it was left for the hospitable hands of Colorado to take him off the doorstep. All the candidates having been exhibited, New York, which had presented none, now asked to be called again. She announced that her delegates had been directed to consult with the leaders from all parts of the country to find out what might be best for the party; that they had become convinced that the voice of the party favored Bryan; and that they were now sure that the same voice had pronounced for Kern.

Kern had been selected because he was a good Democrat, an active campaigner, and came from a doubtful state. The candidate was born on December 20, 1849, near Kokomo, Indiana. Kokomo was noted for its production of natural gas. It was also the birthplace of Tod Sloan, the jockey. The townspeople regarded as a third glory the circumstance that it was the native city of that warm-hearted and very popular politician, John W. Kern.

This gentleman was fortunate, electorally speaking, in his family, circumstances, and personal characteristics. He could be pictured to the masses as a poor boy who became famous, as of distinguished but not aristocratic ancestry, a true Democrat, yet fitted to mingle with the educated and wealthy and actually doing so. Mr. Kern's father, the founder of Kernstown, Virginia, was a descendant of Robert Burns; his mother was a sister of President William Henry Harrison of Tippecanoe and log-cabin fame. He had ridden ten miles a day to attend a normal school and had worked summers to pay for his education. The classes and the intelligentsia could be told that he was a graduate of the Law Department of the University of Michigan, that he was a man of reading and travel, that he was a resident of Indianapolis, the political and social center of the state, and that he dwelt in the same quarter of the city as the late President Benjamin Harrison, Vice-President Fairbanks, and Senator Beveridge.

Kern and Fairbanks lived only three blocks apart and were on excellent personal terms. Care was taken to show that Kern had not become a Croesus. The same article that mentioned the propinquity of Kern and Fairbanks, stated that Kern's home was "modest"; and Kern had publicly called attention to the great difference between himself and his wealthy neighbor. The spring before the nomination, Mr. Bryan had visited Kern at Indianapolis and the Democrats of the city gave him a dinner. In his speech the visitor showed his appreciation of their hospitality by referring to his host as a possible Democratic nominee for Vice-President. Kern called to him to stop that. "It is rumored that it is costing my neighbor, Charles Warren Fairbanks, $50,000 a year. I am too poor to think of running for Vice-President. At that rate I could only afford to stop in Washington a day." Thereupon the generous Mr. Bryan offered Kern a part of the White House rent free.

Like his opponent, Mr. Sherman, Kern was marked by his whiskers but he followed American, not foreign style. E. J. Lewis wrote: "As for Mr.

Kern's whiskers that will probably become noted, he long has worn chin-whiskers. He emerged with them from the whisker days when, in Indiana, not to wear whiskers was considered a physical defect, and the days of the smooth-faced mania which swept Indiana and the West and spared in that state but few whiskers, passed without having touched Kern's wind-breakers."

Supporters praised Kern's kindliness and his good feeling for political opponents. One of them told how in 1904, shortly after he had been defeated for Governor, Kern, uninvited, attended a Republican celebration of the success of Roosevelt and Fairbanks and paid a beautiful tribute to his fellow-townsman, the Vice-President-elect. Kern's opponents accused him of the weakness that sometimes accompanies gentleness, and of a partisanship which, if not malicious, was yet blind. One unfriendly critic said of him: "He has no convictions that are not readily reversed by a majority vote. He opposed free silver and yet was its ardent defender. His political law is to be always regular." Another compared him to Booth Tarkington's creation, Daniel Vorhees Pike. Like Pike, he "parts from" Kokomo, Indiana, was a long, lean, country lawyer—a sort of David Harum of the law as practiced and mixed with politics in the old time Hoosier county seats.

In the campaign the *Nation,* true to its tradition of independence, criticized both candidates for the Vice-Presidency. It said that the nominations were "a proof of the flippant way in which Americans set about filling the highest offices in the government. In either case, it is not personality but geography that has been the decisive factor. At Denver, also, New York might have had its Vice-President had she wished." The *Nation* thought that it was a mistake to nominate a man so eager as Sherman was to get corporate and "undesirable" subscriptions to the campaign fund, and that even Mr. Sherman's friends would not claim that he was fit to be President. It described Sherman as "a plodding Congressman like any other. Outside of his own state he has been known merely as an excellent Parliamentarian. As a practiced Chairman of the Committee of the Whole House he has been an excellent presiding officer; and if the only function of the Vice-President were to be President of the Senate, the choice of Mr. Sherman would be thoroughly justified. But the possibility that he may become President of the United States seemingly never occurred to the Convention."

The nomination of Bryan drove some conservative Democrats to the support of Taft and, on the other hand, attracted back into the Democratic fold some of the liberal wing who had strayed away to the party of Roosevelt. The result of a contest between a party led by the twice defeated Bryan and one led by Secretary Taft, upon whose head President Roosevelt had solemnly poured the oil of anointment, was, as realized by seasoned politicians like Murphy of New York, predetermined. Taft swept the country to gain an almost two to one advantage in the electoral college over his opponent.

Mr. Taft's term as President closed in political disaster. The Roosevelt wing felt that he had deserted the good cause and the man who made him, for "the interests." Mr. Roosevelt decided to seek a nomination by the Republicans. There was a bitter fight, and many seats in the convention were claimed by rival delegations. The direct primary, a product of the "progressive" age, was now for the first time an important factor in determining the make-up of a national party convention. Roosevelt had scored to a large extent though the use of this new device in the Middle Western States. The Taft men, through the aid of the National Committee, controlled the convention at its opening and then decided most of the contests in favor of their friends, though it was recognized that this would result in a bolt which would give the victory to the Democrats.

Under such circumstances, there was little desire for the Vice-Presidency. After the nomination of Taft, most of the Roosevelt delegates had left the convention and, meeting in another hall as a new "third party," nominated their leader for the Presidency. Consequently, when the roll of the states was called for Vice-Presidential nominations, there was, in some cases, no response since whole delegations had bolted. Alabama yielded to New York and J. Van Vechten Olcott, a member of that delegation, nominated Sherman in a one-minute speech. The galleries were empty. There was a bare ripple of applause. What was the mere nomination of a Vice-President to weary delegates, compared with the cataclysmic events which had just gone before? When the roll was called, there were scattering votes for Borah of Idaho, Hadley of Missouri, C. E. Merriam of Illinois, and others; but the regulars stood by Sherman, and when his total was found to be 597, he was declared the nominee of the party.

Far different was the situation in the Democratic camp; there, the hosts met in full assurance of victory. Mr. Bryan announced that because of the personal opposition which he had aroused, he would not accept either place on the ticket. But, like Mr. Roosevelt, if he could not lead the party, he might defeat it by a bolt, and he had a large following in the convention itself. There were two chief contenders for the nomination, Mr. Champ Clark of Missouri, Speaker of the House of Representatives, and Dr. Woodrow Wilson, formerly the able president of Princeton, now the reforming but politically well-managed Governor of New Jersey. Mr. Bryan constantly tried to make it plain that the conservative party was well represented in the convention and would attempt to control it. He concluded that those interests were behind the Clark candidacy, and threw all his great powers as a political manager into the contest against them. Clark soon attained a majority vote. On the tenth ballot Murphy dramatically delivered the ninety votes of New York to Clark. A stampede was expected, but the Wilson forces braced and held. Through many weary ballots the lines remained substantially as they were, but with a perceptible weakening on the Clark side and strengthening on that of his opponent. On the twenty-seventh ballot, Tom Taggart, the Indiana leader, switched twenty-nine of the thirty votes of his state from

Governor Marshall, whom they had steadily supported from the beginning, to Wilson. This was the straw which indicated the direction of the wind. Thereafter the Clark votes steadily dissipated, and Wilson was nominated on the forty-fifth ballot.

Tom Taggart's switch to Wilson nominated the President, and the Vice-Presidency eventually came to the Indiana favorite son of the day. Gratitude is a practical political virtue, and it may have been present in this coincidence. William Gibbs McAdoo, one of the original Wilson-for-President men and later his Secretary of the Treasury, was one of those leaders at the Baltimore convention, primarily responsible for the staying of the Clark drive and the success of the Wilson cause. In his *Reminiscences,* he has given an account of the choosing of Marshall for Vice-President. At four o'clock of the afternoon of July 2 the convention, immediately following the nomination of Governor Wilson, took a recess to meet at nine that evening. The platform, which was still in the hands of the Committee on Resolutions, would be presented at that time, and the Vice-Presidential nomination be made.

McAdoo states:

> "During the recess I had got in touch with Governor Wilson and told him that the convention would nominate anyone he desired for the Vice-Presidency. He said he did not care to offer a suggestion: that he would prefer to have the convention exercise complete freedom of action about the Vice-Presidential nomination. I told the Governor that his friends in the convention would want an indication of his preference and that if he failed to point the way for them there was no telling what might happen. He then asked me to suggest the best available man. I suggested Thomas R. Marshall, of Indiana, whom I did not know personally, but only by reputation. The reason I suggested Marshall was because he was the Governor of a mid-western state; because his reputation was that of a liberal, and because he seemed to be generally well regarded. I thought that his nomination would balance the ticket well, so far as political considerations went. Governor Wilson authorized me to say that Marshall would be acceptable to him.
>
> "I conveyed this information immediately to Taggart. He was immensely pleased. A listless convention, yawning and looking at time-tables, voted Marshall in for second place. Then we went home."

When the roll of the states was called, there were nominations of a half dozen or more men. A delegate from the District of Columbia named Mr. Bryan and the latter, in voicing his declination, took this as an opportunity to deliver his valedictory and formally hand over the leadership of the party to Woodrow Wilson. His work was done, the party had nominated a liberal, and presented the most liberal platform ever adopted by a major political party. He urged the convention to follow this up with the nomination of a liberal for Vice-President, and he ended by seconding the nominations of Governor John Burke of North Dakota, and George E. Chamberlain of Oregon. Mayor G. V. Menzies of Indianapolis nominated Governor Marshall, and received a cheer. On the first ballot, Marshall and Burke ran close, with Chamberlain a strong third. On the second ballot, there was a large accession to the Marshall vote, but Burke also gained. No one had secured a two-thirds vote. But the tired delegates had had enough of balloting; Burke withdrew in favor of Marshall and the latter was nominated by acclamation.

Thomas Riley Marshall, unlike the Indiana Vice-President who immediately preceded him, was a native of the state. His grandfather had settled there when it was a primeval forest. He became the first clerk of Grant County, and his house was used as the meeting place of the courts for several years. His father obtained such education as the frontier afforded, turned to the study of medicine, and spent his life as a country practitioner. The future Vice-President was born at North Manchester, Wabash County, March 14, 1854. Four years later his family joined the caravan of settlers to bleeding Kansas and settled at Osawatomie, the home of John Brown and the center, for the time, of the border warfare of that disturbed territory. Soon convinced that Kansas was a "dark and bloody ground, that it opened up opportunities for all sorts of vicious men to commit all sorts of crimes and have their commission attributed to the political controversies of the day," the senior Marshall led his family eastward toward the Hoosier State. After a year and a half at the turbulent town of La Grange, Missouri, they landed in the old home community on the eve of the Civil War.

The young Marshall was in due time sent to college at Wabash College, and after graduation there, studied law with Judge Walter Olds, later a Justice of the Supreme Court of Indiana. In 1875, he was admitted to the bar and a year later settled down to the practice of law in Columbia City. In this rural county seat of between three and four thousand people, he remained for thirty-three years, until inaugurated as Governor of Indiana in 1909. The humdrum practice of a rural attorney for a third of a century was hardly a school for statesmen, at least for the type of statesmen demanded by the present age. The Indiana Constitution then, as now, permitted any man to practice law if of "good moral character." Mr. Marshall, in his *Recollections,* retorts to those critics in other states, who make light of this provision, by saying that "it is far better to have less learning and more moral character in the practice of law than it is to have great learning and no morals." To this may be added the consideration of Indiana's reputation as the training ground extraordinary of politicians and statesmen.

Mr. Marshall was entirely frank about his law practice; his sense of humor did not permit him to idealize his life in Columbia City as a divinely appointed means of training him for the career of a statesman destined to save his country in a crisis. Fist fights, he tells in his *Recollections,* were the common means of settling difficulties in his community. "For a long while I eked out a precarious existence with these assault-and-battery cases. I did not know that they were just a phase in the evolution of the civilization of Indiana society. They furnished me a livelihood, and I am not quite sure that I felt any compunctions of conscience or shame at civilization when I saw a couple of husky fellows hammer each other, down in front of my office. . . . . But let us never be discouraged about the lack of something to fight— something to overcome, and something out of which to make a living in this life of ours. Scarcely had we reached the point where these fist fights ceased, and it looked as though I might be compelled to seek some other calling than the law, when the railroads began to cut off arms and legs and opened up a new source of revenue. There is hardly a good lawyer of the ancient days of northern Indiana who did not build himself an atrocious brick house out of the contingent fee which he collected from lawsuits prosecuted against railroad companies for mutilating and killing our citizens."

Mr. Marshall was a hereditary Democrat. His grandfather, a fiery Virginian, had once announced that he was "willing to take his chance on Hell but never on the Republican party." His father was a devoted Douglas Democrat. Although interested in politics since his college days, Mr. Marshall had never participated, except in a local way, until he was nominated for Governor in 1908. Even then, he was not over-zealous to trade the quiet, prosperous life of his small town for the uncertainties of state politics. He states: "This adventure for me upon new and uncharted seas was an experiment. As a Presbyterian I was willing to leave it in the hands of God; as a Democrat, on the knees of the gods; as a politician, to the good wishes of the people."

Mr. Marshall was successful in the 1908 election and went in with an increased majority in 1910. His administration generally received the reputation of being "liberal," but this quality consisted more in measures designed to bring about efficiency and honesty in the government, than in laws based on advanced theories of social welfare. Marshall described himself as "a Liberal with the brakes on." He was, in fact, conservative in his social philosophy, but this was colored by a deeply sympathetic, tolerant, and equalitarian attitude toward his fellowmen. Although it was running counter to some of the best cherished tenets of the fellow-liberals of his party, he did not personally favor additional anti-corporation laws, the making mandatory of suffrage for women in the proposed new Indiana Constitution, or the new devices of the Initiative and Referendum. Of the last-named, he said: "I don't believe in it. At least, I don't believe we need it in Indiana. But that's no reason why the people should be barred from having it if they want it."

Marshall's nomination was generally well received throughout the country. The conservative New York *Times* was enthusiastic and took occasion in its encomium to read into Mr. Marshall's thoughts and character something of its own desires. "The Democratic candidate for Vice-President has one qualification for the office that is not usually demanded or obtained—he is quite fitted to perform the duties of President should he be called upon to do so. He was not only seriously proposed by his own state for the first place, but his qualifications as a candidate, as to character, as to ability, and as to popularity where he is best known, rank with those of his associate on the ticket. Indeed, it may be said, with entire respect to Governor Wilson, that had Governor Marshall deemed it his duty to go before the people of the country as freely, he would have impressed them to such a degree that the deadlock in the convention might have resulted differently."

After commending his opposition to the recall of judges, the Initiative and the Referendum, and Federal legislation to curb the trusts, the *Times* discovered still other virtues in the Vice-Presidential nominee:

> "Governor Marshall is an advocate of tariff for revenue only, and he thinks that this can be gradually reached without injury to legitimate interests. His views, on this matter, are deeply imbued with his earnest faith in individualism, a faith that has all the fervor of religion, tempered with common sense. He has very little use for the modern theories of social action or inspired politics. He thinks that representative government, at every stage of evolution, has pretty fairly reflected the voters that have administered it, and that for its faults or its evils the voters are primarily responsible. It is with the voters, therefore, and not with the machinery they use, that true reform must begin.
>
> "Governor Marshall has a peculiar and happy way of saying things. As he is a clear and deliberate and candid thinker, the things he has to say are worth listening to, and he presents them in a concrete and impressive fashion. . . . Governor Marshall undoubtedly represents the sober and intelligent Democratic view of the affairs of the Nation. His nomination strengthens the ticket. We trust that he will be enabled to take a prominent part in the campaign."

Here was a foil for the liberal Presidential nominee who did take stock both in "social action" and in "inspired politics." A little dash of Hoosier conservatism would add just the right ingredient to the Democratic salad.

The New York *Outlook* commented: "In some respects, Mr. Marshall is a counterpart of Mr. Sherman, the present Vice-President and Republican candidate to succeed himself. Both men belong to that old-fashioned school of rather rhetorical politicians who are inclined to 'point with pride' or 'view with alarm' . . . . There is also a homely homespun fervor about Governor Marshall's speeches. Not only has he an unusual capacity for phrase-making, of stating truths concisely and sententiously, but he effectively limits candor with fervidness. . . . . Politically, Mr. Marshall may be termed a Jeffersonian individualist." All in all, the *Outlook* concluded, despite certain personal and political limitations, the Democratic party might in its search for a Vice-Presidential candidate, "have gone very much farther and rated very much worse."

For the first time since the Civil War, there was a "third party" which rivaled the two old ones in vigor; indeed, it eventually polled above a half-million more popular votes than the Republican party, and came forward as the more dangerous antagonist of the Democrats. As related above, the seceding delegates from the Republican convention at Chicago met in an adjoining hall, laid plans for a permanent organization, and offered the Presidential nomination to Theodore Roosevelt. Governor Hiram W. Johnson of California, was made field-marshal and chief organizer. Some days later a call was sent out for a delegate convention to meet in Chicago, August 8. Here, a platform was adopted and Roosevelt was nominated by acclamation. Hiram W. Johnson was nominated for Vice-President by acclamation with the same fervor.

Governor Johnson's nomination was hailed in some quarters as another of those rare instances in which the Vice-Presidential candidate was chosen on the basis of personal fitness, rather than to placate a disappointed faction. The Rooseveltian *Outlook* stated that he might well be regarded as a "pioneer in the development of self-government. Under his administration, the state of California experienced the greatest change in the fundamental character of its government that any state of the Union has probably ever undergone in so short a time."

Governor Johnson was born September 2, 1866, at Sacramento, California. He attended the University of California, but did not remain to graduate, became a newspaper reporter for a short time, read law in his father's office, and was admitted to the bar. He leaped into national prominence when he became an attorney for the state in the prosecution of the corrupt political gang of San Francisco headed by Abe Ruef, taking the place of Francis Heney after he had been shot down in the court room. As a militant progressive he won the Republican nomination for Governor in 1910 and was elected. Under his leadership, the corrupt corporation control on the State Government was broken, and new codes of law regulating corporations and establishing new rights and conditions of labor were enacted. The new devices of the direct primary and the Initiative and the Referendum were made a part of the governmental machinery. His nomination for the second place on the Progressive ticket was indeed consistent with the announced principles of that party and the confession of faith of its standard-bearer. The Democrats had shied away from the nomination of the radical Governor Burke of North Dakota as Wilson's running-mate, choosing the Hoosier conservative; the Progressives went the whole distance.

Roosevelt's attempt to organize the Progressive party in the South was a complete failure. His party remained throughout the campaign substantially what it had been at Chicago—a fragment from the Republican party. A spirited three-sided campaign followed, but it was not necessary for the Democrats to exert themselves to the utmost. With the ancient enemy divided, the outcome was never in doubt. Wilson and Marshall polled considerably less than a majority of the popular votes, but under the working of the electoral system received 435 electoral votes to ninety-six for their opponents.

President Wilson secured the enactment of valuable laws, but he was caught in the whirlwind of the Great War, and bitterly attacked by some as pro-German, by others as pro-English, and was also accused of being a mere reed, shaken by every wind. But there were many who, for various reasons, took up the cry, "He has kept us out of war," and when the Democratic convention met at St. Louis on June 12, 1916, the President's renomination was assured. Marshall's fate was in doubt and the correspondent of the New York *Times* wrote that this was just what the leaders wanted, in order that the nomination might not seem to have been made in a twilight sleep, and also to prevent the convention from hurrying home.

St. Louis had paid well for having it come there and in return she had been promised at least four days to pluck the golden fruit. But with delegates signing on the dotted line in matters of platform and President, how was the pledge to be kept unless there was a fight over the Vice-Presidency? Fortunately the hour found the man. Henry Morgenthau, a wealthy Jewish banker and former Ambassador to Turkey, appeared at St. Louis to oppose Marshall and he let it be known that Jacob Schiff, a mighty power in the financial world, agreed with him. The bankers did not specially object to anything Marshall had done, but said that he was lacking in force. Morgenthau's action stimulated several little boomlets, but they soon faded.

The delegation from Illinois was instructed in favor of Roger Sullivan, but it was said that he did not expect or care for the nomination, but was using his boom to help him in an attempt to get the Illinois Senatorship; and it was even alleged that Sullivan's seeming effort to wear the Senatorial toga was not serious, but was chiefly intended to impress Wilson with his power in Illinois, which the President seemed inclined to forget.

Richard Oulahan, of the New York *Times,* quoted a saying attributed to the brilliant J. Hamilton Lewis some years before, "Many a candidate comes to a convention with a Presidential bee so that he may go home and run for the Legislature."

Secretary of War Baker, and Senator Owen of Oklahoma were mentioned, but neither desired the Vice-Presidency. Senator Chamberlain of Oregon, whose championship of a policy of national defense was very popular on the Pacific Coast, at one time appeared likely to win the prize. Governor Elliott W. Major of Missouri was strongly supported by the delegation from his state. Although the pre-convention boomlets of these men persisted during the early days of the convention, the result had already been determined by the enemy. Word had come to the Democratic leaders some weeks before the convention that the Republicans would nominate ex-Vice-President Fairbanks, and when the Democrats met at St. Louis, this had already been accomplished. To save Indiana, it had been decided by the Administration to select a Hoosier to match him. After the convention had been permitted a reasonable length of time to play with the aspirations of other candidates, the predetermined renomination of Marshall was carried through.

The Republican convention had met at Chicago, June 7, in much perplexity. It wished to get the votes of Roosevelt men who believed that Wilson had crouched shamefully before the Kaiser, and also Pacifists and pro-Germans. Finally it adopted a platform declaring for the enforcement of protection to every American citizen, "at home and abroad, by land and sea," and coupled with this a pronouncement in favor of a "strict and honest neutrality between the belligerents in the great war in Europe."

It nominated for President that very upright conservative reformer, Charles Evans Hughes, Governor of New York two terms and then a Justice of the United States Supreme Court. The impending renomination of Marshall for the Vice-Presidency drove the Republicans to Fairbanks. Indiana was unusually important that year. It was not simply that her vote for President was at stake, but two Senators were to be chosen. If the Republicans won both seats, there was a fighting chance for them to control the next Senate. Otherwise, the Democrats would retain control by a slim majority. The casting vote of the Vice-President might even be decisive in the organization of the Senate as it once had been in the time of Chester A. Arthur.

The nomination of Fairbanks for the Vice-Presidency was generally taken for granted by Republican politicians before the convention assembled at Chicago. His name was put forward by the conservative wing, which was agreeable to Hughes; and even the Progressives, who were now once more back in the fold and hoped for the nomination of Roosevelt for the Presidency, announced that Fairbanks would be acceptable to them for the second place. Only one other name, that of ex-Senator Burkett of Nebraska, was placed before the convention. Fairbanks received an overwhelming majority on the first ballot and was declared unanimously nominated.

He soon issued a statement to the effect that he had not been a candidate, that he had instructed the chairman of the Indiana delegation to withdraw his name if presented, but that the convention had adjourned before he could apprise it of his disinclination to accept. Under the circumstances, however, he regarded it as his duty to accept the commission which the party had so generously and unanimously placed in his hands.

For the only time in United States history, the candidates of the leading parties for Vice-President came from the same State. Both were worthy men of fair ability, but were nominated chiefly for geographical reasons. Oulahan in a mildly sarcastic letter to the *Times* described Fairbanks as a type of the state from which he came. The letter was written from Chicago just after the Republican Convention had adjourned; the *Times* was Democratic in sympathy and the Republican candidate was favored with most of the irony. Oulahan said:

"The Republicans have turned again to Indiana, mother of Vice-Presidents and candidates for Vice-President. The State is 'doubtful'; two seats in the Senate are to be fought for; the Hon. Charles Warren Fairbanks, bland, popular, eirenic, a reconciler who has done much to patch up the feud between the Hoosier Republicans and the Progressives, aspires once more to the honor which he wore gracefully, if a little uneasily, in the Second Consulship of Mr. Roosevelt. Milk and thunder can not be friends (hence the uneasiness) . . . . He is a born temporary chairman, polite, correct, just, safe, dignified, solemn. He is a good mixer.[1] He had the fortune to be born on a farm, the writers of his legend say, in a log cabin. He is a man of education who has honorably risen to great place. He was a respectable member of the Senate for eight years, and served acceptably on the Joint High Commission of 1898. He is the Giant Oak as Dan Voorhees was the Tall Sycamore of the Wabash.

"And he has never shown any disposition to set that Hoosier Amazon on fire. He is prudent. He is judicious. He walks warily. He takes heed to his conversation. He is as cautious as Martin Van Buren or William Boyd Allison. He treads the beaten path of speech. It is his strength. Brilliancy is perilous. The obvious is seldom resented. Mr. Fairbanks is not *too* anything. He is moderation. His expressions of opinion are discreet. There is wisdom in storing unexpressed opinions. . . . . A harmonious nature, the greatest common moderator in the Republican party. A respectable, a tranquilizing figure.

"Mr. Fairbanks' character is unblemished even according to the exacting standards of Indiana. What more impressive evidence could be given of the jealous fondness of Indiana for this Favorite Son than the alarm of hosts of the good at the intrusion of the cocktail, drained by other lips than his at a feast of the mighty in his home.[2] If any remembrance of the heat of the Drys, and the blamelessness of Mr. Fairbanks as to personal looking upon the wine

---

[1]This statement is very surprising but Fairbanks is said to have been cordial with his friends and popular with the newspaper men.

[2]Mr. Fairbanks had been injured in his canvass for the Republican Presidential nomination in 1908 by stories of a cocktail being served at a reception which he gave to President Roosevelt in Indianapolis. Probably it was obtained from a neighboring club when asked for by a guest.

cup, and his association with a blameless buttermilk lingers in the mind of his German-American admirers, doubtless he will be able to satisfy their demands on more important subjects, foreign and domestic. A worthy, excellent gentleman, who, in spite of his high visibility, wears modestly a perfectly neutral tint."

Some weeks later the *Times* depicted the Democratic Vice-Presidential candidate as another Indiana type: "Marshall illustrates the Will Carleton or Farm Ballad side of her; homely apothegms, old fashioned philosophy; farmer plainness and wit, the prairie, in short: the James Whitcomb Riley phase. As for *Fairbanks,* Indiana never did anybody any harm and neither did *Fairbanks.* She has other characteristics, more salient ones, sharper ones, but Fairbanks does not illustrate these. Sometimes she is silent and would rest; her ideas have given out for the moment; then she can turn to *Fairbanks* and see her mood embodied. . . . . She can take refuge in the cool silence of Fairbanks or hear another side of herself in Tom Marshall's Moody and Sankey speech."

Each of the leading candidates for the Vice-Presidency, in his acceptance of the nomination, seemed to be fishing for the neutrality vote. Marshall's speech was Pacifist in tone and contained keen thrusts at the opposition leaders. In reply to a demand of Hughes for Americanism, he asked to be informed as to his partner in the call. "Does the firm consist of Hughes and Roosevelt, of Hughes and Hohenzollern or of Hughes, surviving partner of the firm of Hughes and Huerta?" Roosevelt had decided to support Hughes, and Marshall accused him of not leading his followers to Armageddon, but deserting them at Bull Moose Run.

Of the speech of acceptance of Mr. Fairbanks, the *Times* said that "his eloquence was in his choicest funereal form." He began by defending protection, as might be expected from a representative of the Middle West; he opposed ship subsidies. He angled for the Pacifist and German vote without saying anything essentially unpatriotic. He accused Wilson of vacillating in his treatment of Mexico, and declared that there was no merit in keeping us out of war when no one wished to attack us. He asserted that "there never was a time when it was more important for us as Americans to avoid creating lines of cleavage in this country based upon place of birth or occupational status. We can not properly censure Americans of foreign birth for sympathy with the nations which once claimed their allegiance as against the nations with which they are fighting, and the attempt to impute treasonable motives to any class of our citizens, because of their original nationality, or the sympathies which go with it, so long as these do not interfere with their paramount loyalty to this republic, or in any way infringe it, is severely to be condemned. The greatest menace to this country is not so much the man who loves two countries, as the man who loves no country at all."

Both Marshall and Fairbanks took the stump, but the latter had a severe attack of gastritis about the middle of September while speaking at Oklahoma City, and was obliged to withdraw from the canvass.   Marshall, as chief spokesman for the Administration, carried the fight to the enemy throughout the Middle West. At a concluding rally in Philadelphia he vigorously attacked the trust and tariff policies of the Roosevelt and Taft administrations.   The Democratic campaign slogan, "He kept us out of war," was a powerful argument in the Middle Western and Pacific States.   Perhaps it was the consideration which turned the tide.

Marshall, throughout the campaign, played skillfully on this key.   In his acceptance speech he had made an effective appeal: "The one bright peaceful spot under the sun this day is America, and it is so because the President pleads guilty to the charge of using words rather than shot and shrapnel. Three years ago we thought that the age of brute force had passed and that the brain and heart of man were to rule the world. . . . . In this hour of world darkness, I have faith that humankind is going upward to the heights, and not downward to the vales.   The judgment of the American people is not to make a martyr of the man who brooded over the Republic in storm-stressed times and by mere words spoke peace to the troubled seas of international politics."

Neither major party received a majority of the popular votes, but the Democratic ticket received almost 600,000 more than did Hughes and Fairbanks, and this carried with it a slim electoral margin of 277 to 254.   Indeed, the outcome of the contest was unknown until an official canvass of the close election in California showed that the Democrats had won the thirteen electoral votes of that State.

CHAPTER XIX.

Post-Bellum Vice-Presidential Nominations and Elections: 1920-1932

CIVILIZATION has substituted voting for armed rebellion as the instrument by which a dissatisfied people may overthrow a governmental *régime*. The four national elections in the United States since the close of the World War were held in a time of profound peace; yet two of them exhibited a mass revulsion against the government in power so marked that had it been expressed in force rather than by the innocuous ballot, the event would have been recorded by the historian as a revolution of the first magnitude. In 1920, the Republican Warren G. Harding, backed by sixty per cent. of those voting, ousted the Wilson administration, a mass movement yet unmatched since the Civil War. In 1932, twelve years later, the Democratic Franklin D. Roosevelt led a movement ending only a little less decisively the twelve-year rule of the Republicans. Four years earlier, the Republican hold on power had been reaffirmed by a popular percentage only slightly smaller. Only the election of 1924 might be considered as of normal significance, and yet the Coolidge majority had been equalled but twice in sixty years.

But this great oscillation of the voting masses between the two parties was not the only evidence of a fundamental disturbance in the old and traditional political allegiances. The election of 1928 broke six States loose from the "solid" Democratic South and two, Massachusetts and Rhode Island, from the "solid" Republican North. It may well be that these are premonitory of a time in the not far distant future when the political combinations growing out of the Civil War and the industrial age which followed will be superseded by others based on new interests and new loyalties.

The second Wilson administration had been dominated almost entirely by the World War and its consequent problems. The American part in the war had been well conducted. There were no substantial accusations of corruption and incompetence; the civil population had undergone a minimum of suffering; and American arms had triumphed. Yet it was perfectly clear to politicians in the months following the Armistice that the tide was running strongly against the party in power. It was the heir to all the accumulated dissatisfactions of the war era. Business men who had found their usual channels of production and sale displaced, farmers who had incurred heavy indebtedness for more land and equipment at fantastic prices, families whose sons did not return from the battlefields, and foreign groups which believed that President Wilson had not dealt justly with their native lands in the Peace Settlement, added their antagonisms to the scale. Then there was a mass phenomenon, less concrete but irresistible in its power. For two years the populace had been held to an emotional pitch in which feelings of group loyalty, self-sacrifice, and lofty idealism in general were dominant. The Armistice broke this spell. Again the cry was each man for himself, and it was discovered that many had profited exceedingly while their brethren were on the battlefield. There was a swing to an individualism more extreme than that which had preceded the war—a desire for the old routine which the Republican nominee for President sensed when he promised the populace a return to "normalcy." The political concomitant of this emotional reaction was a surge of voters from the Democratic to the Republican party.

By 1920, the direct primary had been established in a large number of the Middle Western and Pacific States. General Leonard Wood, Governor Frank Lowden, and Senator Hiram W. Johnson had entered these, won a large number of pledged delegates, and so assumed dominant positions in the forthcoming Republican National Convention. Nevertheless, when it met at Chicago, June 8, there was much uncertainty as to the outcome of the contest. The Senatorial junto which had so successfully led the party fight against President Wilson since the close of the war, were clearly in control of the convention and not Wood, Lowden, nor Johnson was on their preferred list of candidates. Wood and Lowden entered the contest with well over two hundred delegates each. Both men were personally honorable, but their lieutenants had been using money and promises of office in an impolitic, if not corrupt, way. Their conduct had been made public by a Senatorial investigation, and the revelations dealt a fatal blow to the hopes of two able, honest, and worthy men. As for Johnson, his cause was hopeless from the beginning. A leader of the revolt in 1912, a highly advertised radical or liberal, the overwhelming conservatism of the 1920 convention created an atmosphere in which his candidacy could not thrive.

The voting went on monotonously through two unbearably hot days with Lowden and Wood deadlocked and both unable to gain. The truth of the matter was that those leaders who held the control of the delegates were unwilling that any of the leading contenders should be nominated. Among those who had foreseen such a deadlock, was one Harry K. Daugherty of Ohio, campaign and general political manager of Senator Warren Gamaliel Harding of Ohio. Shortly before the Ohio Presidential primaries in April, he had made this statement to one of his friends: "At the proper time after the Republican National Committee meets, some fifteen men, bleary-eyed with loss of sleep and perspiring profusely with the excessive heat, will sit down in seclusion around a big table. I will be with them and will present the name of Senator Harding to them, and before we get through they will put him over."

It fell out substantially as Daugherty had foretold. Twenty-four hours before the convention's adjournment, it was the general talk that Harding's opportunity, if ever he had had one, was past. He seemed to have accepted that judgment when, at two minutes before twelve o'clock, midnight, in the last minutes of grace, he had filed down at Columbus his papers for candidacy for reëlection to the United States Senate. But the little conference in the Blackstone Hotel led by Republican Senators had arranged the setting for a new picture. Their work was facilitated by the heat, the high cost of hotel living, and the proximity of Sunday, which would have necessitated an adjournment over for a day.

The ninth roll-call late in the afternoon of Saturday showed decisively the results of the hotel conference, when Harding jumped into the lead. On the tenth he went over.

During these days of deadlock, the Vice-Presidential nomination had been handled as usual from the standpoint of bringing about a Presidential nomination. There were several avowed candidates. Colonel Henry W. Anderson of Virginia was conceded to have considerable strength if Lowden should secure the nomination for the first place. Samuel Adams, Massachusetts born, owner of a farm in Virginia, claimed a large vote for the first ballot. Michael Doliasky of Michigan, a perennial candidate, had arrived early and plastered the hotels with his posters. He was famous in his home State for having once in a State convention nominated himself for Governor. Governor Johnson probably would have been accorded a second place on the ticket by any of the leading candidates, but such offers were promptly refused. Once, when so approached, he said: "There isn't a thing under the sun that I haven't been offered during the past week. It is singular that the very gentlemen who have been equally insistent on my taking the Vice-Presidency had been equally insistent that I was utterly unfit to be President, although there is only a heart-beat between the two." Senator Borah, too, could have had the nomination but it was well known that he would not consider it. Henry Allen of Kansas, Calvin Coolidge of Massachusetts, and Irvine L. Lenroot of Wisconsin were all designated as acceptable to the ruling junto, but the last-named was their first choice. On the call of the roll, the organization promptly placed Lenroot in nomination and there were seconds from various of their members. Massachusetts passed, but when Oregon was called, Judge Wallace McCamant of that State nominated Coolidge. The popularity of his name among the delegates was soon apparent, and there was a rush on the first ballot, which soon assured him a large majority.

Mr. Coolidge in his *Autobiography* describes the nomination as a popular and unplanned achievement. The coterie of United States Senators had manœuvered the convention into adopting a platform and nominating a President "in ways that were not satisfactory to a majority of the delegates. When the same forces undertook for a third time to dictate the action of the convention in naming a Vice-President, the delegates broke away from them and literally stampeded to me."

It was a triumph of men who make the backbone of the Republican party —prosperous, industrious farmers and the substantial middle class, business and professional men, of the cities and towns. They were tired of excitement and confusion, and even of idealism, and wished to be allowed to move on quietly in their old respectable stay-at-home way. Mr. Coolidge had recently put down a strike of the Boston police which seemed to terrified property holders, small as well as large, to threaten the very foundation of the social structure. The trouble arose over an attempt of the police to affiliate with a labor union; and Governor Coolidge's declaration, "There is no right to strike against the public safety, by anybody, anywhere, any time," thrilled the country. There was then a wide-spread condemnation of labor unions, which was not confined to employers. The soldiers came home from the World War feeling that while they were suffering and fighting, the working men at home had been profiteering. It was said that Coolidge had put labor in its place, and hundreds of thousands were grateful to him. Coolidge was a "small town" man who had come from the farm; his words and ways, as well as his works, appealed to the West. Four years before, a trustee at Amherst, Frank Stearns, had been a voice in the wilderness preaching Coolidge and calling on the Republicans to nominate him for President. The prophet was received with laughter, but he persevered. He and a few other fellow-collegians got out a seventy-thousand-volume edition of papers and speeches of Coolidge and sent it far and wide, carefully choosing recipients whose conversion would be useful. In 1920, Massachusetts presented Coolidge for President. The delegates felt it to be a mere gesture, and they made it most unenthusiastically. When Harding's nomination was assured, and Coolidge's friends planned to get him the Vice-Presidency, the Massachusetts delegates accepted the advice to nominate Lenroot, some indeed with great pleasure, and their leaders, like those from other states, went to their hotels. But the generals should not leave the field until the last gun has been fired. The delegates who remained behind had read the Coolidge book; they said to themselves: "Here is an honest, cautious man who thinks and feels as we do. We want him"; and they nominated him. Even Western delegates who suspected anything coming from "the state of the Cabots and the Lodges" were much pleased by the accounts of Coolidge's work as Governor and were ready to support him.

The managers were terrified at the selection of a provincial who had never been in Washington in his life, but on the whole the nomination was well received. The New York *Sun and Herald* remarked that with right-thinking, sound-living Americans, Coolidge had come to occupy something of the character of Abraham Lincoln, and this made him an outstanding man in these days of "high-pressure living and high-speed acting." The St. Paul *Pioneer Press* said: "Calvin Coolidge, the resolute little Massachusetts Governor, with his great gift of common sense, his fine power of expression, and his splendid record on the side of law and order during the riots attending the Boston policemen strike, has fired the public imagination as few public men of recent years have succeeded in firing it, and at first blush it seems strange to find his name second rather than first on the ticket." A Democratic paper, the Richmond *Times-Despatch,* made a similar comment. It said: "Coolidge, a political accident, outgrowth of the Boston police strike, stands for at least one definite thing, law and order, and in this respect he gives the ticket a Kangaroo character, with a colorless candidate and a platform which says anything or nothing." Another Democratic paper, the New York *Times,* declared that "Governor Coolidge for Vice-President really shines by comparison with the head of the ticket. He at least is a man of achievement; he is known to the party and to the Nation."

Calvin Coolidge was born July 4, 1872, in the rural town of Plymouth Notch, Vermont. The Coolidge family had settled there about 1780 and three generations of them, preceding Calvin, had lived the usual life of the New England farmer. His father, Colonel John Calvin Coolidge, had combined with farming the business of a country storekeeper. Typically, he had held several offices such as notary public, constable, and selectman, and he had represented his town in both houses of the State Legislature. Calvin received his elementary education in the public schools of his community; he was prepared for college at the Black River Academy in the neighboring town of Ludlow, and he attended Amherst College, graduating in 1895. Soon thereafter, he began to "read law" in the firm of Hammond and Field of Northampton, and two years later was admitted to the bar.

The superstitious might easily be forgiven for believing that there was some foreordained significance in the coincidence of the natal days of the American Republic and of Calvin Coolidge; for the latter, after reaching maturity, was almost continuously, in some capacity, in the service of the former. Soon after his admission to the bar, he was elected to the City Council of Northampton. Some years later he was elected its city attorney, and then followed the county position of clerk of courts. In turn, he served in the Massachusetts House of Representatives, as mayor of Northampton, in the State Senate, of which he was president for two terms, and as Lieutenant-Governor. In 1918, he was elected Governor of the Commonwealth and gained nation-wide fame through his handling of the Boston police strike. At a time when the conservative elements of the Nation were uneasy because of various sporadic radical movements which had flared up in different parts of the country, his telegram to Samuel Gompers with its ringing phrase seemed to mark him as the man of the hour. In 1919 he had been reëlected Governor.

Various explanations have been ventured by his contemporaries to account for the almost continuous political advancement of Mr. Coolidge. As with all successful men, there exist the two extremes of critics: the one of which attributes to him the most meagre of abilities, the other of which regards him as the type of strong, silent man, of almost unfathomable power, who directs the government of which he is in charge with a sure, powerful, and irresistible hand to the goal which he has set. Somewhere between the two lies the truth. Mr. Coolidge undoubtedly was possessed of a very high degree of political sense. He made no glaring mistakes which could be laid hold of by his political opponents, to his discredit with the voters. He was frugal, taciturn, honest, unostentatious. He never acted impulsively and without due consideration of the facts which he would have to face. He was not moved by every popular wind which blew. Perhaps, as some of his opponents maintained, he drew a larger amount of that thing called "luck" than the average politician. Mr. Ralph Hemenway, his law partner, is said to have remarked on receiving word of his nomination for the Vice-Presidency: "With Cal's luck, I'd hate to be in Mr. Harding's shoes." But, as one of his biographers remarks, always when Luck came round the corner, Mr. Coolidge was there ready to take her by the arm.

It is undoubtedly true that Mr. Coolidge's qualities of character were more appreciated by the Nation in the particular years in which he was given his opportunity than they would have been at any time in the two decades preceding and the one following. Mr. Alfred P. Dennis, who knew him well in his Northampton days, offers this plausible explanation of the Coolidge "cult":[1] "Mr. Coolidge kept faith with the homely virtues of our ancestors. In our restless, complex, high-keyed Western civilization we can not forget the slow grave men of our early, half-starved beginnings in the wildernesses of the New World. The fundamental instinct is the instinct for self-preservation, and that instinct has made our democracy workable. That instinct tells us that we are not to be saved by pomp and show, rhetoric and luxury, but by honesty, frugality and simplicity of character. We live in an extravagant, money-spending, pampered, high-powered age. We must balance excess by moderation. Mr. Coolidge is eighteenth century—frugal, simple, honest, hard-bitten—set down in a twentieth-century age of jazz, extravagance in speech, dress, mad desire for pleasure. As a Nation our craving is to be saved from ourselves. The yearning of the mass mind, whether in religion or politics, is for something to hold to—something to hold us—something to which the poor tentacles of self may cling, as we are carried along by the heedless current of years. Not alone to the poor, the insecure, the insignificant, but to the rich and powerful, comes the yearning for the shelter of a great rock in a weary land."

---

[1]A. P. Dennis: *Gods and Little Fishes,* p. 155.

Mr. Coolidge's rural upbringing and his own life history after maturity made it inevitable that he should be an individualist in his social philosophy. The ordering of the conduct of the citizens in details by government never could have appealed to him. His dislike for governmental interference in matters of business and commerce, again, made him acceptable to a large majority of the population in that period of industrial advance immediately following the World War. It was this note which he sounded at Boston in opening the Republican campaign of 1920. The chief need of the day, he said, was individual culture and self-restraint. "While there ought to be no limit to the duty of obedience to law, there is a very distinct limit as to what can be accomplished by law and the agency of the government. The finer things of life are given voluntarily by the individual, or they are not given at all. The law can impress the body, but the mind is beyond control. Discipline, faithfulness, courage, charity, industry, character and the moral power of the Nation are not created by Government. These virtues the people must provide for themselves." It was the glory of the Republican party, he assured his hearers, that it subscribed to this view.

When the Democratic Convention met at San Francisco, June 28, it was not with the rosiest of prospects. Not only had there been marked indications that popular favor had been withdrawn from that party, but those internal difficulties based on the sharp divergencies of the two wings—one led by the old-fashioned Democracy of the South, the other by the new Democracy of the great cities of the Northeast—had begun to show themselves. There was also the question of who was to receive the favor of the occupant of the White House for the succession. The leading contenders were Attorney-General A. Mitchell Palmer, William G. McAdoo, the President's son-in-law and his Secretary of the Treasury until late in 1918, and Governor James M. Cox of Ohio. McAdoo went into the lead on the second ballot, but the opposition to him led by Charles F. Murphy and his New York delegation was always strong enough to have prevented his securing the necessary two-thirds vote. Palmer eventually dropped out and Cox received the nomination on the forty-third ballot.

A half dozen men had been prominently considered for the Vice-Presidency throughout the period of the Convention, but naturally no decision could be made until it should be known who would best "balance" the ticket. The Palmer leaders were favorable to Governor Alfred E. Smith for the second place. Others in the running were David R. Francis of Missouri, ex-Ambassador to Russia, Senator J. Hamilton Lewis of Illinois, Brigadier-General Lawrence Tyson of Tennessee, Senator Gilbert M. Hitchcock of Nebraska, and Governor Samuel V. Stewart of Montana.

The defeat of the McAdoo organization and the nomination of Cox was in general a victory for the Democracy of the cities of the Northeast. The heart of McAdoo's strength had been in the South. A proper balancing of the ticket would mean conceding the Vice-Presidential nomination to a

McAdoo supporter. Prominent among the New York delegates, all of whom under the unit rule had cast their votes for Cox, was young Franklin D. Roosevelt. Although following the lead of Murphy, as in duty bound by the rules of the convention, he had worked throughout the balloting for the cause of McAdoo. He had been in opposition to Tammany on this point—a qualification that would be popular outside of New York—but he had not broken with that organization. Furthermore, he came from the pivotal State of New York, often a sufficient qualification in itself. Lastly, and a matter whose importance was not unrecognized and undervalued at the time, he bore the magic name of Roosevelt, a vote-getting device whose potency is well understood by all experienced with electoral machinery. Mr. Roosevelt, therefore, presented an almost flawless "availability," and this could not have escaped the observation of such experts as Charles F. Murphy, George E. Brennan of Illinois, and E. H. Moore of Ohio.

Before the Convention was called together for its final session, these men and other leaders had agreed upon Roosevelt, but not unduly to discourage other Vice-Presidential ambitions, it was agreed that the nominations of the standing candidates should be made. Everything went ahead as planned, the nominating and seconding speeches, and the demonstrations. Then, as if at a signal, Alfred Smith of New York mounted the platform, and in an emphatic and authoritative manner, seconded the nomination of Mr. Roosevelt. Sponsors of the various candidates scrambled to be the first to withdraw the names of their favorites and within fifteen minutes the nomination of Roosevelt had been accomplished by acclamation.

The new Roosevelt, who was now given a major rôle in the political scene, was born at Hyde Park, New York, January 30, 1882. His father, James Roosevelt, was a man of wealth and important business interests. He had retired early from business affairs and devoted himself to his family and estate at Hyde Park. He married when past middle life, Sara Delano, the daughter of Warren Delano, who had an estate across the Hudson. Franklin, their only son, was reared in surroundings of wealth. He never attended the public schools, but received his elementary education through tutors, and was prepared for college at Groton School. He matriculated at Harvard in September, 1900, just as his fifth cousin, Theodore Roosevelt, was warming up for his Vice-Presidential campaign, and duly graduated four years later. He entered the law school of Columbia University the next fall, was admitted to the bar in 1907, and began the practice of law in New York City. Early in his law school course, he had been married to a distant cousin, Anna Eleanor Roosevelt, a niece of the President.

Election to the Upper House of the State Legislature in 1910 on the Democratic ticket marked the beginning of Mr. Roosevelt's political career. In this session he was the leading spirit in an insurgent movement against the Democratic organization which had scheduled the election of William F. Sheehan to the United States Senate. The battle-cry of the twenty-nine-year-old and inexperienced Roosevelt was not at first regarded seriously by the veteran Murphy, but it ultimately proved sufficient to deadlock the Legislature and force the choice of a compromise candidate, James A. O'Gorman. The escapade brought for the first time some national prominence to this Democratic Roosevelt. In 1912 he was reëlected to the State Senate.

Roosevelt had entered politics as a liberal and this is doubtless what led him, as early as 1911, to join with the forces desiring the nomination of Woodrow Wilson to the Presidency. Shortly before the inauguration of Wilson as President, Roosevelt was offered a choice of the positions of Assistant Secretary of the Treasury and Collector of the Port of New York. Both of these he refused but when later he was offered the position once held by his illustrious cousin, the Assistant Secretaryship of the Navy, he accepted and resigned his place in the New York Assembly. In this position he remained during the eight years of the Wilson administration and, due to the World War, found it far from the political sinecure which it normally is in times of peace.

Both Vice-Presidential candidates took an active part in the campaign. A certain sensitiveness on the part of Mr. Harding, doubtless due to the wide acclaim on the nomination of Mr. Coolidge and the coolness towards his own, is shown in the statement which he issued late in June. "I think the Vice-President," he said, "should be more than a mere substitute in waiting. In reëstablishing coördination between the Executive office and the Senate, the Vice-President can and ought to play a big part, and I have been telling Governor Coolidge how much I wish him to be not only a participant in the campaign, but how much I wish him to be a helpful part of a Republican Administration. The country needs the counsel and the becoming participation in government of such men as Governor Coolidge."

Mr. Coolidge opened the Republican national campaign at Boston, August 12, and throughout September and into October spoke at various places in New England. About the middle of October, he started on a tour which took him through the Middle Atlantic States and as far south as North Carolina. Mr. Harding, he assured one audience, was a "sound man, tried in the fire of public service, unwarped and unafraid." Throughout the campaign he cautiously followed the lead of his chief in his commitments on issues. Like him, he was favorable to an "association" of nations but not to the League of Nations; for less governmental interference in business and "more reliance of the people on themselves"; for the independence of Congress and against a great concentration of power in the Executive (and on this point he remarked that it was ever easy for an individual "to believe himself divinely chosen to save the people"). He was for more attention to home affairs and less to international. He told a Philadelphia audience: "When my countrymen turn their attention again to the commonplace, I shall know that American institutions are secure." To another one, while speaking on his favorite subject of thrift, he confided that he himself had not bought a suit of clothes in eighteen months and a pair of shoes in two years.

His rival, Mr. Roosevelt, participated in the campaign to a degree never before attempted by a Vice-Presidential candidate unless it was by his cousin in 1900. Even before his acceptance, the tenth of August, he had made several speeches, and immediately after that event started on a series of stumping tours which continued without cessation until the night before election. He formally opened the Democratic campaign at Chicago, August 11; swung Northwest through the northern tier of States to the Pacific Coast, returning through California, Utah, Nebraska, and so eastward; and the first week of September found him campaigning in Maine. Another tour took him through the Middle Western and Border States as far west as Kansas, and he finished at New York City with a record of twelve speeches in one day.

Like his rival, Mr. Coolidge, he followed pretty closely the lead of his chief. He appealed to progressives in general to support the Democratic cause, since Mr. Harding represented the reactionary interests. He spoke consistently against national isolation and for the League of Nations. The latter, he argued, was a "practical solution of a practical problem." Entering it, "we shall grow—sanely, humanly, honorably, happily." In various communities, he turned a sympathetic ear to the local grievances. At Fargo, North Dakota, he told the farmers that they did not receive enough for their wheat and that the consumers paid too much—a theory dear to the hearts of the farming population. At a western point, he promised a greater naval development on the Pacific coast. At Yakima, Washington, in the irrigation belt, he hailed reclamation as the key to the high cost of living problem, and promised to work for an annual appropriation of $40,000,000 for that purpose. In California, he assured his audience that Cox was the Hiram Johnson of the East. Speaking to the Mormons in their Salt Lake Tabernacle, he said that the Democrats did not consider Prohibition a national issue. He reminded the Kansas farmers that the Eastern capitalists had exploited their country in the past, and asked what possibility there would be of cheap tractors in the future from a party thus dominated. All these expressions of sympathy were well received, but there was one bad slip at Butte, Montana. Replying to the oft-repeated Republican argument that Great Britain would have six votes in the League of Nations whereas we would have but one, Roosevelt in a burst of frankness assured his audience that the United States would have twelve votes and enumerated Haiti, Santo Domingo, Panama, Cuba, and the Central American Republics. He, himself, he confided, had written the constitution of Haiti and regarded it as a good job. His opponents at once saw the opening. Roosevelt, posing as a liberal, had revealed himself as a cynical, ultra-imperialist. As for themselves, the Republicans disclaimed all intention of interfering with the independence of nations, no matter how small and weak.

Whether Mr. Roosevelt at any time in the campaign had hope of success is doubtful, but it is certain that he did his utmost to further the party's cause, and at the same time established contacts with local party leaders throughout the Nation which would be of incalculable value in case he later aspired to national political honors.

The outcome, as generally had been predicted, was an overwhelming victory for the Republicans, and the worst defeat for a Democratic ticket since the Civil War. The Republicans received over sixty per cent. of the popular votes and 404 of the 531 electoral votes.

President Harding served less than a year and a half of his term, when through the intervention of death, he was succeeded by Vice-President Coolidge. The years of this administration were prosperous ones and again the electoral prospects looked gloomy for the Democrats. Their chief hope lay in a possible popular revulsion against the party in power because of the Teapot Dome scandal in which Secretary of the Interior, Albert B. Fall, had been party to a cession of oil lands of the public domain to certain great interests under questionable circumstances. The resulting investigation had led to the Secretary's resignation and his criminal prosecution in the Federal courts. Congressional pressure had led also to the resignation of two other Cabinet members under circumstances not creditable to the administration. Economic well-being, however, is an ace card which no mere Jack of Scandals can trump. President Coolidge rode out the storm, generally regarded as sinned against rather than sinning and as the champion of frugality, honesty, and prosperity.

The Republican Convention met at Cleveland, June 11, and President Coolidge received the scheduled renomination. The Senate did not care for him. He made no attempt to rule Congress or to rally the people to him *a la* Roosevelt, or even in the more dignified way of Wilson and his friends. But the masses of the orthodox Republicans approved of him, though they did not rush into the streets and cheer. There was no outstanding man to take the lead against him. If he had failed to make friends at Washington, he had not made active enemies; and when the convention met his unanimous nomination was assured.

The Vice-Presidency was as much seeking as being sought. There was unusual interest in the nomination, for the disabling illness of President Wilson and the death of President Harding had made men realize the importance of the office.

The administration candidate was Judge Kenyon of Iowa, who after eleven years of distinguished service in the United States Senate had been appointed by President Harding in 1922 to the United States Circuit Court of Appeals, Eighth District. Judge Kenyon was a fair representative of the progressive wing of the Mid-Western Republican party, and yet a man of political sanity, who had never championed measures of the extreme type.

CALVIN COOLIDGE, MASSACHUSETTS, TWENTY-NINTH
VICE-PRESIDENT OF THE UNITED STATES, 1921-1925.

His nomination would have been popular throughout the Middle West and Pacific states, and would not have given serious offense even in conservative quarters.

Probably the favorite of the convention was Frank Lowden of Illinois. He had been a vigorous champion of the agricultural interests and was, therefore, strong with the farmers. He was also well liked by the Progressives, and it was most important to keep them away from La Follette. Lowden had announced that he would not accept the Vice-Presidency; but there was a belief that if it were tendered to him unanimously, he would regard it as his duty to obey the call to serve.

Senator Borah of Idaho was considered more of a vote-getter than most of the men from the pivotal states who had been mentioned for the place. But he decidedly preferred to remain in the Senate. Another possible draftee was the Secretary of Commerce. Of him Oulahan said: "And there is Herbert Hoover. Organization politicians do not like him, but it is generally acknowledged that he would be a tower of strength as a Vice-Presidential candidate. Nothing has yet appeared to indicate that he is under consideration for President Coolidge's running mate; but this has not caused any surprise for the reason that it is acknowledged that he is one of the most valuable members of the Cabinet whose displacement from executive office would be a severe loss to the administration."

Not all possibilities were crying *noli episcopari*. Governor Hyde of Missouri had the endorsement of his State and was frankly a candidate. Of him Oulahan said: "He is attractive in appearance and an excellent campaigner, an especial qualification for a Vice-President." Senator Theodore E. Burton of Ohio, an elderly man of long service in Congress, of excellent character and ability, was at least a receptive candidate. The same might be said of Charles G. Dawes of Ohio.

Before the balloting began, Oglesby of Illinois informed the convention that Lowden had told him that his decision not to run was firm and irrevocable. Yet Lowden received 222 votes to 172 for Kenyon, 149 for Dawes, and 39 for Burton. At the close of the second ballot Lowden was far ahead and the change of a few Minnesota votes in his favor started the usual landslide. "Suddenly men were standing on their chairs all over the house, demanding recognition. Indiana, faithful to its tradition, wanted to be first to climb on the bandwagon, but these matters go by favor and Chairman Mondell recognized Senator James W. Wadsworth of New York, who announced that his State had changed its vote to 1 for Burton and 86 for Lowden." Other chairmen demanding opportunity to change the votes of their delegations were rapidly recognized in turn, and in the end Lowden had received 766 of the 1,109 votes.

But Lowden played the part of Silas Wright. A previous telegram from him, sent in anticipation of his nomination, thanking the convention for the honor which it had done him but declining to accept, was read at the insistence of Senator William M. Butler, who was acting as the representative of President Coolidge. A few minutes later came a telegram saying that Lowden had made this statement to the Associated Press: "I thank the convention, but I must decline the honor. So far, I have always kept my word to the public when I have given it. I shall do so now. I'll not go back on my word. I thank the convention but I will not accept."

All this seemed perfectly definite, yet it was not a refusal made to the convention itself after a nomination. The leaders gathered on the platform and agreed that Acting Chairman Mondell should communicate with Lowden. A recess was then taken until nine in the evening. Nine the next morning would have been a more natural time, but it is said that the leaders feared that the convention might drag on until the following day. A telegram was soon received from Mr. Lowden confirming his declination of the nomination and the leaders at once gathered to agree on a candidate. There was a strong current in favor of Secretary Hoover, but it was known that his declination was in the hands of the California delegation, and besides the New York and the Pennsylvania delegations were opposed to him. There was also some opposition to Hoover in the wheat states because of his keeping down the price of grain during the war.

There remained on the available list the name of Brigadier-General Charles G. Dawes, whose cause had from the start been kept before the convention by the Nebraska delegation. Organized labor was said to be opposed to him, but his friends in New York and Pennsylvania argued that this was unimportant because, if a third party were formed (as then seemed probable), the labor vote would probably be cast for its candidate in any event. Everett Sanders of Indiana was considered, but rejected because he was little known, and because he was said to be a Ku Klux. Dawes was then agreed upon as the most available.

At almost ten o'clock the convention met again. The question of greatest interest to the delegates was met by the Secretary's reading the time and schedule of departing trains. Lowden's declination was then read and accepted. The Secretary started to call the roll for the third ballot and it was soon evident that Dawes would receive a large majority on this ballot. When it was through Governor Channing Cox of Massachusetts, seconded by Senator James Watson of Indiana, moved that the nomination be made unanimous, and this was carried with only a few faint noes to gainsay it.

Charles Gates Dawes was born at Marietta, Ohio, August 27, 1865. He is a direct descendant in the paternal line of that William Dawes who, on the same fateful night as the more celebrated Paul Revere, rode to Concord to apprise the villagers of the coming of the British but, unlike the latter, succeeded in avoiding capture. He graduated from Marietta College in 1884, studied law at the Cincinnati Law School, and began the practice of law at Lincoln, Nebraska, in 1886. In a few years he entered the field of business and became eminently successful. In 1894 he removed to Evanston, Illinois. In 1896 he managed McKinley's campaign in the State of Illinois and after the latter's election, served as his Comptroller of the Treasury from 1901 to 1908. At the outbreak of war with the Central Powers in 1917, Dawes enlisted in the 17th Railway Engineers and was commissioned a major. Before long he was made General Purchasing Agent for the American Army in France. In 1921 President Harding appointed him Director of the Budget, the first to hold that position under the new National Budget and Accounting Act. In 1924 he served as chairman of the Experts' Committee on Reparations, and the plan which that body drafted for the settlement of German Reparations was known as the Dawes Plan.

The nomination of General Dawes was widely acclaimed as another like that of 1920, when the Republicans lived up to their obligations to the public by naming a Vice-Presidential candidate eminently qualified, if necessary, to step into the first place. Successful in business, experienced in politics, public-spirited, as shown by his services in the late war, justly famed by reason of his leading part in the Reparations settlement, and possessed withal of a striking personality, the choice seemed an ideal one. Dawes' rugged personality, his outspoken characteristic, and impassioned way of speaking were, indeed, such as are generally associated with the typical reformer of a liberal stripe. Such an attitude, however, was not to be expected from a man of his business connections; and labor was quick to sense in an organization of his contrivance, the "Minute-men of the Constitution," something Fascist in character and inimical to their interests. William Hard, writing in the New York *Nation,* remarked that the tails of all the tickets seemed to have stings to them:

> "Dawes at the tail of the Republican ticket will devote himself, with a poisonousness which Coolidge could not possibly command, to the stinging of 'demagogues.' Suave, kindly, neat, dapper, sociable, musical, aesthetic, amiable, domestic, Dawes is a honey-bee who is full of honey and sweet charm till he sees demagogues.
>
> "Himself, in fact, one of our very best demagogues and delightfully and ingenuously given to passionate appeals to the class feelings of his own class, he is driven frantic when he sees other demagogues making passionate appeals to the class feelings of other classes. He stings them, he threatens to sting them, and he will sting them. . . . . There is no more unconsciously and instinctively perfect platform performer in this country than Charles G. Dawes of Illinois."

The Democratic convention met at Madison Square Garden, in New York City, June 24. Even before its assembling the beating of the war drums had begun. The two chief contenders for the Presidential nomination were William G. McAdoo of California, and Governor Alfred E. Smith of

New York, the one backed by the rural Anglo-Saxon, dry South, the other by the Democracy of the Northern cities, of wet, newer immigrant stock. Through two and a half hot weeks the balloting continued, the bitterness of the two wings becoming more pronounced as the days went on; and on July 10, after the nomination had ceased to be of real value to any person, John W. Davis, formerly of West Virginia but now of New York, was nominated on the one hundred and third ballot. An attempt was made by the weary delegates immediately to nominate by acclamation for the second place the long-suffering and popular Permanent Chairman of the Convention, Senator Thomas J. Walsh of Montana. Only by an appeal not to use snap judgment was the nomination averted and at four o'clock an adjournment taken till eight that evening in order that an agreement might be reached on the Vice-Presidency.

As usual there had been several avowed candidates for the nomination. Major George L. Berry of Tennessee, President of the National Pressmen's Union, had opened headquarters, and his pictures had been placed about the hotels. He had toured the country in his own behalf and was supposed to have considerable support from organized labor and from the American Legion. A. M. Owsley of Dallas, Texas, past commander of the Legion, also was an avowed candidate. Shortly before the assembling of the convention, Congressman Upshaw of Georgia, an ultra-dry, had announced his candidacy.

The way in which the Vice-Presidential nomination was settled in this case, which is more or less typical of such nominations by both parties, illustrates the dangers to the well-being of the Republic inherent in the present nominating and electoral system. An account was given the author by a participant in the council, one of the leaders of the party of that day. It is substantially as follows: "Thirty or forty leaders met after the adjournment in a room underneath the platform of the auditorium. We soon decided to offer the place to Senator Thomas J. Walsh of Montana. He was not easily found and so there was considerable delay before his refusal was made known. We then decided on E. T. Meredith of Iowa and messengers were sent to get in touch with him. There was a long delay and the impromptu committee adjourned to meet after dinner. When we assembled, there was still no word from Meredith and when it came, it was a refusal. It was then about a quarter till eight o'clock, time for the coming of Mr. Davis, who was to appear before the convention on the hour. When Meredith's refusal was announced, we stood around for a few minutes confused, not knowing what to do. I can see W. J. Bryan yet, draped against the wall on the far side of the room. Through the door of an adjoining room his brother Charles, in his skull cap, was visible. Finally some one, I never knew who, shouted out: 'Mr. Bryan, why not persuade your brother to take the nomination,' and he answered: 'It might not take much persuading.' This man then went to Charles Bryan and broached the proposition to him and he readily agreed. The committee members stood about aimlessly seeming to acquiesce—at least no one voiced an objection. At that moment, the door opened and in came Mr. Davis with his escort. Bryan was brought forward and introduced to him as his running-mate. It was a crucial moment for Davis. He had only a split second in which to think. If he refused, the powerful Bryan element would be alienated; if he acceded, Charles Bryan would surely be the candidate. Mr. Davis did not know, of course, that the Bryan nomination had not been formally planned by the caucus. So far as I know, there never was any more planning than this. The caucus hastily dispersed to their respective delegations and there was soon a buzz all over the hall that C. W. Bryan was to be the candidate. He was placed in nomination."

The Bryan brothers, strange to say, had emphatically opposed the choice of Mr. Davis as a compromise candidate on the grounds that he was "reactionary" and a tool of the "interests." Perhaps they were now willing to make the most of a bad situation. William Jennings' explanation of "Brother Charley's" nomination differs only in details from that already given above. He frankly admitted that he was third choice. "But much to my surprise, Mr. Davis favored the nomination of Governor Bryan, not because he was my brother, but because he filled the requirements set forth by Mr. Davis, who desireu, first, a man from the West, second, a man who was progressive, and third, a man who was dry. . . . . It just happened that Governor Bryan is the Chief Executive of a State near the center of the agricultural section. He is progressive, and he is dry."

The nomination of Bryan was received throughout the Nation and particularly in the East where he was little known, with something less than enthusiasm. Some papers, however, were inclined to give him considerable credit as an able and practical executive, not burdened by the high-flown theories for which his elder brother was best known. The general run of commentators doubtless would have agreed with the New York *Times* in its comments that "once again the hazards of mortality have been ignored" and that it was clearly a nomination "that would not have been made for the Presidency." William Hard, writing in the New York *Nation,* in a backhanded way, paid Mr. Bryan a compliment for practicality. "Whatever, therefore, is deficient in Davis because of his excess of brains we may expect to see happily and successfully supplied by Bryan because of his lack of them. This writer, after long experience with highly intelligent public men who can see clearly that nothing can be done about anything, welcomes in Bryan a man so dull and so useful that he cannot see it. The tail of the Davis ticket may be its unthinking, but it is also its working, end." The *Nation* editorially concluded that "Governor Bryan's nomination was a shrewd and successful political trick to capture the William J. Bryan influence. That, not the interest of the Republic, was the aim." The Democratic Dallas *Morning News* remarked that the party had nominated Bryan "to convince themselves that they are undivided and to make sure that William Jennings Bryan doesn't go mugwumping off with La Follette or sulking in his tent." The Philadelphia *Record,* however, found in him "qualifications of fitness and character" in a marked degree; he was sure to command the confidence of that "great element of our population whose economic distress has moved the Republican party only to sympathy, unaccompanied by adequate alleviative action."

Charles Wayland Bryan was born at Salem, Illinois, February 10, 1867. He attended the public schools of the locality and later the neighboring Illinois College, but did not remain to graduate. In 1891 he followed his elder brother to Nebraska and at the time of the famous "Cross of Gold" speech, was a commercial traveler for a wholesale house of Omaha. During the campaign of 1896, he removed to Lincoln and became a sort of secretary and political and business manager for his brother. He worked quietly in this capacity until the latter moved to Florida in 1907. During the greater part of that period he was business manager and associate editor of the *Commoner,* of which his brother was founder and editor. After the latter's departure for Florida, he entered municipal politics and in 1915 was elected a city commissioner and was designated as mayor. Through his leadership, free legal aid and employment bureaus and a public coal market were established by the municipality. When the coal market was closed through a decision of the State Supreme Court, he continued it as a private enterprise for the benefit of the people.

In 1918 he received the nomination of his party for Governor but was defeated by his Republican opponent. Four years later, however, he was more successful and as Governor continued the policy of securing for the general public lower prices for essential commodities. In the matter of coal, alone, he claimed an annual saving for the consumers of one million dollars; that for gasoline was only slightly less. An indisputable achievement was the reduction, in a time of rising prices, of the State taxes by thirteen per cent.

Mr. Bryan, at the time of his nomination, was fifty-seven years of age, but was described by a contemporary as looking nearer fifty. "The Governor is a big man, with the bald Bryan dome, and piercing dark eyes. . . . . He possesses a physical and mental vigor which is simply terrific. He is quick, restless, rapid in speech, and sudden in his movements." As compared with his more famous brother he was more dynamic and alert. Those who knew both men were positive that he was not a mere shadow of William Jennings. He is said to have planned and written the resolution which the latter introduced at the Baltimore Convention, repudiating Tammany control and condemning any candidate which that organization might support, since regarded as the master stroke which defeated Champ Clark and made possible the nomination of Woodrow Wilson. A Democratic neighbor who knew the two brothers well thus characterized them: "William has principles and Charley has policies. William conceives an ideal, and goes out to fight for it until the people accept it. Charley finds out what the people want, and then goes out and fights for it until they accept him as their champion."

"Brother Charley's" skull cap was the joke of the campaign and doubtless was no more effective as a vote-getter than the pictures sent throughout the Nation showing his running-mate clad in golf clothes. To the curious, Mr. Bryan explained that the cap served the purpose of protecting his head from the light, which affected the sensitive nerves of his head and caused headaches. A contemporary writer observed that Mr. Bryan was not the skull cap type at all. "Nothing could be more inappropriate. He is as hard and rough and combative as an Airedale."

For the first time since 1912 a third party was in the field and of sufficient strength to cause worry to both major ones. Senator Robert M. La Follette of Wisconsin, long a leader in the liberal faction of the Republican party, was nominated for President by a convention of Progressives, at Cleveland, July 4th. He hoped to gather together the liberals of all parties under his leadership. The scandals that had occurred in the administration during the past four years he hoped would have generated a sufficient indignation to bring about a revolt cutting across party lines. At his request, Senator Burton K. Wheeler of Montana, who, like himself, had taken a leading part in the Teapot Dome investigation, was nominated for the Vice-Presidency.

Burton Kendall Wheeler was born in Hudson, Middlesex County, Massachusetts, February 27, 1882. He was educated in the public schools of the town and took a law course at the University of Michigan, graduating there in 1905. In the same year he migrated to Montana, was admitted to the bar, and began the practice of law. He was elected to the Lower House of the State Legislature in 1910, and with the incoming of the Democratic administration in 1913 was appointed to the post of United States District Attorney for Montana. He ran for Governor of the State in 1920 and was defeated, but in 1922 was successful in his race for the United States Senate.

William Hard described him as a mere youth, still engaged in writing his juvenilia:

> "He writes them in the spirit appropriate to his years. He is not an old young man. He is a young young man. He is politically romantic. He is pugnacious. He is adventurous. He hails from the East—from Massachusetts. He cannot say cool-lidge, to rhyme with too. He says cull-idge, to rhyme with full. The long "oo" is too much for him. He has a Massachusetts accent and a Montana temperament. The temperament led him inevitably to Montana. He would have made a great prospector in the old Montana mining days. Or he might have made a great gambler. Taking chances is no bother to him. It is no anxiety to him. . . . .
>
> "He had an iron heart and a brass forehead. Also he has one of the most charming of smiles—a boyish smile, a cool and deadly smile. He could have put his shooting-irons on the table and smiled handsomely and happily at his fellow-gamblers in the old Montana

days. . . . . Personally he is hard-boiled, hard-bitten, hard-headed, hard-fisted, with a tinge in him of the handsome, sword-crossing, heart-breaking soldier of fortune."

A half dozen minor parties had candidates in the field. For the first time there was a Communist national ticket with William Z. Foster of Illinois and Benjamin Gitlow of New York as Presidential and Vice-Presidential candidates, respectively. Both had been outstanding agitators for their cause, the latter having run afoul of the criminal syndicalism law of his State.

When General Dawes was nominated, it was with the idea that he would bear the brunt of the campaigning. After his speech of acceptance on August 19, he was almost constantly on the road. The greatest fear of the Republican managers, remembering the experience of 1912, was that the La Follette candidacy would divide the party and either lead to Democratic success in the electoral college through such a schism, or else throw the election into the House of Representatives. Dawes accordingly confined his campaigning chiefly to the States of the agricultural Middle West, particularly Minnesota, Wisconsin, Iowa, Indiana, and Illinois, and directed his fire at the party doctrines of La Follette. The issue, he repeatedly told his audiences, was between those who would pull down the Constitution and the Supreme Court and the Republican Administration defending them. Many times his attacks were too severe to please the party managers. Senator Brookhart, in the midst of the campaign, demanded that he resign his place on the ticket. To the inquiry of a heckler in Iowa as to what he had to say regarding Brookhart, he answered: "The voices of the demagogues are like the faint plaintive cries of the peewit in the wilderness." His denunciations of the Ku Klux Klan in States ridden by that organization were regarded as needlessly severe. Perhaps some mild degree of pressure was exerted on him by party managers to moderate his statements. At least, as the campaign was drawing to a close, there were rumors that he had been gagged, and he told an audience that attempts to muzzle him during the campaign had come from the men and not the women of the party.

The Democratic Vice-Presidential candidate evidently was not regarded by his National Committee as a distinct asset in the campaign. Perhaps the ridicule engendered by the skull cap had something to do with it, but more likely his liberal and proletarian utterances and his record of attacks on private business enterprise were more influential in creating that attitude. Immediately after the nomination, without awaiting for a conference with his chief, he yielded to the entreaties of the reporters and gave out his own platform. He summarized it by saying: "I believe in applying business principles to Federal, municipal, and State Government, and in preventing the larger, richer, and more powerful members of society from imposing on the weaker." His campaigning activities were confined almost exclusively to small towns in Nebraska, Kansas, Oklahoma, and Illinois.

The only hope of a Democratic victory had been the La Follette movement, but as the campaign progressed this was seen to be less of a threat than had been anticipated. The fact of general economic well-being as epitomized in the slogan of "Keep Cool with Coolidge" was more in the minds of the voters than the wrong-doing of certain Republican leaders of the past four years. Coolidge and Dawes received a plurality of more than seven million popular votes and a total of 382 in the electoral college as compared with 136 for the Democratic candidates and 13 for La Follette and Wheeler.

The four years of the second Coolidge administration did not greatly change the political picture. There had been no great scandals involving officers in high places as in the previous four years and, what is more important in forecasting voting behavior, the country had gone steadily forward into a wave of economic prosperity which was marred only by the unsatisfactory condition of agriculture in some regions. President Coolidge, in spite of the third term tradition, doubtless could have had the nomination in 1928 had he indicated that he would accept it. However, he left all aspiring candidates on the anxious seat until August 2, 1927, when he handed out to the newspaper men at his summer camp in the Black Hills the enigmatic statement: "I do not choose to run for President in 1928." Although this left the way open for the "Draft Coolidge" movement which promptly developed, the various aspirants were prompt to accept it as an avowal that he had eliminated himself from consideration. Vice-President Dawes, for instance, immediately announced: "President Coolidge enjoys the confidence and respect of the American people and his decision will be received with regret by millions of his countrymen."

General Dawes had kept himself constantly before the public in such ways as to give the general impression that he was a candidate for the nomination. He had taken an important part in the farm-relief legislative program and had considerable strength in the grain States of the Middle West. His good friend, ex-Governor Frank Lowden, however, had been in the field first, was strong in the same region, and Dawes would not make any move which might be construed as disloyalty to him. A dialogue at the annual Gridiron Dinner in Washington in December of 1932, however, is indicative of the newspaper men's conception of his aspirations. After the manner of the celebrated Mr. Dooley one asked: "D'ye think he'll iver run f'r Pris-dint?" "I dunno," said Mr. Flannigan, "Dawes is sthrong f'r farm ray-lief an' that's bound t' be th' la-aden issue in the campaign of 1932."

As the year 1928 drew nearer, the chances of both Lowden and Dawes grew less. The latter had not been regarded as entirely loyal to the Administration; President Coolidge is said never to have forgiven him for his absence from the Senate when his casting vote would have saved the nomination of Charles B. Warren as Attorney-General, from defeat. Senator Simeon D. Fess, leader of the "Draft Coolidge" movement, openly stated that Dawes could never be nominated, that no one could ride to the leadership of the

Republican party on a "wave of discontent." Lowden was regarded as still "unavailable" because of the revelation of the undue expenditure of funds by his lieutenants in the Missouri primaries campaign in 1924; and he apparently had never forgiven some fellow Republicans their blatant "exposure" of this incident at the time of the 1924 Convention.

This left the field pretty well to Secretary of Commerce Herbert C. Hoover, who proceeded to conduct a vigorous pre-convention campaign for delegates. He was not popular with the party leaders in general and they attempted to checkmate him through the scheme of running "favorite sons" in the various State primaries. He lost such contests to Senators Guy Goff in West Virginia, James Watson in Indiana, George W. Norris in Nebraska, Charles Curtis in Kansas, and ex-Governor Lowden in Illinois. Hoover won in Ohio by default, Senator Willis of that State having died during the campaign, but too late to have his name taken from the ballot Under these circumstances, there seemed to be a fair prospect of deadlocking the Convention and so bringing in a favorite son or a dark horse. Of all the Hoover rivals, Curtis of Kansas seemed the best situated to carry off the nomination.

The first week in June, at a conference in Chicago, a "Voluntary Farm Committee" was formed, ostensibly to formulate a plank favorable to the farm interests, but actually to devise means to head off the Hoover nomination. Dominating it were the "Allies" or their representatives. Curtis, Goff, Lowden, Watson, and, significantly enough, National Committeeman Charles D. Hilles of New York, a "Draft Coolidge" advocate, joined them. After appointing an executive committee, they adjourned.

The Convention met at Kansas City, June 12, and it was soon apparent that Secretary Hoover had gathered even more strength than had been anticipated. Nevertheless, Curtis issued a formal statement warning the Convention that it could not afford to nominate anyone because of whom the party would "be on the defensive from the day he is named until the close of the polls on election day." He had meanwhile been stressing the necessity for the nomination of a "real Republican." The reference to Mr. Hoover in these statements was hardly veiled. On the evening of the 13th there was a meeting of three hundred Oklahoma delegates and visitors, which was addressed by Goff, Watson, and Curtis, the latter telling them that if the gentlemen from the East had had a little backbone, they might have had a ticket "that the whole party would have been proud of," but assuring them that he would support the nominee even if "he started off to London."

Mr. Hoover received a decisive majority on the first ballot and shortly before midnight of the 14th was declared nominated. Mr. Curtis, who had received the solid vote of his own State and Oklahoma, at once called him on the telephone and pledged his support. The Convention then adjourned till noon of the next day and the Vice-President-makers prepared to spend the small hours of the night in doing their work.

The first impression was that Mr. Curtis, through the earnestness of his own efforts for the Presidential nomination, had made himself unavailable as a running-mate for Hoover. John Q. Tilson of Connecticut, Alvan T. Fuller and Channing Cox of Massachusetts, Chase S. Osborn of Michigan, Samuel A. Baker of Missouri, besides Curtis and Dawes, were considered. The list was finally narrowed down to Curtis, Dawes, and Cox, and it was then tentatively agreed to give Dawes the first chance. But there was the matter of his "unsoundness" on the McNary-Haugen Farm Bill, which President Coolidge had recently vetoed. When called on the telephone and asked as to his position on that measure, he agreed to take the position that the veto had shelved it for four years. The leaders were still afraid of him, however, fearing that like Lowden in 1920, he would stage a sensational refusal. He was called again and asked if he would make a public statement to the effect that this bill had been disposed of; and when he refused to do so, his name was dropped. Mr. Borah now entered the conference and insisted on the elimination of Governor Cox on the grounds that he was unknown in the West; that his connection with the Sacco-Vanzetti affair would do the ticket harm with the foreign-born of the large cities; and that, anyway, the Smith danger in the East, which the nomination of Cox was designed to offset, was less to be feared than the agricultural discontent of the West. He urged the nomination of Curtis and threatened to take the matter to the floor of the Convention if Cox was insisted upon.

The leaders were much impressed with these arguments and with the strength Curtis had shown in the Convention. Hoover, when consulted by telephone, was non-committal, and the decision was made for Curtis.

When the Convention assembled at the appointed time, Mr. Curtis was placed in nomination by Senator Borah, as were four other favorite sons by their respective delegations. Curtis received all but a unanimous vote on the first ballot.

The nomination of Senator Curtis was generally received with approval. There were dissentients, of course. Oswald Garrison Villard referred to him as "the apotheosis of mediocrity," a "regular of the regulars," and "faithful and as devoted to his party as he is dull and dumb." The Democratic New York *Times* commented: "In its political aspects, the nomination of Senator Curtis for the Vice-Presidency must be considered a fine piece of strategy. He is devoted to the grass roots of Kansas, but the overwhelming demand for his acceptance came from the great industrial States of the East and, indeed, from all parts of the country. Mr. Curtis is well-liked in the Senate, even by his political opponents. Should he be called to preside in the Senate chamber, he will do it with a better knowledge of the rules and customs and sensibilities of the Senate than most of his predecessors have brought to the chair. . . . . . Since the nomination for the Vice-Presidency was bound to go to one of the discontented farmer States, it is just as well that it should have gone to so well qualified a man as Charles Curtis of Kansas. His name is, politically speaking, a fit pendant on the ticket for that of Secretary Hoover." The New York *Independent* remarked: "For a

Vice-Presidential candidate, whatever his qualities, must necessarily submit to the duty of mopping up, leaving all sword play and gallantry to the leader of the ticket. His duty is that of a squire. Once in a blue moon a Dawes sets out to make the minor candidacy into a brilliant part, but a Dawes is a source of worry to party leaders and a threat to party harmony. If it were otherwise, Mr. Dawes might have fared better at Kansas City last June. Senator Curtis, always a party regular, plays a competent second fiddle."

The country at large is interested chiefly in the nomination for the Presidency, but when the news of the work of the Convention reached a far corner of Oklahoma, there was a celebration inspired entirely by the Vice-Presidential choice. A group of painted Kaw braves, the elders of the tribe, dressed in the aboriginal costume of the prairies, came together to feast and dance. Had not one of their brethren been chosen to sit at the right hand of the Great White Father and, should he fall in the battle, step forward to take his place as the great chief of the entire nation? Will Rogers, the political humorist, himself of Cherokee blood, congratulated Curtis on being the first American to run for that high office, and added: "Come on, Injun, if you are elected, let's run the white people out of the country."

There were few men in high public office in 1928 whose lives so faithfully epitomized the whole course of American national history as did that of Charles Curtis. His life span—and it was a long one, as he was past sixty-eight years of age when nominated to stand as the heir apparent of Herbert Hoover—began with the colonizing era of the Great Plains region and came to its fulfillment when the United States had reached its high stage of urbanization and industrialization. William Allen White, a fellow Kansan, distinguishes the threads of heredity, experience, and environment which together make up the fabric of his character:[1]

> "In his veins are three potent strains of inheritance—Indian, French and New England. In the early part of the nineteenth century, Curtis's great-grandfather, a Frenchman living near St. Louis, married the daughter of White Plume, a Kaw Indian chief. She was the granddaughter of Chief Pawhuskie of the Osage tribe. Julie Conville, the daughter of this Indian woman, married Louis Pappan, a French trader near St. Louis, in the middle of the century, and the Pappans moved with the Kaw Indians to their reservation in Kansas. Senator Curtis's grandmother, Julie Conville Pappan, had an Indian allotment—a farm near North Topeka, Kansas, where Curtis was born, the child of Ellen Pappan and Capt. O. A. Curtis.
>
> "Now the Curtises were from Indiana out of New England,— old New England. His grandmother, Permelia Hubbard, came with her New England conscience from New Hampshire, and her people,

[1]William Allen White: "The Man Who Rules the Senate," in *Collier's Weekly,* October 3, 1925, p. 10.

CHARLES CURTIS, KANSAS, THIRTY-FIRST VICE-PRES-
IDENT OF THE UNITED STATES, 1929-1933.

the Hubbards, came from Massachusettts, where they appeared in 1621. Ten years later the Curtises landed in New York. With the adventurers of freedom who rushed into Kansas in the mid-fifties, came in '56 O. A. Curtis, who married the Indian girl Ellen Pappan, went to the Civil War, and returned a brave soldier and a captain after the war of the 'sixties was over.

"No mere political happen-so is this man Curtis. The scion of two Indian chieftains of more than local fame was probably going to be a leader of his fellows.

"The grandson of a Frenchman was going to have a certain charm and romantic flare in his life. And that Hubbard blood doomed him inexorably to a life-term servitude of details—dry, hard details that under his imagination were bound to take some definite shape in a constructive form.

"The French and Indians got him first. His early career was romantic. His mother died when he was three years old, and he went to the Kaw reservation sixty miles west of Topeka, with his grandmother, Julie Pappan, who was living with her mother's people—reservation Indians. The illimitable prairie was there; hunting was a part of the child's daily life. Dogs and horses were the companions of his babyhood and boyhood, and at eight Charles Curtis was a jockey, riding races at the fairs. At ten he had a name in the State and at twelve he was a figure in his part of the world— a lithe, handsome, black-haired, black-eyed boy, the Indian jockey —'ol' Cap Curtis's boy.'

"After the Cheyenne Indian raid in 1868, Charles Curtis went back to his father's people and lived with his father's parents in Topeka, Kansas. When the Government sent the Kaw Indians from Morris County, Kansas, to the Indian Territory—where Oklahoma now is—the little Curtis boy desired to go with his grandmother Pappan. He joined the tribal hegira. But the first trek out of Topeka, Julie Pappan came to him late at night and told him to go back,—and he did so. He walked to Topeka. In the winter he went to school; in the summer and fall he followed the races. When he was sixteen years old he had a winter contract for riding,—a good one, worth more money to him than his father could have made. But again a wise woman's voice spoke to him—his Curtis grandmother, Permelia Hubbard Curtis of New Hampshire, persuaded him to quit the track and go to school. So he went through the grades of the common school and began life on his own.

"The New England blood was forever calling him, and in the livery stable he spent his spare hours with his books. He got a job on a North Topeka paper and in the late 'teens went about writing and soliciting subscribers."

It is interesting to set Curtis' career alongside that of two men of New England, to whose positions he eventually succeeded. Henry Cabot Lodge, ten years his senior and preceding him by six years in the Senate leadership, was a student at Harvard College while Curtis was touring the Southwest with Tilden, a famous race-horse of the day. He was editing the *North American Review* and had received three academic degrees at the time Charles Curtis went pell-mell through the fence of the Topeka track on the back of a new mount, Headlight.[1] Calvin Coolidge, twelve years his junior and eight years preceding him in the Vice-Presidential office, was a freshman at Amherst at the moment Curtis was nominated for his first term in Congress. He had just received attention nationally as a figure in politics at the time Curtis was Republican whip in the Senate. During his second term as President, it was chiefly with Mr. Curtis as Republican Floor Leader that he had to reckon in dealing with that body.

At seventeen years of age, Curtis left the race track and continued his education in the public schools, supporting himself by various kinds of work. For two years he drove a night hack, pursuing his studies between hours and fares. In this way he met many of the politicians who frequented the old Copeland Hotel, a circumstance which soon was to prove of great value. At the age of nineteen, he began the study of law under these conditions, and was admitted to the bar at twenty-one.

Almost immediately he became active in local politics. For this, he had great natural talents. As Mr. White remarks, he could remember names and faces; he knew hundreds of the farmers of his county; he had a "blessed gift as a hand-shaker" and that "indefinable thing called charm, which binds men to one forever." Mr. White continues: "He was a handsome lad in that day—slight, with the jockey's litheness, with affectionate black, caressing eyes and a curling black moustache." Add to this "a gentle, ingratiating voice and an easy flow of innocuous conversation unimpeded by pestiferous ideas, and you have a creature God sent into politics."

With Mr. Curtis' election as prosecuting attorney of Shawnee County at the age of twenty-four, he began a career of office-holding rivaling that of Calvin Coolidge in continuity, but much exceeding it in length of span. After four years in this office, he retired to the practice of law. After another four years, during which he had been constantly active in local party politics, he was nominated and elected to the National House of Representatives. Here he served eight successive terms at the end of which, in 1907, he was elected to fill out the unexpired term of a United States Senator who had resigned. Except for two years, 1913 to 1915, when the Bull Moose rebellion disturbed the established order in Kansas, he was in the Senate continuously until he assumed the duties of the office of Vice-President in 1929. After the death of Mr. Lodge in 1924, he succeeded to the Republican leadership of the Senate.

---

[1]W. A. DuPuy, quoted in the *Literary Digest,* p. 47, January 3, 1925.

Mr. Curtis' success in the Senate was not due primarily to his work as a debater—the *Record* shows few of his speeches extending beyond a paragraph —but to his work as a member of important standing committees and his ability as a contact man. Important bills of a contentious nature he preferred to have others introduce, while he quietly made the arrangements by which they carried through. Charles Merz once stated in the New York *Independent*: "Curtis does not make policies: he unveils them. It is his business to sound out the opposition, plan a campaign, arrange a compromise if one is necessary, and muster the votes when the skies are stormy." From the beginning of his career, he recognized the value of working with the regular organization of the party, and remaining unswervingly loyal to the party and its policies, a policy which left him out of office two years in forty. Coupled with a natural courage and a highly developed political sense was an urbanity which made it possible for him to oppose policies and men and yet retain their friendship. For a man of conservative, hard money, and protectionist principles to remain almost continuously for forty years the representative of a purely agricultural State is an achievement which bears eloquent testimony to the ability of the man.

The Democratic leaders had learned something from the Madison Square Garden battle of 1924. A war to extinction between the two natural divisions of the party might gratify the feelings of certain *bloc* leaders and give comfort to the Republicans, but it meant disaster to the party as a whole. During the four years of the second Coolidge administration, the Smith organization quietly extended its area of control and consolidated its hold in its original home territory. Certain Southern leaders were now convinced that the urban wing must be given its chance in spite of its wetness and the Catholicism of its leader. No doubt they were influenced by the mathematics of the proposition. A Democratic nominee, no matter what his principles, would win the solid South—there had been no exception to that rule since Reconstruction days; and, if wet, he would have a great advantage over his Republican opponent in all the great populous states of the Northeast. The dry Middle West might then be conceded to the Republican and success still be sure.

An indication of this agreement occurred in the Senate early in January of 1928. After Senator Thomas Heflin had indulged in one of his tirades against the Democratic leader, Mr. Smith, and the Catholic Church, Joseph Robinson of Arkansas arose and gave him a terrific verbal castigation. He then called for a Democratic caucus for the next morning and asked for a vote of confidence, and this was given with only one dissenting vote.

The Democratic Convention, which assembled at Houston, Texas, June 26, was completely in control of the Smith organization and his nomination, as had generally been foreseen, was accomplished on the first ballot. There remained the delicate matter of conciliating the South, many of whose delegates had only sullenly accepted the decision. With this end in view, the South was conceded the Permanent Chairmanship of the Convention, which was given to Robinson of Arkansas, a dry but with the saving grace, so far as Prohibition was concerned, of a firm adherence to states' rights. Carter Glass, of Virginia, was given the chairmanship of the resolutions or platform committee and that body framed a plank with a declaration of dryness, a concession which was doubtless the *sine qua non* of the South's acceptance of the Smith nomination. Smith, however, ate his pie and had it, too, by sending a telegram of acceptance just as the Convention was breaking up, reaffirming his belief that the Prohibition Amendment should be repealed and, by a "fearless application" of the principles of Jeffersonian democracy, the matter be sent back to the states for their care.

It was the general belief when the Convention was assembling, that the South would be conceded the second place on the ticket. For a proper balance, the nominee should also be a dry and a Protestant. Senators Alben W. Barkley of Kentucky, James A. Reed of Missouri, and D. U. Fletcher of Florida, were reported as receptive candidates for the honor, and there was talk of Mrs. Nellie Tayloe Ross, ex-Governor of Wyoming, and Mr. Evans Woollen of Indiana.

But these booms were mostly complimentary and diplomatic. It was generally believed even before the assembling of the Convention that Robinson had been designated for the place. His part in lining up the Southern leaders for Smith, his outspoken utterances against religious bigotry, his dryness, his Protestantism, and his ability as a campaigner all combined to give him the first place in availability. The only objection, and it was only feebly voiced, was that the nomination of a Southerner would make difficult the lining up of the negroes of the Northern cities for the Democratic cause. Two days before the Convention opened, Robinson issued a "harmony" statement; and the declaration of Smith's intimate friend and political *confrère,* Mayor Frank Hague of Jersey City, that he had 128 votes from the Northeast for Robinson for Vice-President, was sufficient indication to the initiated that Robinson had been chosen.

When the Convention assembled at half past ten in the morning of the fourth and last day, it was significant that Chairman Robinson was absent from his place and Franklin D. Roosevelt in the chair. When the roll of the states was called, Arizona yielded to New Mexico and Robinson was placed in nomination by Senator Sam G. Bratton of that State. The hand of Tammany, therefore, was not on him. He received a vote approaching unanimity on the first ballot.

Popular interest in the nomination of Robinson was almost swallowed up in that over the nomination of the vivid personality heading the ticket. Democratic papers, however, generally voiced their approval. The Wheeling *Register,* for instance, said: "Senator Robinson is keen, aggressive, honest. He is well qualified to be first officer on the Ship of State under Captain Smith." The New York *Times,* on the other hand, more cautiously remarked that Senator Robinson's nomination was according to plan. "That plan now appears pretty obvious. It was to do everything to mollify the South. It was in the Southern states that the strongest and most bitter opposition to Governor Smith revealed itself." The Republican Chicago *Tribune* saw the nomination as only one in a mixture of strange unharmonious elements. "Carter Glass swallowing Al Smith, Senator Robinson in bad for urging religious toleration. The Methodist Church, South, on a trip to the night clubs. . . . It lacks only Tom Heflin as chairman of the committee to notify the nominee at Albany and receive his acceptance."

Joseph Taylor Robinson was born near the village of Lonoke, in the State of Arkansas, August 26, 1872. He was educated in the public schools and the University of Arkansas, and studied law at the University of Virginia. He was admitted to the bar in 1895, and commenced the practice of law in his native town. He was elected a member of the State Assembly in 1894, to the United States House of Representatives in 1902, and served nearly five continuous terms there. He was elected Governor of his State in 1912, and served less than two months when he was elected to the United States Senate, in which body he has been continuously since. In 1923, upon the retirement of Senator Oscar W. Underwood of Alabama, he was chosen Democratic leader of the Senate.

Mr. Robinson is a man of great physical strength; a contemporary has described him as "undoubtedly the most vigorous and formidable member of the Senate," his voice as "tremendous, hard metallic," carrying "almost to the other end of the Capitol Building." He was a firm supporter of President Wilson during his administration, standing by him loyally to the end in his fight for the League of Nations Covenant.

There were several "third party" tickets in the field, but none comparable in strength to that of the Progressive party of four years before. The Socialist party nominated Mr. James H. Maurer of Pennsylvania for Vice-President, to run with Norman Thomas of New York. The Communists renamed their old ticket of 1924.

The campaign of 1928 was one of unusual intensity, for which the two issues of Prohibition and the Catholic adherence of the head of the Democratic ticket were mainly responsible. That the two nominees for the Vice-Presidency were both men of unusual qualifications for that office was quite overlooked. Never before had the respective leaders of the Senate faced each other in a campaign for the Presidency of that body. Not since the Civil War had a Southern man received a nomination for either of the two places on the ticket of a major political party—this much the South had won by assuming an attitude of uncertainty in a national election. Never before had one of the Great Plains states received from one of the major political parties a Presidential or a Vice-Presidential nomination—this much the farmers of the Middle West had won by their wavering allegiance to the Grand Old Party.

Both candidates took an active part in the campaign. Their acceptance speeches were much as might have been expected. Curtis outlined a program deeply sympathetic with the plight of the farmers and staunchly for Prohibition. Not too much was said about his favorite doctrine of protection. The Governor of Arkansas proclaimed a State-wide holiday for the Robinson notification ceremonies; and Senator Robinson, directing his talk in effect to the disaffected South, explained that there had always been room in the Democratic party for those who differed "as to the best means of promoting temperance and of suppressing the traffic in alcoholic beverages." He reminded them that President Wilson had vetoed the Volstead Act. As for Mr. Smith, his honest convictions that temperance and respect for law could best be promoted by "changes in the existing system," coupled with his promise to enforce the existing law so long as it was in force, were not so much "nullification" as was the failure of the Republicans for eight years to enforce the law. Mr. Curtis ignored the opposing party and candidates, while Mr. Robinson went vigorously to the attack. A commentator in the New York *Independent* remarked that Senator Robinson had made his notification ceremony at Hot Springs, Arkansas, "equal in excitement to the eruption of a new geyser in the Yellowstone," but that this might have been due to the fact that "both climate and natural phenomena make for warmth."

Curtis, as had been planned, did the major part of his campaigning in the grain regions of the Middle West and the Northwest, and in the border State of Oklahoma, but extended it to Ohio, New York, and New Jersey. Robinson concentrated his efforts on the South and the border states, but extended his efforts as far West as Idaho and through the disaffected grain regions of the middle and upper Mississippi River regions.

There were some startling results in the election of 1928. First, next to that of Cox and Roosevelt in 1920, it was the most overwhelming defeat of any party since the Civil War, the Republican ticket receiving over fifty-eight per cent. of the popular and 444 of the electoral votes. Secondly, there were breaks in the party ranks in certain regions which might be interpreted as of lasting significance. The Republicans carried all of the border states and four of the "solid" South, while the Democrats, in spite of the adverse landslide, captured two states of the "solid" North, Massachusetts and Rhode Island. It was running true to form, too, that both Vice-Presidential candidates fulfilled the parts which had been assigned to them, in carrying their respective states in spite of the local spirit of disaffection for their respective parties.

President Hoover had less than a year in which to fully enjoy the popular favor as evidenced by his triumph in the electoral college. Late in October, 1929, there was a catastrophic break in the prices of securities on the New York Stock Exchange. This was but the outward sign of the beginning of the depressive stages of an economic cycle. There was a progressive decline in commodity prices extending throughout his administration. The demand for manufactured goods and agricultural products fell off, factories closed, wages declined, and the number of the unemployed became the greatest in the history of the country. American loans to Europe already had ceased and with this there followed a sharp recession in the demand for American raw and manufactured products. With both domestic and foreign trade shrunk to a small percentage of normal, the American people, as a whole, were faced by an unexampled lowering in the standard of living and, in case of the less fortunate millions, by a degree of want and privation hitherto unknown.

It is the invariable rule in a democracy that the government in power at the moment must accept responsibility when economic misfortunes come to the masses of the voters, just as it claims the credit when they prosper. This holds even though economic dislocations throughout the world are the basic cause, rather than the misdeeds of the political régime. It was evident to the most casual observer throughout 1931 that nothing less than a sharp reversal in the tide of business could prevent a great disaster to the Republican administration in 1932 elections. Just as the party of Woodrow Wilson in 1920 faced a tremendous accumulation of hostile attitudes drawn from a multitude of sources, many of them unrelated, so the Republicans would find converging against them the combined forces of the unemployed, the owners of worthless stocks and bonds, those dispossessed of farms and homes, and those more fortunate millions who found unlowered taxes levied upon greatly reduced incomes. Votes thus lost by the logic of misfortune could only be won back by the logic of prosperity.

There was another element of similarity between the situation of the respective administrations in 1920 and in 1932—the element of revulsion which comes when masses believe themselves to have been misled by a false idealism or hopes improvidently raised. In the first case, the people had been worked up to a pitch of idealism and feeling of social solidarity and sacrifice far above their normal habits, and the "war to end war" had culminated in a series of eminently practical and hard-driven bargains among the nations associated with us. In the second, the Republican party had put Mr. Hoover forward as one capable of ensuring to the United States a continuance and an extension of the great advance in the material standard of living which had begun with the coming of peace and the Harding administration. The promises in both cases were honestly made, but upon failure of fulfillment, something more than the ordinary popular reaction was to be expected.

The Republican Convention met at Chicago, June 14, with Congress still in session and at grips with the most pressing problems of legislation since the World War. Had there been any such inclination, the party could not, in the face of the Democratic threat, have failed to give Mr. Hoover the customary renomination. The chief question of uncertainty was the framing of the plank on Prohibition. Since a nation-wide poll conducted on a gigantic scale by the New York *Literary Digest* a few weeks earlier had shown a tremendous swing of popular sentiment to the "wet" side, politicians of both parties were convinced that the party sails should be trimmed to catch the new current. ˏThe plank finally adopted by the Republicans reaffirmed the party faith in obedience to and the enforcement of law, but favored a submission to the states of a resolution repealing the Eighteenth Amendment, and substituting in its place one retaining in the Federal Government some power over the traffic, perhaps in the direction of protecting dry states and regulating the retail sale of liquors in those which chose to bring it back. Mr. Hoover received the nomination on the first ballot with only a few scattering votes in opposition.

Mr. Curtis, however, did not face the Chicago convention with the same assurance as did his chief. Generally speaking, political events are perhaps more against the renomination of a Vice-President than for it. Since the nomination is primarily dictated by the exigency of placating or winning a doubtful section, State, or group of voters, it might very well happen that the danger point to a ticket should in four years' time shift from one spot to another. In no case where a new Presidential nomination was made and the old Vice-President had served but one term, was he renominated; and in only one case did a Republican President running for his second term have with him his original running-mate—that of Taft and Sherman in 1912. Lincoln ran with Andrew Johnson in 1864 rather than with Hannibal Hamlin; General Grant had Henry Wilson in the place of Schuyler Colfax; and Benjamin Harrison, Whitelaw Reid, in the place of Levi P. Morton. The coupling of Charles W. Fairbanks with Charles Evans Hughes in 1916, eight years after he had retired from the Vice-Presidential office, stands alone as an example of that kind.

Just as the Republican Convention was assembling, sentiment among party leaders against the renaming of Curtis became apparent. This arose, not from personal or political antagonism to Mr. Curtis, but was born of the general hopelessness of the Republican cause. Conceding the political unpopularity of those who had been in office during the past few years, might it not be possible to place a name on the ticket which might have something of the appeal of the new and the untried which was bound to go with the Democratic nominees? But in order to shelve a man of the personal popularity and political ability of Charles Curtis, there must be a visible rival around whom the hostile forces might group themselves. It was thought that ex-Vice-President Charles G. Dawes might prove to be the man of the hour. He had been out of office during the four years of the depression, and he had not otherwise been closely enough identified with the administration to have shared the popular emotional reaction against it. His was a colorful and forceful personality, and he had a campaigning ability which might be that heaven-sent gift which only could prevent a disastrous defeat in November.

Creager, chairman of the Texas delegation, came to the Convention with his delegation lined up for Mr. Dawes. When the latter had been approached by those promoting his candidacy, he had requested that he be not embarrassed by having his name presented. But, according to Mr. Creager, there had been no categorical refusal to run, and there were good reasons for believing that he would accept if drafted. The Dawes boom grew rapidly. Its promoters announced that twenty-four state delegations, including several large states of the industrial Northeast, had given their adherence, and that six more were wavering. Iowa, of the Corn Belt, which region Curtis was supposed primarily to represent, had been the first state to join the Texas revolutionists. The plan was that, upon the call of the roll, Arkansas should yield to Texas and Dawes' name would be presented to the Convention. Competent observers at this point reported that only the personal intervention of President Hoover could save Mr. Curtis. And about this intervention there was grave doubt. A prominent member of the Cabinet, upon his arrival at Chicago, pointed out that both Curtis and Dawes were good friends of the President, and that he did not desire to be placed in the position of dictating to the Convention as between the two.

But these plans so carefully laid were to be completely wrecked. Late in the day of June 15, Mr. Dawes gave out a statement that he had given the matter "considerable thought," and had decided that he "could not accept the nomination if made." Whether this action was taken solely upon his own initiative or as a result of a decision by President Hoover and his intimate counsellors to support Mr. Curtis, is not yet generally known. Sober second thought might well have led them to conclude that more was to be gained by going before the country with an appeal for the "old ticket," than by taking chances of a greater loss through an offense to the Curtis following and the doubtful gains which Mr. Dawes or any similar candidate might have brought.

The Texans, although irked at the embarrassment of being left with a deflated boom on their hands, announced that they would continue the fight for another candidate. Such men were considered as Secretary of the Treasurer Ogden Mills, Secretary of War Patrick Hurley, Representative Bertrand Snell of New York, and Walter E. Edge of New Jersey, Ambassador to France. Since all these were close friends of the administration, it was not seriously believed that any would lend his support to an anti-Curtis movement. The Iowa delegation began agitation for Mr. Hanford MacNider, ex-National Commander of the American Legion; but while his anti-bonus attitude might have been pleasing to the administration, the nomination would have been a needless provocation to an already alienated Legion.

The Dawes refusal discouraged, but came far from causing the Curtis opposition to lose hope. The roll-call for nominations brought forth five other names and that for votes disclosed a scattering among thirteen. Mr. Charles F. Scott of the Kansas delegation placed Curtis in nomination in a speech which betrayed something of a defensive attitude. Mr. Curtis' "long road from an Indian reservation to the Vice-Presidency of the United States" was one which had had few parallels in American annals. He reminded the audience of his continued industry and loyalty to the party under all conditions, of the nation-wide campaign which he made in 1928, as "custom imposes upon the candidate for Vice-President." Because of Mr. Curtis' unusual qualifications for the office through his positions as party whip and leader in the Senate, he had given to the Vice-Presidency greater usefulness, leadership, and real power than it ever before exercised or enjoyed. His consummate skill as a parliamentary and political leader had always been at the command of the President and his colleagues in the House and Senate.

Governor Alvan Fuller of Massachusetts was placed in nomination by the delegation of that State; Jay N. Darling, the cartoonist, speaking for the Iowa delegation, nominated Hanford MacNider; and Newman T. Miller, of the Florida delegation, nominated Mr. Replogle, of that State, but also, as his party affiliation might suggest, of Pennsylvania and New York. The feature nomination was the dramatic attempt of the persistent Mr. Creager of Texas to defeat Curtis through creating a stampede for another candidate. Standing on the platform near its presiding officer, Bertrand Snell of New York, he turned without warning toward him and announced that Texas "nominates Bertrand H. Snell of New York." There was the expected cheer, but the quick-witted Snell was equal to the occasion. Pounding for order, he announced that he would not accept the honor and motioned for Charles H. Tuttle to come forward with the nomination of General Harbord, a deploying of administration forces much better designed to hold the Curtis lines than a simple, direct disclaimer in his favor.

On the roll-call, the administration's cue was given when California, the fourth State on the list, cast its solid vote of forty-seven for Curtis. There were actors on the stage, however, who were less interested in the officially planned drama than in their own productions. The key states of New York, Pennsylvania, and Massachusetts cast either all or the bulk of their votes for favorite sons. Illinois gave the major part of its strength to MacNider. All in all, thirteen candidates were voted for. Just as the last State was called and it was seen that Mr. Curtis had $19\frac{1}{4}$ votes short of a majority, Pennsylvania announced the switch of its seventy-five votes from General Edward Martin to Mr. Curtis, and his nomination was accomplished. There were said to be more administration votes which could have been switched if necessary. The usual motion to make the action unanimous was made and carried.

The Democratic Convention met at Chicago, June 27, in a hall which the Republicans left all equipped except that the icons must of necessity be changed. Down came the images of Hamilton, Lincoln, Grant, Roosevelt, Coolidge, and McKinley, and in their places appeared those of Jefferson, Jackson, Cleveland, Wilson, Smith, and the new Roosevelt. It was generally realized in advance that there would be a real contest for the Presidential nomination, with its outcome uncertain. Franklin D. Roosevelt, Democratic Vice-Presidential nominee of 1920, would start with a full majority of the votes but Alfred Smith, the nominee of four years before, was again an active candidate, with nearly two hundred votes pledged and more held in reserve. Some months before, there had been a political break between this Damon-and-Pythias combination in politics, Smith on one occasion publicly referring to Roosevelt as a "demagogue." The plan of the Smith forces was, in conjunction with the other candidates holding scattering votes, to cause a deadlock and thus, through the operation of the two-thirds rule, force the nomination if not of Smith, then of some "dark horse" candidate.

As the Convention was assembling, Mr. James Farley, for the Roosevelt organization, began an attack on the historic two-thirds rule. He proposed a revision that would permit a bare majority of the delegates to nominate and when this met a storm of opposition, modified it to retain the two-thirds rule for the first half dozen ballots or so and thereafter a simple majority. This meeting with no greater favor, the first was abandoned at the express request of Mr. Roosevelt.

John N. Garner, Speaker of the House of Representatives, entered the contest with the solid delegations of Texas and California totaling ninety votes pledged to him. Governor Albert C. Ritchie of Maryland had twenty-one. The real threat to the Roosevelt cause, however, was in neither of these men, but in the under-cover strength of an Ohioan, Mr. Newton D. Baker, Secretary of War under Wilson. Should the contest go much beyond six ballots, it was generally expected that his strength would begin to appear. The campaign in Mr. Baker's behalf had been quietly but skillfully conducted. There had been no embarrassing contests for delegates in the various primaries and conventions. He had never given outward encouragement to the movement, nor had he outwardly discouraged it. To observers it had seemed significant that such utterances on public questions as he had made all contributed toward his "availability." His stand for the outright repeal of the Eighteenth Amendment antedated the late conversion of the Convention leaders. His devotion to the cause of the League of Nations had long been an insuperable barrier to further national party honors, but this was in measure removed by a statement early in the year that he regarded the League as no longer an issue. While the contest over the repeal of the two-thirds rule was on, he stood with the Smith forces in condemning opposition to the change.

Some of the Roosevelt delegations were "shaky." Already on the third ballot there had been slight defections, and it was evident that they would not stand up beyond a few ballots more. At this juncture entered the tall form of William Gibbs McAdoo, now of California, the rival whose Presidential aspirations had been blasted by the Smith forces in the stalemate in Madison Square Garden in 1924. As California was called on the fourth ballot, Mr. McAdoo announced that his State had come to Chicago not to produce a deadlock, but to nominate a candidate. The import of his words was soon gathered by the galleries, whose sympathies were loudly pro-Smith. It required the intervention of Mayor Cermak of Chicago to quiet them sufficiently for McAdoo to finish his speech and announce that both California and Texas had released their votes from Garner to Roosevelt. These were just sufficient to give him the necessary two-thirds. Many other states rushed to the Roosevelt bandwagon, but the 190 die-hard Smith votes remained true to him to the end.

Even while McAdoo was on the platform, during the din which followed, Senator Cordell Hull of Tennessee exclaimed: "Speaker Garner has been offered the Vice-Presidential nomination and will accept." After the night session which had nominated Roosevelt, the Convention adjourned to meet in the afternoon. It was called to order at shortly before two o'clock by Senator Walsh of Montana. The delegates, as usual, had given little thought to the Vice-Presidency and the decision of the leaders to award the second place to Mr. Garner was readily accepted. In the code of the politician, the release of his delegates to the winner at a critical moment had amply earned for him the second place should he desire it. When the roll of the states was called, Alabama yielded to Texas and Representative Sam Rayburn of that State mounted the platform and in turn introduced Representative John McDuffie of the former State, Democratic whip of the House, who made the nominating speech for Mr. Garner. He described him as a "red-blooded" man who was "calm enough for any crisis, cool enough for any emergency, brave enough for any battle," and as "sane, safe, sound in the fundamentals of American government." Several states had had favorite son choices for the Vice-Presidency. Oregon had Milton A. Miller; New Jersey, Mary T. Norton; and Iowa, General Matt A. Tinley. None of these, however, was placed in nomination except the last named. As the roll-call ended, showing a clean sweep for Garner, General Tinley mounted the platform and moved that it be made unanimous; to which motion, when placed, there was no dissent.

William Randolph Hearst, owner of a vast chain of daily newspapers scattered from coast to coast, had had no small part in the thwarting of the plans of both the Smith and the Baker followings. Like many other political observers, he had realized six months previously that Mr. Smith would attempt to deadlock the Convention in order to defeat Roosevelt and that Mr. Baker would be a likely recipient of the Presidential nomination in that event. His political feud with the former dated back ten years, and that with Mr. Baker still further to the Wilson administration. As an offset, he decided to groom some other man for the nomination, which plan would at least result in segregating a block of votes beyond the reach of Smith and Baker, and which might at the moment of the deadlock be thrown to Mr. Roosevelt or some other candidate friendly to Hearst.

His choice fell upon the newly elected Speaker of the House, the veteran John Nance Garner of Texas. Early in January of 1932, a series of biographical articles were prepared and run in all the newspapers of his chain. Garner, the obscure, now became one of the best known of the Democratic leaders. His candidacy began to be taken seriously.

John Nance Garner was born November 22, 1868, in a log cabin at Blossom Prairie, a rural community near the village of Detroit, Red River County,

Texas, in the Northeast corner of that State. His formal elementary education was obtained in a rural school, but it ended at the fourth grade. Thereafter, he received some instruction from an aunt. Like many country youths of the time, he began early to earn his own livelihood. He worked for a time in his uncle's store at the village of Detroit, but was chiefly employed on the farm, attaining in time to the dignity of a cow-puncher. His higher education consisted of one term at Vanderbilt University. After this, he located at the county seat, Clarksville, where he studied law with a local attorney, and at the age of twenty-one was admitted to the bar. He set up a law office, ran for city attorney, and was defeated. At about the same time, he developed symptoms of tuberculosis and to combat it, removed to Uvalde, a county town in the dry southwestern part of the State.

At Uvalde, Mr. Garner regained his health and soon began to prosper. He invested in cattle and in farm and ranch lands, became the owner and editor of a weekly newspaper and, in time, the principal owner of two banks. His investments in land, cattle, and banks have increased with the years until he is now a "man of property," according to the standards of the Rio Grande country.

Like his chief rival, Mr. Curtis, he began office-holding early in life. He was first appointed to fill out the unexpired term of county judge, and then was elected to the place. In 1898, he was chosen a member of the Texas legislature and served two terms there. As chairman of the Redistricting Committee, he brought about the separation of his county from the old Seventh Congressional District and with others it went to form the new Fifteenth. He was promptly nominated for Congressman from this district and elected. He entered upon his duties in November of 1903, and has served continuously since.

Mr. Garner's Fifteenth District, comprising twenty-two counties, is almost a kingdom in itself, stretching for nearly four hundred miles along the Rio Grande River, from Brownsville and the Gulf to beyond Eagle Pass. It is, roughly, the region beyond the Nueces River, over which the United States and Mexico went to war in 1846, but which resulted in the acquisition of the much more valuable territory of California. Strangely enough, California showed the old affinity in the Democratic Convention in 1932 by coming forward to win the Vice-Presidential honors for the ruler of the realm beyond the Nueces. Long known as the disputed territory, the title is now strangely inappropriate since the district brooks no rivals to Mr. Garner, and it is said he has not found it necessary to make a campaign speech there in twenty years.

In another respect Mr. Garner resembles his chief rival; he has made very few speeches in the House, having served there eight years before he made such an attempt. He has risen to power chiefly through his work on standing committees. In 1913, he was placed at the foot of the powerful

Ways and Means Committee; through the efflux of time he became, in 1923, its ranking Democratic member; and in 1931, through Republican electoral misfortunes, its Chairman. In 1928, when Representative Finis Garrett left the House, he succeeded him as Floor Leader. Republican defeats and deaths gave the Democrats a tenuous majority in the Seventy-second Congress, and Mr. Garner again stepped up, this time as Speaker of the House.

Mr. Garner is a man of medium height and build and has been described by one observer as in appearance "the most humble and artless person on Capitol Hill." The *Literary Digest* thus characterizes him: "A stocky, white-haired man, his most conspicuous characteristics are his heavy white eye-brows and pink face. He has a short hawk-like nose, wide cheek-bones, and bright blue eyes. Decisive in manner, he is not blunt nor aggressive but a friendly appearing person . . . ." Mr. Roy T. Tucker, writing in the New York *Outlook* described him as, in short, "the frontiersman come to Congress. With a gun in each fist, he would delight the heart of an artist as a model for Deadwood Dick."

Opinions by contemporaries as to the statesmanlike qualities of Mr. Garner naturally vary. Owen P. White wrote in *Collier's* that "with his lucid mind, his rare skill in handling men, his large experience of Washington, the Speaker would make a great President." George Milburn, in *Harper's,* expresses an entirely different view: "Not once in his entire career has he risen above the level of a smart county-seat politician. Not a single piece of important legislation graces his lifetime record in Congress. Throughout his long years in Congress he has kept one of his hands dipping into the pork barrel, and he has kept his other hand busy scratching backs." The Democratic New York *Times* referred to him as a "statesman in homespun" and conceded that there was "no more astute practical politician" in Washington.

In spite of his proletarian appearance, Mr. Garner's record is not that of a pronounced progressive. He regards himself as an old-fashioned Jeffersonian, but this seems to be more evidenced in a devotion to its symbols and trappings than to concrete equalitarian measures. For instance, while Mr. Longworth was Speaker of the House, he was a constant critic of the government's provision for him of an official car and chauffeur, and when he himself succeeded to the Speakership, he declined the perquisite. He opposed adoption of both the Prohibition and the woman's suffrage amendments. Earlier voicing opposition to the principle of the protective tariff, he later came to advocate a "modified and equalized protection," so that each region should receive its proportionate share of the benefits. This, of course, would not differ in practice from the system in use for several generations. He hesitatingly appeared before the Ways and Means Committee in the fateful last session of the Seventy-second Congress in 1932 and testified in favor of the sales tax, a measure not specially designed for the underdog. Throughout the Coolidge administration, however, he was a constant thorn in the side of

Secretary Mellon and succeeded in forcing a modification in the tax bill presented by the latter in 1923 in favor of the smaller incomes. Although a man of wealth himself, his constant denunciation of the "interests" as represented by Mellon, Rockefeller, and Morgan, has served to align him in the popular mind with the cause of the propertyless.

There were five minor parties in the field, only one of which, the Socialist, represented a significant popular following. Norman Thomas, heading this ticket, had as his running-mate, Mr. James H. Maurer of Pennsylvania, for sixteen years President of the Federation of Labor of that State. Verne L. Reynolds of New York for President, and John W. Aiken of Massachusetts for Vice-President, represented the Socialist-Labor party; the venerable Jacob S. Coxey of Ohio for President and Julius J. Reiter of Minnesota for Vice-President, the Farmer-Labor party. Mr. William Z. Foster was again given the Presidential nomination by the Communist party and for the first time in American history a Vice-Presidential candidate of the Negro race was named, Mr. James W. Ford of Alabama, a graduate of Fisk University.

In the campaign, the Republicans were on the defensive from the beginning. President Hoover made a half dozen or more speeches in the large centers of population and one in the Corn Belt at Des Moines, Iowa, and these were broadcast by the national radio chains. The Democratic campaign was aggressive. Mr. Roosevelt followed closely the tactics of his Vice-Presidential campaign in 1920. He appeared in almost all sections of the country, in cities large and small, and having previously ascertained the particular grievances of each region, offered to redress them should he be elected President.

The acceptance pronunciamentos of the two Vice-Presidential candidates were indicative of the place which each was to be given in the campaign. Mr. Curtis paid tribute to the leadership of both parties in standing behind the President during the trying times of the depression. In spite of all that had happened, he reaffirmed his belief in the need for the "American system of protection" in order to keep out European goods which come into competition with American-made goods. He reviewed the farm legislation of the past decade, stating that nearly thirty bills for its relief had been passed, but acknowledged that most of them had not come up to the expectations of those who introduced and supported them. He advocated a system of national coöperative marketing as promising the best way out. He reviewed the efforts of President Hoover's administration to alleviate the conditions in general caused by the depression. While acknowledging the right of any Republican to stand on either side of the Prohibition question, he reaffirmed his own opposition to the return of the saloon and the repeal of the Eighteenth Amendment.

Mr. Garner added another innovation to that of Mr. Roosevelt in flying to the Convention which had nominated him and addressing it before its adjournment. He refused to countenance the expense of the usual elaborate ceremony of notification and acceptance and so received the notification from the chairman of the committee, A. W. Barkley of Kentucky, by mail and by the same means sent his acceptance.

In this letter, he harked back to the Jeffersonian ideas of national decentralization and states' rights; he found the cause of many of our ills in the steady encroachment of the Federal government on the rights and duties of the states. He reaffirmed his faith in the ancient tenets of individualism and *laissez faire*. Like Adam Smith and Tom Paine, he recognized only two legitimate functions of Government: "The first is to safeguard the lives and properties of our people; the second, to insure that each of us has a chance to work out his destiny according to his talents." Nearly all our social ills, he believed, had arisen from government's departure from its "legitimate" functions. Strangely inconsistent with this stand was his condemnation of the government for not raising its heavy hand to stop speculation in 1929, and for its inadequate legislation following the economic collapse, and for its failure to see that "the evolutionary processes of government must go forward to meet ever-changing human needs." Efforts of the "slim Democratic majority in the House" to effect economies and balance the budget, he said, had been thwarted by the Hoover administration. (No mention here was made to his own efforts to increase that deficit by over four billions of dollars.) He went on record as opposed to the Smoot-Hawley tariff and to the cancellation of the war debts owed this country by its late allies, and condemned the Republicans for having already scaled them down by forty per cent. He stood unequivocally for the repeal of the Eighteenth Amendment.

As was the case four years before, for the Republican ticket Mr. Curtis bore the brunt of the campaigning. On September 17, he delivered the principal address at the opening rally of the party in Pennsylvania at the village of Fogelsville. Thereafter, he was almost continuously on the move until the close of the campaign, making formal speeches in the larger centers and rear-platform speeches at numerous smaller places. These trips carried him into the Border states of the South and through the Northwest to the Pacific states, but with the most intensive campaigning in the agricultural states of the Middle West. In general, he stood by his guns on the Protective tariff, explaining how it had been fashioned to aid the interests of the farmers, and attempted to demonstrate how greatly the administration had softened the severity of the depression.

Mr. Garner, unlike his Republican rival, figured very little in the contest. There was a reason for it. It had been made an important part of the Republican strategy that their fire should be concentrated on the rival Vice-Presidential nominee as the most vulnerable sector in the opposing line. These tactics were dictated by his record in the session of the Congress just closed.

The session of a Congress immediately preceding a Presidential election normally is chiefly concerned with the manufacturing of issues for the coming campaign, and the one ending in June, 1932, was no exception. In the December preceding, Mr. Garner had been inducted into the office of Speaker, backed by the support of a bare majority. The other law-making authorities, the Senate and the President, were controlled by the Republicans. The economic condition of the country at the time, however, was so desperate that public opinion demanded a closing up of ranks and a pull together so that proper alleviative measures might be devised. A Constitution which permits such a division of responsibility as existed in the Government at the time of this crisis is obviously defective, but for this defect neither party was to blame. It was incumbent upon the Democrats of the House to present a program with which they could go before the country, and the same responsibility rested with President Hoover and the Senate. This was performed after a manner in both cases, but the advantage of position being with the Republicans, the program of the President dominated. Bowing to the necessity of some legislation, Mr. Garner helped further considerable parts of the Hoover program and in so doing laid himself open to criticism from his fellow Democrats. By vitriolic words outside the House session, however, he kept the record straight as to his fundamental disagreement with the Hoover administration and all its works. If this had not been sufficient, his support of three major pieces of legislation which were anathema to the President would have rounded it out. The first was a bill which provided that the veterans of the World War should be paid at once the value of their adjusted compensation certificates by the issuance of $2,400,000,000 in Treasury certificates; another, the authorization of $1,000,000,000 to be added to the capital of the Reconstruction Finance Corporation to be used for making loans to stimulate employment; and the third, the issuing of bonds in the amount of $1,000,000,000 to be used for the construction of public buildings and works in 2300 specified cities, villages, and rural communities. The first was defeated by the Republican Senate, and the second and third passed the House. The second was rewritten in conference between the two Houses in conformance with the views of the President. The third did not survive his denunciation as the "most gigantic pork barrel ever proposed to the American Congress," and it perished. Late in March Mr. Garner, alarmed at the failure of the House to agree on a tax program looking to a balancing of the budget, left the Speaker's chair and, after the manner of an evangelist in a revival meeting, asked all those willing to coöperate in balancing the budget to rise in their seats. There was a unanimous response to the invitation. His championship of these three measures calling for an expenditure of well over four billion dollars and a consequent bankrupt Treasury or fiat currency seemed hardly consistent. Perhaps it had the effect of putting the President "in a hole" with the American Legion and other beneficiaries of the acts, but it did shock the conservative leaders of his own party. Obviously the Garner leadership in the House was the most hopeful issue the Republicans could find in an otherwise dismal setting.

Soon after the Chicago Convention, Mr. Garner expressed the intention of carrying the issue between himself and President over the relief program into the campaign. On his way back to Uvalde he stopped off at Dallas, Texas, where a home-coming welcome had been prepared for him, and delivered·a speech in his direct, forthright manner. Frankly he confessed that he had had no Presidential aspirations; but, when his Texas and California friends had insisted that he was "fit timber to deal with Herbert Hoover," he had assented. "I think now," he continued, "I may be big enough for that job, considering his weakness and vacillation. I hold the most powerful position in this Government excepting that of President of the United States. I accepted the proposed Vice-Presidential nomination with much hesitancy, for already we have whipped Hoover three times in Congress."

This speech, well enough designed for the home community in which it was delivered, brought spasms of fear to Democratic headquarters. Was the party again to live up to its tradition of bungling tactics and so lose what seemed a sure election? The alarmed New York *Times* in its most chilly manner remarked: "Without any warning, but doubtless after deep thought, Mr. Garner is attempting to enhance the importance of a candidate for Vice-President. In this pleasing task, he seems to forget that he is not actually running for President. . . . Unless he is capable of amending his peculiar style of talk, his talents would best be employed in the Philippines." Probably no one else was more surprised than Mr. Garner himself at the unfriendly attitude of the managers of his own party at his amiable attempt to help along the cause. He retired to Uvalde in silence, and thereafter took no part in the fray which had not beforehand been planned by the Democratic board of strategy.

At about the middle of August, Mr. Garner was in New York to consult with his chief and the party managers, after which he announced that he favored a campaign of "silence." He denounced the "bigotry" which had led his native State in 1928 to desert the Smith ticket and vouched for his own regularity at the time. To that individual he paid a visit in an attempt to persuade him to come out openly for the election of Roosevelt, dropping the word to the newspaper men as he left that he was a "great American" and "worth more to the ticket than any other one man." Mr. Garner also expressed regret that he himself was considered a handicap to the ticket in the East, but laid it to the bigotry of his section in 1928.

The policy of silence which had evidently been decided upon for Mr. Garner was, with a few exceptions, faithfully followed. A Republican orator, with Mr. Roosevelt's speech on "The Forgotten Man" in mind, referred to Mr. Garner late in the campaign as its real forgotten man. Only when

JOHN NANCE GARNER, TEXAS, THIRTY-SECOND VICE-
PRESIDENT OF THE UNITED STATES, 1933-19—.

President Hoover in his Des Moines speech attacked his legislative record, did Mr. Garner venture forth to address a public audience. He made only one radio address and then from the studio, rather than before an audience. This was at the height of the drive to convince the business interests that the Democratic party was safe and sane. "I know I have been represented in certain partisan arguments as a dangerous radical," he said, "either without the disposition to understand great public questions or with a Satanic desire to turn things topsy-turvy with some wild idea of destruction. Actually, I am a plain business man who has happened to have had a long legislative experience in the representation of a conservative community. This experience has endowed me with a fair realization, I hope, of the problems of government." No champion of the under-dog, or Wild West "Cactus" Jack irresponsibility about this, but only the orthodox business man! Two days previously, he had met a representative group of business men at a dinner in New York, where assurance was given that he was an advocate of sound money as represented by the gold standard, and not an economic menace.

Toward the end of the campaign, Mr. Alfred Smith, speaking from Newark, New Jersey, made an appeal over a nation-wide radio hook-up, for the election of the Democratic ticket, and that ended the only serious worry of the party managers. The Republican attempt to give their opponents the stamp of "unsound" and "radical," because of the Garner record, failed; the economic distress continued unabated; the hoped-for last-minute reaction toward the Republican cause failed to appear; and the Democrats rode into power on a tidal wave of votes. The electoral vote was the largest received by any national ticket since the Civil War and the popular vote, a fraction of one per cent. larger than that of Mr. Hoover four years before, was exceeded in that period only by Mr. Harding in 1920.

On the second Wednesday in February, in the presence of the two Houses, Vice-President Curtis opened the electoral votes and announced his own defeat and the victory of his rival. On the fourth of March, at about a quarter to twelve, Mr. Garner, as Speaker, declared the House of Representatives adjourned *sine die* and led them into the Senate chamber to witness the valedictory of Mr. Curtis. He ascended to the rostrum and there received the oath from his erstwhile rival and delivered his inaugural speech as Vice-President of the United States and President of the Senate. Within thirty minutes he had exchanged a place of some dignity and much power for one of great dignity and little power. How expeditiously the cow-man from beyond the Nueces will adjust himself to this turn in fortune is left to the future. It were kindlier, too, not to refer to the inward pain of this Prometheus of the political world, chained to the rock for four years, and prohibited from expressing his anguish except in the robot phrase, "Does the Senator from X yield to the Senator from Y?"

CHAPTER XX.

Conclusion

ONE warm day in August, 1787, some one in the Grand Committee of the States of the Philadelphia Constitutional Convention suggested that an elective heir apparent be provided for the President of the proposed new government of the American states. That suggestion was ultimately adopted and so it was foreordained that through one hundred and forty-four years thirty upright citizens should while away their time in the United States Senate awaiting, but not daring to hope for, one of those contingencies by which the Executive Chair is made vacant. Six of them received the summons and so saved the country from the turbulence which normally attends an interregnum or a disputed title to the succession; seven died in office, one resigned, and the other sixteen served out the allotted term as the presiding officer of the Senate.

Through unnumbered centuries until recent years, the human race has existed under political institutions which were not planned but which arose, flourished, and fell by accident and chance. Only when a civic consciousness impelled by the dogmas of human equality and popular sovereignty arose, were there attempts to substitute state planning for the hit or miss method of unguided political events. The philosopher Burke justly remarks that it is easy to establish a government if only power and authority are desired, and easy to set up a régime of freedom if peace and order are sacrificed. But to form a *free government,* "to temper together these opposite elements of liberty and restraint in one consistent work, requires much thought, deep reflection, a sagacious, powerful, and combining mind." It is generally acknowledged that the leadership in the planning commission of the American people which held its sessions at Philadelphia in the summer of 1787, was of this type. Has the Vice-Presidential institution worked true to the plan of the designers?

Its chief and most obvious purpose was to provide a succession to the executive headship of the Nation which would be free of legal doubt, and prompt and automatic in operation. There were incidents in Anglo-Saxon history which pointed to the necessity for such an institution. William Rufus, an early king, one day sat down to a jovial feast with boon companions, after which all went to hunt deer in the New Forest. That evening the corpse of the king was found by a poor woodman. No one was able to account for the arrow through the heart and it remains one of the world's unsolved crimes. The Red King's eldest brother was in France at the time of the accident and the youngest, Henry, nearby in England. Something other than law was to determine the succession. The latter at once galloped to the capital, seized the treasury, and with that in hand secured from the national council an acknowledgment of his succession to the throne.

In not one of the six cases of the death of a President was there a dispute as to the right of the Vice-President to take over his duties. True it was that in the first one, the death of General Harrison, the Whig Senate attempted to give Tyler the title of Acting President only, but this was soon foregone. Andrew Johnson, a citizen of a Southern State, claimed the succession at a time when the country bristled with military forces and the Congress was in control of an overwhelming majority of Republican Unionists; yet there was no opposition. The public generally looked with aversion and distrust upon the succession of Mr. Arthur to the place of President Garfield, yet everywhere there was a loyal resolve to support him in his difficult position. In only one case, that of Mr. Tyler, was there an interregnum which amounted to more than a few hours. It remained for the defective electoral system devised by the Fathers, rather than the Vice-Presidency, to give rise to the only two disputes over the title to the Presidency serious enough to cause talk of the use of armed force—the Jefferson-Burr contest of 1800 and the Hayes-Tilden contest of 1876.

But what of the success of the administrations of the six heirs who succeeded to the Presidency? In the first of these cases, President Tyler, a man of mediocre ability, soon found himself at odds with the leaders of his party on almost every major issue, and this lack of coherence in the administration lasted throughout the four years. The basis of the trouble, however, lay in the fact that the Whig party, itself, had no real unity of organization or principle. Mr. Tyler, known to be a Jeffersonian and States' Rights man, had been offered the Vice-Presidential nomination by a party dominated by the nationalists, Henry Clay and Daniel Webster, and he had accepted it. In this, both Mr. Tyler and the conservative Whigs were culpable, but the former won the cast of the die. The perfected organization of the political parties since the Civil War makes unlikely the repetition of such a nomination and its attendant unfortunate consequences. The death of President Taylor and Mr. Fillmore's accession to his place must be reckoned as, on the whole, a loss; but the administration which followed struck about an average in its virtues and faults. The death of Mr. Lincoln brought into being the most unfortunate of all the administrations since the adoption of the Constitution. Mr. Johnson's two resplendent virtues of honesty and courage were not sufficient to overcome the handicaps imposed upon him by Nature and his early environment. After four years in which there had been stupendous losses in lives and materials, the North had emerged from the war victorious. Problems of a social, constitutional, and economic nature, greater than had been encountered in any other period, confronted the Nation. Mr. Johnson made the mistake of attempting to settle large questions of a legislative nature by executive decree. Common sense should have dictated that Congress would not permit itself to be superseded in any such manner. Johnson persisted and thereby played into the hands of the most radical and vindictive members of Congress. His bad temper and bad judgment only added to the flame, and the country for two generations dearly paid for the misfortune of his accession to the Presidency.

The succession of Mr. Arthur in 1881 and of Calvin Coolidge in 1921, added two more to the list of mediocre administrations: the first, perhaps falling somewhat below what might have been expected of Mr. Garfield, and the latter somewhat above that of Mr. Harding. It remained for Theodore Roosevelt to restore the balance in favor of the Vice-Presidents as desirable heirs to the Chief Magistracy, which had been so completely upset by Andrew Johnson. Mr. Roosevelt proved himself to be a political leader of great power and vision, and his administration must be ranked among the six or eight most notable.

It must be concluded, then, that the work of the Vice-Presidents upon becoming President has struck about an average for the office, one administration representing the extreme of ineffectiveness, another standing among the ablest, and four thrown in with the colorless mediocre. In respect to planning a satisfactory succession, therefore, the Fathers seem to have planned well.

The second object which the Framers had in mind in establishing the Vice-Presidency was to facilitate the election of a fit man to the Presidency.

It is to be remembered that those who wrote the Constitution had no thought of permitting the popular election of a Chief Magistrate, nor did they visualize the existence of political parties, nor their agency in such an election. The foundation of the system of election which they adopted was the principle of states' rights and states' sovereignty. Each state was allotted as many electoral votes as it had senators and representatives in the National Congress. It was believed that the electors of each state would vote solidly on candidates just as one expects the delegates of each Nation sent to an international conference to do. The only party lines anticipated, if they might be so designated, would be the coalitions of the large and the small states, respectively. It was expected that the electors of each state would normally vote for some one from their own state, which would, of course, result in no one's receiving a majority of the electoral votes. It was provided that in such a contingency, the House of Representatives, voting by states, should choose a President from the five receiving the highest number of electoral votes. The vote of the states' electors, therefore, would serve as a sort of nomination, with the large states having somewhat the better of it, while the election would be in the House, all states there being given equal power.

But it was thought that something should be added in order to give a chance for the election of a "continental character" rather than one known only in his own state. Consequently the expedient was adopted of requiring the electors to vote for two men, one of whom must be a citizen of a state other than their own. It was believed that this clever device would ensure, if not the election, at least the nomination, of men honored throughout the Union. It is to be noted that no one was voted for as *Vice-President;* both men presumably were voted for as President. But the provision ran that "in every case, after the choice of the President, the person having the greatest number of votes of the electors shall be the Vice-President." A majority was not required. Indeed, Mr. Adams, the first Vice-President, was chosen by only a plurality vote. Presuming the non-existence of concerted action through political parties and the continued solidarity of the states electoral votes, it must follow that the Vice-President would always be the person most desired for President after the one actually elected. And this is exactly what happened in the first three elections. Adams in two instances rivaled Washington, and Jefferson in the other rivaled Adams.

By 1800, however, true political parties had appeared and the concert of action was so perfect that two Democrats, Jefferson and Burr, received the same number of electoral votes. Burr had been voted for by the Democratic electors equally with Jefferson, but with the mental reservation that he should be Vice-President. They had put him forward because he might carry the doubtful State of New York. Soon, thereafter, the Twelfth Amendment was adopted, which frankly acknowledged the party system and the veiled popular election. Thenceforward, the Vice-President was not the person who happened to have received the second greatest number of votes for President, but he was a person chosen beforehand for the second place. The Federalists correctly argued in Congress that this changed the original conception of the office, and they backed a constitutional amendment abolishing it. They argued that hereafter mediocre characters would be nominated for the place and it would be awarded solely from the view-point of gaining votes for the President. There was much in the contention.

In the thirty-three elections since the adoption of the Twelfth Amendment, it is difficult to find even one Vice-Presidential nomination that was not made primarily from the standpoint of its utility in carrying a doubtful state or region, or in satisfying a disgruntled faction of the party. The choice of Mr. Coolidge in 1920 is as near an exception as any; the Republicans were sure of success beforehand and permitted the delegates to have their own way in taking Mr. Coolidge rather than the one who had been slated by the leaders. In a number of cases, very little consideration was given to the abilities of the man chosen. The present electoral system, with its emphasis on states' rights and the consequent undivided electoral vote of each State, calls for a campaign strategy based on the capturing of large states rather than on the winning of popular majorities throughout the Nation. This has given a political power to the large and doubtful states out of all relation to their place in the Union. A Governor of New York State, for instance, no matter what his calibre, is almost as a matter of course a candidate for the Presidential nomination of his party or, at the very least, for its Vice-Presidential nomination. The extent of this advantage to New York is shown in the fact that in only one of the seventeen elections since the Civil War has that state failed to have one or more of the four positions at the head of the two main parties. If the party leaders agree that New York is to be granted the Vice-Presidency when the first place has gone to some other state, it is customary to leave the choice of the man to the state delegation—a method which does not commend itself to the thoughtful citizen as a sound method of choosing the person whom chance may make President of the United States. It was the New York delegation which in caucus turned down Vice-President Levi P. Morton for re-nomination with President Benjamin Harrison in 1888 because he had offended some local politicians, and substituted Whitelaw Reid. They were offered the opportunity to name the Vice-Presidential candidate in 1908, but "Boss" Murphy scornfully declined. Occasionally, however, the delegation leaders use a commendable conservatism in choosing the person who is to receive the blessing. In 1900, for instance, a good Tammany man, William Sulzer, had arrived at Kansas City ahead of "Boss" Croker and was pushing his claims for the Vice-Presidency. But when the latter arrived and Sulzer broached the matter to him, he promptly punctured the boom with the remark: "Bryan and Sulzer! Huh! How long before everybody would be saying 'Brandy and Seltzers!'" Ohio and Indiana are two other states which have profited considerably from the even strength of the parties within their borders.

Greater care on the part of party managers in the choosing of Vice-Presidential candidates is needed. Nothing would contribute more to the accomplishment of this end than the substitution of some form of direct popular election in the place of the present outgrown electoral system. So long as the nomination is only a pawn in the winning of a doubtful State, little change in the spirit of making it is to be expected. The memories of politicians are notoriously short. Many Republicans regretted exceedingly the nomination of Andrew Johnson and his rise to power in a critical time. Their resolve not to repeat the error led in 1868 to the most spirited contest for the Vice-Presidential nomination in the history of that party; but by 1880 the lesson had been entirely forgotten.

Not often do those dominating a convention show as much spirit and foresight as did Mark A. Hanna with his 1896 Republican Convention. Timothy Woodruff, a ridiculous New York politician, approached him for the Vice-Presidential nomination.[1] "Do you think that the Convention would nominate you for the Presidency?" Mr. Hanna asked in his blunt way. Mr.

---

[1] Herbert Croly: *Marcus Alonzo Hanna*, 310.

Woodruff had to confess that there was no such possibility. "Then," continued Mr. Hanna, "don't you know that there is only one life between the Presidency and the Vice-Presidency and that it would be foolhardy to nominate a man for Vice-President who would not be big enough to be President?"

What of the character of the men who have been brought forward for the Vice-Presidency in the thirty-seven quadrennial elections? Hegel lays it down as a principle that "the course of empire is from East to West" and so it falls out that the hundred-forty-four-year procession of Vice-Presidents and Vice-Presidential candidates begins with John Adams of Quincy, Massachusetts, and ends with Charles Curtis of Kansas, and John Nance Garner of Uvalde, Texas. Approximately eighty candidates have been nominated by the two major parties of the time, or by an occasional strong "third party," and so may be considered as having come within a reasonable distance of the office. How many of these are known to the American public today, and how many even to the student of history? What do the names of John E. Howard, Daniel D. Tompkins, Richard Stockton, James Sergeant, Francis Granger, William O. Butler, W. R. King, George Pendleton, William H. English, Adlai Stevenson, John W. Kern, and Henry Gassaway Davis mean to the reader today?

But set over against the unknowns are such names as John Adams, Thomas Jefferson, Rufus King, Elbridge Gerry, John C. Calhoun, Edward Everett, Whitelaw Reid, Theodore Roosevelt, Calvin Coolidge, and Franklin D. Roosevelt.

But even though nine-tenths of the Vice-Presidential candidates have faded into oblivion, that in itself is not complete proof of their unfitness for the Presidential office. The only absolute proof of such inability is the man faced with the task. It is not hard to believe that had Abraham Lincoln, rather than William L. Dayton, won out in the Vice-Presidential contest in 1856, he would not have won more enduring fame than did his rival. Nor is it difficult to believe that if the names of a strong one-half of the Presidents of the United States were not listed on the rolls of the office, their oblivion would now be as complete as that of sixty or seventy of the Vice-Presidents and Vice-Presidential candidates.

The roll of nominees comprises with a few exceptions men of high character, and of long experience in political life, or of eminence in other fields. In few if any of the cases would the government have fallen into the hands of reckless or irresponsible men. Some might have risen to heights equalled only by a half-dozen Presidents; the rest would doubtless have struck the average of a Van Buren, a Polk, or a Hayes.

A third, but incidental, purpose of the Vice-Presidency, was to provide a presiding officer for that great Council of the States, the United States Senate, and one who should act as an arbiter when the states were equally divided.

Here again the failure of the Founding Fathers to foresee the coming of party government led to another miscarriage of the original purpose of the Vice-Presidency. The solidarity of state delegations has never existed in Congress, and so there has never been an opportunity for the Vice-President to act as an arbiter among the states. Nor has there existed the expected division between the large and the small states. The Vice-President, on the other hand, has often served to augment in general the power and the voting strength of his party in the Senate. Never, however, has it been feasible for him to assume a frankly partisan attitude, since his position as presiding officer is weak and vulnerable.

Party government, on the whole, has served to weaken his position. Party leadership in the Senate demands a more vigorous attitude than a presiding officer, not chosen by that body, could ever hope to offer. Then again, it often happens that the Vice-President's party loses control of the Senate at the middle of the quadrennium, which leaves him in the unenviable situation of acting as the servant of a body with whose purposes he is out of sympathy.

The political weakness of the Vice-President both in the Senate and in his party organization is reflected by the former's attitude toward its presiding officer. He has never exerted a substantial control over the work of the standing committees. True it is that for the greater part of the time from 1823 to 1845 their appointment was in his hands; but the unwritten law required that he take his place in the Senate chair several days after the beginning of a session, so that a President *pro tempore* might be chosen and the committees be formed; and that even in the filling up of vacancies in the committees during the session, he follow the list of the party leaders. Today he appoints to committees only by virtue of *ad hoc* resolutions and even these are confined to routine special committees whose membership is dictated by the customs of the Senate. Furthermore, the attitude of the Senators has been such that he has only very cautiously exerted that most elementary of the powers of a moderator—the maintenance of order and decorum in debate. Vice-President Calhoun, sensing the attitude of the Senate, contributed largely to this result. In an argument, after his most logical manner, he went on to prove that he had no constitutional power to call one of the delegates of the sovereign states to order; that duty rested entirely with the individual senators themselves. In 1828, the Senate rules were revised to confer on him this specific power, but it was unhappily received by Calhoun and never vigorously used by any subsequent Vice-President.

Custom and, perhaps, the Constitution, forbid the Vice-President to engage in debate in the Senate. If he is wise, he will never attempt openly to exert influence on its organizational and legislative affairs. A few, like Mr. Curtis, have wielded real power, but it has been done chiefly outside the formal sessions. Mr. Dawes stands unique in his open challenge of Senate methods and rules and his country-wide campaign to win his cause. Born partly of an ignorance of the full significance of the rules, and of a desire to carry over the technique and autocratic standards of the business world into the conduct of public affairs, it was foredoomed to failure from the beginning. Within six months, his attempt to reform the rules ceased to be taken seriously and was generally regarded as an attempt to relieve the tedium of his office and perhaps keep him in the running for the Presidential nomination in 1928.

In short, throughout almost a century and a half, the Vice-Presidents have not only failed to establish for themselves a place of power in legislation, but they have lost something of what they held in the first three decades of the office. Now that there is always a President *pro tempore* in existence, there is no substantial reason for the faithful attendance of the Vice-President at Senate sessions, and most of them of late years have deliberately absented themselves some hours of each day and occasionally for days and weeks at a time. The mere existence of the Vice-President as an outside constitutional presiding officer not chosen by the Senate itself has, on the other hand, contributed to its looseness of organization, and informality and freedom of debate; by the same token, it has been saved from the reverse, the legislative steamroller of the type found at the other end of the Capitol.

The growing burden of the President's office has often brought out the suggestion that the Vice-President should be called upon to act as his assistant or deputy. Various political considerations, however, have led the Presidents to prefer to delegate such powers to those whom they may directly control, such as the Heads of the Executive Departments, an unofficial political adviser, a special agent (in foreign affairs), or even a Private Secretary. To this there is one conspicuous exception. As the second in rank in the land, the Vice-President has been found a convenient and proper person on whom to unload the performance of a mass of duties of a social, ceremonial, and political nature. Such duties seem trivial to the average voter, but they must be performed if powerful interests at home and abroad are not to be alienated. The Vice-President's contribution in this report to the lightening of the President's work is a substantial one.

A change which bids fair to increase the dignity of the Vice-Presidential office and compensate it for its loss of prestige in the Senate, was instituted by President Harding in 1920, when he invited Mr. Coolidge to a place in the Cabinet. The latter in turn extended the invitation to Mr. Dawes, but he refused on the grounds of sound administrative policy. Mr. Curtis sat throughout the four years in Mr. Hoover's Cabinet and the newly elected Vice-President, John Nance Garner, occupies the same position in the Roosevelt administration. This innovation has the sound argument behind it that it will tend to bring a better understanding and perhaps a closer coöperation between the President and the Senate; against it are no potent general principles. If it becomes the means of making the Vice-Presidency attractive to statesmen of the first rank, it will constitute the most important modification in that office since the adoption of the Twelfth Amendment.

INDEX

Index